Tuscany

Damien Simonis

LONELY PLANET PUBLICATIONS
Melbourne • Oakland • London • Paris

TUSCANY

Adriatic Sea

Rimini

San Marino

San Marino

Ravenna

Forlì

Imola

EMILIA-ROMAGNA

Bologna

LE MARCHE

UMBRIA

AREZZO
The fresco cycle at the Chiesa di San Francesco and the magnificent façade of the Pieve di Santa Maria

THE CHIANTI REGION
A patchwork quilt of vineyards, fallow fields and olive groves, with seams of cypress and pine

Alpe della Luna

Pieve San Stefano

Sansepolcro

Arezzo

Castiglion Fiorentino

Cortona

Monte San Savino

Asciano

Poppi

Bibbiena

Montevarchi

Radda in Chianti

Siena

Parco Nazionale delle Foreste Casentinesi, Monte Falterona, Campigna

Monte Falterona (1654m)

Alpe di S. Benedetto

Borgo San Lorenzo

Dicomano

Pontassieve

Rufina

Riserva Naturale di Vallombrosa

Monti del Chianti

Fiesole

Florence

Impruneta

Greve in Chianti

San Casciano in Val di Pesa

Poggibonsi

Firenzuola

Prato

FLORENCE
The treasures of the Uffizi, Renaissance architecture from the dome of the Duomo to the Basilica di San Lorenzo, and Michelangelo's sublime David

Certaldo

Castelfiorentino

San Gimignano

Volterra

Pomarance

Empoli

Monsummano

Pontedera

Ponsacco

Montecatini Terme

Pistoia

Monti Albano

San Marcello Pistoiese

Abetone

Castelnuovo di Garfagnana

Barga

Borgo a Mozzano

Lucca

Pisa

APUAN ALPS
Breathtaking views and some of the region's best walking

PISA
Romanesque splendour and the gravity-defying Leaning Tower

Riserva Naturale dell'Orecchiella

Parco Regionale delle Alpi Apuane

Pania della Croce (1858m)

Massa

Carrara

Seravezza

Pietrasanta

Viareggio

Parco Naturale Migliarino San Rossore Massaciuccoli

Rosignano Mattimo

Cecina

Livorno

Ligurian Sea

Gorgona

SIENA
Home of the famous Palio horse race and one of Italy's greatest Gothic cathedrals

LIGURIA

Passo Cerreto

Pontremoli

Fivizzano

Aulla

La Spezia

Magra River

LUNIGIANA

GARFAGNANA

PITIGLIANO
Extraordinary town of tiny winding lanes, rising dramatically from a rocky outcrop

POPULONIA
Etruscan tombs, medieval settlements and picturesque beaches

ELBA
Idyllic little beaches and coves and stunning views from Monte Capanne

PARCO NATURALE DELLA MAREMMA
The forest-covered Monti dell'Uccellina and a magnificent stretch of unspoilt coastline

LAZIO

ROME

Chiusi
Montepulciano
Pienza
Abbadia San Salvatore
Monte Amiata (1738m)
Pitigliano
Montalcino
Massa Marittima
Grosseto
Monte dell'Uccellina
Parco Naturale della Maremma
Lagoon Orbetello
Orbetello
Porto S Stefano
Monte Argentario
Giglio Porto
Giglio
Il Telegrafo (635m)
Lago di Burano
Giannutri
Lago di Bolsena

Capraia
Monte Arpagna (410m)
Populonia
Piombino
Golfo di Baratti
Rio Marina
Porto Azzurro
Elba
Portoferraio
Monte Calamita (413m)
Monte Capanne (1018m)
Pianosa
Montecristo

Golfo di Follonica

Tyrrhenian Sea

SS1
SS2
SS146
SS223
SS223
SS322
SS322
SS323
SS74
SS1
SS73
SS1
S1
SS312
SS571
SS1
SS2
A12
SS675

ELEVATION

| 1500m |
| 1000m |
| 500m |
| 200m |
| 100m |
| 0 |

National Parks

0   15   30 km
0   9   18 miles

Tuscany
1st edition – July 2000

Published by
Lonely Planet Publications Pty Ltd A.C.N. 005 607 983
192 Burwood Rd, Hawthorn, Victoria 3122, Australia

Lonely Planet Offices
Australia PO Box 617, Hawthorn, Victoria 3122
USA 150 Linden St, Oakland, CA 94607
UK 10a Spring Place, London NW5 3BH
France 1 rue du Dahomey, 75011 Paris

Photographs
Most of the images in this guide are available for licensing from
Lonely Planet Images.
email: lpi@lonelyplanet.com.au

Front cover photograph
The 12th-century Abbazia di Sant'Antimo, nestled in the hills of Siena
Province (Joe Cornish, Tony Stone Images)

ISBN 0 86442 733 6

text & maps © Lonely Planet 2000
photos © photographers as indicated 2000

Printed by SNP Offset (M) Sdn Bhd

Contents – Text

1

Contents – Maps

MAP LEGEND – SEE BACK PAGE

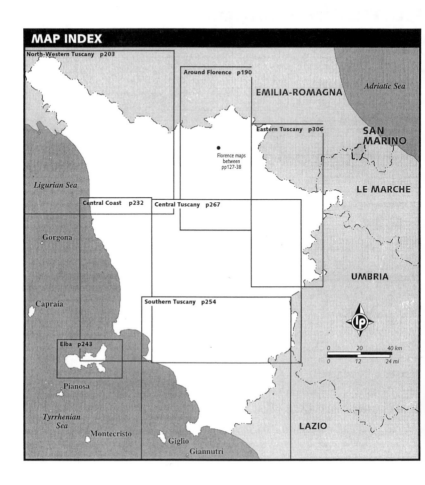

MAP INDEX

North-Western Tuscany p203

Around Florence p190

EMILIA-ROMAGNA

Adriatic Sea

Eastern Tuscany p306

SAN MARINO

Florence maps between pp127-38

Ligurian Sea

LE MARCHE

Central Coast p232

Central Tuscany p267

Gorgona

UMBRIA

Capraia

Southern Tuscany p254

0   20   40 km
0   12   24 mi

Elba p243

Pianosa

Tyrrhenian Sea

LAZIO

Montecristo

Giglio

Giannutri

The Author

Damien Simonis

With a degree in languages and several years' reporting and sub-editing on Australian newspapers (including the *Australian* and the *Age*), Sydney-born Damien left the country in 1989. He has since lived, worked and travelled extensively throughout Europe, the Middle East and North Africa. Since 1992, Lonely Planet has kept him busy writing *Jordan & Syria*, *Egypt & the Sudan*, *Morocco*, *North Africa*, *Italy*, *Spain*, *The Canary Islands*, *Barcelona*, *Venice* and *Florence*. No sooner had he wrapped up *Tuscany* than he was back in Spain working on several titles, including Lonely Planet's new guide to Madrid. He has also written and snapped for other publications in Australia, the UK and North America. When not on the road, Damien resides in splendid Stoke Newington, deep in the heart of north London.

FROM THE AUTHOR

Increasingly the creation and maintenance of Lonely Planet's books is a collective effort. I owe a lot to my colleagues in Italy, Helen Gillman, Stefano Cavedoni and Sally Webb, for information pooled and traded. Thanks also to the guys in the London office for their input, editorial and otherwise.

On the ground, various people came up with ideas or simply tagged along and helped make work almost seem like fun. The crowd at No 62, led by fearless Julie, were a good crew to live with and often had ideas on potential venues – for work and play. Thanks to Tiarna, Andrew, Georgina and, above all, the New York Boyz (Camille and Laura). Thanks also to DB, GB and the Villa gang for the timely fashion hints.

I owe a great deal to Ottobrina Voccoli – *a te vorrei dedicare i risultati modestissimi di questo lavoro.* 'Otto' and her band of pals (Silvia, Ruggero, Claudia, Michela, Barbera, Anna *et al*) helped make my time on the Arno more than just an assignment. Thanks also to Monica Fontani – next time we'll actually hang out!

This Book

This 1st edition of *Tuscany* was researched and written by Damien Simonis and is based on the relevant chapter of Lonely Planet's *Italy* guide.

From the Publisher

This edition of *Tuscany* was produced in Lonely Planet's London office. Sam Trafford coordinated the editing and proofing, with invaluable assistance from Claire Hornshaw, Amanda Canning and Lynn Bresler. Ed Pickard coordinated the mapping and design, and produced the colour pages and cover, assisted by Marcel Gaston, Sara Yorke, Angie Watts and Gadi Farfour. Sara produced the climate charts, Claudia Martin compiled the index and Adam McCrow made last-minute design corrections. The illustrations were drawn by Jane Smith. Quentin Frayne provided input for the Language chapter and information on the Tuscan dialect, and Imogen Franks and Anna Sutton chipped in with additional research. Big thanks to Tim Ryder for his wise words and encouragement, and above all, for his patience.

Foreword

ABOUT LONELY PLANET GUIDEBOOKS

The story begins with a classic travel adventure: Tony and Maureen Wheeler's 1972 journey across Europe and Asia to Australia. Useful information about the overland trail did not exist at that time, so Tony and Maureen published the first Lonely Planet guidebook to meet a growing need.

From a kitchen table, then from a tiny office in Melbourne (Australia), Lonely Planet has become the largest independent travel publisher in the world, an international company with offices in Melbourne, Oakland (USA), London (UK) and Paris (France).

Today Lonely Planet guidebooks cover the globe. There is an ever-growing list of books and there's information in a variety of forms and media. Some things haven't changed. The main aim is still to help make it possible for adventurous travellers to get out there – to explore and better understand the world.

At Lonely Planet we believe travellers can make a positive contribution to the countries they visit – if they respect their host communities and spend their money wisely. Since 1986 a percentage of the income from each book has been donated to aid projects and human rights campaigns.

Updates Lonely Planet thoroughly updates each guidebook as often as possible. This usually means there are around two years between editions, although for more unusual or more stable destinations the gap can be longer. Check the imprint page (following the colour map at the beginning of the book) for publication dates.

Between editions up-to-date information is available in two free newsletters – the paper *Planet Talk* and email *Comet* (to subscribe, contact any Lonely Planet office) – and on our Web site at www.lonelyplanet.com. The *Upgrades* section of the Web site covers a number of important and volatile destinations and is regularly updated by Lonely Planet authors. *Scoop* covers news and current affairs relevant to travellers. And, lastly, the *Thorn Tree* bulletin board and *Postcards* section of the site carry unverified, but fascinating, reports from travellers.

Correspondence The process of creating new editions begins with the letters, postcards and emails received from travellers. This correspondence often includes suggestions, criticisms and comments about the current editions. Interesting excerpts are immediately passed on via newsletters and the Web site, and everything goes to our authors to be verified when they're researching on the road. We're keen to get more feedback from organisations or individuals who represent communities visited by travellers.

Lonely Planet gathers information for everyone who's curious about the planet – and especially for those who explore it first-hand. Through guidebooks, phrasebooks, activity guides, maps, literature, newsletters, image library, TV series and Web site we act as an information exchange for a worldwide community of travellers.

7

Research Authors aim to gather sufficient practical information to enable travellers to make informed choices and to make the mechanics of a journey run smoothly. They also research historical and cultural background to help enrich the travel experience and allow travellers to understand and respond appropriately to cultural and environmental issues.

Authors don't stay in every hotel because that would mean spending a couple of months in each medium-sized city and, no, they don't eat at every restaurant because that would mean stretching belts beyond capacity. They do visit hotels and restaurants to check standards and prices, but feedback based on readers' direct experiences can be very helpful.

Many of our authors work undercover, others aren't so secretive. None of them accept freebies in exchange for positive write-ups. And none of our guidebooks contain any advertising.

Production Authors submit their raw manuscripts and maps to offices in Australia, USA, UK or France. Editors and cartographers – all experienced travellers themselves – then begin the process of assembling the pieces. When the book finally hits the shops some things are already out of date, we start getting feedback from readers, and the process begins again ...

WARNING & REQUEST

Things change – prices go up, schedules change, good places go bad and bad places go bankrupt – nothing stays the same. So, if you find things better or worse, recently opened or long since closed, please tell us and help make the next edition even more accurate and useful. We genuinely value all the feedback we receive. Julie Young coordinates a well-travelled team that reads and acknowledges every letter, postcard and email and ensures that every morsel of information finds its way to the appropriate authors, editors and cartographers for verification.

Everyone who writes to us will find their name in the next edition of the appropriate guidebook. They will also receive the latest issue of *Planet Talk*, our quarterly printed newsletter, or *Comet*, our monthly email newsletter. Subscriptions to both newsletters are free. The very best contributions will be rewarded with a free guidebook.

Excerpts from your correspondence may appear in new editions of Lonely Planet guidebooks, the Lonely Planet Web site, *Planet Talk* or *Comet*, so please let us know if you *don't* want your letter published or your name acknowledged.

Send all correspondence to the Lonely Planet office closest to you:

Australia: PO Box 617, Hawthorn, Victoria 3122
UK: 10A Spring Place, London NW5 3BH
USA: 150 Linden St, Oakland CA 94607
France: 1 rue du Dahomey, Paris 75011

Or email us at: talk2us@lonelyplanet.com.au

For news, views and updates see our Web site: www.lonelyplanet.com

HOW TO USE A LONELY PLANET GUIDEBOOK

The best way to use a Lonely Planet guidebook is any way you choose. At Lonely Planet we believe the most memorable travel experiences are often those that are unexpected, and the finest discoveries are those you make yourself. Guidebooks are not intended to be used as if they provide a detailed set of infallible instructions!

Contents All Lonely Planet guidebooks follow roughly the same format. The Facts about the Destination chapter or section gives background information ranging from history to weather. Facts for the Visitor gives practical information on issues like visas and health. Getting There & Away gives a brief starting point for researching travel to and from the destination. Getting Around gives an overview of the transport options when you arrive.

The peculiar demands of each destination determine how subsequent chapters are broken up, but some things remain constant. We always start with background, then proceed to sights, places to stay, places to eat, entertainment, getting there and away, and getting around information – in that order.

Heading Hierarchy Lonely Planet headings are used in a strict hierarchical structure that can be visualised as a set of Russian dolls. Each heading (and its following text) is encompassed by any preceding heading that is higher on the hierarchical ladder.

Entry Points We do not assume guidebooks will be read from beginning to end, but that people will dip into them. The traditional entry points are the list of contents and the index. In addition, however, some books have a complete list of maps and an index map illustrating map coverage.

There may also be a colour map that shows highlights. These highlights are dealt with in greater detail in the Facts for the Visitor chapter, along with planning questions and suggested itineraries. Each chapter covering a geographical region usually begins with a locator map and another list of highlights. Once you find something of interest in a list of highlights, turn to the index.

Maps Maps play a crucial role in Lonely Planet guidebooks and include a huge amount of information. A legend is printed on the back page. We seek to have complete consistency between maps and text, and to have every important place in the text captured on a map. Map key numbers usually start in the top left corner.

Although inclusion in a guidebook usually implies a recommendation we cannot list every good place. Exclusion does not necessarily imply criticism. In fact there are a number of reasons why we might exclude a place – sometimes it is simply inappropriate to encourage an influx of travellers.

Introduction

If the requirements for nationhood were cultural wealth, variety of landscape, quality of food, natural beauty, fashion and industriousness, Tuscany would probably be counted among the great nations. Like a fine wine, Tuscany has been some time in the making. More than 10,000 years of history have gone into shaping this, perhaps one of the most representative and varied of the Italian regions.

The Etruscans left behind them an impressive artistic tradition that Rome could do little more than copy and adapt. Cities that sprang out of the landscape thousands of years ago still thrive today. From Arezzo to Volterra, the Etruscan origins of the region are never far out of sight.

Out of the confusion of the early Middle Ages emerged a series of fiercely independent city states that spent centuries engaged in an at times deadly game of one-upmanship. Of these, Florence emerged the victor and capital of Tuscany. Today it is possibly the single greatest repository of Renaissance art in the world. In its palaces and churches, its galleries and cloisters, a seemingly endless treasure chest of extraordinary paintings, sculpture, frescoes and other art splashes forth. The true art lover could spend many weeks in Florence alone.

However, visitors to Tuscany come for many reasons. Many are in search of some of the finest art created since the death of Christ, while others choose to explore the countryside, which in itself seems a work of art. Gourmets and wine buffs descend on the place to delight their palate. Walkers don their boots for mountain hikes. Summer vacationers head for the coast and islands.

Where to begin beyond the banks of the Arno? From the haunting Gothic majesty of Florence's most bitter rival, Siena, through to the Romanesque splendour of the onetime maritime power Pisa, the roll call of *città d'arte* (cities of art) in Tuscany is daunting. Arezzo, Cortona and Lucca are among the more striking of the other cities.

The more you come to know the region and strike out beyond the main urban centres, the more extraordinary Tuscany appears. Centuries-old villages huddle for protection atop lonely hills. Sprawling churches lie scattered about in the most unlikely places. From the patchwork quilt hills of the Chianti region to the rain-swept heights of the Apuan Alps, from the cypress-sprinkled fields of the Crete south of Siena to the rugged gorges around Pitigliano, the variety of the Tuscan countryside seems endless.

With all the tourists you could be forgiven for thinking there was nowhere to turn for a quiet moment. Nothing could be further from the truth. Whether in the rough lands of the Lunigiana to the north-west or the deep forests of the Casentino, whether in the plains of the Maremma or on the slopes of Monte Amiata, Tuscany remains full of scope for escaping the madding crowd. Indeed, the contrast between such rural retreats and the chaos of a place like Florence is astounding.

Cruise along a Chianti ridgeback in mid-autumn and drool at the mere thought of the olives and grapes you see ripening. They will go to make some of the finest wines and most exquisite virgin olive oil in the world. Whether at the end of the day or at lunch, both will accompany wonderful meals – good food is part of the Tuscan experience. Simple and honest fare means that you can generally be sure of eating well – Tuscans are obsessive about using only the freshest ingredients and cooking them just right.

While in the countryside, leave the roads and get into your stride. Country lanes and mule tracks criss-cross much of the region, offering the walker unlimited options for wandering about in the fields and hills. Sooner or later you will stumble upon an old church or Etruscan tomb. Little villages emerge around bends in your path, fortress walls loom menacingly in the distance.

In the Apuan Alps in particular the walker can get in some more serious leg exercise, while the most ambitious of walkers could choose to follow the grand excursion along the Apennines across the length of the region.

The patient walker can also indulge in a little bird and animal watching – the remarkable variety of birds, in winter especially, makes excursions to some of the region's nature reserves worthwhile. Those along the coast, such as the Parco Naturale della Maremma, are particularly tempting.

Tuscany also offers enough beach activity to keep summer holiday-makers happy. Better still than most beaches on the mainland coast are the islands, led by the former home of the exiled Emperor Napoleon, Elba.

In the cooler months something a little warmer is in order. Right across Tuscany, but especially in the south and north-west, hot springs have been exploited for their medicinal and recreational value since Roman times. People feeling the need to take the waters can choose from several centres around the region, or freer spirits can head for open springs and cascades.

Many have suggested that, by the manner in which Tuscans have shaped and moulded their land, they have long displayed an innate artistic sensibility. That thought reflects what at least seems like a real local affinity with beauty. There is no doubt that Tuscans like to present well, and they always have done. And even today, Tuscany and its people have lost none of their seductive power.

Facts about Tuscany

HISTORY
Etruria Rules

More than two million years ago, the site where Florence now stands was virtually on the coast. As the waters receded, life came to the region that we now know as Tuscany (Toscana).

Evidence suggests the first Neolithic tribes, Ligurians from northern Italy, moved in to the area around the 10th century BC. They were later joined by other tribes, among them the Etruscans, who appear to have founded settlements as early as the 9th century BC. By the beginning of the 6th century the Etruscans had become the dominant power in central Italy. Territory in their control stretched from Rome in the south to the Apennines (Appennini).

Etruria, encompassing much of modern Tuscany and parts of Latium (the Latin name for Lazio) and Umbria, was by no means a monolith. The Etruscan settlements were largely independent of one another and they are said to have formed a league, the 12-city Dodecapolis, for the celebration of annual religious festivities more than anything else. In times of conflict with other tribes they generally helped each other out.

Among the senior members of the league were Fiesole (the northernmost town), Chiusi, Cortona, Arezzo, Roselle, Populonia, Volterra, Sovana, Saturnia, Vetulonia, Tarquinia and Veio (the last two in Latium). Each city was ruled by a chief or *lucumones*.

Just where the Etruscans came from remains a 64,000 dollar question. The Greek historian Herodotus claimed they migrated in waves from Asia Minor in the wake of the Trojan Wars. Linguistic evidence, based largely on funerary inscriptions, suggests their language was neither Indo-European nor Semitic. It was still spoken until the 2nd century AD, allowing the Roman emperor Claudius to write a history of Etruria. Unfortunately the manuscript has not survived.

A more recent theory has the Etruscans, along with the Basques (in northern Spain) and other tribes, migrating from northern Africa as long as 6000 years ago in the face of worsening desertification. These tribes, according to the theory, headed for the Canary Islands, the Iberian peninsula, Italy, Sicily and Sardinia.

To the Greeks the Etruscans came to be known as the Tyrsenoi or Tyrrhenoi, a name that survives in that of the Tyrrhenian Sea off Italy's west coast. The Romans, who in the 6th century had barely embarked on the urbanisation of what would be the most powerful city in the world, called the Etruscans' homeland Tuscia, from which comes to us the regional name of Tuscany.

Etruria on the March

Starting in the late 7th century BC, the Etruscans embarked on repeated campaigns of conquest across the peninsula. They marched south into Latium, taking the village of Rome and proceeding into Campania, where they were brought to a halt by the Greeks at Cumae in 535 BC. That date is seen by many as the beginning of the end for Etruria.

In the same period, Etruscan warrior bands marched across the Apennines and burst into the Po valley, where they quickly came to rule the roost. With help from Carthage (the Phoenician outpost in North Africa) they also ousted the Greeks from Corsica.

Etruria had by now reached the apogee of its power. In Rome, the Etruscans were in complete control and furnished at least three of its kings. The backward Latin tribes had much to learn from their culturally superior Etruscan overlords.

The Romans Rebel

The Etruscans helped make Rome the centre of power in Latium. Etruscan influence on art and architecture mixed with that of Greek traders from the south. The Etruscans also reformed the military, creating a disciplined infantry organised into heavily armed centuries (units of 100 men).

Indeed, Rome owed the Etruscans a considerable debt. The classic Roman town plan, based on two perpendicular main streets, the *decumanus* and *cardo*, is said to have been inherited from the Etruscans. The Roman toga and even the she-wolf symbol of Rome are further borrowings. They also passed on their knowledge of engineering and tunnelling to the Romans.

The monarchy was toppled in 509 BC but the Etruscans, many of whom continued to live in Rome, had already helped elevate the city to a level of importance that later generations of Etruscans would come to regret. In any event, whatever control the Etruscans may have had over the Latin towns evaporated. Within 10 years Rome rose to head the Latin League (a loose alliance of towns in Latium), and top of their list of enemies were the Etruscans.

In 392 BC the Romans took Veio, an Etruscan stronghold about 15km north of Rome. This marked the start of a limited campaign of conquest, and soon all of southern Etruria was under Roman influence. The Etruscans had good cause to be worried, for the Gauls had invaded northern Italy and ejected their cousins from the Po valley. Several attempts to regain control of southern Etruria failed and in 351 BC the Etruscans sued for peace.

Rome spent the following years warring and putting out fires across Latium and south into Campania, where they were having mixed success against the Samnites. At various moments during the Samnite wars, and even afterwards, the Etruscan cities chose to break their peace treaties with Rome in the hope of winning back territory. They always came off second best. By 265 BC, all of Etruria was firmly bound up in the Roman system of compulsory alliances.

Upheaval and civil war around 88 BC impelled Rome to grant full Roman citizenship to subordinate territories throughout much of the Italian peninsula. The violence of the civil wars also left a trail of destruction across Etruria. While citizenship assured the few Etruscans who had survived the carnage equal rights, it also spelled the final stage of the eradication of local culture and language (although the latter hung on for another couple of centuries).

Another result of the civil wars was a policy of Roman colonisation. Caesar founded Florentia (today Florence) in 59 BC as a military settlement for war veterans, choosing a trading post on the narrowest crossing of the river Arno as the site. In 20 BC, Romans began to arrive at the military colony of Saena Julia (today Siena). No-one could know then that more than 1000 years later the two settlements would be flourishing city states and bitter rivals. Other towns founded by the Romans included Pisa (an important river port), Pistoia, Lucca (base of the triumvirate of Julius Caesar, Crassus and Pompey) and Empoli. They also drove major roads, such as the Via Aurelia north from Rome along the coast, through the region.

The Early Middle Ages

Towards the end of the 3rd century AD, the Tetrarchy, which had been in command in Rome since AD 293, decided to reorganise the administration of the peninsula. As part of this, the administrative province of Regio VII Etruria was converted into the Regio Tuscia et Umbria. Thus the name by which this part of central Italy had been known for more than 10 centuries was consigned to the dustbin of history.

The Romans themselves were not far behind. By the 6th century their mighty empire had collapsed into an ignominious heap and most of central Italy had been put to the torch by the criss-crossing barbarian and Byzantine armies. The latter were sent in by Justinian, the eastern emperor in Constantinople (now Istanbul), to retake Italy. Tuscia hence came under their control, ruled through the Exarchy of Ravenna. By this time Christianity was well installed as the majority religion in Tuscan towns. Florence already had a martyr, St Minius (San Miniato).

This state of affairs didn't last long, as the invading Lombards wrested control of

Tuscia from Byzantine forces in 570. They turned it into a duchy with its capital in Lucca and remained in control until 774. Little documentation from this period survives, but it appears Tuscia was relatively peaceful through these centuries.

In the last century of Lombard rule, the Via Francigena, entering Tuscia at the Cisa pass and dropping south through the Lunigiana to Lucca and on to San Gimignano and Siena, was one of the busiest pilgrim routes to Rome in the country. The road took its name from the Franks, who under Charlemagne arrived in 774. Charlemagne, who in 800 would be crowned Holy Roman Emperor, took over the running of Tuscia indirectly, installing as lieutenants a series of margraves. By the end of the 11th century, particularly under the administration of Countess Matilda Canossa, the duchy had achieved considerable independence from the empire. Florence, with a population of 20,000, had supplanted Lucca as a robust and flourishing regional capital.

When hostilities broke out between emperor Henry IV and Pope Gregory VII, Matilda allied herself with the pope, setting a precedent that would long resonate through Florentine history. Henry tried to have the pope deposed in 1076 but instead found himself at Matilda's castle at Canossa, in Emilia, imploring him to lift an order of excommunication.

That was little more than a truce, and this round of the papal–imperial struggle only ended when Henry was deposed by his son, Henry V, in 1105. Matilda meanwhile managed to keep control of the duchy of Tuscany for another 10 years. Her death spelled the end of Tuscany as a political unit. In a confusing free-for-all, each of the Tuscan cities sought independence as an individual mini-state.

The City States

Less than 50 years later the Holy Roman Emperor, Frederick I, better known as Barbarossa (Redbeard), granted the river-port city of Pisa control of the coast from Portovenere (in Liguria) to Civitavecchia (in Lazio), as well as Sardinia. With control over Tuscany's sea trade, Pisa was, from that point on, to be long in the driver's seat. For a time Pisa was able to compete with Genoa and Venice for Mediterranean trade and it was in this golden age that much of the great Pisan monuments were completed. The cathedral had already been started, the Leaning Tower was begun and artisans flocked to this flourishing port.

The city councils *(comunes)* of Prato and Pistoia became independent with the promulgation of their own statutes in 1140 and 1117. Lucca followed suit and would remain an independent republic until the age of Napoleon.

Siena, meanwhile, had become the dominant city of central Tuscany, slowly extending its power southwards into the Maremma. Only 70km to the north, however, its nemesis was already bracing itself for conflict.

The Rise of Florence

Only eight years after the death of Matilda, Florence's city fathers undertook the conquest of nearby Fiesole. In 1173 emperor Frederick was in town dictating terms to the Florentines and restricting their jurisdiction to their own city limits. Florence, like the rest of Tuscany, paid him little heed.

Although skirmishes had been taking place for years between Florence and Siena in the Chianti region, it was not until the bloody Battle of Monteaperti in 1260 that the two sides clashed head on. By this time Florence and many other Tuscan cities had been divided into two main factions, the pro-empire Ghibellines and the pro-pope Guelphs.

Supposedly the division was between those who backed imperial influence in Italy and those who preferred papal supremacy. Often, however, the papal–imperial conflict was more of a pretext for local feuding than anything else. The Ghibellines dominated Florence until 1250, when the Guelphs turfed them out.

The Battle of Monteaperti, although a resounding defeat for Guelph Florence, was only a temporary setback. Within 10 years Florence had managed to impose a Guelph governorship on Siena, after the Battle of Colle di Val d'Elsa.

Florence got lucky with Pisa too. The port town was heavily defeated at sea by Genoa at the Battle of Meloria in 1284, signalling the end of Pisa as a dominant trading city and weakening it enough for Florence to have a Guelph in power there too. Five years later, Florentine Guelph troops, Dante among them, crushed Arezzo. It and other Tuscan towns were all soon obliged to accept Guelph leadership.

By the turn of the century Florence counted 100,000 inhabitants, making it one of the five biggest cities in Europe. Pisa, Siena and Lucca each had fewer than half that number.

Rival Conquests

Although Florence was emerging as the leading city in Tuscany, its bigger rivals were not exactly subordinate, Guelph governors or not. In 1335, for instance, Siena completed the takeover of Grosseto and Massa Marittima.

Indeed this was Siena's golden age, a period in which much of the cathedral was completed, the Torre del Mangia was raised in the Palazzo Pubblico and many of the fine works of art by Duccio and others were commissioned. In short, it was in this period that the Gothic masterpiece you see today was largely formed.

In 1348 disaster struck. The Black Death swept across Tuscany, decimating urban populations and stunning the countryside. It was a blow from which Siena would never really recover, while Florence managed to bounce back and capture Prato just three years later. In 1384 Florence simply bought Arezzo.

In the meantime, the Visconti rulers of Milan had brought Pisa and Siena into their orbit and so threatened to complete their domination of Tuscany by encircling Florence. This city had more lives than a cat, however, and the problem was solved by the timely death in 1402 of Gian Galeazzo Visconti. Only four years later, Florence had taken control of Pisa, Livorno, Cortona and Montepulciano. Siena remained one of

the few significant Tuscan centres not under direct Florentine control.

Enter the Medicis

The attempt at democratic republican rule in Florence had always been something of a farce. The city governors, or priors, elected every two months, tended to be carefully selected and elections gerrymandered by the competing wealthy merchant and banking families that called the shots in Florence by the end of the 14th century.

One of these families was the Medici clan. Having successfully become God's bankers (being the Vatican's top financiers), this family had risen to be among the most powerful in the city by the time Cosimo de' Medici was in charge of its affairs in 1429. Although discreet, Cosimo's desire to rule by proxy was clear enough to some and the rival Albizi clan plotted his removal. The move backfired and by the time Cosimo returned from a brief exile in 1434, Florence was effectively his.

The Medici family crest was made up of six balls *(palle)*, which must have been

JANE SMITH

The Medici family's balls can be seen on coats of arms across Tuscany.

cause for some mirth through the years as Medici supporters would clatter around on horseback crying out: 'Balls! Balls! Balls!' The word has the same less than decorous meaning in Italian as in English. Be that as it may, the Medicis were here to stay and their balls can be seen on stone coats of arms in towns across Tuscany to this day.

Cosimo tended to remain in the background, believing discretion to be the better part of valour. Few were fooled. In the 1450s, Pope Pius II actually dubbed Cosimo 'master of all Italy'. The Medici clan kept the government stacked with its own people and, when dissenting voices were raised, found indirect means to silence them, such as special taxes and other rulings to ruin their opponents financially. The Medicis were not beyond tinkering with the constitution to head off potential opposition.

Foreign policy came close to undoing Cosimo. His unswerving allegiance to the Milanese usurper, Francesco Sforza, brought upon Florence the enmity of Venice and the kingdom of Naples.

Opposition to the ensuing war was strong and things were looking a trifle dodgy when Neapolitan forces breached the Tuscan frontier in 1450. Cosimo remained unperturbed and the doubters were proved wrong. Venice was too concerned with threats from Turkey, and the other Italian states worried lest a French army march into Italy to aid Florence.

As so often in the peninsula, the boys put away their toys and signed a pact in 1454 aimed at creating unity in the face of potential outside aggression. Ten years of peace followed.

It was also under Cosimo, a passionate patron of the arts, that the humanist revolution in thinking and the accompanying Renaissance (Rinascimento) in the visual arts took off. The process had been under way since the previous century, as witnessed by the work of artists such as Giotto. But the generous patronage of the Medici family was a catalyst that would turn Florence into the most innovative centre of the arts in all of Europe.

Lorenzo the Magnificent (il Magnifico)

continued his grandfather's work, expanding the city's power and maintaining its primacy in the artistic realm. Lorenzo, who took up the reins of power in 1469, narrowly escaped assassination shortly afterwards. His enemies didn't give up there and Lorenzo was soon faced with invasion by papal and Neapolitan troops. Things could have gone horribly wrong but Lorenzo managed to negotiate his way out of trouble and turn the tables.

His death and his succession by his nasty son Piero in 1492, the year Columbus discovered the Americas, spelled the temporary end of Medici rule and the start of heated times for Florence.

Ups & Downs

In 1494, Piero abjectly bowed to a muscle-bound invasion force led by the diminutive French king Charles VIII. Piero and his family, increasingly disliked by the people of Florence, fled the city and were replaced by the rather humourless theocracy of a dour, droopy-lipped Dominican monk by the name of Girolamo Savonarola.

Savonarola's spiritual austerity program and slavish pro-imperialism went down fine for a while, but as the city's economy stagnated and Savonarola directed a growing portion of his fire-and-brimstone sermons at papal and Church corruption, he found himself increasingly friendless. So much so that he ended up on an Inquisitorial bonfire in 1498. Over the following 14 years Florence remained a republic along pre-Medici lines, but this family was not so easily discouraged.

It took some time and a good deal of bloodshed, but Giovanni de' Medici returned home in 1512 backed by a Spanish-led army. He set about restoring the position of his family in Florence, which should have been further strengthened when he was elected Pope Leo X three years later.

But the Medici name had lost much of its lustre. Florence in any case was not the same city as in the days of Cosimo. Most of its banks had failed and business was not so good. A series of Medici lads, culminating in the illegitimate (and utterly useless)

Ippolito and Alessandro, managed to so alienate the Florentines that when Pope Clement VII (another Medici) was cornered in Rome by an uncompromising imperial army, the people rejoiced and threw the Medici out.

Of course deals were done and the imperial forces subsequently promised to reinstate the Medici in Florence if the pope recognised imperial suzerainty of all Italy. Florence, which had enjoyed a few short Medici-free years, was weakened by siege in 1530. Alessandro and Ippolito returned and the former was made duke, bringing to an end even the pretence of a republic. The jealousy of an unhinged cousin, Lorenzino, saved Florence from too protracted a rule by Alessandro: Lorenzino killed him and ran away. Florence breathed a sigh of relief and waited for the next exciting instalment in the Medici soap opera.

The Grand Duchy of Tuscany

Cosimo (a descendant of the original Cosimo's brother) succeeded Alessandro in 1537. Although in many respects Florence and its Tuscan dominions had by now been eclipsed on the European stage by the emergence of powerful nation states such as France, Cosimo was determined to keep a key role for Florence in the affairs of a still-fractured Italy.

A key moment came in 1555 when a Florentine army entered Siena after a year-long siege. The city and all its possessions across southern Tuscany passed into Florentine hands. Four years later Cosimo's victory was confirmed by the peace of Cateau-Cambrésis. In 1569 Pope Pius V conferred upon Cosimo the title of Cosimo I, Grand Duke of Tuscany.

Florence was now the capital of most of Tuscany. Only Lucca and its modest possessions in the Garfagnana, the Lunigiana (held by the Hapsburg empire), Piombino and most of Elba (together forming a separate principality) and the coastal area around Orbetello and Monte Argentario (the Spanish-controlled military outposts or *presidios*) remained out of the Grand Duke's control.

In his long reign from 1537 to 1574, Cosimo I was no doubt a despot, but a comparatively enlightened one. He sorted out the city's finances, built a fleet (which participated in the crushing defeat of the Turkish navy in the Battle of Lepanto in 1571) and promoted economic growth across Tuscany, with irrigation programs for agriculture and mining.

Cosimo I was a patron of the arts and sciences, and he also reformed the civil service, building the Uffizi in Florence to house all government departments in a single, more easily controlled building. He and his family also acquired and moved into the Palazzo Pitti.

The Medici of the Grand Duchy

From the death of Cosimo until that of the dissolute lout Gian Gastone de' Medici in 1737, the once glorious family continued to rule over Tuscany with uneven results.

Cosimo I's two immediate successors, Francesco and Ferdinando I, between them managed to keep Tuscany out of trouble and go some way to stimulating the local economy and promoting agriculture, building hospitals and bringing some relief to the poor. Cosimo II invited Galileo Galilei to Florence, where the scientist could continue his research under Tuscan protection and undisturbed by the bellyaching of the Church.

Ferdinando II was ineffectual if well meaning – during the three terrible years of plague that scourged Florence from 1630, he stayed behind when anyone else who could was hightailing it to the countryside.

Next in line was Cosimo III, a dour, depressing man if ever there was one. Perhaps he had read his Savonarola. Not exactly a fun date, he was also an ill-educated bigot. Persecution of the Jews was one of his contributions to Tuscan society and he also backed the Inquisition in its opposition to virtually any kind of scientific learning. Inevitably, sex was one of his biggest bugbears. A little stretch on the rack was the prescribed tonic for horizontal jogging outside marriage, while buggery was punished with decapitation.

Busy as Cosimo III was overseeing the mores of his subjects, they were either dying or going hungry. The population of Tuscany was in decline, the economy was a mess and taxes were skyrocketing.

Before the next in the Medici line, the drunkard Gian Gastone, had kicked (or rather stumbled over) the bucket, the European powers had decided the issue of the 'Tuscan succession' and appointed Francis, Duke of Lorraine and husband of the Austrian empress Maria Theresa, Grand Duke of Tuscany.

The last significant act of the Medicis came six years after the death of Gian Gastone. His sister Anna Maria, who died in 1743, bequeathed all the Medici property and art collections to the grand duchy of Tuscany, on condition that they never leave Florence.

Austrians in Charge
The imperial Austrian couple popped down for a three-month sojourn in Florence and liked it well enough, but from then until 1765 the city and grand duchy were to be ruled by regents (the Reggenza).

The regents brought a feeling of (mostly) quiet discontent to their subjects. It is true that much-needed reforms swept away glaring inequities in taxation, somewhat streamlined civil administration and bridled the Inquisition. At the same time, however, the regents' main task seemed to be the systematic plunder of Tuscany's resources for the greater glory of the Austrian Empire.

Things looked up a little in 1765, when Pietro Leopoldo became Grand Duke and moved down from Vienna. He threw himself into his task with considerable vim and vigour. The list of his reforms and initiatives is impressive, even if some proved less than satisfactory. The Grand Duke abolished torture and the death penalty, suppressed the Inquisition, embarked on a school building program for the poor, busied himself with agricultural issues and prodded Florence's city council to clean up the city, improve lighting and introduce street names. He also saw to it that at least some of the art and furnishings that had

been removed to Austria under his predecessor were returned.

Pietro Leopoldo, as heir to the Austrian throne, had to up himself and leave Tuscany upon the death of his brother, Emperor Josef II, in 1790. Until Grand Duke Ferdinando III arrived the following year, Tuscany was put under a Regency Council that within weeks found itself struggling to put down food riots in Florence.

Napoleon
The revolutionary events that had so profoundly rocked France in the meantime could not fail to have an impact, sooner or later, on the rest of Europe. Napoleon Bonaparte marched into Italy at the head of his ill-equipped but highly motivated republican army in 1796 and on 24 March 1799 occupied Florence. Within a couple of days Grand Duke Ferdinando III had been courteously handed his hat and the French tricolour was flying over Palazzo Pitti.

This first round of French occupation of the northern half of Italy was as fleeting as the invasion had been spectacular. By the end of July, Ferdinando III was again Grand Duke, although he was hedging his bets back in Vienna.

Good job really, because the following year Napoleon was back, not as a republican general but as consul and virtual ruler of France. He retook Florence and made it capital of his newly coined kingdom of Etruria, which for the following nine years was run by Louis, son of the Bourbon Duke of Parma, and his wife the Infanta Maria Luisa of Spain.

In 1809 Napoleon, by now emperor, handed Tuscany over to his sister Elisa, who remained Grand Duchess for the five years left to Napoleon as warrior emperor. Before the year 1814 was out, Grand Duke Ferdinando III was back in town.

Towards Italian Unity
Grand Duke Ferdinando III proved to be one of the more popular of the Tuscan overlords. He pushed through a raft of reforms at every level of city and grand ducal administration and by all accounts was an

all-round good fellow. He eschewed many of the trappings of his position and mingled freely with his subjects.

His death in 1824 was greeted with dismay, not least because no-one knew what to expect from his gloomy son Leopoldo.

Grand Duke Leopoldo II actually proved more up to the task than many had thought. Under his rule the first long-distance rail line (Florence-Pisa-Livorno) and the first telegraphic link (Florence-Pisa) were both opened in the 1840s. In 1847, he had the pleasure of seeing Lucca transferred to the control of the grand duchy, ending centuries of Luccan independence.

It was in this period that some of the most important infrastructural reforms in Tuscany took place. The road system, both inside Tuscany and connecting it with other, particularly northern, regions, was improved (often using plans laid out under Napoleonic rule). The drainage and population of much of the lowland coast, especially the Maremma, was accelerated. For centuries the coast had been sparsely populated for several reasons, including malaria and fear of attack by North African pirates. The last such assault by Tunisian raiders took place on the Monte Argentario coast as late as 1815!

As the years wore on, however, the task of reforming the city grew steadily more onerous. The independence of the grand duchy was menaced not only by more direct interference from Vienna, but also by growing calls for a united Italian state.

A whirlwind of plotting and a few turns of the wheel of fortune brought events to a head in 1859, when a combined French–Piedmontese army marched against the Austrians and defeated them in two bloody battles at Magenta and Solferino in June.

Two months earlier, Leopoldo had been convinced of the wisdom of leaving Tuscany after mass demonstrations were held against him and in favour of a united Italy.

On 15 March 1860, the provisional government in Florence announced the adhesion of the grand duchy to what was still the Savoy kingdom of Sardinia. After other parts of the peninsula also joined, a united Italy under a constitutional monarch was born in the following year.

In February 1865, King Vittorio Emmanuele and the national government took up residence in Florence. Turin had been the first seat of the national parliament but was deemed too far north to remain capital.

The natural choice would have been Rome, but the Eternal City was yet to be wrenched from papal hands. And so an 'army' of 30,000, including bureaucrats and their families, descended on Florence, a city of around 115,000.

The incorporation of Rome into the kingdom and the end of fighting throughout the peninsula finally came in 1870 and the government shifted there the following year.

When one considers that the last of the Medici rulers had left behind them a region in a pitiful economic state a century and a half before, it is not surprising that most Tuscans still led a hand-to-mouth existence at the time of unification. The wars and crises following, the tendency towards heavy taxation and the consequent lack of local investment in any kind of production all helped keep the region in check. An 1892 report on Florence suggested that, of a total population of 180,000 in the city, 72,000 were officially poor.

In the 10 years prior to the outbreak of WWI, Florence became something of a cultural cauldron in Italy. Numerous literary, political and free-thinking newspapers and reviews opened at this time.

Florentine politics was becoming more radical too. By 1914 the Socialists had almost 3000 party members in Florence, and the year before, when universal male suffrage was granted, almost 30% of Tuscan votes went to the Socialists. Tuscany was also turning into a fulcrum of anarchist activity.

WWI & Fascism

Italy's decision to enter WWI on 24 May 1915 had little initial direct impact on Tuscany, tucked far away from the front lines in the north. Like the rest of the country, however, Tuscany paid a high price in the lives of its young men sacrificed as cannon fodder.

By 1917, the situation on Italy's home front had become grim too. All basic products were strictly rationed and that winter, a harsh one, brought intense hardship as heating fuel was virtually unavailable.

Italy, like the rest of Europe, emerged from the war in a state of collective shock. The fighting had cost the fledgling country dear in lives and resources and the political turmoil that ensued was inevitable.

By 1920, Benito Mussolini's Fascists had established branches in Florence, which in less than two years would become one of the Blackshirts' key strongholds. Tuscany became one of the single biggest sources of card-carrying Fascist members.

Almost perversely, Livorno was the site in 1921 of the ill-fated Italian Socialist Party's congress, where a split led to the birth of the Partito Comunista Italiano (PCI; the Italian Communist Party).

On 28 October 1922, Mussolini rolled the dice and marched on Rome. Had the King been truly opposed to the Fascists, it is likely they would have failed in this endeavour, but in the event Mussolini emerged the victor.

The Florentine version of Fascism was particularly virulent. In 1924, after the assassination in Rome of the Socialist Giacomo Matteotti had particularly aroused anti-Fascist sentiment, the Blackshirt squads (squadre) set about terrorising anyone suspected of antipathy towards their glorious movement. The violence became so alarming that Mussolini sent people in to shake out the local organisation and put a brake on the bloodshed.

WWII

For Italy, the real tragedy began in June 1940, when Mussolini decided to take the plunge and join Hitler's European tour. Things went Germany's way for a while, but for the Italians the difficulties began almost from the outset. One disaster led to another and by 8 September 1943, when Italy surrendered to the Allies, the latter's troops were about to land at Salerno, south of Naples. They were a long way from Tuscany, which now became occupied territory

under the Germans and a nasty band of diehard Italian Fascists.

Resistance groups began to operate in Tuscany almost immediately, and the mountainous and hilly countryside was frequently the stage for partisan assaults and German reprisal. Allied bombers meanwhile caused heavy damage to coastal cities such as Piombino and Livorno. Pisa too was badly bombed, while raids on Florence were comparatively light.

By July 1944, Free French troops occupied the island of Elba. At the same time, Allied forces approached the German lines near Florence. At this point, the German high command decided to blow the city's bridges, sparing only the Ponte Vecchio (some say it was Hitler who ordered it be spared). Early in the morning of 4 August, the other bridges (along with those in Pisa farther down river) went up in smoke. Allied troops moved in to the city later that day, but the bulk of their forces opted to envelop it rather than engage in close combat. Pisa and Lucca both fell to the Allies in the first days of September.

The Germans, meanwhile, had fallen back to one of their planned defensive lines, the so-called Gothic Line, which stretched from the Versilia coast across the Apuan Alps and Garfagnana, and on across the Apennines to Rimini on the Adriatic coast. The Allies first breached the line in heavy fighting in November and December, but winter delayed their advance and they did not finally break through to the Po valley and force the Germans north until April 1945.

Since WWII

In the 1946 referendum on whether to institute a republic or a monarchy, 71.6% of Tuscans voted for a republic. The monarchy, discredited by its association with Fascism, only gained solid support in southern Italy and was swept aside.

For more on Tuscan politics since WWII, see Government & Politics later in this chapter.

The big international headline of the postwar period was the disastrous flood in

Florence when the Arno burst its banks after torrential rains in November 1966. Some 14,000 families were left homeless and the impact on the city's art treasures was incalculable.

The clean-up process was long and arduous, but more complex still was the restoration of monuments, paintings and manuscripts that had been damaged but not lost. Funds and experts poured in from around the world to help out. If anything good can be said to have come the flood, then it was the great advances made in art restoration. Florence remains a world centre in this field to this day.

GEOGRAPHY

If you regard Tuscany's coast as the base, the region forms a rough triangle covering 22,992 sq km. Crammed within that triangle is a remarkable variety of land forms, from mountains in the north and east to flat plains in the south, from islands off the coast to hill country in the interior sliced up by river valleys.

Much of the coast facing the Tyrrhenian (to the south) and Ligurian seas is flat, with the major exception of a stretch immediately south of Livorno and parts of the Monte Argentario peninsula.

The northern flank of the region, which runs roughly east–west (with a gradual southward drop), is closed off by the Apennines, which it shares with Emilia (part of the Emilia-Romagna region) and the Apuan Alps. These latter mountains in the northwest corner of the region are particularly known for their white marble deposits (see the Carrara entry in the North & Western Tuscany chapter).

Lower hill ranges rise farther south in the region, such as those of Monte Albano south of Pistoia and Monte Pratomagno in Arezzo province to the east. Separating them is a series of low river valleys, the most important of which is the Arno. In all, two-thirds of Tuscany is mountainous or hilly.

The most extensive lowlands are the Maremma Pisana, one-time swamps south of Pisa and in from the coast, and its

southerly extension, the Maremma, which covers a wide area down to the regional boundary with Lazio.

The Arno river, at 240 windy kilometres long, is Tuscany's main river, although it is hardly one of the world's great natural wonders. It rises in Monte Falterona in the Apennines, flows south to Arezzo and then meanders north-west for a while. By the time it passes through Florence it is on a westward course towards Pisa and finally the Ligurian Sea. Once an important trade artery, traffic on the river today is virtually non-existent.

Of the seven islands scattered off Tuscany's coast, the central and eastern parts of Elba, along with Giannutri and parts of Giglio, are reminders of a great Apennine wall that collapsed into the sea millions of years ago. Capraia, Montecristo, western Elba and parts of Giglio are the creation of volcanic activity. The islands are surprisingly varied, from the unexciting flatness of Pianosa to the rugged and rocky coastline of much of Elba, broken up here and there by small but often enchanting little coves and beaches.

CLIMATE

Tuscan summers can be hot and oppressive. Inland especially the heat can be suffocating. The Chianti hills and the valleys are the worst. Being in Florence in July and August is akin to sticking your head into a smelter oven. Temperatures along the coast are marginally lower. Some hill and mountains areas are also cooler.

The Vallombrosa and Camaldoli forests and especially the Apuan Alps can be a real relief from the heat – although even here you can easily strike very hot weather. In general, daytime highs of 35°C are more the norm than the exception. You can expect this kind of weather from late June to well into September.

Spring and autumn are the most delightful times of year, although the latter can be wet. Rainfall in October and especially November is heavy. Average daytime highs around 20–25°C are pleasant and ideal for countryside walks, such as in the Chianti region.

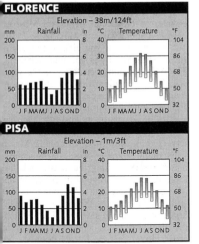

FLORENCE

Elevation – 38m/124ft

Rainfall

Temperature

PISA

Elevation – 1m/3ft

Rainfall

Temperature

On the subject of walking, the Apuan Alps tend to be cooler than much of the rest of the region. They also happen to be the wettest zone in Tuscany, receiving up to 3000mm a year. The south-western side of this range enjoys a predominantly Mediterranean climate, warm in summer and mild in winter. The northern side and the Apennines, on the other hand, are colder in winter, with the temperature frequently plunging below zero, bringing regular snowfalls.

On the subject of winter, it is generally pretty chilly across the region – more than you might expect. Snowfalls and minimum temperatures around and below zero are common in inland hilly areas (such as Siena and Cortona). The coast enjoys a milder climate, and Florence doesn't get snow too often.

ECOLOGY & ENVIRONMENT

Probably one of the greatest ecological headaches is the question of marble extraction in the mountains of the Apuan Alps. The great white scars that from the seaside almost look like snowfalls are the result of many centuries' work.

But never has the stone been removed at such a pace as today. Some 1.5 million tonnes a year are scraped away and trundled down to the coast on heavy trucks. Before WWII, the level of incursion was much slighter and marble miners eased blocks down to nearby villages with complex pulley systems. The extraction is disfiguring part of what is considered a nature reserve, the waste produced is creating disposal problems and the heavy truck traffic is itself an ecological disaster. Everyone knows this, but no one dares seriously object to one of Tuscany's prestige industries. Carrara marble is sought after worldwide by everyone from architects to sculptors.

Heavy industry never really came to Tuscany, so the problems of air and water pollution associated with industry elsewhere in Italy are not as great as here. That said, the medium and light industrial areas of Livorno, Piombino, suburban Florence and along the Arno are far from hazard free. Heavy road traffic makes clean air a distant dream in Florence and in much of the heavily populated Prato-Pistoia area.

The landscape of Tuscany has long seemed something of a work of art, with farmers alternating a patchwork quilt of farmland with stretches of forest. The postwar crisis in agriculture saw many farmers leave the land and in more remote spots, where wringing results from the earth was always a challenge at best, forest or scrub is reclaiming its territory. Sometimes this uncontrolled regrowth has a downside, helping propagate bushfires as happened in 1998.

FLORA

Tuscan farmland has long been appreciated as a visual treat, a pleasing mix of orderly human intervention and natural 'chaos'. In among the ubiquitous olive groves (olives were introduced in Etruscan times from the Middle East) and vineyards, a feast of trees and smaller plants thrives.

Tall, slender cypress and the odd flattened cluster pines (or *pino marittimo*, mainly on the coast) are among the most striking of Tuscany's call-sign trees. Driving down a cypress-lined country road on the way to a little village or vineyard is one of those pleasant daydreams that frequently become reality for the cross-country tourist in Tuscany. The cypress was introduced from Asia Minor in Roman times precisely for its decorative qualities.

Beech trees are common in the mountainous territory of the Apuan Alps, often competing for attention with chestnuts. Hunting for chestnuts is a favourite pastime on November weekends. Heating them up for eating is the next stage, although they are something of an acquired taste. In the Casentino and Vallombrosa areas of eastern Tuscany, deep, thick forests of pine, oak (one species of which is the cork, whose bark is all-important to the wine industry) and beech still cover important tracts of otherwise little-touched land. Other species include maple, hazelnut, alder and imported eucalyptus.

Springtime is obviously the brightest time of year, when whole valley floors and upland plains are bathed in a technicolour sea of wildflowers. They can include jonquils, crocuses, anemones, gentians and orchids.

Coastal and island areas boast typical Mediterranean scrub, or *macchia*.

Flower spotters should equip themselves with specialist books such as *Mediterranean Wild Flowers*, by M Blamey and C Grey Wilson.

FAUNA

Cinghiale, or wild boar, has been on Tuscan menus since the days of the Etruscans, and the hills and coastal areas of the region still teem with these beasts. The only difference is that today most of them are the offspring of eastern European boar imported to make up for the depletion of local species. Although common enough, you will probably not spot them on walks in the countryside. They are busy avoiding their nastiest enemy – the Tuscan hunter.

Among other animals fairly common in the Tuscan countryside are squirrels, rabbits, foxes, martens, weasels, hares and the black-and-white-quilled *istrice,* a porcupine supposedly imported from North Africa by the ancient Romans, for whom it was a particularly tasty morsel.

On a more slithery note, you can encounter several kinds of snake. Most are harmless and, if you are walking, will glide out of your way if you give them warning (by treading heavily as you approach them). The only poisonous customer is the viper, which can be identified by its diamond markings. Rocky areas and the island of Elba are among its principal habitats.

Birdlife is varied in Tuscany. The best time of year for fully appreciating that variety is from November to around March when many migratory species hang about in nature reserves along the coast, including Lago di Burano, Laguna di Orbetello and Monti dell'Uccellina. As many as 140 species of our winged friends call Tuscany home or use it as a stopover. They include the blackbird, black-winged stilt, buzzard, crow, dove, falcon, hawk, hoopoe, jay, kestrel, kingfisher, osprey, thrush, tit, woodpecker and wren.

The hunting season extends from early September to sometime in January. The opening and closure dates depend in part on what you want to hunt. Limits are imposed on how many of any given type of bird or animal you can bag in one day, and hunters are required to arm themselves with a licence and practise the activity in designated areas. Some game animals, such as wild boar, are considered pests and culled as such.

GOVERNMENT & POLITICS

Tuscany is one of 20 regions in Italy. With the exception of the five regions with special autonomous powers (Friuli-Venezia Giulia, Sicily, Sardinia, Trentino-Alto Adige and Valle d'Aosta), government at this level is rather flimsy.

From unification in 1861 until 1948, Italy was governed as a centralised state, particularly under Fascism. That year, the above named regions received special autonomous statutes either on ethnic or particular political grounds. They thus gained wide administrative powers, albeit within limits set by the state.

The remaining regions, among them Tuscany, only received statutes in 1970, and on a much reduced level.

The PCI (Italian Communist Party) won the first regional assembly elections in 1970 with 42.3% of the votes. The Democristiani (Christian Democrats), who until the late 1980s dominated Italian national politics, came in second with 30.6% of the vote, and the Socialists third with 8.8%. Indeed, while Florence often votes right, the region tends to lean to the red.

Tuscany's regional government (giunta regionale) is formed after elections (every four years) to the regional parliament (consiglio regionale). The Presidente della Regione acts as much as anything as a link between the region and the central state.

The regional government has no revenue-raising powers. It receives funds from the state and can legislate on a limited range of issues, such as tourism and the hospitality industry, agriculture and forests, museums and libraries, some areas of professional training, markets and fairs and so on. In an effort to reduce needless duplication of bureaucracy, the regional government tends to act simply as a coordinator, delegating many of its tasks to provincial and local government.

Tuscany and other regions in the course of the 1990s increased pressure on the state to adopt a federalist line and transfer more power to the regions. The 1997 Bassini law was supposed to help in this direction. It is thought that in coming years the regions will acquire more power, including the right to raise revenue. In Rome it is hoped that any transfer of power to the regions can be accomplished quietly, without the need to alter the constitution.

Tuscany is subdivided into 10 provinces, which are in turn separated into a total of 287 comuni (town or city councils). If the regional government is the coordinator, the provincial government (consiglio provinciale) does all the nuts-and-bolts work, in conjunction with its town councils. These latter function much as local governments anywhere, providing local transport, civic services (such as rubbish collection and street cleaning) and so on. The town council's government (giunta comunale) is headed up by a sindaco or mayor.

ECONOMY

Tuscany hit its economic peak in the Middle Ages. The countryside supplied many of the raw materials needed by the cities, from farm produce and meat through to metals and marble. The cities in turn became, to a greater or lesser extent, thriving trade and banking centres.

Florence emerged as the front runner but, until crushed by its jealous rival, Siena too was a flourishing banking centre (the Monte dei Paschi di Siena bank remains one of Italy's senior financial institutions). Smaller towns also thrived. Prato, for instance, became and long remained an important wool and textile centre. Arezzo was famed for its gold.

The gradual eclipse of Florence as a power in the wake of the Renaissance brought overall decline to Tuscany too. By the 18th century, Tuscany had largely been reduced to a rural backwater. At the end of the 19th century, 57% of the workforce worked the land, mostly along traditional lines. The bulk of farmers were mezzadri, working the big landholders' land and taking a share of the profit.

Farm machinery had been tried out but largely failed to take off, partly due to the difficulty of the terrain in some areas. Even in the flatlands of the Maremma, drained and reclaimed over the previous two centuries, agriculture remained largely labour-intensive, mostly because landowners did not wish to invest in machinery and the farmers themselves could not afford to.

Industry was noticeable mostly by its absence, although mining (iron on Elba, marble in the Apuan Alps and copper, mercury, lignite and other raw materials around the region) benefited from a growing demand, especially from more rapidly industrialising countries abroad.

All told, however, Tuscany remained a predominantly agricultural economy until the mid-1950s. Even then, although small-scale manufacturing spread (the main areas being the suburbs of Florence, the north-western towns and Livorno on the coast), Tuscany never really experienced an industrial revolution.

Instead, the 'Tuscan model' was born. Amid much doom-mongering on the part of trade unions and business groups, small light-industrial firms sprang up and spread across the region. The pessimists, who might have hoped for massive industrialisation and phalanxes of smoke stacks, saw in this phenomenon a precarious and short-term solution to Tuscany's undoubted backwardness.

In fact, at a time when agriculture was in crisis and a flood of labour flowed towards the urban centres and the coast, this micro-industrial expansion saved Tuscany's bacon. In the period from the end of WWII to 1970, employment in the non-agricultural sector grew by 70%, industrialisation by 115%, and the Tuscan model spread to other parts of central and north-eastern Italy, leaving the heavy industry to the north-west.

As if in recognition of a centuries-old tradition of family business, small and medium-sized enterprises became the motor of Tuscany's economic regeneration. Tradition wasn't the only spur, however. Heavy state interference in big industry and a desire to sidestep militant unionism through diffusion of employment influenced the tendency.

For most observers, Tuscany was already a 'post-industrial' society by the end of the 1970s. For alongside the small-scale industry, the service sector was growing fast. Fashion, tourism, financial services and the like began to make up a growing slice of the income pie.

Tourism is one of the central pillars of the modern Tuscan economy. Other sources of income include the production and export of quality textiles, clothes and shoes, leather goods, furniture and jewellery. Of course quality agricultural products are also up there, including wine and olive oil. In Florence food-processing, rubber goods and chemicals are among the other light-industrial products to power the local economy.

Bearing in mind that at the close of WWII farming was still the centrepiece of the Tuscan economy, it is a measure of how radical change has been that now only 4.2%

of the Tuscan labour pool works the land. The light industrial sector takes up 34.3% while 61.5% are occupied in other sectors (principally tourism, banking and other services). Unemployment, at 12.3% of the total workforce of 1.5 million, remains a concern.

Total exports out of the region in 1997 were 30% higher than imports, but relied largely on the success of the fashion, textiles and leather industries.

POPULATION & PEOPLE

The total population of Tuscany was just over 3.5 million at the last count. Most live in the north-west in an area bounded by Florence, Livorno, Massa and Pistoia. Prato province is the most crowded, with 614 people per square kilometre.

By comparison, the centre, south and east have a good deal more breathing space. Siena province has 66 people per square kilometre, while Grosseto has just 48.

The make-up of the family unit is perhaps surprising in view of the traditional child-friendliness associated with Italians in general. In line with a national trend (Italy's birth rate is, with that of another kid-loving Catholic country, Spain, the lowest in Europe), 35% of Tuscan families are childless, while 8% have single parents. The 'traditional' model accounts for 57% of Tuscan families.

EDUCATION

Florence, Siena and Pisa are the main university centres in Tuscany. Pisa's university is the oldest, although it has had a chequered history. Galileo Galilei taught there for a while before getting better offers elsewhere.

Florence's main centre of study is the Università degli Studi di Firenze. It traces its history back to the Studium Generale established in 1321. Pope Clement VI granted this institution permission to issue full degrees in 1349, after the universities of Bologna and Paris. Italy's first theology faculty was also founded in Florence. In successive centuries the various faculties were split up and spread across the city and

Pisa. In 1860, the Istituto di Studi Pratici e di Perfezionamento (Institute for Practical Studies and Further Education) was established in Florence under the auspices of the newly united Italy. It was finally elevated officially to university status in 1923.

The other main university town is Siena, perhaps best known today for its Università per Stranieri (University for Foreigners; see also the Siena section later in this book).

Illiteracy is barely an issue in Tuscany. The national Italian average of 97% literacy can be accepted as standard for this part of the country too.

ARTS

The undisputed beauty of the Tuscan countryside is matched by the extraordinary artistic output of its people. From the Middle Ages through to the Renaissance in particular, Tuscany's cities were hives of such creativity that it is hardly surprising they have not been able to match, in either quality or quantity, the output of those troubled but glorious centuries. From the visual arts to literature, although less so in music, the Tuscans left an indelible mark on the culture of Italy, and indeed all Europe.

Architecture

Etruscan & Roman Comparatively few ancient reminders of Etruscan and Roman civilisation remain today in Tuscany.

Of the Etruscans, the most common reminders of their presence are tombs scattered about the Tuscan countryside, particularly in the south. A rare exception is the archaeological site of Poggio Civitate, near Murlo (south of Siena), consisting of a couple of buildings – one dating back to the 7th century BC (the site is closed to visitors).

Of the tombs, two general types emerge. The first is cut deep into a rock wall, with a steep declining walkway or steps to the entrance. The tomb is generally formed of an atrium and burial chamber. Others created more in the open were surrounded by a low wall and covered with a low dome or vault, above which was heaped a mound of earth. Good examples of both can be seen in Populonia, on the coast just north of Piombino.

Another outstanding and well known site is Sorano, in southern Tuscany.

It is perhaps more surprising that so little evidence of Roman times remains. In Volterra, Arezzo and Fiesole you can admire Roman amphitheatres but that's about it. Virtually nothing remains of Roman Florentia (modern-day Florence).

Romanesque Out of the confusion of the collapse of the Roman Empire and the early medieval centuries of barbarian invasion and foreign rule, several fairly simple building styles emerged in Italy.

Of course we are talking about monumental buildings – churches, government palaces and mansions for the rich and powerful. Your average citizen lived in flimsy, precarious wooden housing so utterly dwarfed by the solid stone and/or brick public edifices that they probably could not conceive what it might be like to live in such luxury.

Byzantine models, drawing on examples in Constantinople and the eastern empire, which in turn looked to their classical Roman heritage, made little impression on Tuscany. The Romanesque style, which emerged in the northern Lombard plains of Italy, was characterised by a beguiling simplicity. Few nonreligious buildings from this period have survived, either in Italy or anywhere else in Europe.

The standard church ground plan, generally composed of a nave and two aisles, no transept and between one and five apses, topped by a simple dome, followed that used in Roman-era basilicas. Initially at any rate, churches tended to be bereft of decoration except for the semi-circular apses and arches above doorways and windows. Such churches were most commonly accompanied by a free-standing square-based bell tower, also adorned with layers of semi-circular arched windows.

In Tuscany, the early rediscovery of that favourite of Roman building materials, marble, led to a rather more florid decorative style, the best examples of which you can see in Pisa and Lucca, to the north-west of Florence. The key characteristics of the

Tuscan variant are the use of two-tone marble banding and complex rows of columns and loggias in the facade. In Carrara the cathedral, begun in the 11th century, was one of the first medieval buildings to be constructed entirely of marble from the Apuan Alps.

The Battistero in Florence, embellished in its marble casing, is a fine example of the pure lines of the Romanesque style. Compare it with the Gothic mass of the Duomo next door. Also in Florence, the Chiesa di San Miniato al Monte is a splendid example of the style. The Pieve di Santa Maria in Arezzo is another fine version, although in this instance lacking the refinement of a marble facing.

The Tuscan countryside and its villages are littered with Romanesque churches of greater or lesser beauty – some are mentioned in the appropriate regional chapters of this guide.

Gothic The transition across Europe from Romanesque to the massive forms of the Gothic was uniformly spectacular but extraordinarily varied in its results. Compared with their humble Romanesque predecessors the Gothic versions are colossal. The process began in the Île de France area around Paris, where the first truly Gothic churches were built from the 12th century – at a time when elsewhere in Europe Romanesque was still the predominant style.

The one element most Gothic structures have in common is their great height. Soaring structures, it was felt, would lift mortal eyes to the heavens and at the same time remind people of their smallness compared with the greatness of God. These complex structures were perfected using pillars, columns, arches and vaulting of various kinds to support high ceilings. Rather than relying on the solidity of mass and building thick, heavy walls, priority was given to an almost diaphanous light pouring though tall pointed windows. The whole thing was topped by an almost obsessive desire to decorate. These churches are bedecked with pinnacles, statues, gargoyles and all sorts of baubles – the busier the better.

Most of us, when thinking of Gothic have in mind the improbable lace stone work of the great Gothic cathedrals o northern Europe, from the Notre Dame churches of Paris and Amiens to the pow erful hulk of the Cologne Dom in Germany or the great churches of English Gothic However, examples of that northern European style are few and far between in Italy and non-existent in Tuscany.

Among Tuscany's great Gothic churches are Florence and Siena cathedrals, along with Florence's Santa Croce and Santa Maria Novella churches, built for the dominant preaching orders of the time, the Franciscans and Dominicans respectively Although both the cathedrals are full of rich artworks, they are architecturally relatively spartan inside. Outside, they are both layered in rich marble decoration, which had become something of a Tuscan trademark. In terms of volume they are every bit as impressive as their northern counterparts.

Florence's Duomo was designed by Arnolfo di Cambio (1245–1302), the first great master builder in Florentine architectural history. Striking because it is something of a one-off is Arnolfo's Palazzo Vecchio in Florence. Built of pietra forte (literally 'hard stone') with the rusticated surface typical of many later grand buildings in Florence, it is one of the most imposing of government buildings of the medieval Italian city states.

It is easily matched by Siena's Palazzo Pubblico, which with its slender Torre del Mangia is one of the finest examples of civil Gothic construction in Tuscany. Built at the end of the 13th and the beginning of the 14th centuries, this elegant seat of Sienese government was expanded in the following decades.

Bad Boy Brunelleschi Enter Filippo Brunelleschi (1377–1446), one of the hotter tempers in the history of Italian architecture. After failing to win the 1401 competition to design a set of bronze doors for Florence's Battistero (see later in this chapter), Brunelleschi left in a creative huff for Rome. His intention had been to study and continue with sculpture, but his interests moved to mathematics and architecture. He and his sculptor pal Donatello spent much of their time taking measurements of ancient Roman monuments, research that later would come to spectacular fruition. Locals, however, thought they were using bizarre divining methods to look for buried treasure!

Brunelleschi launched the architectural branch of the Renaissance in Florence. It manifested itself in a rediscovery of simplicity and purity in classical building, with great attention paid to perspective and harmonious distribution of space and volume. His single most remarkable achievement was solving the conundrum of the dome in Florence's Duomo. He proposed to build the octagonal-based dome without the aid of scaffolding, unheard of at the time. Brunelleschi's double-skinned dome, raised in sections, was the greatest feat of its kind since ancient times. In later years Michelangelo, when commissioned to create the dome for St Peter's (San Pietro) in Rome, observed with undisguised admiration, *'Io farò la sorella, già più gran ma non più bella'* (I'll make its (the Brunelleschi dome's) sister, bigger yes, but no more beautiful).

That feat alone was tremendous but Brunelleschi's importance goes beyond the splendid dome. He 'created' the role of architect. Rather than act as a foreman, guiding construction as it progressed and to some extent making it up as he went along, Brunelleschi devised formulae of perspective and balance that allowed him to create a completed concept at the drawing board.

Other examples of Brunelleschi's keen sense of proportion, all in Florence, are the portico of the Ospedale degli Innocenti (1419), considered the earliest work of the Florentine Renaissance, the Sagrestia Vecchia (Old Sacristy) in San Lorenzo (1428) and the Cappella dei Pazzi in Santa Croce (1430).

Perhaps more importantly, Brunelleschi was also called upon to design the Basilica di San Lorenzo (1420) and the Basilica di Santo Spirito (designed in 1436). A quick wander inside both might lead you to think they are identical. The use of Corinthian columns, simple arches, a coffered ceiling over the wide nave (merely painted in Santo Spirito) and two-tone (grey pietra serena, literally meaning 'tranquil stone', and white plaster on the trim) colouring are common elements, but closer inspection soon reveals differences. Brunelleschi had planned for Santo Spirito to be lined with semi-circular chapels jutting out into the square around it, but these were walled in by his successors. Santo Spirito is an altogether heavier, more massive church in its feel, while San Lorenzo oozes a light elegance.

Brunelleschi more than once flounced out of meetings and dropped projects if he did not get his own way. But it was he who launched a new era in building design and philosophy, so he can probably be forgiven his short fuse.

Florence & the Renaissance Brunelleschi did little outside Florence and, under the patronage of the Medici and other senior families, it was in Florence that the Tuscan Renaissance flourished. Not that things weren't happening elsewhere in the region, but the growing power of Florence in the coming centuries effectively meant that most of the artistic impulses came from what was to become the capital.

Other cities in fact remained immune to the Renaissance for some time. Well into the 15th century, for example, Siena's architects and artists were still well rooted in the Gothic.

It was in Florence, thus, that the Renaissance truly took off. It is generally accepted that Cosimo de' Medici commissioned Michelozzo di Bartolomeo Michelozzi (1396–1472) to build a new residence in keeping with the family's importance. Three hefty storeys, with the air of a fortress, are topped by a solid roof with eaves jutting far out from the walls. The lowest storey features rustication (which can also be seen on the Palazzo Vecchio). This describes the rough-hewn, protruding blocks of stone used to build it, as opposed to the smoothed stone of the upper storeys.

This set the tone for civil building in Florence.

The acclaimed theorist of Renaissance architecture and art was Leon Battista Alberti (1404–72). Born in Genoa into an exiled Florentine family, he contributed the facade of the Palazzo Rucellai, a development on the style started with Michelozzo.

Other Renaissance palaces represent variations on the style and lend Florence its uniquely stern yet elegant feel. One example is the palace of the Strozzi family, designed by Benedetto da Maiano (1442–97) with facade work by Giuliano da Sangallo (1445–1516). This particular aspect of Florentine Renaissance building is echoed in buildings in other parts of Tuscany, especially the nearby northern towns of Prato, Pistoia and Pisa – and often many years after the Renaissance had been left behind.

Francesco di Giorgio (1439–1502) was about the only architect of any note to come out of Siena during the Renaissance. An accomplished painter and sculptor as well, his only lasting building is the Chiesa di Santa Maria del Calcinaio, a few kilometres outside Cortona. His was an original vision – he dropped the use of pillars and columns to separate aisles from a central nave. Instead, the building is a solid two-storey construction with tabernacle windows on the second level. Had this been a private mansion, the upper storey would have been the *piano nobile*, or nobles' storey.

Michelangelo Born in to a poor family, Michelangelo Buonarroti (1475–1564) got a lucky break early on, entering the Medici household as a privileged student of painting and sculpture. In later years he also turned his attention to building design, although his architectural activities in Florence were not extensive. Indeed, much of his greatest work was done in Rome, where the majesty of the High Renaissance left even Florence gasping in the dust.

In Florence, Michelangelo worked on the Sagrestia Nuova (New Sacristy) in the Basilica di San Lorenzo, intended as part of the funerary chapels for the Medici family. Although not completed as planned, this was as close as Michelangelo got to realising one of his architectural–sculptural whims.

Another of Michelangelo's tasks in the same church was the grand staircase and entrance hall for the Biblioteca Medicea Laurenziana (Laurentian Library). Michelangelo never saw it completed, as he returned to Rome. It is a startling late Renaissance creation, with columns recessed into the walls (and thus deprived of their natural supporting function) and other architectural oddities since seen as precursors of Mannerism.

Mannerism The High Renaissance ended around 1520. Certainly by 1527, with the sack of Rome, it was all over, if only because war and suffering had depleted the funds and snuffed out the desire to continue creating in such quantity.

What follows is generally called Mannerism, although this intermediate phase between the Renaissance and baroque is not easily defined. For many, Michelangelo's work in San Lorenzo is a clear precursor to the Mannerist period. For others, the Mannerists were a fairly unimaginative lot, fiddling around the edges of what had been the core of Renaissance thinking in architecture without making substantive innovations.

Antonio da Sangallo il Giovane (1485–1546), son of another Florentine architect and sculptor, Antonio da Sangallo il Vecchio (1455–1534), worked mostly in Rome, although he returned briefly to Florence to build the Fortezza da Basso in 1534 for Alessandro de' Medici. His father had worked on several projects in Rome and around Tuscany, including the Chiesa della Madonna di San Biagio and several civic buildings in Montepulciano, as well as the Fortezza Vecchia in Livorno.

Bartolomeo Ammannati (1511–92) expanded Florence's Palazzo Pitti into a suburban palace for the Medici dukes and designed the Ponte Santa Trinita. He also had a hand in the design of the Giardino di Boboli.

Arezzo-born Giorgio Vasari (1511–74)

left his mark in Florence with the creation of the Uffizi and the Corridoio Vasariano that links Palazzo Vecchio with Palazzo Pitti across the Arno. Bernardo Buontalenti (1536–1608) succeeded Vasari as architect to the Grand Duke of Tuscany. He designed the Forte di Belvedere and the Palazzo Nonfinito on Via del Proconsolo, which differs from Renaissance predecessors principally in decorative flounces on the facade.

Don't Baroque the Boat The 17th century brought a construction slowdown throughout Tuscany. This was the era of baroque, which often had more impact on decor than on architectural design. At its most extreme, particularly in Rome, such decoration was sumptuous to the point of giddiness – all curvaceous statuary, twisting pillars and assorted baubles. These are the exception rather than the norm in Tuscany, but some excellent examples of the style can be found in Florence, like the inside of the Basilica di Santa Maria del Carmine. Other good examples of the style are the Chiesa di San Gaetano and the facade for the Chiesa di Ognissanti. The former, finished by Gherardo Silvani (1579–1675), is considered the finest piece of baroque in Florence and a demonstration of the restraint typical of the city.

Occasionally you will bump into bursts of baroque while touring around the region. Some of the villas near Lucca fall into this category, as does the cathedral in Pescia.

Urban Renewal The first tentative moves towards urban renewal in some Tuscan cities came early in the 19th century. Under Napoleon's representative, Elisa Baciocchi, for instance, Lucca's walls were turned into the velvet green garden area surrounding the old city that you see today.

In Florence, public works programmes also got under way. The space around the southern flank of the Duomo was cleared and fronted by neoclassical buildings. The architect behind that project was Gaetano Baccani (1792–1867). East and west of the town centre two new bridges went up on the Arno, the Ponte San Niccolò and the Ponte Vittoria. French engineers raised them and in so doing introduced to Florence the use of metals in construction.

By the end of the century the walls had been torn down and replaced by a series of *viali* (boulevards) that still carry the bulk of the city's traffic today. Perhaps worst of all, the core of old Florence around what had been the Roman forum was flattened to make way for the grandiloquent Piazza della Repubblica in the 1890s.

The Mercato Centrale (finished in 1874) is a rare Florentine example of the late-19th-century passion for iron-and-glass structures, designed by Giuseppe Mengoni (1829–77), the Bologna-born architect responsible for Milan's Galleria.

The 20th Century To the Italians, the Art Nouveau style that took hold of the architectural imagination in Europe from the 1880s through to the interwar period is known as Liberty (after the London store of that name). Examples of it are dotted about the main cities of Tuscany, although often they are rather modest reminders. In central Florence one of the best examples is the Casa Galleria by Giovanni Michelazzi (1879–1920) at Borgo Ognissanti 26.

Viareggio is crammed with Liberty buildings. In an area stretching back four or five blocks from the seashore the buff can feast on forty or so edifices with at least some Liberty traces.

Elsewhere the pickings are slimmer and often consist of little more than a few modest decorative leftovers. The determined Art Nouveau hunter can turn up a few items of interest in all the main towns of Tuscany. To help in the process, you can pick up a pink booklet available in tourist offices around the region, *Le Stagioni del Liberty in Toscana* (available in several languages).

The Fascist era also left its stamp, especially in the train station and the main soccer stadium in Florence, but otherwise the 20th century has hardly been inspirational in Tuscany. Cities and towns like Livorno, which were heavily damaged during WWII, were generally at the receiving end of an unsympathetic postwar reconstruction boom. Florence, as Tuscany's capital, has been plagued by uncontrolled urban sprawl, particularly to the west. Nothing could be further from the ideals of Brunelleschi's finest structures than the soulless, fast-buck housing and light industrial zones that now virtually fill the area between Florence and Prato.

Painting

The painting to emerge in medieval Europe – and Tuscany was no exception – was not so much a response to an aesthetic need, as a means of keeping alive in the minds of the faithful the stories of the Bible and teachings of the church. Art was devotional and instructive, as most people, even among the wealthiest classes, were illiterate or as near as dammit. For this reason, as you will soon come to notice the more you study the paintings that fill churches and galleries across Tuscany, many themes became standard and crop up repeatedly. The bulk of Romanesque, Byzantine and Gothic art was commissioned (although not always paid for) by the Church for religious institutions. The clergy generally had a clear idea of what they wanted and gave precise instructions to painters. The latter were viewed much as tradespeople are today. There was little exaltation of their skills and until the dawn of the Renaissance few artists even signed their work.

As greater individuality and an aesthetic appreciation of painting, apart from its didactic or devotional purposes, emerged with the Renaissance, so its practitioners gained in social standing. In Florence especially, but also elsewhere in Tuscany and beyond, lay people began to commission art, either for public places or their own homes. This promoted a broadening of themes, but even through the Renaissance and beyond, much of the output remained faithful to a series of frequently stock religious icons. Innovation was not always easy under such conditions.

Still, other themes developed too. Battle scenes, portraits (generally busts) and scenes from classical mythology gained ground during the Renaissance.

Renaissance Florence was the uncontested centre of Tuscan art, and indeed for a while could be said to have held primacy in all Italy. With the passing of the Renaissance, Florence and Tuscany as a whole stagnated and the great revolutions in Western art, whether in painting or sculpture, took place on other stages. That remains the case to this day.

Antiquity It is difficult to talk of 'Etruscan art' and perhaps more appropriate to view it

Oh Madonna!

As so much of the art of medieval and Renaissance Europe falls into distinct thematic groups, the titles of many paintings in particular are nearly always the same. You will rarely see such stock titles translated into English while in Tuscany, so a handful of clues follows.

A *Crocifissione* (Crucifixion) represents the crucifixion of Christ, one of the most common subjects of religious art. Another is the *Deposizione* (Deposition), which depicts the taking down of the body of Christ from the cross, while the *Pietà*, a particularly popular subject for sculptors, shows the lifeless body of Christ in the arms of his followers – the characters can vary, but the theme remains the same. Before all the nastiness began, Christ managed to have an *Ultima Cena* or Last Supper with the Apostles.

Perhaps the most favoured subject is the *Madonna col Bambino/Bimbo* (Virgin Mary with Christ Child). The variations on this theme are legion. Sometimes they are depicted alone, sometimes with various *santi* (saints), *angeli* (angels) and other figures. The *Annunciazione* (Annunciation) is yet another standard episode, when the Angel Gabriel announces to Mary the strange honour that has been bestowed upon her. When the big event occurred, lots of people, including the *Magi* (Wise Men) came to participate in the *Adorazione* (Adoration) of the newly born Christ.

as art created in Etruscan territory. What has been preserved comes largely from tombs. Painted ceramics, statues and the like from around the 8th century BC are all marked by an eastern predilection for geometrical designs.

Greek influence was also strong, particularly along the southern coast of Etruria (modern Tuscany and into Lazio), where there was direct contact with Greek traders. Fresco painting in tombs seems to have started in Tarquinia (Lazio) and was later developed in the Chiusi area. It is worth noting that the greatest concentration of Greek ceramics found in Italy turned up on Etruscan territory.

As Roman expansion gathered pace, Etruscan artistic activity declined, although it knew one final creative spurt in the last two centuries BC. The Romans were a rather coarse lot who began to embark on artistic endeavours only around the 2nd century BC. Heavily influenced by the Etruscans and, hence, indirectly by the Greeks, there was little original about their early output. In any case, precious little has been left to us in Tuscany. The great frescoes of Pompei or mosaics of Roman towns from Sicily to Syria are but a distant dream.

Emerging from the Middle Ages Not until the 13th century does any original artistic activity seem to get underway again in Tuscany. As the cities freed themselves from imperial or feudal control in the course of the 12th century, so art seems to have begun to free itself from the inherited rigidity of Romanesque and Byzantine norms.

Lagging behind sculptural activity (described later in the chapter), the earliest surviving paintings appeared in churches ranging from Lucca's San Michele in Foro to Santa Croce in Florence. Other works began to appear in Arezzo, Siena and smaller centres such as Pescia. The Florentine Coppo di Marcovaldo (c.1225–80), imprisoned in Siena, ended up painting his *Madonna del Bordone* in the Chiesa di Santa Maria dei Servi before moving on to Orvieto and Pistoia.

In Tuscany Pisa was in the ascendant. Master of Sardinia and a busy sea trade port, Pisa was more open to external influences and artistic interchange than inland cities such as Florence. The first artist of note to make an impact in Florence was Cimabue (c.1240–1302). He began in Pisa but later moved all over Tuscany. Vasari identifies him as the catalyst for change in painting from the rigidity of Gothic and Byzantine models. In Florence, his *Maestà* (in the Uffizi) amply demonstrates the transition from Byzantine-style iconography to a fresh exploration of expression and lifelike dimension.

Giotto di Bondone (c.1266–1337), born in the Mugello north of Florence, was the key figure in the artistic revolution that was gathering pace in the run-up to the Renaissance explosion. Most of his Florentine contemporaries were to some degree influenced by him, and his is one of the pivotal names in the Italian artistic pantheon.

In Giotto the move from the symbolic, other-worldly representations of Italo-Byzantine and Gothic religious art to something more real, more directly inspired by observed truth than the desire to teach 'truths', is clear. His figures are essentially human and express feeling, something alien to earlier phases of art in Christian Europe.

He is better known for his work in other towns, such as Assisi (Basilica di San Francesco) and Padua (Cappella degli Scrovegni). However, he left behind several works in Florence, among the most important of which are the frescoes in the Peruzzi and Bardi chapels in the Basilica di Santa Croce. Fresco painting involves painting directly onto wet plaster, a tricky business.

The Sienese School Although the focus of artistic life in Tuscany was already shifting to Florence, its southern rival Siena enjoyed a brief period of glory.

Guido da Siena (active in second half of 13th century), who seems to have been influenced by Coppo di Marcovaldo, left behind few works. The only signed one was the *Madonna col Bambino* in the Palazzo Pubblico.

The only artist in Siena to hold a candle to Giotto was Duccio di Buoninsegna (c.1255–1318). Although still much attached to the Byzantine school, he mixed it with Gothic ideas and introduced a degree of fluidity and expressiveness that have led some to compare him with Cimabue. Various examples of his work can be seen in Siena cathedral and Florence's Uffizi. Duccio's star pupil was Simone Martini (c.1284–1344). Perhaps his most celebrated work is the *Annunciazione*, created for the cathedral in Siena but now hanging in the Uffizi.

Other artists of note in Siena included the brothers Pietro (c.1290–c.1348) and Ambrogio Lorenzetti (?–c.1348). Both worked in Siena and elsewhere – Pietro was particularly active in Assisi. Ambrogio's best-known work is the startling *Effetti del Buon e del Cattivo Governo* (Allegories of Good and Bad Government) in Siena's Palazzo Pubblico.

As you trawl through the palazzi and galleries of Siena, it will sooner or later hit you that, for all the beauty of the masterpieces by Siena's greatest artists, they seem to stand still in time. While the Renaissance and subsequent movements gripped Florence, Siena remained supremely indifferent and plugged on with largely Byzantine and Gothic models. You can see this in the work of such painters as Taddeo di Bartolo (1362–1422) and even Giovanni di Paolo (1395–1482), who remained anchored in Late Gothic while in Florence people such as Uccello, Verrocchio and Filippo Lippi were turning painting on its head.

Giotto's Successors Confirmation of Giotto's influence comes in the work of several other painters active at the same time. Maso di Banco's (active prior to 1348) *Storie di San Silvestro* (Stories of St Sylvester) series (in Florence's Basilica di Santa Croce) reflects in its luminosity and simplicity the long shadow of his master, Giotto. The human faces also have a fullness and naturalness of expression that one might expect from Giotto, although they retain a Gothic stiffness in movement.

Andrea di Cione Orcagna (active from 1343 to 1368), represents something of a Gothic throwback. His most important remaining works are the tabernacle and other statuary inside the late Gothic Orsanmichele and a polyptych in the Basilica di Santa Maria Novella. Flattened profiles and garish colouring fly in the face of the groundwork laid by Giotto.

Indeed, Gothic was anything but dead as the new century dawned and the two tendencies appeared in direct competition. One of Gothic's principal exponents in the first quarter of the 15th century in Florence was the Sienese painter Lorenzo Monaco (c.1370–c.1424). Several of his works are in the Uffizi.

Il Quattrocento & the Renaissance

The young Masaccio (1401–28) can probably be given a good deal of the credit for the definitive break with Gothic in Florentine painting. Born in an Arno village at the dawn of the 15th century (what the Italians call the Quattrocento, or the 'four hundreds'), his brief but dynamic career made him to painting what his contemporaries, the older Brunelleschi and Donatello, were to architecture and sculpture. You don't need to look long and hard at his Florentine masterpieces, such as his frescoes in the Cappella Brancacci (Basilica di Santa Maria del Carmine), to recognise his genius. His best-known image, the *Cacciata dei Progenitori* (Expulsion) in the Cappella Brancacci, depicts all the anguish and shame of Adam and, especially, Eve. Such raw and believable human emotion was a novelty in painting.

Following in Masaccio's footsteps were two masters who in temperament could not have been more different from one another. Fra Angelico (c.1395–1455), a Dominican monk later known as Beato (Blessed) Angelico for his noted piety, for a while dominated the Florentine art world. His work, much of it done for the Convento di San Marco, is suffused with a diaphanous light aimed at emphasising the good in humankind. Although a friar, Fra Filippo Lippi (c.1406–69) had an appetite for sex, drink and general carousing that left him the father of two by a nun. Fra Filippo left some fine pieces behind in Florence. A *Madonna col Bambino* in the Uffizi and another in Palazzo Pitti (in the Sala di Prometeo) demonstrate his mastery of light and shadow, a weighty reality about the characters and an eye for detail.

A strange bird was Paolo Uccello (1397–1475). More preoccupied with perspective studies than making a living, Uccello did manage to crank out a few lasting pieces. They include the *Diluvio* (Deluge) fresco in the Basilica di Santa Maria Novella and the *Battaglia di San Romano* (Battle of San Romano) done for the Medici family and now (in part) in the Uffizi.

Antonio del Pollaiolo (c.1431–98) had a predilection for scenes of tension or struggle. His *Ercole e Anteo* (Hercules and Anteus), now in the Uffizi, amply demonstrates the emphasis on human movement, expressed with a freedom rarely witnessed until then.

The painting of Andrea del Verrocchio (1435–88), who is perhaps better known for his sculpture (see later in this chapter), presents difficulties as it is often impossible to distinguish his work from that of his pupils. Among the latter was Leonardo da Vinci, with whom Verrocchio did the *Battesimo di Cristo* (now in the Uffizi).

Born in the remote south-east Tuscan town of Sansepolcro, Piero della Francesca (c.1415–92) went to Florence to learn from his predecessors and contemporaries but did the bulk of his work in his own neck of the woods, particularly in Arezzo and the Montefeltro court in Urbino. His *Leggenda della Vera Croce* (Legend of the True Cross) fresco cycle in the Chiesa di San Francesco in Arezzo is a masterpiece.

Luca Signorelli (1450–1523), born in Cortona, was a pupil of Piero della Francesca. He went on to become one of the great figures of the late Renaissance, specialising above all in grand, complex works, of which his fresco cycle in the cathedral in Orvieto (Umbria) is the uncontested masterpiece.

Sandro Botticelli (1445–1510) is remembered most for works such as *Nascita di Venere* (Birth of Venus) and *Primavera* (Spring), both in the Uffizi. In these and other paintings of their ilk, wispy, ethereal figures seem to float serenely across the canvas in an idealised evocation of classical Greece.

Fra Filippo's son, Filippino Lippi (1457–1504), worked in Botticelli's workshop for a time but Lippi was more directly influenced by Leonardo da Vinci and Flemish artists. His frescoes of *Storie di San Giovanni Evangelista e San Filippo* (Stories of St John and St Philip) in the Cappella Strozzi in the Basilica di Santa Maria Novella reveal a move away from the humanist ideals of Quattrocento painting.

Leonardo da Vinci Born in a small town west of Florence, Leonardo da Vinci (1452–1519), stands apart from all his contemporaries. How do you categorise a man who hardly belonged in his own time? Painter, sculptor, architect, scientist and engineer, Leonardo brought to all fields of knowledge and art an original touch, often opening up whole new branches of thought. If one had to sum up what made him tick, it might be 'seeing is believing'. In the thousands of pages of notes he left behind, he repeatedly extolled the virtue of sight and observation. Paying little heed to received wisdoms, either Christian or classical, Leonardo barrelled along with unquenchable curiosity.

All his studies took up much of Leonardo's time, but he found plenty more to devote to what he saw as the noblest art, painting. Leonardo did much of his work outside Florence (he stayed in Milan for 20 years). One of his outstanding early works, the *Annunciazione*, now in the Uffizi (under restoration at the time of writing), already revealed his concern with light and shadow.

Michelangelo While Leonardo was in Milan, Michelangelo Buonarroti (1475–1564) was asserting himself as a rival painter, albeit of a very different ilk. In contrast to Leonardo's smoky, veiled images, Michelangelo demonstrated a greater clarity of line. As a young lad he was taken in by Lorenzo de' Medici, who could spot talent when it presented itself. His greatest painting project was the ceiling of the Sistine Chapel in Rome. In Florence relatively little of his can be seen, but the *Doni Madonna* in the Uffizi provides stunning insight into his craft. Details of his sculpture are given later in this chapter.

High Renaissance to Mannerism Fra Bartolomeo (1472–1517) stands out for such paintings as the *Apparizione della Vergina a San Bernardo* (Vision of St Bernard), now in the Galleria dell'Accademia, Florence. A follower of Savonarola, Fra Bartolomeo's is a clearly devotional art, with virtually all incidental detail eliminated in favour of the central subject. Piero di Cosimo (c.1461–1521), on the other hand, was interested in nature and mythology. Several of his works can be seen in Florence's Palazzo Pitti.

The torment associated with the likes of Jacopo Pontormo (1494–1556) makes his work emblematic of Mannerism, that troubled search for a freer expression. In his

The World Turns

'Eppur si muove', Galileo is supposed to have muttered after having been compelled to recant his teachings on astronomy before the Inquisition in Rome in 1633. 'And yet it *does* move.' He was referring to the Earth, whose exalted position at the centre of the universe he so inconveniently maintained was a falsehood. The Earth, along with other planets, rotated around the Sun, just as Copernicus had claimed.

As long ago as 1616 Galileo had been ordered not to push this theory, which conservative Vatican elements not overly well disposed to the 'new learning' saw as a potential threat to the very Church. If teachings long held dear about the position of the world in God's universe were condemned as balderdash, there was a threat that the Church could be subject to the kind of unforgiving inquiry that Galileo and others were engaged in to understand better the world around them. The growing insistence on humankind's capacity to reveal what makes things tick, rather than simply remaining awestruck by the divine majesty of it all, was singularly inconvenient to those intent on maintaining the Church's position of pre-eminence in worldly and spiritual affairs.

Galileo was born in Pisa on 15 February 1564, the son of a musician. He received his early education at the monastery of Vallombrosa near Florence and later studied medicine at the University of Pisa. During his time there he became fascinated by mathematics and the study of motion, so much so that he is regarded as the founder of experimental physics. He became professor of mathematics in Pisa and then moved to Padua for 18 years to teach and research there.

Having heard of the invention of the telescope in 1609, he set about making his own version, the first used to scan the night skies. In the coming years he made discoveries that led him to confirm Copernicus' theory that the planets revolve around the Sun. In 1610 he moved to Florence, where the Grand Duke had offered him permanent residence to continue his research. Galileo had many supporters, but not enough to prevent his works on the subject being placed on the index of banned books in 1616.

For the next seven years he continued his studies in Florence, where he lived mainly at Bellosguardo. The 1616 edict declaring his teachings on astronomy blasphemous was softened in 1624 to the extent that he was given permission to write an 'objective study' of the various proposed models. His study was a triumph of argumentation in favour of his own theory, culminating nevertheless in the obligatory disclaimer that remained imposed on him. It was in the wake of this that the Inquisition summoned him to Rome in 1632. From then on he was confined to internal exile in Florence until his death in 1642. Until his last days, even after blindness had beset him in 1637, he continued to study, experiment, correspond with other scientists across Europe and write books. He lies buried in the Basilica di Santa Croce.

Visitazione (Visitation) in the SS Annunziata in Florence, the figures seem almost furtive or preoccupied.

Il Rosso Fiorentino (the Florentine Redhead; 1494–1540) also worked on the SS Annunziata frescoes and several other projects elsewhere in Tuscany before heading to Rome. In his works, too, one detects a similar note of disquiet, although his style is different. The flashes of contrasting light and dark create an unreal effect in his characters.

A student of Pontormo, Il Bronzino (1503–72) begins in his later works to move away from Mannerism. Employed by the Medici family, his approach lacked the agitation evident in his master. Rather he fixed images in a static fashion, reflecting perhaps his employers' desire to convey the sureness of their sovereignty, however spurious. His greatest achievement was the chapel done for Eleonora de Toledo in the Palazzo Vecchio.

Down in Siena, Domenico Beccafumi (c.1484–1551) was perhaps one of the leading exponents of Tuscan Mannerism. Among his better known works, the *Caduta degli Angeli* (Fall of the Angels) is replete with disquiet and movement – to the point of blurring his images. It can be seen in the Pinacoteca Nazionale in Siena. Around the same time, Il Sodoma (1477–1549) was producing works of an altogether smokier style. Some critics see in him a follower, initially at least, of Leonardo da Vinci and later of Raffaello – his paintings have a matt quality suffused with Mediterranean light. You can compare several of his works with those of Beccafumi in Siena's Pinacoteca Nazionale.

The works of Giorgio Vasari (1511–74) and his students litter Florence, some better than others. His particular boast seems to have been speed – with an army of helpers he was able to plough through commissions for frescoes and paintings with great alacrity, if not always with equal aplomb. He is perhaps most important in the history of Renaissance art as the author of *Lives of the Artists*, a rich compendium of fact and fiction about Italian art up to his own day.

Vasari & co were largely responsible for the decoration of the Palazzo Vecchio.

Baroque & Neoclassicism Flocks of artists continued to work in Florence as the new century wore on, but few of enormous note. Giovanni da San Giovanni (1592–1636) was the leading light of the first half of the century, and some of his frescoes remain in the Palazzo Pitti. One much underestimated painter of the period was Cecco Bravo (1601–60), whose canvasses combine Florentine tastes of the period with a rediscovery of the soft nebulous colours of Venice's Titian.

The arrival of artists from out of town, such as Pietro da Cortona and the Neapolitan Luca Giordano (1634–1705), brought the winds of baroque taste to Florence. Where the Mannerists had searched, often rather stiffly, for ways of breaking with Renaissance conventions, the baroque bounded headlong into a hedonistic riot of colour and movement, leaving any semblance of reality behind.

At any rate, Florence was by now no longer the centre of artistic creation it had been.

The Macchiaioli The Florentine art scene remained sterile until the first signs of Impressionism wafted across from Paris, around the middle of the 19th century. In Florence anti-academic artists declared that painting real life scenes was the only way forward. Their Macchiaioli movement lasted until the late 1860s and received its name (which could be translated as the 'stainers' or 'blotchers') in a disparaging newspaper article in 1862.

The Macchiaioli released Florentine, indeed Italian, art from the sclerosis that had set in over the previous century. They abandoned the religious and historical themes to which painting, no matter how innovative in style, had largely been bound for centuries. Then they dropped chiaroscuro effects in favour of playful use of colour plus light and/or colour plus shade.

Although the hub of their activity was Florence, a good number of the Macchiaioli had come from all over Italy. You can see some of the works of various of these artists, such as Livorno-born Giovanni Fattori (1825–1908), Neapolitan Giuseppe Abbati (1836–68) and the Emilian painter Silvestro Lega (1826–95), in Florence's Galleria d'Arte Moderna.

By 1870 the movement had run out of steam. Splinter tendencies emerged separating the realism of subject from questions of style.

20th Century Florence's decline as a centre of artistic ferment seems to have been compounded during the 20th century. Futurism had little impact here in the years before WWI, while the Novecento movement, which preached a return to order in the wake of various avant-garde tendencies, also bore precious little fruit in Tuscany.

One of the few Tuscan stars of the 20th century international art scene was undoubtedly the Livorno-born Amedeo Modigliani (1884–1920), although he spent most of his adult life in Paris. His portraits and nudes are often a celebration of strong colour and are the best-known part of his opus.

Sculpture
Etruscans & Romans Although bronze sculptures found in Etruscan tombs go back to the 8th century BC, production of greater quality and in increased quantity dates to the 5th century BC. It is to this period that such fine pieces as the Arezzo *Chimera* (now housed in the Museo Archeologico in Florence) can be dated. Another good place to see Etruscan bronze work is Volterra.

Although Etruscan cities began to fall to Rome about this time, it took centuries to extinguish local culture completely. From the 4th century BC onwards, the Etruscans were making stone and, later, terracotta funerary urns and sarcophagi. You can see a fine collection in Florence's Museo Archeologico. A close look at the relief sculptures on these reveals that influences from the Eastern Mediterranean and even beyond seem still to have made their way across to Etruria.

As with painting, the Romans took most of their cues from elsewhere, initially from the Greek-influenced Etruscans and later directly from the Greeks. Comparatively little has been found in Tuscany. Much of the Roman statuary collected by the Medici (and on show in the Uffizi and the Loggia della Signoria in Florence) came from Rome. In the archaeological museums of Florence, Siena, Arezzo and elsewhere you can see some modest examples of Roman bronze and stone statuary.

Medieval Sculptors As the straightforward simplicity of Romanesque began to give way to the grandeur of Gothic, so the first of the Tuscan master sculptors began to emerge.

Nicola Pisano (c.1215–c.1278), who left behind some of his best work in the Battistero in Pisa and the pulpit in Siena cathedral, was something of a master to all who followed in Tuscany. Despite his nickname (Pisano) he was actually born in southern Italy. He was succeeded by his son Giovanni Pisano (c.1248–c.1314), who worked on the cathedral in Siena.

Arnolfo di Cambio (c.1245–1302), a student of Nicola Pisano, is best known as the architect of the Duomo and Palazzo Vecchio in Florence. He also had the task of decorating the facade of the Duomo. Some of this sculpture remains in the Museo dell'Opera del Duomo, but the bulk of his work was destroyed in the 16th century.

Another outstanding sculptor was Andrea Pisano (c.1290–c.1348), who left behind him the bronze doors of the south facade of the Florence Battistero. The realism of the characters combines with the fine linear detail of a Gothic imprint, revealing that this century was one of transition.

Il Quattrocento In 1401 Lorenzo Ghiberti (1378–1455) won a competition to design a second pair of doors for the Florence Battistero. He was later called on to do another set of doors on the east side and ended up dedicating 17 years of his career to what an admiring Michelangelo (and it was not his wont to admire anything much) would later dub the Porta del Paradiso (Heaven's Door).

Ghiberti's workshop was a prestige address in Florence, and one of the lucky young hopefuls to be apprenticed there was Donatello (c.1386–1466). As the Renaissance gathered momentum in the 1420s and 30s, Donatello burst his banks and produced a stream of sculpture hitherto unparalleled in its dynamism and force. The results swing from his rather camp bronze *David*, the first nude sculpture since classical times, to the racy *Cantoria*, a marble and mosaic tribune where small choirs could gather, created for the Duomo (now in the Museo dell'Opera del Duomo).

Meanwhile, Siena's Jacopo della Quercia (1374–1438) was cutting a temperamental swathe across Tuscany, working above all in Lucca and Siena, where he designed the Fonte Gaia in Il Campo.

Although he would subsequently be best known for his decorative, glazed terracotta, Luca della Robbia (c.1400–82) for a while showed promise as a sculptor, as examination of his exquisite *Cantoria*, now in Florence's Museo dell'Opera del Duomo, will reveal. His nephew Andrea (1435–1525) and the latter's son Giovanni (1469–1529) continued the successful family terracotta business. The pretty terracotta medallions and other more complex pieces adorning buildings all over Florence and beyond came to be known as *robbiane*. A good collection can be admired up close in the Bargello.

Desiderio da Settignano (c.1430–64) was a master of marble. Little of his work remains in Florence aside from the tomb of Carlo Marsuppini in the Basilica di Santa Croce. A pupil of Desiderio, Mino da Fiesole (1429–84) was busy in Florence and as far afield as Naples. His most important work was a new tomb for Ugo, the early medieval count of Tuscany, in Florence's Badia.

Although also active as a painter, Andrea del Verrocchio is best remembered for his sculpture. His virtuosity can be admired in the tomb monument to Piero and Giovanni de' Medici in the Basilica di San Lorenzo in Florence. His masterpiece, however, is the bronze equestrian statue of Colleoni in Venice.

The Fiery Florentine A passionate republican, Michelangelo Buonarroti was most prolific as a sculptor. And while he painted and built in Florence, his greatest gifts to the city were those he crafted from stone.

After a stint in Rome, where he carved the remarkable *Pietà*, Michelangelo returned to Florence in 1501 to carry out one of his most striking commissions, the colossal statue of *David*. By now, Michelangelo had long established himself as the champion of full nudity. The body, he argued, was a divine creation and its beauty without peer.

In 1516, after another long stint in Rome, Michelangelo was back in Florence. Among his last great works, not quite completed, are the statues in the Sagrestia Nuova of San Lorenzo.

Il Cinquecento (16th Century) Other sculptors during Michelangelo's lifetime included Benvenuto Cellini (1500–71) and Bartolommeo Ammannati (1511–92). The former, trained as a goldsmith, produced the bronze *Perseo e Medusa* (now standing in the Loggia della Signoria in Florence) – technically fine, but it lacks life. Ammannati is perhaps best known for the nearby *Fontana del Nettuno* (Neptune Fountain) in Piazza della Signoria.

Another name associated with Florence was Giambologna (Jean de Boulogne; 1529–1608). Some consider him the herald of baroque. He was at any rate the dominant force in Florentine sculpture towards the end of the 16th century. His *Ratto della Sabina* (Rape of the Sabine Women), placed in the Loggia della Signoria, is one of his best known efforts. It is typical of his lust for movement – the figures seem to be caught up in a veritable whirlwind.

Lean Centuries One of Florence's senior court sculptors, Giovanni Battista Foggini (1652–1725), immersed himself in the baroque circles of Rome when sent there by the Medici to copy statues of antiquity. He returned and put to use his new found knowledge in reliefs and other decoration in several churches, among them the Basilica di Santa Maria del Carmine.

One of the dominant figures in the 19th century was Lorenzo Bartolini (1777–1850). Born in Prato, he studied in France before settling in Florence, where he became the grand man of sculpture. He and his contemporaries, however, were to some extent bound up in the rediscovery of the masters of the 15th century, and so produced little that was exciting or innovative.

20th Century Possibly even more so than with painting, Tuscan sculpture has remained in the doldrums. Perhaps the awe-inspiring legacy of the great masters has been too great a burden to shake off.

This is not to say activity ground to a complete halt. The Pescia-born Libero Andreotti (1875–1933) and the tormented Florentine Evaristo Boncinelli (1883–1946) were among the prominent figures in the first half of the century, while Pistoia-born Marino Marini (1901–80) is doubtless the torch-bearer of 20th-century Tuscan sculpture. You can admire his work in the museum dedicated to him in Florence.

Literature

First Stirrings Long after the fall of Rome, Latin remained the language of learned discourse and writing throughout Italy. The elevation of local tongues to literary status was a long and weary process, and the case of Italian was no exception.

In the mid-13th century, Tuscan poets started to experiment with verse and song in the local tongue, inspired by the troubadours of Provence and a Sicilian tradition that had grown out of the Provencal experience. Such early poets included Chiaro Davanzati (?–1303) and Guittone d'Arezzo (c.1235–94), whose writings also included political and moral treatises in verse. Brunetto Latini (1212–94) was not only recognised as one of Florence's finer poets, he was Dante's instructor.

Dante the Master All the poetry, song, didactic and religious literature of 13th-century writers in Tuscany, and indeed beyond, would appear to be nothing before the genius of the Florentine Dante Alighieri (1265–1321). Dante wrote on many subjects and often in Latin, but when he decided to compose the *Divina Commedia* (Divine Comedy) in the 'vulgar' tongue of his countrymen, he was truly inspired.

The protagonist is escorted on a journey through hell, purgatory and heaven in a work so dense with subtext that scholars are still beavering away at it today. At once a religious work and cautionary tale, it also operates on a far more complex level.

The gloomy circles of Dante's hell do not serve merely to remind his readers of the wages of sin. Far more interestingly, they become an uneasy resting place for a parade of characters, many of them his contemporaries, whom he judged worthy of an uncomfortable time in the next life. Political and religious figures of all persuasions get short shrift, but others come out looking better in his vision of purgatory and heaven.

Dante himself would not take all the credit. He was full of praise for the poet Guido Cavalcanti (c.1250–1300), inventor of the *dolce stil nuovo* (sweet new style) in Tuscan that Dante turned into the tool of his most exalted writings.

Dante's extraordinary capacity to construct and tell stories within stories would have ensured him a place in the pantheon of scribblers regardless of his language of delivery. But his decision to write in the Tuscan dialect was a bold step. In doing so he catapulted Italian, or at least a version of it, to the literary stage. Scholars have been enthusing ever since that Italian was 'born' with Dante's *Commedia*.

Petrarch & Boccaccio Dante does not stand completely alone, and two Tuscan successors form with him the triumvirate that laid down the course for the development of a rich Italian literature.

Petrarch (Francesco Petrarca; 1304–74), born in Arezzo to Florentine parents who had been exiled from their city about the same time as Dante, actually wrote more in Latin than in Italian. *Il Canzoniere* is the distilled result of his finest poetry. Although the core subject is the unrequited love for a girl called Laura, the whole breadth of human grief and joy is treated with a lyrical quality hitherto unmatched. So striking was his clear, passionate verse, filtered through his knowledge of the classics, that a phenomenon known as *petrarchismo* emerged across Europe – the desire of writers within and beyond Italy to emulate him.

Contemporary and friend of Petrarch was the Florentine Giovanni Boccaccio (1303–75), who ended his days in Certaldo, outside Florence. His masterpiece was the *Decameron*, written in the years immediately following the plague of 1348, which he survived in Florence. His ten characters each recount a story in which a vast panorama of personalities, events and symbolism is explored.

The Renaissance Even as the Renaissance in the fine arts was getting under way, writers were amusing themselves with language too. Burchiello (1404–49), a Florentine barber, would play host to writers, painters and other creative types in his shop, where they fooled around with verse. The sonnets that have remained often seem to make little sense, leaping from one subject to another, with references to people and events by now unknown even to scholars. The importance of his verse lies more in the extent to which it shows writers actively searching for new forms of expression. Such a search fits in nicely with the age.

Lorenzo the Magnificent dominated the second half of the 15th century in Florence and was handy with a pen himself. His enlightened approach to learning and the arts created a healthy atmosphere for writers.

Angelo Ambrogini (1454–94), born in Montepulciano and known as Il Poliziano, is considered one of Italy's most important 15th-century poets in Latin and Italian. His major work in the latter is the allegorical tale in verse *Stanze per la Giostra* (Verses for the Joust) penned to celebrate the vic-

tory of Giuliano de' Medici at such a contest.

Another outstanding writer of the Florentine Renaissance is Niccolò Machiavelli (1469–1527). He is known above all for his work on power and politics, *Il Principe* (see also the boxed text 'Machiavelli's Manoeuvres' overleaf). But he was a prolific writer in many fields. His *Mandragola* is a lively piece of comic theatre and a virtuoso example of Italian literature.

A little more staid is the principal work of Francesco Guicciardini (1483–1540), a wily statesman and historian. His *Storia d'Italia* (History of Italy) might never have been written had Cosimo I de' Medici not dispensed with his services shortly after becoming duke in 1537.

17th to 19th Centuries Few writers of great standing emerged in these centuries, although the occasional name is worth mentioning.

Theatre The first signs of change in theatre away from the Commedia dell'Arte, which had become something of a fixture in the Italian repertoire since the early 16th century, emerged in Florence. Giovanni Battista Fagiuoli (1660–1742) was among those who made the first tentative steps away from the old forms, but it would fall to the Venetian Carlo Goldoni to start a true revolution in the theatre.

Novels Although plenty of lesser scribblers were busy over the course of these centuries, Tuscany cannot really claim to have produced any outstanding names. There is, as usual, at least one exception to the rule. Carlo Lorenzini (1826–90), better known to Italians of all ages under the pseudonym of Carlo Collodi, was the creator of *Le Avventure di Pinocchio*. Outside Italy Pinocchio has come to be known more in his saccharine Walt Disney guise, but in Italy this best seller of 'children's literature' has been a source of amusement and instruction for both children and adults for generations.

Considerably less well known to posterity are writers such as Renato Fucini

Machiavelli's Manoeuvres

JANE SMITH

Born in 1469 into a poor branch of what had been one of Florence's leading families, Niccolò Machiavelli got off to a bad start. His father was a small-time lawyer whose practice had been all but strangled by the city authorities as he was a debtor. Young Niccolò missed out on the best schools and could consider himself lucky that his father was at least rich in books. His prospects were not sparkling.

Somehow he managed to swing a post in the city's second chancery at the age of 29, and so embarked on a colourful career as a Florentine public servant. His tasks covered a range of internal dealings in Florence and some aspects of foreign affairs and defence. Our man must have shown early promise, as by 1500 he was in France on his first diplomatic mission. A couple of years later he married Marietta Corsini, with whom he would have five children in the following 12 years.

Impressed by the marshal success of Cesare Borgia and the centralised state of France, Machiavelli came to the conclusion that Florence needed a standing army. The city, like many others across the length and breadth of the Italian peninsula, had a habit of employing mercenaries to fight their wars. The problem with that system was that mercenaries had few reasons to fight and die for anyone. They took their pay and as often as not did their level best to avoid mortal combat.

Machiavelli managed to convince his rulers of the advantages of an army raised to defend hearth and home and so in 1506 formed a conscript militia. In 1509 he got to try it out on the rebellious city of Pisa, whose fall was in large measure attributed to the troops led by the wily statesman. He was back in Pisa two years later to dismantle a French-backed schismatic council there.

Florence, however, was not Rome's flavour of the month and troops from the Holy See and its allies marched on the city. Machiavelli was now defending not only his hearth but his future – to no avail.

The return of the Medici family to power was a blow for Machiavelli, who was promptly removed from all posts. Suspected of plotting against the Medici, he was even thrown into the dungeons in 1513 and tortured. He maintained his innocence and was freed, but reduced to penury as he retired to his little property outside Florence.

It was in these years that he produced his greatest writing. *Il Principe* (The Prince) is his classic treatise on the nature of power and its administration. In it he developed his theories not only on politics and power but on history and human behaviour. Thus Machiavelli turned what was a thoroughly demoralising time to good account for generations to come. This work and other writings reflect the confusing and corrupt times in which he lived, and his desire for strong and just rule, in Florence and beyond.

He ached to get back into active public life too, but in this he was never to be truly satisfied. He was commissioned to write an official history of Florence, the *Istorie Fiorentine,* and towards the end of his life appointed to a defence commission to improve the city walls and join a papal army in its ultimately futile fight against imperial forces. By the time the latter had sacked Rome in 1527, Florence had again rid itself of the Medici. Machiavelli hoped that he would be restored to a position of dignity, but by now he was as suspected almost as much by the Medicis' opponents as he had been years before by the Medici. He died frustrated and, as in his youth, on the brink of poverty, in 1527.

(1843–1921) and Mario Pratese (1842–1921), both of whom tend to be classed with realist novelists.

Poetry Giosue Carducci (1835–1907) was one of the key figures of Tuscan 19th-century literature. Born in the Maremma, he actually spent the second half of his life in Bologna. Probably the best of his poetry was written in the 1870s. It ranged in tone from pensive evocation of death (such as in *Pianto Antico*) or memories of youthful passion *(Idillio Maremmano)* to a kind of historic nostalgia. In many of these latter poems he harked back to the glories of ancient Rome.

Early 20th Century Florence's Aldo Palazzeschi (1885–1974) was in the vanguard of the Futurist movement during the pre-WWI years. In 1911 he published arguably his best (although at the time little-appreciated) work, *Il Codice di Perelà* (Perelà's Code), an at times bitter allegory that in part becomes a farcical imitation of the life of Christ.

A contemporary of Palazzeschi's, now all but forgotten, was Ardengo Soffici (1879–1964), a painter and writer who, after some hesitation, embraced Futurism. After WWI he moved closer to Fascism.

The Mussolini Years By the 1920s and 30s Florence was bubbling with activity as a series of literary magazines flourished, at least for a while, in spite of the Fascist regime. Magazines such as *Solaria*, which lasted from 1926 to 1934, its successor *Letteratura* (which began circulating in 1937) and *Il Frontespizio* (1929–40) gave writers from across Italy a platform from which to launch and discuss their work.

These were not the easiest of times, and most of the magazines, including Vasco Pratolini's short-lived *Campo di Marte*, fell prey sooner or later to censorship. That some lasted as long as they did is remarkable enough.

One of the founding authors of *Letteratura* was Alessandro Bonsanti (1904–84), much of whose writings are in essays and criticism. A contributor on *Letteratura* was Guglielmo Petroni (born 1911), from Lucca. Although a poet of some note in his day, his novel *Il Mondo è una Prigione* (The World Is a Prison, 1948), a vivid account of political prison, was thought to be one of the best accounts of the Italian Resistance. Mario Tobino (born 1910), from Viareggio, uses his experience as director of a lunatic asylum to great effect in *Le Donne Libere di Magliano* (Free Women of Magliano) which looks at life inside one such institution.

One of the most controversial figures in Italian letters of these years was Prato-born Curzio Malaparte (1898–1957). An early member of the Fascist party, from which he was later turfed out, Malaparte was a showy and tempestuous character. His most enduring works were novels, including *Maledetti Toscani* (Damned Tuscans), written in and about the tough immediate postwar period in Italy.

To the Present Few Tuscan writers of the 20th century gained a particularly high profile. One exception was Vasco Pratolini (1913–91), son of a manual labourer and self-taught writer who dabbled successfully in theatre and cinema as well as the novel and poetry. Among his most enduring works is the trilogy *Una Storia Italiana* (An Italian Story), whose first part *Metello* set off a heated debate in Italian literary circles. Those who liked this novel saw in it a mature departure from neo-realism to a more robust realism. Pratolini's detractors considered him still caught in a rigid and limited ideological trap. The trilogy follows the lives of working- and middle-class Florentines, through whom Pratolini analyses a variety of political, social and emotional issues.

A minor novelist is Catholic writer Carlo Cocciolo, born in Livorno in 1920, whose themes recall those of Georges Bernanos. Arrigo Benedetti (1910–76) in such novels as *Il Passo dei Longobardi* (The Passage of the Lombards), showed a keen eye for day-to-day detail, which he mixed with a sense of the fantastic and mythological.

One of Italy's leading postwar poets was

the Florentine Mario Luzi (born 1914). His poetry concentrates on the anguish arising from the contrast between the individual and the broader universe.

Few women writers have reached the limelight in Tuscany, but an important exception was Anna Banti (1895–1985). Her prose approach is psychological, delving deep into the minds of her characters and analysing the position of women in society.

Dacia Maraina (born 1936) is with little doubt Tuscany's most prominent contemporary female author, with some 10 novels to her credit. An interesting one is *Voci* (Voices), in which the main character, a female journalist, embarks on the investigation of a murder. The journalist has little to go on – the corpse of a young girl and a pair of blue running shoes. Why, she asks herself, do women seem so readily disposed to open their homes to whomever knocks at the door? It is a mystery laced with disturbing social comment.

Pisa-born Antonio Tabucchi (born 1943) is emerging as a writer of some stature, with more than a dozen books to his name. Possibly one of his most endearing works is *Sostiene Pereira*, set in prewar Lisbon and made into a charming film starring Marcello Mastroianni.

Music

While Florence may have been the epicentre of the greatest explosion in the world of fine arts and the birthplace of literary Italian, music was not a strong point either there or anywhere else in Tuscany.

The Roman-born composer Jacopo Peri (1561–1633) moved to Florence in 1588 to serve the Medici court. He and Florentine writer Ottavio Rinuccini (1562–1621) are credited with having created the first opera in the modern sense, *Dafne*, in 1598. They and Giulio Caccini (1550–1618) also wrote *Euridice* a couple of years later. It is the oldest opera for which the complete score still exists. All three men were part of a Florentine group of intellectuals known as the Camerata, which worked to revive and develop ancient Greek musical traditions in theatre.

Florence's next musical contribution was a key development, although it came at the hands of a Paduan resident on the Arno. In 1711 Bartolomeo Cristofori (1655–1731) invented the pianoforte.

In 1632, Giovanni Battista Lulli was born in Florence. That may not ring too many bells until we add that he moved to France where he would dominate the musical life of the court of Louis XIV as Jean-Baptiste Lully. With Molière he created new dramatic genres such as the comedy-ballet. He also gave instrumental suites their definitive form.

Another Florentine export to Paris was the composer Luigi Cherubini (1760–1842), who somehow managed the tricky feat of keeping his head attached to his torso through the French Revolution, the Napoleonic era and the Restoration.

Contemporary Music On a quite different note, one of Italy's leading pop bands, Litfiba, happens to be a Florentine product. The country's most popular rap singer in recent years, Jovanotti, is also Tuscan.

Indeed Tuscany has produced plenty of bands and musicians, ranging from Marasco – a gritty, folksy singer from Florence who was big in the 1950s, through to Dirotto Su Cuba, a trip hop band that has attracted a lot of attention around the country.

Film

The Italian cinema has known periods of enormous productivity and contributed some of Europe's proudest gems on film. Most people think of the postwar period of neo-realism as the apogee of Italian filmmaking, and there is no doubting the richness of the output at that time. It didn't end there, and Italy has continued to produce good directors ever since.

Tuscany and its capital, Florence, have had remarkably little impact on the world of movies. Greatness might have come Florence's way from the outset. Filoteo Alberini had created his *kinotegrafo* (cinema projector) in 1895, a year before the Lumière brothers patented their version in Paris. No-one in Florence was interested and Alberini moved to Rome, where he created the

Cines, which would grow to command the stage of Italian cinema.

A second chance came in the 1920s, when a Florentine gent by the name of Giovanni Montalbano set up studios in Rifredi to create historical blockbusters. The enterprise pumped out some pretty poor flicks and soon went belly up.

An early Florentine film-maker of note was Gianni Franciolini (1910–60). After spending about 10 years in France learning journalism and then film, Franciolini returned to Italy in 1940, from which time he turned out a film almost every year until his death. An early flick, *Fari Nella Nebbia* (Headlights in the Mist; 1941) shows the French influence on his ideas, but also presages the prolific period of Italian film-making that lay just around the corner – neo-realism.

The biggest name to come out of Tuscany is with little doubt Franco Zeffirelli (born 1923). His varied career took him from radio and theatre to opera productions and occasional stints as aide to Luchino Visconti on several films. His film directing days began in earnest in the late 1970s. Some of you may remember his TV blockbuster *Jesus of Nazareth* (1977). Many of his productions have been non-Italian. A couple of his more interesting ones were *Young Toscanini* (1988) and *Hamlet* (1990), a British–US co-production. He was in his hometown of Florence to do *Tea with Mussolini*, starring Maggie Smith, which hit the screens in 1999.

Neri Parenti (born 1950) started directing in 1979. Since 1980 he has been kept busy directing the comedian Paolo Villaggi in a seemingly endless stream of films starring Fantozzi, Villaggio's best known comic character. Fantozzi is a sort of thinking man's cross between Mr Bean and Benny Hill. The humour can swing pretty low, but he's popular.

Two of Italy's modern success stories are Tuscan. Light-hearted comedy is a forte of Leonardo Pieraccioni (born 1965). His *Il Ciclone* (1996), about the effects of the arrival of a small flamenco troupe on the lads of a small Tuscan town, was a big hit.

Humour with considerably greater depth is, however, the department of Roberto Benigni (born 1952). Long established as one of Italy's favourite comedic actors, he must be the first director to try to get a laugh out of the Holocaust – and succeed. He picked up three Oscars in 1999, including Best Actor, an honour rarely bestowed by Hollywood upon anyone but its own, for his *La Vita è Bella* (Life is Beautiful; 1998). The flick, which he directed and starred in, is the story of an Italian Jewish family that ends up in the camps, where the father tries to hide its horrors from his son by pretending it's all a game. Arezzo-born Benigni was already known to cinema-goers outside Italy for his appearances in Jim Jarmusch's *Down by Law* and *Night on Earth*. Charlie Chaplin's daughter, Geraldine, declared months after the Oscars that Benigni had inherited her father's cinematic poetry. Quite an accolade.

The city of Florence became something of a star in James Ivory's 1985 rendition of the EM Forster classic, *A Room with a View*, starring Helena Bonham Carter.

SOCIETY & CULTURE

Tuscans are particularly attached to their home ground and family. These ties continue to influence how people do things in this part of the world. Many businesses are relatively small, family enterprises. From the great names in wine, such as the Antinori, through to the flower-producing industry of Pescia, most 'industries' are run by families who pass on the business from generation to generation. In some respects this has contributed to a degree of immobility in Tuscan society. The readiness with which Anglo-Saxons seem disposed to shift from one city or one country to another often leaves Tuscans perplexed – mind you, their home ground is a pretty tough one to leave!

This is not to say they don't move around. Ever since the Middle Ages, when urban Tuscan families were at the head of some of the most advanced and dynamic of European trading and banking enterprises, living and working abroad was for many a rite of passage. Most, however, sooner or later returned home.

The family remains the cornerstone of Tuscan society. Although the big extended families of the past are in most cases little more than a distant memory, family ties remain tight. Children still typically remain at home with their parents until they reach their 30s, often only leaving when they get married. And from then on, weekly visits home to *mamma* and *babbo* are the norm for most.

The stereotypical perceptions foreigners tend to have of Italians in general, while they inevitably contain a grain of truth, do not tell much of the story. The image of the animated, gesticulating people seemingly with plenty of time to kill is some distance from the truth.

If anything the Tuscans have more in common with the image many have of the Scots – who can become pretty animated themselves! Thrifty and hard-working, the Tuscans can also be a fairly reserved lot. To be swept up into Tuscan social life (as opposed to circles of resident Italians from other parts of the country) is no mean feat and a sign of considerable success.

Dos & Don'ts

Tuscans perhaps even more than other Italians take particular pride in their dress and appearance. To many outsiders such concerns can seem a trifle overdone. In some cases, however, those outsiders seem to abandon any standards they might normally adhere to at home as soon as they hit the holiday trail.

Leaving aside the sartorial spectacle of the loud-shirts-and-shorts brigade, there are those who seem to think walking around with precious little on is the only way to fly. Your average Tuscan in heavily touristed centres such as Florence has grown accustomed to the odd ways of the *stranieri* (foreigners), but in restaurants, cafes and bars it doesn't hurt to at least put your shirt back on!

Many churches will not allow you entry if you are deemed to be inadequately attired. No one's suggesting you bring your Sunday best along, but a little common sense and sensitivity go a long way.

Topless sunbathing, while not uncommon on some Tuscan beaches, is not *de rigueur* – women should look around before dropping their tops. Nude sunbathing is likely to be offensive anywhere but on appropriately designated beaches (there's a couple on Elba).

The standard form of greeting is the handshake. Kissing on both cheeks is generally reserved for people who already know one another. There will always be exceptions to these rules, so the best thing on being introduced to locals is probably not to launch your lips in anyone's general direction unless you are pretty sure they are welcome. If this is the case, a light brushing of cheeks will do.

The police (*polizia* and *carabinieri*; see also Dangers & Annoyances in the Facts for the Visitor chapter) have the right to arrest you for 'insulting a state official' if they believe you have been rude or offensive – so be diplomatic in your dealings with them!

RELIGION

As elsewhere in Italy, Catholicism is the dominant religion. It became the state religion of the new Italian nation when unity was completed in 1871. Only when the 1929 Lateran Treaty between the Vatican and the Italian state was modified in 1985 did Catholicism lose that status.

Still, as many as 85% of Italians profess to be Catholic, and roughly the same figure can probably be applied to Tuscany. There is also a small Protestant population, made up of various denominations and consisting mostly of the expat community. Florence, interestingly, is one of the country's biggest centres of Buddhism, which has about 5000 followers throughout Tuscany.

Religiosity among the Italians appears often to be more a matter of form. First communions, church weddings and religious feast days are an integral part of Italian ritual. In the same way the Royal Family is a part of the ritual scenery in the life of many Britons, so the Papacy is a kind of royal family to Italians.

LANGUAGE

Many Italians speak some English because they studied it in school. Clearly in heavily touristed centres such as Florence and, to a lesser extent, Pisa and Siena, you will find that many hotel, restaurant and shop staff members speak at least a little English. In 'Chiantishire' you will often come across locals with some knowledge. Nevertheless, in these places as elsewhere in Tuscany you will be better received if you at least attempt to communicate in Italian. See the Language chapter for an introduction to the language and vocabulary.

Facts for the Visitor

SUGGESTED ITINERARIES

You could organise yourself to cover quite a bit of ground, especially with your own vehicle, in as little as a week, although ideally you would need at least two weeks to make the most of the following suggestions. Taking Florence as a natural focal point, various itineraries spring to mind.

After a few days in Florence (to do the place any justice at all you need at least four days), you could set out southwards. Your main objective would be Siena, with a detour en route to San Gimignano and Volterra, south-west of Florence. From Siena you could scoot east to Cortona and then head south-west to the charming towns of Montepulciano, Pienza, Montalcino and a series of abbeys scattered about the Sienese countryside.

At a more leisurely pace, you could easily spend a few days weaving your way south to Siena through the Chianti region, stopping in at Greve, Radda, Monteriggioni and so on.

Another fairly obvious option from Florence would be to move westward to take in the towns of Prato, Pistoia, Lucca and Pisa, making one of the latter two an overnight stop. From Pisa you might want to pop along to one of the beaches around nearby Viareggio. Although nothing amazing, they certainly bring relief to the heat of a summer's day. Carrara, the centre of Tuscany's white marble industry, is a worthwhile stop and in the north-western corner of the region you could easily lose yourself for several days. The main attraction is the walking in the Garfagnana, the mountains of the Apuan Alps and in the still less visited Lunigiana.

If you have ended up in Pisa, you could choose to take the coastal option. This might see you travelling along the ridge inland from the coast south towards Piombino. The road gets more interesting the further you go, towns such as Suvereto and Campiglia Marittima are highlights. One of

the prettiest spots along the Tuscan coast is the Golfo di Baratti, backed by the Etruscan ruins of Populonia and the likenamed medieval borgo nearby. With a few days more to pare, it is tempting and easy to proceed to Piombino and get the ferry for Napoleon's one time island exile, Elba.

Heading into the little-travelled east you could happily spend a week or so exploring the Vallombrosa area and the remoter still Casentino, with a swing south to Arezzo and Cortona.

In the south, several days or more could be profitably spent moving from the Monte Argentario peninsula on the coast inland through relatively untouristed country, bespattered with ancient Etruscan sites around the hill towns of Magliano in Toscana, Manciano, Pitigliano, Sovana and Sorano.

PLANNING
When to Go

The best time to visit Tuscany is in the low season, from April to June and in September/October, when the weather is usually good, prices are lower and there are fewer tourists. Late July and August is the time to avoid the place: the sun broils, prices are inflated and you can't see the place for the swarms of holiday-makers. Most of Italy goes on vacation in August, abandoning the cities (and leaving many shops, hotels and restaurants closed) and packing out the coast and mountains. Finding a place to stay by the sea or in the hills without booking months in advance can be especially difficult at this time.

June and September are the best months for walking in the Apennines (like everything else, walking trails and *rifugi* (refuges) are crowded in August). During these months the weather is generally good, although you should always allow for cold snaps.

You may prefer to organise your trip or itinerary to coincide with one or more of the many festivals that festoon the Tuscan calendar – an obvious choice is Il Palio in Siena. To help start planning around such events, turn to the Special Events section later in this chapter.

What Kind of Trip

Apart from simply making a tour of the main towns and cities, several other approaches suggest themselves. Many people choose to rent a villa in the countryside for a week or two. Generally in this case you should hire a car to allow you to potter around the area and visit some of the towns and cities that interest you.

More energetic types might opt to build their visit around walking routes. The most challenging walking is in the Apuan Alps, but for gentler walking there are plenty of trails criss-crossing the Chianti region and other parts of Tuscany. Cycling (for the fit – there is not a lot of flat country in Tuscany) is another option.

You might even consider a low-level week of skiing in Abetone coupled with visits to Florence and other relatively close-by cities. Bear in mind that the slopes are not exactly first rate – the idea would be a kind of cake-and-eat-it option allowing you to make excursions to the great cities of Florence, Pisa, Lucca and so on and still manage to get in a little snow fun. Perhaps a week of culture followed by a local week of skiing might be the way to go.

Tuscany is really not beach country. If you are looking for an essentially sea and sun holiday, this is not the place to come.

Some people opt to build their stay around some kind of course, whether language, cooking or art history. Such courses abound in Florence and to a lesser extent in other towns, and in some cases in the countryside too.

Maps

Road Atlases If you are driving around Tuscany and beyond, the AA's *Big Road Atlas – Italy*, available in the UK for UK£9.99, is scaled at 1:250,000 and includes 39 town maps. In Italy, de Agostini's *Atlante Stradale d'Italia* (1:600,000) contains city plans and sells for L24,500. For L43,000 the same publisher offers the more comprehensive *Atlante Turistico Stradale d'Italia* (1:250,000). The Touring Club Italiano (TCI) publishes an *Atlante Stradale d'Italia* (1:200,000), divided into three parts – Nord, Centro and Sud. Each costs L34,000.

euro currency converter L10,000 = €5.16

Regional & Provincial Maps Michelin's map No 430, *Italia Centro*, on a scale of 1:400,000, includes Tuscany and parts of surrounding regions.

The TCI produces a regional map of Tuscany at a scale of 1:200,000, while several other publishers do them at 1:250,000. For greater scale detail, you have to revert to provincial maps (the region is divided up into 10 provinces). Edizioni Multigraphic Firenze publishes a series of provincial maps. Ask for the *Carta Stradale Provinciale* of the province(s) you want. They are scaled at 1:100,000. Beyond that they subdivide into road maps at 1:50,000 (*Carta Turistica e Stradale*) and, for walkers (see also below), the *Carta Turistica dei Sentieri e Rifugi* (Tourist Trails and Refuges Map). These are done at 1:50,000 and 1:25,000. A couple of other publishers produce comparable maps.

City Maps City maps in this book, combined with tourist office maps, are generally adequate. More detailed maps are available at good bookshops (such as Feltrinelli) or newspaper stands.

The quality of city maps available commercially varies considerably, depending on the city. The TCI has a good foldout map of Florence and, handier still, a small ringbound book version. The latter covers the whole city on a scale of 1:11,000 and the centre at 1:5500. A full street index follows at the back. It costs L15,000. For suggestions on the maps for the main cities covered in this book, refer to each destination.

Walking Maps More information on maps useful for walkers is given in the special section 'Tuscany on Foot' after this chapter.

What to Bring

Pack as little as possible. A backpack is an advantage since petty thieves prey on luggage-laden tourists with no free hands. Backpacks whose straps and openings can be zipped inside a flap are less awkard and more secure than the standard ones.

Suitcases with portable trolleys may be fine in airports but otherwise you won't get far on foot with them. If you must carry suitcase/bag, make sure it is lightweight and not too big. Remember that most everyday necessities can be found easily in Italy – there is no need to stock up in advance and drag it all around with you.

A small pack (with a lock) for day trips and sightseeing is preferable to a handbag or shoulder bag.

Clothes Tuscany is hot in summer but can be ice cold in winter, especially at higher altitudes. You probably won't need so much as a light jacket in July and August, but in winter you will need a decent coat, hat, gloves and scarf.

Italians dress up just to do the daily food shopping, so if you plan to hang around in cafes and bars or enjoy some of the nightlife you'll feel more comfortable with a set of casually dressy clobber. Jeans and T-shirts will give you the decided air of a bum by local standards.

You'll need a pair of hardy, comfortable walking shoes with rubber soles – trainers are fine except for going out, so something a little more presentable, though casual, might cover all bases.

People planning to hike in the mountains should bring the necessary clothing and equipment, in particular a pair of walking boots (lightweight and waterproof). Even in high summer you would be advised to have some warm clothing on long hikes – it can get chilly high up.

Unless you plan to spend large sums in dry-cleaners and laundries, pack a portable clothesline. Many *pensioni* (boarding houses) and hotels ask guests not to wash clothes in the room, but such rules are rarely enforced. Consider packing a light travel iron or crease-proof clothes.

Useful Items Apart from any special personal needs, consider the following:

• an under-the-clothes money belt or shoulder wallet, useful for protecting your money and documents in cities
• a towel and soap, often lacking in cheap accommodation
• a small Italian dictionary and/or phrasebook

a Swiss army knife

minimal unbreakable cooking, eating and drinking gear if you plan to prepare your own food and drinks

a medical kit

a padlock or two to secure your luggage to racks and to lock hostel lockers

a sleeping sheet to save on sheet rental costs if you're using youth hostels (a sleeping bag is unnecessary unless you're camping)

an adapter plug for electrical appliances

a torch (flashlight)

an alarm clock

sunglasses

a universal sink plug

Basic drugs are widely available and indeed many items requiring prescriptions in countries such as the USA can be obtained easily over the counter in Italy. If you require specific medication, it's easier to bring it with you. Condoms can cost L30,000, or more, for 12 but as little as L12,000 in supermarkets.

RESPONSIBLE TOURISM

It would be nice to see travellers moving around with a little more awareness than some do. Visitors all too often ignore local sensibilities and seem to leave manners and common sense at home. In the main tourist centres locals are by now used to the sight of men wandering around in little more than a pair of shorts and (maybe) sandals. But you have to ask yourself – if you wouldn't walk around like that at home, why do so in someone else's town? Sun scorched bellies do not a pretty sight make, and less still to a people known for their preoccupation with dressing well.

When visiting monuments, treat them with respect. At ancient sites such as the Roman amphitheatre in Fiesole or Etruscan tombs and similar locations, don't go clambering over everything where you are asked not to or have no need to. By leaving things alone you do your little part to help preserve them.

Don't use the flash when photographing artworks in museums, churches and so on. The burst of light only damages the art.

The sheer volume of people visiting a place like Florence, and to a slightly lesser extent towns like Siena, San Gimignano, Cortona and Pisa, puts enormous pressure on the infrastructure of those places. For a local trying to get anything done in central Florence it can be a nightmare. Try to be aware while wandering around and staring at things that some people around you are trying to get places!

Bongos are big in Florence. Why is that? A handful of young travellers appear to believe that the rhythmic thudding of their questionable musical prowess is just what central Florence needs – all day and all night.

The moral of the story is, simply, respect the monuments and works of art, the towns and their people, as you would your own most prized possessions. Tread softly. And enjoy.

TOURIST OFFICES
Local Tourist Offices

There is no regional tourist office in Tuscany. Instead you will find an Azienda di Promozione Turistica (APT) in all the provincial capitals. Generally they can provide information only on that province, usually including the city itself, but little or nothing on the rest of the region. In Florence you have a choice of three different offices, but the main APT on Via Cavour is the best stocked – it's amazing what they dig up for you if you ask the right questions. Since tourism isn't exactly new to Tuscany you'll generally find English, and sometimes other languages, spoken.

The next rung down are local city or town tourist offices. These come under various names but most commonly are known as Pro Loco. They may deal with a town only, or in some cases the surrounding countryside.

Things you may want to ask for include: a map *(pianta della città)*; a list of hotels *(elenco degli alberghi)*; and information on the major sights *(informazioni sulle attrazioni turistiche)*. Many will help you find a hotel.

Some of the bigger APT offices will respond to written and telephone requests – for example, information about hotels or apartments for rent.

The addresses and telephone numbers of tourist offices are listed under towns and cities throughout this book.

Tourist Offices Abroad

Information on Tuscany is available from the Italian State Tourist Office (Web site www.enit.it) in the following countries:

Australia
(☎ 02-9262 1666, fax 9262 5745) c/o Italian Chamber of Commerce, Level 26, 44 Market St, Sydney, NSW 2000
Austria
(☎ 01-505 16 39) Kaerntnerring 4, 1010 Vienna
Canada
(☎ 514-866 7668, ✉ initaly@ican.net) Suite 1914, 1 Place Ville Marie, Montreal, Quebec H3B 2C3
France
(☎ 01 42 66 66 68, ✉ 106616.131@ compuserve.com) 23 rue de la Paix, 75002 Paris
Germany
Berlin: (☎ 030-247 83 97, ✉ enit-berlin@ t-online.de) Karl Liebknecht Strasse 34, 10178 Berlin
Frankfurt: (☎ 069-25 93 32, ✉ enit.ffm@ t-online.de) Kaiser Strasse 65, 60329 Frankfurt am Main
Munich: (☎ 089-53 13 17) Goethe Strasse 20, 80336 Munich
The Netherlands
(☎ 020-616 82 44) Stadhouderskade 2, 1054 ES Amsterdam
Spain
(☎ 91 559 9750) Gran Via 84, Edificio Espagna 1, 28013 Madrid
Switzerland
(☎ 01-211 79 17, ✉ enit@bluewin.ch) Urania Strasse 32, 8001 Zürich
UK
(☎ 020-7408 1254, ✉ enitlond@globalnet.co.uk) 1 Princes St, London W1R 8AY
USA
Chicago: (☎ 312-644 0996, ✉ enitch@ italiantouism.com) 500 North Michigan Ave, Chicago, IL 60611
Los Angeles: (☎ 310-820 1819) Suite 550, 12400 Wilshire Blvd, Los Angeles, CA 90025
New York: (☎ 212-245 4822, ✉ enitny@bway.net) Suite 1565, 630 Fifth Ave, New York, NY 10111

Sestante-CIT (Compagnia Italiana di Turismo), Italy's national travel agency, also has offices throughout the world (known a CIT or Citalia outside Italy). Staff can provide extensive information on travelling i Italy and will organise tours, as well a book individual hotels. CIT can also mak train bookings. Offices include:

Australia
Melbourne: (☎ 03-9650 5510) Level 4, 227 Collins St, Melbourne, Victoria 3000
Sydney: (☎ 02-9267 1255), 263 Clarence St, Sydney, NSW 2000
Canada
Quebec: (☎ 514-845 4310, 800 361 7799) Suite 750, 1450 City Councillors St, Montreal Quebec H3A 2E6
Toronto: (☎ 905-415 1060, 800 387 0711) Suite 401, 80 Tiverton Court, Markham, Toronto, Ontario L3R 0G4
France
(☎ 01 44 51 39 00) 5 blvd des Capucines, Paris 75002
Germany
(☎ 0211-69 00 30) Geibel Strasse 39, 40235 Düsseldorf
UK
(☎ 020-8686 0677, 8686 5533) Marco Polo House, 3–5 Lansdowne Rd, Croydon CR9 1LL
USA
Los Angeles: (☎ 310-338 8615) Suite 980, 6033 West Century Blvd, Los Angeles, CA 90045
New York: (☎ 212-730 2121) 10th floor, 15 West 44th St, New York, NY 10036

Italian cultural institutes in major cities throughout the world have extensive information on study opportunities in Italy. See also Useful Organisations later in this chapter.

VISAS & DOCUMENTS
Passport

Citizens of the 15 European Union (EU) member states can travel to Italy with their national identity cards alone. People from countries that do not issue ID cards, such as the UK, must have a valid passport. All non-EU nationals must have a full valid passport.

If your passport is stolen or lost while in

taly, notify the police and obtain a statement, and then contact your embassy or
consulate as soon as possible.

Visas

Italy is one of 15 countries that have signed
the Schengen Convention, an agreement
whereby all EU member countries (except
the UK and Ireland) plus Iceland and Norway have agreed to abolish checks at internal borders by the end of 2000. The other
EU countries are Austria, Belgium, Denmark, Finland, France, Germany, Greece,
Luxembourg, the Netherlands, Portugal,
Spain and Sweden. Legal residents of one
Schengen country do not require a visa for
another Schengen country. In addition, nationals of a number of other countries, including the UK, Canada, Ireland, Japan,
New Zealand and Switzerland do not require visas for tourist visits of up to 90 days
to any Schengen country.

Various other nationals not covered by
the Schengen exemption, can also spend up
to 90 days in Italy without a visa. These include Australian, Israeli and US citizens.
However all non-EU nationals entering
Italy for any reason other than tourism
(such as study or work) should contact an
Italian consulate as they may need a specific visa. They should also insist on having
their passport stamped on entry as, without
a stamp, they could encounter problems
when trying to obtain a *permesso di soggiorno* (see under Permits later in this section). If you are a citizen of a country not
mentioned in this section, you should check
with an Italian consulate whether you need
a visa.

The standard tourist visa issued by Italian
consulates is the Schengen visa, valid for up
to 90 days. A Schengen visa issued by one
Schengen country is generally valid for
travel in all other Schengen countries. However individual Schengen countries may impose additional restrictions on certain
nationalities. It is therefore worth checking
visa regulations with the consulate of each
Schengen country you plan to visit.

It's mandatory that you apply for a visa
in your country of residence. You can apply

for no more than two Schengen visas in any
12 month period and they are not renewable
inside Italy.

Study Visas Non-EU citizens who want to
study at a university or language school in
Italy must have a study visa. These visas
can be obtained from your nearest Italian
embassy or consulate. You will normally
require confirmation of your enrolment and
payment of fees as well as proof of adequate funds to support yourself. The visa
will then cover only the period of the enrolment. This type of visa is renewable
within Italy but, again, only with confirmation of ongoing enrolment and proof that
you are able to support yourself – bank
statements are preferred.

Permits

EU citizens supposedly do not require any
permits to live, work or start a business in
Italy. They are, however, advised to register
with a *questura* (police station) if they take
up residence – in accordance with an anti-
mafia law that aims at keeping a watch on
everyone's whereabouts in the country.
Failure to do so carries no consequences, although some landlords may be unwilling to
rent out a flat to you if you cannot produce
proof of registration. Those considering
long-term residence will want to get a permesso di soggiorno, a necessary first step to
acquiring a *carta d'identità,* or residence
card. See the following Permesso di Soggiorno section. While you're at it, you'll
need a *codice fiscale* (tax file number) if
you wish to be paid for most work in Italy.

Work Permits Non-EU citizens wishing
to work in Italy will need to obtain a work
permit *(permesso di lavoro).* If you intend
to work for an Italian company and will be
paid in lire, the company must organise the
permesso and forward it to the Italian consulate in your country – only then will you
be issued an appropriate visa.

If non-EU citizens intend to work for a
non-Italian company or will be paid in foreign currency, or wish to go freelance, they
must organise the visa and permesso in their

euro currency converter L10,000 = €5.16

country of residence through an Italian consulate. This process can take many months – so look into it early.

Some foreigners prefer simply to work 'black' in areas such as teaching English, bar work and seasonal jobs. See the section on Work later in this chapter.

Permesso di Soggiorno Visitors are technically obliged to report to a questura if they plan to stay at the same address for more than one week (this does not apply to holiday-makers), to receive a permesso di soggiorno (residence permit). Tourists who are staying in hotels are not required to do this, because hotel-owners are required to register all guests with the police.

A permesso di soggiorno only becomes a necessity if you plan to study, work (legally) or live in Italy. Obtaining one is never a pleasant experience, although for EU citizens it is straightforward. Other nationals will find it involves enduring long queues, rude police officers and the frustration of arriving at the counter (after a two-hour wait) to find that you don't have all the necessary documents.

The exact requirements, such as documents and official stamps *(marche da bollo)*, vary from city to city. In general, you will need a valid passport, containing a visa stamp indicating your date of entry into Italy; a special visa issued in your own country if you are planning to study; four passport-style photographs; and proof of your ability to support yourself financially.

It is best to go to the questura to obtain precise information.

Travel Insurance

Don't, as they say, leave home without it. It will cover you for medical expenses, theft or loss of luggage, and for cancellation of and delays in your travel arrangements. Ticket loss is also covered by travel insurance, but keep a separate record of your ticket details (see also Photocopies later in this section).

Travel insurance papers, and the international medical aid numbers that generally accompany them, are valuable documents,

so treat them as carefully as you would a tickets and passports. Keep the details (photo copies or handwritten) in a separate part of your luggage.

Paying for your ticket with a credit car often provides limited travel accident in surance, and you may be able to reclaim th payment if the operator doesn't delive Ask your credit card company what it wi cover.

You may prefer a policy that pays doctor or hospitals directly rather than your havin to pay on the spot and claim later. If yo have to claim later make sure you keep a documentation. Some policies ask you t call back (reverse charges) to a centre i your home country where an immediate as sessment of your problem is made.

Check that the policy covers ambulance or an emergency flight home.

Driving Licence & Permits

EU member states' pink-and-green drivin licences are recognised in Italy. If you hol a licence from other countries you are sup posed to obtain an International Drivin Permit too. See under Car & Motorcycle i the Getting There & Away chapter for mor information.

Hostel Cards

A valid HI hostelling card is required in al associated youth hostels (Associazione Ital iana Alberghi per la Gioventù) in Italy. Yo can get this in your home country or a youth hostels in Italy. In the latter case yo apply for the card and must collect si stamps in the card at L5000 each. You pa for a stamp on each of the first six night you spend in a hostel. With six stamps yo are considered a full international membe HI is on the Web at www.iyhf.org.

Student, Teacher & Youth Cards

These cards can get you worthwhile dis counts on travel, and reduced prices at som museums, sights and entertainments. Th International Student Identity Card (ISIC for full-time students, and the Internationa Teacher Identity Card (ITIC), for full-tim teachers and professors, are issued by mor an 5000 organisations around the world – mainly student travel-related, and often selling student air, train and bus tickets too. The cards entitle you to a range of discounts, from reduced museum entry charges to cheap airfares. You also get use of an international help line. You call reverse charges to the UK (☎ 020-8666 205).

Student travel organisations such as STA (Australia, UK & USA), Council Travel (UK & USA) and Travel CUTS/Voyages Campus (Canada) can issue these cards. See under Air in the Getting There & Away chapter for some addresses, phone numbers and Web sites.

Anyone under 26 can get a Euro<26 card. This gives similar discounts to the ISIC and are issued by most of the same organisations. The Euro<26 has a variety of names including the Under 26 Card in England and Wales.

CTS (Centro Turistico Studentesco e Giovanile) youth and student travel organisation branches in Italy can issue ISIC, ITIC and Euro<26 cards. You have to become a member of the CTS first however, which costs L45,000.

Seniors' Cards

Seniors over 60 or 65 (depending on what they are seeking a discount for) can get many discounts simply by presenting their passport or ID card as proof of age. For discounted international rail travel in Europe, you could apply for a Rail Europe Senior card.

Photocopies

Make photocopies of important documents, especially your passport. This will help speed replacement if they are lost or stolen. Other documents to photocopy might include your airline ticket and credit cards. Also record the serial numbers of your travellers' cheques (cross them off as you cash them in). Leave extra copies with someone reliable at home. If your passport is stolen or lost, notify the police and obtain a statement, and then contact your embassy or consulate as soon as possible.

EMBASSIES & CONSULATES

It's important to realise what your own embassy – the embassy of the country of which you are a citizen – can and can't do to help you if you get into trouble.

Generally speaking, it won't be much help in emergencies if the trouble you're in is remotely your own fault. Remember that you are bound by the laws of the country you are in. Your embassy will not be sympathetic if you end up in jail after committing a crime locally, even if such actions are legal in your own country.

In genuine emergencies you might get some assistance, but only if other channels have been exhausted. For example, if you need to get home urgently, a free ticket home is exceedingly unlikely – the embassy would expect you to have insurance. If you have all your money and documents stolen, it might assist with getting a new passport, but not with a loan for onward travel.

Italian Embassies & Consulates

The following is a selection of Italian diplomatic missions abroad. As a rule, you will need to approach a consulate rather than an embassy (where both are present) on visa matters. Also bear in mind that in many of the countries listed below there are further consulates in other cities.

Australia
Embassy: (☎ 02-6273 3333, fax 6273 4223, @ ambital2@dynamite.com.au) 12 Grey St, Deakin, Canberra, ACT 2600
Consulate: (☎ 03-9867 5744, fax 9866 3932, @ itconmel@netlink.com.au) 509 St Kilda Rd, Melbourne, Vic 3004
Consulate: (☎ 02-9392 7900, fax 9252 4830, @ itconsyd@armadillo.com.au) Level 43, The Gateway, 1 Macquarie Place, Sydney, NSW 2000
Austria
Embassy: (☎ 01-712 51 21, fax 713 97 19, @ ambitalviepress@via.at) Metternichgasse 13, Vienna 1030
Consulate: (☎ 01-713 5671, fax 715 40 30) Ungarngasse 43, Vienna 1030
Canada
Embassy: (☎ 613-232 2401, fax 233 1484, @ italcomm@trytel.com) 21st floor, 275

euro currency converter L10,000 = €5.16

Slater St, Ottawa, Ontario K1P 5H9
Consulate: (☎ 514-849 8351, fax 499 9471,
❻ consitmtl@cyberglobe.net) 3489 Drum-
mond St, Montreal, Quebec H3G 1X6
Consulate: (☎ 416-977 1566, ❻ consolato.it@
toronto.italconsulate.org) 136 Beverley St,
Toronto, Ontario M5T 1Y5

France
Embassy: (☎ 01 49 54 03 00, fax 01 45 49 35
81, ❻ stampa@dial.oleane.com) 7 rue de
Varenne, Paris 75007
Consulate: (☎ 01 44 30 47 00, fax 01 45 66 41
78) 5 blvd Augier, Paris 75116

Germany
Embassy: (☎ 030-247 83 97,❻ enit.berlin@
t-online.de) Karl Liebknecht Strasse 34, 10178
Berlin
Consulate: (☎ 069-25 93 32, ❻ enit.ffm@
t-online.de) Kaisertstrasse 65, 60329 Frankfurt
am Main
Consulate: (☎ 089-53 13 17) Goethe Strasse
20, 80336 Munich

Ireland
Embassy: (☎ 01-660 1744, fax 668 2759,
❻ italianembassy@tinet.ie) 63/65
Northumberland Rd, Dublin 4

The Netherlands
Embassy: (☎ 070-302 1030, fax 361 4932,
❻ italemb@worldonline.nl) Alexanderstraat
12, 2514 JL The Hague
Consulate: (☎ 020-550 2050, fax 626 2444,
❻ consital@euronet.nl) Herengracht 581,
1017 Amsterdam

New Zealand
Embassy: (☎ 04-473 53 39, fax 472 72 55,
❻ ambwell@xtra.co.nz) 34 Grant Rd,
Thorndon, Wellington

Slovenia
Embassy: (☎ 061-126 21 94, fax 125 33 02)
Snezniska Ulica 8, Ljubljana 61000

Spain
Embassy: (☎ 91 577 6529, fax 575 7776,
❻ ambital.sp@nauta.es) Calle de Lagasca 98,
Madrid 28006
Consulate: (☎ 93 467 7305, fax 467 7306,
❻ conbarc@olivet.com) Carrer de Mallorca
270, Barcelona 08037

Switzerland
Embassy: (☎ 031-352 41 51, fax 351 10 26
❻ ambital.berna@spectraweb.ch) Elfenstrasse
14, Bern 3006
Consulate: (☎ 022-839 67 44, fax 839 67 45)
14 rue Charles Galland, Geneva 1206

UK
Embassy: (☎ 020-7312 2209, fax 7312 2230,
❻ emblondon@embitaly.org.uk) 14 Three
Kings Yard, London W1Y 2EH

Consulate: (☎ 020-7235 9371, fax 7823 1609
38 Eaton Place, London SW1X 8AN

USA
Embassy: (☎ 202-328 5500, fax 328 5593,
❻ itapress@ix.netcom.com) 1601 Fuller St,
NW Washington, DC 20009
Consulate: (☎ 213-820 0622, fax 820 0727,
❻ cglos@aol.com) Suite 300, 12400 Wilshire
Blvd, West Los Angeles, CA 90025
Consulate: (☎ 212-737 9100, fax 249 4945,
❻ italconsny@aol.com) 690 Park Ave, New
York, NY 10021-5044
Consulate: (☎ 415-931 4924, fax 931 7205)
2590 Webster St, San Francisco, CA 94115

Embassies & Consulates in Rome

Most countries have an embassy (and ofte
a consulate) in Rome, many also maintai
consulates elsewhere in the country. Pass
port enquires should be addressed to th
Rome-based offices:

Australia
Embassy: (☎ 06 85 27 21) Via
Alessandria 215

Austria
Embassy: (☎ 06 844 01 41) Via Pergolesi 3
Consulate: (☎ 06 855 29 66) Viale Liegi 32

Canada
Embassy: (☎ 06 44 59 81) Via G B de Rossi 2
Consulate: (☎ 06 44 59 81) Via Zara 30

France
Embassy: (☎ 06 68 60 11) Piazza Farnese 67
Consulate: (☎ 06 68 30 73 14) Via Giulia 25

Germany
Embassy: (☎ 06 49 21 31) Via San Martino
della Battaglia 4

Ireland
Embassy: (☎ 06 697 91 21) Piazza Campitelli

The Netherlands
Embassy: (☎ 06 322 11 41) Via Michele
Mercati 8

New Zealand
Embassy: (☎ 06 441 71 71) Via Zara 28

Slovenia
Embassy: (☎ 06 808 10 75) Via L Pisano 10

Spain
Embassy: (☎ 06 68 32 168) Largo Fontanella
Borghese 19
Consulate: (☎ 06 687 14 01) Via Campo
Marzio 34

Switzerland
Embassy: (☎ 06 80 95 71) Via Barnarba
Oriani 61
Consulate: (☎ 06 808 83 61) Largo Elvezia 1

K

:mbassy: (☎ 06 482 54 41) Via XX
ettembre 80a

;A

:mbassy: (☎ 06 4 67 41) Via Vittorio
/eneto 119a-121

onsulates in Florence

may be handier for some to go to their
nsulate in Florence. Quite a few countries
ve consular reps here, including:

ance (☎ 055 230 25 56) Piazza Ognissanti 2.
Office hours are from 9 am to noon Monday
o Friday.
:rmany (☎ 055 29 47 22) Lungarno Vespucci
i0. Office hours are from 9.30 am to 12.30 pm
Monday to Friday.
ie Netherlands (☎ 055 47 52 49) Via
Cavour 81
vitzerland (☎ 055 22 24 34) Piazzale Galileo 5
K (☎ 055 28 41 33) Lungarno Corsini 2
;A (☎ 055 239 82 76) Lungarno Vespucci 38.
Office hours are from 9 am to 12.30 pm and
2.30 to 3.30 pm Monday to Friday.

USTOMS

1 July 1999 duty-free sales within the
U were abolished. Under the rules of the
ngle market, goods bought in and ex-
•rted within the EU incur no additional
ixes, provided duty has been paid some-
here within the EU and the goods are for
:rsonal consumption.

Travellers coming from outside the EU,
the other hand, can import, duty free:
)0 cigarettes, 1L of spirits, 2L of wine,
)mL of perfume, 250mL of toilet water,
id other goods up to a total value of
340,000 (€175); anything over this limit
ust be declared on arrival and the appro-
iate duty paid (it is advisable to carry all
ceipts).

1ONEY

combination of travellers cheques and
edit or cash cards is the best way to take
iur money.

urrency

ntil the euro notes and coins are in circu-
ition, Italy's currency will remain the lira
•lural: lire). The smallest note is L1000.

Other denominations in notes are L2000,
L5000, L10,000, L50,000, L100,000 and
L500,000. Coin denominations are L50,
L100 (two types of silver coin), L200, L500
and L1000.

Remember that, like other continental
Europeans, Italians indicate decimals with
commas and thousands with points.

Exchange Rates

country	unit		lire
Australia	AS$1	=	L1295
Canada	C$1	=	L1280
euro	€1	=	L1940
France	1FF	=	L290
Germany	DM1	=	L975
Ireland	£IR1	=	L2460
Japan	¥100	=	L15
New Zealand	NZ$1	=	L1127
UK	UK£1	=	L2804
USA	US$1	=	L1772

Exchanging Money

If you need to change cash or travellers
cheques, be prepared to queue (this is when
you'll wish you had a credit/debit card to
stick in the nearest friendly ATM!).

You can change money in banks, at the
post office or in special change offices.
Banks are generally the most reliable and
tend to offer the best rates. However, you
should look around and ask about commissions. These can fluctuate considerably and
a lot depends on whether you are changing
cash or cheques. While the post office
charges a flat rate of L1000 per cash transaction, banks charge L2500 or even more.
Travellers cheques attract higher fees. Some
banks charge L1000 per cheque with a
L3000 minimum, while the post office
charges a maximum L5000 per transaction.
Other banks will have different arrangements again, and in all cases you should
compare the exchange rates too.

You should keep a sharp eye open for
commissions at exchange booths. By way
of example, Exact Change charges 9.8% on
foreign currency travellers cheques. Another booth was charging 5% on cash or
cheques along with a set fee (L1000 for

Introducing the Euro

Since 1 January 1999, the lira and the euro – the new currency in 11 EU countries – have both been legal tender in Italy. Euro coins and banknotes have not been issued yet, but you can already get billed in euros and opt to pay in euros by credit card. Essentially, if there's no hard cash involved, you can deal in euros. Travellers should check bills carefully to make sure that any conversion has been calculated correctly.

The whole idea behind the current paperless currency is to give euro-fearing punters a chance to limber up arithmetically before euro coins and banknotes are issued on 1 January 2002. The same euro coins (one to 50 cents, €1 and €2) and banknotes (€5 to €500) will then be used in the 11 countries of what has been dubbed Euroland: Austria, Belgium, Finland, France, Germany, Ireland, Italy, Luxembourg, the Netherlands, Portugal and Spain. The lira will remain legal currency alongside the euro until 1 July 2002, when it will be hurled on the scrapheap of history.

Until then, the 11 currencies have been fixed to the euro at the following rates: AS13.76, BF40.34, 5.95 mk, 6.56FF, DM1.96, IR£0.79, L1936, flux40.34, f2.2, 200$48 and 166.39 ptas. The Lonely Planet Web site at www.lonelyplanet.com has a link to a currency converter and up-to-date news on the integration process. Or have a look at europa.eu.int/euro/html/entry.html.

Euro exchange rates include:

country	unit		euro
Australia	A$1	=	€0.62
Canada	C$1	=	€0.65
Japan	¥100	=	€0.91
New Zealand	NZ$1	=	€0.50
UK	UK£1	=	€1.56
USA	US$1	=	€0.95

cash and L3000 for travellers cheques). Thomas Cook charges 4.5% (L5500 minimum) for cash or cheques (except Thomas Cook travellers cheques, which are free of commission).

Cash Don't bring wads of cash from hom (travellers cheques and plastic are mu safer – see below). Wandering around wi pounds and dollars in your pockets is ju asking to be made instantly poor by rubbe fingers. It is, however, an idea to keep emergency stash separate from other val ables in case you should lose your travelle cheques and credit cards. You will ne cash for many day-to-day transactio (many small pensioni, eateries and sho take cash only). Try not to carry aroun more than you need at any one time – much the same way as you try to avo doing so at home!

Travellers Cheques These protect yo money because they can be replaced if th are lost or stolen. They can be cashed most banks and exchange offices. Americ Express (Amex) and Thomas Cook a widely accepted brands. If you lose yo Amex cheques, you can call a 24 hour to free number (☎ 800 87 20 00) anywhere Italy.

It doesn't matter whether your chequ are denominated in lire or in the curren of the country you buy them in: Italian e change outlets will change most no obscure currencies. Get most of yo cheques in fairly large denominations (t equivalent of L100,000 or more) to save any per-cheque commission charges. Am exchange offices charge no commission change travellers cheques (even oth brands).

It's vital to keep your initial receipt, a a record of your cheque numbers and t ones you have used, separate from t cheques themselves. Take along your pas port when you go to cash travelle cheques.

Credit/Debit Cards Carrying plast (whether a credit or debit card) is the si plest way to organise your holiday fund You don't have large amounts of cash cheques to lose, you can get money aft hours and at weekends and the exchan rate is sometimes better than that offered f travellers cheques or cash exchanges.

rranging for payments to be made into our card account while you are travelling, ou can avoid paying interest.

Major credit/debit cards, such as Visa, MasterCard, Eurocard, Cirrus and Eurocheques cards, are accepted throughout taly.

They can be used for many purchases (inluding in some supermarkets) and in hotels nd restaurants (although pensioni and maller *trattorie* and *pizzerie* tend to accept ash only). Credit cards can also be used in ATMs *(bancomat)* displaying the appropriate sign or (if you have no PIN number) to btain cash advances over the counter in nany banks – Visa and MasterCard are mong the most widely recognised for such ransactions. Check charges with your bank ut, as a rule, there is no charge for purhases on major cards and a minimum harge on cash advances and ATM transacions in foreign currencies. For larger withrawals this charge rarely exceeds 1.5%.

It is not uncommon for ATMs in Italy to eject foreign cards. Don't despair or start vasting money on international calls to our bank. Try a few more ATMs displayng your credit card's logo before assuming he problem lies with your card rather than vith the local system.

If your credit card is lost, stolen or swalowed by an ATM, you can telephone tollree to have an immediate stop put on its se. For MasterCard the number in Italy is ☎ 800 87 08 66, or make a reverse-charges all to St Louis in the USA on ☎ 314-275 6 90; for Visa, phone ☎ 800 87 72 32 in aly.

Amex is also widely accepted (although ot as common as Visa or MasterCard). The ffice in Florence has an express cash mahine for cardholders. If you lose your mex card you can call ☎ 800 86 40 46.

nternational Transfers One reliable way o send money to Italy is by 'urgent telex' through the foreign office of a large Italian ank, or through major banks in your own ountry, to a nominated bank in Italy. It is nportant to have an exact record of all deils associated with the money transfer.

The money will always be held at the head office of the bank in the town to which it has been sent. Urgent-telex transfers should take only a few days, while other means, such as telegraphic transfer, or draft, can take weeks.

It is also possible to transfer money through Amex and Thomas Cook.

A speedier option is to send money through Western Union (toll-free ☎ 800 46 44 64 or ☎ 800 22 00 55). The sender and receiver have to turn up at a Western Union outlet with passport or other form of ID and the fees charged for the virtually immediate transfer depend on the amount sent. For sums up to US$400, Western Union charges the *sender* US$20; the money can supposedly be handed over to the recipient within 10 minutes of being sent. This service functions through several outlets in Tuscany.

Another service along the same lines is MoneyGram, which operates mainly through Thomas Cook. Like Western Union, however, they are expanding their network of agents.

Security

Keep only a limited amount as cash, and the bulk in more easily replaceable forms such as travellers cheques or plastic. If your accommodation has a safe, use it. If you have to leave money in your room, divide it into several stashes and hide them in different places.

For carrying money on the street the safest thing is a shoulder wallet or under-the-clothes money belt. An external money belt attracts rather than deflects attention from your valuables.

Costs

Tuscany is expensive. Accommodation charges (especially in high season) and high entrance fees for many sights keep daily expenditure high. A *very* prudent backpacker might scrape by on around L80,000 a day, but only by staying in youth hostels, eating one simple meal a day (at the youth hostel), buying a sandwich or pizza slice for lunch, travelling slowly to keep transport costs

euro currency converter L10,000 = €5.16

down and minimising visits to museums and galleries.

One rung up, you can get by on L150,000 per day if you stay in the cheaper pensioni or small hotels, and keep sit-down meals and museum visits to one a day. Lone travellers may find even this budget hard to maintain.

If money is no object, you'll find a plethora of ways to burn it. In the cities especially there's no shortage of luxury hotels, expensive restaurants and shops to wave wads at. Realistically, a traveller wanting to stay in comfortable lower to mid-range hotels, eat two square meals a day, not feel restricted to one museum a day and be able to enjoy the odd drink and other minor indulgences should reckon on a minimum daily average of L250,000 a day – more if you have a car.

Ways to Save If you could it would be nice to avoid paying the extra charged by many pensioni for compulsory breakfast – a coffee and brioche in a cafe cost less and are better. The sad reality is that most places only offer the one price on rooms that automatically includes breakfast.

In bars, prices can double (sometimes even triple) if you sit down and are served at the table. Stand at the bar to drink your coffee or eat a sandwich.

Read the fine print on menus (usually posted outside eating establishments) to check the cover charge *(coperto)* and service fee *(servizio)*.

Aerograms (on sale only at the post office for L900) are the cheapest way to send international mail.

Tipping
You are not expected to tip on top of restaurant service charges, but it is common to leave a small amount. If there is no service charge, the customer might consider leaving a 10% tip, but this is by no means obligatory. In bars, Italians often leave any small change as a tip, often only L100 or L200. Tipping taxi drivers is not common practice, but you should tip the porter at higher class hotels.

Taxes & Refunds
Value-added tax, known as IVA (Imposta e Valore Aggiunto) is slapped on to just abou everything in Italy and hovers around 19%. Tourists who are residents of countries outside the EU may claim a refund on this ta if the item was purchased for personal us and cost more than a certain amour (L300,000 in 1999). The goods must be cai ried with you and you must keep the fisca receipt.

The refund only applies to items pui chased at retail outlets affiliated to the sys tem – these shops display a 'Tax-free fc tourists' sign. Otherwise, ask the shop keeper. You must fill out a form at the poir of purchase and have the form stamped an checked by Italian customs when you leav the country. You then return it by ma within 60 days to the vendor, who wi make the refund, either by cheque or t your credit card. At major airports an some border crossings you can get an im mediate cash refund at specially marke booths.

Receipts
Laws aimed at tightening controls on th payment of taxes in Italy mean that the onu is on the buyer to ask for and retain receipi for all goods and services. This applies t everything from a litre of milk to a haircu Although it rarely happens, you could b asked by an officer of the Fiscal Polic (Guardia di Finanza) to produce the receip immediately after you leave a shop. If yo don't have it, you may be obliged to pay fine of up to L300,000.

POST & COMMUNICATIONS
Post
Italy's postal service is notoriously slov unreliable and expensive.

Stamps *(francobolli)* are available at po: offices and authorised tobacconists (loc for the official *tabacchi* sign: a big 'T often white on black). Main post offices i the bigger cities are generally open fro around 8 am to at least 5 pm. Many open c Saturday morning too. Tobacconists kee regular shop hours.

Rates Postcards and letters up to 20g sent air mail cost L1400 to Australia and New Zealand, L1300 to the USA and L800 to EU countries (L900 to the rest of Europe). Aerograms are a cheap alternative, costing only L900 to send anywhere. They can be purchased at post offices only.

A new service, *posta prioritaria* (priority post – a little like the UK's 1st class post), began in 1999. For L1200, postcards and letters up to 20g posted to destinations within Italy, the EU, Switzerland and Norway are supposed to arrive the following day.

Sending letters express *(espresso)* costs a standard extra L3600, but may help speed a letter on its way.

If you want to post more important items by registered mail *(raccomandato)* or by insured mail *(assicurato)*, remember that they will take as long as normal mail. Raccomandato costs L4000 on top of the normal cost of the letter. The cost of assicurato depends on the value of the object being sent (L6000 for objects up to L100,000 value) and is not available to the USA.

Sending Mail If you choose not to use posta prioritaria (see Rates above) an airmail letter can take up to two weeks to reach the UK or the USA, while a letter to Australia will take between two and three weeks.

The service within Italy is not much better: local letters take at least three days and up to a week to arrive in another city.

Parcels *(pacchetti)* can be sent from any post office. You can buy posting boxes or padded envelopes from most post offices. Stationery shops *(cartolerie)* and some tobacconists also sell padded envelopes. Don't tape up or staple envelopes – they should be sealed with glue. Your best bet is not to close the envelope or box completely and ask at the counter how it should be done. Parcels usually take longer to be delivered than letters. A different set of postal rates applies.

Express Mail
Urgent mail can be sent by the post office's express mail service, known as *posta celere*

or CAI Post. Letters up to 500g cost L30,000 in Europe, L46,000 to the USA and L68,000 to Australia. A parcel weighing 1kg will cost L34,000 in Europe, L54,000 to the USA and Canada, and L80,000 to Australia and New Zealand. CAI post is not necessarily as fast as private services. It will take three to five days for a parcel to reach the USA, Canada or Australia and one to three days to European destinations. Ask at post offices for addresses of CAI post outlets.

Couriers Several international couriers operate in Italy: DHL has the toll-free number ☎ 800 34 53 45; for Federal Express call toll-free ☎ 800 12 38 00; for UPS call toll-free ☎ 800 82 20 54. Look in the telephone book for addresses. Note that if you are having articles sent to you by courier in Italy, you might be obliged to pay IVA of up to 20% to retrieve the goods.

Receiving Mail
Poste restante is known as *fermo posta*. Letters marked thus will be held at the counter of the same name in the main post office in the relevant town. Poste restante mail should be addressed as follows:

> John SMITH,
> Fermo Posta,
> Posta Centrale
> 50100 Florence
> Italy

Postcodes are provided throughout this guide. You will need to pick up your letters in person and present your passport as ID.

Amex card or travellers cheque holders can use the free client mail-holding service at Amex offices. Take your passport when you go to pick up mail.

Telephone
The partly privatised Telecom Italia is the largest phone company in the country and its orange public pay phones are liberally scattered all over the place. The most common accept only telephone cards *(carte/schede telefoniche)*, although you will still

Emergency Numbers

Military Police (Carabinieri)	☎ 112
Police (Polizia)	☎ 113
Fire Brigade (Vigili del Fuoco)	☎ 115
Highway Rescue	
(Soccorso Stradale)	☎ 116
Ambulance (Ambulanza)	☎ 118

find some that accept cards and coins (L100, L200 and L500). Some card phones now also accept special Telecom credit cards and even commercial credit cards.

Phones can be found in the streets, train stations and some big stores as well as in unstaffed Telecom centres, a few of which also have telephone directories for other parts of the country.

You can buy phonecards at post offices, tobacconists, newspaper stands and from vending machines in Telecom offices. To avoid the frustration of trying to find fast-disappearing coin telephones, always keep a phonecard on hand. They come with a value of L5000, L10,000 and L15,000. Remember to snap off the perforated corner before using them.

Public phones operated by a new telecommunications company, Infostrada, can be found in airports and train stations. These phones accept Infostrada phonecards (available from post offices, tobacconists and newspaper stands), which come with a value of L3000, L5000 or L10,000. Infostrada's rates are slightly cheaper than Telecom's for long-distance and international calls but you cannot make local calls from these phones.

Costs Rates, particularly for long-distance calls, are among the highest in Europe. The cheapest time for domestic calls is from 6.30 pm to 8 am. It is a little more complicated for international calls but, basically, the cheapest off-peak time is 10 pm to 8 am and all of Sunday, depending on the country called.

A local call *(comunicazione urbana)* from a public phone will cost L200 for three to six minutes, depending on the time of day

you call. Peak call times are 8 am to 6.3 pm Monday to Friday and 8 am to 1 pm Sa urday.

Rates for long-distance calls within Ital *(comunicazione interurbana)* depend on th time of day and the distance involved. A the worst, one minute will cost about L34 in peak periods.

If you need to call overseas, beware of th cost – even a call of five minutes to Aus tralia after 10 pm will cost around L10,00 from a private phone (more from a publi phone). Calls to most of the rest of Europ (except UK, which is cheaper) cost L76 per minute (the first minute costs L1245 and closer to L1200 from a public phone.

Travellers from countries that offer direc dialling services paid for at home countr rates (such as AT&T in the USA and Telstr in Australia) should think seriously abou taking advantage of them.

Domestic Calls Since July 1998 are codes have become an integral part of th phone number. The codes all began with and consisted of up to four digits. You mus now dial this whole number even if callin from next door. Thus, any number you cal in the Florence area will begin with 055.

Toll-free numbers *(numeri verdi)* that unti February 1999 began with the digits 16 have been changed to 800 numbers (bringin Italy into line with an international trend).

Mobile-telephone numbers begin with four digit prefix such as 0330, 0335, 0347 etc

For directory enquiries within Italy, dia ☎ 12.

Note Not content to make the area cod part of the phone number, it is planned t convert the initial 0 into a 4 by the end o 2000. Thus any number in the Florence are will start with 455.

International Calls Direct internationa calls can easily be made from public tele phones by using a phonecard. Dial 00 to ge out of Italy, then the relevant country and cit codes, followed by the telephone number.

Useful country codes are: Australia 6 Canada and USA 1, New Zealand 64 and

e UK 44. Codes for other countries in Euope include: France 33, Germany 49,
reece 30, Ireland 353 and Spain 34. Other
odes are listed in Italian telephone books.

To make a reverse charges (collect) in-
rnational call from a public telephone,
ial ☎ 170.

Easier, and often cheaper, is using the
ountry Direct service in your country. You
ial the number and request a reverse
narges call through the operator in your
ountry. Numbers for this service include
e following (note that in some countries
e number of options grows as more com-
anies and plans emerge – there are seven
ptions for the USA!):

Australia (Optus)	☎ 172 11 61
Australia (Telstra)	☎ 172 10 61
Canada (AT&T)	☎ 172 10 02
Canada (Teleglobe)	☎ 172 10 01
France	☎ 172 00 33
Germany	☎ 172 00 49
Ireland	☎ 172 03 53
The Netherlands	☎ 172 00 31
New Zealand	☎ 172 10 64
UK (BT)	☎ 172 00 44
UK (BT Automatic)	☎ 172 01 44
USA (AT&T)	☎ 172 10 11
USA (IDB)	☎ 172 17 77
USA (MCI)	☎ 172 10 22
USA (Sprint)	☎ 172 18 77

or international directory enquiries call
☎ 176.

nternational Phonecards The Lonely
lanet eKno Communication Card (visit its
Veb site at www.ekno.lonelyplanet.com
or details) is aimed specifically at inde-
endent travellers and provides budget
nternational calls, a range of messaging
ervices, free email and travel information
for local calls, you're usually better off
vith a local card. You can join online, or by
hone from Italy by dialling ☎ 800 875691.
Once you have joined, to use eKno from
taly dial ☎ 800 875683.

Check the eKno Web site for joining and
ccess numbers from other countries and
pdates on super budget local access num-
ers and new features.

A growing army of private companies
now distribute international phonecards,
some linked to US phone companies such
as Sprint and MCI. The cards come in a
variety of unit sizes and are sold in some
bars, tobacconists, newspaper stands and
other shops – look out for signs advertising them.

Telecom itself has brought out its Welcome Card, which costs L25,000 for 100
units and is certainly cheaper than making
international calls on a standard phonecard,
but may not stand up to some of the competition. Other new Telecom cards can be
used in several countries as well as Italy.

Another competitor in Italy is Infostrada.
They sell various cards, some of which are
only good in the very limited number of Infostrada phones around. The best for international calls cost L20,000 and can be used
from private or public phones (you dial a
toll-free access number and then key in a
provided code).

A further possibility for long-distance
calls are privately run call centres. Yellow
Point at Via Santa Elisabetta 5 in Florence
is a newcomer to Italy. You pay for a card
to use in one of their phones. When you
have finished, they check what you have
left on the card and pay you the difference.
They claim the rates work out cheaper than
dialing with Telecom.

Calling Tuscany from Abroad Call the
international access code (00 in most countries), followed by the code for Italy (39)
and the full number – remember to include
the initial zero (for example – 00 39 055
555 55 55). If calling a mobile phone you
must drop the initial 0.

Telegram

These dinosaurs can be sent from post offices or dictated by phone (☎ 186) and are
an expensive, but sure, way of having important messages delivered by the same or
next day.

Fax

There is no shortage of fax offices in Italy
but the country's high telephone charges

make faxes an expensive mode of communication. Some offices charge per page and others charge per minute, and still others charge for both! In all cases, prices vary considerably from one office to another. However, in general, to send a fax within Italy you can expect to pay L4000 for the first page and L1500 for each page thereafter, or L3000 for the first minute and L1500 for subsequent minutes. International faxes can cost from L8000 for the first page and L5000 per page thereafter, depending on the destination. Per minute, a fax to an EU country can cost L7000 for the first minute and L3500 thereafter; to the USA it can cost L9000 for the first minute and L4500 thereafter. Faxes can also be sent from some Telecom public phones. It usually costs about L1000 per page to receive a fax.

Email & Internet Access

Italy has been a little slower than some parts of Western Europe to march down the information highway. Nevertheless, email has definitely arrived. If you plan to carry your notebook or palmtop computer with you, buy a universal AC adapter, which will enable you to plug it in anywhere without frying the innards. You'll also need a plug adapter – it's easiest to buy these before you leave home.

Also, your PC-card modem may or may not work once you leave your home country – and you won't know for sure until you try. The safest option is to buy a reputable 'global' modem before you leave home, or buy a local PC-card modem if you're spending an extended time in Italy. The telephone socket will sometimes be different from that at home, so have at least a US RJ-11 telephone adapter that works with your modem. You can almost always find an adapter that will convert from RJ-11 to the local variety. For more information on travelling with a portable computer, see www.teleadapt.com or www.warrior.com.

Major Internet service providers (ISPs), such as CompuServe (www.compuserve .com) and IBM Net (www.ibm.net), have dial-in nodes in Italy; download a list of the dial-in numbers before you leave home –

and read the fine print. Often you pay a extra fee for use of a local node.

Some Italian servers can provide short term accounts for Internet access. Flashn (☎ 06 66 05 41) offers 20-hour renewab subscriptions for L30,000 (valid for on year); www.flashnet.it (Italian only) has list of authorised sales points in Italy. Ago (☎ 06 699 17 42) has subscriptions for tw months for L84,000. These providers hav English-speaking staff.

If you intend to rely on cybercafes, you' need to carry three pieces of informatio with you to enable you to access your In ternet mail account: your incoming (POP IMAP) mail server name, your accou name and your password. Your ISP or ne work supervisor will be able to give yo these. Armed with this information, yo should be able to access your Internet ma account from any Net-connected machin in the world. Another option to collect ma through cybercafes is to open a free eKn Web-based email account on line www.ekno.lonelyplanet.com. You can the access your mail from anywhere in th world from any Net-connected machin running a standard Web browser.

You'll find plenty of cybercafes in Flo ence, but they are not so common in othe parts of Tuscany. You can expect to pa from L10,000 to L15,000 an hour.

INTERNET RESOURCES

The World Wide Web is a rich resource fo travellers. You can research your trip, hun down bargain air fares, book hotels, chec on weather conditions or chat with local and other travellers about the best places t visit (or avoid!).

One of the best places to start your We explorations is the Lonely Planet Web sit (www.lonelyplanet.com).

ATAF Online All you ever wanted to know, an probably quite a few things you didn't, abou Florence's public transport system. www.comune.firenze.it/ataf
Chianti A useful site devoted to this popula wine region. www.chianti.it
Chiantinet An excellent site with lots of info

e cluttered Ponte Vecchio in Florence looks much as it did when constructed in 1345.

e Leaning Tower of Pisa looms precariously – but it's quite safe to get off the bus.

ena offers an amazing concentration of historic buildings.

Motorini – nip around Florence in style.

The Piazza, Pienza, designed by Rossellino

Meander slowly through the Tuscan countryside.

The old fishing port of Portoferraio, Elba

mation about the Chianti area and links to other sites.

www.chiantinet.it

Citylife A site full of more or less useful listings information and a host of links.

www.firenze.net

CTS Village Useful information from CTS, Italy's leading student travel organisation. Italian only.

www.cts.it

Excite Reviews Call this site up and key in Italy and it will give you a long selection of sites related to Italy, as well as brief reviews and ratings.

www.excite.com

Excite Travel This site contains a farefinder and booking facilities and links to maps, restaurant tips and the like.

city.net/countries/italy/florence

Ferroive dello Stato This is the official site of the Ferrovie dello Stato, the Italian railways. You can look up fare and timetable information here, although it can be a little complicated to plough through.

www.fs-on-line.com

Go Tuscany This site is aimed at the expat community and English-speaking visitors to the region. It contains tips on places to stay and eat in and outside Florence, itineraries in Tuscany, classified ads and an events calendar.

www.firenze.net/events

Informacittà Here you can check out the latest on what's happening in and around Florence.

www.informacitta.net

Internet Cafe Guide At this site you can get a list of Internet cafes in Florence (and around Italy). It's not as up to date as you might expect such a site to be, but it is a start.

www.netcafeguide.com/frames

Italink This is a busy site with info on everything from emergency telephone numbers to airline reservation contacts, with stuff on Florence events, nightlife, cinema, study and so on. It also boasts some good links and claims to be updated weekly.

www.italink.com/fbnet.htm

Parks.it This is the place to look for basic information on all of Italy's national and regional parks, along with any other protected areas. Naturally all of Tuscany's parks are here.

www.parks.it

Siena All From this page you can fan out in search of all sorts of Siena- and Tuscany-related links. Everything from books to events, museum timetables to notes on the life of Santa Caterina can be located here. Italian only.

www.novamedia.it/sienall

Siena Online At this address you can open a

series of Web pages and search links for items on Siena.

www.sienaol.it

Siena Tourist Office The provincial Siena tourist office site has useful info on tourist offices throughout the province, as well as other items of interest. Italian only.

www.siena.turismo.toscana.it

BOOKS

Most books are published in different editions by different publishers in different countries. As a result, a book might be a hardcover rarity in one country while it is readily available in paperback in another. Your local bookshop or library is best placed to advise you on the availability of the following recommendations.

Lonely Planet

If you intend to spend most of your time in Florence, the guide *Florence*, with more in-depth information on the city, may be useful. Travellers planning to move around more widely should consider *Italy*. The *Italian phrasebook* lists all the words and phrases you're likely to need when travelling in Italy.

Lonely Planet's *World Food Italy* is a full-colour book with information on the whole range of Italian food and drink. It includes a useful language section, with the definitive culinary dictionary and a handy quick-reference glossary.

Guidebooks

If you like density, the ultimate guides are the red hardbacks published in Italian by the Touring Club Italiano. Look for *Toscana* and *Firenze e Provincia*. To give you an idea of what you are in for, the latter is some 800 closely printed pages. The TCI, perhaps realising that not everyone can get their heads around this sort of thing, also puts out a much more user-friendly, green soft cover series.

Travel

An endless stream of foreign wallahs has poured into Tuscany over the centuries to soak in the beauty and express an opinion. Many barely got past the expat communities of Florence and some of their opinions are remarkable more for their pomposity than for any insight. Numerous exceptions confirm that harsh rule.

Two Grand Tour classics are Johann Wolfgang von Goethe's *Italienische Reise* (*Italian Journey*, 1786-88), and Henry James' *Italian Hours*. DH Lawrence wrote three short travel books while living in Italy, now combined in one volume entitled *DH Lawrence and Italy*. The relevant one is *Etruscan Places*, in which Lawrence fairly writhes in ecstasy over this ancient people. Something about their phallic knowledge – what was Lawrence's problem?

A brief, readable, insightful and highly opinionated account of Florence, its past and its foibles is *The Stones of Florence* by Mary McCarthy.

Italian History & People

Edward Gibbon's *History of the Decline and Fall of the Roman Empire* (available in six hardback volumes, or an abridged, single-volume paperback) remains the masterwork on that subject in English.

For a general look at Italy, try *History of the Italian People* by Giuliano Procacci. Other options to help you get started include *Italy: A Short History* by Harry Hearder and *Concise History of Italy* by Vincent Cronin. *A History of Contemporary Italy: Society and Politics 1943-1988*, by Paul Ginsburg, is an absorbing analysis of the country's post-WWII travails.

Tuscan History & People

It is damned near impossible to find a general history of Tuscany. Time and again you will be offered histories of Florence. It is even fairly difficult to come across histories of other Tuscan cities. The following will get you started.

Christopher Hibbert's *The Rise and Fall of the House of Medici* is an acknowledged classic on the fortunes of Florence's most famous family. For a more general history of the city, try his *Biography of Florence*, which sweeps you along at a brisk pace through the political, social and artistic highs and lows of the city. Hibbert's racy

narrative style makes both books a good initial investment.

Leaning more to the artistic side of the story of Florence is Michael Levey's *Florence – A Portrait*. Not as full of intriguing anecdote as Hibbert's books, it is still an excellent and highly readable treatment.

A rather more ponderous general history of the city is Marcello Vanuzzi's multi-volume *Storia di Firenze*. The quirky text has been condensed into an English version, *The History of Florence*. The information is in there, but the often overly lyrical style is a little peculiar, not to say highly irritating at some points.

Ferdinand Schevill's *Siena – The History of a Medieval Commune* was penned at the beginning of the 20th century. Some of the writer's assertions should be read with a pinch of salt, but it remains one of the only accounts of the city in English.

For an excursion into the day-to-day life of a Tuscan merchant family, get hold of Iris Origo's *The Merchant of Prato*, a splendid synthesis of the reams of documentation that have survived from the 14th century.

Art & Architecture

An attractive coffee table book with serious content is *History of Italian Renaissance Art* by Frederick Hartt. He concentrates on Florence, but does not overlook art and architecture elsewhere in Tuscany. He of course also deals with the greats of Roman and Venetian art too. Hartt was one of the most distinguished authorities on Renaissance art in the 20th century.

A good general reference work covering the Renaissance in all its facets is JR Hale's *Concise Encyclopedia of the Italian Renaissance*.

Charles Avery's *Florentine Renaissance Sculpture* is a comprehensive study of this aspect of Florence's glittering artistic legacy.

Bruno Nardini's *Incontro con Michelangiolo* has been translated as *Michelangelo – Biography of a Genius*, a compelling account of the artist's life.

If you think you are up to it, you can pick up Giorgio Vasari's classic *Le Vite de' Eccellenti Architetti, Pittori, et Scultori Ital-*

ani, da Cimabue, insino a' Tempi Nostri, better known to English readers simply as *Lives of the Artists*, available in several editions and translations.

Children

Bambini alla Scoperta di Florence (translated as *Florence for Kids*) is a brightly presented book for young people obliged by their elders to explore the city. It is an entertaining, informative approach, with quizzes and other learning prompts. Adults can learn quite a lot about the city too. It is published by Fratelli Palomb Editori.

Maureen Wheeler's *Travel with Children* gives practical information and advice to make travel as stress-free as possible.

Cuisine

The Food of Italy by Waverley Root is an acknowledged classic covering Italian cuisine in general. For more specifically Tuscan cooking, you could try *Il Libro della Cucina Fiorentina e Toscana*, a prettily illustrated job by Elisabetta Piazzesi that has been translated into several languages – you can find it in bookshops in Florence. For information on *World Food Italy*, Lonely Planet's guide to Italian cuisine, see earlier in this section.

Stephanie Alexander and Maggie Beer's *Tuscan Cooking* is a beautifully illustrated coffee table tome. Another more suited to the coffee table than the kitchen is Jeni Wright's *Tuscan Food and Folklore*.

For some fine traditional recipes, you will enjoy Slow Food Editore's *Ricette di Osterie di Firenze e Chianti* – if you read some Italian.

Wine buffs may want to get a hold of Luca Maroni's *Guide to Italian Wines* or *Italian Wines*.

Walking

For information on books describing walking in Tuscany, see the special section 'Tuscany on Foot' after this chapter.

NEWSPAPERS & MAGAZINES

You can easily find a wide selection of national daily newspapers from around Europe and the UK at newsstands all over central Florence and in most towns of consequence throughout Tuscany. The *International Herald Tribune*, *Time*, The *Economist*, *Le Monde*, *Der Spiegel* and a host of other international magazines are also available.

Italian National Press

There is no 'national' paper as such, but rather several important dailies published out of the major cities. These include Milan's *Corriere della Sera*, Turin's *La Stampa* and Rome's *La Repubblica*. This trio forms what could be considered the nucleus of a national press, publishing local editions up and down the country. Politically speaking, they range from centre-left *(La Repubblica)* to establishment right *(La Stampa)*.

Most daily papers cost L1500, unless there is a weekly magazine *inserto* of one sort or another, in which case the cost sometimes rises to L2200.

Local Press

The main regional broadsheet is the Florence-based *La Nazione*. Compared with the likes of the *Corriere della Sera* it is pretty poor on both national and foreign news, but if you are more interested in what's happening locally, it's probably the paper of choice. It is published in provincial editions, so the one you buy in Florence won't be exactly the same as the one you pick up in Grosseto. You will find a fairly decent cinema and theatre listings section in it too. Along the coast you will see *Il Tirreno*, again with local editions. Most provinces have at least one other local competition rag.

Useful Publications

The multi-lingual *Chianti News* sometimes has interesting articles but is directed more at local expats than passing interlopers.

RADIO

You can pick up the BBC World Service on medium wave at 648kHz, short wave at 6195kHz, 9410kHz, 12095kHz, 15575kHz, and on long wave at 198kHz, depending on where you are and the time of day. Voice of

America (VOA) can usually be found on short wave at 15205 kHz.

There are three state-owned stations: RAI-1 (1332 AM or 89.7 FM), RAI-2 (846 AM or 91.7 FM) and RAI-3 (93.7 FM). They combine classical and light music with news broadcasts and discussion programmes.

Many of the local stations are a little bland. For a good mix of contemporary music you could try Controradio on 93.6 AM or Nova Radio on 101.5 FM in Florence.

TV

The three state-run stations, RAI-1, RAI-2 and RAI-3 are run by Radio e Televisione Italiane. Historically, each has been in the hands of one of the main political groupings in the country, although those waters have been muddied in the past few years of musical chairs down in Rome.

Of the three, RAI-3 tends to have some of the more interesting programmes. Generally, however, these stations and the private Canale 5, Italia 1 and Rete 4, tend to serve up a diet of indifferent news, tacky variety hours (with lots of near-naked tits and bums, appalling crooning and vaudeville humour) and game shows. Talk shows, some interesting but many nauseating, also abound.

Other stations include TMC (Telemontecarlo), on which you can see CNN if you stay up late enough (starting from as late as 5 am), and a host of local channels.

VIDEO SYSTEMS

If you want to record or buy video tapes to play back home, you won't get a picture if the image registration systems are different. TVs and nearly all prerecorded videos on sale in Italy use the PAL (Phase Alternation Line) system common to most of Western Europe and Australia, incompatible with France's SECAM system or the NTSC system used in North America and Japan.

PHOTOGRAPHY
Film & Equipment

A roll of 100 ASA Kodak film costs around L7000/8000 for 24/36 exposures. Develop-

ing costs around L11,000/14,000 for 24/36 exposures in standard format. A roll of 36 slides costs L10,000 to buy and L8000 for development.

TIME

Italy operates on a 24-hour clock. Daylight-saving time starts on the last Sunday in March, when clocks are put forward one hour. Clocks are put back an hour on the last Sunday in October.

European countries such as France, Germany, Austria and Spain are on the same time as Italy. Greece, Egypt and Israel are one hour ahead. When it's noon in Florence, it's 11 pm in Auckland, 11 am in London, 6 am in New York, 7 pm in Perth, 3 am in San Francisco, 9 pm in Sydney and 6 am in Toronto.

ELECTRICITY
Voltages & Cycles

Electric current in Florence is 220V, 50Hz, as in the rest of continental Europe. Several countries outside Europe (such as the USA and Canada) have 60Hz, which means that appliances from those countries with electric motors (such as some CD and tape players) may perform poorly. It is always safest to use a transformer.

Plugs & Sockets

Plugs have two round pins, again as in the rest of continental Europe.

WEIGHTS & MEASURES

The metric system is used (see the inside back cover for a conversion chart). Basic terms for weight include *un etto* (100g) and *un chilo* (1kg). Like other continental Europeans, the Italians indicate decimals with commas and thousands with points.

LAUNDRY

Coin laundrettes, where you can do your own washing, are catching on in Italy. You'll find plenty in Florence and one or two in Siena and Pisa. A load will cost around L8000. Dry-cleaning *(lavasecco)* charges range from around L6000 for a shirt to L12,000 for a jacket.

TOILETS

Public toilets are not exactly widespread in Italy. Most people use the toilets in bars and cafes – although you might need to buy a coffee first!

HEALTH
Medical Services

If you need an ambulance anywhere in Italy call ☎ 118.

The quality of medical treatment in public hospitals varies in Italy. Simply put, the farther north, the better the care.

Private hospitals and clinics throughout the country generally provide excellent services but are expensive for those without medical insurance. That said, certain treatments in public hospitals may also have to be paid for, and in such cases can be equally costly.

Your embassy or consulate in Italy can provide a list of recommended doctors in major cities; however, if you have a specific health complaint, it would be wise to obtain the necessary information and referrals for treatment before leaving home.

The public health system is administered along provincial lines by centres generally known as Unità Sanitarie Locali (USL) or Unità Soci Sanitarie Locali (USSL). Increasingly they are being reorganised as Aziende Sanitarie Locali (ASL). Through them you find out where your nearest hospital, medical clinics and other services are. Look under 'U' or 'A' in the telephone book (sometimes the USL and USSL are under 'A' too, as Azienda USL).

Under these headings you'll find long lists of offices – look for Poliambulatorio (Polyclinic) and the telephone number for Accetazione Sanitaria. You need to call this number to make an appointment: there is no point in just rolling up. Clinic opening hours vary widely, with the minimum generally being about 8 am to 12.30 pm Monday to Friday. Some open for a couple of hours in the afternoon and on Saturday mornings too.

Each ASL/USL area has its own Consultorio Familiare (Family Planning Centre) where you can go for contraceptives, pregnancy tests and information about abortion (legal up to the 12th week of pregnancy).

For emergency treatment, go straight to the *pronto soccorso* (casualty) section of a public hospital, where you can also get emergency dental treatment. Sometimes hospitals are listed in the phone book under Aziende Ospedaliere. In major cities you are likely to find doctors who speak English, or a volunteer translator service. Often, first aid is also available at train stations, airports and ports.

Medical Cover

Citizens of EU countries are covered for emergency medical treatment in Italy on presentation of an E111 form. Treatment in private hospitals is not covered and charges are also likely for medication, dental work and secondary examinations, including X-rays and laboratory tests. Ask about the E111 at your local health services department a few weeks before you travel (in the UK, the form is available at post offices).

Australia also has a reciprocal arrangement with Italy so that emergency treatment is covered – Medicare in Australia publishes a brochure with the details. The USA, Canada and New Zealand do not have reciprocal arrangements and citizens of these countries will be required to pay for any treatment in Italy themselves. Advise medical staff of any reciprocal arrangements *before* they begin treating you. Most travel insurance policies include medical cover. See Travel Insurance under Visas & Documents earlier in this chapter.

General Preparations

Make sure you are healthy before you leave home. If you are embarking on a long trip, make sure your teeth are OK, because dental treatment is particularly expensive in Italy.

If you wear glasses, take a spare pair and your prescription. If you lose your glasses, you will be able to have them replaced within a few days by an *ottico* (optician).

Travellers who require a particular medication should take an adequate supply as well as the prescription, with the generic rather than the brand name, which will make getting replacements easier. Basic drugs are widely available and indeed many items requiring prescriptions in countries such as the USA can be obtained over the counter in Italy. Tampons and condoms are available in pharmacies and supermarkets.

No vaccinations are required for entry into Italy unless you have been travelling through a part of the world where yellow fever or cholera is prevalent.

Basic Rules

Stomach upsets are the most likely travel health problem, but in Italy the majority of these will be relatively minor and probably due to overindulgence in the local food. Some people take a while to adjust to the regular use of olive oil in the food.

Water Tap water is drinkable throughout Italy, although Italians themselves have taken to drinking the bottled stuff. The sign *acqua non potable* tells you that water is not drinkable (you may see it in trains and at some camping grounds). Water from drinking fountains is safe unless there is a sign telling you otherwise.

Everyday Health Normal body temperature is 37°C or 98.6°F; more than 2°C (4°F) higher indicates a 'high' fever. Normal adult pulse rate is 60 to 100 beats per minute (children 80 to 100; babies 100 to 140). As a general rule, the pulse increases by about 20 beats per minute for each °C (2°F) rise in fever.

Environmental Hazards

Heatstroke This serious and sometimes fatal condition can occur if the body's heat-regulating mechanism breaks down and the body temperature rises to dangerous levels. Long, continuous periods of exposure to high temperatures can leave you vulnerable to heatstroke. Avoid excessive alcohol or strenuous activity when you first arrive in Italy during mid-summer.

The symptoms of heatstroke are feeling unwell, not sweating much or at all and a high body temperature (39 to 41°C or 102 to 106°F). Where sweating has ceased, the skin becomes flushed. Severe, throbbing headaches and lack of coordination will also occur. The sufferer may become confused or aggressive. Eventually the victim will become delirious or convulse. Hospitalisation is essential and, meanwhile, get patients out of the sun, remove their clothing, cover them with a wet sheet or towel and then fan them continuously.

Hypothermia Too much cold can be just as dangerous as too much heat. If you are trekking at high altitudes, particularly at night, be prepared.

Hypothermia occurs when the body loses heat faster than it can produce it and the core temperature of the body falls. It is surprisingly easy to progress from very cold to dangerously cold due to a combination of wind, wet clothing, fatigue and hunger, even if the air temperature is above freezing. It is best to dress in layers: silk, wool and some of the new artificial fibres are all good insulating materials. A hat is important, as a lot of heat is lost through the head. A strong, waterproof outer layer (and a 'space' blanket for emergencies) is essential. Carry basic supplies, including food containing simple sugars to generate heat quickly and fluid to drink.

Symptoms of hypothermia are exhaustion, numb skin (particularly toes and fingers), shivering, slurred speech, irrational or violent behaviour, lethargy, stumbling, dizzy spells, muscle cramps and violent bursts of energy. Irrationality may take the form of sufferers claiming they are warm and trying to take off their clothes.

To treat mild hypothermia, first get the person out of the wind and/or rain, remove their clothing if it's wet and replace it with dry, warm clothing. Give them hot liquids – not alcohol – and some high-kilojoule, easily digestible food. Do not rub victims; instead, allow them to slowly warm themselves. This should be enough to treat the early stages of hypothermia. The early recognition and treatment of mild hypothermia is the only way to prevent severe hypothermia, which is a critical condition.

Motion Sickness Eating lightly before and during a trip will reduce the chances of motion sickness. If you are prone to motion sickness, try to find a place that minimises disturbance – near the wing on aircraft, close to midships on boats, near the centre on buses. Fresh air usually helps; reading and cigarette smoke don't. Commercial anti-motion-sickness preparations, which can cause drowsiness, have to be taken before the trip commences. Ginger (available in capsule form) and peppermint (including mint-flavoured sweets) are natural preventatives.

Prickly Heat Prickly heat is an itchy rash caused by excessive perspiration trapped under the skin. It usually strikes people who have just arrived in a hot climate. Keeping cool by bathing often, using a mild talcum powder or even resorting to air-conditioning may help until you acclimatise.

Sunburn At high altitude in the Alps you can get sunburnt surprisingly quickly, even through cloud. Use a sunscreen, a hat and some barrier cream for your nose and lips. Calamine lotion is good for soothing mild sunburn. Protect your eyes with good-quality sunglasses.

Infectious Diseases

Diarrhoea Despite all your precautions, you may still have a bout of mild travellers' diarrhoea. Dehydration is the main danger with any diarrhoea, particularly for children and the elderly, so fluid replenishment is the number-one treatment. Weak black tea with a little sugar, soda water or soft drinks allowed to go flat and diluted 50% with water are all good. With severe diarrhoea, a rehydrating solution is necessary to replace minerals and salts and you should see a doctor. Stick to a bland diet as you recover.

Hepatitis Hepatitis is a general term for inflammation of the liver. The symptoms are fever, chills, headache, fatigue, feelings of weakness and aches and pains, followed by loss of appetite, nausea, vomiting, abdominal pain, dark urine, light-coloured faeces, jaundiced (yellow) skin and the whites of the eyes may turn yellow. Hepatitis A is transmitted by contaminated food and drinking water. You should seek medical advice but there is not much you can do apart from resting, drinking lots of fluids, eating lightly and avoiding fatty foods. People who have had hepatitis should avoid alcohol for some time after the illness as the liver needs time to recover.

Hepatitis B is spread through contact with infected blood, blood products or body fluids – for example, through sexual contact, unsterilised needles, blood transfusions or contact with blood via small breaks in the skin. Other risk situations include getting a tattoo and body piercing. Hepatitis B may lead to long-term problems.

There is no treatment for hepatitis, but vaccination against the disease is readily available in most countries. The problem has been complicated in recent years by the discovery of a plethora of new strains of the disease: C, D, E and a rumoured G. Recent reports have shown a sharp rise in Italy in the incidence of hepatitis C through sexual contact.

Rabies Rabies is still found in Italy, but only in isolated areas of the Alps. It is transmitted through a bite or scratch by an infected animal. Dogs are noted carriers. Any bite, scratch or even lick from a mammal in an area where rabies does exist should be cleaned immediately and thoroughly. Scrub with soap and running water and then clean with an alcohol solution. Medical help should be sought immediately.

Sexually Transmitted Diseases If you require treatment or tests for a suspected STD or for HIV/AIDS, contact the provincial ASL (see the earlier Medical Services section). The Human Immunodeficiency Virus (HIV) may develop into Acquired Immune Deficiency Syndrome (AIDS). Exposure to infected blood, blood products or bodily fluids may put the individual at risk. In Italy, transmission is most likely through sexual contact with homosexual or bisexual males, or via contaminated needles shared by IV drug users. Apart from abstinence, the most effective preventative is always to practise safe sex using condoms. It's impossible to detect the HIV-positive status of an otherwise healthy-looking person without a blood test.

HIV/AIDS can be spread through infected blood transfusions, but in Italy blood is screened and they are safe. It can also be spread by dirty needles – acupuncture, tattooing and ear and nose piercing can potentially be as dangerous as intravenous drug use if the equipment isn't clean. The needles used in Italian hospitals are reliable. Fear of HIV infection should never preclude treatment for serious medical conditions.

Insect-Borne Diseases
Leishmaniasis This is a group of parasitic diseases transmitted by sandflies and found in coastal parts of Italy. Cutaneous leishmaniasis affects the skin tissue, causing ulceration and disfigurement; visceral leishmaniasis affects the internal organs. Avoiding sandfly bites by covering up and using repellent is the best precaution against this disease.

Lyme Disease Lyme disease is an infection transmitted by ticks that can be acquired throughout Europe, including in forested areas of Italy. The illness usually begins with a spreading rash at the site of the tick bite and is accompanied by fever, headache, extreme fatigue, aching joints and muscles and mild neck stiffness. If untreated, these symptoms usually resolve over several weeks but, over subsequent weeks or months, disorders of the nervous system, heart and joints may develop. Treatment works best early in the illness. Medical help should be sought.

Bites & Stings
Jellyfish Italian beaches are occasionally inundated with jellyfish. Their stings are painful but not dangerous. Dousing in vinegar will deactivate any stingers that have not fired. Calamine lotion, antihistamines and analgesics may reduce the reaction and

relieve the pain. If in doubt about swimming, ask locals if any jellyfish are in the water.

Snakes Italy's only dangerous snake, the viper, is found throughout Tuscany. To minimise your chances of being bitten, always wear boots, socks and long trousers when walking through undergrowth where snakes may be present. Don't put your hands into holes and crevices and do be careful when collecting firewood.

Viper bites do not cause instantaneous death and an antivenene is widely available in pharmacies. Keep the victim calm and still, wrap the bitten limb tightly, as you would for a sprained ankle, and attach a splint to immobilise it. Then seek medical help, if possible with the dead snake for identification. Don't attempt to catch the snake if there is even a remote possibility of being bitten again. Tourniquets and sucking out the poison are now comprehensively discredited.

Ticks Always check your body if you have been walking through a tick-infested area. In recent years there have been several reported deaths in Sardinia related to tick bites. Health authorities have yet to pinpoint the cause.

WOMEN TRAVELLERS
Tuscany is not a dangerous region for women, but women travelling alone will sometimes find themselves plagued by unwanted attention from men. This attention usually involves catcalls, hisses and whistles and, as such, is more annoying than anything else.

Lone women may at times also find it difficult to remain alone. It is not uncommon for Italian men to harass foreign women in the street, while drinking a coffee in a bar or trying to read a book in a park. Usually the best response is to ignore them, but if that doesn't work, politely tell them that you are waiting for your husband *(marito)* or boyfriend *(fidanzato)* and, if necessary, walk away. Florence can be a pain in this way, especially in the bars. It

an also be an issue in some of the coastal
esorts and on Elba.

Avoid becoming aggressive as this almost always results in an unpleasant con-
frontation. If all else fails, approach the
nearest member of the police or *carabinieri*
(military police force).

Basically, most of the attention falls into
the nuisance/harassment category. However,
women on their own should use their common sense. Avoid walking alone on deserted
and dark streets and look for centrally located hotels within easy walking distance of
places where you can eat at night. Women
should avoid hitchhiking alone.

Recommended reading is the *Handbook
for Women Travellers* by M & G Moss.

GAY & LESBIAN TRAVELLERS
Homosexuality is legal in Italy and well tol-
erated in the northern half of the country in
general. The legal age of consent is 16.

Gay discos and the like can be tracked
down through local gay organisations (see
below) or the national monthly gay magazine *Babilonia* which, along with the annual
Guida Gay Italia, is available at most newsstands. You can also read *Babilonia* on the
net at www.babilonia.net. Be warned, however, that outside Florence's limited scene
there ain't a lot happening on this front in
Tuscany.

International gay and lesbian guides
worth tracking down are the *Spartacus
Guide for Gay Men* (the Spartacus list also
includes the comprehensive *Spartacus National Edition Italia*, in English and German), published by Bruno Gmünder Verlag,
Mail Order, PO Box 61 01 04, 10921
Berlin; and *Places for Women*, published by
Ferrari Publications, Phoenix, AZ, USA.

Organisations
The national organisation for gay men is
ArciGay and its equivalent for lesbians, Ar-
ciLesbica (☎ 051 644 70 54, fax 644 67 22),
at Piazza di Porta Saragozza 2, 40123
Bologna.

You'll find any number of Italian gay
sites on the net, but some are all but useless.
ArciGay (www.gay.it/arcigay, Italian only)

has general information on the gay and lesbian scene in Italy and plenty of useful
links. For lesbians, the equivalent is Ar-
ciLesbica Nazionale (www.women.it/
~arciles).

In Florence, Azione Gay e Lesbica Finisterrae (☎/fax 055 67 12 98) is at Via Manara 6. It has a phone health consultation line
(☎ 055 48 82 88). It is also possible to
arrange to have HIV tests here. Their Web
site is at www.agora.stm.it/gaylesbica.fi.

DISABLED TRAVELLERS
The Italian State Tourist Office in your
country may be able to provide advice on
Italian associations for the disabled and
what help is available in the country. It may
also carry a small brochure, *Services for
Disabled People*, published by the Italian
railways, which details facilities at stations
and on trains. Some of the better trains,
such as the ETR460 and ETR500 trains,
have a carriage for passengers in wheel-
chairs and their companions.

The UK-based Royal Association for
Disability & Rehabilitation (RADAR) publishes a useful guide called *Holidays &
Travel Abroad: A Guide for Disabled
People*, which provides a good overview
of facilities available to disabled travellers throughout Europe. Contact RADAR
(☎ 020-7250 3222), Unit 12, City Forum,
250 City Rd, London EC1V 8AS.

Another organisation worth calling is Holiday Care Service (☎ 01293-774535). They
produce an information pack on Italy for disabled people and others with special needs.

Organisations
In Italy itself you may also be able to get
help. Co.In. (Cooperative Integrate) is a national voluntary group with links to the government and branches all over the country.
It publishes a quarterly magazine for disabled tourists, *Turismo per Tutti* (*Tourism
for All*) in Italian and English. They have information on accessible accommodation,
transport and attractions. Co.In. (☎ 06 23 26
75 05) is at Via Enrico Giglioli 54a, Rome.
Web site at andi.casaccia.enea.it/hometur
.htm.

SENIOR TRAVELLERS

Senior citizens are entitled to discounts on public transport and on admission fees at some museums in Tuscany. It is always important to ask. The minimum qualifying age is generally 60 years. You should also seek information in your own country on travel packages and discounts for senior travellers, through senior citizens' organisations and travel agents.

TRAVEL WITH CHILDREN

Successful travel with children can require a special effort. Don't try to overdo things by packing too much into the time available, and make sure activities include the kids as well. Remember that visits to museums and galleries can be tiring, even for adults. Allow time for the kids to play, either in a park or in the hotel room.

Discounts are available for children (usually under 12 years of age) on public transport and for admission to museums, galleries etc.

Always make a point of asking at tourist offices if they know of any special family or children's activities and for suggestions on hotels that cater for kids. Families should book accommodation in advance, where possible, to avoid inconvenience.

Chemists *(farmacie)* sell baby formula in powder or liquid form as well as sterilising solutions, such as Milton. Disposable nappies are widely available at supermarkets, chemists (where they are more expensive) and sometimes in larger stationary stores. A pack of around 30 disposable nappies (diapers) costs around L18,000. Fresh cow's milk is sold in cartons in bars (which have a 'Latteria' sign) and in supermarkets. If it is essential that you have milk you should carry an emergency carton of UHT milk, since bars usually close at 8 pm. In many out-of-the-way areas the locals use only UHT milk.

USEFUL ORGANISATIONS

The Istituto Italiano di Cultura (IIC), with branches all over the world, is a government-sponsored organisation aimed at promoting Italian culture and language. They put on classes in Italian and provide a library and information service. This is good place to start your search for places t study in Italy. The library at the Londo branch – 39 Belgrave Square, London SW (☎ 020-7235 1461) – has an extensive reference book collection, with works on th arts and history, a range of periodicals an videos. Other IIC branches include:

Australia
(☎ 03-9866 5931) 233 Domain Rd, South Yarra Melbourne, Vic 3141
(☎ 02-9392 7939) Level 45, Gateway Macquarie Place, Sydney, NSW 2000
Web site: www.iicmelau.org
Canada
(☎ 416-921 3802) 496 Huron Street, Toronto Ontario M5R 2R3
(☎ 514-849 3473) 1200 Penfield Drive, Montreal, Quebec H3A 1A9
Web site: www.iicto-ca.org/istituto.htm
France
(☎ 01 44 39 49 39) Hôtel Galliffet, 50 rue de Varenne, 75007 Paris
Web site: www.italynet.com/cultura/istcult
Germany
(☎ 030-261 7875) Hildebrandstrasse 1, 10785 Berlin
(☎ 089-764563) Hermann Schmidt Strasse 8 80336 Munich
Ireland
(☎ 01-676 6662) 11 Fitzwilliam Square, Dublin 2
Switzerland
(☎ 01-202 4846) Gotthardstrasse 27, 8002 Zürich
USA
(☎ 212-879 4242) 686 Park Ave, New York, NY 10021-5009
(☎ 310-443 3250) 1023 Hildegard Ave, Los Angeles, CA 90024
(☎ 202-387 5261) 1717 Massachussets Ave S104, NW, Washington, DC 20036
Web site: www.italcultny.org

Centro Turistico Studentesco e Giovanile (CTS) is the main Italian student and youth travel organisation. They act mainly as a travel agent, but you can also obtain ISIC, Euro<26 and Youth Hostel cards at their branches if you haven't already done so abroad. Note, however, that you will generally be obliged to pay a joining fee of L45,000. CTS has 13 branches scattered in the main centres across Tuscany.

DANGERS & ANNOYANCES
Theft
This is the main problem for travellers in Tuscany, although it is not as troublesome as in other parts of the country.

Pickpockets and bag-snatchers operate in the most touristy parts of the bigger cities and some of the coastal resort towns. Paying a little attention should help you avoid unpleasantness.

Wear a money belt under your clothing. Keep all important items, such as money, passport, other papers and tickets, in your money belt at all times. If you are carrying a bag or camera, wear the strap across your body and have the bag on the side away from the road to deter snatch thieves who operate from motorcycles and scooters. Thankfully motorcycle bandits aren't common in Tuscany, even in Florence.

In Florence especially you should also watch out for groups of dishevelled-looking women and children. They generally work in groups of four or five and carry paper or cardboard which they use to distract your attention while they swarm around and riffle through your pockets and bag. Never underestimate their skill – they are as fast as lightning and very adept.

Parked cars are also prime targets for thieves, particularly those with foreign number plates or rental company stickers. *Never* leave valuables in your car – in fact, try not to leave anything in the car if you can help it.

In case of theft or loss, always report the incident at the questura within 24 hours and ask for a statement, otherwise your travel insurance company won't pay out.

Traffic
Italian traffic can at best be described as chaotic, at worst downright dangerous, for the unprepared tourist. Drivers are not keen to stop for pedestrians, even at pedestrian crossings, and are more likely to swerve. Italians simply step off the footpath and walk through the (swerving) traffic with determination – it is a practice which seems to work, so if you feel uncertain about crossing a busy road, wait for the next Italian. In many cities, roads that appear to be for one-way traffic have special lanes for buses travelling in the opposite direction – always look both ways before stepping out.

LEGAL MATTERS
For many Italians, finding ways to get around the law (any law) is a way of life. They are likely to react with surprise, if not annoyance, if you point out that they might be breaking a law. Few people pay attention to speed limits, few motorcyclists and many drivers don't stop at red lights – and certainly not at pedestrian crossings. No-one bats an eyelid about littering or dogs pooping in the middle of the footpath – even though many municipal governments have introduced laws against these things. But these are minor transgressions when measured up against the country's organised crime, the extraordinary levels of tax evasion and corruption in government and business.

The average tourist will probably have a brush with the law only after being robbed by a bag snatcher or pickpocket.

Drugs
Italy's drug laws are lenient on users and heavy on pushers. If you're caught with drugs that the police determine are for your own personal use, you'll be let off with a warning – and, of course, the drugs will be confiscated. If, instead, it is determined that you intend to sell the drugs, you could find yourself in prison. It's up to the police to determine whether or not you're a pusher, since the law is not specific about quantities. The sensible option is to avoid illicit drugs altogether.

Drink Driving
The legal limit for blood alcohol level is 0.08% and breath tests are now in use. See Road Rules in the Getting Around chapter for more information.

Police
To call the *polizia* (police) dial the toll-free emergency number ☎ 113 or the carabinieri on ☎ 112. Addresses of police stations are given in destination sections throughout the book.

euro currency converter L10,000 = €5.16

The police are a civil force and take their orders from the Ministry of the Interior, while the carabinieri fall under the Ministry of Defence. There is a considerable duplication of their roles, despite a 1981 reform intended to merge the two forces.

The carabinieri wear a dark-blue uniform with a red stripe and drive dark-blue cars with a red stripe. They are well trained and tend to be helpful. Their police station is called a *caserma* (barracks).

The police wear powder-blue trousers with a fuchsia stripe and a navy-blue jacket and drive light blue cars with a white stripe, with 'polizia' written on the side. Tourists who want to report thefts, and people wanting to get a residence permit, will have to deal with them. Their headquarters are called the questura.

Other varieties of police in Italy include the *vigili urbani*, basically traffic police, who you will have to deal with if you get a parking ticket, or your car is towed away; and the *guardia di finanza*, who are responsible for fighting tax evasion and drug smuggling.

Your Rights Italy still has some anti-terrorism laws on its books that could make life difficult if you happen to be detained by the police. You can be held for 48 hours without a magistrate being informed and you can be interrogated without the presence of a lawyer. It is difficult to obtain bail and you can be held legally for up to three years without being brought to trial.

BUSINESS HOURS

Generally shops are open from around 9 am to 1 pm and 3.30 to 7.30 pm (or 4 to 8 pm) Monday to Friday. Some stay closed on Monday mornings. Big department stores, such as Coin and Rinascente, and most supermarkets have continuous opening hours, from 9 am to 7.30 pm Monday to Saturday. Some even open from 9 am to 1 pm on Sunday. Smaller shops will open on Saturday morning until about 1 pm.

All of this has become more flexible since opening times were liberalised under new trading hours laws that went into effect in April 1999. At the time of writing it was difficult to determine what effect this would have on day to day practicalities.

Banks tend to open from 8.30 am to 1.30 pm and 3.30 to 4.30 pm Monday to Friday, although hours can vary. They are closed at weekends, but it is always possible to find an exchange office open in the larger cities and in major tourist areas.

Major post offices open from 8.30 am to 6 or 7 pm Monday to Saturday. Smaller post offices generally open from 8.30 am to 2 pm Monday to Friday and on Saturday from 8.30 am to midday.

Pharmacies are usually open from 9 am to 12.30 pm and 3.30 to 7.30 pm. They are always closed on Sunday and usually on Saturday afternoon. When closed, pharmacies are required to display a list of pharmacies in the area which are open.

Bars (in the Italian sense, ie coffee-and-sandwich places) and cafes generally open from 7.30 am to 8 pm, although some stay open after 8 pm and turn into pub-style drinking and meeting places. Discos and clubs might open around 10 pm, but often there'll be no-one there until midnight. Restaurants open roughly from midday to 3 pm and 7.30 to 11 pm. Restaurants and bars are required to close for one day each week, which varies between establishments.

Museum and gallery opening hours vary, although there is a trend towards continuous opening hours from around 9.30 am to 7 pm. Many close on Monday.

PUBLIC HOLIDAYS

Most Tuscans take their annual holidays in August, deserting the cities for the cooler seaside or mountains. This means that many businesses and shops close for at least a part of the month, particularly during the week around Ferragosto (Feast of the Assumption) on 15 August. Cities such as Florence are left to the tourists, who may be frustrated that many restaurants and shops are closed until early September. The Easter break (Settimana Santa) is another busy holiday period for Italians. To give you an idea of when this period will fall in the next

[continued on page 86]

THE TUSCAN TABLE

For some, arrival in Tuscany means having reached the pearly gates of food heaven. For others, Tuscan cuisine is rather over-rated.

The truth lies somewhere between the two. As with many (but not all) of the Mediterranean cuisines, it is essentially the result of poverty. Simple, wholesome ingredients have traditionally been thrown together to produce healthy but hardly fascinating meals. The extraordinary excesses we read about of the tables of medieval barons or later on of the Medici and their pals were not passed down to us through the ages. One can only drool and dream about what concoctions must have been served up at such Festivals of Bacchus.

Most common folk had to make do with limited ingredients. This is what has come down to us today. It has been refined and enriched, particularly with other dishes and combinations from more widely flung parts of Italy. And all told it is very good – one of the keys remains the quality and freshness of the ingredients, upon which great store is placed. The use of herbs such as basil, thyme, parsley and rosemary is liberal.

Gourmands will miss something though – adventure. In Tuscany as elsewhere in Italy, tradition still controls much of what the cook does. They can tweak and fiddle (perhaps best exemplified in a growing daring in the preparation of pasta sauces) but all in all must remain faithful to the old ways. There are those in Tuscany (and again, throughout the country) who can solemnly state exactly what kind of sauce will go with which kind of pasta – any deviation from the rules meets with scorn. Undoubtedly many of these 'rules' are sound, but at times they are merely oppressive.

Carping aside, it is unlikely you will quickly get sick of Tuscan cuisine and other Italian dishes on offer throughout Tuscany. Add to the food some of the finest wines produced in the country and you will want to come with your taste buds fully braced for action.

MEALS IN TUSCANY
When to Eat

Breakfast *(colazione)* is generally a quick affair taken on the hop in a bar on the way to work.

For lunch *(pranzo)*, restaurants usually operate from 12.30 to 3 pm, but many are not keen to take orders after 2 pm. In the evening, opening hours for dinner *(cena)* vary but people start sitting down to dine around 7.30 pm. You will be hard-pressed to find a place still serving after 10.30 pm.

Bars (in the Italian sense, ie coffee-and-sandwich places) and cafes generally open from 7.30 am to 8 pm, although some stay open after 8 pm and turn into pub-style drinking and meeting places.

Many restaurants and bars shut one or two days a week, but others don't. In some parts of Italy at least one day off is mandatory but ultimately the decision on whether or not to enforce that rule rests with the comune. The Florence comune, for instance, does not care what restaurateurs do (unless they close for three days or more in a week) so that some skip the weekly break altogether.

Where to Eat

Bars Some bars known as *vinai* are good places to either snack or put together a full meal from a range of enticing options on display. This is more of a lunchtime choice than for your evening meal.

Restaurants, Trattorie & Osterie, Fiaschetterie & Pizziccherie

The standard name for a restaurant is *ristorante*. Often you will come across something known as a *trattoria*, by tradition at least a cheaper, simpler version of a ristorante. On pretty much the same level is the *osteria*. The *pizzeria* needs no explanation.

A *fiaschetteria* may serve up small snacks, sandwiches and the like, usually at the bar while you down a glass of wine or two. It is a particularly Tuscan phenomenon. A *tavola calda* (literally 'hot table') usually offers cheap, pre-prepared meat, pasta and vegetable dishes in a self-service style.

Wine lovers should look out for their local *enoteca*. These places offer snacks and sometimes full meals to accompany a selection of wines. Their primary business is the latter – food is viewed as an accompaniment to your chosen tipple(s). Generally the idea is to try the wines by the glass.

The problem with all this is that nowadays all the names seem to have become interchangeable. It would appear restaurant owners consider it more enticing for punters to call their places osterie (or even *hostarie*, the olde worlde version).

In all cases, it is best to check the menu, usually posted by the door, for prices.

Don't judge an eatery by its tablecloth. You may well have your best meal at the dingiest little establishment imaginable.

Occasionally you will find places with no written menu. This usually means they change the menu daily. Inside there may be a blackboard or the waiter will tell you what's on – fine if you speak Italian, a little disconcerting if you don't. Try to think of it as a surprise. If you encounter this situation in an overtly touristy area, you should have your rip-off antenna up.

Most eating establishments have a cover charge, which ranges from L1500 up to L10,000 (!). You usually have to factor in a service charge of 10% to 15%.

Where Not to Eat

You may not wish to know this but many of the touristy restaurants – especially in the centre of cities like Florence – have a rather ruthless attitude to food, customers and employees. How does it make you feel to know that a number of pizzerie employ foreigners without papers at slave rates to churn out pre-prepared pizzas? The base and sauce is ready to go, just tip canned mushrooms on the top, heat and serve. Delicious. The process with other dishes in some trattorie (perhaps they should be called 'trap-orie') is similar. Mountains of already cooked pasta get the reheat treatment – you can be sure most if not all ingredients are canned and your hosts will do their best to make sure the elements of your salad have been well aged.

Didn't want to spoil your appetite, but this is the state of affairs. How to recognise these places before it's too late? It's not always easy. Many of those in the most touristed areas (such as Piazza della Signoria in Florence and on the waterfront in many of the coastal resorts), especially if they have outdoor dining, tend to fall roughly into this category. If no locals are eating in the place you are considering, ask yourself why. If you see tour groups gobbling down identical meals – stay away! Places that need to advertise themselves loudly or that display menus in a variety of languages are often suspect. Unfortunately, there are some noble exceptions to these rules, so at the end of the day you need something of a sixth sense and a small portion of good luck.

What to Eat

Breakfast Italians rarely eat a sit-down breakfast. They tend to drink a cappuccino, usually *tiepido* (warm), and eat a croissant *(cornetto)* or other type of pastry (generically known as a *brioche*) while standing at a bar.

Snacks A few bars serve filling snacks with lunch-time and pre-dinner drinks. At others you can pick up reasonable *panini* (filled rolls or sandwiches). Otherwise snack food is more the preserve of the *trippai* and occasional *vinai* – (see the boxed text 'Fast Food Florence Style' in the Florence chapter). You'll also find numerous outlets where you can buy pizza by the slice *(a taglio)*.

Another option is to go to an *alimentari* (delicatessen) and ask them to make a *panino* with the filling of your choice. At a *pasticceria* you can buy pastries, cakes and biscuits.

Lunch & Dinner Lunch *(pranzo)* is traditionally the main meal of the day and some shops and businesses close for two or three hours every afternoon to accommodate it.

Many Italians grab a cappuccino and brioche at a bar to start the day.

A full meal will consist of an *antipasto*, which can vary from vegetables to a small offering of fried seafood. Next comes the *primo piatto*, often a pasta or risotto (although in Tuscany pasta has a modest place in traditional cooking), followed by the *secondo piatto* of meat or fish. This Italians usually accompany with a *contorno* (vegetable side-dish), although in some cases these latter are eaten separately. *Insalate* (salads) have a strange position in the order here. They are usually ordered as separate dishes and in some cases serve as a replacement for the primo.

ANE SMITH

Although most restaurants offer a range of desserts, Italians some-times prefer to round off the meal with fruit and *caffè*, the latter often at a bar on the way back to work.

Numerous restaurants offer a *menù turistico* or *menù a prezzo fisso*, a set price lunch that can cost as little as L10,000 to L15,000 (usually not including drinks). Generally the food is breathtakingly unspectac-ular (and sometimes just plain bad), with limited choices. From your tastebuds' point of view (if you are not overly hungry) you'd be better off settling for a good primo or secondo at a decent restaurant. On the other hand, if you look at lunch as a mere refuelling stop, this could be the way to go.

The evening meal *(cena)* was traditionally a simpler affair, but habits are changing because of the inconvenience of travelling home for lunch every day.

Gelati At the tail end of lunch and dinner you can opt for a house dessert, but at least once or twice you should head for the nearest *gelateria* (ice-cream parlour) to round off the meal with some excellent *gelati*, followed by a *digestivo* (di-gestive liqueur) at a bar. Many Italians actually skip the gelato altogether. They tend to see it as a sum-mertime treat and/or something for the kids.

Kid or not, a gelato always goes down well.

JANE SMITH

TUSCAN CUISINE
Staples

In the dark years of the barbarian invasions of what was left of the Roman empire, times got exceedingly difficult for the bulk of the people in Tuscany. Salt became a scarce commodity and *pane sciocco* (unsalted bread) became the basis of nutrition. Or at least that is one story. Unsalted bread (which doesn't necessarily appeal to everyone!) has in any case remained a feature of local cooking ever since.

The other single most important staple product, although not one that would do you a lot of good on its own, is olive oil. Some of the best extra virgin olive oil, with its limpid emerald appearance, looks good enough to drink. Since Etruscan times farmers have grown olives. Harvest time is around late November, and certainly not later that 13 December (the Festa di Santa Lucia) they say. In Tuscany olives are still largely harvested by hand and sent to presses. After an initial crush-ing, the resulting mass is squeezed. The most prized oil is extra virgin, extracted on the first round of squeezing and without any additives.

Antipasti (Starters)

You have the option of starting a meal with a 'pre-meal'. The classic in Tuscany are *crostini*, lightly grilled slices of unsalted bread traditionally

JULIET COOMBE

BETHUNE CARMICHAEL

BETHUNE CARMICHAEL

DAMIEN SIMONIS

Top: Keep your strength up for more sightseeing: shop window, Florence

Middle Left: Sandwich-and-a-half: bread shop, Florence

Middle Right: *Gelato* – an Italian tradition (so it'd be rude not to indulge…)

Bottom: Like all things in life, pasta comes in all shapes and sizes.

DAMIEN SIMONIS

JUDY WILLOUGHBY

DAMIEN SIMONIS

BETHUNE CARMICHAEL

Top: Grapes ripe for the picking in the Chianti region

Middle: Chianti wine, ready for sampling

Bottom: Complement the local wines with some fresh goat's and sheep's cheese.

covered in a chicken liver pâté. Other toppings have become equally popular – diced tomato with herbs, onion and garlic is a popular version virtually indistinguishable from the Pugliese *bruschetta*.

The other classic is *fettunta*, basically a slab of toasted bread rubbed with garlic and dipped in olive oil.

Another favourite, *prosciutto e melone* (ham and rockmelon), is known well beyond the confines of Tuscany. Other cured meats and sausages are popular.

Primi Piatti (First Courses)

You may be surprised to learn that pasta does not occupy a place of honour in traditional Tuscan menus. Some believe it was the Arabs who introduced pasta to Sicily in the early Middle Ages. By the 14th century its use had definitely spread to Florence, but without displacing local favourites.

A light summer dish is *panzanella*, basically a cold mixed salad with bread crumbs. Tomato, cucumber, red onions and lettuce are tossed into a bowl with stale bread that has been soaked and broken up. Mix in lots of oil, vinegar and basil and stick it in the fridge.

The winter equivalent is *ribollita*, another example of making use of every last scrap. Basically a vegetable stew, again with bread mixed in, it is a hearty dish for cold winter nights. *Pappa di pomodoro* is a bread and tomato paste served hot. Along the Maremma coast water was for centuries about the only thing in abundance in the swamps, and so *acqua cotta* (literally 'cooked water') was the mainstay of the average peasant family: a few vegetable leaves, onion, stale bread bits and a grating of pecorino cheese thrown together to make a thin broth. The modern restaurant version is considerably tastier, with a richer variety of elements.

Pasta did take hold in Tuscany, and among the dishes that have long kept locals munching happily are: *pappardelle sulla lepre* (ribbon pasta with hare), *pasta e ceci* (a pasta and chick pea broth) and *spaghetti allo scoglio* (spaghetti with seafood – pretty much a national dish). *Ravioli* and *tortelli*, both kinds of filled pasta, are also popular. Try the Maremma version of *tortelli*, large packets of fresh pasta filled with spinach and ricotta cheese and bathed in a sauce of your choice (the *burro e salvia* – butter and sage – is a good match). In Siena and other parts of central Tuscany you will come across *pici*, basically a rough, thick version of spaghetti. Their greater consistency allows cooks to match them up with heavier sauces and you feel like you are getting your teeth into something more substantial than with standard spaghetti.

Note It appears certain culinary stereotypes have gone too far. Many people seem to believe that *parmigiano* (parmesan cheese) should be scattered atop all pasta dishes, no matter what the sauce. Nothing could be further from the truth. You should never use it with any kind of seafood sauce, for the simple reason that the cheese kills the flavour rather than enhancing it! If your waiter doesn't offer you the cheese, 99 times out of 100 there will be a perfectly good reason. It seems some dinner guests feel they are being ripped off if they don't get their parmesan!

Secondi Piatti (Second Courses)

In keeping with the simplicity for which local cuisine is known, meats and fish tend to be grilled. Meat eaters will sooner or later want to try *bistecca alla fiorentina*, a slab of Florentine steak. It should not cost more than L50,000-60,000 a kilogram, which is usually sufficient for two. Traditionally the meat was taken from bovines in the Val di Chiana, but often this is no longer the case.

Cuisines born of poverty found a use for everything. As a result, animal innards became an integral part of the local diet. *Rognone*, a great plate of kidneys, is one favourite, although you might find it a little much. Tripe is particularly prized by some, and you can get it at roadside stands (in Florence's Cascine park for example). *Trippa alla fiorentina* is prepared with carrot, celery, tomato and onion mix. For the true tripe fans, locals distinguish between various parts of the gut. One particular part of the tripe is known as *lampredotto*, just in case you are contemplating having some on a roll without knowing what it is.

Tuscany is hunting territory, and wild boar *(cinghiale)* along with other game meats finds its way to many restaurant tables. Indeed for some the game meats form the basis of the best in Tuscan cooking. Among the possible choices of side order are *fagiolini alla fiorentina*, string beans prepared with tomatoes, fennel seeds, onion and garlic.

Not surprisingly, seafood dominates along the coast and on the islands. One dish that stands out is *cacciucco*. It is basically a hot pot stew of whatever seafood came to hand, and when prepared well nowadays can be a cornucopia of delights from the depths. When dining in this part of Tuscany ask if the seafood is fresh – if it is, stick with seafood pasta dishes and mains. The meat dishes you can try out when you are further inland.

Dolci (Desserts)

Apart from the classic gelati (see under What to Eat earlier in this section), you will find no shortage of house desserts.

Tiramisù, a rich mascarpone dessert, has become something of a worldwide dessert favourite among lovers of Italian food. It is actually a Venetian speciality, but is pretty commonly available in Tuscan eateries.

More in the Tuscan tradition are almond-based biscuits, such as Siena's *cantucci* or *biscottini di Prato*, best chomped while you sip Vin Santo, a dessert wine. Lighter but also using almonds are *brutti ma*

buoni ('ugly but good'). *Schiacciata con l'uva* is
covered in crushed red grapes.

Panforte is a classic of the Tuscan table. It is a dens
an almond base but bursting with other ingredients includi
figs, mixed dried fruits such as orange and lemon, mixed s
cluding cinnamon, coriander, and even white pepper, honey
cocoa. Done properly, the result is divine and seems purpose designe
for the region's Vin Santo (see under Tuscan Wines later in this section).
From Pontremoli in the Lunigiana comes a vaguely similar pie filled
with a chocolate and almond mix.

Zuppa Inglese, invented by Sienese cooks and originally known as
zuppa ducale, is a sugar bomb of chocolate, cream, rum and *savoiar-
di* biscuits. It acquired its present name because in the Florence of the
18th century it was a favourite among British expats who used to
gobble it down at Caffè Doney (long gone).

WINE
Wine in Italy

Wine *(vino)* is an essential accompaniment to any meal. Tuscans are
justifiably proud of their wines and it would be surprising for dinner
time conversation not to touch on the subject at least for a moment.

Prices are reasonable and you will rarely pay more than L15,000 for
a drinkable bottle of wine, although prices range up to more than
L40,000 for the better stuff. If you want an exceptional *riserva* (aged
wine) you can pay up to L150,000.

For something to merely wash down your meal, you will generally
be safe spending L8000 or so in a supermarket.

You will often see many wines from other Italian regions on sale, but
only rarely from beyond Italy.

Since the 1960s, wine in Italy has been graded according to four
main classifications. *Vino da tavola* indicates no specific classification;
Indicazione Geografica Tipica (IGT) means that the wine is typical of a
certain area; *Denominazione di Origine Controllata* (DOC) wines are
produced subject to certain specifications (regarding grape types,
method and so on); and *Denominazione d'Origine Controllata e
Garantita* (DOCG), which shows that wine is subject to the same requirements as normal DOC but that it is also tested by government in-
spectors. These indications appear on labels.

A DOC label can refer to wine from a single vineyard or an area.
DOC wines can be elevated to DOCG after five years consistent ex-
cellence. Equally, wines can be demoted.

Further hints come with indications such as *superiore*, which can
denote DOC wines above the general standard (perhaps with greater
alcohol or longer ageing). *Riserva* is applied only to DOC or DOCG
wines that have aged for a specified amount of time.

In general, however, the presence or absence of such labels is by no
means a cast-iron guarantee of anything. Many notable wines fly no

IGT wine is so denominated simply
not to adhere to the regulations
times include prestige wines.

erally only stock a limited range of
nts present a carefully chosen selec-
me osterie in particular concentrate
e wines than on the food. *Enoteche*
an enormous range of wines and a

he house wine (*vino della casa*) by the
glass, half litre a perfectly acceptable table wine to
accompany your food.

Tuscan Wines

Tuscany, perhaps surprisingly to some readers, actually ranks third
(behind Il Veneto and Piedmont) in the production of classified wines.
In total volume it comes in eighth out of the 20 regions, largely
because the lay of the land is restrictive.

Six of Italy's DOCG wines come from Tuscany. They are Brunello,
Carmignano, Chianti, Chianti Classico, Vernaccia di San Gimignano
(the only white) and Vino Nobile di Montepulciano.

There was a time when the bulk of wine coming out of Tuscany was
rough and ready, if highly palatable, Chianti in flasks. The Chianti
region remains the heartland of Tuscan wine production, but for a
good generation winemakers have been concentrating more on quality
rather than quantity.

The best of them, Chianti Classico, comes from seven zones in many
different guises. The backbone of the Chianti
reds is the Sangiovese grape, although other grape types
are mixed in varying
modest quantities
to produce

JANE SMITH

A glass or two of
Chianti is the perfect
accompaniment for
local cheese.

different styles of wine. Chianti Classico wines share the Gallo Nero (Black Cock) emblem that once symbolised the medieval Chianti League. Chianti in general is full and dry, although ageing requirements differ from area to area and even across vineyards.

The choice doesn't stop in the Chianti region. Among Italy's most esteemed and priciest drops is the Brunello di Montalcino (in Siena province). Until not so long ago only a handful of established estates produced this grand old red, but now everyone seems to be at it. At one reckoning some 60 producers turn out good product, which as usual varies a great deal in style depending on soil, microclimate and so on. Like the Chianti reds, the Sangiovese grape is at the heart of the Brunello. It is aged in casks for four years and then another two years after in bottles.

Another Sangiovese-based winner is Vino Nobile di Montepulciano, another hilltop town in Siena province. The grape blend and conditions here make this a quite distinctive wine too, but it is not aged for as long as the Brunello.

Tuscany is largely, but not exclusively, about reds. Easily the best known white is the Vernaccia of San Gimignano. Some of the best is aged in barriques (small barrels), while others are sometimes oaked.

An important development since the end of the 1980s has been the rise of Super Tuscans. Departing from the norms imposed by DOC and DOCG requirements, certain vineyards are finally doing the kind of thing that Australian and Californian vintners have been doing for ages – experimenting with different mixes. So now alongside the Sangiovese they are growing sauvignon, merlots and other grape varieties and mixing them with the Sangiovese. The results are some first class wines that promise to shake the wine establishment as the public is weaned off DOC-dependence. Some have been classed among the best wines in all Italy. By all means try the classics. But then experiment yourselves with these emerging wines and enjoy the difference. Long may they prosper side by side.

A regional speciality that will appeal to the sweet tooth is Vin Santo (Holy Wine), a dessert wine also used in Mass. Malvasia and Trebbiano grape varieties are generally used to produce a strong, aromatic and amber-coloured wine, ranging from dry to very sweet (even the dry retains a hint of sweetness). A good one will last years and is traditionally served with almond-based Cantucci biscuits.

For hints on particular vineyards you might want to invest in a wine guide. Burton Anderson's hardback pocket guide, *Wines of Italy*, is a handy little tool to have with you.

[continued from page 76]

few years, Good Friday is April 13 in 2001 and March 29 in 2002.

National public holidays include the following:

New Year's Day (Anno Nuovo) 1 January – The celebrating takes place on New Year's Eve (Capodanno)

Epiphany (Befana) 6 January

Good Friday (Venerdì Santo) March/April

Easter Monday (Pasquetta/Giorno dopo Pasqua) March/April

Liberation Day (Giorno della Liberazione) 25 April – which marks the Allied victory in Italy and the end of the German presence and Mussolini

Labour Day (Giorno del Lavoro) 1 May

Feast of the Assumption (Ferragosto) 15 August

All Saints' Day (Ognissanti) 1 November

Feast of the Immaculate Conception (Concezione Immaculata) 8 December

Christmas Day (Natale) 25 December

St Stephen's Day (Boxing Day, Festa di Santo Stefano) 26 December

Individual towns also have public holidays to celebrate the feasts of their patron saints. See the following section.

SPECIAL EVENTS

Tuscany's calendar is full to bursting with events, ranging from colourful traditional celebrations, with a religious and/or historical flavour, through to festivals of the performing arts, including opera, music and theatre. Some appear in the following list:

February
Carnevale

During the period before Ash Wednesday many towns stage carnivals and enjoy their last opportunity to indulge before Lent. The popular carnival celebrations held at Viareggio are among the best known in all Italy, second only to the extravaganza of Venice.

April
Easter (Pasqua)

Holy Week in Tuscany is marked by solemn processions and passion plays. In Florence the Scoppio del Carro is staged in the Piazza del Duomo at noon on Easter Saturday. This event features the explosion of a cart full of fireworks – a tradition dating back to the Crusades and seen as a good omen for the city if it works.

May
Maggio Musicale Fiorentino

Starting in late April and spilling over into June Florence's Musical May was inaugurated in 1933. It is a high point on the musical calendar with top names performing opera, ballet and classical music at venues across the city. Tickets can be hard to come by.

Palio della Balestra

The Palio of the Crossbow, held in Gubbio (Umbria) on the last Sunday in May, is a crossbow contest between the men of Gubbio and Sansepolcro, who dress in medieval costume and use antique weapons. There is a rematch at Sansepolcro on the first Sunday in September.

Balestro del Girifalco

This crossbow competition takes place in Massa Marittima on the first Sunday after 19 May.

June
Regatta di San Ranieri

This boat race, held on 16–17 June, in Pisa is preceded by the *Luminaria*, a torchlit procession.

Festa di San Giovanni

The spectacular fireworks *(fuochi artificial)* let off in Piazzale Michelangelo on 24 June, the feast day of Florence's patron saint, is the culmination of the city's festivities. In the four or five preceding days, teams from the city's four historical districts battle it out in the *Gioco del Calcio Storico* (Historical Soccer Game). On the first day the game is preceded by a procession of hundreds of people in traditional costume in Piazza Santa Croce, which becomes the football pitch for the matches.

Palio delle Quattro Antiche Repubbliche Marinare (Historical Regatta of the Four Ancient Maritime Republics)

This event sees a procession of boats and a race between the four historical maritime rivals – Pisa, Venice, Amalfi and Genoa. The event rotates between the four towns and is due to be held in Pisa again in 2002.

Giostra del Saracino (Joust of the Saracen)

On the second last Sunday of June, four ancient quarters of the city of Arezzo present teams of knights armed with lances who compete in Piazza Grande for the Lanza d'Oro (the Golden Lance). The joust has its origins in the early 16th century and in its present form commemorates Christian efforts to hold back the tide of Islam in the 14th century. The joust is staged again in September.

Gioco del Ponte (Game of the Bridge)

Two groups in medieval costume contend for

the Ponte di Mezzo, a bridge over the Arno river, in Pisa on the third Sunday of the month.

July

Il Palio (The Banner)
The pride and joy of Siena, this famous traditional event, held on 2 July, sees the town's beautiful central square, Piazza del Campo, turned into a scene of equine mayhem. It involves a dangerous bareback horse race around the piazza, preceded by a parade of supporters in traditional costume. There is a replay in August.

Giostro dell'Orso
Pistoia hosts this so-called Joust of the Bear on 25 July.

Anfiteatro delle Cascine
Nightly free concerts to keep Florence humming through the summer. It largely attracts a young crowd.

Festa di San Paolino
This torchlit procession in Lucca is accompanied by a crossbow competition on the third Sunday of the month.

Florence Dance Festival
A series of performances of dance – from classical ballet to modern – held in Piazzale Michelangelo.

Pistoia Blues
One of Italy's bigger music events, held in Pistoia around the middle of the month.

August

Luminaria di Santa Croce
This is a torchlight procession through Lucca on 14 August.

Festa del Grillo (Cricket Festival)
This festival is held in Le Cascine on 15 August.

Il Palio
16 August sees a repeat of Siena's famous horse race.

Bravio delle Botti
The streets of Montepulciano rattle and thunder to the sound of barrel races.

September

Festa delle Rificolone (Festival of the Paper Lanterns)
Processions, mostly of lantern-bearing children, converge on Florence's Piazza Santissima Annunziata to celebrate the eve of Our Lady's birthday on 7 September. A food fair is held in the same square in the week prior to the festival.

Giostro del Saracino
Good old-fashioned medieval jousting in Arezzo on the first Sunday of the month, this is a re-run of the June event.

Festa degli Omaggi
A parade in traditional dress through the streets of Prato, held on 8 September.

Festa della Santa Croce
This incorporates a religious procession through Lucca.

Palio della Balestra
A rematch of the crossbow competition between Gubbio and Sansepolcro is held at Sansepolcro on the second Sunday of the month.

October

Rassegna Internazionale Musica dei Popoli
Local and international musicians come together in Florence to perform traditional and ethnic music from all over the world. The festival goes on for most of the month.

November

Festa di Santa Cecilia
A series of concerts and exhibitions takes place in Siena to honour the patron saint of musicians.

ACTIVITIES

If the museums, galleries and sights are not enough for you there are numerous options for getting off the beaten tourist track.

Cycling

This is a good option for people who can't afford a car but want to see some of the more out-of-the-way places. The only problem is that much of Tuscany is hilly, so you will need some stamina and a good bike. You can either bring your own bike or buy or hire one in Tuscany.

Popular are the areas near Florence and Siena, from where you could explore the hills around Fiesole, San Gimignano and in the Chianti, just to name a few possibilities.

Skiing

The Tuscan ski option is centred on Abetone, on the border with the region of Emilia-Romagna. It gets pretty packed on winter weekends.

Walking

The Apuan Alps have well-marked and challenging trails for the serious walker. If you want something a little more easy-going, there is plenty of pleasant walking in the Chianti area or out towards San

Gimignano. See the special walking section 'Tuscany on Foot' after this chapter.

Water Sports

Windsurfing and sailing are extremely popular in Italy, and at most Tuscan beach resorts it is possible to rent boats and equipment. On Elba you will find plenty of outfits willing to take your money for diving courses and windsurfing instruction.

COURSES

Studying Italian in Tuscany is big business. Universities and private schools all over the region offer tuition, although the two main magnets are Florence and Siena. It's a great way to get a feel for the place.

Individual schools and universities are listed under the relevant towns throughout this book. Accommodation can usually be arranged through the school.

Many schools also offer courses in painting, art history, sculpture, architecture and cooking; however, all these courses can be expensive at an average of L600,000 to L800,000 a month.

It is also possible to undertake serious academic study at a university, although obviously only if you have a solid command of the language.

Italian cultural institutes (see Useful Organisations earlier in this chapter) will provide information about study in Tuscany, as well as enrolment forms to some schools.

In England, an organisation called Italian Study Tours (☎ 020-7916 7323, fax 7916 7327, ✉ bonallack@compuserve.com), 35 Murray Mews, London NW1 9RH, organises small-group courses in art and architecture, painting and cooking in a farmhouse near Lucca, in Tuscany. Courses run in spring and autumn and cost around L835,000 for seven days, including food and accommodation. Their Web site at www.vallicorte.demon.co.uk contains full course details.

For the hefty sum of L5,900,000 you can learn the art of Tuscan cuisine in a 9th-century former monastery in the Chianti area with Lorenza de' Medici (☎ 0577 74 94 98, fax 74 92 35, ✉ cuisineint@aol.com) and you get to sleep in a monk's cell to boo

At a more moderate L1,950,000 you ca spend a week in a restored Chianti ston farm house combining a cookery and win course with language lessons. For informa tion write, call or fax: Podere Le Ros (☎ 055 29 45 11, fax 055 239 68 87), Poggi San Polo 2, 53010 Lecchi-Gaiole (SI), Italia

WORK

It is illegal for non-EU citizens to work i Italy without a work permit, but trying t obtain one can be time consuming. EU cit izens are allowed to work in Italy, but the still need to obtain a permesso di soggiorn from the main questura in the town wher they have found work. See the Visas & Documents section earlier in this chapte for more information about these permits.

Au Pair

Babysitting is a possibility, as is au pai work, organised before you come to Tus cany. A useful guide is *The Au Pair anc Nanny's Guide to Working Abroad* by S Griffith & S Legg. *Work Your Way Arounc the World* by Susan Griffith is also useful.

English Tutoring

The easiest source of work for foreigners is teaching English, but even with full qualifi cations an American, Australian, Canadian or New Zealander might find it difficult to secure a permanent position. Most of the larger, more reputable schools will hire only people with a permesso di lavoro, but their attitude can become more flexible if de mand for teachers is high and they come across someone with good qualifications. The more professional schools will require at least a TEFL (Teaching English as a For eign Language) certificate. It is advisable to apply for work early in the year, in order to be considered for positions available in Oc tober (language school years correspond roughly to the Italian school year: late Sep tember to the end of June).

Some schools hire people without work permits or qualifications, but the pay is usu ally low (around L15,000 an hour). It is more lucrative to advertise your services and pick up private students (although rates vary wildly, ranging from as low as L15,000 up to L50,000 an hour). Although you can get away with absolutely no qualifications or experience, it might be a good idea to bring along a few English grammar books (including exercises) to help you at least appear professional.

Most people get started by placing advertisements in shop windows and on university notice boards.

Street Performers

Busking is common although, theoretically, buskers require a municipal permit. Italians tend not to stop and gather around street performers, but they are usually quite generous.

Other Work

There are plenty of markets around the country where you can set up a stall and sell your wares, although you may need to pay a fee. Selling goods on the street is illegal unless you have a municipal permit and it is quite common to see municipal police moving people along. Another option is to head for beach resorts in summer, particularly if you have handicrafts or jewellery to sell.

Some people manage to swing work in the kitchens of more touristy restaurants, particularly in Florence.

ACCOMMODATION

Prices for accommodation quoted in this book are intended as a guide only. There is generally a fair degree of fluctuation in hotel prices, depending on the season and whether establishments raise prices when they have the opportunity. It is not unusual for prices to remain fixed for years on end, and in some cases they even go down. But it is more common that they rise by around 5% or 10% annually. Always check room charges before putting your bags down.

Reservations

It's a good idea to book a room if you are planning to travel during peak tourist periods such as summer. Hotels usually require confirmation by fax or letter, as well as a deposit. Tourist offices will generally send out information about hotels, camping, apartments and so on, if you need more suggestions than we provide. Another option is to use one of the Florence-based hotel booking services.

Camping

Most camping facilities in Tuscany are major complexes with swimming pools, tennis courts, restaurants and shops. Even the most basic camp sites can be surprisingly dear once you add up the various charges for each person, a site for your tent or caravan and a car, but they generally still work out cheaper than a double room in a one-star hotel. Prices range from L8000 to L18,000 per adult, L6000 to L15,000 for children aged under 12, and L10,000 to L20,000 for a site. You'll also often have to pay to park your car and there is sometimes a charge for use of the showers, usually around L2000.

In the cities camp sites are often a long way from the historic centre. The inconvenience, plus the additional cost of needing to use public transport, should be weighed up against the price of a hotel room. Some, but by no means all, camp sites are on pleasant country or beachside locations.

Independent camping is generally not permitted and you might find yourself disturbed during the night by the carabinieri. But, out of the main summer tourist season, independent campers who choose spots not visible from the road, don't light fires, and who try to be inconspicuous, shouldn't have too much trouble. Always get permission from the landowner if you want to camp on private property. Camper vans are popular in Italy (see under Car & Motorcycle in the Getting There & Away chapter for more details).

The Touring Club Italiano publishes an annual book listing all camp sites in Italy, *Campeggi in Italia* (L32,000), and the Istituto Geografico de Agostini publishes the annual *Guida ai Campeggi in Europa*, sold together with *Guida ai Campeggi in Italia* (L29,900).

euro currency converter   L10,000 = €5.16

Hostels

Ostelli per la Gioventù, of which there are six in Tuscany, are run by the Associazione Italiana Alberghi per la Gioventù (AIG), which is affiliated to Hostelling International (HI). You need to be a member, but can join at one of the hostels. For details on how to get a card see Hostel Card in the Visas & Documents section earlier in this chapter. Nightly rates vary from L16,000 to L24,000 including breakfast. A meal will cost L14,000.

Accommodation is in segregated dormitories, although some hostels offer family rooms (at a higher price per person).

Hostels are generally closed from 10 am to 3.30 pm, although the Florence and Marina di Massa ones open all day. Check-in is from 6 to 10.30 pm, although some hostels will allow you a morning check-in, before they close for the day (it is best to confirm beforehand). Curfew is 11.30 pm or midnight. It is usually necessary to pay before 9 am on the day of your departure, otherwise you could be charged for another night.

Pensioni & Hotels

Prices quoted in this book are intended as a guide only. Hotels and pensioni are allowed to increase charges twice a year, although many don't. Travellers should always check on prices before deciding to stay. Make a complaint to the local tourist office if you believe you're being overcharged. Many proprietors employ various methods of bill-padding, such as charging for showers, or making breakfast compulsory.

There is often no difference between a *pensione* and an *albergo* (or hotel); in fact, some establishments use both titles. However, a pensione will generally be of one to three-star quality, while an albergo can be awarded up to five stars. *Locande* (similar to pensioni) and *alloggi*, also known as *affittacamere*, are generally cheaper, but not always. Locande and affittacamere are not included in the star classification system.

Quality of accommodation can vary a great deal. One-star alberghi/pensioni tend to be basic and usually do not have an en-suite bathroom. Standards at two-star place are often only slightly better, but rooms wil generally have a private bathroom. Onc you arrive at three stars you can assum that standards will be reasonable, althoug quality still varies dramatically. Four- an five-star hotels are sometimes part of group of hotels and offer facilities such a room service, laundry and dry-cleaning. Fo the average traveller it is really an unneces sary expense to go above three-star hotels

Prices are highest in Florence and o Elba (in July and August).

A single room *(camera singola)* will al ways be expensive. Although there are few pokey exceptions, you should reckon on a minimum of L40,000. In Florence yo will generally not pay less than L60,000. A double room with twin beds *(camer doppia)*, and a double with a double be *(camera matrimoniale)* cost from aroun L70,000. It is much cheaper to share wit two or more people. Proprietors will ofte charge no more than 15% of the cost of double room for each additional person.

Tourist offices have booklets listing a pensioni and hotels, including prices (al though they might not always be up t date). Ask about locande and affittacamere too.

Agriturismo

This is a holiday on a working farm and i particularly popular in Tuscany. Tradition ally the idea was that families rented ou rooms in their farmhouses, and it is stil possible to find this type of accommoda tion. However, more commonly it is restaurant in a restored farm complex, wit rooms available for rent. All *agriturism* establishments are operating farms and yo will usually be able to sample the local pro duce.

Increasingly this is becoming a popula choice with travellers wanting to enjoy th peace of the countryside. Generally yo need to have your own transport to get t and away from these places.

In Florence three organisations can pro vide information on this kind of accommo dation in Tuscany: Agriturist Toscan

☎ 055 28 78 38) at Piazza San Firenze 3, with a Web site at www.agriturist.it; Terranostra (☎ 055 28 05 39) at Via Magazzini 2, with a Web site at www.terranostra.it (Italian only) and Turismo Verde Toscano (☎ 055 234 49 25) at Via Verdi 5.

Convents & Monasteries

Many of the more than 50 convents and monasteries scattered about Tuscany offer some form of accommodation to outsiders. The nature of it varies greatly between institutions, often being single sex and relatively spartan. As a rule the institutions are looking for guests hoping to plug into their religion more closely or at least spiritually recharge their batteries. In many cases you are asked to take part in monastic life and respect the hours and practices of the order while you stay. Tourists just looking for a cheap sleep are not generally welcome. Nevertheless, if you were looking at a different kind of tourism, it would be possible to tour much of the region (slowly!) as a pilgrim.

You generally need to call ahead rather than turning up. A handy book available in good travel bookshops in Tuscany (such as Florence's Il Viaggio – see the Florence chapter) is *Guida ai Monasteri d'Italia*, by Gian Maria Grasselli and Pietro Tarallo. To get the best out of it you really need to read Italian. In the worst case you can at least make out the phone numbers and call to see whether you can get into your chosen monastery.

Villas

To some, a villa will sound more like the ticket. People wanting to rent a villa in the countryside can seek information from specialist travel agencies in their own country, or contact an organisation in Italy directly. One major Italian company with villas in Tuscany is Cuendet. This reliable firm publishes a booklet listing all the villas in its files, many with photos. Prices for a villa for four to six people range from around US$400 a week in winter up to US$1200 a week in August. For details, write to Cuendet & Cie spa, Strada di Strove 17, 53035

Monteriggioni, Siena (☎ 0577 57 63 10, fax 0577 30 11 49, ✉ cuede@tin.it), and ask them to send you a copy of their catalogue (US$15).

In the UK, you can order Cuendet's catalogues and make reservations by calling ☎ 0800 891 573 toll-free. In the USA, Cuendet bookings are handled by Rentals in Italy (☎ 805-987 5278, fax 482 7976), 1742 Calle Corva, Camarillo, CA 93010.

Another reputable purveyor of self-catering villas is Invitation to Tuscany (☎ 01481-727298, fax 713473), PO Box 527, TSB House, Le Truchot, St Peter Port, Guernsey GY1 3AA, Channel Islands, UK. Properties, many with pool, can cost anything from UK£400 to UK£1200 a week for four to eight people. They have representatives in the UK, USA, Australia and New Zealand. Visit their Web site at www.invitationtotuscany.com.

Cottages to Castles (☎ 01622-726883, fax 729835, ✉ tuscany@tcp.co.uk), 351 Tonbridge Rd, Maidstone, Kent ME16 8NH, UK, also has an enticing collection of properties to choose from. Prices are comparable to those of Invitation to Tuscany. They also have an office in Australia (☎ 03-9853 1142, fax 9853 0509, ✉ cottages@vicnet.net.au), 11 Laver St, Kew, Victoria 3101. Their Web site is www.cottagestocastles.com.

CIT offices throughout the world also have lists of villas and apartments available for rent in Tuscany.

Rifugi

If you are planning to hike in the Apuan Alps, obtain information on the network of *rifugi* (refuges). The most common are those run by the Club Alpino Italiano (CAI) and accommodation is generally in bunk rooms sleeping anything from two to a dozen or more people. Half board (dinner, bed and breakfast) includes a set evening meal prepared by the *gestore* (manager) and their assistants. Food is plentiful and good. Half board costs from L45,000 to L53,000 per person, while lunch can cost up to L18,000.

In addition to CAI rifugi there are some

euro currency converter L10,000 = €5.16

private ones and the occasional *bivacchio*, a basic, unstaffed hut. In general, rifugi remain open from mid-June to mid-September, but some at lower altitudes may remain open longer.

If you are counting on staying in a rifugio, always call ahead or have someone do so for you to check it is open and has room for you. Where possible, let staff know approximately when you expect to arrive.

Student Accommodation
People planning to study in Italy can usually organise accommodation through the school or university they will be attending. Options include a room with an Italian family, or a share arrangement with other students in an independent apartment.

Rental Accommodation
Finding rental accommodation in the cities can be difficult and time-consuming, but not impossible. Rental agencies will assist, for a fee. A one-room apartment with kitchenette in Florence's city centre will cost from L600,000 to L1,000,000 a month (long term). Renting in other towns can be considerably cheaper.

You can look for rental ads in the advert rags such as Florence's *La Pulce* (L2800; three times a week) and *Il Mercato della Toscana* (L2500). You'll find few ads for share accommodation though.

Short-term rental is inevitably more expensive, but many locals are keen to rent to foreigners for brief periods.

FOOD
Eating is one of life's great pleasures for Italians and Tuscany is no exception. For a food glossary, see the Language chapter towards the end of this book. See the special section 'The Tuscan Table' for information on when, where and what to eat in Tuscany, as well as some pointers on Tuscan wine.

Vegetarian Food
Vegetarians will have few problems eating in Tuscany, although vegans may make heavier weather of it. While few restaurants are strictly vegetarian, vegetables are a staple of the Italian diet. Most eating establishments serve a good selection of *antipasti* and *contorni* (vegetable side orders prepared in a variety of ways).

Self-Catering
If you have access to cooking facilities, it is best to buy fruit and vegetables at open markets, and salami, cheese and table wine at *alimentari*, which are a cross between grocery stores and delicatessens. *Salumerie* and *pizziccherie* sell sausages, meats and sometimes cheeses. For quality wine search out an *enoteca*. Fresh bread is available at a *forno* or *panetteria* (bakeries that sell bread, pastries and sometimes groceries) and usually at alimentari. Most towns also have supermarkets.

DRINKS
Nonalcoholic Drinks
Coffee The first-time visitor to Italy is likely to be confused by the many ways in which the locals consume their caffeine. As in other Latin countries, Italians take their coffee seriously. Consequently they also make it complicated!

First is the pure and simple *espresso* – a small cup of very strong black coffee. A *doppio espresso* is a double shot of the same. You could also ask for a *caffè lungo*, but this may end up being more like the watered down version with which Anglos will be more familiar. If you want to be quite sure of getting the watery version, ask for a *caffè americano*.

Enter the milk. A *caffè latte* is coffee with a reasonable amount of milk. To most locals it is a breakfast and morning drink. The stronger version is a *caffè macchiato*, basically an espresso with a dash of milk. Alternatively, you can have *latte macchiato*, a glass of hot milk with a dash of coffee. The *cappuccino* is basically a frothy version of the caffè latte. You can ask for it *senza schiuma* (without froth), which is then scraped off the top. It tend to come lukewarm, so if you want it hot, ask for it to be *molto caldo*.

In summer, the local version of an iced coffee is a *caffè freddo*, a long glass of cold offee, sometimes helped along with ice ubes.

To warm up on those winter nights, a *corrtto* might be for you – an espresso 'corcted' with a dash of grappa or some other oirit. Some locals have it as a heart starter.

After lunch and dinner it wouldn't occur ◗ Italians to order either caffè latte or a capuccino – espressos, macchiatos and corttos are perfectly acceptable. Of course, if ou want a cappuccino there's no problem but you might have to repeat your request couple of times to convince disbelieving vaiters that they have heard correctly.

An espresso or macchiato can cost from n Italy-wide standard of L1400 or L1500 tanding at a bar to L5000 sitting outside at iilli in Florence.

ea Italians don't drink a lot of tea *(tè)* and enerally only in the late afternoon, when ley might take a cup with a few *pasticcini* small cakes). You can order tea in bars, allough it will usually arrive in the form of cup of warm water with an accompanying :a bag. If this doesn't suit your taste, ask or the water molto caldo or *bollente* (boilig). Good-quality packaged teas, such as 'winings tea bags and leaves, as well as ackaged herbal teas, such as camomile, are ften sold in alimentari and some bars. You an find a wide range of herbal teas in a erbalist's shop *(erboristeria)*, which somemes will also stock health foods.

⟩ranita *Granita* is a drink made of crushed ⟩e with fresh lemon or other fruit juices, or vith coffee topped with fresh whipped ream. It is a Sicilian speciality but you'll ⟩e it in Tuscany in the summer months too.

⟩oft Drinks The usual range of internaional soft drinks are available in Tuscany, ⟨though they tend to be expensive. There re some local versions too, along with the ather bitter acquired taste of Chinotto.

⟩Vater While tap water is reliable through⟩ut the country, most Italians prefer to drink ⟩ottled mineral water *(acqua minerale)*. It vill be either sparkling *(frizzante)* or still

(naturale) and you will be asked in restaurants and bars which you would prefer. If you want a glass of tap water, ask for *acqua dal rubinetto*, although simply asking for *acqua naturale* will also suffice.

Alcoholic Drinks

Beer The main Italian labels are Peroni, Dreher and Moretti, all very drinkable and cheaper than the imported varieties.

Italy also imports beers from throughout Europe and the rest of the world. Several German beers, for instance, are available in bottles or cans; English beers and Guinness are often found on tap *(alla spina)* in *birrerie* (bars specialising in beer). You can even find Australia's XXXX if you are so inclined.

Wine See the special section 'The Tuscan Table' earlier in this chapter.

Liquors & Liqueurs After dinner try a shot of grappa, a strong, clear brew made from grapes. It originally comes from the Grappa region in the Veneto region of north-eastern Italy, but they make it in Tuscany too now. Or you could go with an *amaro*, a dark liqueur prepared from herbs. If you prefer a sweeter liqueur, try an almond-flavoured *amaretto* or the sweet aniseed *sambuca*.

ENTERTAINMENT
Bars & Pubs

Italians cannot be said to have a 'drinking culture' but, in the bigger cities especially, you'll find plenty of bars all over. You can get a beer, wine or anything else at practically any bar where you could also get a cup of coffee. They range from workaday grungy through to chic places to be seen. Those places operating first and foremost as nocturnal drinking establishments can be expected to stay open until about 1 am in most cases, sometimes later.

The Italian version of the Irish pub has taken off in a big way. Basically places where you can get Guinness on tap or select from a wide range of international beers, they are becoming more numerous by the month, especially in Florence.

Perhaps one reason why Italians don't tend to wander out of bars legless is the price of a drink. A tiny glass of beer can start at around L4000! For a pint you are looking at an average of L8000.

Discos & Clubs

Discos (what Brits think of as clubs) are expensive: entrance charges hover around L20,000, which sometimes includes a drink. Tuscany is not the most happening clubland in Europe, but you'll find some reasonable places in Florence and coastal spots such as Viareggio. Some are enormous, with several dance spaces catering to a variety of tastes.

Outside Florence and the summer resorts the pickings are slim. Often the clubs are well out in the countryside and if you aren't in the know and don't have wheels they can remain pretty much out of reach. The theory appears to be that at least the city and town dwellers don't have their sleep ruined.

Rock

The world's major performers are constantly passing through Italy and sometimes poke their noses into Tuscany. Keep an eye on local newspapers. In June and early July Arezzo stages Arezzo Wave, a rock festival featuring some known acts and emerging bands. Lucca's Summer Festival is held in July. It attracts some class acts, which in 1999 included Elton John, the Backstreet Boys, James Taylor and Bill Wyman.

Jazz

Italians love jazz and in Tuscany the biggest jazz event is Siena Jazz, held in July and August.

Classical Music

The main concert seasons are usually during the winter months, although there are always plenty of classical music concerts included in major summer entertainment festivals.

Cinemas

There is no shortage of cinemas in Tuscany, but quite a dearth of original language ones.

In Florence several cater to an extent to the market for subtitled, original langua (mostly English) movies but even there the choice is usually limited. Beyond Floren your chances are close to zero. It cos around L13,000 to see a movie, althoug that can come down to L6000 on the chea day, which is often Wednesday.

Theatre

If you can understand Italian, you'll ha several options in places such as Florenc Pisa and Siena. Performances in languag other than Italian are hard to come b Tourist offices should be able to help o with information.

SPECTATOR SPORT
Football (Soccer)

Il calcio excites Italian souls more than po itics, religion, good food and dressing up a put together. Tuscany's only Serie A (pr mier league) reps are Florence's Fiorentin They finished high up the ladder in th 1998–99 season but have won the champio ship only twice since the side was formed 1926.

SHOPPING

Shopping in Tuscany is probably not wh you are used to back home. Most shops ar small businesses, and large departme stores and supermarkets tend to be thin o the ground.

If you need necessities such as underwea tights, pyjamas, T-shirts or toiletries head f one of the large retail stores such as COIN Rinascente. Otherwise, you can pick up u derwear, tights and pyjamas in a haberdas ery *(merceria)*, toiletries and condoms in pharmacy *(farmacia)* or sometimes in an a imentari, and items such as T-shirts in a no mal clothing store. Supermarkets also stoc toiletries and condoms. For air-mail pape note pads, pens, greeting cards etc try paper-goods shop *(cartoleria)*.

Ceramics

You'll find plenty of locally made stuff ar if you get the chance you should visit Mo telupo, west of Florence, which has been famed centre of ceramics production since medieval times. Cortona, in the south-east, is another good place to look for pottery.

Clothing & Leather

Italy is synonymous with elegant, fashionable and high-quality clothing. The problem is that most of the better quality clothes are very expensive. However, if you can manage to be in the country during the summer sales in July and August and the winter sales in December and January, you can pick up incredible bargains. By mid-sale, prices are often slashed by up to 60% and 70%.

In Tuscany, Florence is probably the place to be. All the big name stylists have outlets here, although what's on offer tends to stick to the straight and narrow. For deals, try Gucci's and Prada's wholesale outlets on the road linking Florence and Arezzo (see Shopping in the Florence chapter).

Florence is also known for leather goods. You can spend a fortune on shoes, bags, wallets and just about anything else that can conceivably be fashioned from animal hides. It was always said that you could pick up good stuff cheaply too, but prices have tended to sneak upwards over the years. In Florence's San Lorenzo street market there is plenty of cheap and cheerful stuff on sale, but you need to watch the quality.

Shoes are a big attraction to the compulsive shopper, but expect to have a little trouble finding larger sizes. Again, the time to be looking is during the sales.

Jewellery

Popular jewellery tends to be chunky and cheap-looking, but if they can afford it, Italians love to wear gold. The best-known haunt for tourists wanting to buy gold in Italy is the Ponte Vecchio in Florence, lined with tiny shops full of both modern and antique jewellery.

That said, the gold capital of Tuscany is actually Arezzo.

Souvenirs & Handicrafts

The beautiful Florentine paper goods, with their delicate designs, are reasonably priced and make wonderful gifts. Specialist shops are dotted around Florence, although it is possible to buy these paper goods in stationary shops throughout the region.

TUSCANY ON FOOT

As all of Italy plunged into the Dark Ages that followed the collapse of the western Roman Empire, anyone who wanted to get around tended to walk. Under the Lombards and then the Franks, an important pilgrim route known as the Via Francigena (or Via Romea) turned into something of a highway across Tuscany. Starting down the River Magra valley through the wild Lunigiana territory of the north-west, the trail hugged the coast for a while before cutting inland to Siena via San Gimignano and then turning south to the Christian capital, Rome.

Although the bulk of the pilgrims and other travellers walking this road weren't doing it for fun, Tuscany is eminently suited to walking. The beautiful patchwork countryside of the centre, the wilder valleys and hills of the east, south and north-west and finally the Apuan Alps and Apennine ranges offer a colourful variety of opportunities to the traveller with time and a desire to move on foot.

A truly ambitious walker could undertake the 24-stage Grande Escursione Appenninica, an arc that takes you from Passo dei Due Santi above La Spezia south-east to Sansepolcro. A few suggestions on somewhat less demanding options follow.

When to Walk

The most pleasant (and safest) time to go walking in the Apuan Alps and other mountain areas (such as Monte Cetona in the south-east or the small Orecchiella reserve in the north) is summer. *Rifugi* (mountain refuges) tend to open from June to September, which gives you an idea of when you can best afford to go walking. August is perhaps not ideal, as many locals are on holiday and trails get busy.

Depending on your experience, weather conditions and where exactly you walk, you probably get away with some walks well into the autumn, but by November you risk dealing with snow and ice, not to mention limited light – not a happy combination.

Conversely, walking at low altitude or even on the Chianti hills and similar terrain is pretty much a year-round option. Obviously in the depths of winter you are unlikely to be keen on difficult day-long walks, but plenty of pleasant country strolls of a few hours are often just the ticket on a bright crisp winter's day.

The height of summer is not the ideal time for such walks. Inland (especially) the heat is oppressive, making even a crawl to the nearest air-conditioned bar a bit of a strain.

Spring is undoubtedly the prettiest period, especially when the wild flowers are in full bloom. Easter and holidays around 25 April and 1 May are to be avoided if possible.

The colours of autumn have their own special attraction. Given that summertime continues into late October, you have lots of light for longer walks. After Tuscany's mad summer tourist rush, things begin to ease off by late September – all the more so out in the countryside.

Top Left: The hilltop village of Lucchio is typical of the kind of place you'll stumble across when exploring the Tuscan hills.

Top Right: Make hay while the sun shines: the Tuscan farmland around Siena is perfect for gentle strolls.

Middle: Portoferraio on Elba, a good starting point for the island's network of walking trails

Bottom: Walking in Tuscany you may come across ancient relics such as these Etruscan tombs the Parco Archeologico di Baratti e Populonia, Livorno Province.

JOHN HAY

JUDY WILLOUGHBY

JUDY WILLOUGHBY

Top: The elegant Abbaz
di Sant'Antimo, on one
of the walking routes
south of Siena.

Middle: The Chianti
countryside, waiting to
be explored, unfolds
below the medieval tow
of Monteriggioni.

Bottom: An early-
morning start for a
day's walking around
Mont Amiata

What to Take

For your average walks in the Chianti area, further south around Pitigliano and in many of the parks you will need only a minimum of items. Firstly, a good pair of comfortable trainers (gym shoes) should be sufficient, although of course there is nothing to stop you taking along your walking boots. A change of socks is handy for the end of the day. A small daypack

JANE SMITH

could contain an extra layer of clothing should temperatures drop and some kind of wet-weather gear (like a poncho). Depending on the season, sunblock, sunglasses and a hat are recommended. Obviously you need a map of the area you are walking in and a compass should be a standard item in any walker's pack.

If you are not sure how long you will be out and about, a water flask and some food are essential. Mixed nuts and dried fruit are good, although you may want to prepare a picnic lunch for day-long walks, especially if you cannot be sure of happening on an eatery at the right moment.

You may laugh, but if you encounter difficulties while off the beaten track a mobile phone can come in handy.

In the Apuan Alps and other mountainous areas things are a little tougher and you need to kit yourself out properly. This means first and foremost sturdy walking boots. You can find yourself in loose scree and other tough terrain where a pair of trainers will be of no use at all.

Free camping is not permitted in the mountains. That may seem like bad news to some, because you need to plan your overnight stops around the availability of beds in rifugi (see Walking in the North-West below). The upside is that you can leave tents, cooking gear and the like at your base accommodation. Bring your sleeping bag along as extra insurance against the cold.

On the subject of cold, you need to be prepared for all kinds of weather in the mountains. You may start the day in splendid sunshine and heat, but that can easily change to cold and wet – bear in mind that the Apuan Alps get the greatest concentration of rainfall in Tuscany. Take a pair of soft shoes to change into at the end of the day's march.

A minimum of equipment is needed for walks in the gentle Chianti, but walks in the tougher Apuan Alps take a bit more planning.

Information

Maps Nothing like the UK's Ordnance Survey maps really exists in Italy. Several publishers produce maps of varying quality that cover certain parts of Tuscany.

First off, about the best regional map is the Touring Club Italiano's (TCI's) 1:200,000 scale map. It is detailed and a more than sufficient tool for navigating around the region on wheels.

The next level down, but still not detailed enough for walking, are individual provincial maps (there are 10 provinces in Tuscany). Edizioni Multigraphic Firenze publishes a series. Ask for the *Carta Stradale Provinciale* of the province(s) you want. They are scaled at 1:100,000.

Edizioni Multigraphic also publishes a couple of series designed for walkers and mountain-bike riders (mule trails, or *mulattiere*, are especially good for mountain bikes), which are scaled at 1:50,000 and 1:25,000. Where possible you should go for the latter. Ask for the *Carta dei Sentieri e Rifugi* or *Carta Turistica e dei Sentieri*. Its maps concentrate mainly on the Apennines, but they have one at 1:50,000 covering the Apuan Alps (or two covering roughly the same area at 1:25,000), and others at 1:25,000 on the Monti del Chianti and San Gimignano Volterra. They cost around L10,000 a sheet.

Another publisher is Kompass, which produces 1:25,000 scale maps of various parts of Italy, including Tuscany. In some cases it covers areas that Edizioni Multigraphic does not. Occasionally you will come across useful maps put out by the Club Alpino Italiano (CAI) as well. As a rule of thumb, you can get a hold of maps for the area you are in at local newsstands and bookshops. Otherwise you could try the Libreria Il Viaggio (☎ 055 24 04 89), Borgo degli Albizi 41r, in Florence. It has a good, though incomplete, range of maps.

Books You are unlikely to want to have too many books with you. An excellent one that includes over 50 walks and hikes of a not-too-strenuous nature is *Walking in Tuscany* by Gillian Price (the text spills over into neighbouring Umbria and Lazio). This covers an ample selection taking you from Chianti country to the island of Elba, and to plenty of lesser explored parts of the region too.

Price does not cover the more arduous trekking possibilities in the Apuan Alps in Tuscany's north-west. A couple of good suggestions for this area appear in Lonely Planet's *Walking in Italy*, along with several other walks in Tuscany. The guides published by Cicerone Press, Cumbria, are also worth a try. Otherwise your choices in English are virtually nil. Tim Jepson's *Wild Italy* has some information on the Apuan Alps, but if your Italian is up to it you should go for one of several Italian guides on the mountains, such as *Alpi Apuane: Guida al Territorio del Parco* by Frederick Bradley and Enrico Medda. The series of *Guide dei Monti d'Italia*, grey hardbacks published by the TCI and Club Alpino Italiano (CAI), are exhaustive walking guides containing maps. You might also like to consult the *A Piedi...* series, which includes *A Piedi nel Chianti* and *A Piedi in Toscana*.

Walking and Eating in Tuscany and Umbria by James Lasdun and Pia Davis provides 40 varied itineraries across these two central regions of Italy.

Where to Walk

Walking in the Chianti Region & Around The walking options in this gentle and blessed country are virtually limitless and in most cases require only a moderate level of fitness.

The classic walk would take you rambling over several days (perhaps as many as five or six) from Florence to Siena. The variations on this theme are numerous, so you can expand or contract it as suits. One way of looking at it is as a stroll through Chianti Classico territory – the heartland of Chianti's best wine country. SELCA in fact puts out a map in several languages, *The Black Rooster Roads*, at 1:70,000. If you intend to search out vineyards while walking, this map marks all member vineyards of the Chianti Classico consortium, whose symbol is the black rooster (or cockerel).

You could start your walk in the Oltrarno area of Florence but ideally you would choose a more enticing start position such as Strada in Chianti. From here you head south along a variety of routes, either following minor roads or paths, and making the Badia di Passignano your objective and then turning east to make for Greve in Chianti. A route dropping roughly south and then edging south-east would keep you in mild hill country, on country lanes and passing through such villages as Panzano and Radda in Chianti.

Another, longer, walk would follow the walking route from, say, San Donato in Collina and wind across several low hill ranges and valleys to Greve and then by one of several routes south to Siena. History buffs may choose to pass as far south as Monteaperti, site of Siena's crushing victory over Florence in 1260, before swinging west for the final leg to Siena. In either case a little planning is necessary as you need to arrange your accommodation for your nights on the trail. Between hotels and *affittacamere* (places with rooms to rent) in the villages and

Walking in the Chianti region has some obvious benefits...

JANE SMITH

ʒ on a working farm) options in the countryside,
e problem so long as you think, and preferably book,

ᵃnti territory, another popular option is to walk from
ᵇ Volterra. The start and end points are fascinating
mediᵉ.............. see the Central Tuscany chapter) and have the advantage of sure transport in and out (say to Florence or Siena) and plenty of accommodation.

Although most tend to walk *from* San Gimignano, there is no reason not to do it in reverse. It is about 30km, so advisable to split into a two-day walk (a further one-day extension would add the stretch between San Gimignano and Certaldo to the north).

Walking in Elba Walkers should pick up a copy of *Trekking all'Elba*, which lists walking trails and details each itinerary. You can also get information on hiking at Il Genio del Bosco – Centro Trekking Isola d'Elba (☎ 05 65 93 03 35) at Portoferraio. The Comunità Montana at Viale Manzoni 4 has contour maps of the island, with paths clearly marked. For a decent general map of the island, try Marco Polo's *Leisure Map – Elba* (L12,500), which is scaled at 1:30,000 and fine for navigating roads. Walking trails are not so clear. The Kompass map is similar.

The island is a splendid little spot to undertake comparatively short walks. You will generally be able to plan your own routes quite easily or in any case arrange it so that you arrive somewhere where accommodation is assured or buses can be caught to a more central point.

The western half of the island, dominated by Monte Capanne, boasts some of the most attractive walking (and mountain-biking) country. You could cross vaguely north to south from Marciana Marina to Marina di Campo choosing from a variety of routes. Even if you end up resorting to following the asphalted road over the hilliest parts you should enjoy it for the thick woods in the high central crossing and the wonderful views over the sea that are frequently offered up as a reward for your troubles. Other areas that attract are the south-eastern corner around Capoliveri and Monte Calamita, and the rougher and comparatively neglected north-eastern corner to the north of Rio nell'Elba.

At the end of most hikes you can, without too much clever planning required, reward yourself with a dip in the Med at the day's end.

Walking in the Centre & South-East Unfortunately there's too little space here to detail the myriad of options open to the walker in central and south-eastern Tuscany.

In the centre, south of Siena, you can compose your own hikes, such as a loop taking in Murlo, or a stroll from Montalcino to Sant'Antimo. A circuit around the Orcia river valley is particularly attractive. None of these walks need take longer than half a day. The main thing you need to bear in mind is transport to and from wherever you make base.

Further south, the wild gorges around Pitigliano and Sovana are also highly appealing. You can combine some magnificent nature and ancient history by stopping by the Etruscan Necropoli di San Rocco along the way.

Further east, there are some fine walks in and around Cortona, as well as around Monte Cetona, an area little bothered by foreign tourists at any time of year.

Walking in the National Parks Tuscany has several national parks and nature reserves. The most interesting is the Parco Naturale della Maremma along the coast south of Piombino. Here you can choose from several walks along strictly marked trails through the region's most diligently protected nature reserve. Walks in several other small parks are also an option. None are particularly strenuous and all are a matter of day trips to and from the parks. In some cases one of the main attractions is the possibility of bird-watching, as Parco Naturale della Maremma is on a main route for migrating birds. More details appear in the appropriate chapters of this guide.

Walking in the North-West The most serious walking you can hope to undertake in Tuscany is in the north-west, particularly in the Apuan Alps. To a lesser extent, the Apennine region bordering the region of Emilia is also promising, especially in the Reserva Naturale dell'Orecchiella.

The Apuan Alps offer a variety of walking possibilities, from relatively easy strolls to challenging treks that can even require Alpine and rock-climbing skills. For the latter you will need the appropriate experience and equipment. A reasonable level of fitness is necessary for the more challenging walks, as well as sturdy walking boots and all-weather clothing. Remember that at higher altitudes abrupt changes of weather for the worse are the norm.

One of the best-known objectives is the **Pania della Croce** peak (1858m) in the southern reaches of the park. The tree line is made up mainly of beech, above which the stony ground, in some areas with surface karst, creates a dramatic, stark walking environment. Several approaches and walks suggest themselves.

One almost circular and solid two-day trek gives you a good feel for this part of the Apuan Alps. A good starting point is Stazzema, which is accessible by bus from Pietrasanta (see the Pietrasanta & Around section in the North-West Tuscany chapter) on the coast. You will probably end up staying overnight prior to your walk in one of the many coastal hotels at Pietrasanta and around.

The first day of this walk takes you east from Stazzema to the Rifugio Forte dei Marmi and then swings north past Monte Procinto (1147m). Along the northward walk towards Pania della Croce, you will pass the strange natural arch called Monte Forato ('mountain with a hole in it'), from where you follow a jagged ridge to Pania della Croce. You can climb the peak or leave it for the following day, staying overnight at the **Rifugio Rossi alla Pania** (☎ 0583 71 03 86). The return leg to Pontestazzemese (from where there are buses to

Pietrasanta) is mostly easy downhill going. On each leg you are looking at around five hours' walking time.

There are plenty of variations on this theme. Many walkers drive to towns as close as they can get to Pania della Croce (such as Piglionico) and walk up to the Rifugio Rossi alla Pania, which they then use as a base for several excursions.

A side trail leads east and downhill a few kilometres from Pania della Croce to the village of Fornovalasco, from where a road winds about 1.5km north towards Trimpello. Just before Trimpello you reach the **Grotta del Vento**, caves with stalagmites, stalactites and crystal-encrusted lakes – see the Apuan Alps section in the North-West Tuscany chapter for more details.

Another exciting area to consider for walking is around the **Pizzo d'Uccello** peak (1781m) in the north of the park.

You can take on the services of guides in the park, but they don't come cheap. You are generally looking at L200,000 per day for the guide, plus accommodation and food costs if the walk lasts more than a day. Lists of accredited guides are available at the information centres for the park.

Where to Sleep

Walks in the Apuan Alps won't take you higher than around 1800m, but many walkers tend to spend a few days on the trails in these mountains. Since wild camping is forbidden, the only sleeping options are the mountain rifugi or *bivacchi* (huts), mostly operated by the CAI. A *rifugio* can be quite cosy with beds, a restaurant and a small supplies store. A *bivacchio* is generally an extremely basic option to doss down for the night, often without a guardian.

The CAI operates eight rifugi and three bivacchi in the Apuan Alps. One non-CAI rifugio also operates in the same area. Non-CAI members pay about double what members pay to sleep in these rifugi. Fees vary depending on the type of rifugio and the services provided. You can be looking at anything up to L36,000 a night for a bed with blankets. A heating supplement of up to L7000 per person may apply. A meal can cost anything up to L20,000. As a rule, lights out is between 10 pm and 6 am.

Most rifugi are open daily from mid-June to mid-September. During the rest of the year they are often closed, although some open on weekends and holidays. You need to call ahead to find out if they are open and have space for you. You can obtain information on the park, including a list of rifugi, from one of three visitors centres. The main one is in Castelnuovo di Garfagnana (see the Garfagnana section in the North-West Tuscany chapter). The others are in Seravezza (☎ 0584 75 61 44), Via Corrado del Greco 11, and Forno (☎ 0585 31 53 00). You can also check out the park's Web site at www.parks.it/parco .alpi.apuane. One of the tourist offices in the area (in Lucca or Viareggio, for example) can also provide you with a list of rifugi.

Getting There & Away

AIR

Competition on intercontinental routes between the airlines means you should be able to pick up a reasonably priced fare, even if you are coming from as far away as Australia. If you live in Europe, you can go overland to Tuscany easily enough, but don't ignore the flight option, as enticing deals frequently pop up.

Airports & Airlines

Tuscany's main hub is Pisa's Galileo Galilei airport, which is where the bulk of European scheduled and charter flights for the area land. Intercontinental flights use Rome's Leonardo da Vinci (Fiumicino) airport, to the south of Tuscany. The small Amerigo Vespucci airport, just outside Florence, takes some European flights. Both the Florence and Pisa airports are used for domestic flights from other parts of Italy too.

Many European and international carriers compete with the country's national airline, Alitalia.

Buying Tickets

Global aviation has never been so competitive, making air travel better value than ever, but you have to research the options carefully to make sure you get the best deal. The Internet is a useful resource for checking air fares: many travel agencies and airlines have Web sites (included later in this chapter).

Some airlines now sell discounted tickets direct to the customer, and it's worth contacting airlines anyway for information on routes and timetables. However, sometimes there is nothing to be gained by going direct to the airline – specialist discount agencies often offer fares that are lower and/or carry fewer conditions than the airline's published prices. You can expect to be offered a wider range of options than a single airline would provide and, at worst, you will just end up paying the official airline fare.

The exception to this rule is the new breed of 'no-frills' carriers, which mostly sell direct. Unlike the 'full-service' airlines, the no-frills carriers often have one-way tickets available at around half the return fare, making it easy to stitch together an open-jaw itinerary. Regular airlines may also offer open-jaw tickets, particularly if you are flying in from outside Europe.

If you're booking a charter flight, remember to check what time of day or night you'll be flying: many charter flights arrive late at night. If you miss your charter flight, you've lost your money.

Round-the-world (RTW) tickets are another possibility, and are comparable in price to an ordinary return long-haul ticket. RTWs start at about UK£800, A$1800 or US$1300 and can be valid for up to a year. They can be particularly economical if you're flying from Australia or New Zealand. Special conditions might be attached to such tickets (such as not being able to backtrack on a route). Also beware of cancellation penalties for these and other tickets.

You may find that the cheapest flights are being advertised by obscure agencies. Most such firms are honest and solvent, but there are some rogue fly-by-night outfits around. Paying by credit card generally offers protection since most card issuers will provide refunds if you don't get what you've paid for. Similar protection can be obtained by buying a ticket from a bonded agent, such as one covered by the Air Transport Operators Licence (ATOL) scheme in the UK. If you feel suspicious of a firm it's best to steer clear, or only pay a deposit before you get your ticket, then ring the airline to confirm that you are actually booked on the flight before you pay the balance. Established outfits such as those mentioned in this chapter offer more security and are about as competitive as you can get.

The cheapest deals are available at certain times of the year only or on weekdays. Always ask about the route: the cheapest tickets may involve an inconvenient stopover.

Air Travel Glossary

Cancellation Penalties If you have to cancel or change a discounted ticket, there are often heavy penalties involved; insurance can sometimes be taken out against these penalties. Some airlines impose penalties on regular tickets as well, particularly against 'no-show' passengers.

Courier Fares Businesses often need to send urgent documents or freight securely and quickly. Courier companies hire people to accompany the package through customs and, in return, offer a discount ticket which is sometimes a phenomenal bargain. However, you may have to surrender all your baggage allowance and take only carry-on luggage.

Full Fares Airlines traditionally offer 1st class (coded F), business class (coded J) and economy class (coded Y) tickets. These days there are so many promotional and discounted fares available that few passengers pay full economy fare.

Lost Tickets If you lose your airline ticket an airline will usually treat it like a travellers cheque and, after inquiries, issue you with another one. Legally, however, an airline is entitled to treat it like cash and if you lose it then it's gone forever. Take good care of your tickets.

Onward Tickets An entry requirement for many countries is that you have a ticket out of the country. If you're unsure of your next move, the easiest solution is to buy the cheapest onward ticket to a neighbouring country or a ticket from a reliable airline which can later be refunded if you do not use it.

Open-Jaw Tickets These are return tickets where you fly out to one place but return from another. If available, this can save you backtracking to your arrival point.

Overbooking Since every flight has some passengers who fail to show up, airlines often book more passengers than they have seats. Usually excess passengers make up for the no-shows, but occasionally somebody gets 'bumped' onto the next available flight. Guess who it is most likely to be? The passengers who check in late.

Promotional Fares These are officially discounted fares, available from travel agencies or direct from the airline.

Reconfirmation If you don't reconfirm your flight at least 72 hours prior to departure, the airline may delete your name from the passenger list. Ring to find out if your airline requires reconfirmation.

Restrictions Discounted tickets often have various restrictions on them – such as needing to be paid for in advance and incurring a penalty to be altered. Others are restrictions on the minimum and maximum period you must be away.

Round-the-World Tickets RTW tickets give you a limited period (usually a year) in which to circumnavigate the globe. You can go anywhere the carrying airlines go, as long as you don't backtrack. The number of stopovers or total number of separate flights is decided before you set off and they usually cost a bit more than a basic return flight.

Transferred Tickets Airline tickets cannot be transferred from one person to another. Travellers sometimes try to sell the return half of their ticket, but officials can ask you to prove that you are the person named on the ticket. On an international flight tickets are compared with passports.

Travel Periods Ticket prices vary with the time of year. There is a low (off-peak) season and a high (peak) season, and often a low-shoulder season and a high-shoulder season as well. Usually the fare depends on your outward flight – if you depart in the high season and return in the low season, you pay the high-season fare.

Ticketless travel, whereby your reservation details are kept on an airline computer, is becoming more common.

Student & Youth Fares Full-time students and people aged under 26 have access to better deals than other travellers. The better deals may not always be cheaper fares but can include more flexibility to change flights and/or routes. You have to show a document proving your date of birth or a valid International Student Identity Card (ISIC) when buying your ticket and boarding the plane.

Frequent Fliers Most airlines offer frequent-flier deals that can earn you a free air ticket or other goodies. To qualify, you have to accumulate sufficient mileage with the same airline or airline alliance. Many airlines have blackout periods, or times when you cannot fly for free on your frequent-flier points (Christmas and Chinese New Year, for example).

Courier Flights Courier flights are a great bargain if you're lucky enough to find one. Air freight companies expedite delivery of urgent items by sending them with you as your baggage allowance. You are permitted to bring along a carry-on bag, but that's all. In return, you get a steeply discounted ticket. There are other restrictions and you should be sure before you fly which apply to your ticket.

Booking a courier ticket takes some effort. They are not readily available and arrangements have to be made a month or more in advance. Courier flights are occasionally advertised in the newspapers, or you could contact air freight companies listed in the phone book, although they aren't always keen to give out information over the phone. *Travel Unlimited* (PO Box 1058, Allston, MA 02134, USA) is a monthly travel newsletter that publishes many courier flight deals from departure points worldwide. A 12-month subscription to the newsletter costs US$25, or US$35 for those resident outside the USA.

Travellers with Special Needs
If you have a broken leg, are a vegetarian or require a special diet (such as kosher food), are travelling in a wheelchair or have some other special need, let the airline know so they can make arrangements. You should call to remind them of your requirements at least 72 hours before departure and remind them again when you check in at the airport. It may also be worth ringing round the airlines before you make your booking to find out how they can handle your particular needs. Some airlines publish brochures on the subject. Ask your travel agency for details.

Guide dogs for the blind will often have to travel in a specially pressurised baggage compartment and are subject to quarantine laws (six months in isolation and so on) when entering, or returning to, countries currently free of rabies such as the UK and Australia. Deaf travellers can ask for airport and in-flight announcements to be written down for them.

Children aged under two travel for 10% of the standard fare (or free on some airlines), as long as they don't occupy a seat. They don't get a baggage allowance. Skycots, baby food and nappies (diapers) should be provided by the airline if requested in advance. Children aged between two and 12 can usually occupy a seat for half to two-thirds of the full fare and do get a baggage allowance. Pushchairs (strollers) can often be carried as hand luggage.

Departure Tax
The departure tax payable when you leave Italy by air is factored into your airline ticket.

The Rest of Italy
Travelling by plane is expensive within Italy and it makes much better sense to use the efficient and considerably cheaper train and bus services. In any case, only a handful of domestic airports offer flights to Florence. The domestic lines are Alitalia (☎ 800-050350) and Meridiana (☎ 0789 6 93 00); their Web sites are at www.alitalia .it (with an English-language site at www .alitalia.co.uk) and www.meridiana.it respectively. In Florence, call ☎ 055 3 29 61 for Meridiana.

euro currency converter L10,000 = €5.16

There are flights from Bari, Cagliari, Milan and Rome into Florence's Amerigo Vespucci airport. You can get to Pisa from Catania, Milan and Rome. Domestic flights can be booked through any travel agency. Journeys from Milan and Rome are both cheaper and just as easy (indeed often more convenient) by train.

Alitalia offers a range of discounts for young people, families, the elderly and weekend travellers, as well as occasional special promotional fares. It should be noted that airline fares fluctuate and that special deals sometimes only apply when tickets are bought in Italy, or for return fares only.

Meridiana has flights to Florence and Pisa from Catania and Palermo, as well as flights from Cagliari to Florence. It also runs a handful of international flights to Florence from Amsterdam, Paris (Charles de Gaulle) and London (Gatwick). The fare system is similar to that of Alitalia and is just as expensive.

One-way fares and standard returns (basically just two one-way tickets) are expensive. If you get a return, purchasing an Apex (or even better a Super Apex) fare will bring the price down considerably in exchange for respecting certain conditions.

One-way air fares to Florence (Vespucci) include:

origin	fare (L)	duration
Bari	270,000	1½ hours direct/three hours via Rome
Cagliari	260,000	3½ hours via Rome
Milan	165,000	55 minutes
Rome	165,000	1¼ hours

One-way air fares to Pisa (Galileo Galilei) include:

origin	fare (L)	duration
Catania	315,000	1½ hours direct/up to four hours via Rome
Milan	165,000	1¼ hours
Rome	165,000	one hour 10 minutes

A return Apex fare to Florence (Vespucci) from Rome, however, comes to L180,000. From Cagliari it would be L310,000. Even then, in the case of the Rome trip it is much simpler to get the train (which can take as little as 1½ hours)!

The UK & Ireland

Discount air travel is big business in London. Advertisements for many travel agencies appear in the travel pages of the weekend broadsheets, in *Time Out*, the *Evening Standard* and the free magazine *TNT*. Those with access to Teletext will find a host of travel agencies advertising.

For students and for travellers aged under 26, popular travel agencies in the UK include STA Travel (☎ 020-7361 6161), 86 Old Brompton Rd, London SW7, whose Web site is at www.statravel.co.uk, and Usit CAMPUS (☎ 0870 240 1010), 52 Grosvenor Gardens, London SW1, whose Web site is at www.usitcampus.co.uk. Both of these agencies have branches throughout the UK, and sell tickets to all travellers but cater especially for young people and students.

Other recommended bucket shops include Trailfinders (☎ 020-7937 5400), 215 Kensington High St, London W8, Web site www.trailfinders.co.uk; Bridge the World (☎ 020-7734 7447), 4 Regent Place, London W1, Web site www.b-t-w.co.uk; and Flightbookers (☎ 020-7757 2000), 177–178 Tottenham Court Rd, London W1, Web site www.ebookers.com.

As fare competition in Europe grows, a gaggle of small airlines jostles for custom. British Airways' low-budget subsidiary airline, Go (☎ 0845 6054321 in the UK, ☎ 147 88 77 66 in Italy), flies to several Italian destinations from London Stansted. The nearest to Tuscany are Rome and Bologna. Standard returns (no changes, no refunds) start at UK£100 including taxes. You can book by phone, or online at www.go-fly.com.

The only Italian destination for the low-cost airline Buzz is Milan. A standard one-way ticket from London Stansted costs £80 including taxes. You can book by phone (☎ 0870 240 7070 in the UK or ☎ 02 6968 2222 in Italy) or online at www.buzzaway.com.

The Irish airline Ryanair (☎ 0870 3331250 in the UK, ☎ 050 50 37 70 in Italy) as two flights a day (except Saturday, when only one goes) to Pisa. At the time of writing the fare was UK£85 return, but silly deals are frequently available. Visit its Web site at www.ryanair.ie.

Virgin Express (☎ 020-7744 0004 in the UK, ☎ 800 097097 in Italy) also flies to Rome from Gatwick, Heathrow and Stansted. At the time of writing, one-way fares started at UK£90. You can book online at www.virgin-express.com.

The two principal airlines linking the UK and Italy are British Airways (BA; ☎ 020-7434 4700, 0845 222111 for a 24-hour localrate line), 156 Regent St, London W1R, and Alitalia (☎ 08705 448259), 4 Portman Square, London W1. High-season fares on a scheduled Alitalia flight to Pisa range from UK£119 to UK£169 return (plus UK£27 departure tax). The cheaper the ticket, the shorter the validity of the return ticket. A standard one-way ticket costs around UK£260 and it's hard to think of any reason for buying one. Alitalia has no direct flights to Florence's Amerigo Vespucci airport – to fly there you must change in Milan. Return fares range from UK£119 to UK£199. A standard one-way costs UK£268.

Italy Sky Shuttle (☎ 020-8748 1333), 227 Shepherd's Bush Rd, London W6, specialises in charter flights to 22 destinations in Italy, including Pisa. Prices are largely determined by availability and ranged from UK£169 to UK£209 at the time of writing.

The Charter Flight Centre (☎ 020-7565 6755), 15 Gillingham St, London SW1, has return flights to Pisa valid for up to four weeks in the high season for around UK£149. They have a direct flight to Florence with Meridiana, which costs UK£259 plus taxes. You're better off with the cheaper flights into Pisa. Another specialist in flights and holidays to Italy is Skybus Italia (☎ 020-7631 3444), 37 Harley St, London W1.

If you're coming from Ireland, it might be worth comparing the cost of flying direct with the cost of travelling to London first and then flying on to Italy.

Youth Passes Alitalia offers people aged under 26 (and students aged under 31 with a valid ISIC) a Europa Pass from London and Dublin. The pass is valid for up to six months and allows unlimited one-way flights to the airline's European and Mediterranean destinations for UK£59 per flight, with a minimum of four flights. The first flight must be *to* Italy and the last flight back to the UK or Ireland *from* Italy. Internal flights in Italy on this pass cost UK£53 a pop. In the UK, contact CTS (☎ 020 7636 0031) for more details. Lufthansa Airlines, British Midland and Scandinavian Airlines (SAS) have a similar pass called Young Europe Special (YES). Eight Italian destinations are included in the program. The Alitalia deal is better if you plan to do most of your flying and travelling in Italy.

Continental Europe

Air travel between the rest of continental Europe and Italy is worth considering if you are pushed for time. Short hops can be expensive, but good deals are available from some major hubs.

Several airlines, including Alitalia, Qantas Airways and Air France, offer cut-rate fares on legs of international flights between European cities. These are usually cheap, but often involve flying at night or early in the morning.

France The student travel agency OTU Voyages (☎ 01 44 41 38 50) has a central Paris office at 39 ave Georges Bernanos and another 42 offices around the country. The Web address is www.otu.fr. Usit-Voyages (☎ 01 42 44 14 00) is a safe bet for reasonable student and cut-price travel. It has four addresses in Paris, including 85 blvd St Michel, and other offices around the country. STA Travel's Paris agent is Voyages Wasteels (☎ 01 43 25 58 35).

Occasionally you can dig up a good flight deal from Paris. One low-season option at the time of writing was a return to Florence for 1414FF, flying with Meridiana. You needed to book 10 days ahead and stay at least one weekend. This can work out better than the train, and it's certainly quicker.

Air Littoral (☎ 0803 834 834) operates

flights between Nice and Florence, with connections from other airports in France.

Germany Munich is a haven of bucket shops and more mainstream budget travel outlets. Council Travel (☎ 089-39 50 22), Adalbertstrasse 32, near the university, is one of the best. STA Travel (☎ 089-39 90 96), Königstrasse 49, is also good.

In Berlin, Kilroy Travel-ARTU Reisen (☎ 030-310 00 40), Hardenbergstrasse 9, near Berlin Zoo (with three branches around the city), is good. There is also an STA branch (☎ 030-311 09 50, fax 313 09 48) at Goethestrasse 73.

In Frankfurt-am-Main, you could try STA Travel (☎ 069-70 30 35), Bockenheimer Landstrasse 133.

At the time of writing, Alitalia offered discount return fares starting at DM400 from Munich/Berlin to Florence.

The Netherlands The student travel agency NBBS Reiswinkels (☎ 020-620 5071), Rokin 66, Amsterdam, offers reliable and reasonably low fares. Compare with the bucket shops along Rokin before deciding. Another recommended travel agency in Amsterdam is Malibu Travel (☎ 020-626 3230), Prinsengracht 230. At the time of writing, adult returns to Florence with Meridiana started at f580.

Spain In Madrid one of the most reliable budget travel agencies is Viajes Zeppelin (☎ 91 547 79 03), Plaza de Santo Domingo 2. Adult returns to Florence with Air France started at 60,000 ptas at the time of writing.

The USA

The North Atlantic is the world's busiest long-haul air corridor and the flight options are bewildering. Flights from the USA to either Florence or Pisa are possible with European airlines such as Lufthansa and Air France, and sometimes work out cheaper and more convenient than getting an Alitalia flight. Whichever you opt for, you will almost certainly have to change flights.

Given that Florence is a fairly easy train ride from Rome, you could consider looking at flight options to the capital and making the connection by train. This will increase your flight options but be aware that often the difference in ticket prices is negligible.

Discount travel agencies in the USA are known as consolidators. San Francisco is the ticket-consolidator capital of America although some good deals can be found in Los Angeles, New York and other big cities. Consolidators can be found through the *Yellow Pages* or the major daily newspapers. The *New York Times*, the *Los Angeles Times*, the *Chicago Tribune* and the *San Francisco Examiner* all produce weekly travel sections in which you will find a number of travel agency ads. Watch out for their SOT number – if they have one of these they are probably legitimate.

Council Travel (☎ 800 226 8624), 205 E 42 St, New York, NY 10017, is America's largest student travel organisation and has around 60 offices in the USA. Call for the office nearest you or visit the Web site at www.ciee.org. STA Travel (☎ 800 777 0112) has offices in Boston, Chicago, Miami, New York, Philadelphia, San Francisco and other major cities. Call the toll-free 800 number for office locations or visit its Web site at www.statravel.com.

At the time of writing, you could get return fares from Los Angeles to Rome or Florence for around US$530 with Lufthansa via Frankfurt-am-Main in the low season (roughly January to March). With a little luck you can do better still from the east coast. KLM, for instance, was offering return fares of around US$300 from New York to Milan in the low season. After March, prices begin to rise rapidly and availability declines.

Discount and rock-bottom options from the USA include charter flights, stand-by and courier flights. Stand-by fares are often sold at 60% of the normal price for one-way tickets. Airhitch (☎ 212-864 2000, ☎ 800 326 2009 toll free), 3rd floor, 2641 Broadway, New York, NY 10025, specialises in this. Have a look at their Web site at www.airhitch.org. You will need to give a general idea of where and when you need to o, and a few days before your departure ou will be presented with a choice of two r three flights.

A New York to Rome return on a courier light can cost about US$300 (more from ne west coast). Now Voyager (☎ 212-431 616), Suite 307, 74 Varrick St, New York, JY 10013, specialises in courier flights, but ou must pay an annual membership fee around US$50) that entitles you to take as nany courier flights as you like. The Colorado-based Air Courier Association ☎ 303-215 9000) is similar.

Europe by Air coupons (☎ 888 387 2479) re also worth considering. Their Web site an be found at www.eurair.com. You pur- hase a minimum of three US$90 coupons efore leaving North America. Each cou- on is valid for a one-way flight within the ombined system of 10 participating re- ional airlines in Europe (exclusive of local axes, which you will be charged when you nake the flight). The coupons are valid for 20 days from the day you make your first light. A few words of caution – using one f these coupons for a one-way flight won't lways be better value than local alter- atives, so check them out before commit- ing yourself to any given flight.

If you can't find a particularly good deal, t is always worth considering a cheap trans- tlantic hop to London to prowl around the ucket shops there. See The UK & Ireland ection earlier in this chapter.

Canada

Both Alitalia and Air Canada have direct lights to Rome and Milan from Toronto nd Montreal. Scan the budget travel agen- cies' ads in the *Toronto Globe & Mail*, the *Toronto Star* and the *Vancouver Province*.

Canada's main student travel organisa- ion is Travel CUTS (☎ 800 667 2887) and t has offices in all major cities. It is known as Voyages Campus in Quebec. Its Web address is www.travelcuts.com. For courier lights originating in Canada, contact FB On- oard Courier Services (☎ 514-631 2077).

Low-season return fares from Toronto to Rome start from around C$630 for students nd other young types. From Montreal,

KLM had a student deal for C$540 at the time of writing.

Australia

Cheap flights from Australia to Europe generally go via South-East Asian capitals, involving stopovers at Kuala Lumpur, Bangkok or Singapore. If a long stopover between connections is necessary, transit accommodation is sometimes included in the price of the ticket. If it's at your own ex- pense, it may be worth considering a more expensive ticket that does include accom- modation.

Many European airlines throw in a return flight to another European city – so, for in- stance, BA may fly you return to London with a London-Rome-London flight in- cluded in the price.

Quite a few travel offices specialise in discount air tickets. Some travel agencies, particularly smaller ones, advertise cheap air fares in the travel sections of weekend newspapers, such as the *Age* in Melbourne and the *Sydney Morning Herald*.

Two agencies that are well known for cheap fares are STA Travel and Flight Cen- tre. STA Travel (☎ 03-9349 2411), 224 Faraday St, Carlton, Melbourne 3053, has offices in all major cities and on many uni- versity campuses. Call ☎ 131 776 Australia- wide for the location of your nearest branch or visit its Web site at www.statravel .com.au. Flight Centre (☎ 131 600 Aus- tralia-wide), 82 Elizabeth St, Sydney, has dozens of offices throughout Australia. Its Web address is www.flightcentre.com.au. Compagnia Italiana di Turismo (CIT) can also help out with cheap fares (see Tourist Offices Abroad in the Facts for the Visitor chapter for details).

Discounted return fares on mainstream airlines through reputable agents can be sur- prisingly cheap. A low-season return fare can be as low as A$1300 with an airline such as Garuda Indonesia. In the high sea- son you could be looking at around A$2500.

Qantas and Alitalia fly from Melbourne and Sydney to Rome three times a week. Flights from Perth are generally a few hun- dred dollars cheaper.

euro currency converter L10,000 = €5.16

For courier flights try Jupiter (☎ 02-9317 2230), Unit 3, 55 Kent Rd, Mascot, Sydney 2020.

New Zealand

RTW and Circle Pacific fares for travel to or from New Zealand are usually the best value. Depending on which airline you choose, you may fly across Asia, with possible stopovers in India, Bangkok or Singapore, or across the USA, with possible stopovers in Australia, Honolulu or one of the Pacific Islands.

The *New Zealand Herald* has a travel section in which travel agencies advertise fares. Flight Centre (☎ 09-309 6171) has a large central office in Auckland at National Bank Towers, on the corner of Queen and Darby Sts, and many branches throughout the country. STA Travel (☎ 09-309 0458), 10 High St, Auckland, has other offices in Auckland as well as in Hamilton, Palmerston North, Wellington, Christchurch and Dunedin. The Web address is www.statravel.com.au.

Asia

Although most Asian countries are now offering fairly competitive air fare deals, Bangkok, Singapore and Hong Kong are still the best places to shop around for discount tickets.

In Bangkok try STA Travel (☎ 02-236 0262), 33 Surawong Rd. In Hong Kong many travellers use the Hong Kong Student Travel Bureau (☎ 2730 3269), 8th floor, Star House, Tsimshatsui. You could also try Phoenix Services (☎ 2722 7378), 7th floor, Milton Mansion, 96 Nathan Rd, Tsimshatsui. In Singapore a safe bet is STA Travel (☎ 737 7188), Orchard Parade Hotel, 1 Tanglin Rd.

Africa

Nairobi and Johannesburg are probably the best places in East and South Africa to buy tickets. Flight Centres (☎ 02-21 00 24), Lakhamshi House, Biashara St, Nairobi, has been in business for many years. In Johannesburg, the South African Student's Travel Services (☎ 011-716 30 45) has an office at the University of the Witwaters-

rand. STA Travel (☎ 011-447 55 51) has an office on Tyrwhitt Ave in Rosebank.

LAND

There are plenty of options for reaching Tuscany by train, bus or private vehicle. Bus is generally the cheapest, but services are less frequent and considerably less comfortable than the train.

If you are travelling by bus, train or car to Italy, check whether you require visas for the countries you intend to pass through.

Bus

Eurolines The easiest way to book tickets is through Eurolines, a consortium of coach operators with offices all over Europe (see under The UK or Continental Europe later in this section) or visit their Web site at www.eurolines.com. Their Italian headquarters (☎ 055 35 71 10, fax 055 35 05 65) are at Via Mercadante 2B, 50144 Florence. The Florence ticket office (☎ 055 21 51 55) is at the Autostazione, Piazza Stazione 1, on the corner of Piazza Adua.

Eurolines Pass Eurolines offers the Eurolines Pass, a useful option for travellers planning to pack in a lot of kilometres touring Europe. A pass valid for 30/60 days costs UK£199/249 (UK£159/199 for those aged under 26 and senior citizens), and allows unlimited travel between up to 30 European cities, including Florence. Prices on all these passes rise by between UK£30 and UK£50 from June to September.

The Rest of Italy Long-haul travel is generally more comfortably done by train, particularly if you're travelling around the north of Italy. This is true for Rome and Naples too. If you're travelling from the south the bus is sometimes a sensible alternative.

Lazzi (☎ 055 35 10 61 in Florence, automated nationwide service in Italian on ☎ 166 845010) is responsible for long-haul bus services from other parts of Italy, mostly on routes where train services are either nonexistent or painfully slow. They include Potenza and Matera (Basilicata) and some places in Puglia and Calabria. SITA (☎ 055

78 21) also offers a handful of long-distance services, all from southern Italy. Generally you must book these tickets in advance. A one-way fare will cost around L80,000 from the most distant places and the trip can take 12 hours.

In collaboration with SITA, Lazzi also operates a service called Alpi Bus, which runs extensive routes to the Alps. These buses depart from numerous cities and towns throughout Tuscany for most main resorts in the Alps. A brochure detailing the services is available from the Lazzi office. Destinations likely to interest travellers in Tuscany are hardly numerous. Lazzi has a bus to Perugia at 5 pm from Monday to Saturday. The fare is L19,000 and the trip takes about 1¾ hours. It also goes to Assisi.

The same company also operates the Freccia dell'Appennino (Apennine Arrow) service, with buses connecting Florence, Siena and Montecatini with destinations in The Marches (such as Ascoli Piceno) and in Abruzzo (such as Chieto and Pescara). These services tend to stop in Perugia, where you sometimes have to change bus.

The UK Eurolines (☎ 0990 143219), 52 Grosvenor Gardens, Victoria, London SW1 (the terminal is a couple of blocks away), runs buses to Florence (and on to Rome) via Milan on Monday, Wednesday and Friday (up to three extra buses a week operate in summer). The trip takes 30 hours. The one-way/return fares are UK£88/125 (UK£78/112 for those under 26 and senior citizens). The standard one-way adult fare going the other way is L222,000. Fares rise in the peak summer season (July and August) and in the week before Christmas.

Continental Europe Sample fares given here are to/from Florence. You will find Eurolines' main European offices at:

France (☎ 08 36 69 52 52) 28 ave du Général de Gaulle, Paris. The high-season return fare from/to Paris is 830FF.
Germany (☎ 089-545 87 00) Deutsche Touring GmbH, Arnulfstrasse 3 (Stamberger Bahnhof), Munich. Services run from/to many German

cities. From/to Cologne you'd pay DM350 or DM180 from/to Munich.
The Netherlands (☎ 020-560 8788) Rokin 10, Amsterdam. The return fare from/to Amsterdam is f300.
Spain (☎ 91 528 1105) Estación Sur de Autobuses, Calle de Méndez Alvaro 83, Madrid. The return fare from/to Madrid is 30,000ptas.

Train

The *Thomas Cook European Timetable* has an extensive listing of train schedules. It is updated monthly and available from Thomas Cook offices and agents worldwide.

On overnight hauls you can book a couchette *(cuccetta)* for around UK£10 to UK£15 on most international trains. In 1st class there are four bunks per cabin and in 2nd class there are six.

It is always advisable, and sometimes compulsory, to book seats on international trains to and from Italy. Some of the main international services include transport for private cars – an option worth examining to save wear and tear on your vehicle before it arrives in Italy.

The Rest of Italy The principal north–south train line into Tuscany passes through Florence on a route that runs from Milan through Bologna and on to Rome via Arezzo. Another line from Rome hugs the coast as it heads into Tuscany, before passing through Grosseto, Follonica (branch to Piombino), Livorno, Pisa (branch to Florence), Viareggio and on along the coast to La Spezia and Genoa (Liguria).

Information For information on trains you can call ☎ 147 888088 anywhere in Italy. The service is automated and in Italian only. In train stations in Tuscany you can sometimes find the handy *In Treno Toscana* booklet of timetables, which covers journeys to other parts of Italy from Florence.

Main train timetables generally display arrivals *(arrivi)* on a white background and departures *(partenze)* on a yellow one. Impending arrivals and departures also appear on electronic boards. You will notice a plethora of symbols and acronyms on the main timetables, some of which are useful for identifying the kind of train concerned (see Types of Train in this section).

It is possible to get a paperback-sized timetable with details of all the main services from selected outlets outside Italy. In the UK, for instance, you can find it at Italwings (☎ 020-7287 2117), 162/168 Regent St, London W1. The same timetable is available at many newsstands in Italy.

Types of Train A wide variety of trains circulates around Italy. They start with slow all-stops *locali*, which generally don't travel much beyond their main city of origin or province. Next come the *regionali*, which also tend to be slow but cover greater distances, sometimes going beyond their region of origin. *Interregionali* cover greater distances still and don't necessarily stop at every last station.

From this level there is a leap upwards to InterCitys (IC), faster long-distance trains operating between major cities and for which you generally have to pay a *supplemento* on top of the normal cost of a ticket. EuroCity (EC) trains are the international version. They can reach a top speed of 200km/h (but rarely get the chance!). Comfort and speed on the most important lines have been provided for the past few years by the *pendolino* trains, so-called because they 'lean' up to 8° into curves, increasing the overall speed of a standard InterCity by up to 35%. On high-speed track the fastest Italian trains zoom along at more than 300km/h.

Services using top-of-the-range locos are now collectively known as Eurostar Italia (ES). ES trains connect Florence with Rome (1¾ hours) up to 25 times a day and with Milan (2¾ hours) 16 times daily. Seven Eurostar trains proceed from Rome to Naples and five others connect Florence with Venice (one goes on to Trieste). Other main lines for this premier service include one connecting Milan with Venice and another from Milan to Ancona (on the Adriatic) via Bologna.

Other train types you may encounter are the *diretto* (D) and *espresso* (E). They are slow and gradually disappearing. Night trains *(notturne)* are either old *espressi* c increasingly, InterCity Notte (ICN) se vices. You generally have the option of couchette (one of four or six fold-dow bunkbeds in a compartment), or a prope bed in a sleeping car *(vagone letto)*. A plac in the latter tends to be much more expen sive than in a simple couchette. The inte national version is the EuroNight (EN).

Train Passes It is not worth buying a Eura or InterRail pass if you are going to trav only in Italy, since train fares are reasonab cheap. The FS offers its own discount passe for travel within the country. CIT office around the world (see Tourist Office Abroad in the Facts for the Visitor chapte can also sell them.

Two useful passes are the Italy Railcar and Italy Flexi Rail (both of which can b purchased in Italy and the UK). With bo passes, prices include supplements fc travel on Intercity trains but not for E trains. You should have your passport fc identification when purchasing either pas Italy Railcard, valid for eight/15/21/3 days, costs L438,000/717,000/635,00C 1,500,000 (1st class) or L292,000/477,00C 423,000/657,000 (2nd class). Italy Flex Rail, valid for four/eight/12 days of trave within one month, costs L356,000/627,00C 641,000 (1st class) or L237,000/387,00€ 427,000 (2nd class).

The Euro-Domino pass, known as a Free dom pass in the UK, is available for any on of 28 European countries, including Italy, an is valid for three, five or 10 days of trave over a month. For Italy, a 1st class, 10-da pass costs UK£265. Second class is UK£182 and for those aged under 26 it's UK£140.

Tickets The cost of train travel is lower i Italy than in most of the rest of Wester Europe. Fares are traditionally calculate according to distance travelled, but the na tional government is currently implement ing a new price structure that will take othe factors, such as service, into account. Th changes are due to be completed in 2001 For further details, see the Web site a www.fs-on-line.com.

breathtaking view of a breathtaking city – Florence from the Piazza Michelangelo

he 'Big White Thing' – the Neptune fountain in Piazza della Signoria, Florence

DAMIEN SIMONIS

Giotto's Gothic Campanile, Florence

JOHN HAY

Popular with the birds: bust of Cellini, Ponte Vecchio, Florenc

JULIET COOMBE

Neptune in the Boboli Gardens, Florence

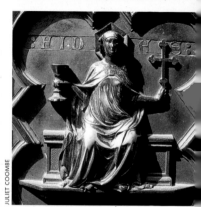
JULIET COOMBE

Detail of the south doors of Florence's Baptistr

JULIET COOMBE

The modern face of art, by Florence's Palazzo P

There are many ticketing possibilities. Apart from the standard division between 1st and 2nd class on the faster trains (generally you can get only 2nd-class seats on locali and regionali), you usually have to pay a supplement for being on a fast train.

As with tickets, the price of the supplement is in part calculated according to the length of the journey. You can pay the supplement separately from the ticket. Thus if you have a 2nd-class return ticket from Florence to Rome, you might decide to avoid the supplement one way and take a slower train, but pay a supplement for the return trip to speed things up a little. Whatever you decide, you need to pay the supplement before boarding the train.

You can buy rail tickets (for major destinations on fast trains at least) from most travel agents. If you choose to buy them at the station, there are automatic machines that accept cash. If you queue at the windows, watch out for those displaying the Eurostar sign – they will only sell you tickets on ES trains.

It is advisable, and in some cases obligatory, to book long-distance tickets in advance, whether international or domestic. In 1st class, booking is often mandatory (and free). Where it is optional (which is more often, but not always, the case in 2nd class), you may pay a L5000 booking fee. Tickets can be booked at the windows in the station or at most travel agencies.

The following prices are approximate, standard, 2nd-class, one-way fares (+ supplement) on IC trains from Florence. ES fares are higher, and the trains are faster and make fewer stops.

destination	fare (L)	duration
Bologna	8200 (+5500)	one hour
Milan	25,500 (+13,000)	three hours 20 minutes
Naples	42,000 (+17,500)	four hours
Rome	25,500 (+13,000)	one hour 55 minutes
Venice	22,000 (+12,000)	three hours
(with change in Bologna)		

Other long-haul destinations within Italy for which there is at least one direct connection from Florence include Bolzano, Palermo, Reggio Calabria, Siracusa, Trieste and Udine.

Rules & Fines When you buy a ticket you are supposed to stamp it in one of the yellow machines scattered about all stations (usually with a *convalida* sign on them). Failure to do so will be rewarded with an on-the-spot L40,000 fine by the conductor. If you buy a return ticket, you must stamp it each way (each end of the ticket). One of the several Italian verbs for this operation of stamping your ticket is *obliterare* – it makes for a wonderful translation into English: 'Ladies and gentlemen, please obliterate your tickets before boarding the train'.

The ticket you buy is valid for two months until stamped. Once stamped it is valid for 24 hours if the journey distance (one-way) is greater than 200km (six hours if it is less). For a return ticket, the time is calculated separately for each one-way journey (ie, on a short return trip you get six hours from the time of stamping on the way out and the same on the way back).

All seats on ES trains on Friday and Sunday must be booked in advance. On other days waggons for unbooked seats are set aside. If you board an ES train on a Friday or Sunday without a booking, you pay a L10,000 fine.

UK The Channel Tunnel makes land travel possible between Britain and continental Europe. The Eurostar passenger train service (☎ 0990 186186) travels between London and Paris and London and Brussels. Visit its Web site at www.eurostar.com. Vehicles can be taken on the Eurotunnel service (for more details see the Car & Motorcycle section later in this chapter).

Alternatively, you can get a train ticket that includes the Channel crossing by ferry or SeaCat hovercraft. After that, you can travel via Paris and southern France or by heading from Belgium down through Germany and Switzerland.

The cheapest standard fares to Florence on offer at the time of writing were

euro currency converter L10,000 = €5.16

UK£74/143 one-way/return for students and those under 26, while the full adult fares were UK£93/153.

For information on international rail travel (including Eurostar services), call European Rail (☎ 020-7387 0444) or go to the Wasteels office opposite platform 2 at Victoria station. You can also get information on Eurostar and rail passes from the Rail Europe Travel Centre (☎ 08705 848848) at 179 Piccadilly, London W1, or see their Web site at www.raileurope.co.uk. For Eurostar you can also make enquiries and buy tickets at Waterloo station, from where the trains depart.

Continental Europe Train lines cross the Italian frontier at several points from France, Switzerland, Austria and Slovenia. Unless you are following the coast from France, in which case you can get to Florence via Genoa (Liguria) and Pisa, you will almost certainly end up heading to Florence from Bologna. The main high-speed international runs follow the Milan-Bologna-Florence-Rome route. If you are approaching from Austria or Eastern Europe, you will either join the line at Bologna or have to change trains there.

France Your quickest option from Paris to Florence is a morning departure on a TGV to Milan (8.12 am or 11.12 am), changing there for the onward trip. You are looking at about 10½ hours travel and 650FF one way in 2nd class. Some 2½ hours slower is the trip via Lausanne (Switzerland), also starting with a TGV. About the cheapest one-way ticket available from Paris is 500FF, for people under 26. You have to add a little for the couchette, as the ticket is for the overnight sleeper train.

As many as three trains do an overnight run from Paris, one direct to Florence but the others involve early-morning changes at either Milan or Pisa.

Switzerland, Germany & Austria The comfiest way by rail from Switzerland into Italy is with the modern Cisalpino (CiS) service. The bulk of these services go to Milan, starting at Basle, Bern, Geneva or Zürich. One service connects Zürich directly with Florence, via Milan. That trip costs Sfr140 one way or Sfr260 return and takes a little less than seven hours.

In Switzerland you can connect with fast services from Germany, from places such as Stuttgart, Frankfurt-am-Main and Cologne.

Up to three daily direct trains connect Innsbruck and Munich with Florence via the Brenner Pass. Three other trains go from Vienna via Bologna and Venice. If you're travelling from other German cities, you will generally have to make connections along the way (although there is one overnight train between Dortmund and Florence).

Spain Direct overnight trains run from Barcelona to Milan (12¾ hours), from three to seven days a week depending on the season. The cheapest sleeper costs 29,000 ptas (L207,100), or you can get a seat for 22,000 ptas (L166,400). At Barcelona you can connect with trains from other points in Spain. To Florence, you need to allow at least 17 hours (including the change of trains at Milan).

Car & Motorcycle

From the UK, you can take your car across to France by ferry or the Channel Tunnel car train, Eurotunnel (☎ 0990 353535), Web site www.eurotunnel.com. The latter runs between terminals in Folkestone and Calais, with crossings lasting 35 minutes. The service runs around the clock, with up to four crossings an hour in high season. You pay for the vehicle only and fares vary according to time of day and season. The cheapest economy fare (January to May) is around UK£170 return (valid for a year) and the most expensive (May to late September) is around UK£220, if you depart during the day Friday to Sunday.

Europe is made for motorcycle touring and Tuscany is no exception. Motorcyclists literally swarm in during summer to tour the winding, scenic roads. Motorcyclists rarely have to book ahead for ferries. You will be able to enter restricted traffic areas in Italian cities without any problems and Italian traffic police generally turn a blind eye to motorcycles parked on footpaths.

The main points of entry to Italy are: the Mont Blanc tunnel from France at Chamonix (90FF; closed at the time of writing but due to reopen late 2000; up-to-date information is available from the Chamonix Mont Blanc Tourist Office on ☎ 04 50 53 00 24) which connects with the A5 for Turin and Milan; the Grand St Bernard tunnel from Switzerland (Sfr27), which also connects with the A5; and the Brenner Pass from Austria (AS130), which connects with the A22 to Bologna. Mountain passes in the Alps are often closed in winter and sometimes in autumn and spring, making the tunnels a less scenic but more reliable way to arrive in Italy. Make sure you have snow chains in winter.

Roads are generally good throughout the country and there is an excellent network of *autostrade* (motorways). The main north–south link, which skirts Florence, is the Autostrada del Sole, which extends from Milan to Reggio di Calabria (called the A1 from Milan to Naples and the A3 from Naples to Reggio di Calabria). The A11 heads west via Pistoia and Lucca towards Pisa and Livorno and meets the A12 to La Spezia and Genoa. Apart from the A1, you can follow the SS1 south from Livorno to Rome via Grosseto. Where it is still single carriageway it can be a little hairy, but progress on the parallel A12 extension continues.

Several back mountain roads allow you to cross the Apennines from Emilia-Romagna in far more picturesque style. One example is the SS302, or Via Faenza, from that town south to Borgo San Lorenzo in the Mugello. From there you are a fairly short drive from Florence. From Perugia (Umbria), the SS75b west along the north of Lago Trasimeno puts you on the road to Siena, intersecting the A1 on the way.

Drivers usually travel at high speeds in the left-hand fast lane on the autostrade, so use that lane only to pass other cars. You have to pay a toll to use the autostrade – for example, it will cost you approximately L30,000 from Rome to Bologna, L50,000 from Rome to Milan and L18,000 from Milan to Bologna.

You can pay tolls with a credit card (including Visa, Master[...], press and Diners Club) o[...] in northern Italy. Another w[...] buy a Viacard (at toll booths an[...] vice stations and tourist offices). [...] sent it to the attendant as payment or [...] it into the appropriate Viacard machine [...] you exit an autostrada. Left-over credit is not refundable on leaving Italy.

Travellers with time to spare could consider using the system of state roads *(strade statali)*, which are sometimes multi-lane dual carriageways and are toll-free. They are represented on maps as 'S' or 'SS'. The provincial roads *(strade provinciali)* are sometimes little more than country lanes, but provide access to some of the more beautiful scenery and the many towns and villages. They are represented as 'SP' on maps.

An interesting Web site loaded with advice for people planning to drive in Europe is www.ideamerge.com/motoeuropa. If you want help with route planning, try out www.euroshell.com.

For information on road rules, paperwork and car rental see the Getting Around chapter.

Paperwork & Preparations Proof of ownership of a private vehicle should always be carried (Vehicle Registration Document for UK-registered cars) when driving through Europe. All EU member states' driving licences (not the old-style UK green licence) are fully recognised throughout the Union, regardless of your length of stay. Those with a non-EU licence are supposed to obtain an International Driving Permit (IDP) to accompany their national licence. In practice you will probably be OK with national licences from countries such as Australia, Canada and the USA. If you decide to get the permit, your national automobile associations can issue them.

Third-party motor insurance is a minimum requirement in Italy and throughout Europe. The Green Card, an internationally recognised proof of insurance obtainable from your insurer, is mandatory. Also ask your insurer for a European Accident Statement form, which can simplify matters in

ign state-
ıd – insist
y if it's ac-

ance policy
ıe AA Five
r the RAC's
ce (☎ 0990
ı be obtained
Italiano. See
Road Assistance   r & Motorcycle heading in the Getting Around chapter
for details.

Every vehicle travelling across an international border should display a nationality plate of its country of registration. A warning triangle (to be used in the event of a breakdown) is compulsory throughout Europe. Recommended accessories are a first-aid kit, a spare-bulb kit and a fire extinguisher.

Rental There is a mind-boggling variety of special deals and terms and conditions attached to car rental. Here are a few pointers to help you through.

Multinational agencies – Hertz, Avis, Budget and Europe's largest rental agency, Europcar – will provide a reliable service and good standard of vehicle. However, if you walk into an office and ask for a car on the spot, you will always pay high rates, even allowing for special weekend deals. National and local firms can sometimes undercut the multinationals, but be sure to examine the rental agreement carefully (although this might be difficult if it is in Italian).

Planning ahead and pre-booking a rental car through a multinational agency before leaving home will enable you to find the best deals. Pre-booked and pre-paid rates are always cheaper. Fly/drive packages are worth looking into – ask your travel agency for information, or contact one of the major rental agencies.

Holiday Autos sometimes has good rates for Europe, for which you need to pre-book – its main office is in the UK (☎ 0870 400 0011). At the time of writing they were charging UK£332 (all-inclusive) for a small car (such as a Renault Twingo) for two weeks, with the option of one-way rental. Car Rental Direct (☎ 020-7625 7166) is another possibility – have a look at their Web site at www.car-rental-direct.com.

If you don't know exactly when you will want to rent, you could call back home from Italy (more or less affordable to the UK and the USA) and reserve through an agency there. This way you get the benefits of booking from home.

Make sure you understand what is included in the price (unlimited kilometres, tax, insurance, collision damage waiver and so on) and what your liabilities are. Insurance can be a thorny issue. Are you covered for theft, vandalism and fire damage? Since the most common and convenient way to pay for rental is credit card, check whether or not you have car insurance with the credit card provider and what the conditions are. The extra cover provided may pick up the slack in any local cover. The minimum rental age in Italy is 21 years.

Motorcycle and moped rental is possible in Tuscany. For instance there are several specialist rental agencies in Florence (see the Car & Motorcycle section under Getting Around in the Florence chapter).

Purchase It is illegal for nonresidents to purchase vehicles in Italy. The UK is probably the best place to buy second-hand cars (prices there are not competitive for new cars though). Bear in mind that you will be getting a left-hand-drive car (with the steering wheel on the right).

If you want a right-hand-drive car and can afford to buy new, prices are relatively low in Belgium, the Netherlands and Luxembourg. Paperwork can be tricky wherever you buy.

Camper Van Travelling in a camper van can kill several birds with one stone, taking care of eating, sleeping and travelling in one package. Among Europeans it is quite a popular way to get around.

London is a good place to buy. Look in *TNT* magazine or the ads paper *Loot*, or go to the daily van market in Market Rd, London N7 (near Caledonian Road tube sta-ion). Expect to spend at least UK£2000. The most common camper is the VW based on the 1600cc or 2000cc Transporter, for which spare parts are widely available in Europe.

There are drawbacks. Campers can be expensive to buy in spring and hard to get rid of in autumn. They are difficult to manoeuvre around towns. A car and tent may do just as well for some people. If you want to rent, organise it before reaching Tuscany, as the options there are limited.

SEA
Ferries connect Italy with countries all over the Mediterranean, but if you want to reach Tuscany directly by sea, the only options are the ferry crossings to Livorno from Sardinia and Corsica. See the Livorno section of the Central Coast chapter for more details.

ORGANISED TOURS
Options for organised travel to Tuscany abound. The Italian State Tourist Office (see under Tourist Offices Abroad in the Facts for the Visitor chapter) can provide a list of tour operators, with notes of what each specialises in. Tours can save you hassles, but they rob you of independence and generally do not come cheap.

General
A couple of big specialists are Magic of Italy (☎ 020-8748 7575), 227 Shepherd's Bush Rd, London W6 7AS, and Alitalia's subsidiary, Italiatour (☎ 01883-621900). Between them they offer a wide range of tours, city breaks and resort-based holidays covering the whole region. Sestante-CIT (aka CIT or Citalia), with offices worldwide (see Tourist Offices Abroad in the Facts for the Visitor chapter), organises many types of tour.

Short Breaks
Kirker Travel Ltd (☎ 020-7231 3333), 3 New Concordia Wharf, Mill St, London SE1 2BB, specialises in short breaks from London. Such a trip starts at about UK£390 per person for three nights in twin accommodation with air fare, transfers and breakfast in-

Warning

The information in this chapter is particularly vulnerable to change: Prices for international travel are volatile, routes are introduced and cancelled, schedules change, special deals come and go, and rules and visa requirements are amended. Airlines and governments seem to take a perverse pleasure in making price structures and regulations as complicated as possible. You should check directly with the airline or a travel agent to make sure you understand how a fare (and ticket you may buy) works. In addition, the travel industry is highly competitive and there are many lurks and perks.

The upshot of this is that you should get opinions, quotes and advice from as many airlines and travel agents as possible before you part with your hard-earned cash. The details given in this chapter should be regarded as pointers and are not a substitute for your own careful, up-to-date research.

cluded. Depending on the hotel you choose, the price can rise considerably. Prices also go up in summer.

Walking & Cycling
Several companies offer organised walking tours in Tuscany. Explore Worldwide (☎ 01252-319448), 1 Frederick St, Aldershot, Hants GU11 1LQ, is one. Also in the UK, Alternative Travel Group (☎ 01865-315678) offers a series of escorted and unescorted walking and cycling tours. With the unescorted version, accommodation is pre-booked and luggage forwarded on while you walk or cycle. Prices for the unescorted tours start at around UK£300 for eight days (excluding flights). Headwater (☎ 01606-813333), 146 London Rd, Northwich, Cheshire CW9 5HH, also does cycling tours in Tuscany.

Cooking
More focused possibilities abound. Tasting Places (☎ 020-7460 0077), Unit 40, Buspace Studios, Conlan St, London W10 5AP, offers one-week trips led by cooking

instructors. You cook and eat your way to a better understanding of Tuscany. You won't get much change from UK£1000.

You can find more details of cookery courses and tours in the Courses section of the Facts for the Visitor chapter.

Under-35s

Top Deck Travel (☎ 020-7370 4555), 131–135 Earls Court Rd, London SW5 9RH, and Contiki Travel Ltd (☎ 020-7637 0802), c/o Royal National Hotel, Bedford Way, London WC1H 0DG, do a range of coach tours for young people across Europe – they are generally aimed at the high-speed, party-minded crowd.

In the USA, New Frontiers (☎ 800 366 6387), 12 East 33rd St, New York, offer rail-travel packages and other tours in Italy.

Tours for Seniors

For people aged over 60, Saga Holidays offers holidays ranging from cheap coach tours to luxury cruises. You will find offices in Britain (☎ 0800 300456), Saga Building, Middelburg Square, Folkestone, Kent CT20 1AZ; the USA (☎ 800 343 0273), 222 Berkeley St, Boston, MA 02116; and Australia (☎ 02-9957 4266), Level 1, Suite 2, 110 Pacific Highway, North Sydney, Sydney 2061.

Getting Around

AIR

There are no direct flights between cities in Tuscany.

BUS

Unless you have your own wheels, bus is often the only way to get around Tuscany. Where there is a train, you should probably take it, but there are some exceptions. One of them is the Florence–Siena run, which is much quicker and more convenient by rapid SITA bus. Other buses also run from Florence and Siena to Poggibonsi, where there are connecting buses to San Gimignano and Volterra.

Direct buses also run from Florence to Arezzo, Castellina in the Chianti region, Marina di Grosseto and other smaller cities throughout Tuscany.

Lazzi has buses from Florence to parts of Tuscany, mostly in the north-west, including Pisa, Lucca and Pistoia. The CAP and COPIT companies serve towns in the north-west.

In general, separate bus companies operate services in each province, radiating from the provincial capital. Frequently services overlap into neighbouring provinces.

Services can be frequent on weekdays but between smaller towns often drop to a few or even none on Sundays and public holidays. If you are depending on buses to get around, always keep this in mind, as it is easy to get stuck in smaller places on the weekend.

To give you an idea of the cost and time involved for making bus journeys around Tuscany, a few sample one-way trips from Florence follow. Further information appears in the destination chapters in the course of the guide.

destination	one-way (L)	duration
Arezzo	9900	130 minutes
Empoli	5000	70 minutes
Forte dei Marmi	11,400	185 minutes
Greve in Chianti	5000	65 minutes
Lucca	8600	1¼ hours
Marina di Carrara	12,000	2¾ hours
Marina di Massa	12,200	2½ hours
Montecatini	5800	50 minutes
Montelupo	4200	55 minutes
Pisa	11,200	three hours
Pistoia	5000	50 minutes
Poggibonsi	5800	80 minutes
Prato	3500	45 minutes
Radda in Chianti	6200	100 minutes
San Gimignano (change at Poggibonsi)	10,000	1½ hours
Siena	7800	130 minutes
Siena *(rapido)*	11,000	1¼ hours
Viareggio	10,600	two hours
Volterra	7800	130 minutes
Volterra *(rapido)*	11,000	1¼ hours

TRAIN

Some of the long distance trains that run across the country can be used to get around Tuscany. Destinations such as Arezzo and Chiusi, on the Bologna–Florence–Rome line, are easily reached this way.

The lines radiating west towards Pisa (and on to Livorno) and Viareggio are also fairly reliable, with regular services.

The Florence–Pisa run is a good example of where you should choose rail over bus. The train via Empoli takes little over an hour, while the bus stops frequently and takes up to three hours (and costs more into the bargain).

The Viareggio line is the one to take for Prato, Pistoia and Lucca. If you get an all-stops commuter train on either of these lines the going can be a little slow.

The coastal rail line (between Rome and Genoa) is the easiest way to reach most major points along the Tuscan coast (and a branch line cuts inland to Florence). To proceed to smaller towns a little way inland you will often need to make a bus connection.

Several minor lines spread out across the Tuscan countryside too, but services can be limited and slow. The Florence–Siena service is a good example. Others include Siena–Grosseto, Siena–Chiusi, Arezzo–Sinalunga, Lucca–Pisa, Volterra–Cecina (with a couple of connections to Pisa). Another line winds north from Pontassieve via Borgo San Lorenzo across the north-east of the region to Faenza in Emilia-Romagna.

An added inconvenience of numerous Tuscan towns is their hilltop position. When you arrive at the train station in places like Siena, Cortona and Volterra, you still have to get a local bus to take you up to the town.

Some sample one-way, 2nd-class fares and times follow. Bear in mind that times vary considerably depending on what kind of train you end up on and the number of stops made (for information on types of trains see the section under Land in the Getting There & Away chapter):

from	to	cost (L)	duration
Florence	Arezzo	8000	85 minutes
Florence	Borgo San Lorenzo	5700	55 minutes
Florence	Lucca	7300	75 minutes
Florence (via Empoli)	Pisa	8000	65 minutes
Florence	Pistoia	4200	40 minutes
Florence	Prato	2400	25 minutes
Florence	Siena	8800	75 minutes
Florence	Viareggio	10,100	105 minutes
Siena	Chiusi	8000	75 minutes
Siena	Grosseto	10,100	75 minutes

CAR & MOTORCYCLE

Touring Tuscany with your own wheels gives you maximum flexibility. The main highways are good if often busy. The traffic around Florence, on the *autostrade* (four- to six-lane motorways) and the *superstrada* (up to four-lane motorways) between Florence and Siena can be intense (to say the least).

Remember that the autostrade are toll roads. There aren't too many of these. The A1 (aka Autostrada del Sole) from Bologna heads down northern Tuscany to swing in a wide loop to the west and south of Florence before veering south-east to pass (at some distance) Arezzo, Cortona and Chiusi before proceeding on to Rome. The A12 slithers down the Ligurian coast from Genoa and La Spezia through Viareggio and Pisa to Livorno. It will eventually go to Rome, but at this point peters out just south of

Rosignano Marittima. The A11 connects Florence with Pisa and the A12.

There are a couple of four-lane, toll-free superstrade as an alternative to the autostrade. The SS1 (Via Aurelia) along the coast is four lanes almost all the way from Livorno Sud (south) to Tuscany's border with Lazio. From Livorno Nord (north) it's mostly two-lane only and often clogged with traffic. The SGC highway (also known as the Fi-Pi-Li) connects Florence, Pisa and Livorno. The other important one is the SS2, which links Florence with Siena.

When you get away from the main centres, the smaller back roads offer frequently pretty drives, but be prepared to take your time. Progress around the winding hill country of Tuscany can be slow. The most congested areas are in the north-west in and around the towns of Prato, Pistoia, Lucca, Pisa and Viareggio.

JANE SMITH

Motorini – easier to park than a car and less effort than a bike...

The Car & Motorcycle section of the Getting There & Away chapter covers paperwork and ways of getting your car to Tuscany from other parts of Italy and abroad.

Road Maps & Atlases

See the beginning of the Facts for the Visitor chapter for information on road maps.

Road Rules

In general, standard European road rules apply. In built-up areas the speed limit is usually 50km/h, rising to 90km/h on secondary roads, 110km/h on main roads (caravans 80km/h) and up to 130km/h (caravans 100km/h) on autostrade.

Motorcyclists must use headlights at all times. Crash helmets are obligatory on bikes of 125cc or more.

Vehicles already on a roundabout often have right of way. However, this is not always the case and working out which type you are confronted with is best done by paying careful attention to local example!

The blood-alcohol limit is 0.08%. Random breath tests are conducted – penalties range from on-the-spot fines to confiscation of your driving licence.

Petrol

Petrol *(benzina)* in Italy is among the dearest in Western Europe, and the price has been increasing steadily of late with the run-away dollar fuelling the problem. Super costs L2040 a litre; unleaded *(senza piombo)* L1940 a litre; and diesel (or *gasolio*) L1560 a litre. These prices can drop by up to L50 in some service stations, especially those with *fai da te* (DIY) promotions, where you serve yourself rather than wait for an attendant. Stations on autostrade charge about L20 more per litre.

If you are driving a car that uses liquid petroleum gas (LPG), you will need to buy a special guide to service stations that have *gasauto* or GPL. By law these must be located in nonresidential areas and are usually in the country or on city outskirts, although you'll find plenty on the autostrade. GPL costs around L900 a litre (although it can come down to L850).

122 Getting Around

Sign Language

You can save yourse
by learning what s(
signs mean:

entrata – entrance (for example onto autostrada)
incrocio – intersection/crossroads
lavori in corso – roadworks ahead
parcheggio – parking lot
passaggio a livello – level crossing
rallentare – slow down
senso unico – one-way street
senso vietato – no entry
sosta autorizzata – parking permitted (during times displayed)
sosta vietata – no stopping/parking
svolta – bend
tutte le direzioni – all directions (useful when looking for town exit)
uscita – exit (for example from autostrada)

You can pay with most credit cards at the great majority of service stations. Those on the autostrade open 24 hours a day. Otherwise, opening hours are generally from around 7 am to 12.30 pm and 3.30 to 7.30 pm (7 pm in winter). Up to 75% are closed on Sundays and public holidays, and those that open then close on Monday. Don't assume you can't get petrol if you pass a station that is closed. Quite a few have self-service pumps that accept banknotes. It is illegal to carry spare fuel in your vehicle.

Road Assistance

As a rule, holders of motoring insurance with foreign organisations such as the RAC, AA (UK) or AAA (USA) will be provided with an emergency assistance number to use while travelling in Italy. You can also get road assistance and a tow with the Automobile Club Italia (ACI) by calling ☎ 116. If you have the appropriate insurance you should probably be covered. It is likely in any case that, whichever number you use, an ACI truck will arrive.

ving

...le of thumb, in most cities you will ...to park your car and forget about it. Dri-...ng in the historic centre of most towns is either banned or restricted, and finding a legal parking spot can be a nightmare. Until you know your way around, park in a designated meter parking area or parking station. If you leave the car farther away from the centre you can generally find free street parking.

When you do drive around in the cities, you'll probably find it a little chaotic and unnerving initially. Road rules and traffic lights are generally respected though.

Never leave anything visibly unattended in your car. Where possible, never leave anything in the car at all.

Rental

All the big companies have outlets in the main cities and at the airports. In Florence you can rent a motorbike for up to L180,000 a day at Alinari (☎ 055 28 05 00), Via Guelfa 85r.

If you decide to rent a motorhome while in Florence, one of Italy's few rental outlets specialising in these is based about 20km south of Florence. Laika Viaggi (☎ 055 805 82 00, fax 055 805 85 00) is at Via B Cellini 210/214 at Tavarnelle Val di Pesa. Their low season rates for a week's rental start at L204,000 with unlimited kilometres. Note that you have to pay a L2,500,000 deposit. Its Web site is at www.laikaviaggi.com.

BICYCLE

If you plan to bring your own bike, check with the airline about any hidden costs. It will have to be disassembled and packed for the journey.

Cycle touring across Tuscany is becoming increasingly popular. UK-based cyclists planning to do some of this might want to contact the Cyclists' Touring Club (☎ 01483-417217), Cotterell House, 69 Meadrow, Godalming, Surrey GU7 3HS, UK. It can supply information to members on cycling conditions, itineraries and cheap insurance. Route and information sheets include: *Emilia-Romagna & Tuscany*; *Tuscany & Umbria*; *Circular Tour of Tuscany*; and *Day Rides from Sambuca*. Membership costs UK£25 per annum.

Once in Italy, it is possible to transport your bicycle on many trains. Those marked on timetables with a bicycle symbol have a carriage set aside for the transport of bicycles. Otherwise you need to dismantle it and pack it. You may not take your bike on Eurostar Italia services requiring a booking. In all cases where you are allowed to take the bike, you must pay a *supplemento* of L5000 to L10,000.

You can hire bicycles, including mountain bikes, from several outlets in Florence and other towns around the region (see regional chapters for details).

HITCHING

Hitching is never entirely safe and we don't recommend it. Travellers who decide to hitch should understand that they are taking a small but potentially serious risk. People who do choose to hitch will be safer if they travel in pairs and let someone know where they are planning to go.

To get out of Florence you need to start at one of the highway exits. The chances of anyone stopping for you on autostrade are close to zero – try the more congested toll-free highways (such as the SS2 heading south towards Siena, the SS65 north to Bologna or the SS435 west to Lucca).

BOAT

Regular ferries connect Piombino with Elba. In summer, excursions depart from Portoferraio on Elba for the island of Capraia, and since 1999 other excursions have been organised to the tiny island of Pianosa from Marina di Campo. From Livorno ferries run to Capraia via the prison island of Gorgona. You can reach the island of Giglio from Porto Santo Stefano. Summer excursions (May to September) also leave the same port for the island of Giannutri. See the relevant chapters for more details.

LOCAL TRANSPORT

All cities and major towns have a reasonable local bus service (local buses are genrally orange). Usually you won't need to use them, as the towns are compact, with sights, hotels, restaurants and long-distance transport stations within walking distance of each other. The only probable exceptions might be Florence, Siena and Pisa.

Buses and trains connect Pisa's Galileo Galilei airport with Pisa and Florence, while buses link Amerigo Vespucci airport with central Florence.

ORGANISED TOURS

Guided tour options of individual cities abound (local tourist offices generally have details). They can be illuminating, but generally you can get around any of the towns under your own steam with no difficulty. From cities such as Florence and Siena it is possible to join tours of towns and areas (such as the Chianti region) in the vicinity.

Florence (Firenze)

postcode 50100 • pop 461,000

Situated on the banks of the Arno river in a valley and set among low hills covered with olive groves and vineyards, Florence is immediately captivating. Cradle of the Renaissance and home of Machiavelli, Michelangelo and the Medici, the city seems unfairly burdened with art, culture and history.

Despite the implausible traffic, stifling summer heat, pollution and industrial sprawl on the city's outskirts, Florence attracts millions of tourists each year. The French writer Stendhal was so dazzled by the magnificence of the Basilica di Santa Croce that he was barely able to walk for faintness. He is apparently not the only one to have felt thus overwhelmed by the beauty of Florence – they say Florentine doctors treat a dozen cases of 'stendhalismo' a year.

You will need at least four or five days to do Florence any justice at all.

HISTORY

The Etruscan city of Fiesole founded Florence as a colony in about 200 BC. It later became the Roman Florentia, a strategic garrison whose purpose was to control the Via Flaminia linking Rome to northern Italy and Gaul. Along with the rest of northern Italy, the city suffered during the barbarian invasions of the Dark Ages. In the early 12th century it became a free *comune* (city state) and by 1138 was ruled by 12 consuls, assisted by the Consiglio di Cento (Council of One Hundred). The council members were drawn mainly from the prosperous merchant class. Agitation among differing factions in the city led to the appointment of a foreign head of state, known as the *podestà*, in 1207.

The first conflicts between the pro-papal Guelphs (Guelfi) and the pro-imperial Ghibellines (Ghibellini) started towards the middle of the 13th century, with power passing from one faction to the other for al-

Highlights

- Gorge yourself on the art treasures of the Uffizi and Bargello
- Climb to the top of the Campanile for wonderful views of the city
- Hang out in the hip Rex Caffè for a cocktail or two
- Take in the views with a drink at Piazzale Michelangelo
- Come to know the work of Brunelleschi, the genius of Renaissance architecture whose work ranges from the dome of the Duomo to the Basilica di San Lorenzo
- Stand slack-jawed before the sublime reality of Michelangelo's David
- Loosen the purse strings and hit the fashion shops around Via de' Tornabuoni

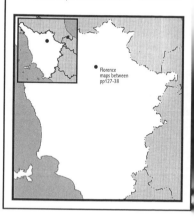

Florence
maps between
pp127-38

most a century. The Guelphs eventually formed a government, known as the Primo Popolo, but in 1260 were ousted after Florence was defeated by Ghibelline Siena at the Battle of Monteaperti. The Guelphs regained control in 1289.

If you thought that was complicated, it got worse in the 1290s as the Guelphs split into two factions: the Neri (Blacks) and

Bianchi (Whites). When the latter were defeated in 1302, Dante was among those driven into exile. As the nobility lost ground, the Guelph merchant class took control. But trouble was never far away. The great plague of 1348 halved the city's population and the government was rocked by growing agitation from the lower classes.

During the latter part of the 14th century, Florence was ruled by a caucus of Guelphs under the leadership of the Albizi family. Among the families opposing them were the Medici, whose influence grew as they became the papal bankers.

In the 15th century Cosimo de' Medici emerged as the head of the opposition to the Albizi and eventually became Florence's ruler. His eye for talent and his tact in dealing with artists saw the likes of Alberti, Brunelleschi, Lorenzo Ghiberti, Donatello, Fra Angelico and Filippo Lippi flourish under his patronage. Many of the city's finest buildings are testimony to his tastes.

Cosimo was eventually followed by his grandson, Lorenzo the Magnificent ('il Magnifico'), whose rule (1469–92) ushered in the most glorious period of Florentine civilisation and of the Italian Renaissance. His court fostered a great flowering of art, music and poetry, and Florence became the cultural capital of Italy. Lorenzo favoured philosophers, but he maintained family tradition by sponsoring artists such as Botticelli and Domenico Ghirlandaio; he also encouraged Leonardo and the young Michelangelo, who was working under Giovanni di Bertoldo, Donatello's pupil.

Not long before Lorenzo's death in 1492, the Medici bank failed and, two years later, the Medici were driven out of Florence. The city fell under the control of Girolamo Savonarola, a Dominican monk who led a puritanical republic until he fell from public favour and was fried as a heretic in 1498.

After Florence's defeat by the Spanish in 1512, the Medici returned to the city but were once again expelled, this time by Emperor Charles V, in 1527. Two years later they had made peace, and Charles not only

allowed the Me but married h great-grandson whom he made The Medici th years, during w trol of all Tusca

In 1737 the passed to the House of Lorraine, which retained control (apart from a brief interruption under Napoleon from 1799 to 1814) until it was incorporated into the kingdom of Italy in 1860. Florence became the national capital a year later, but Rome assumed the mantle permanently in 1875.

Florence was badly damaged during WWII by the retreating Germans, who blew up all its bridges except the Ponte Vecchio. Devastating floods ravaged the city in 1966, causing inestimable damage to its buildings and artworks. However, the salvage operation led to the widespread use of modern restoration techniques that have saved artworks throughout the country.

ORIENTATION

Whether you arrive by train, bus or car, the central train station, Stazione di Santa Maria Novella, is a good reference point. Budget hotels and *pensioni* are concentrated around Via Nazionale, to the east of the station, and Piazza Santa Maria Novella, to the south. The main route to the city centre is Via de' Panzani and then Via de' Cerretani, about a 10-minute walk. You'll know you've arrived when you first glimpse the Duomo.

Most of the major sights are within easy walking distance – you can stroll from one end of the city centre to the other in about 30 minutes. From Piazza San Giovanni around the Baptistry, Via Roma leads to Piazza della Repubblica and continues as Via Calimala then Via Por Santa Maria to the Ponte Vecchio. Take Via de' Calzaiuoli from Piazza del Duomo for Piazza della Signoria, the historic seat of government. The Uffizi is on the piazza's southern edge, near the Arno. Cross the Ponte Vecchio, or the Ponte alle Grazie farther east, and head south-east to Piazzale Michelangelo for a fantastic view over the city.

reasonably priced public ...und the imposing Fortezza da ...st north of the train station and a ...0-minute walk to the historic centre ...g Via Faenza.

Florence has two street-numbering systems: red or brown numbers indicate commercial premises and black or blue numbers denote a private residence. When written, black or blue addresses are denoted by the number only, while red or brown addresses usually carry an 'r' (for *rosso*, or 'red') after the number. It can be confusing as the black and blue numbers tend to denote whole buildings, while the others may refer to one small part of the same building. When looking for a specific address, keep your eyes on both sets of numbers and accept that backtracking is sometimes inevitable.

INFORMATION
Tourist Offices

The main APT tourist office (☎ 055 29 08 32, fax 055 276 03 83) is just north of the Duomo at Via Cavour 1r. It is open from 8.15 am to 7.15 pm Monday to Saturday and from 8.45 am to 1.45 pm on Sunday between April and October. It is open until 1.45 pm and closed on Sunday during the other months. The branch at Amerigo Vespucci airport (☎ 055 31 58 74) opens from 8.30 am to 10.30 pm daily. Check out the APT's Web site at www.firenze .turismo.toscana.it.

The Comune di Firenze (Florence's city council) operates a tourist office (☎ 055 21 22 45) at the southern end of the series of ATAF (Azienda Trasporti Area Fiorentina) bus stops between Piazza Adua and Piazza della Stazione, just outside the south-east exit from the train station. It generally opens from 8.15 am to 7.15 pm Monday to Saturday in summer. The hours are cut to 9 am to 1.45 pm in winter. There is another office (☎ 055 234 04 44) at Borgo Santa Croce 29r, which opens at the same times.

Inside the train station you can pick up basic information at the Consorzio ITA office (☎ 055 28 28 93). Their main role is to book hotels. The office is open from 8.30 am to 9 pm daily. See also Places to Stay later in the chapter for details about hotel booking services.

APT staff speak English, French, Spanish and German, and have extensive useful information about the city and its services, from language and art courses to car and bike rental. From April to October the APT also offers a special service known as Firenze SOS Turista (☎ 055 276 03 82). Tourists needing guidance on matters such as disputes over hotel bills can phone from 10 am to 1 pm and 3 to 6 pm Monday to Saturday.

One of the handiest commercial maps of the city is the ring-bound *Firenze*, published by the Touring Club Italiano. It costs L15,000. There are plenty of cheaper ones around too.

Foreign Consulates

Check the Embassies & Consulates in Italy section in the Facts for the Visitor chapter.

Money

A number of banks are concentrated around Piazza della Repubblica. Thomas Cook has an exchange office (☎ 055 28 97 81) at Lungarno degli Acciaioli 6r, near the Ponte Vecchio. It opens from 9 am to 7 pm Monday to Saturday and from 9 am to 1 pm on Sunday. American Express (Amex) is at Via Dante Alighieri 22r (☎ 055 5 09 81). It opens from 9 am to 5.30 pm Monday to Friday and from 9.30 am to 12.30 pm on Saturday. If you've lost travellers cheques or credit cards you can call ☎ 800 87 20 00 or ☎ 800 86 40 46 respectively out of hours.

Post & Communications

The main post office is in Via Pellicceria, off Piazza della Repubblica, and is open from 8.15 am to 7 pm daily. Another big one is on the corner of Via Giuseppe Verdi and Via Pietrapiana. Poste restante mail should be addressed to 50100 Florence.

The main post office operates a fax poste restante service. You can have faxes sent to

[continued on page 139]

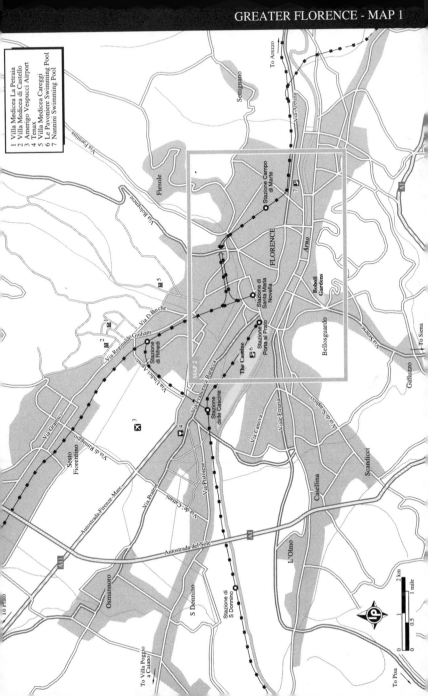

GREATER FLORENCE - MAP 1

1 Villa Medicea La Petraia
2 Villa Medicea di Castello
3 Amerigo Vespucci Airport
4 Tenax
5 Villa Medicea Careggi
6 Le Pavoniere Swimming Pool
7 Nannini Swimming Pool

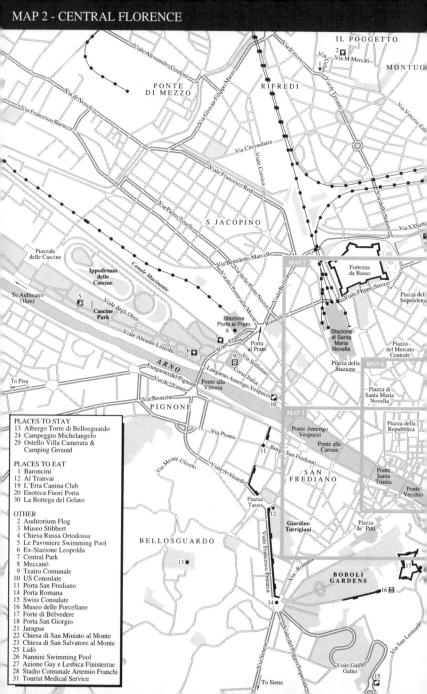

MAP 2 - CENTRAL FLORENCE

IL POGGETTO

MONTUG

RIFREDI

PONTE
DI MEZZO

S JACOPINO

Piazzale
delle Cascine

Ippodromo
delle
Cascine

To Anfiteatro
(1km)

Cascine
Park

To Pisa

ARNO

PIGNONE

Fortezza
da Basso

Piazza del
Inipenden

Stazione
di Santa
Maria
Novella

Piazza
del Mercato
Centrale

Piazza della
Stazione

Stazione
Porta al Prato

Porta
al Prato

Ponte alla
Vittoria

Piazza di
Santa Maria
Novella

Piazza della
Repubblica

Ponte Amerigo
Vespucci

Ponte alle
Carraia

Ponte
Santa
Trinita

Ponte
Vecchio

SAN
FREDIANO

Piazza
Tasso

Piazza
de' Pitti

Giardino
Torrigiani

BELLOSGUARDO

BOBOLI
GARDENS

To Siena

PLACES TO STAY
13 Albergo Torre di Bellosguardo
24 Campeggio Michelangelo
29 Ostello Villa Camerata &
   Camping Ground

PLACES TO EAT
1 Baroncini
12 Al Tranvai
19 L'Erta Canina Club
20 Enoteca Fuori Porta
30 La Bottega del Gelato

OTHER
2 Auditorium Flog
3 Museo Stibbert
4 Chiesa Russa Ortodossa
5 Le Pavoniere Swimming Pool
6 Ex-Stazione Leopolda
7 Central Park
8 Meccanò
9 Teatro Comunale
10 US Consulate
11 Porta San Frediano
14 Porta Romana
15 Swiss Consulate
16 Museo delle Porcellane
17 Forte di Belvedere
18 Porta San Giorgio
21 Jaragua
22 Chiesa di San Miniato al Monte
23 Chiesa di San Salvatore al Monte
25 Lidò
26 Nannini Swimming Pool
27 Azione Gay e Lesbica Finisterrae
28 Stadio Comunale Artemio Franchi
31 Tourist Medical Service

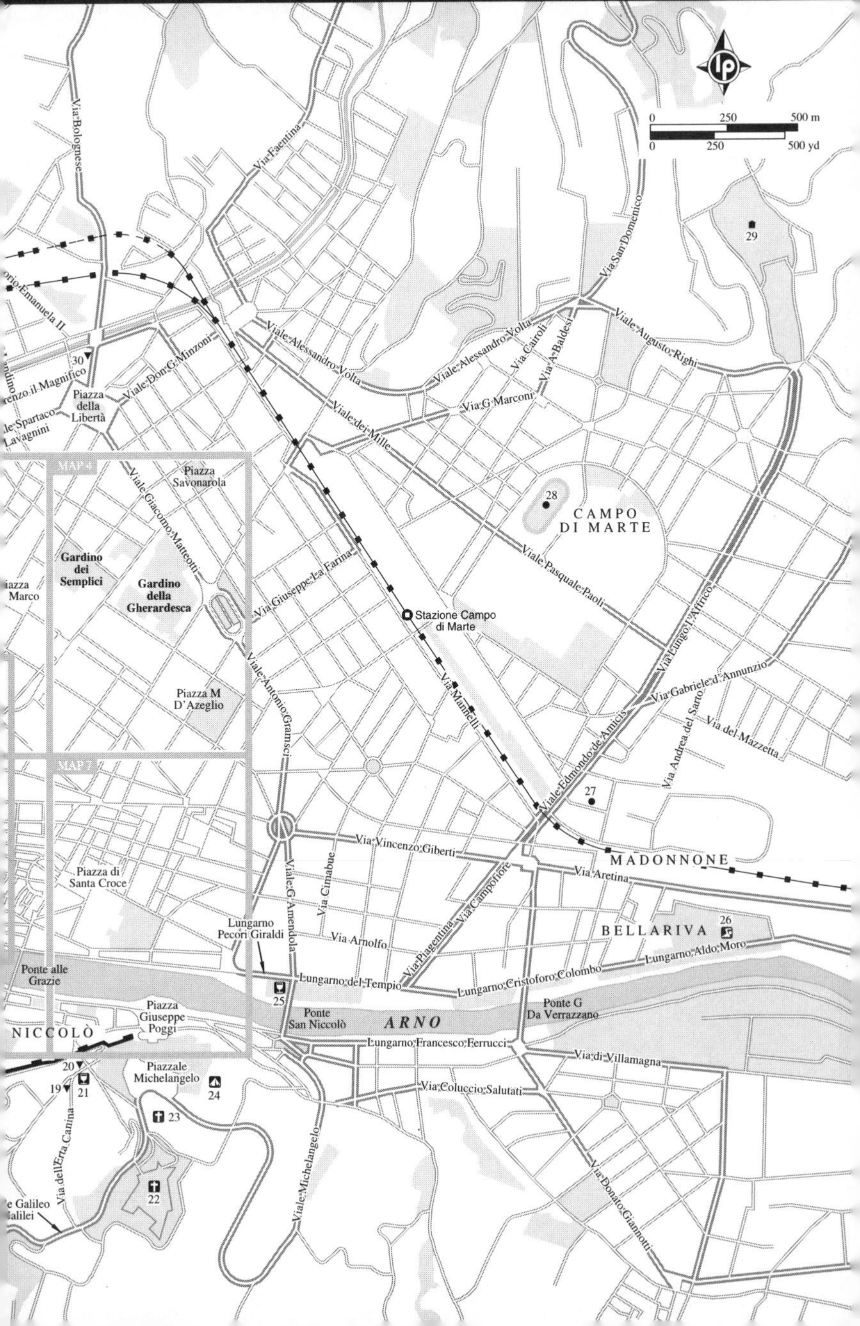
0
250
500 m
0
250
500 yd
29
Via Bolognese
Via Faentina
Via San Domenico
orio Emanuela II
30
renzo il Magnifico
Piazza
della
Libertà
le Spartaco
Lavagnini
Viale Don G Minzoni
Viale Alessandro Volta
Viale Alessandro Volta
Via Cairoli
Via A Baldesi
Viale Augusto Righi
Via G Marconi
Viale dei Mille
MAP 4
Piazza
Savonarola
Viale Giacomo Matteotti
28
CAMPO
DI MARTE
Gardino
dei
Semplici
Gardino
della
Gherardesca
iazza
Marco
Via Giuseppe La Farina
Viale Pasquale Paoli
Stazione Campo
di Marte
Via Lungo l'Affrico
Viale Antonio Gramsci
Via Mannelli
Via Gabriele d'Annunzio
Piazza M
D'Azeglio
Viale Edmondo de Amicis
Via Andrea del Sarto
Via del Mazzetta
MAP 7
27
Via Vincenzo Giberti
MADONNONE
Piazza di
Santa Croce
Via Cimabue
Viale G Amendola
Via Aretina
Via Campofiore
Lungarno
Pecori Giraldi
Via Arnolfo
BELLARIVA
26
Via Piagentina
Lungarno Aldo Moro
Ponte alle
Grazie
Lungarno del Tempio
Lungarno Cristoforo Colombo
25
Piazza
Giuseppe
Poggi
Ponte
San Niccolò
ARNO
Ponte G
Da Verrazzano
NICCOLÒ
Lungarno Francesco Ferrucci
20
Piazzale
Michelangelo
Via di Villamagna
19
21
24
Via Coluccio Salutati
23
Via dell'Erta Canina
Viale Michelangelo
Via Donato Giannotti
22
e Galileo
alilei

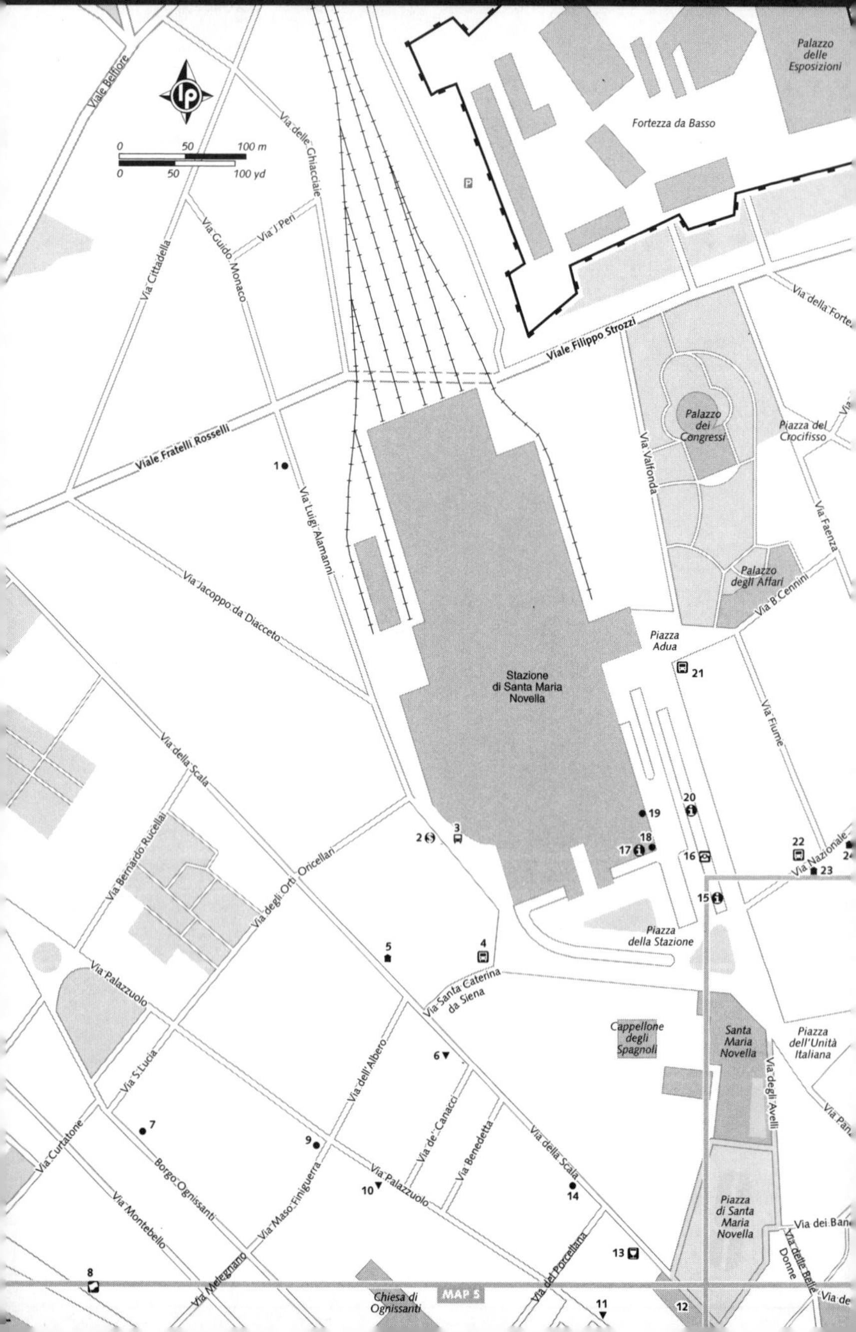

MAP 3

Palazzo
delle
Esposizioni

Fortezza da Basso

Via della Forte

Viale Battore

Via delle Chiascaie

Via J' Peri

Via Guido Monaco

Via Cittadella

Viale Filippo Strozzi

Viale Fratelli Rosselli

Via Luigi Alamanni

1

Palazzo
dei
Congressi

Via Valfonda

Piazza del
Crocifisso

Via Faenza

Palazzo
degli Affari

Via B Cennini

Via Jacoppo da Diacceto

Piazza
Adua

21

Via Fiume

Stazione
di Santa Maria
Novella

Via della Scala

Via Bernardo Rucellai

Via degli Orti Oricellari

20

19

18

17   16

22

Via Nazionale

23

2   3

15

Piazza
della Stazione

Via Palazzuolo

Via S. Lucia

4

5

Via Santa Caterina
da Siena

Cappellone
degli
Spagnoli

Santa
Maria
Novella

Piazza
dell'Unità
Italiana

Via degli Avelli

Via Pan

Via Curtatone

Via dell'Albero

6

7

Via de' Canacci

Via Benedetta

Via della Scala

Borgo Ognissanti

9

Via Palazzuolo

10

14

Piazza
di Santa
Maria
Novella

Via dei Ban

Via dei Ban

Via Montebello

Via Maso Finiguerra

Via del Porcellana

13

Via delle Belle
Donne

Via de

8

Via Melegnano

Chiesa di
Ognissanti

MAP 5

11

12

MAP 3

Via delle Mantellate

Via Duca d'Aosta

Viale Spartaco Lavagnini

Via Enrico Poggi

Via G. Dolfi

Via Filippo Strozzi

Via di Barbano

Via C. Ridolfi

Via F. Bartolommei

Via S. Caterina d'Alessandria

Via Zanobi

Via Bonifacio Lupi

Via Zara

🛏 35

Police Station

Via di Camporeggi

Via Salvestrina

34 ▼
33 ●

Via delle Ruote

Via Santa Reparata

Piazza della Indipendenza

Via Fortezza

Via XXVII Aprile

32 ●

Via San Gallo

Via Guelfa

Via Nazionale

31 ■

30 ●

Via Zanobi

Via Santa Reparata

Cenacolo di Sant'Apollonia

Via degli Arazzieri

Via Cavour

Chiesa di San Marco

▼ 36
📷 37

Piazza San Marco

Via La Pira

Università degli Studi di Firenze

📷 38

Via Panicale

Via S. Orsola

Via Taddea

Via Guelfa

39 📷

Via Cesare Battisti

Galleria dell'Accademia

Via Ricasoli

27

Mercato Centrale

Via dell'Ariento

Piazza del Mercato Centrale

Via Rosina

▼ 40
▼ 41

42 ■

Via degli Alfani

43 ●

MAP 4

MAP 6

Via Sant'Antonino

Via Faenza

Via dell'Amorino

Melarancio

Piazza Madonna degli Aldobrandini

Cappelle Medicee

Via del Canto de' Nelli

Piazza San Lorenzo

Basilica di San Lorenzo

Borgo la Noce

Via della Stufa

Via de' Ginori

Palazzo Medici-Riccardi

Via de' Gori

Via Cavour

Via Ricasoli

44 🛏
45 📷
46 📷

Piazza Brunelleschi

Via de' Servi

Giglio

Via dell'Alloro

Via de' Conti

Via F. Zanetti

Borgo San Lorenzo

Via de' Martelli

Via de' Biffi

Via de' Pucci

Ospedale di Santa Maria Nuova

Via Bufalini

47 ●

Piazza di Santa Maria Nuova

Rondinelli

Via de' Cerretani

Piazza del Duomo

Baptistry

Duomo

Museo dell'Opera del Duomo

Via Sant' Egidio

MAP 5

MAP 3

PLACES TO STAY
5   La Romagnola
23   Pensione Le Cascine
24   Ostello Spirito Santo
27   Nuova Italia
28   Albergo Azzi
29   Ostello Archi Rossi
31   Pensione Ausonia & Rimini
42   Hotel Il Guelfo Bianco

PLACES TO EAT
6   La Grotta di Leo
10   Trattoria il Contadino
11   Amon
26   Ristorante Lobs
34   Il Vegetariano
36   La Bodeguita
40   Mario
41   Ristorante ZàZà

OTHER
1   Box Office
2   Exact Change
3   ATAF Local Bus Stop
4   SITA Bus Station
7   Avis Car Rental
8   German Consulate
9   Hertz Car Rental
12   Loggia di San Paolo
13   The Chequers Pub
14   Mail Boxes Etc
15   Comune di Firenze
       Tourist Office
16   Telecom Booths
17   Consorzio ITA
18   Farmacia Comunale
       (24-Hour Pharmacy)
19   Deposito
       (Left Luggage)

20   ATAF Ticket & Information
       Office; ATAF Bus Stop for
       Nos 7, 13, 62 & 70
21   Lazzi Bus Station &
       Ticket Office
22   CAP & COPIT Bus Station
25   Centro Lorenzo de' Medici
30   Alinari Bike Rentals
32   Firenze & Abroad
33   Florence By Bike
35   Swedish Consulate
37   CyberOffice
38   Internet Train
39   Mondial Net
43   Wash & Dry Laundrette
44   Bebop
45   Belgian Consulate
46   Danish Consulate
47   Scuola Leonardo da Vinci

BETHUNE CARMICHAEL

Terracotta medallions on the facade of Europe's first orphanage, the Spedale delgi Innocenti.

JULIET COOMBE

From the pavement to the Uffizi, there's hardly a corner free of art in Florence.

MAP 4

Ospedale
Militare

PLACES TO STAY
2 Pensione Losanna;
  Pensione Donatello
3 Hotel Le Due Fontane

PLACES TO EAT
5 Caffellatte

OTHER
1 Norwegian Consulate
4 Wash & Dry
6 WWW.Village
7 Paperback Exchange
  Bookshop
8 Jazz Club

Via F. Valori

Piazza
Savonarola

Via Fra Buonvicini

Via M. Ficino

Via G. Benivieni

Via Gustavo Modena

Piazza I
Del Lungo

Via Pier Capponi

Piazza
A. Conti

Via Venezia

Via Alfonso Lamarmora

Via Luigi Salvatore Cherubini

Viale Giacomo Matteotti

Via della Robbia

Via La Pira

Via Pier Antonio Micheli

Via Cino Capponi

Via degli Artisti

**Giardino
dei Semplici**

Museo
Botanico

Palazzo
Capponi

Gardino
della
Gherardesca

Piazzale
Donatello

⌖ 1

Borgo Pinti

Cimitero
degli
Inglesi

Chiesa di
SS Annunziata

Via Giuseppe Giusti

Piazza
della SS
Annunziata

Viale Antonio
Gramsci

Via della Colonna

Via Laura

Spedale
degli
Innocenti

Museo
Archeologico

Via Vittorio Alfieri

2 ●

Via degli Alfani

Via della Pergola

Piazza
Massimo
d'Azeglio

● 4

Borgo Pinti

5 ▼

Via della Colonna

Via Nuova de' Caccini

6 ⌂

Via Luigi Carlo Farini

8 ⌂   7 ●

Via de' Pilastri

Teatro
della
Pergola

Via G. B. Niccol

MAP 7

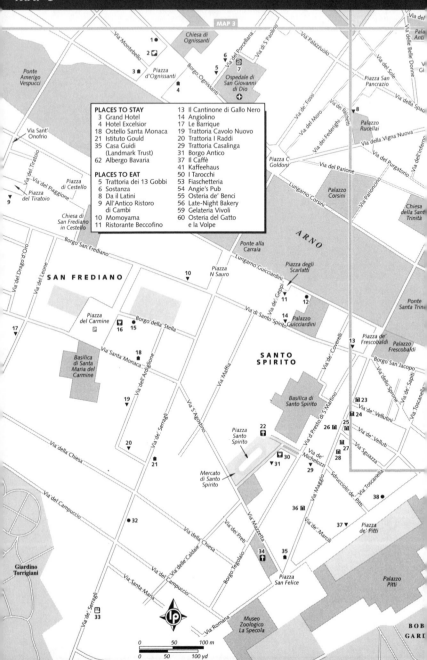

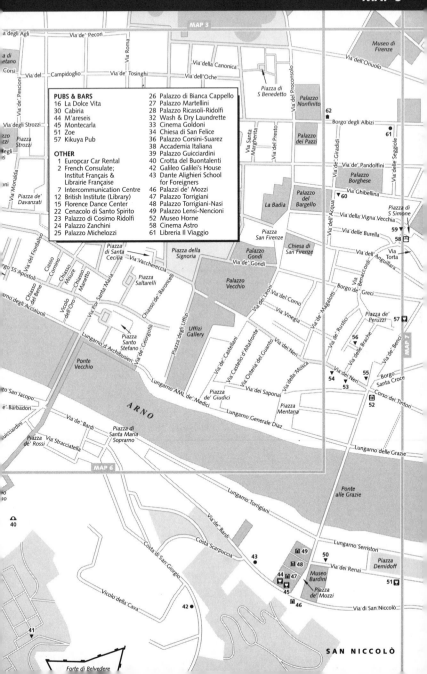

MAP 3

PUBS & BARS
16 La Dolce Vita
30 Cabiria
44 M'areseis
45 Montecarla
51 Zoe
57 Kikuya Pub

OTHER
1 Europcar Car Rental
2 French Consulate;
  Institut Français &
  Librairie Française
7 Intercommunication Centre
12 British Institute (Library)
15 Florence Dance Center
22 Cenacolo di Santo Spirito
23 Palazzo di Cosimo Ridolfi
24 Palazzo Zanchini
25 Palazzo Michelozzi

26 Palazzo di Bianca Cappello
27 Palazzo Martellini
28 Palazzo Ricasoli-Ridolfi
32 Wash & Dry Laundrette
33 Cinema Goldoni
34 Chiesa di San Felice
36 Palazzo Corsini-Suarez
38 Accademia Italiana
39 Palazzo Guicciardini
40 Crotta del Buontalenti
42 Galileo Galilei's House
43 Dante Alighieri School
   for Foreigners
46 Palazzi de' Mozzi
47 Palazzo Torrigiani
48 Palazzo Torrigiani-Nasi
49 Palazzo Lensi-Nencioni
52 Museo Horne
58 Cinema Astro
61 Libreria Il Viaggio

MAP 6

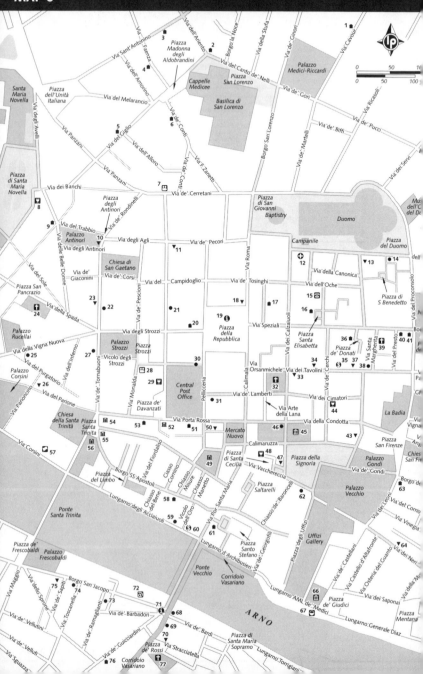

MAP 6

PLACES TO STAY

1	Hotel Le Casci
2	Giada
3	Hotel Globus
4	Pensione Accademia
5	Giotto
6	Hotel Bellettini
9	Pensione Ferretti
16	Hotel Brunelleschi; Torre della Pagliazza
17	Maxim
20	Pendini
36	Albergo Firenze
40	Pensione Maria Luisa de' Medici; Centro Linguistico Sperimentale
41	Brunori
51	Pensione TeTi & Prestige
53	Hotel Porta Rossa
58	Hotel Alessandra
61	Aily Home
63	Bernini Palace
76	Pensione la Scaletta

PLACES TO EAT

10	Cantinetta Antinori
11	Ristorante Self-Service Leonardo
13	Hostariail Caminetto
18	Gilli
23	Procacci
26	Trattoria Coco Lezzone
33	Gelateria Perchè No?
34	Ristorante Paoli
37	Trattoria del Pennello
43	Vini e Vecchi Sapori
47	Rivoire
50	Trattoria Pasquini
64	Eito
65	Trattoriada Benvenuto
70	Le Volpi e l'Uva
75	Osteria del Cinghiale Bianco

PUBS & BARS

8	Fiddler's Elbow
29	Yab
44	Andromeda
48	Tabasco

OTHER

7	Astra Cinehall
12	Misericordiadi Firenze Ambulances
14	Istituto Europeo
15	Yellow Point Phone Centre
19	Tourist Help Point
21	TWA
22	Internazionale Seeber Bookshop
24	Chiesa di San Pancrazio; Museo Marino Marini
25	Loggia dei Rucellai
27	Gucci
28	Odeon Cinehall
30	Chiosco degli Sportivi
31	City Centre Intertravel (Lufthansa)
32	Chiesa di Orsanmichele
35	American Express Office
38	Casa di Dante (Dante's House)
39	Chiesa di Santa Margherita
42	Palazzo del Bargello; Museo del Bargello
45	Raccolta d'Arte Contemporanea Alberto della Ragione
46	Molteni (24-Hour Pharmacy)
49	Palazzo dei Capitani di Parte Guelfa
52	Palazzo Davanzati; Museo dell' Antica Casa Fiorentina
54	Palazzo Bartolini-Saltimbeni
55	Palazzo Buondelmonti
56	Palazzo Spini-Ferroni; Ferragamo
57	UK Consulate
59	Alitalia
60	Thomas Cook Exchange Office
62	Loggia della Signoria (Loggia dei Lanzi)
66	Museo di Storia delle Scienze
67	Arno Boat Tour Departure Point
68	Torre dei Mannelli
69	Torre degli Ubriachi
71	Tourist Help Point
72	Internet Train
73	Torre de' Belfredelli
74	Torre dei Marsili
77	Chiesa di Santa Felicita

JULIA WILKINSON

e upper section of the facade of the Basilica di Santa Maria Novella, designed by Alberti.

MAP 7

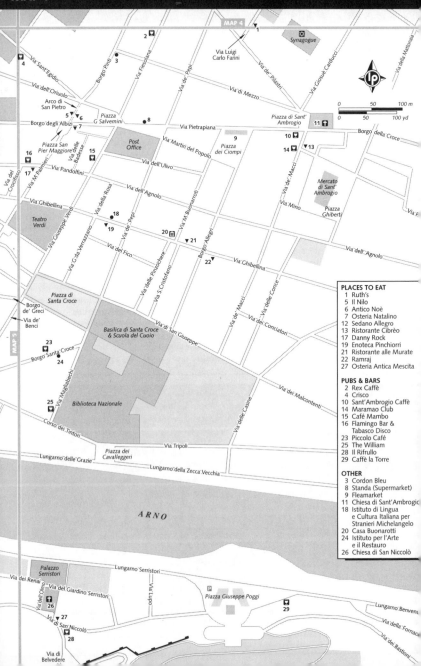

PLACES TO EAT
1   Ruth's
5   Il Nilo
6   Antico Noè
7   Osteria Natalino
12 Sedano Allegro
13 Ristorante Cibrèo
17 Danny Rock
19 Enoteca Pinchiorri
21 Ristorante alle Murate
22 Ramraj
27 Osteria Antica Mescita

PUBS & BARS
2   Rex Caffè
4   Crisco
10 Sant'Ambrogio Caffè
14 Maramao Club
15 Café Mambo
16 Flamingo Bar &
    Tabasco Disco
23 Piccolo Café
25 The William
28 Il Rifrullo
29 Caffè la Torre

OTHER
3   Cordon Bleu
8   Standa (Supermarket)
9   Fleamarket
11 Chiesa di Sant'Ambrogio
18 Istituto di Lingua
    e Cultura Italiana per
    Stranieri Michelangelo
20 Casa Buonarroti
24 Istituto per l'Arte
    e il Restauro
26 Chiesa di San Niccolò

continued from page 126]

ou at Fax Fermo Posta. To retrieve the fax ou will need a passport or some other hoto ID. You pay L2000 for the first page ceived and L500 for each page thereafter. sk in the telegrams office (off to the right hen you reach the main hall of the post ffice). Send faxes to 055 21 49 45. The PT has a list of private fax services in lorence.

Amex customers can have mail forarded to the Amex office (see under loney earlier in the chapter).

You will find Telecom phones in the post ffice building (open the same hours), as ell as several booths near the ATAF information booth outside the train station. The nstaffed office at Via Cavour 21r is open aily from 7 am to 11 pm and has phone ooks.

mail & Internet Access

laces to get online are mushrooming in lorence. The cheapest deal in town is Il airo Phone Center (☎ 055 263 83 36) at ia de' Macci 90r. You can sign up for a lock of 10 hours (useable any time) for 50,000. Down the road at No 8r, Net Bar ☎ 055 247 94 65) is open for Internet business until midnight (closed Sunday). It osts L14,000 an hour (L10,000 for students).

Internet Train has three branches, at Via ell'Oriuolo 25r (☎ 055 263 89 68), Via iuelfa 24a (☎ 055 21 47 94) and Borgo San acopo 30r (☎ 055 265 79 35). It costs 12,000 (L10,000 for students) to hook up r an hour.

Another option is Intercommunication entre (☎ 055 267 88 28), Via del Porcellana 0r. Yet another is The Netgate (☎ 055 234 9 67) at Via Sant'Egidio 10r. You could lso try WWW.Village (☎ 055 247 93 98) at ia degli Alfani 13r. Mondial Net (☎ 055 65 75 84) is at Via de' Ginori 59r. Cyberffice (☎ 055 21 11 03), Via San Gallo 4r, ets you online for L10,000 an hour.

Amex clients can arrange to receive mail at the Amex office (see under Money arlier in the chapter).

Travel Agencies

Sestante has offices at Via Cavour 56r (☎ 055 29 43 06) and CIT at Piazza della Stazione 51r (☎ 055 28 41 45). At either you can book train and air fares, organise guided tours etc.

CTS (☎ 055 28 95 70) is at Via de' Ginori 25r.

Bookshops

The Paperback Exchange, Via Fiesolana 31r, has a vast selection of new and secondhand books in English. Feltrinelli International, Via Cavour 12r, opposite the APT, has a good selection of books in English, French, German, Spanish, Portuguese and Russian. Internazionale Seeber, Via de' Tornabuoni 70r, also has books in those languages, as well as a fine selection of art books.

Libreria Il Viaggio (☎ 055 24 04 89), at Borgo degli Albizi 41r, sells walking maps.

Gay & Lesbian Information

In Florence, Azione Gay e Lesbica Finisterrae (☎/fax 055 67 12 98) is at Via Manara 6. They have a Web site at www.agora .stm.it/gaylesbica.fi and a phone health consultation line (☎ 055 48 82 88). It is also possible to arrange to have HIV tests done here.

At the Libreria delle Donne (☎ 055 24 03 84), Via Fiesolana 2b, you can get information to tune you into the lesbian scene in Florence.

Laundry

The Wash & Dry laundrette chain (☎ 800 23 11 72) has seven branches across the city. You pay L6000 for 8kg of washing and L6000 for drying. They open from 8 am to 10 pm (last wash at 9 pm). Addresses include: Via Nazionale 49, Via della Sole 52–54r and Via dei Servi 105r. There are several other laundrettes around town.

Medical Services

The main public hospital is Ospedale Careggi (☎ 055 427 71 11), Viale Morgagni 85, north of the city centre. There is also the

FLORENCE

A Recipe for Stendhalismo

Any list of 'must sees' in Florence is going to incite cries of protest. How can you recommend that a tour cover the Galleria degli Uffizi, the Duomo and the Battistero, without including the Museo del Bargello, the Convento di San Marco and the churches of Santa Maria Novella, Santa Croce and SS Annunziata? And what about Masaccio's fresco cycle in the Basilica di Santa Maria del Carmine? Or Michelangelo's *David* in the Galleria dell'Accademia and his Medici tombs in the family chapel attached to the Basilica di San Lorenzo?

Plan carefully, or you could end up with a severe case of Stendhalismo – about which see the introduction to the Florence chapter. And make sure you carry plenty of L100, L200 and L500 coins for the machines to illuminate the frescoes in the churches.

Ospedale Santa Maria Nuova (☎ 055 2 75 81), Piazza Santa Maria Nuova 1, just east of the Duomo.

The Tourist Medical Service (☎ 055 47 54 11), Via Lorenzo il Magnifico 59, is open 24 hours and doctors speak English, French and German. The APT has lists of doctors and dentists of various nationalities.

Twenty-four-hour pharmacies include the Farmacia Comunale (☎ 055 21 67 61) inside the Stazione di Santa Maria Novella, and Molteni (☎ 055 28 94 90), in the city centre at Via de' Calzaiuoli 7r.

There is an ambulance station (☎ 055 21 22 22) in Piazza del Duomo.

Police

The police station (☎ 055 4 97 71) is at Via Zara 2. You can report thefts and so on at the Foreigners Office here. There's another police station (☎ 055 29 34 62) at Piazza del Duomo 5.

Dangers & Annoyances

The most annoying aspect of Florence is the crowds, closely followed by the summer heat. Pickpockets are active in crowds and on buses. Beware of the numerous bands of dishevelled women and childre carrying newspapers or cardboard. A fe will distract you while the others rifle yo bag and pockets.

THINGS TO SEE & DO

Florence is the proverbial chocolate bo All cliches apply. Like 'all good thing come in small packages'. We won't eve try to compete with the battalions of lite ary greats and other important person who have spilled rivers of ink in the searc for an original superlative. Florence jammed with monuments and sights, mo of them mercifully confined to a sma area.

Opening Times

Museums and monuments tend to close o Monday in Italy. Given the hordes c tourists that pour into Florence year roun quite a few places *do* open on Monday you can get a list of them from the AP tourist office.

Opening times vary throughout the yea although many monuments stick to vague alternating summer/winter time table. In the case of state museums, sum mer means the six months 1 May to 3 October. For other sights it can be mor like Easter to the end of September. It impossible to be overly precise, if only be cause many of the timetables change fro year to year anyway.

Details of further variations at some c the most important sights are given in th course of the chapter but be warned that considerable amount of confusion reign Many museums alter the timetables eac year, so that even a detailed account of th 1999 summer and winter situation coul easily reveal itself wide of the mark i 2000. Museum staff members themselve only find out about changes at the la minute.

Warning At most sights the ticket windo shuts up to half an hour before the adve tised closing time. Also, in some of thes places (the Uffizi and Cappella Brancacc to name a couple of the culprits), actuall

Queue Jumping

If time is precious and money is not a prime concern, you can skip some of the museum queues in Florence by booking ahead.

For a L2000 fee, you can book a ticket to the Uffizi by phoning Firenze Musei (☎ 055 29 48 83). You are given a booking number and agree the time you want to visit. When you arrive at the gallery, follow the signs to a separate entrance for those with pre-booked tickets, which you pick up and pay for on the spot without queuing.

You can book any of the state museums this way. They include the Palazzo Pitti, the Bargello, Galleria dell'Accademia and Cappelle Medicee.

If you prefer the electronic age, Weekend a Firenze is an online service where you book tickets for the same museums and galleries. For this you pay L8270 on top of the ticket price of L12,000. You must book at least five days in advance. You will get an email confirmation that you will have to print out and present at the cashier's desk on the day you go. You can also book to visit the Corridoio Vasariano, which costs L38,500. Check it out at www.weekendafirenze.com.

Many of the bigger hotels will also book these tickets for you.

When you go to the Uffizi or other of the sights with prepaid tickets, email confirmation or whatever, head for the designated entrance for those with booked tickets, and smile smugly at the suffering hordes lined up outside the other entrance.

shuffle you out at least 15 minutes before closing time. For the attendants closing time means not when you have to start heading out the door, but when the door has to be bolted shut.

Carnet dei Musei Fiorentini

If you intend to see a good number of the museums in Florence, this set of 10 vouchers for L10,000 is worth considering. You get an explanatory booklet and discounts of up to 50% on 10 sights. Some of these are pretty minor, but others you will probably want to visit. They include (in order of interest): Palazzo Vecchio, Cappella Brancacci, the museum and cloisters in the basilica di Santa Maria Novella, Museo Gibbert, Museo Bardini, Museo di Firenze, Museo Marino Marini, Fondazione Romano (Cenacolo di Santo Spirito), Raccolta Alberto della Ragione and Galleria Rinaldo Carnielo. The carnet is valid for a year from the date of purchase.

For information on phone and Internet bookings to major sights, see the 'Queue Jumping' boxed text.

Piazza del Duomo & Around

The Duomo (Map 6) When you first come upon it from the crowded streets around the square, you will likely stop momentarily in your tracks, taken aback by the ordered vivacity of its pink, white and green marble facade. You had probably already espied Brunelleschi's sloping, red-tiled dome – the predominant feature of Florence's skyline and at the time a unique stroke of engineering genius.

The great temple's full name is Cattedrale di Santa Maria del Fiore and it is the world's fourth-largest cathedral. Begun in 1296 by Arnolfo di Cambio, it took almost 150 years to complete. It is 153m long and 38m wide, except the transept, which extends 90m.

The facade was only raised in the late 19th century. Its architect, Emilio de Fabris, was inspired by the design of the cathedral's flanks, which largely date to the 14th century.

From the facade, you should do a circuit of the church to take in its splendour before heading inside.

The south flank is the oldest and most clearly Gothic of the Duomo. The second doorway here, the **Porta dei Canonici** (Canons' Door), is a mid-14th-century High Gothic creation (you enter here to climb up inside the dome). Wander around the trio of apses, designed to appear as the flowers on the stem that is the nave of the church (and so reflecting its name – Santa Maria del Fiore, St Mary of the Flower).

The first door you see on the north flank after the apses is the early-15th-century **Porta della Mandorla** (Almond Door), so named because of the relief of the Virgin Mary contained within an almond-shaped frame.

Much of the decorative sculpture that graced the flanks of the cathedral has been removed for its own protection to the Museo dell'Opera del Duomo, in some cases to be replaced by copies.

The Interior The Duomo's vast and spartan interior comes as a surprise after the visual assault outside. Down the left aisle you will see two immense frescoes of equestrian statues dedicated to two mercenaries or *condottieri*, who fought in the service of Florence (for lots of dosh of course). The one on the left is Niccolò da Tolentino (by Andrea del Castagno) and the other is Giovanni Acuto, better known to the English as Sir John Hawkwood (by Paolo Uccello).

Although Florence had exiled him, Dante and the world that he created in the *Divina Commedia* (Divine Comedy) fascinated subsequent generations of Florentines, who revered him. Domenico di Michelino's *Dante e I Suoi Mondi* (Dante and His Worlds), the next painting along the left aisle, is one of the most reproduced images of the poet and his verse masterpiece.

The festival of colour and images that greets you as you arrive beneath Brunelleschi's dome is the work of Giorgio Vasari and Frederico Zuccari. The fresco series depicts the *Giudizio Universale* (Last Judgement). Below it is the octagonal **Coro** (choirstalls). Its low marble 'fence' also encloses the altar, above which hangs a crucifix by Benedetto da Maiano.

From the choirstalls, the two wings of the transept and the rear apse spread out, each containing five chapels. The pillars delimiting the entrance into each wing and the apse are fronted by statues of Apostles,

as are the two hefty pillars just west of the choirstalls.

Between the left (north) arm of the transept and the apse is the **Sagrestia del Messe** (Mass Sacristy), whose panelling a marvel of inlaid wood created b Benedetto and Giuliano da Maiano. Th fine bronze doors were executed by Luc della Robbia, showing he could turn h hand to other material as well as glazed te racotta. That said, the top of the doorway decorated with one of his 'robbiane', as the **Sagrestia Nuova** (New Sacristy) by th right transept (no access). By the way, was through della Robbia's doors tha Lorenzo de' Medici fled in the uproar fo lowing the assassination by the Pazzi con spirators of his brother Giuliano durin Mass in 1478.

Some of the finest stained-glass window in Italy, by Donatello, Andrea del Castagn Paolo Uccello and Lorenzo Ghiberti, ador the windows.

A stairway near the main entrance of th Duomo leads down to the 'crypt', actuall the site where excavations have unearthe parts of the 5th-century Chiesa di San Reparata. Brunelleschi's tomb is also i here. Admission to the excavations L5000. Apart from the remaining floor m saics, typical of early Christian churches i Italy and recalling their Roman heritag the spurs and sword of Giovanni de Medici were dug up here. Otherwise the r mains give only a vague idea of what th Romanesque church might have been lik and still dimmer a clue of what the church Roman predecessor might have been.

You can enter the Duomo and 'crypt', e cept during Mass, from 10 am to 5 pm dai (from 1 to 5 pm on Sunday).

The Dome You can climb up into the don to get a closer look at Brunelleschi's eng neering feat. You enter by the Porta d Canonici from outside the south flank of th cathedral. The view from the summit ov Florence is breathtaking.

The dome is open from 8.30 am 6.20 pm daily except Sunday (until 5 pm c Saturday) and the climb costs L10,000.

On 8 September every year, a walkway at stretches around the sides and facade the dome is opened to the public. You cess it by the same entrance as to the me.

ampanile (Map 6) Giotto designed and gan building the graceful and unusual mpanile (Bell Tower) next to the Duomo 1334, but died only three years later. Andrea Pisano and Francesco Talenti ntinued the work. The first tier of bas-liefs around the base, carved by Pisano but ssibly designed by Giotto, depicts the eation of Man and the arts and industries *tività umane)*. Those on the second tier pict the planets, cardinal virtues, the arts d the seven sacraments. The sculptures the prophets and sibyls in the niches of e upper storeys are actually copies of orks by Donatello and others – the origi-ls are in the Museo dell'Opera del uomo.

The bell tower is 84.7m high and you can mb its 414 stairs between 8.30 am and 50 pm daily (9 am and 5.20 pm in Oct-er; 9 am and 4.20 pm from November to arch). Admission costs L10,000.

arning People with heart conditions or ho are otherwise unfit should not under-ke this climb. There is *no* lift should you t into difficulties.

useo dell'Opera del Duomo (Map 6) is museum, behind the cathedral at Pi-za del Duomo 9, features most of the art asures from the Duomo, Baptistry and ampanile.

Displays include the equipment used by runelleschi to build the dome, as well as s death mask. Perhaps its best piece is ichelangelo's *Pietà*, which he intended r his own tomb.

The collection of sculpture is considered e city's best after that in the Museo del argello. Note in particular Donatello's rving of the prophet Habakkuk (taken om the Campanile) and his wooden im-ession of Mary Magdalene.

Ghiberti's original *Porta del Paradiso*

from the Battistero is being restored and parts of it are now on display. It will, how-ever, be some years before the doors in their entirety can go on show.

The museum is open from 9 am to 6.50 pm (6.20 pm in winter) daily except Sunday. Admission costs L10,000. The mu-seum re-opened in March 2000 after restoration and reorganisation work.

Baptistry (Map 6) The Romanesque Bap-tistry (Battistero) may have been built as early as the 5th century on the site of a Roman temple. It is one of the oldest build-ings in Florence and dedicated to St John the Baptist (San Giovanni Battista).

The present structure, or at least its fa-cade, dates to about the 11th century. The stripes of white and green marble that be-deck the octagonal structure are typical of Tuscan Romanesque style.

More striking still are the three sets of bronze doors, conceived as a series of pan-els in which the story of humanity and the Redemption would be told.

The earliest set of doors, now on the south side, was completed by Andrea Pisano in 1336.

Lorenzo Ghiberti toiled away for 20 years to get his set of doors, on the north flank, just right. The top 20 panels recount episodes from the New Testament, while the eight lower ones show the four Evange-lists and the four fathers of the Church.

Good as this late Gothic effort was, Ghib-erti returned almost immediately to his workshops to turn out the east doors. Made of gilded bronze, they took 28 years to com-plete, largely because of Ghiberti's intran-sigent perfectionism. The bas-reliefs on their 10 panels depict scenes from the Old Testament. So extraordinary were his exer-tions that, many years later, Michelangelo stood before the doors in awe and declared them fit to be the *Porta del Paradiso* (Gates of Paradise), which is how they remain known to this day.

Most of the doors are copies. The origi-nal panels are being removed for restoration and are due to be placed in the Museo dell'Opera del Duomo as work is completed.

euro currency converter L10,000 = €5.16

Interior Inside, one is reminded of the Pantheon in Rome. The two-coloured marble facing on the outside continues within, made more arresting by the geometrical flourishes above the Romanesque windows.

The single most arresting aspect of the decoration are the mosaics. Those in the apse were started in 1225 and are looking a little jaded. The glittering spectacle in the dome is, however, a unique sight in Florence. It was carried out by Venetian experts over 32 years from 1270, to designs by Tuscan artists, including Cimabue.

Donatello carved the tomb of Baldassare Cossa, better known as John XXIII the Antipope, which takes up the wall to the right of the apse.

The Baptistry is open from noon to 6.30 pm daily. Admission costs L5000.

Loggia del Bigallo (Map 6) This elegant marble loggia was built in the second half of the 14th century for the Compagnia del Bigallo, which had been formed in 1244 to help old people, orphans and beggars. Lost and abandoned children were customarily placed here so that they could be reclaimed by their families. At the time of writing it was completely hidden by scaffolding.

Museo di Firenze (Map 5) This is mildly interesting for those who want to get an idea of how the city developed, particularly from the Renaissance to the modern day. Paintings, models, topographical drawings (the earliest dating to 1594) and prints help explain the history of the city.

The museum is at Via dell'Oriuolo 24 and is open from 9 am to 2 pm daily except Thursday (8 am to 1 pm on Sunday and holidays). Admission costs L5000.

From the Duomo to Piazza della Signoria (Map 6)

What follows is a rather serpentine meander across the heart of old Florence. You could do it in a million ways, so don't take the following order too much to heart.

Via del Proconsolo Bernardo Buontalenti started work on the **Palazzo Nonfinito**, a residence for members of the Strozzi family, in 1593. Buontalenti and others completed the 1st floor and courtyard, whi is Palladian in style, but the upper floor were never completely finished, hence the building's name. The obscure **Museo de l'Antropologia e Etnologia** (Museum Anthropology and Ethnology) is hous here. It opens from 10 am to noon daily e cept Tuesday, and admission costs L600C

Across Borgo degli Albizi stands the equally proud **Palazzo dei Pazzi**, whi went up a century earlier and is clearly i fluenced by the Palazzo Medici-Riccardi. now houses offices, but you can wand into the courtyard.

La Badia The 10th-century Badia Fiore tina (Florence abbey) was built on th orders of Willa, who was the mother of o of the early Margraves of Tuscany, Ug Willa was inspired to this act by calls f greater piety in the church, which at th time was coming under hefty attack fro some quarters for corruption of all kind Ugo continued the work of his mother, i vesting considerably in the Benedicti monastery and church. He was eventual buried here.

Palazzo del Bargello Just across Via d Proconsolo from the Badia is this gra mansion, also known as the Palazzo c Podestà. Started in 1254, the palace w originally the residence of the chief magi trate and was then turned into a police st tion. During its days as a police comple many people were tortured near the well the centre of the medieval courtyard. I deed for a long time the city's prisons we located here.

It now houses the **Museo del Bargel** and the most comprehensive collection Tuscan Renaissance sculpture in Italy. Th museum is absolutely not to be missed.

You enter the courtyard from Via Ghi ellina and turn right into the ticket offic From here you end up in the ground-flo Sala del Cinquecento (the 16th-Centu Room), dominated by early works Michelangelo. His drunken *Bacco* (Ba

room with a view in Via del Duomo, Lucca

Romanesque meets Gothic in Carrara cathedral

at leaning feeling: the Bell Tower, Pisa

Pisa cathedral's elegant 11th-century facade

BETHUNE CARMICHAEL

A panoramic view over Lucca's rooftops

DAMIEN SIMONIS

The exquisite facade of Lucca's cathedral

DAMIEN SIMONIS

Puccini's favourite – the Liberty-style Gran Caffè Margherita in Viareggio, north-western Tuscany

us), executed when the artist was 22, a marble bust of *Brutus* and a tondo of the *Madonna col Bambino* (Madonna and Child) are among his best here. Other works f particular interest are Benvenuto Cellini's rather camp marble *Ganimede* (Ganymede) and *Narciso* (Narcissus), along with Giambologna's *Mercurio Volante* (Winged Mercury).

Upstairs is the majestic Salone del Conglio Generale (Hall of the General Council). At the far end, housed in a tabernacle, s Donatello's famed *San Giorgio* (St George), which once graced the Orsanmichele. David (as in David and Goliath) was a favourite subject for sculptors. In this hall you can see both a marble version by Donatello and the fabled bronze he did in later years. The latter is extraordinary – more so when you consider it was the first free standing naked statue done since classical times. This *David* doesn't appear terribly warrior-like.

Up on the 2nd floor you will find a bronze collection that includes two masterpieces: Antonio Pollaiuolo's *Ercole e Anteo* (Hercules and Anteus) and Cellini's *Ganimede*.

The museum is open from 8.30 am to 1.50 pm Tuesday to Saturday and on alternating Sundays and Mondays. Admission costs L8000.

San Firenze The small medieval parish church of San Firenze is no longer recognisable in this baroque complex that is today home to law courts. The original church of San Firenze, on the right, was reduced to an oratory when the church on the left, dedicated to San Filippo Neri (St Phillip Neri) was built. The late baroque facade that unites the buildings was completed in 1775.

Across the piazza (on the west side) is the main facade of **Palazzo Gondi**, once the site of the merchants' tribunal, a court set up to deal with their quarrels.

Casa di Dante & Around The house on the corner of Via Dante Alighieri and Via Santa Margherita was built in the early 20th century, so you can be quite sure the claim

that Dante lived here is utterly spurious. The display inside could be of mild interest to those with a thing for Dante but it is basically a bit of a rip-off. It is open from 10 am to 4 pm daily except Tuesday (until 2 pm on Sunday and holidays and until 6 pm from May to September). Admission costs L5000.

Just up Via Santa Margherita is the small **Chiesa di Santa Margherita**, which dates at least to 1032. Some claim that it was in this small single-nave church with a timber ceiling that Dante met his muse, Beatrice Portinari, although he himself said he bumped into her in the Badia.

Orsanmichele Originally a grain market, this church was formed when the arcades of the granary building were walled in during the 14th century and the granary was moved elsewhere. The granary was built on a spot known as Orsanmichele, a contraction of Orto di San Michele (St Michael's Garden). Under the Lombards, a small church dedicated to St Michael and an adjacent Benedictine convent had indeed been graced with a pleasant garden. The *signoria* (the city's government) cleared the lot to have the granary built. It was destroyed by fire 20 years later and a finer replacement constructed. This was considered too good to be a mere granary, and so it was converted into a church.

The signoria ordered the guilds to finance the decoration of the oddly shaped house of worship, and they proceeded to commission sculptors to erect statues of their patron saints in tabernacles placed around the building's facades.

The statues, commissioned over the 15th and 16th centuries, represent the work of some of the Renaissance's greatest artists. Some of the statues are now in the Museo del Bargello. However, many splendid pieces remain, including Giambologna's *San Luca* (St Luke, third on the right on Via Calzaiuoli), a copy of Donatello's *San Giorgio* (St George, last on the right on Via Orsanmichele) and Ghiberti's bronze *San Matteo* (St Matthew, first on the left on Via Arte della Lana).

euro currency converter L10,000 = €5.16

The main feature of the interior is the splendid Gothic tabernacle, decorated with coloured marble, by Andrea Orcagna. It is an extraordinary item, and to look at the convulsed, twisting columns you could swear you are looking at a scale prototype for the cathedral in Orvieto (Umbria).

Occasionally classical music recitals are held here.

The church is open from 9 am to midday and 4 to 6 pm daily (closed the first and last Monday of the month). There is also a small museum inside, for which you have to join a guided visit at 9, 10 or 11 am. Admission is free.

Opposite Orsanmichele on Via Calzaiuoli is the humble little **Chiesa di San Carlo dei Lombardi**. The church, built in the 14th century, though technically Gothic, still bears Romanesque trademarks in its simple, squat facade.

Piazza della Repubblica Ever since this square was ruthlessly gouged from the city centre in the years following Italian unity in 1860, all and sundry have continued to execrate it.

To create the piazza and restructure the surrounding areas, 26 ancient streets and a further 18 lanes disappeared, along with 341 residential buildings, 451 stores, 173 warehouses and other buildings and services... 5822 residents were forcibly relocated to other parts of the city. The entire Mercato Vecchio, which had inherited its function as the central market from the Roman forum, and the nearby lanes of the small Jewish ghetto were simply wiped from the map. Nice one.

If you want to get some idea of what this part of town looked like before the 'squalor' was wiped away, the Museo di Firenze has a model, maps and late-19th-century pictures of the area.

Mercato Nuovo If you stroll south down Via Calimala you arrive at this loggia, built to cover the merchandise (including wool, silk and gold) traded here at the 'New Market' under Cosimo I in the mid-16th century. Nowadays the goods on sale are aimed

exclusively at tourists and range from trashy statuettes and other souvenirs to leather goods of mixed quality.

At its southern end is a bronze statue of a boar known as the *fontana del porcellino* (piglet's fountain), an early 17th-century copy of the Greek marble original that is now in the Uffizi. They say that if you chuck a coin into the small basin and rub the critter's snout you will return to Florence.

Palazzo dei Capitani di Parte Guelfa Just off to the south-west of the Mercato Nuovo, this 'Palace of the Guelph Faction' Captains' was built in the early 13th century and later tinkered with by Brunelleschi and Vasari. The leaders of the Guelph faction raised this fortified building in 1265, taking up land and houses that had been confiscated from the Ghibellines.

Palazzo Davanzati About a block west is this remarkable 14th-century mansion at Via Porta Rossa 13. Inside, the **Museo dell'Antica Casa Fiorentina** aims to transmit an idea of what life was like in a medieval Florentine mansion. It has been closed for some time for restoration.

Ponte Vecchio See the entry below under Oltrarno.

Piazza della Signoria (Map 6)
The Piazza The hub of the city's political life through the centuries and surrounded by some of its most celebrated buildings, the piazza has the appearance of an outdoor sculpture gallery.

Throughout the centuries, whenever Florence entered one of its innumerable political crises, the people would be called here as a *parlamento* (people's plebiscite) to rubber-stamp decisions that frequently meant ruin for some ruling families and victory for others. Scenes of great pomp and circumstance alternated with others of terrible suffering – here the preacher-leader Savonarola was hanged and fried along with two supporters in 1498. A bronze plaque marks the spot.

Ammannati's huge *Fontana di Nettuno* (Neptune Fountain) sits beside the Palazzo Vecchio. Although the bronze satyrs and divinities frolicking about the edges of the fountain are quite delightful, Il Biancone ('the Big White Thing'), as locals derisively refer to it, is pretty universally considered a bit of a flop.

Flanking the entrance to the palace are copies of Michelangelo's *David* (the original is in the Galleria dell'Accademia) and Donatello's *Marzocco*, the heraldic Florentine lion (the original is in the Museo del Bargello). To the latter's right is a 1980 copy of Donatello's bronze *Giuditta e Oloferne* (Judith Slays Holofernes) – the original is in the Sala dei Gigli inside the palace.

A bronze equestrian statue of Cosimo I de' Medici, created by Giambologna in 1594–98, stands towards the centre of the piazza.

Palazzo Vecchio Formerly known as the Palazzo della Signoria and built by Arnolfo di Cambio between 1298 and 1314, this is the traditional seat of Florentine government. Its **Torre d'Arnolfo** is 94m high and, with its striking crenellations, is as much a symbol of the city as the Duomo.

Built for the *priori* (city government) who ruled Florence (in two-month turns), it came to be known as the Palazzo della Signoria as the government took on this name.

In 1540, Cosimo I de' Medici moved from the Palazzo Medici into this building, making it the ducal residence and centre of government. Cosimo commissioned Vasari to renovate the interior, creating new apartments and decorating the lot. In a sense it was all in vain, because Cosimo's wife, Eleonora de Toledo, was not so keen on it and bought Palazzo Pitti.

The latter took a while to expand and fit out as Eleonora wanted (she died before the work was finished), but the Medici family moved in anyway in 1549. Thus the Palazzo Ducale (or della Signoria for those with a nostalgic bent) came to be called the Palazzo Vecchio (Old Palace) as it still is today. It remains the seat of the city's

power, as this is where the mayor does his thing.

Coming in from Piazza della Signoria, you arrive first in the courtyard, reworked in early Renaissance style by Michelozzo in 1453. The decoration came more than a century later when Francesco de' Medici married Joanna of Austria. The cities depicted are jewels in the Austrian imperial crown.

From here you pass into the **Cortile della Dogana** (Customs Courtyard), off which you'll find the ticket office.

A stairway leads up to the magnificent **Salone dei Cinquecento**, also known more simply as the Sala Grande (Big Hall). It was created within the original building in the 1490s to accommodate the Consiglio dei Cinquecento (Council of 500) called into being in the republic under Savonarola. Cosimo I de' Medici later turned the hall into a splendid expression of his own power. The elevated tribune at one end was where Cosimo held audiences. In the 1560s the ceiling was raised 7m and Vasari added the decorations.

From the Salone dei Cinquecento you enter the **Quartiere di Leone X** by another door. The so-called 'Leo X Area' is named after the Medici pope. Upstairs is the **Quartiere degli Elementi** (Elements Area), a series of rooms and terraces dedicated to pagan deities. The original *Putto col Delfino* (Cupid with Dolphin) sculpture by Verocchio (a copy graces the courtyard of the building) is in the Sala di Giunone.

From here a walkway takes you across the top of the Salone dei Cinquecento into the **Quartiere di Eleonora**, the apartments of Cosimo I's wife. The room most likely to catch your attention is Eleonora's chapel just off to the right as you enter the apartments. Bronzino's decoration represents the acme of his painting career.

You pass through several more rooms until reaching the **Sala dell'Udienza** (Audience Room), where the priori administered medieval Florentine justice.

The following room is the **Sala dei Gigli**, named after the lilies of the French monarchy that decorate three of the walls (the

French were traditionally well disposed to Florence). Domenico Ghirlandaio's fresco on the far wall was supposed to be matched by others. Donatello's restored original bronze of *Giuditta e Oloferne* stands in here. A small, bare study off this hall is the chancery, where Machiavelli worked for a while. The other room off the hall is a wonderful maproom. The walls are covered by 16th-century maps of all the known world.

Exiting the Sala dei Gigli you can climb stairs to the **battlements**, from where you have fine views of the city.

The palace is open from 9 am to 7 pm daily (to 2 pm only on Thursday). Admission costs L10,000.

Loggia della Signoria Built in the late 14th century as a platform for public ceremonies, this loggia eventually became a showcase for sculptures. It also became known as the Loggia dei Lanzi, as Cosimo I used to station his Swiss mercenaries (or *Landsknechte*), armed with lances, in it to remind people of who was in charge around here.

To the left of the steps normally stands Benvenuto Cellini's magnificent bronze statue of Perseus holding the head of Medusa. It has been under restoration since 1997. To the right is Giambologna's Mannerist *Ratto delle Sabine* (Rape of the Sabine Women), his final work. Inside the loggia proper is another of Giambologna's works, *Ercole col Centauro Nesso* (Hercules with the Centaur). Among the other statues are some Roman representations of women.

Raccolta d'Arte Contemporanea Alberto della Ragione The collection may awaken mild interest in the art buff with a passion for the Italian 20th-century product. Most of the painters on view worked in the first half of the 20th century. A few Giorgio Morandis in Room IX are worth a quick look. There's even a modest De Chirico in the same room.

The collection was donated to Florence by the Genoese collector Alberto della Ragione on his death in 1970.

The museum is open from 8.30 am to 1.30 pm daily except Tuesday. Admission costs L4000.

The Uffizi (Map 6)

Designed and built by Vasari in the second half of the 16th century at the request of Cosimo I de' Medici, the Palazzo degli Uffizi originally housed the city's administrators, judiciary and guilds. It was, in effect, a government office building (*uffizi* meant offices).

Vasari also designed the private corridor that links the Palazzo Vecchio and the Palazzo Pitti, through the Uffizi and across the Ponte Vecchio. Known as the **Corridoio Vasariano**, it was recently opened to the public (see later in this section).

Cosimo's successor, Francesco I, commissioned the architect Buontalenti to modify the upper floor of the Palazzo degli Uffizi to house the Medicis' growing art collection. Thus, indirectly, the first steps were taken to turn it into an art gallery.

The gallery now houses the family's private collection, bequeathed to the city in 1743 by the last of the Medici family, Anna Maria Ludovica, on condition that it never leave the city. Over the years, sections of the collection have been moved to the Museo del Bargello and the city's Museo Archeologico. In compensation, other collections, such as that put together by the Count Augusto Contini-Bonacossi in the 1930s, have joined the core group. Paintings from Florence's churches have also been moved to the gallery. It is by no means the biggest art gallery around (this is no Louvre), but in all, the Galleria degli Uffizi still houses the world's single greatest collection of Italian and Florentine art.

Sadly, several of its artworks were destroyed and others badly damaged when a car bomb planted by the Mafia exploded outside the gallery's western wing in May 1993. Six people died in the explosion. Documents cataloguing the collection were also destroyed.

Partly in response to the bombing, but even more to the gallery's immense popularity (a staggering 1.5 million visitors arched through in 1998, compared with 00,000 in 1950!), restoration and reorganation will lead to what promoters have abbed the 'Grandi Uffizi'. It is hoped that y 2001 all the damaged rooms and others reviously closed off will be open to the ublic.

While these changes are made the displays remain in a state of flux. However, the principal lines remain the same – the gallery is arranged to illustrate the evolving story of talian and, in particular, Florentine art. Those rooms marked with an asterisk (*) were closed at the time of writing.

It has to be said that, especially when rowded in summer, visiting the Uffizi can e a singularly unpleasant experience. The allery tends to be hot and stuffy and the rowds render the chances of enjoying anything of what is on display a challenge to ay the least. To queue and then suffer inide seems more like a modern-day act of eligious abnegation than a desirable opportunity to contemplate beautiful art. On he other hand, the queuing is in part due to n effort to limit the maximum number inide at any time to 660 people.

To avoid some of the pain, try to arrive in he morning when the gallery first opens, or luring lunchtime or the late afternoon. Alernatively, book ahead (see the boxed text Queue Jumping' earlier in the chapter).

The extraordinary wealth of the collecion and the sheer number of famous works neans one visit is not enough – if you are going to come down with 'stendhalismo', it night well be here! If you are in Florence or three or four days and can afford the adlitional cost, try to spend at least two blocks of three or so hours in the gallery, spread over a few days.

Several guidebooks to the gallery are on ale at vendors all over the city, and outside he entrance.

The Gallery Before heading upstairs, visit he restored remains of the 11th-century Chiesa di San Piero Scheraggio. The hurch's apse was incorporated into the tructure of the palace but most of the rest lestroyed. At the time of writing it was closed, but you can get a fractional idea from what remains on the exterior the north wall of the palace. Room 1, devoted to archaeological finds, was also closed.

On the 1st floor is a small **Galleria dei Disegni e delle Stampe** (Drawing and Print Gallery), in which sketches and initial drafts by the great masters are often shown. They tend to rotate the display frequently, as prolonged exposure can damage the drawings.

Upstairs in the gallery proper, you pass through two vestibules, the first with busts of several of the Medici clan and other grand dukes, the second with some Roman statuary.

The long corridor has been arranged much as it appeared in the 16th century. Below the frescoed ceilings is a series of small portraits of great and good men, interspersed with larger portraits, often of Medici family members or intimates. The statuary, much of it collected in Rome by the Medicis' agents, is either Roman or at least thought to be.

The first rooms feature works by Tuscan masters of the 13th and early 14th centuries. Room 2 is dominated by three paintings of the *Maestà* by Duccio di Buoninsegna, Cimabue and Giotto. All three were altarpieces in Florentine churches before being placed in the gallery. To look at them in this order is to appreciate the transition from Gothic to the precursor of the Renaissance. Also in the room is Giotto's polyptych *Madonna col Bambino Gesù, Santi e Angeli* (Madonna with Baby Jesus, Saints and Angels).

Room 3 traces the Sienese school of the 14th century. Of particular note is Simone Martini's shimmering *Annunciazione*, considered a masterpiece of the school, and Ambrogio Lorenzetti's triptych *Madonna col Bambino e Santi* (Madonna and Child with Saints). Room 4 contains works of the Florentine 14th century.

Rooms 5 and 6 house examples of the international Gothic style, among them Gentile da Fabriano's *Adorazione dei Magi* (Adoration of the Magi).

Room 7 features works by painters of the

early-15th-century Florentine school, which pioneered the Renaissance. There is one panel (the other two are in the Louvre and London's National Gallery) from Paolo Uccello's striking *La Battaglia di San Romano* (Battle of San Romano). In his efforts to create perspective he directs the lances, horses and soldiers to a central disappearing point. Other works include Piero della Francesca's portraits of *Battista Sforza* and *Federico da Montefeltro*, and a *Madonna col Bambino* painted jointly by Masaccio and Masolino. In the next room is Fra Filippo Lippi's delightful *Madonna col Bambino e due Angeli* (Madonna and Child with Two Angels). One of those angels has the cheekiest little grin. Have you ever noticed how rarely anyone seems to be smiling in the religious art of this or other periods?

The Botticelli Room, Nos 10 to 14, is considered the gallery's most spectacular. Highlights are the *La Nascita di Venere* (Birth of Venus) and *Allegria della Primavera* (Joy of Spring). His *Calunnia* (Calumny) is a disturbing reflection of the artist's loss of faith in human potential that came in later life.

Room 15 features Da Vinci's *Annunciazione*, painted when he was a student of Verrocchio. Perhaps more intriguing is his unfinished *Adorazione dei Magi*. Rooms 16* and 17* are fairly minor.

Room 18, known as the Tribuna, houses the celebrated *Medici Venus*, a 1st-century BC copy of a 4th-century BC sculpture by the Greek sculptor, Praxiteles. The room also contains portraits of various members of the Medici family.

The great Umbrian painter, Perugino, who studied under Piero della Francesca and later became Raphael's master, is represented in Room 19, as well as Luca Signorelli. Room 20 features works from the German Renaissance, including Dürer's *Adorazione dei Magi*. Room 21 has works by Giovanni Bellini and his pupil, Giorgione. Peek through the railings to see the 15th- to 19th-century works in the Miniatures Room and then cross into the western wing, which houses works of Italian masters dating from the 16th century.

The star of Room 25 is Michelangelo dazzling *Tondo Doni*, which depicts th Holy Family. The composition is highl unusual, with Joseph holding Jesus o Mary's shoulder as she twists around watch him. The colours are so vibrant, th lines so clear as to seem almost phot graphic. This masterpiece of the High R naissance leaps out at you as you ente demanding attention.

In the next room are works by Raphae including his *Leo X* and *Madonna d Cardellino*. The former is remarkable f the richness of colour (especially the red and detail. Room 27 is dominated by th sometimes disquieting works of Florence two main Mannerist masters, Pontormo an Rosso Fiorentino.

Room 28 boasts seven Titians, includin *Venere d'Urbino* (Venus of Urbino). Hi presence signals a shift in the weightin here to representatives of the Venetia school.

Rooms 29 and 30 contain works by com paratively minor northern Italian painters but Room 31 is dominated above all b Venice's Paolo Veronese, including his *Sacr Famiglia e Santa Barbara* (Holy Famil with St Barbara). In Room 32 it is Tin toretto's turn. He is accompanied by a fe Jacopo Bassano canvasses. Rooms 33 an 34 were open but still being organised at th time of writing. Room 35 is closed pendin reorganisation.

For some reason the counting starts at N 41* after this. This room is given ove mostly to non-Italian masters such a Rubens and Van Dyck. The beautifully de signed Room 42, with its exquisite coffere ceiling and splendid dome, is filled wit Roman statues.

Caravaggio dominates Room 43*, whil Rembrandt and Jan Breughel the Elder fea ture in Room 44*. In Room 45* are 18th century works by Canaletto, Guardi an Crespi, along with a smattering of foreign ers such as the Spaniard Goya.

Between rooms 25 and 34 is an entranc (not open to the public) into the Corridoi Vasariano, which at the time of writin could be visited in a separate guided tou

...m Palazzo Vecchio (see the Corridoio ...sariano section).

...mission The gallery is open from 8.30 ...1 to 10 pm Tuesday to Saturday (to ...30 pm in winter) and to 8 pm on Sunday ...50 pm in winter). Admission costs ...2,000 and the ticket office closes 55 min- ...es before closing time.

...rridoio Vasariano When Cosimo I de' ...edici's wife bought the Palazzo Pitti and ...e family moved into their new digs, they ...anted to maintain their link – literally – ...ith what from then on would be known as ...e Palazzo Vecchio. And so Cosimo com- ...issioned Vasari to build this enclosed ...alkway between the two palaces that ...ould allow the Medicis to wander between ...e two without having to deal with the pub- ...c.

The corridor, lined with phalanxes of ...rgely minor art works, has changed con- ...derably over the years. Its present aspect ...ates to 1923, but it is possible that many of ...e paintings hung here will be moved to ...e Grandi Uffizi (see 'The Uffizi' earlier in ...e chapter) in the coming years.

Be that as it may, the corridor was opened ...the public in a rather limited fashion in ...999. Let's say right away that, given the ...ifficulty and cost of getting in here, many ...isitors are likely to be disappointed. To ap- ...reciate it at all you will want to have a gen- ...ine interest in Florentine history and/or a ...unger for relatively obscure art. Your av- ...rage three-day visitor who has done little ...r no reading on Florence will *not* be inter- ...sted in this.

In 1999 it opened from March to May ...nd again from September to October. It ...as unclear what the situation would be in ...oming years. People seem to have caught ...'asari Fever – the September to October ...eriod in 1999 was fully booked up by the ...*eginning* of September. During those ...nonths it was open Tuesday to Thursday ...nd Saturday. Visits are by guided tour ...generally in Italian), which lasts a long 2½ ...ours. Tours start at 9 am, 10.30 am, 1 pm ...nd 2.30 pm. A maximum of 35 people go

through in any one visit. You start in the Corte Dogana in the Palazzo Vecchio and emerge in the Palazzo Pitti. You need to book ahead for this by calling ☎ 055 265 43 21 between 8.30 am and 1.30 pm, Monday to Saturday. You can also book online (see the boxed text 'Queue Jumping'). You pick up your tickets, which cost a whopping L38,500, at the prebooked ticket desk in the Uffizi.

What you can expect is the following. The first part of the tour takes you first to the Salone dei Cinquecento in the Palazzo Vecchio (see earlier in the chapter). From here the tour follows a route upstairs via the Quartiere di Leone X and into the Quartiere di Eleonora. With much unbolting of doors and ceremony you are then ushered in through the first part of the corridor (which houses offices) across to the Uffizi, where you emerge at the beginning of the gallery. Here the tour continues, stopping at certain points of the Uffizi (but without scope for looking at the art) until another door is un- locked to allow you into the main stretch of the corridor. This first part of the tour takes an hour, and for those who have already visited the Palazzo Vecchio and the Uffizi and done some research, you can get the feeling that you'll never get down to busi- ness.

Museo di Storia delle Scienze Tele- scopes that look more like works of art, the most extraordinarily complex-looking in- struments for the measurement of distance, time and space, and a room full of wax and plastic cutaway models of the various stages of childbirth are among the high- lights in this odd collection, in this Museum of the History of Science.

Given the admission price, you may want to think twice about it. If you have a gen- uine interest in the history of science, then you will almost certainly find at least some of the exhibits intriguing.

The museum is open from 9 am to 1 pm daily except Sunday. In winter it opens from 2 to 5 pm as well on Monday, Wednesday and Friday. Admission costs L10,000.

euro currency converter L10,000 = €5.16

FLORENCE

Santa Maria Novella & Around

Basilica di Santa Maria Novella (Map 6) Just south of Stazione de Santa Maria Novella in the piazza of the same name, this church was begun in the late 13th century as the Florentine base for the Dominican order. Although mostly completed by around 1360, work on its facade and the embellishment of its interior continued until well into the 15th century.

The lower section of the green and white marble facade is transitional from Romanesque to Gothic, while the upper section and the main doorway were designed by Alberti and completed in around 1470. The highlight of the Gothic interior is Masaccio's superb fresco of the *Trinità* (1428), one of the first artworks to use the then newly discovered techniques of perspective and proportion. It is about halfway along the north aisle.

The first chapel to the right of the choir, the Cappella di Filippo Strozzi, features lively frescoes by Filippino Lippi depicting the lives of St John the Evangelist and St Philip the Apostle. Another important work is Domenico Ghirlandaio's series of frescoes behind the main altar, painted with the help of artists who may have included the young student Michelangelo. Relating the lives of the Virgin Mary, St John the Baptist and others, the frescoes are notable for their depiction of Florentine life during the Renaissance. Brunelleschi's crucifix hangs above the altar in the **Cappella Gondi**, the first chapel on the left of the choir.

To reach the **Chiostro Verde** (Green Cloister), exit the church and follow the signs to the Museo. The porticoes' arches are propped up by massive octagonal pillars. Three of the four walls are decorated with fading frescoes recounting Genesis. The cloister actually takes its name from the green earth base used for the frescoes. The most interesting artistically, by Paolo Uccello, are those on the party wall with the church. Outstanding is *Il Diluvio Universale* (the Great Flood).

Off the next side of the cloister is the **Cappellone degli Spagnoli** (Spanish Chapel; Map 3), which was set aside for the Spanish retinue that accompanied Eleonora di Toledo, Cosimo I's wife, to Florence. It contains well-preserved frescoes by Andrea di Bonaiuto and his helpers.

On the western side of the cloister is the museum itself, which in two rooms that used to be the convent's foyer and refectory contains vestments, relics and some art belonging to the Dominicans.

The museum is open from 9 am to 2 pm daily except Friday (8 am to 1 pm on Sunday and public holidays). Admission cost L5000.

Chiesa d'Ognissanti (Map 5) This 13th-century church was much altered in the 17th century and has a baroque facade but inside are 15th-century works by Domenico Ghirlandaio and Botticelli. Of interest is Ghirlandaio's fresco above the second altar on the right of the Madonna della Misericordia, protector of the Vespucci family. Amerigo Vespucci, who gave his name to the American continent is supposedly the young boy whose head appears between the Madonna and the old man.

Ghirlandaio's masterpiece, the *Ultima Cena* (Last Supper), covers most of a wall in the former monastery's refectory, or *cenacolo*. The church is usually open from 8 am to midday and 4 to 6 pm daily, but at the time of writing it was closed for restoration. Access to the refectory is from 9 am to noon only.

The Cascine (Map 2) Before we turn our steps back to the centre of Florence, you might want to bear in mind that about 10 minutes' walk to the west along Borgo Ognissanti brings you to the **Porta al Prato**, part of the walls that were knocked down in the late 19th century to make way for the ring of boulevards that still surrounds the city.

A short walk south from here towards the Arno brings you to the eastern tip of Florence's great green lung, the Cascine. The Medici dukes made this a private hunting reserve, but Pietro Leopoldo opened it to e public in 1776, with boulevards, fountains and bird sanctuaries (Le Pavoniere, now a swimming pool). In the late 19th century horse racing began here (a British import it seems, since the locals referred to the sport as *le corse inglesi* – the English races). Queen Victoria was a fan of Florence and toddled along to the Cascine during her stays – whether or not she had a flutter at the races we don't know.

Palazzo Rucellai (Map 6) Designed by Alberti, the Palazzo Rucellai is in Via della Vigna Nuova. The palace houses a photographic museum dedicated to the vast collection compiled by the Alinari brothers. It was closed at the time of writing. The facade is curious for a few reasons, not least for the seating originally intended for employees of the Rucellai family but now quite handy for anyone passing by. Across the small triangular square is the family loggia, also designed by Alberti and now used for occasional exhibits. Any family worth its salt aimed to have a loggia in addition to the family residence.

Chiesa di San Pancrazio & Museo Marino Marini (Map 6) As early as the 9th century a church stood here. The shabby-looking version you see today is what remains of the building from the 14th and 15th centuries. The church was deconsecrated in the 19th century and now houses the museum donated to the city of Florence by the Pistoia-born sculptor Marino Marini (1901–80).

Among the 200 works this artist left behind are sculptures, portraits and drawings. The overwhelmingly recurring theme seems to be man and horse, or rather man on horse. The figures are in some cases simple-looking chaps in various poses suggesting rapture or extreme frustration, while the horses too seem to express a gamut of emotion. On the other extreme, the two partners are barely distinguishable from one another.

The museum opens from 10 am to 5 pm daily except Tuesday (to 1 pm on Sunday and holidays). It closes all of August. In the

other summer months (from May to September) it also remains open until 11 pm on Thursday evenings. Admission costs L8000, which is rather a lot unless you are particularly taken with this guy.

Via de' Tornabuoni & Around (Map 6)
If from Palazzo Rucellai you skittle on down Via del Purgatorio and make a right down the narrow Via Parioncino you reach Via Corsini on the Arno.

For the best view of the Arno-side of the **Palazzo Corsini** you should head across the bridge. This grandiose late-baroque edifice will probably seem a little curious – the U-shaped courtyard isn't in the middle. It would have been had the project been completed. The wing nearest Ponte alla Carraia was originally supposed to mirror the right wing. The building had belonged to the Medici family but they sold it in 1640. From then until 1735 work on the exterior (the mighty facade on Via del Parione is a worthy counterpoint to the Arno frontage) dragged on at a snail's pace. By the time work was finished, the Corsini family was in the ascendant, with Lorenzo Corsini in the driving seat in Rome as Pope Clement XII. The most interesting feature of the inside is the spiral staircase known as the *lumaca* (literally, 'the slug').

Head east for the **Ponte Santa Trinita**, a harmonious and charming crossing for the river. Cosimo I de' Medici put Vasari in charge of the project and he in turn asked Michelangelo for advice. In the end, the job was handed over to Ammannati, who finished it in 1567. The statues of the seasons are by Pietro Francavilla.

Turning inland to the piazza of the same name, you arrive at the 13th-century **Chiesa della Santa Trinita**. Although rebuilt in the Gothic style and later graced with a Mannerist facade of indifferent taste, you can still get some idea of what the Romanesque original looked like by looking at the facade wall from the *inside*. Among its more eye-catching art are frescoes depicting the life of St Francis of Assisi by Domenico Ghirlandaio in the Cappella Sassetti (in the right transept).

Across Via de' Tornabuoni from it is the forbidding **Palazzo Spini-Ferroni**, built in the 14th century with Guelph battlements and now owned by the Ferragamo shoe empire. The street itself, often referred to as the 'Salotto di Firenze' (Florence's Drawing Room) actually follows the original course of the Mugnone tributary into the Arno.

Piazza Santa Trinita is also faced by the **Palazzo Buondelmonti**. The family of the same name was at the heart of the Guelph-Ghibelline feud in Florence. More imposing is the **Palazzo Bartolini-Saltimbeni**, an example of High Renaissance with a Roman touch (columns flanking the main door and triangular tympana).

By far the most impressive of the Renaissance mansions is the earthy-coloured **Palazzo Strozzi**, a great colossus of rusticated *pietra forte* (literally 'hard stone') raised by one of the most powerful of the Medicis' rival families. It now houses offices and is occasionally used for art exhibitions.

Two blocks north stands the clearly baroque facade in pietra forte of the **Chiesa di San Gaetano**. The church had been around since the 11th century, but from 1604 it was rebuilt. The facade only went up in 1683. Opposite and a few strides north, the **Palazzo Antinori** was built in the 15th century by Giuliano da Maiano.

San Lorenzo Area (Map 6)

Basilica di San Lorenzo The Medici commissioned Brunelleschi to rebuild this church in 1425, on the site of a 4th-century basilica. It is considered one of the most harmonious examples of Renaissance architecture. Michelangelo prepared a design for the facade that was never executed, which is why this, as so many other Florentine churches, appears unfinished from the outside.

It was the Medici parish church and many family members are buried here. The church is a masterstroke of Brunelleschi's style. The nave is separated from the two aisles by columns in *pietra serena* (literally 'tranquil stone') and crowned with Corinthian capitals.

Rosso Fiorentino's *Sposalizio del Vergine* (Marriage of the Virgin Mary) dominates the second chapel on the right aisle after you enter. As you approach the transept, you will see two pulpits o *pergami* (they look like treasure chests of Ionic columns) in dark bronze – or at least what appears to be dark bronze. Some of the panels on each have been attributed to Donatello. Others, added later, are supposedly made of wood (money was obviously running short) made to seem like bronze.

You enter the **Sagrestia Vecchia** (Old Sacristy) to the left of the altar. It was designed by Brunelleschi and mostly decorated by Donatello.

From the main body of the church you can also enter the peaceful cloisters, off the first of which a staircase leads up to the **Biblioteca Medicea Laurenziana**. It was commissioned by Cosimo de' Medici to house the Medici library and contains 10,000 volumes. The real attraction is Michelangelo's magnificent vestibule and staircase. He also designed the main reading hall. The library is normally open from 9 am to 1 pm daily except Sunday. At the time of writing it was, however, closed for restoration work. Admission is free.

The entrance to the church is in the busy Piazza San Lorenzo, off Borgo San Lorenzo. The church is open from 7 am to midday and 3.30 to 6.30 pm daily.

Cappelle Medicee A separate entrance on Piazza Madonna degli Aldobrandini takes you to the Medicean chapels. After buying your ticket you first enter a crypt. The stairs from this take you up to the **Cappella dei Principi** (Princes' Chapel), which comes as something similar to a blow over the head with a mallet.

Conceived not as a place of religious reflection, the so-called chapel is rather the triumphalist mausoleum of some (but by no means all) the Medici rulers.

It is sumptuously decorated top to bottom with various kinds of marble, granite and other stone. Breaking up the colossal splendour of the stone are the decorative tableaux made from painstakingly chosen and cut emi-precious stones, or *pietre dure*. It was or the purpose of decorating the chapel that Ferdinando I ordered the creation of the Opificio delle Pietre Dure.

Statues of the grand men were supposed to be placed in the still empty niches, but no one quite got around to finishing the project. Only the bronze of Ferdinando I and partly gilt bronze of Cosimo II were done.

A corridor leads from the Cappella dei Principi to the **Sagrestia Nuova** (New Sacristy), so-called to distinguish it from the Sagrestia Vecchia. In fact it was the Medicis' funeral chapel.

It was here that Michelangelo came nearest to finishing an architectural commission. His haunting sculptures, *Notte e Giorno* (Night and Day), *Aurora e Crepusculo* (Dawn and Dusk) and the *Madonna ol Bambino* adorn Medici tombs including that of Lorenzo il Magnifico.

The chapels are open from 8.30 am to 5 pm Monday to Saturday and until 1.50 pm on Sunday and holidays. Admission costs L13,000.

Palazzo Medici-Riccardi When Cosimo de' Medici felt fairly sure of his position in Florence, he decided it was time to move house. He entrusted Michelozzo with the design in 1444.

What Michelozzo came up with was ground-breaking and would continue to influence the construction of family residences in Florence for years to come. The fortress town houses with their towers that characterised Gothic Florence were no longer necessary. Cosimo's power was more or less undisputed. Instead Michelozzo created a self-assured, stout but not inelegant pile on three storeys.

The ground floor is characterised by the bulbous, rough surface (known as rustication) in pietra forte. The upper two storeys are less aggressive, maintaining restrained classical lines already a feature of the emerging Renaissance canon and topped with a heavy timber roof whose eaves protrude well out over the street below.

The Medicis stayed here until 1540 and the building was finally acquired and somewhat remodelled by the Riccardi family in the 17th century.

You can wander inside to the courtyard and up to some of the rooms upstairs, although much of the building is now given over to public administration offices. The main hall you will want to inspect is the **Galleria** on the 1st floor. It is a rather sumptuous example of late baroque designed for the Riccardi family. The room glisters with gold leaf and bursts with curvaceous figures looming out at you, especially from the ceiling frescoes by Luca Giordano, after which the room is now usually named **Sala Luca Giordano**.

The highlight, however, is the **Cappella dei Magi**, a chapel with striking frescoes by Benozzo Gozzoli. You have to buy a ticket first from the office off the second internal courtyard. They rotate 15 people through the chapel every 15 minutes as it is rather squeezy inside. Make an effort to see this jewel.

The palazzo is open Monday to Saturday (closed Wednesday) from 9 am to 1 pm and 3 to 6 pm (in summer daily from 9 am to 7 pm) and on Sunday and holidays to 1 pm. Admission to the chapel costs L6000, but the remainder is free.

Mercato Centrale (Map 3) Built in 1874, the city's central produce market seems to disappear amid the confusion of makeshift stands of the clothes and leather market that fill the surrounding square and streets during the day. The iron and glass architecture was something of a novelty in Florence when the market was first built.

San Marco Area
Galleria dell'Accademia (Map 3) Take Via Cesare Battisti from Piazza SS Annunziata to Piazza San Marco; the entrance to the gallery is to the left on Via Ricasoli. For many visitors to Florence, the gallery is pretty much unavoidable, if only because it contains the original of one of the greatest (and most trumpeted) masterpieces of the Renaissance, Michelangelo's giant statue of *David*.

When you enter the museum you are

obliged to turn left into a long hall, at the end of which you can make out the *David*. Try to contain the urge to hurtle off in the giant-slayer's general direction and have a look at the four *Prigioni* (Prisoners or Slaves) and the statue of *San Matteo* (St Matthew) between the two Prigioni on the right. The latter was created about 1506, while the four others were executed in 1530. All five have in common the feature of not being completed. The experts will tell you completion is in the eye of the beholder. In the case of Michelangelo in particular, it is said he left many works 'unfinished' deliberately. The statues are interesting if only because they show us a little of how the artist went about extracting such beauty from lumps of marble.

Now the *David* is finished. Carved from one block of marble and weighing in at 19 tonnes, it's an exquisite, powerful figure that beggars description. While the statue still stood in Piazza della Signoria, the left arm actually fell off and killed a peasant.

In the surrounding rooms there is a mixed collection of paintings and sculpture ranging from a triptych by Orcagna through to a plaster model of Giambologna's *Ratto delle Sabine* (Rape of the Sabine Women).

Upstairs is a further collection of 13th- and 14th-century art and Russian icons.

The gallery is open from 8.30 am to 9 pm Tuesday to Friday (to midnight on Saturday and 8 pm on Sunday). Closing time is usually 6.50 pm (1.50 pm at the weekend) in winter. Admission costs L12,000.

Museo di San Marco (Map 5) The museum is housed in the now deconsecrated Dominican convent and the Chiesa di San Marco. Back in 1481 a rather ugly and intense little Dominican friar, Girolamo Savonarola, turned up here as *lector* and later ended up the de facto head of a short-lived theocracy in Florence before frying on an Inquisitorial bonfire.

The piazza is the centre of the university area. The church was founded in 1299, rebuilt by Michelozzo in 1437, and again remodelled by Giambologna some years later.

It features several paintings, but they pale comparison to the treasures contained in th adjoining convent.

Famous Florentines who called the con vent home include the painters Fra (Beato) Angelico and Fra Bartolommeo. now serves as a museum of Fra Angelico works, many of which were moved there the 1860s, and should be up there on ever art lover's top-priority hitlist.

You find yourself in the **Chiostro di San Antonio**, designed by Michelozzo in 144 when you first enter the museum. Tur immediately to the right and enter the **Sal dell'Ospizio**. Paintings by Fra Angelic that once hung in the Galleria dell'Acc demia and the Uffizi have been brough together here. Among the better-know works are the *Deposizione di Cristo* and th *Pala di San Marco*, an altarpiece for th church paid for by the Medici family. It di not fare well as a result of 19th-centur restoration.

The eastern wing of the cloister, former the monks' rectory, contains works by var ious artists from the 14th to the 17th cen turies. Paintings by Fra Bartolommeo ar on display in a small annex off the refector rooms. Among them is a celebrated portra of Savonarola.

You reach the upper floor by passin through the bookshop. This is the real trea Fra Angelico was invited to decorate th monks' cells with devotional frescoe aimed as a guide to the friars' meditatio Some were done by Fra Angelico, others b aides under his supervision. You can pee into them today and wonder what sort o thoughts would swim through the minds o the monks as they prayed before thes images.

The true masterpieces up here are, how ever, on the walls in the corridors. Alread at the top of the stairs you climbed to the 1 floor is an *Annunciazione*, faced on the op posite wall with a *Crocifisso* featuring Sa Domenico (St Dominic). One of Fra An gelico's most famous works is the *Madonn delle Ombre* (Madonna of the Shadows), t the right of cell No 25.

The museum is open from 8.30 am t

.50 pm Tuesday to Saturday (as well as alternating Mondays and Sundays). Admission costs L8000.

iazza della SS Annunziata (Map 4) iiambologna's equestrian statue of the irand Duke Ferdinando I de' Medici commands the scene from the centre of this quare. Some observers find it the city's oveliest square. Certainly part of Florence's ankie community seem to like it in the vening.

hiesa di SS Annunziata The church that ives the square its name was established in 250 by the founders of the Servite order nd rebuilt by Michelozzo and others in the nid-15th century. It is dedicated to the Virin Mary and in the ornate tabernacle, to our left as you enter the church from the trium, is a so-called miraculous painting of ne Virgin.

The painting, no longer on public view, s attributed to a 14th-century friar, and leend says it was completed by an angel. Also of note are frescoes by Andrea del Castagno in the first two chapels on the left f the church, a fresco by Perugino in the ifth chapel and the frescoes in Michelozzo's atrium, particularly the *Nascita ella Vergine* (Birth of the Virgin) by Anrea del Sarto and the *Visitazione* by Jaopo Pontormo. The church is open from .30 am to 12.30 pm and 4 to 6.30 pm aily.

pedale degli Innocenti This 'hospital of he innocents' was founded on the southastern side of the piazza in 1421 as Euope's first orphanage.

Brunelleschi designed the portico, which Andrea della Robbia then decorated with erracotta medallions of a baby in swaddling clothes. Under the portico to the left f the entrance is the small revolving door vhere unwanted children were left. A good umber of people in Florence with surames such as degli Innocenti, Innocenti nd Nocentini, can trace their family tree nly as far back as the orphanage. The idea f the orphanage was in itself no novelty –

this place was built in response to the growing numbers of foundlings. Undoubtedly life inside was no picnic, but the Spedale's avowed aim was to care for and educate its wards until they turned 18.

A small gallery on the 2nd floor features works by Florentine artists. If you are already overdosing on the seemingly endless diet of art in Florence, you could skip this stop. Those truly interested will find it worthwhile. The most striking piece is Domenico Ghirlandaio's *Adorazione dei Magi* at the right end of the hall.

The gallery is open from 8.30 am to 2 pm daily except Wednesday. Admission costs L5000.

Museo Archeologico (Map 4) About 200m south-east of the piazza along Via della Colonna is the Museo Archeologico, considered one of Italy's best. A good deal of the Medici family's horde of antiquities ended up here. Further collections have been added in the centuries since.

For those interested in antiquity, this museum offers a surprisingly rich collection of finds. Many items were damaged in the floods of 1966 and even today parts of the museum are still being worked on. All up, the museum is well worth the effort.

On the 1st floor you can either head left into the ancient Egyptian collection, or right into the section on Etruscan and Greco-Roman art.

The former is an impressive collection of tablets inscribed with hieroglyphics, statues and other sculpture, various coffins and a remarkable array of everyday objects – it is extraordinary to ponder on how sandals, baskets and all sorts of other odds and ends have survived to this day.

In the Etruscan section you pass first through two rooms dominated by funeral urns. Particularly noteworthy is the marble *Sarcofago delle Amazzoni* (Amazons' Sarcophagus) from Tarquinia and the alabaster *Sarcofago dell'Obeso* (Sarcophagus of the Fat Man) from Chiusi.

From the funerary urns you pass into a hall dedicated to bronze sculptures, ranging from miniatures depicting mythical beasts through to the life-size *Arringatore* (Orator). Dating to the 1st century BC, the figure, draped in clearly Roman garb, illustrates the extent to which Rome had come to dominate the Etruscans at this point. By the time the statue was made, Etruria had been under the Roman thumb for a good 200 years. Other outstanding works include the statue of *Minerva* from Arezzo, a Roman copy of a Greek original, and the *Chimera*, a beast of classical mythology.

From this display you enter an enclosed corridor lined on one side by ancient rings, pendants and amulets, many made of chalcedony. When you reach the end you swing left and walk back along another corridor with windows overlooking the museum's gardens. Here you can admire a selection of the museum's treasure of ancient gold jewellery.

Downstairs is space for temporary exhibits.

The 2nd floor is taken up with an extensive collection of Greek pottery from various epoques. Again it is surprising for its sheer extent. Although most of the exhibits have had to be meticulously reassembled from the shards discovered on excavation sites, the collection is varied and certainly intriguing to anyone interested in this kind of thing.

It is open from 9 am to 2 pm Tuesday to Saturday and to 1 pm on Sunday. Admission costs L8000.

Santa Croce Area

Piazza di Santa Croce (Map 7) The Franciscan Basilica di Santa Croce stands haughty watch over the piazza of the same name. The square was initially cleared in the Middle Ages primarily to allow hordes of the faithful to gather when the church itself was full (Mass must have been quite an event in those days). On a more sober religious note, the piazza was used in Savonarola's day for the execution of heretics.

Such an open space inevitably found other uses and from the 14th century on it was often the colourful scene of jousts,

festivals and *calcio storico* matches. The latter was like a combination of football (soccer) and rugby with no rules. They still play it today (see Festivals in the Facts for the Visitor chapter). Below the gaily frescoed facade of the **Palazzo dell'Antella** on the south side of the piazza is a marble stone imbedded in the wall – it marks the halfway line on this, one of the oldest soccer pitches in the world. Today the square is lined with the inevitable souvenir shops.

Curiously enough, the Romans used to have fun in much the same area centuries before. The city's 2nd-century amphitheatre took up the area facing the western end of Piazza di Santa Croce. To this day, Piazza de' Peruzzi, Via Bentaccordi and Via Torta mark the oval outline of the north, west and south sides of the theatre.

Basilica di Santa Croce (Map 7) Attributed to Arnolfo di Cambio, Santa Croce was started in 1294 on the site of a Franciscan chapel, but was not completed until 1385. The name stems from a splinter of the Holy Cross donated to the Franciscans by King Louis of France in 1258. Today the church is known as much for the celebrities buried here as for its captivating artistic treasures.

The magnificent facade is actually a neo-Gothic addition of the 19th century, as indeed is the bell tower. Rather austere compared with the contemporary job done on the Duomo, the main source of jollity is the variety of colour in the different types of marble used. The statue in front of the left end of the facade is of Dante.

The church's massive interior is divided into a nave and two aisles by solid octagonal pillars. The ceiling is a fine example of the timber A-frame style used occasionally in Italy's Gothic churches.

Heading down the right aisle you see first, between the first and second altar, Michelangelo's tomb, designed by Vasari. The three muses below it represent his three principal gifts – sculpting, painting and architecture. Next up is a cenotaph to the memory of Dante, followed by a tomb sculpted by Antonio Canova in 1810.

After the fourth altar is Machiavelli's tomb.

After the next altar is an extraordinary piece of sculpture of the *Annunciazione* by Donatello. You won't see many other sculptures in grey pietra serena, brightened here by some gilding. Between the sixth and seventh altars you can peer out the doorway into the cloister and get a look at Brunelleschi's Cappella de' Pazzi (see later in this chapter).

Dogleg round to the right as you approach the transept and you find yourself before the delightful frescoes by Agnolo Gaddi in the **Cappella Castellani**. By the way, the church is covered in more than 2500 square metres of frescoes. Taddeo Gaddi did the frescoes, depicting the life of the Virgin, and the stained-glass window in the adjacent **Cappella Baroncelli**. Next a doorway designed by Michelozzo leads into a corridor off which is the **Sagrestia**, an enchanting 14th-century room dominated on the right by Taddeo Gaddi's fresco of the *Crocifissione*.

Through the next room, which now serves as a bookshop, you can get to the **Scuola del Cuoio**, a leather school where you can see things being made and also buy finished goods. At the end of the Michelozzo corridor is a Medici chapel, featuring a large altarpiece by Andrea della Robbia.

Back in the church, the transept is lined by five minor chapels on either side of the **Cappella Maggiore**. The two chapels nearest the right side of the Cappella Maggiore are decorated with partly fragmented frescoes by Giotto. In the ninth chapel along, you can see a glazed terracotta altarpiece by Giovanni della Robbia, while the final chapel is frescoed by Maso di Banco. These frescoes, among them the *Miracolo del Santo che Chiude le Fauci del Drago e Risuscita due Maghi Uccisi Dall'Alito del Mostro* (Miracle of the Saint who Shuts the Dragon's Jaws and Brings Back to Life the Magi Killed by the Monster's Breath – how's that for a title), burst with life.

From the entrance, the first tomb in the left aisle is Galileo Galilei's. You will also have noticed by now that the floor is paved with the tombstones of famous Florentines of the past 500 years. Monuments to the particularly notable were added along the walls from the mid-16th century.

Cloisters & Cappella de' Pazzi Brunelleschi designed the serene **cloisters** just before his death in 1446. His **Cappella de' Pazzi**, at the end of the first cloister, is a masterpiece of Renaissance architecture. The **Museo dell'Opera di Santa Croce**, off the first cloister, features a partially restored crucifix by Cimabue, which was badly damaged during the disastrous 1966 flood, when the Santa Croce area was inundated. Donatello's gilded bronze statue of *San Ludovico di Tolosa* (St Ludovich of Toulouse) was originally placed in a tabernacle on the Orsanmichele facade.

In summer the church is open from 8 am to 6.30 pm Monday to Saturday (closed from 12.30 to 3 pm in winter) and from 3 to 6 pm on Sunday. The museum is open from 10 am to 12.30 pm and 2.30 to 6.30 pm (3 to 5 pm in winter) daily except Wednesday. Admission costs L5000.

Museo del Rinascimento (Map 7)

Guess it was inevitable that Florence should get its own wax museum. Dummies in period costume include Dante with his beloved Beatrice in the heaven he described in the *Divina Commedia*, Masaccio hard at work in the Cappella Brancacci, Leonardo with Mona Lisa, Amerigo Vespucci with his navigational charts and so forth. If you like this sort of thing it's all right, but with so much genuine material to marvel over in this city, you may find it hard to justify the L12,000 outlay. It opens from 10 am to 7 pm daily.

Museo Horne (Map 5)

Herbert Percy Horne was one of those eccentric Brits abroad with cash. He bought this building on Via de' Benci in the early 1900s and installed his eclectic collection of 14th- and 15th-century Italian paintings, sculptures, ceramics, coins and other odds and sods. Perhaps more interesting than many of the paintings is the furniture, some of which is exquisite. On the top floor is the original kitchen. Kitchens tended to be on the top floor to reduce the risk of fire.

The museum is open from 9 am to 1 pm daily except Sunday and holidays. Admission costs L8000.

Ponte alle Grazie (Map 5) In 1237, Messer Rubaconte da Mandella, a Milanese then serving as an external martial *(podestà)* in Florence, had this bridge built – or so Giorgio Villani tells us. It was swept away in 1333 and on its replacement were raised chapels, one of them dubbed Madonna alle Grazie, from which the bridge then took its name. The Germans blew up the bridge in 1944, and the present version went up in 1957.

Teatro Verdi (Map 7) Rather than cross the bridge at this point, we will head back north along Via de' Benci (which becomes Via Verdi after Piazza Santa Croce). At the intersection with Via Ghibellina stands this 19th-century theatre on the site of the 14th-century prison, Le Stinche, which had also been used as a horse-riding school. The theatre was built in 1838. We now head east along Via Ghibellina.

Casa Buonarroti (Map 7) Three blocks from the Teatro Verdi at No 70 is the Casa Buonarroti, which Michelangelo owned but never lived in. Upon his death, the house went to his nephew and eventually became a museum in the mid-1850s.

Although not uninteresting, the collections are a little disappointing given what you pay to get in. On the ground floor is a series of rooms on the left used for temporary exhibitions, usually held annually from May to September. To the right of the ticket window is a small archaeological display. The Buonarroti family collected about 150 pieces over the years, many of which were in the Museo Archeologico (see the San Marco Area section earlier in the chapter).

Beyond this room are some paintings done in imitation of Michelangelo's style, along with some fine glazed terracotta pieces by the della Robbia family.

Upstairs you can admire a detailed model of Michelangelo's design for the facade of the Basilica di San Lorenzo – as close as the church came to getting one. By Michelangelo also are a couple of marble bas-reliefs and a crucifix. Of the reliefs, *Madonna della Scala* (Madonna of the Steps) is thought to be his earliest work.

Otherwise, a series of rooms designed by Michelangelo Il Giovane, the genius' grand nephew, are intriguing. The first is full of paintings and frescoes that together amount to a kind of apotheosis of the great man. Portraits of Michelangelo meeting VIPs of his time predominate.

The museum is open from 9.30 am to 1.30 pm daily except Tuesday. Admission costs L12,000.

Piazza Sant'Ambrogio & Around (Maps 4 & 7) From the Casa Buonarroti turn northwards up Via Michelangelo Buonarroti and proceed to **Piazza dei Ciompi**. The piazza was cleared in the 1930s and named after the textile workers who used to meet in secret in the Santa Croce area and whose 14th-century revolt, which had seemed so full of promise, came to nothing. Nowadays it is the scene of a busy flea market.

The **Loggia del Pesce** (Fish Market) was designed by Vasari on the orders of Cosimo I de' Medici for the Mercato Vecchio (Old Market), which was at the heart of what is now Piazza della Repubblica. The loggia was moved to the Convento di San Marco when the Mercato Vecchio and the heart of the town were wiped out towards the end of the 19th century to make way for Piazza della Repubblica. Then in 1955 it was set up here.

A block east along Via Pietrapiana, the plain **Chiesa di Sant'Ambrogio** presents an inconspicuous 18th-century facade on the square of the same name. The first church here was raised in the 10th century, but what you see inside is a mix of 13th-century Gothic and 15th-century refurbishment. The name comes from Sant'Ambrogio (St Ambrose), the powerful 4th-century archbishop of Milan who stayed in an earlier onvent on this site when he visited Florence. The church is something of an artists' graveyard too. Among those who rest in peace here are Mino da Fiesole, Il Verrocchio and Il Cronaca.

Nearby is the local produce market, the **Mercato Sant'Ambrogio**, on Piazza Ghiberti.

A quick nip up Via de' Pilastri off Piazza Sant'Ambrogio and right up Via Luigi Carlo Farini brings us to the **Sinagoga**, the late-19th-century synagogue. It is a fanciful structure with playful Moorish and even Byzantine elements. In the **Museo Ebraico** you can see Jewish ceremonial objects and some old codices. The synagogue and museum are open from 10 am to 1 pm and 2 to 5 pm daily except Friday afternoon and Saturday (to 4 pm in winter). Admission costs L6000.

Oltrarno

Ponte Vecchio (Map 6) The first documentation of a stone bridge here, at the narrowest crossing point along the entire length of the Arno, dates to 972. The Arno looks placid enough, but when it gets mean, it gets very mean. Floods in 1177 and 1333 destroyed the bridge, and in 1966 it came close again. Newspaper reports of the time highlight how dangerous the situation was. One couple who owned a jewellery store on the bridge described afterwards the crashing of the waters just below the floorboards as they tried to salvage some of their goods. Carabinieri on the river bank excitedly warned them to get off, but they retorted that the forces of law and order should *do* something. They did get off in the end, fearful they'd be swept away by the torrential onslaught.

Those jewellers were among several who have inherited the traditional business on the bridge since Grand Duke Ferdinando I de' Medici ordered them here in the 16th century to replace the rather malodorous presence of the town butchers. The latter tended to jettison unwanted leftovers into the river.

The bridge as it stands was built in 1345 and those of us who get the chance to admire it can thank...well, someone...that it wasn't

blown to smithereens in August 1944. The retreating German forces blew all the other bridges on the Arno, but someone (some say Hitler himself) among them must have decided that sending the Ponte Vecchio to the bottom would have been a bridge too far. Instead they mined the areas on either side of the bridge.

As you reach the southern bank, this becomes pretty obvious. Take a halfway careful look at the buildings around Via de' Guicciardini and Borgo San Jacopo – they ain't exactly ancient heritage sites.

A couple of buildings to survive the Nazi's mines are two medieval towers. The first, **Torre dei Mannelli**, just on the southern end of the bridge, looks very odd, as the Corridoio Vasariano was built *around* it, not simply straight through it as the Medici would have preferred. Across Via de' Bardi as your eye follows the Corridoio, you can espy **Torre degli Ubriachi**, the Drunks' Tower. Nice surname!

Chiesa di Santa Felicita (Map 6) About the most captivating thing about the facade of this 18th-century remake of what had been Florence's oldest (4th century) church is the fact that the Corridoio Vasariano passes right across it. The Medici could stop by and hear Mass without being seen by anyone!

Inside, the main interest is the small **Cappella Barbadori**, designed by Brunelleschi, immediately on the right as you enter. Here Pontormo left his disquieting mark with a fresco of the Annunciation and a disturbing *Deposizione*. The latter depicts the taking down of Christ from the Cross in surreal colours. The people engaged in this operation look almost like they have been given a fright by the prying eyes of the onlooker.

The church is open from 9 am to noon and 3 to 6 pm during the week and from 9 am to 1 pm on Sunday and holidays.

Palazzo Pitti (Map 5) When the Pitti, a wealthy merchant family, asked Brunelleschi to design the family home, they did not have modesty in mind. Great rivals of the Medici, there is not a little irony in the fact that their grandiloquence would one day be sacrificed to the bank account.

Begun in 1458, the original nucleus of the palace took up the space encompassing the seven sets of windows on the second and third storeys.

In 1549 Eleonora de Toledo, wife of Cosimo I de' Medici, finding the Palazzo Vecchio too claustrophobic, acquired the palace from a by now rather skint Pitti family. She launched the extension work, which ended up crawling along until 1839! Through all that time the original design was respected and today you would be hard pressed to distinguish the various phases of construction.

After the demise of the Medici dynasty, the palace remained the residence of the city's rulers, the dukes of the Lorraine and their Austrian and (briefly) Napoleonic successors.

When Florence was made capital of the nascent kingdom of Italy in 1865, it became a residence of the Savoy royal family, who graciously presented it to the state in 1919.

The Museums The palace houses five museums. The **Galleria Palatina** (Palatine Gallery) houses paintings from the 16th to 18th centuries, which are hung in lavishly decorated rooms. The works were collected mostly by the Medici and their grand ducal successors.

After getting your ticket you head up a grand staircase to the gallery floor. The first rooms you pass through are a seemingly haphazard mix of the odd painting and period furniture.

The gallery proper starts after the Sala della Musica (Music Room). The paintings hung in the succeeding rooms are not in any particular order. Among Tuscan masters you can see work by Fra Filippo Lippi, Sandro Botticelli, Giorgio Vasari and Andrea del Sarto. The collection also boasts some important works by other Italian and foreign painters. Foremost among them are those by Raphael, especially in the Sala di Saturnio. A close second is Titian, one of the greatest of the Venetian school. Other important artists represented include Tin-

toretto, Paolo Veronese, Ribera, Rube[n] and Van Dyck. Caravaggio is represent[e] with the striking *Amore Dormiente* (Lo[v] Sleeping) in the Sala dell'Educazione Giove.

From the gallery you can pass into t[h] Appartamenti Reali (Royal Apartments), series of rather sickeningly furnished a[n] decorated rooms, where the Medici ar[e] their successors slept, received guests ar[e] generally hung about. The style and di[v] ision of tasks assigned to each room is re[m] iniscent of Spanish royal palaces.

At the time of writing some of the min[e] rooms of the gallery (not mentioned her[e] and a good many of the royal apartmen[ts] were closed.

The other galleries are worth a look you have plenty of time. The **Galleria d'Ar[t]e Moderna** (Modern Art Gallery) cove[r] mostly Tuscan works from the 18th to t[h] mid-20th century, and the **Museo degli A[r]genti** (Silver Museum), entered from t[h] garden courtyard, has a collection of glas[s] ware, silver and semiprecious stones fro[m] the Medici collections. The **Galleria d[e] Costume** (Costume Gallery) has high-cla[s] clothing from the 18th and 19th centurie[s] while the **Museo delle Carrozze** contair[s] ducal coaches and the like.

Opening Times The Galleria Palatina [is] open from 8.30 am to 9 pm Tuesday to Fr[i] day (6.50 pm in winter), until midnight o[n] Saturday (6.50 pm in winter) and to 8 pm o[n] Sunday (1.50 pm in winter).

The Museo degli Argenti and the Galle[r]ia d'Arte Moderna open from 8.30 am t[o] 1.50 pm Tuesday to Saturday and on alte[r]nating Sundays and Mondays. The othe[r] two galleries were closed at the time o[f] writing.

Admission Prices A L20,000 *biglietto cu[mulativo* (cumulative ticket) will get yo[u] entry into everything that is open and th[e] Giardino di Boboli (see the following se[c]tion). But watch the times, as you may b[e] too late for some of the museums.

L12,000 gets you into the Galleri[a] Palatina and Appartamenti Reali alon[e]

Entry into each of the other museums costs L4000. As you can see, the cumulative ticket only makes sense if you plan to see the lot in the same day.

Boboli Gardens (Maps 2 & 5) Take a break in the palace's Renaissance **Boboli Gardens** (Giardino di Boboli), which were laid out in the mid-16th century and based on a design by the architect known as Il Tribolo. Buontalenti's noted artificial grotto, with a *Venere* (Venus) by Giambologna, is interesting.

Inside the garden is the **Museo delle Porcellane** (Map 2), which houses a varied collection of the fine porcelain collected over the centuries by the illustrious tenants of Palazzo Pitti, from Cosimo I de' Medici and Eleonora de Toledo onwards. The exhibits include some exquisite Sèvres and Vincennes pieces. You could skip the museum if the tupperware of the rich and famous leaves you cold. On the other hand, since you have already paid to get into the garden, it can't hurt to get a glimpse of how the other half have lived in this town.

You can get into the **Forte di Belvedere** (Map 2; see later in the chapter) from the south-eastern end of the garden. Also near here is the **Kaffeehaus** (Map 5), a late-19th-century conceit where you can sit down for a L4500 espresso.

The garden is open from 9 am to 4.30 pm daily in winter and up to 8 pm at the height of summer. Admission costs L4000, which includes access to the Museo delle Porcellane. The latter keeps the same timetable as the Museo degli Argenti (see the preceding section).

Chiesa di San Felice (Map 5) This unprepossessing church has been made over several times since the Romanesque original went up in 1066. The simple Renaissance facade was done by Michelozzo. Inside you can admire an early-14th-century crucifix by Giotto's workshop. Opening hours are irregular.

At No 8 on this square is Casa Guidi, where the Brownings lived.

Museo Zoologico La Specola (Map 5) A little farther down Via Romana from Piazza San Felice, this rather fusty museum offers for your delectation, the stuffed animal collection apart, a collection of wax models of various bits of human anatomy in varying states of bad health. An offbeat change from all that art and history anyway! It opens from 9 am to 1 pm daily except Wednesday and admission costs L6000. It sometimes closes on public holidays, but second guessing on this is a hazardous exercise.

To Porta Romana (Map 2) Pilgrims to Rome headed down Via Romana as they left Florence behind them. The end of the road is marked by the Porta Romana, an imposing city gate that was part of the outer circle of city walls knocked down in the 19th century. A strip of this wall still stretches to the north from the gate. If you head along the inside of this wall (the area is now a car park) you will soon come across an entrance that allows you to get to the top of Porta Romana.

Via Maggio (Map 5) No it doesn't mean May St, but rather Via Maggiore (Main St). In the 16th century this was a rather posh address, as the line-up of fine Renaissance mansions duly attests. **Palazzo di Bianca Cappello**, at No 26, has the most eye-catching facade, covered as it is in *graffiti* designs. Bianca Cappello was Francesco I de' Medici's lover and eventually wife. Across the street, a series of imposing mansions more or less following the same Renaissance or Renaissance-inspired style include the **Palazzo Ricasoli-Ridolfi** at No 7, **Palazzo Martellini** at No 9, **Palazzo Michelozzi** at No 11, **Palazzo Zanchini** at No 13 and **Palazzo di Cosimo Ridolfi** at No 15. All were built and fiddled around with over the 14th, 15th and 16th centuries. Another impressive one is the **Palazzo Corsini-Suarez** at No 42.

Piazza Santo Spirito (Map 5) From Via Maggio you can turn into Via de'Michelozzi to reach the lively Piazza Santo Spirito.

At its northern end, the square is fronted by the flaking facade of the **Basilica di Santo Spirito**, designed by Brunelleschi. It's a shame they couldn't get their act together to provide it with a dignified front, but don't let this put you off. The inside is a masterpiece of Florentine Renaissance design.

The church was one of Brunelleschi's last commissions. The entire length of the church inside is lined by a series of 40 semicircular chapels. Unfortunately the architects who succeeded the master were not entirely faithful to his design. He wanted the chapels to form a shell of little apses right around the church, which clearly would have been a revolutionary step. Instead they chose to hide them behind a rather ad-hoc-looking wall, flattening off the flanks of the church in an unsatisfying and untidy fashion.

More than the chapels, the colonnade of 35 columns in pietra serena is particularly striking inside. Not only do they separate the aisles from the nave, they continue around into the transept, creating the optical impression of a grey stone forest.

One of the most noteworthy works of art is Filippino Lippi's *Madonna col Bambino e Santi* in one of the chapels in the right transept. The main altar, beneath the central dome, is a voluptuous baroque flourish rather out of place in the spare setting of Brunelleschi's church. The sacristy *(sagrestia)* on the left side of the church is worth a look, particularly for its barrel-vaulted vestibule.

Santo Spirito is open from 8 am to midday and 4 to 6 pm daily except Wednesday afternoon.

Next door to the church is the **Cenacolo di Santo Spirito**, which is home to the Fondazione Romano. Andrea Orcagna decorated the refectory with a grand fresco depicting the Last Supper and the Crucifixion. In 1946 the Neapolitan collector Salvatore Romano left his sculpture collection to Florence's council, the Comune di Firenze. Among the most intriguing pieces are rare pre-Romanesque sculptures and other works by Jacopo della Quercia and Donatello. Only those with a genuine interest in pre-Romanesque and Romanesque sculptures need enter.

It is open from 9 am to 2 pm Tuesday to Saturday, and from 8 am to 1 pm on Sunday and holidays. Admission costs L4000.

Basilica di Santa Maria del Carmine (Map 5) West of Piazza Santo Spirito, Piazza del Carmine is an unkempt square used as a car park. On its south flank stands the Basilica di Santa Maria del Carmine, high on many art lovers' Florentine list of must-sees because of the **Cappella Brancacci**.

This chapel is a treasure of paintings by Masolino da Panicale, Masaccio and Filippino Lippi. Above all, the frescoes by Masaccio are considered among his greatest works, representing a definitive break with Gothic art and a plunge into new worlds of expression in the early stages of the Renaissance. His *Cacciata dei Progenitori* (Expulsion of Adam and Eve), on the left side of the chapel, is his best-known work. His depiction of Eve's anguish in particular lends the image a human touch hitherto little seen in European painting. In times gone by prudish church authorities had Adam and Eve's privates covered up. Masaccio painted these frescoes in his early 20s and interrupted the task to go to Rome, where he died aged only 28. The cycle was completed some 60 years later by Filippino Lippi.

That you can even see these frescoes today is little short of miraculous. The 13th-century church was nearly destroyed by a fire in the late 18th century. About the only thing the fire spared was the chapel.

The church interior is something of a saccharine baroque bomb. Look up at the barrel-vaulted ceiling above the single nave. It fairly drips with excessive architectural trompe l'oeil fresco painting, with arches, pillars, columns and tympana all colliding into one another in a frenzy of movement. Opposite the Cappella Brancacci is the **Cappella Corsini**, one of the first (and few) examples of the extremes of Roman baroque executed in Florence. The billowy statuary is all a bit much.

The chapel is open from 10 am to 5 pm daily except Tuesday (1 to 5 pm on Sunday and holidays), but you will be thrown out by 4.45 pm. Admission costs L6000. You enter by a side door that takes you through the cloister.

Should you arrive too late for the chapel but find the church still open, you can wander in and get a distant look at the chapel from behind barriers – but the close-up inspection is what you need to appreciate the staggering detail.

Borgo San Frediano (Map 2)

Heading north from Piazza del Carmine you reach Borgo San Frediano. The street and surrounding area retain something of the feel of what they have always been, a working-class quarter where artisans have been beavering away for centuries.

At the western end of the street stands the lonely **Porta San Frediano**, one of the old city gates left in place when the walls were demolished in the 19th century. Before you reach the gate, the unpolished feel of the area is neatly reflected in the undorned brick walls of the **Chiesa di San Frediano in Cestello**, whose incomplete facade hides within a fairly bland, restrained version of a baroque church interior. The church is open from 9 to 11.30 am and 5 to 6 pm Monday to Saturday and from 5 to 6 pm only on Sunday and holidays. The western side of Piazza di Cestello is occupied by granaries built under Cosimo III de' Medici.

Back to Ponte Vecchio (Maps 5 & 6)

From the front of Chiesa di San Frediano in Cestello you can wander along the river back towards the Ponte Vecchio.

Along the way you pass several grand family mansions, including **Palazzo Guicciardini** at Lungarno Guicciardini 7 and the 13th-century **Palazzo Frescobaldo** on the square of the same name. Round this palazzo you continue east along Borgo San Jacopo, on which still stand two 12th-century towers, the **Torre dei Marsili** and **Torre de' Belfredelli**. On Via de' Ramaglianti once stood the old Jewish synagogue.

Ponte Vecchio to Porta San Niccolò

Continuing east away from the Ponte Vecchio, the first stretch of Via de' Bardi shows clear signs of its recent history. This entire area was flattened by German mines in 1944 and hastily rebuilt in questionable taste after the war.

The street spills into **Piazza di Santa Maria Soprarno** (Map 6), which takes its name from a church that has long ceased to exist. Follow the narrow Via de' Bardi (the right fork) away from the square and you enter a pleasantly quieter corner of Florence. The Bardi family once owned all the houses along this street, but by the time the chubby Cosimo de' Medici married Contessina de' Bardi in 1415, the latter's family was well on the decline. They were among the banking dynasties ruined by the habit of debtors like England's King Edward III of defaulting on huge loans. Cosimo and Contessina moved into a Bardi mansion on this street, but it was later pulled down. Buying up the street had clearly been a medieval bargain, as until the de' Bardi family built their mansions the street had been known as Borgo Pidiglioso (Flea St), one of the city's poorer quarters.

Via de' Bardi expires in **Piazza de' Mozzi** (Map 5), which is also surrounded by the sturdy facades of grand residences belonging to the high and mighty. No 2, the south flank of the piazza, is occupied by the **Palazzi de' Mozzi**, where Pope Gregory X stayed when brokering peace between the Guelphs and Ghibellines. The west side is lined by the 15th-century **Palazzo Lensi-Nencioni**, **Palazzo Torrigiani-Nasi** (with the graffiti ornamentation) and the **Palazzo Torrigiani**.

Across the square, the long facade of the **Museo Bardini** is the result of an eclectic 19th-century building project by its owner, the collector Stefano Bardini. The collection is a broad mix ranging from Persian carpets to Etruscan carvings, from paintings by many lesser- and occasionally well-known artists through to sculptures in stone and wood from a wide variety of artists and periods. It was closed for refurbishment at the time of writing.

From here turn east down Via dei Renai past the leafy **Piazza Demidoff**, dedicated to Nicola Demidoff, a 19th-century Russian philanthropist who lived nearby in Via San Niccolò. The 16th-century **Palazzo Serristori** at the end of Via dei Renai was home to Joseph Bonaparte in the last years of his life (he died in 1844). At the height of his career he had been made king of Spain under Napoleon.

Turn right and you end up in Via San Niccolò. The bland-looking **Chiesa di San Niccolò Oltrarno** is interesting if for nothing else than the little plaque indicating how high the 1966 flood waters reached – about four metres. If you head east along Via San Niccolò you emerge at the tower marking the **Porta San Niccolò**, all that is left of the city walls here.

To get an idea of what the walls were like walk south from the Chiesa di San Niccolò Oltrarno through **Porta San Miniato**. The wall extends a short way to the east and quite a deal farther west up a steep hill that leads you to the Forte di Belvedere.

Forte di Belvedere (Map 2) Bernardo Buontalenti helped design the rambling fortifications here for Grand Duke Ferdinando I towards the end of the 16th century. From this massive bulwark soldiers could keep watch on four fronts, and indeed it was designed with internal security in mind as much as foreign attack. The views are excellent.

The main entrance is near Porta San Giorgio, and you can approach, as we have, from the east along the walls or by taking Costa di San Giorgio from up near the Ponte Vecchio. If you take the latter, you will pass, at Nos 17–21 (Map 5), one of the houses where Galileo Galilei lived while in Florence. You can also visit the fort from the Boboli Gardens, which is in fact what most people do (see Boboli Gardens earlier in this section). Entry to the fort is free – in fact there's no-one around to disturb you as you wander inside.

Piazzale Michelangelo (Map 2) From Porta San Miniato (Map 7) you could turn east instead of following the climb up to the Forte di Belvedere. A few twists and turns and you find yourself looking over Ponte San Niccolò. Several paths and stairways lead up from here to Piazzale Michelangelo, a favoured spot for viewing the city.

Local bus No 13, which leaves from Stazione di Santa Maria Novella and crosses Ponte alle Grazie, stops at the piazzale.

Chiesa di San Salvatore al Monte (Map 2) A short steep climb up from the piazzale brings you to this spartan church which you will probably find closed. That is no great disaster as this early 16th-century structure ain't that fascinating inside either.

Chiesa di San Miniato al Monte (Map 2) The real point of your exertions is about five minutes farther up, at this wonderful Romanesque church. It is dedicated to St Minius (San Miniato), an early Christian martyr in Florence who is said to have flown to this spot after his death down in the town.

The church was started in the early 11th century, and the typically Tuscan marble facade features a mosaic depicting Christ between the Virgin and St Minius added 200 years later.

Inside you will see 13th- to 15th-century frescoes on the right wall, intricate inlaid marble designs down the length of the nave and a fine Romanesque crypt at the back below the unusual raised presbytery (*presbiterio*). The latter boasts a fine marble pulpit replete with intriguing geometrical designs. The sacristy, to the right of the church (they suggest you donate L1000 to get in), features marvellously bright frescoes. The four figures in the cross vault are the Evangelists. The **Cappella del Cardinale del Portogallo** to the left side of the church features a tomb by Antonio Rossellino and a ceiling decorated in terracotta by Luca della Robbia.

It is possible to wander through the cemetery outside. Some of Michelangelo's battlements remain standing around here too.

The church is open from 8 am to noon and 4 to 6.30 pm daily. Bus No 13 stops nearby.

North of the Old City
Fortezza da Basso (Map 3) Alessandro de' Medici ordered the construction of this huge defensive fortress in 1534, and the task went to a Florentine living in Rome, Antonio da Sangallo il Giovane. The Medici family in general and Alessandro in particular were not flavour of the month in Florence at the time and construction of the fortress was an ominous sign of oppression. It was not designed to protect the city from invasion – Alessandro had recently been put back in the saddle after a siege by papal-imperial forces. The idea was to keep a watchful eye over the Florentines themselves.

Nowadays it is sometimes used for exhibitions and cultural events.

Chiesa Russa Ortodossa (Map 2)
A couple of blocks east of the fortress, the onion-shaped domes are a bit of a giveaway on this Russian Orthodox church. Built in 1902 for the Russian populace resident here, it was designed in the north Russian style, with two interior levels decorated in part by Florentine artists but mostly by Russian experts in iconography.

Museo Stibbert (Map 2)
Frederick Stibbert was one of the grand wheeler-dealers in the European antiquities market in the 19th century and unsurprisingly had quite a collection himself. He bought the Villa di Montughi with the intention of creating a museum exuding the atmosphere of the various countries and periods covered by his collections. The result is an intriguing mix.

An eye-opener is his collection of armour and arms. In one room, the **Sala della Cavalcata** (Parade Room), are life-size figures of horses and their soldierly riders in all manner of suits of armour from Europe and the Middle East. The exhibits also include clothes, furnishings, tapestries and paintings from the 16th to the 19th centuries.

The museum is at Via Federico Stibbert 26, north of the Fortezza da Basso. It is open from 10 am to 1 pm and 3 to 6 pm daily except Thursday in summer. In winter it opens from 10 am to 6 pm at the weekend and from 10 am to 2 pm on weekdays (closed Thursday). Admission costs L8000.

The No 4 bus from Stazione di Santa Maria Novella takes you as close as Via Vittorio Emanuele II, from where you have a fairly short walk.

South of the Old City
Bellosguardo (Map 2) A favourite spot for 19th-century landscape painters was the hill of Bellosguardo (Beautiful View) south-west of the city centre. A narrow winding road leads up past a couple of villas from Piazza Tasso to Piazza Bellosguardo. You can't see anything from here, but if you wander along Via Roti Michelozzi into the grounds of the Albergo Torre di Bellosguardo, you'll see what the fuss was about. The hotel staff may not be too keen on tourists, but by the time they are aware you are an interloper there ain't much they can do about it. The hotel is the latest guise of what was once a 14th-century castle. Unfortunately no buses run here.

Certosa di Galluzzo About 3km south of Porta Romana, along Via Senese, is Galluzzo, which is home to a quite remarkable 14th-century monastery, the Certosa. Its great cloister is decorated with busts from the della Robbia workshop and there are frescoes by Pontormo in the Gothic hall of the Palazzo degli Studi.

The Certosa is open daily except Monday and can be visited only with a guide from 9 am to midday and from 3 to 6 pm (5 pm in winter). To get there catch bus No 37 from Stazione di Santa Maria Novella. Payment is by offer (try not to be overly stingy).

ACTIVITIES
Swimming
Piscina Nannini (Map 2; ☎ 055 67 75 21) is about 3.5km east of the Ponte Vecchio along Lungarno Aldo Moro in Bellariva

(bus No 14 from Piazza dell'Unità and the Duomo takes you closest to the pool). In summer, when they pull back the movable roof over the Olympic-size pool, it becomes a watery haven on those torrid Florentine days. Opening times tend to change from month to month, but as a rule of thumb it opens from 9 am to 6.30 pm and from 8 to 11.30 pm daily in summer. Standard adult admission costs L10,000, or you can become a member *(socio)* for L10,000 and get blocks of 10 tickets for L71,000. A block of tickets for non-members costs L75,000.

Piscina Le Pavoniere (Map 2; ☎ 055 35 83 27) at Viale degli Olmi in the Cascine opens from May to September. It opens late into the night on some evenings and has a pizzeria and bar.

COURSES

Florence has more than 30 schools offering courses in Italian language and culture. Numerous other schools offer courses in art, including painting, drawing, sculpture and art history, and there are also plenty of schools offering cooking courses.

While Florence is one of the most attractive cities in which to study Italian language or art, it is one of the more expensive. You may want to check out the options in places such as Siena, Perugia and Urbino. Also, as far as learning the language is concerned, Florence is a poor choice – for English speakers at any rate – as most Anglo students find themselves hanging out with other Anglos and never speaking a word of the language. If you are serious about the language, you may want to think about picking a less touristed town.

Brochures detailing courses and prices are available at Italian cultural institutes throughout the world (see Useful Organisations in the Facts for the Visitor chapter). Florence's APT tourist office also has lists of schools and courses, which it will mail on request. You can write in English to request information and enrolment forms – letters should be addressed to the *'segretaria'* (secretary).

Remember that many nationalities must apply for a visa to study in Italy, so chec with the Italian consulate in your country

Language Courses

The cost of language courses in Florenc depends on the school, the length of th course (one month is usually the minimum duration) and its intensity. Local authoritie sometimes run irregular courses, generall for free and aimed at impecunious migrant for a couple of hours a week.

Language courses available in Florenc include those offered at the followin schools:

Dante Alighieri School for Foreigners
(Map 5; ☎ 055 234 29 86) Via de'Bardi 1 50125′. A well-known school for language ar culture classes.

Istituto Europe
(Map 6; ☎ 055 238 10 71) Piazzale delle Pa lottole 1, 50122. Courses here start at L370,00 for two hours a day (one week). A much bett deal is to hang around for four wee (L840,000).

Istituto di Lingua e Cultura Italiana per Stranieri Michelangelo
(Map 7; ☎ 055 24 09 75) Via Ghibellina 8 50122. Here you will pay L890,000 for fou weeks' tuition, but the school will also organi private one-on-one courses, starting L6,230,000 for two weeks (which includ lunch with the teacher – so you'd better lik your teacher!).

Scuola Leonardo da Vinci
(Map 3; ☎ 055 29 44 20) Via Bufalini 3, 5012 Courses offered range from two to 24 week usually averaging four hours of classes a da Basic course costs start at L800,000 for fo weeks.

Other Courses

Many of the schools already listed als offer a programme of courses on art histor cooking, art, music and the like.

Some schools specialise in these sorts c discipline. Art courses range from on month summer workshops (costing fro L500,000 to more than L1,000,000) longer-term professional diploma course These can be expensive – some cost mo than L6,500,000 a year.

Schools will organise accommodation fo

tudents, upon request and at added cost, either in private apartments or with Italian families.

Accademia Italiana

(Map 5; ☎ 055 28 46 16) Piazza de'Pitti 15, 50125. This school offers a wide range of design programmes. They include one-month courses for dilettantes and more rigorous semester courses in painting, graphic arts, fashion design and related fields.

Centro Lorenzo de' Medici

(Map 3; ☎ 055 28 73 60) Via Faenza 43, 50122. This school is popular with American students abroad wishing to learn Italian.

Cordon Bleu

(Map 7; ☎ 055 234 54 68) Via di Mezzo 55r, 50123. This is the place to go if you want to learn some stylish cooking methods.

Florence Dance Center

(Map 5; ☎ 055 28 92 76) Borgo della Stella 23r. Here you can train in classical, jazz and modern dance.
Web site www.florencedance.org

Istituto per l'Arte e il Restauro

(Map 7; ☎ 055 24 60 01) Palazzo Spinelli, Borgo Santa Croce 10, 50122. Here you can learn to restore anything from paintings to ceramics, interior and graphic design, gilding and marquetry. ·

ORGANISED TOURS

Walking Tours of Florence (☎ 055 234 62 5) organises city walks led by historians. It does an introductory walk three days a week for L35,000 starting at 10 am at Caffè Giubbe Rosse in Piazza della Repubblica. You can organise all sorts of specific walks to suit your own needs and tastes – at a price. See the Web site at www.artviva com.

SPECIAL EVENTS

Major festivals include: the Scoppio del Carro (Explosion of the Cart), when a cart full of fireworks is exploded in front of the Duomo on Easter Saturday; the Festa del Patrono (the Feast of St John the Baptist) on 24 June; and the lively Calcio Storico Football in Costume), featuring football matches played in 16th-century costume, held in June in Piazza Santa Croce and ending with a fireworks display over Piazzale Michelangelo.

Every two years Florence hosts the Internazionale Antiquariato, an antiques fair attracting exhibitors from across Europe, at the Palazzo Strozzi, Via de' Tornabuoni. Call ☎ 055 28 26 35 for information. The next fair will be in September/October 2001.

PLACES TO STAY

The city has hundreds of hotels in all categories and a good range of alternatives, including hostels and private rooms. There are more than 200 one- and two-star hotels in Florence, so even in the peak season, it is generally possible – although not always easy – to find a room.

You are, however, advised to book ahead in summer (from mid-April on) and for the Easter and Christmas to New Year holiday periods, and, frankly, it's not a bad idea at any time.

Hotels generally go by the name of *hotel* or *albergo*, essentially the same thing. A *pensione* is generally a smaller, cheaper family-run affair. That said, you will sometimes find that even the tiniest places refer to themselves as hotels. The one- to five-star system is indicative only of the facilities and services available in a hotel – although the rating may give some idea of quality and prices, it is all rather arbitrary. Hoteliers are under little or no obligation to charge any particular rate.

Hotels and pensioni are concentrated in three areas: near the main train station, near Piazza Santa Maria Novella and in the old city between the Duomo and the river.

If you arrive at Stazione di Santa Maria Novella without a hotel booking, head for the Consorzio ITA office (see the Information section near the beginning of the chapter). Using a computer network, the office can check the availability of rooms and make a booking for a small fee – there are no phone bookings. The fee charged ranges from L4500 to L15,000 (for one- to five-star places). The office is open from 8.30 am to 9 pm daily. Several other hotel associations offer booking services for a range of hotels registered with them (see the list in the next section).

You can also contact the APT tourist office for a list of private rooms *(affitta-camere)*, which generally charge from L25,000 per person in a shared room and from L35,000 per person in a single room. Most fill with students during the school year (from October to June), but are a good option if you are staying for a week or longer.

When you arrive at a hotel, always ask for the full price of a room before putting your bags down. Florentine hotels and pensioni are notorious for their bill-padding, particularly in summer. Some may require up to L10,000 extra for compulsory breakfast and others will charge L3000 or more for a shower.

Prices listed here are for the high season and, unless otherwise indicated, are for rooms without bathroom. A bathroom will cost from L10,000 to L30,000 extra, and sometimes all this means is a shower cubicle. Many places, especially at the lower end, offer triples and quads as well as the standard single/double arrangement. If you are travelling in a group of three or four, these bigger rooms are generally the best value.

High season for those hotels that lift their prices (which is most of them) starts on 15 April and fizzles out by mid-October. Some hotels have an intermediate stage starting on 1 March. Others don't bother changing prices much at any time of the year.

It follows that low season (mid-October to the end of February, and for some places also March) is the thinnest time for tourists and so the best for getting the cheapest hotel rates.

Hotel Associations

The following organisations can book you into member hotels. They usually offer a fair range of possibilities, but rarely drop below two stars.

Associazione Gestori Alloggi Privati (AGAP)

(☎/fax 055 28 41 00) Via de' Neri 9. This organisation can get you a room in an affitta-camere.

Consorzio Finestre Sull'Arno

(☎ 800 292773) c/o Hotel Augustus, Vicolo dell Oro 5

COOPAL

(☎ 055 21 95 25, fax 055 29 21 92) Via Il Prato 2r

Florence Promhotels

(☎ 055 57 04 81 or ☎ 800 866022, fax 055 5 71 89, @ info@promhotels.it) Viale Volta 72

Top Quark (incorporating Family Hotels an Sun Ray Hotels)
(☎ 055 462 00 80, fax 055 48 22 88 @ top-quark.fi@mbox.it.net) Via Trieste 5

Places to Stay – Budget

Camping The closest camp site to the city centre is *Campeggio Michelangelo (Map 2 ☎ 055 681 19 77, Viale Michelangelo 80)* just off Piazzale Michelangelo, south of the Arno. It opens from April until the end o October. Take bus No 13 from the trai station.

Villa Camerata (Map 2; ☎ 055 61 03 00 Viale Augusto Righi 2–4) has a camp sit next to the HI hostel (see the next section) There is a camp site at Fiesole, *Campeggio Panoramico (☎ 055 59 90 69, Via Pera monda 1)*, which also has bungalows. Tak bus No 7 to Fiesole from the main trai station.

Hostels The Hostelling International (HI *Ostello Villa Camerata (Map 2; ☎ 055 6 14 51, fax 055 61 03 00, Viale August Righi 2–4)*, is considered one of the mos beautiful hostels in Europe. B&B i L24,000, dinner L14,000, and there is a bar Only members are accepted and the hoste is part of the International Booking Net work (IBN) system, the online booking sys tem for HI (see their Web site at www .iyhf.org for more details). The hostel i open from 7 am to midnight, with a breal from 9 am to 2 pm. Take bus No 17B, whic leaves from the right of the main train sta tion as you leave the platforms. The trip takes 30 minutes.

The private *Ostello Archi Rossi (Map 3 ☎ 055 29 08 04, Via Faenza 94r)* is anothe good option for a bed in a dorm room (L24,000), and it is close to the train station A bed in a smaller room costs L30,00(

Ostello Santa Monaca (Map 5; ☎ 055 26 83 38, Via Santa Monaca 6) is another private hostel. It is a 15- to 20-minute walk south from the train station, through Piazza di Santa Maria Novella, along Via de' Fossi, across the Ponte alla Carraia and directly ahead along Via de' Serragli. Via Santa Monaca is a few blocks from the river, on the right. A bed costs L23,000, and sheets and meals are available.

The Ostello Spirito Santo (Map 3; ☎ 055 39 82 02, Via Nazionale 8) is a religious institution near the main train station. The nuns accept only women and families, and charge L40,000 per person or L60,000 for a double. They seem cagey about accepting bookings over the phone – but do try in any case. The hostel is open from July to October.

Istituto Gould (Map 5; ☎ 055 21 25 76, Via de' Serragli 49) has clean doubles for L39,000. A bed in a quad costs L33,000, while one in a quintuple comes in at L28,000.

Hotels – East of Stazione di SM Novella

Many of the hotels in this area are very well run, clean and safe, but there are also a fair number of seedy establishments. The area includes the streets around Piazza della Stazione and east to Via Cavour. If you have nothing booked and don't wish to tramp around town, the area has the advantage of being close to the station.

The Pensione Bellavista (Map 3; ☎ 055 28 45 28, Largo Alinari 15), at the start of Via Nazionale, is small, but a bargain if you can manage to book one of the two double rooms with balconies and a view of the Duomo and Palazzo Vecchio – they cost L130,000. At the time of writing they said they had no singles.

Albergo Azzi (Map 3; ☎ 055 21 38 06, Via Faenza 56) has a helpful management, which will arrange accommodation for you in other Italian cities. Simple, comfortable singles/doubles are L70,000/100,000, or L140,000 for a double with bathroom. Ask for a room away from the noisy Via Faenza and enjoy breakfast on the hotel's terrace.

At No 24 is the Pensione Ausonia & Rimini (Map 3; ☎ 055 49 65 47), run by an obliging young couple. Singles/doubles cost L70,000/105,000, or L95,000/125,000 with own bath. The price includes breakfast.

Hotel Globus (Map 6; ☎ 055 21 10 62, Via Sant'Antonino 24) is a handy little place with reasonable if unspectacular rooms going for up to L80,000/130,000. You can snag a single for L60,000 in low season, which is about as cheap as this kind of place gets around here. Everything is kept spotlessly clean.

Hotels – Around Piazza di SM Novella

This area is just south of the Stazione di Santa Maria Novella and includes Piazza di Santa Maria Novella, the streets running south to the Arno and east to Via de' Tornabuoni.

Via della Scala, which runs north-west off the piazza, is lined with pensioni. It is not the most salubrious part of town, but if you want to find a place to put your head down quickly after arriving, at least you have plenty of choice.

La Romagnola (Map 3; ☎ 055 21 15 97) at No 40 has large, clean rooms and a helpful management. Singles/doubles are L48,000/84,000. Add L8000 for a room with private bath.

Hidden away on a quiet tiny intersection is the modest Pensione Ferretti (Map 6; ☎ 055 238 13 28, Via delle Belle Donne 17). Simple but quiet rooms start at L66,000/105,000 without own bath or L85,000/125,000 with.

Hotels – Between the Duomo & the Arno

This area is a 15-minute walk south from Stazione di Santa Maria Novella in the heart of old Florence. One of the best deals is the small Aily Home (Map 6; ☎ 055 239 65 05, Piazza Santo Stefano 81), just near the Ponte Vecchio. Rooms cost L35,000/60,000. It has five large rooms, three overlooking the bridge, and accepts bookings. The singles are tiny, but this has to be about the cheapest hotel option in Florence.

Pensione Maria Luisa de' Medici (Map 6; ☎ *055 28 00 48, Via del Corso 1)* is in a 17th-century mansion. They have large rooms and cater for families. Doubles/ triples without own bath cost L101,000/ 140,000 and L139,000/179,000 with. Prices include breakfast.

Albergo Firenze (Map 6; ☎ *055 21 42 03, Piazza de'Donati 4)*, just south of the Duomo, has singles/doubles for L90,000/ 130,000 and breakfast is included. The *Brunori (Map 6;* ☎ *055 28 96 48, Via del Proconsolo 5)* charges up to L102,000 for doubles with a shower. Singles without start at L48,000.

Albergo Bavaria (Map 5; ☎ *055 234 03 13, Borgo degli Albizi 26)* is housed in the fine Palazzo di Ramirez di Montalvo, built around a peaceful courtyard by Ammannati. The hotel has singles/doubles for up to L90,000/120,000. A double with bathroom is L150,000. The *Pensione TeTi & Prestige (Map 6;* ☎ *055 239 84 35, Via Porta Rossa 5)* has singles/doubles for L90,000/130,000 with own shower and a few doubles with full private bathroom for L150,000. The manager is willing to chop off about L20,000 in slack times.

The *Maxim (Map 6;* ☎ *055 21 74 74, Via de' Medici 4)* has singles/doubles/triples from L105,000/140,000/180,000 and offers substantial discounts in the low season.

Elsewhere If things are looking tough in the centre of town, a few possibilities a little farther out suggest themselves.

Pensione Losanna (Map 4; ☎ *055 24 58 40, Via Vittorio Alfieri 9)* lies a few blocks east of the Museo Archeologico as the crow flies and is a well-run establishment where rooms cost L70,000/95,000.

If there is no room at that inn, try upstairs at *Pensione Donatello (Map 4;* ☎ *041 247 74 16)*. The place is a little tattier, but the rooms are spacious, clean and quiet. The bathrooms are on the corridor. The price, which includes breakfast, is L60,000/ 100,000. If no singles are left, the lady running the place will give you a double for L70,000 (which the lady downstairs will not).

Places to Stay – Mid-Range

East of Stazione di SM Novella The
Pensione Le Cascine (Map 3; ☎ *055 21 10 66, Largo Alinari 15)*, near the train station is a two-star hotel with nicely furnished rooms, some with balconies. Singles/ doubles with bathroom cost L140,000/ 300,000, including breakfast.

The *Nuova Italia (Map 3;* ☎ *055 26 84 30, Via Faenza 26)* is a good choice. Its singles/doubles with bathroom cost up to L125,000/185,000. *Pensione Accademia (Map 6;* ☎ *055 29 34 51, Via Faenza 7)* has pleasant rooms and incorporates an 18th-century mansion with magnificent stained glass doors and carved wooden ceilings. The only single costs L130,000 (without own bathroom), while doubles with bath room go for L200,000, breakfast and television included.

Hotel Bellettini (Map 6; ☎ *055 21 35 61 Via de'Conti 7)* is a delightful small hotel with well-furnished singles/doubles with bathroom for L140,000/190,000. Try for one of the rooms with a view.

The *Giotto (Map 6;* ☎ *055 28 98 64, Via del Giglio 13)* has doubles with bathroom for L160,000. The *Giada (Map 6;* ☎ *055 21 53 17, Via del Canto de' Nelli 2)* is in the middle of the open-air leather market. The rooms with bathroom are OK, and you have the rare luxury of breakfast in your room. Rates are L120,000/180,000. *Hotel Le Casci (Map 6;* ☎ *055 21 16 86 Via Cavour 13)* has good rooms for L140,000/ 190,000 with bathroom, breakfast and TV.

Between the Duomo & the Arno The
Hotel Alessandra (Map 6; ☎ *055 28 34 38 Borgo SS Apostoli 17)* has lots of character. Singles/doubles are L100,000/150,000, or L150,000/200,000 with bathroom. The *Pendini (Map 6;* ☎ *055 21 11 70, Via degli Strozzi 2)* is another excellent choice. Its rooms are furnished with antiques and reproductions, and singles/doubles with bath room are L170,000/250,000. The *Hotel Porta Rossa (Map 6;* ☎ *055 28 75 51, Via Porta Rossa 19)* has large singles/doubles for L170,000/285,000.

Oltrarno A good choice if you want to stay south of the river is **Pensione la caletta** (Map 6; ☎ 055 28 30 28, Via de' Guicciardini 13). It has a terrace with excellent views. Rooms with bathroom are L140,000/200,000, which includes breakfast. Some cheaper rooms looking onto the street cost a little less.

Places to Stay – Top End

In this category appear a handful of choices where a single can cost you from L200,000 a night up to more than L620,000 at the very top end of the scale.

East of Stazione di SM Novella In a fine old building right on the square is **Hotel Le Due Fontane** (Map 4; ☎ 055 21 01 85, Piazza SS Annunziata 14). The well-presented rooms cost L200,000/290,000, including breakfast. It's one of the few hotels at this level to have a baby-sitting service.

Hotel Il Guelfo Bianco (Map 3; ☎ 055 28 83 30, fax 055 29 52 03, Via Cavour 27r) has 29 attractively laid-out and comfortable rooms. If you are alone, see if you can get the charming single with its own private terrace. Rooms cost L205,000/235,000.

Around Ognissanti The most expensive hotels in town face each other in self-assured style on Piazza Ognissanti. **Grand Hotel** (Map 5; ☎ 055 28 87 81, fax 055 21 72 78, Piazza d'Ognissanti 1) is every bit as grand as the name suggests. Marble bathrooms and regal furnishings characterise the best rooms with river views. A wander in the glorious ground floor, with its bars and restaurant, is almost nauseating. You are looking at a minimum in high season of L620,000/860,000 for singles/doubles. Deluxe doubles with river views cost L1,062,000.

Hotel Excelsior (Map 5; ☎/fax 055 26 42 01, Piazza d'Ognissanti 3) is the haughtier of the two hotels. Luxury is again the key in the 158 rooms. Prices for singles/doubles in high season start at L566,000/860,000, rising to L1,100,000 for a double with river views.

Between the Duomo & the Arno Set in a historic building, **Bernini Palace** (Map 6; ☎ 055 28 86 21, Piazza San Firenze 29) is an excellent hotel. Its luxurious rooms are L340,000/500,000 for singles/doubles.

Hotel Brunelleschi (Map 6; ☎ 055 21 73 70, fax 055 21 96 53, Piazza Santa Elisabetta 3) is the place to stay if you fancy sleeping in the round tower of a one-time medieval prison. Good, modern rooms with satellite TV, air-con and hairdryers cost L380,000/510,000, including breakfast. Only the penthouse suites are actually in the tower. See the Web site at www.hotel brunelleschi.it.

Oltrarno Worth considering is **Albergo Torre di Bellosguardo** (Map 6; ☎ 055 229 81 45, fax 055 22 90 08, Via Roti Michelozzi 2, ✉ torredibellosguardo@dada.it), if only for its position. Long appreciated as a bucolic escape from the simmering heat of the summertime Florence, the Bellosguardo hill to the south-west of the city centre offers not only enchanting views but enticing accommodation in what started life as a small castle in the 14th century. Rooms cost L340,000/450,000 year-round, and breakfast an extra L35,000.

Landmark Trust

If you fancy staying in the poet Browning's house, **Casa Guidi** (Map 5), in Piazza San Felice, contact the Landmark Trust in the UK. Established as a charity in 1965, the trust restores and conserves a host of architectural marvels in the UK, as well as several abroad. Casa Guidi has been restored and is owned by Eton College. It sleeps six and can cost around UK£1300 a week. For information, get in touch with The Landmark Trust (☎ 01628-825 925, ✉ bookings@landmarktrust.co.uk), Shottesbrooke, Maidenhead, Berkshire SL6 3SW, UK, or see their Web site at www .landmarktrust.co.uk.

Short-Term Rental

If you are travelling in a group and plan to stay in Florence for at least a week or more, it may be worth considering renting an apartment or villa. This is obviously an even more popular option for those choosing to stay in the surrounding countryside. Any Italian tourist office abroad will be able to supply you with mountains of brochures for companies brokering such arrangements. The problem is knowing what you are going to get – not always easy to judge, even if you get to see photos. Remember to find out exactly what the facilities are and what costs extra (such as heating and use of a swimming pool).

One major Italian company with villas in Tuscany is Cuendet. This reliable firm publishes a booklet listing all the villas on its files, many with photos. Prices for a villa for four to six people range from around US$400 a week in winter up to US$1200 a week in August. For details, write to Cuendet & Cie spa, Strada di Strove 17, 53035 Monteriggioni, Siena (☎ 0577 57 63 10, fax 0577 30 11 49, ✆ cuede@tin.it), and ask them to send you a copy of their catalogue (US$15).

In the UK, you can order Cuendet's catalogues and make reservations by calling ☎ 0800 891 573 toll free. In North America, Cuendet is represented by Rentvillas.com (previously Rentals In Italy – and Elsewhere!) (☎ 805-987 5278, fax 482 7976), 1742 Calle Corva, in Camarillo, California They have a Web site at www.rentvillas.com. In Australia, try an organisation called Cottages & Castles (☎ 03-9853 1142, fax 9853 0509, ✆ cottages@vicnet.net.au), 11 Laver St, Kew 3101, Victoria.

Long-Term Rental

If you want an apartment in Florence, save your pennies and, if you can, start looking well before you arrive, as apartments are difficult to come by and can be very expensive. A one-room studio with kitchenette in the city centre will generally cost around L1,000,000 a month. Florence & Abroad (Map 3; ☎ 055 48 70 04), Via Zanobi 58, deals with rental accommodation.

If you decide while in Florence to start looking, be prepared for some degree of frustration. You can look for rental ads in advert rags such as *La Pulce* (L2800, three times a week) and *Il Mercato della Toscano* (L2500). You'll find few ads for share accommodation though.

Another obvious route to follow, especially if you are looking for share housing, is the language and other schools frequented by foreigners in Florence. You can put up your own ad or hopefully get lucky and find some likely candidates to share with.

Other places to look for ads include English bookshops (such as the Paperback Exchange), cybercafes, laundrettes and faculty buildings of the Università degli Studi di Firenze (Map 3).

PLACES TO EAT

There is no shortage of places to eat in Florence, and although Florentines have largely abandoned the city centre to the foreigners, you can still dig up quite a few fine little eateries dotted about the place. Of course, there is room for big spenders too.

Places to Eat – Budget

Eating at a good *trattoria* can be surprisingly economical – a virtue of the competition for customers' attention. The definition of budget eating is as solid as a bowl of soup, so what follows is an arbitrary division. Anywhere you can fairly safely assume you will pay below about L40,000 for a full meal has been classed as 'budget', ranging from sandwich joints (where you might pay around L5000 for a filling roll) through to trattorie serving respectable and good-value set meals *(menù del giorno o menù turistico)* and upwards into the modest categories of restaurant. Anything from around L40,000 up to L80,000 is classed here as mid-range, and everything beyond that as top end. Obviously in that category the sky's the limit.

City Centre The streets between the Duomo and the Arno harbour many *pizzerie* where you can buy takeaway pizza by the slice for around L2000 to L3000.

pending on the weight. All of the restaurants in this section can be found on Map

When it comes to eating a full meal while you pinch pennies, it's hard to go past *Ristorante Self-Service Leonardo* (055 28 44 46, Via de' Pecori 35r), where main courses cost L7500 for lunch or dinner. It is closed Saturday.

Hostaria il Caminetto (055 239 62 4, Via dello Studio 34), south of the uomo, has a small, vine-covered terrace. asta costs around L7000 and a main ourse from L9000 to L10,000. It is closed ednesday.

Trattoria del Pennello (055 29 48 48, a Dante Alighieri 4r) is popular but not as neap as it once was. Pasta starts at 10,000. The place has been serving up ood for the past four centuries! It is closed unday evening and Monday. *Ristorante aoli* (055 21 62 15, Via dei Tavolini 12) as magnificent vaulted ceilings and walls vered with frescoes, and food to match. It fers a L36,000 set menu and pasta from 12,000. It is closed Tuesday.

A tiny but welcoming little corner is rattoria Pasquini (055 21 89 95, Via Val Lamona 2r). The cheerful guy who runs Giacinto, offers a varied menu that includes Tuscan meals such as tripe or biscca alla fiorentina, and a mix of other ational dishes. It is closed Wednesday.

Trattoria da Benvenuto (055 21 48 3, Via Mosca 16r), on the corner of Via dei eri, is hardly an ambient dining experience, but the food is reliable and modestly iced. The main courses include several orentine favourites, including *lampre- tto* and bistecca, while the pasta dishes e an interesting mix, including a decent gatoni alla siciliana. A full meal can cost ound L35,000. It is wise to reserve a table. is closed Sunday.

Among the great little treasures of Florce is *Angie's Pub* (Map 5; 055 239 82 , Via dei Neri 35r), east of the Palazzo ecchio, which offers a vast array of *panini* d *focaccia*, as well as hamburgers, Italian- le with mozzarella and spinach, and real gels. A menu lists the panini, but you n design your own from the extensive

selection of fillings; you should try one with artichoke, mozzarella and mushroom cream. Prices start at around L4000. It is closed Sunday.

Virtually on Piazza San Pier Maggiore is a pleasant, reasonably priced little trattoria, *Osteria Natalino* (055 28 94 04, Borgo degli Albizi 17r). It is closed Monday.

East of Stazione di Santa Maria Novella A small bar and trattoria near Piazza del Mercato Centrale, *Mario* (Map 3; 055 21 85 50, Via Rosina 2r) is open only for lunch and serves pasta for around L6000 to L8000 and main courses for L7000 to L9000. It is very busy, and it is closed on Sunday. A few doors down is *Ristorante Zàtà* (Map 3; 055 21 54 11, Piazza del Mercato Centrale 20), so popular that it's growing. Try the *ravioli al pesto* – an unusual combination that works well. Prices are similar to those at Mario's. It is also closed Sunday.

Vegetarian One of the few veggie options in town is *Il Vegetariano* (Map 3; 055 47 50 30, Via delle Ruote 30r). It is an unassuming little place with a limited (but changing) menu. A meal with wine can cost under L30,000 per person. On weekends it opens for dinner only and it is closed on Monday.

Stazione di SM Novella to Ognissanti Those wanting to spend little *and* switch from Italian fare should make a beeline for *Amon* (Map 3; 055 29 31 46, Via Palazzuolo 6). Here you can pick up cheap Egyptian sandwiches such as felafel or *foul* (fava beans) for around L4000 – a couple of these will fill most reasonable paunches. It is closed Sunday.

La Grotta di Leo (Map 3; 055 21 92 65, Via della Scala 41) is a pleasant trattoria with a L20,000 set menu or pizzas and pasta from L8000. *Trattoria il Contadino* (Map 3; 055 238 26 73, Via Palazzuolo 71r) has a L15,000 set menu, including wine. The food is no great culinary exploit, but it is perfectly edible and at a price hard to beat. It is closed Sunday.

Da il Latini (Map 5; ☎ 055 21 09 16, Via dei Palchetti 4), just off Via del Moro, is an attractive trattoria serving pasta from L6000 and main courses from L14,000. They don't take reservations and the place can get packed – queues are not unusual. So many Florentines can't be wrong. It is closed Monday.

Trattoria dei 13 Gobbi (Map 5; ☎ 055 21 32 04, Via del Porcellana 9r) sets a somewhat artificially bucolic scene inside but in a tasteful fashion. A full meal will set you back around L25,000. It is closed Monday.

Santa Croce & East of the Centre A charming and teeny little place for a long cappuccino over the paper or for a tasty lunch (try the pumpkin soup – *crema di zucca*) is *Caffellatte* (Map 4; ☎ 055 47 88 78, Via degli Alfani 39r). They are into health foods and open until 1 am. It is closed Sunday.

At *Il Nilo* (Map 7; Arco di San Piero 9r) you can pick up fat shawarma and felafel sandwiches for up to L6000. It's open until midnight, but is closed on Sunday.

Need a pastry at 4 am? A couple of *bakeries* open around Florence to sell their wares straight out of the oven. One without a name or street number is at Via del Canto Rivolto (Map 5), just north of Via dei Neri. As you will see they want you to be quiet and get out of there asap. If the neighbours should become vexed by street noise, they may have to stop the practice.

For a cheap and tasty set-lunch menu for just L14,500, head for the vaulted *Caffetteria Piansa* (Map 7; ☎ 055 234 23 62, Borgo Pinti 18r). You basically point and choose from a limited number of dishes. Get in early, as by 2 pm it's all over. It doesn't do dinner and it's closed on Sunday.

Osteria de' Benci (Map 5; ☎ 055 234 49 23, Via de' Benci 13r) is a consistently good bet. They change their menu frequently and serve up honest slabs of *bistecca alla fiorentina*. Food is consistently good and prices are moderate. It is closed Sunday.

Another option for a light lunch is *Antic Noè* (Map 7; ☎ 055 234 08 38, Arco di Sa Piero 6r), a legendary sandwich bar just o Piazza San Pier Maggiore. They have tw sections. The sandwich bar is takeawa only, but next door they run a cosy litt restaurant where you can enjoy fine coo ing to slow jazz and blues tunes. Try the r freshing *farfalle al salmone e pomodo freschi* (butterfly pasta with salmon an fresh tomato). It is closed Monday.

Not far off, *Danny Rock* (Map 7; ☎ 05 234 03 07, Via Pandolfini 13r) does n sound promising, but inside is an im mensely popular place for pizza, pasta an perhaps best of all, their *insalatoni* (hug salads). One of the latter makes a meal i itself.

Osteria del Gatto e la Volpe (Map ☎ 055 28 92 64, Via Ghibellina 151r), c the corner of Via de' Giraldi, has pizz from L7000 and pasta from L7500. It closed Tuesday.

The *Sant'Ambrogio Caffè* (Map ☎ 055 24 10 35, Piazza di Sant'Ambrog 7), along Via Pietrapiana, is a bar an restaurant where you can get a sandwic from L3000 or pasta from L7000. It closed Sunday.

International Cuisine For something little different, you should try out *Ruth* (Map 7; ☎ 055 248 08 88, Via Farini 2a) t the synagogue. They serve tasty kosh Jewish food – it bears a strong resemblanc to other Middle Eastern cuisine and make a good choice for vegetarians. For L16,0 you can have a plate of mixed dips wit couscous, felafel, filo pastry pie and pota salad, quite filling in itself. It is closed Fr day evening and on Saturday.

If meat is OK with you, get yourse down to *La Bodeguita* (Map 3; ☎ 055 78 82, Via San Gallo 16r). Although t people running it aren't Cuban, they put tasty versions of *picadillo* (a spicy minc meat with vegetables and rice) and som good chicken dishes. The *mojitos* are mea It is closed Sunday.

For takeaway tandoori and other Indi specialities drop by at *Ramraj* (Map

DAMIEN SIMONIS

windswept Golfo di Baratti, north of Piombino in Livorno Province

DAMIEN SIMONIS

old centre of Piombino, with the Elba ferry heading out

DAMIEN SIMONIS

dramatic facade of Fortezza Vecchia in Livorno

Napoleon's one-time home: the old port of Portoferraio, Elba

Taking it easy near Marciana Marina, Elba

The enchanting village of Poggio in western Elb

Fast Food Florence-Style

Some habits die hard. When Florentines feel like a fast snack instead of a sit-down lunch, they might well stop by a *trippaio* for a nice tripe burger (well, tripe on a bread roll). It may sound a little nauseating to the uninitiated but it's really not that bad. McDonald's has very definitely arrived in Florence, but the American giant fronted by the silly-looking clown has yet to snuff out local preferences. But then, who knows what a generation fed on the Big Mac might think of tripe rolls in years to come?

Savouring fine wines is one of the great pleasures of the palate in Florence, and for many there is nothing better than a couple of glasses of a good drop accompanied by simple local snacks – sausage meats, cheeses, *ribollita* (vegetable stew) and the like. And the good news is that the tradition of the *vinaio* has won new life in the past few years in Florence. You may never see the word 'vinaio' on the doorway, but the idea remains the same. The old traditional places still exist – often dark little grog shops where you can get a bite to eat too. Look out for the sign 'Mescita di Vini' (roughly, 'wine outlet').

At *Enoteca Fuori Porta* (☎ 055 234 24 83, *Via Monte alle Croci 10r*) the wine list comprises hundreds of different wines (and an impressive roll call of Scotch whiskies and other liqueurs). You can order from a limited list of *primi* ('first dishes') for a pleasant evening meal. The desserts are also good. It's closed on Sunday.

Hidden deep in the San Frediano area *Le Barrique* (☎ 055 22 41 92, *Via del Leone 40r*) offers a limited *menù del giorno* (menu of the day) or, for those just stopping in for a quick drink or two, snacks at the bar. Again the emphasis is on wine, although the pasta dishes are good. It also offers a selection of Tuscan and French cheeses. It's closed on Monday.

At the *Fiaschetteria* (☎ 055 21 74 11, *Via dei Neri 17r*) you can drop by for an excellent ribollita for L11,000, accompanied by a few glasses of wine. It's closed on Monday.

It seems barely conceivable that within about 10 seconds' walk of Piazza della Signoria, which is lined with tourist rip-off restaurants, one of the city centre's last surviving, more or less genuine, *osterie* should remain. In *Vini e Vecchi Sapori* (☎ 055 29 30 45, *Via dei Magazzini 3r*) there is barely room to swing a Florentine rat, but you can eat decently and taste some solid local wines for about L25,000 a head. They also import *fragolino*, a strawberry-flavoured wine made in the north-east of Italy.

Another choice is *Le Volpi e l'Uva* (☎ 055 239 81 32, *Piazza dei Rossi 1r*), hidden away off the Oltrarno end of the Ponte Vecchio, where you can sample cheeses, have a *tramezzino* (sandwich) and try out new wines. It's closed on Sunday and holidays.

---

055 24 09 99, Via Ghibellina 61r). You can eat at the bench if you want to. The food OK if unspectacular, but it is quick and modestly priced. It is closed Monday.

Vegetarian The best place to come for *caloppina di seitan* or a *bavette al gorgonzola* is definitely *Sedano Allegro* (Map 7; ☎ 055 234 55 05, *Borgo della Croce 20r*). Dishes are pretty cheap, ranging from L9000 to L12,000. It is open for lunch and dinner and in the warmer months they open up a garden at the rear. It is closed Monday.

Oltrarno The simple Art Nouveau décor of *Il Caffè (Map 5; ☎ 055 239 62 41, Piazza de'Pitti)* makes it a charming place for breakfast or an afternoon coffee. Should you want to eat, they serve cheap no-nonsense set meals for up to L18,000. It is closed Monday.

The pizzeria *Borgo Antico (Map 5; ☎ 055 21 04 37, Piazza Santo Spirito 6r)* is a great location in summer, when you can sit at an outside table and enjoy the atmosphere in the piazza. They also offer an expensive but tempting menu that changes daily. *Cabiria (Map 5; ☎ 055 21 57 32,*

FLORENCE

Piazza Santo Spirito 4r) is a popular cafe which also has outdoor seating. It is closed Tuesday. See also the listing in the Entertainment section of this chapter.

If you are in need of food of indifferent quality in the wee hours of the morning, about the only choice you have is *Caffè La Torre (Map 7; ☎ 055 68 06 43, Lungarno Benvenuto Cellini 65r)*. It is also listed in the Entertainment section of this chapter.

The gritty working-class San Frediano quarter of the Oltrarno is sufficiently distant from the hurly-burly of the centre to have a quite individual feel. You can dig up a few fairly simple and solid local eateries here. *All'Antico Ristoro di Cambi (Map 5; ☎ 055 21 71 34, Via Sant'Onofrio 1)* is one such place. The food is traditional Tuscan, the bistecca alla fiorentina succulent and the final bill is unlikely to exceed L45,000. It is closed Sunday.

If you don't mind eating elbow to elbow with complete (local) strangers, *Al Tranvai (Map 2; ☎ 055 22 51 97, Piazza Tasso 14r)* is a wonderful rustic Tuscan eatery. They serve up a limited range of pastas as *primi* and specialise in animal innards, including *trippa alla fiorentina* (tripe). It's nothing fancy but it is authentic cooking. You can get away with L30,000 for a full meal. It is closed at weekends.

Osteria del Cinghiale Bianco (Map 6; ☎ 055 21 57 06, Borgo San Jacopo 43), to the right as you cross Ponte Vecchio, specialises in Florentine food. As the name suggests, wild boar is on the menu – the *pappardelle al cinghiale* (a plump kind of pasta in wild boar sauce) are music to your tastebuds on a cold evening. It is closed Tuesday and Wednesday.

Angiolino (Map 5; ☎ 055 239 89 76, Via di Santo Spirito 36r) is an excellent trattoria where you can eat a meal, including bistecca, for around L40,000. If offal doesn't turn you off, you might like their *rognoncino*, a main course of chopped kidney in a balsamic vinegar marinade. The restaurant is closed Monday.

Trattoria Casalinga (Map 5; ☎ 055 21 86 24, Via de'Michelozzi 9r) is a bustling,

popular eating place. The food is great and a filling meal of pasta, meat or vegetable plus wine will cost under L25,000. Don't expect to linger over a meal, as there is usually a queue of people waiting for your table. It is closed Sunday. *Trattoria I Raddi (Map 5; ☎ 055 21 10 72, Via dell' Ardiglione 47r)*, just near Via de' Serragli, serve traditional Florentine meals and has pasta from L8000 and main courses from L14,000. It is closed Sunday.

Il Cantinone di Gallo Nero (Map 5; ☎ 055 41 06 69, Via di Santo Spirito 6r) specialises in *crostini*, starting at L3500. It is something of a Florentine classic for down-to-earth Tuscan cooking, with local dishes accompanied by good Chianti wine. You will pay around L40,000 a head. It is closed Monday.

I Tarocchi (Map 5; ☎ 055 234 39 12, Via de' Renai 12–14r) is a popular pizzeria/trattoria serving excellent pizzas costing around L10,000. The first and second courses each cost about the same, and the former alone are enough to satisfy most people's hunger. The menu changes daily. It is closed Monday.

The *Osteria Antica Mescita (Map 7; ☎ 055 234 28 36, Via San Niccolò 60r)* is a fine little eating hideaway where the kitchen stays open until near after 11 pm. The food is tasty without being spectacular, but throw in a good bottle from their impressive wine collection and the equation is good. You can get away with about L40,000 for a salad, main course, wine and dessert. It is closed Sunday.

Places to Eat – Mid-Range
City Centre At *Procacci (Map 5; ☎ 055 21 16 56, Via de' Tornabuoni 14r)* they have been tickling Florentine (and quite a few foreign) palates for a century with their *panini tartufati* (truffle-filled rolls). Not so much a nutritional exercise as a ritual, these tasty little numbers can be accompanied by a drop of Tuscan wine or even a cup of tea. It's definitely more of a winter scene, when it stays open until about 9 pm (no later than 8 pm in the warmer months). You can also buy wine and foodstuffs, including truffle

take away. It is closed Sunday and Monay.

Trattoria Coco Lezzone (Map 6; ☎ 055 8 71 78, Via Parioncino 26r). *Ribollita* is ne house speciality, but they will do you a enuine bistecca alla fiorentina for L60,000 enough for two in most cases) if you book : ahead. One oddity is that they do not erve coffee in this tiny place tucked away ff Via del Purgatorio. It is closed Sunday nd holidays.

Cantinetta Antinori (Map 6; ☎ 055 29 2 34, Piazza degli Antinori 3r) might be ne place for you if you suddenly have a noment in which you feel both posh and lush. For about L70,000 a head you can njoy a reasonable meal accompanied by ome fine wines – it is for the latter that nost people come here. It's not a bad choice f you have to impress a suit or two. It is losed at the weekend.

International Cuisine A reasonable representative of the Japanese genre is *Eito* Map 6; ☎ 055 21 09 40, Via dei Neri 72r). Wednesday is '*sushi*' day, when you are offered the choice of two set menus, one with 12 pieces of sushi and six of *sashimi* L50,000) and one the other way around L35,000). Both come with miso soup. Otherwise they have quite a broad selecion of dishes, which can be washed down with Kirin or Sapporo beer. It is closed Monday.

East of Stazione di SM Novella An excellent fish restaurant is *Ristorante Lobs* Map 3; ☎ 055 21 24 78, Via Faenza 75). For L60,000 you can enjoy a seafood menu ncluding oysters and Norwegian salmon, and Soave wine from the country's northeast. Otherwise, main courses cost around L32,000. Round off with *sorbetto al vodka*. Another plus about this joint is that they top cooking about 12.30 am – a rare thing n a town where few restaurants serve after 11 pm at the latest.

Stazione di SM Novella to Ognissanti Traditional Tuscan cooking is offered at *Sostanza* (Map 5; ☎ 055 21 26 91, Via del

Porcellana 25r), also one of the best spots in town for bistecca alla fiorentina. Main courses start at L18,000. It is closed at weekends.

Oltrarno Hidden away in a back street, *Trattoria Cavolo Nero* (Map 5; ☎ 055 29 47 44, Via dell'Ardiglione 22) will set you back up to L60,000 a head – try the *carpaccio di Angus con rucola e grana* (carpaccio of Angus steak with rocket and grana cheese). It is closed Sunday.

L'Erta Canina Club (Map 5; ☎ 055 24 22 50, Via dell'Erta Canina 6r) is a strange little place with the look of a misplaced clubhouse. The low-lit atmosphere is tranquil and the food is good. Try the *filetto di manzo lardellato di Brunello*, a beef filet prepared in Brunello wine. It is closed Tuesday.

Ristorante Beccofino (Map 5; ☎ 055 29 00 76, Piazza degli Scarlatti) is a recent addition to the Florentine culinary scene, and a rare breed in this town. The grub is pricey and the surroundings nouvelle chic – no trad bucolics in here thank you. You can sip at the bar and then try a vaguely adventurous style of cooking. Expect to pay out around L70,000 per person. It is closed on Sunday.

International Cuisine Touting itself as a sushi bar offering 'inventive food' *Momoyama* (Map 5; ☎ 055 29 18 40, Borgo San Frediano 10r) technically operates as a club. When you come the first time you will have to fill out a form and possibly show some form of ID to become a member. For Florence it is an original dining experience, with bare minimalist ochrecoloured decor and tables spread over floors reaching well into the back. As you enter you will see a Japanese chef preparing some of the dishes right in front of you. Reckon on a minimum of L70,000 per person. It is closed Monday.

Outside Florence

One of the city's better-known restaurants is *La Capponcina* (☎ 055 69 70 37, Via San Romano 17r, Settignano), up in the hills

FLORENCE

overlooking Florence from the north-east. The kitchen is known in particular for its *tagliata di manzo*, succulent beef filets sliced up and served on a bed of lettuce. Sitting in the garden is a true pleasure in summer, where you are sure of being several degrees cooler than in town. Count on paying about L70,000 per person for a full meal. You can get bus No 10 from the train station, or Piazza San Marco. This service is replaced from 9 pm by the No 67. The restaurant is closed Monday.

Places To Eat – Top End

City Centre One of the city's finest cafes, *Gilli (Map 6;* ☎ *055 21 38 96, Piazza della Repubblica)* is reasonably cheap if you stand at the bar – a coffee at the bar is L1500, but at a table outside it is L5000. It is closed Tuesday.

Rivoire (Map 6; ☎ *055 21 44 12, Piazza della Signoria)* is one of Florence's classic old cafes. True, it is inevitably somewhat touristy because of its position, but if only once this is the place to sip on a cup of sticky *cioccolata* after overdosing on art in the Uffizi. It is closed Monday.

Santa Croce & East of the Centre With an atmosphere of slightly dated elegance, with lots of wood panelling and frosted glass, *Ristorante Cibréo (Map 7;* ☎ *055 234 11 00, Via de' Macci 118r)* and its twin *osteria* combine to form a fine restaurant. At the osteria you can eat well for around L40,000, while a visit to the restaurant is a much more refined and expensive outing. You can book for the latter but the former is first in, first served. It is closed Sunday and Monday.

One of the city's finest restaurants, *Enoteca Pinchiorri (Map 7;* ☎ *055 24 27 77, Via Ghibellina 87)* is noted for its nouvelle cuisine, Italian-style. A meal will cost L180,000 per person. It is closed on Sunday and Monday.

For those in search of elegant dining and equipped with elastic purses – but not quite *that* elastic – head a little farther down the street to *Ristorante alle Murate (Map 7;* ☎ *055 24 06 18, Via Ghibellina 64)*. A full meal here will set you back

about L80,000 per person. The restaurant is closed Monday.

Gelaterie

People queue outside *Gelateria Vivoli (Map 5;* ☎ *055 29 23 34, Via dell'Isola dell Stinche)*, near Via Ghibellina, to delight i the gelati widely considered to be the city' best. It is closed Monday. *Perché No? (Map 6;* ☎ *055 239 89 69, Via dei Tavolini 19r,* off Via de' Calzaiuoli, is excellent. It i closed Tuesday.

La Bottega del Gelato (Map 2; ☎ *055 4 67 76, Via del Ponte Rosso 57r)* is just of Piazza della Libertà and does a particularl' enticing range of fruit-flavoured gelati. It i closed Sunday.

If you're in the area, drop in to *Baroncin (Map 2;* ☎ *055 48 91 85, Via Celso 3r)*. It i one of the best-known gelaterie in town They use fresh fruit in the fruit-flavoure options and also do great yoghurt and *sor betto al limone*. It is closed Wednesday.

Self-Catering

You can save money by getting your ow groceries and throwing your own sand wiches and the like together. A handy cen tral supermarket is *Standa (Map 7; Vi Pietrapiana 42)*.

ENTERTAINMENT

Several publications list the theatrical an musical events and festivals held in the cit' and surrounding areas. The free bimonthl' *Florence Today*, the monthly *Firenze Infor mation* and *Firenze Avvenimenti* (a monthl' brochure distributed by the Comune) are al available (haphazardly) at tourist offices The APT publishes an annual booklet list ing the year's events, as well as monthly in formation sheets.

Firenze Spettacolo, the city's definitiv entertainment publication, is availabl weekly for L3000 at news stands.

Posters at the tourist offices, the univer sity and in Piazza della Repubblica adver tise current concerts and other events.

A handy central ticket outlet is *Box Of fice (Map 3;* ☎ *055 21 08 04)* at Via Luig Alamanni 39. It opens from 3.30 to 7.30 pm

Monday and from 10 am to 7 pm Tues-
y to Saturday. An online ticket service,
cket One (www.ticketone.it) allows you
book tickets for theatre, football and
her events. It also provides a list of out-
ts around town where you can pick up
ckets in person.

ubs & Bars

he APT tourist office's *Firenze per i Gio-
ni* (Florence for Young People) brochure
ovides a list a mile long of bars and clubs.
or a good overview of the latest events
d in-spots in the club and live music
ene, try to get a hold of the local free
ooklet *Zero55*. You can pick it up in the
gger pubs/bars.

Many bars and pubs tend to shut by
round 1 am, but there are enough excep-
ons to this rule to keep you going to 3 am
d sometimes later still. It is a little diffi-
lt to classify all places strictly as either
ars, live music venues or discos/clubs, so
e following subdivision is a little arbi-
ary.

round SM Novella & Ognissanti For-
igners hang about at the *Fiddler's Elbow*
*Map 6; ☎ 055 21 50 56, Piazza Santa
Maria Novella*), one of the better so-called
rish pubs distributed around the city. Not
ar off is another of the Irish clan, *The Che-
uers Pub* (*Map 3; ☎ 055 28 75 88, Via
ella Scala 7–9r*).

ity Centre & Towards Santa Croce
he rather cramped *Kikuya Pub* (*Map 5;
☎ 055 234 48 79, Via Giuseppe Verdi 43r*)
as a long happy hour from 7 to 10 pm,
when the unusually generous cocktails can
ost as little as L5000. You can also hear
ve music here occasionally.

A cool place to hang out in style is *Café
Mambo* (*Map 7; ☎ 055 247 89 94, Via Verdi
7r*). It's a hip little bar with a Latin theme
where you can sidle up for some saucy salsa
essons if you're of a mind to do so. It is
losed Sunday.

Sant'Ambrogio Caffè (*Map 7; ☎ 055 24
0 35, Piazza Sant'Ambrogio 7r*), as well as
eing a place to get snacks, is especially

dedicated to the sipping of cocktails. They
cost L10,000 a hit. See also Places to Eat. It
is closed Sunday.

Another stop on the cocktail circuit, *Rex
Caffè* (*Map 7; ☎ 055 248 03 31, Via
Fiesolana 25r*) is a hip place to sip on your
favourite mixed concoction, or maybe two
in happy hour (from 5 to 9.30 pm). Occasionally you'll strike live music and when
it's vinyl the taste is eclectic. You get a
mixed crowd in here, from arty types
through students and even a sprinkling of
beautiful people. Whether it's a Martini at
the bar or a quiet beer sitting at one of the
metallic tables, this is one of the better
watering holes in town.

The William (*Map 7; ☎ 055 246 98 00,
Via Magliabechi 7r*), is a barn of a place
along Irish pub lines, but it has found quite
a following among young Florentines in
search of a pint of ale.

A fun and buzzy place to hang out until
2 am is *Salamanca* (*Map 7; ☎ 055 234 54
52, Via Ghibellina 40r*). The tapas have a
vaguely Italian flavour about them but
otherwise the place manages to exude a
Spanish atmosphere with plenty of hearty
flamenco rock and South American sounds
to keep punters returning to the bar for more
– it's a favourite with Latin Americans living in Florence. Sangria and Latin American cocktails predominate. It is closed
Tuesday.

Oltrarno A cool corner bar nicely placed
off the main tourist trails is *Il Rifrullo*
(*Map 7; ☎ 055 234 26 21, Via San Niccolò
55r*). The bar snacks are generous and the
evening cocktails good. You can sit by the
bar or wind your way out back to the garden on warm summer nights.

If it seems a little too snooty for your
tastes, you could mosey around to the
nearby *Zoe* (*Map 5; ☎ 055 24 31 11, Via dei
Renai 13r*), which heaves as its squadrons
of punters end up spilling out onto the
street. Although the bar attracts a mixed
crowd, the majority tend to be around 25 or
younger. It is closed Sunday.

Cabiria (*Map 5; ☎ 055 21 57 32, Piazza
Santo Spirito 4r*) is a popular cafe by day

(also listed in the Oltrarno section of Places to Eat) that converts into a hip music bar by night. In summer the buzz extends on to Piazza Santo Spirito, which becomes a stage for an outdoor bar and regular free concerts. Summer and winter, the drinking comes to a halt around 2 am on the square and in Cabiria. It is closed Tuesday.

Just a piazza away, **La Dolce Vita** *(Map 5; ☎ 055 28 45 95, Piazza del Carmine 6r)* attracts a rather more self-consciously select crowd of self-appointed beautiful types. During the week it's a fairly tame affair, with the clientele looking carefully dressy over a cocktail that lasts most of the evening until closing time around 1 am. Things get busier from Thursday night onwards, when the same carefully chic punters hang out in rowdier fashion until about 3 am.

One of the weirder places to get a late-night cocktail (and an indifferent pizza if you have the munchies) is **Montecarla** *(Map 5; ☎ 055 234 02 59, Via de' Bardi 2)*. The place has changed hands a few times but all have remained faithful to the baroque kitsch aesthetic that inspired the place's originator – a prostitute of some fame in years gone by (hence the feminine version of the bar's name). It's all leopard skins, gaudy cushions, plush drapes and moody corners – very warm and cosy on a winter's evening, although it kind of belts you in the eye when you walk in for the first time. Mixed drinks cost around L12,000 and the place is generally open until at least 3 am. It operates a 'membership' policy – you should be able to get away with filling out a card as a pro forma operation. It is closed Wednesday.

For all kinds of music from jazz to Latin rhythms, try **Caffè La Torre** *(Map 7; ☎ 055 68 06 43, Lungarno Benvenuto Cellini 65r)*. This is a great place to just hang out drinking until the wee hours. The tipples are reasonable (around L10,000 for decent mixed drinks) and this is one of the only places in Florence where you can get a bite to eat well after midnight (see the Places to Eat section earlier in the chapter.

Live Music

In some cases you may be asked to pay a membership – this is effectively like paying a one-off cover charge. If you are staying in Florence for any length of time give a local address so that you receive your card – generally valid for a year.

Often people just blag their way into a place. 'Yes, I'm a member but I left my *tessera* (membership card) at home,' must be one of the most oft-used lines in Florence. In some places the request is a formality anyway and if you can't produce a card you will be asked to fill out a new one or some kind of replacement form. Establishments do this to keep their noses clean with the law and maintain their status as 'clubs', which brings tax breaks.

In addition to the places in this section, some of those listed under Discos/Clubs later in the chapter also present live music on occasion. Check out *Firenze Spettacolo* or *Zero55* to see what's happening where.

City Centre & Towards Santa Croce

The **Jazz Club** *(Map 4; ☎ 055 247 97 00, Via Nuova de' Caccini 3)*, is one of Florence's top jazz venues. The atmosphere is low-lit and the music there to be enjoyed without necessarily killing the conversation – a good mix. At the weekend you should book a table if you are going in a group. You pay L10,000 to get in (which is for a year's membership – if you have a local address for them to mail you your card! After that expect to pay around L12,000 a drink (a bottle of unspectacular Chianti will cost L35,000).

Another place where you can catch a little jazz, blues or whatever else they happen to come up with is **Bebop** *(Map 3; ☎ 055 239 65 44, Via dei Servi 76r)*. You head downstairs to a mellow environment and average-priced drinks. Basically the music consists of light covers but can be quite pleasant, and the place doesn't seem to get too crowded. Many nights the music is free, although if they are convinced they have a class act on you may pay as much as L20,000 (including a drink). They close by about 2 am.

ltrarno Later in the week, *M'areseis* *lap 5; ☎ 055 234 39 21, Via de' Bardi -6r)* is a happening place, with live acts of ll types on Wednesday and Thursday, hile on Friday and Saturday the club is ut in the hands of DJs. Earlier on in the eek it is pretty much dead. You have to ay L10,000 membership the first time round.

ther Areas Some of the bigger venues re well outside the town centre. *Tenax Map 1; ☎ 055 30 81 60, Via Pratese 46)* is ne of the city's more popular clubs and is vell out to the north-west of town. It is one f Florence's biggest venues for Italian and nternational acts. Bus Nos 29 and 30 from tazione di Santa Maria Novella will get ou there, but you'll be looking at a taxi to et home.

Another venue for bands is *Auditorium log (Map 2; ☎ 055 49 04 37, Via M Mer-ati 24b)* in the Rifredi area, also north of he centre but a little closer than Tenax. It's ot as big (in any sense) as Tenax but has a easonable stage and dance area. Bus Nos 8 nd 14 go from the train station.

Depending on who is playing at these venues, admission costs from nothing to .20,000. Then the drinks will cost you on op of that – around L10,000 for a mixer. Doors generally open at 10 pm.

Discos/Clubs

Beware of places claiming that entrance is free. Very often late-night bars and clubs operate a rather strange system whereby you pay to leave rather than to enter. This may take several forms and often you get a chit on buying a first drink. You present the chit on your way out.

City Centre & Towards Santa Croce

Maramao Club (Map 7; ☎ 055 24 43 41, Via de' Macci 79r) has all the appearance of a bar but it stays open well past 2 am and the DJs keep the music suitably deafening so that you can at least imagine you're in a club. A fairly small, narrow affair with a minuscule dance area on what could be de-scribed as the poop deck at the back, it can

get packed beyond comfort at the weekend. Entry with one drink is L20,000. Thereafter drinks cost L10,000. This is one of those places where you are given a card on entry that is then exchanged for a different one on purchase of a drink – you need this to get back out again. It's closed Monday and Tuesday.

Yab (Map 6; ☎ 055 21 08 84, Via Sassetti 5r) is in the heart of town near the main post office. It's supposedly an 'in' place with the locals but is really a little sad, with a repu-tation as more of a meat market than a seri-ous dance venue. It's closed Sunday and from late May to September.

Oltrarno Somewhat hidden from the main tourist streams, *Jaragua (Map 2; ☎ 055 234 65 43, Via dell'Erta Canina 24a)* is a cool Latin place where you can admire some pretty slick movers or join in if you think you have rhythm. Sip on a Banana Mama, Jaragua or Culo Bello ('Nice Ass').

The Cascine The city's two main clubs are here. They are quite fun, without exactly being the last word in European nightlife. In both you will be given a card on entry. You use this to get drinks (and food if you want). It is swiped on your way out, which is when you pay. You will be obliged to pay for at least one drink whether you have one or not – this is effectively your admission charge. A word of warning about the Cascine – it is a haunt for prostitutes, pimps and other in-teresting fauna. A taxi is probably not a bad idea when you head home.

Central Park (Map 2; ☎ 055 35 35 05, Via Fosso Macinante 2) is one of the city's most popular clubs. What music you hear will depend partly on the night, although as you wander from one dance area to another you can expect a general range from Latin and pop through to house. In summer you can also opt to dance inside or under the stars. You will be obliged to buy at least one drink at around L15,000. The place gener-ally opens until 6 am. It's closed Monday.

Nearby *Meccanò (Map 2; ☎ 055 331 33 71, Viale degli Olmi)* is right up there in popularity with Central Park. Three dance spaces offer house, funk and mainstream commercial music to appeal to a fairly broad range of tastes. Admission usually costs L15,000 to L20,000 and the club is open until 5 am. It is closed Sunday, Monday and Wednesday.

Other Areas Both *Tenax* and *Auditorium Flog* (see Live Music earlier in this section) usually serve as discos after the bands have finished or when none has been on.

Lidò (Map 2; ☎ 055 234 27 26, Lungarno Pecori Giraldi) is often thought of as a dance club but tends to put on a lot of jazz and soul music too. Sometimes it's live, sometimes it's vinyl. The place can be a little cramped and attracts a fairly young crowd. Things generally kick off around 10 pm and admission is free. It is closed on Monday.

Gay & Lesbian Venues

Florence ain't exactly memorable for gay nightlife, but there are a few places you can head to, some genuinely gay and others 'gay-friendly'.

Bars A relaxed little place to hang out and get acquainted with the remainder of the scene is *Piccolo Café (Map 7; ☎ 055 24 17 04, Borgo Santa Croce 23r)*. You should probably make this your first stop if you are a gay male. Try to pick up a copy of *Il Giglio Fuchsia* (The Pink Lily), a locally produced gay guide to Tuscany. There are usually some lying around the place. The bar is open until 1 am.

Crisco (Map 7; ☎ 055 248 05 80, Via Sant'Egidio 43r) is a strictly men-only club open until 4 am during the week and 6 am on Friday and Saturday. It's closed Tuesday.

Discos/Clubs Florence has only two serious gay clubs where you can dance through the wee hours and then some. *Tabasco (Map 6; ☎ 055 21 30 00, Piazza Santa Cecilia 3r)* boasts a disco, cocktail bar and dark room. Wednesday is leather night. It stays open until 4 am. On Tuesday, Friday and Saturday there is a disco and the place thumps until 6 am.

The alternative is *Flamingo Bar & Tabasco Disco (Map 7; ☎ 055 24 33 56, Via Pandolfini 26r)*. Italy's first gay bar, it is open until 4 am for gay men only. There's a dark room and video room. Thursday to Saturday it stays open until 5 am, with a disco for gay men and women. It is closed Monday.

Both places are free to get in, but you are obliged to have at least one drink (a L12,000).

Classical Music & Opera

Concerts, opera and dance are performed at various times of the year at the *Teatro Comunale (Map 2; ☎ 055 21 11 58, Corso Italia 16)*, on the northern bank of the Arno. In May and June the theatre hosts Maggio Musicale Fiorentina, an international concert festival. Contact the theatre's box office for details.

There are also seasons of drama, opera, concerts and dance at the *Teatro Verdi (Map 7; ☎ 055 21 23 20, Via Ghibellina 101)*, from January to April and October to December.

The Amici della Musica (☎ 055 60 84 20) organise concert series from January to April and October to December at the *Teatro della Pergola (Map 4; ☎ 055 247 96 51, Via della Pergola 18)*.

Several other venues have theatre seasons, including the Teatro della Pergola during the winter.

Cinemas

You have a few choices of venue for seeing movies in their original language *(versione originale)*. The *Odeon Cinehall (Map 6; ☎ 055 21 40 68, Piazza Strozzi)* screens such movies every Monday evening. For films in English most evenings except Monday, try *Cinema Astro (Map 5; Piazza San Simone)*. *Astra Cinehall (Map 6; ☎ 055 29 47 70, Via Cerretani 54r)* screens films in English from Monday to Wednesday. Finally, *Cinema Goldoni (Map 5; ☎ 055 22 24 37, Via de' Serragli)* presents subtitled movies on Wednesday nights.

From June to September you can enjoy outdoor cinema at several locations – check with the APT tourist office.

Theatre & Dance

One of the council's smarter ideas some years back was to convert the Leopolda train station (near the Cascine) into a performance space – in fact several spaces. Theatre, most of it of an avant-garde nature, is frequently the star, although occasionally concerts are put on too at the *Ex-Stazione Leopolda (Map 2; Viale Fratelli Rosselli 5)*. For programmes and tickets it is easiest to go to Box Office (see the start of the Entertainment section) or the tourist office.

Spectator Sport

Football (Soccer) Florentines are as passionate about their football as the next Italian, but their side, AC Fiorentina, has never quite been one of the crème de la crème of the Italian premier league. However, on a good day they can produce the goods – they managed to beat Arsenal at Wembley in a European Cup match in late 1999.

If you want to see a match, tickets, which start at L35,000 and can easily rise beyond L200,000, are available at the Stadio Comunale Artemio Franchi in the Campo di Marte (Map 2; ☎ 055 58 78 58) or at the Chiosco degli Sportivi ticket outlet (Map 6; ☎ 055 29 23 63; while you're at it you can have a flutter on the *Totocalcio* or football pools) on Via Anselmi, just off Piazza della Repubblica. It is open from 9 am to 1 pm and 3 to 7 pm Tuesday to Thursday; from 9 am to 7 pm on Friday; from 9 am to 1 pm and 3 to 8 pm on Saturday; and from 9.30 am to noon on Sunday.

You can also book them through the Box Office ticket outlet or Ticket One (see the start of the Entertainment section).

SHOPPING

It is said that Milan has the best clothes and Rome the best shoes, but Florence without doubt has the greatest variety of goods. The main shopping area is between the Duomo and the Arno, with boutiques concentrated along Via Roma, Via de' Calzaiuoli and Via Por Santa Maria, leading to the gold-

JANE SMITH

The atmosphere alone makes an AC Fiorentina match worth a visit.

smiths lining the Ponte Vecchio. Window-shop along Via de' Tornabuoni, where the top designers, including Gucci, Saint-Laurent and Pucci, sell their wares.

By the way, Gucci and Prada each have massive wholesale stores in the Tuscan countryside. The savings, especially compared with, for example, London and Paris prices, can be considerable. Some Japanese tour companies organise trips that have these stores as their prime objective!

The Gucci outlet (☎ 055 865 77 75) is at Via Aretino 63 (the SS67 highway) at the northern edge of Leccio, about 30–40 minutes south-east of Florence on the road to Arezzo. It is open from 9 am to 7 pm Monday to Saturday.

The Prada outlet (☎ 055 919 05 80), which has the elegance of a high street store with a cafe and taxis waiting, is just outside the village of Levanelle, about another half hour down the same road towards Arezzo. It opens from 9.30 am to 12.30 pm and 1.30 to 6 pm Monday to Friday (2.30 to 6 pm on Saturday) and in the afternoon only on Sunday. The quickest way by car is to take the A1 motorway, leave at the Valdarno exit and follow the signs for Montevarchi.

The open-air market (Map 3), on Monday to Saturday near Piazza del Mercato Centrale, offers leather goods, clothing and jewellery at low prices, but quality varies greatly. You could pick up the bargain of a lifetime, but check the item carefully before paying. It is possible to bargain, but not if you want to use a credit card. The flea market (Map 7), on Monday to Saturday at Piazza dei Ciompi, off Borgo Allegri near Piazza Santa Croce, specialises in antiques and bric-a-brac.

Florence is famous for its beautifully patterned paper, which is stocked in the many stationery and speciality shops throughout the city and at the markets.

GETTING THERE & AWAY
Air

Florence is served by two airports, Amerigo Vespucci (Map 1; ☎ 055 306 17 00), a few kilometres north-west of the city centre at Via del Termine 11, and Galileo Galilei (☎ 055 50 07 07; ☎ 055 21 60 73 at the Florence Air Terminal in the train station) near Pisa and about an hour by train or car from Florence. Vespucci serves domestic and European flights. Galileo Galilei is one of northern Italy's main international and domestic airports and has regular connections to London, Paris, Munich and major Italian cities.

A few airlines are represented in Florence itself. Alitalia (Map 6; ☎ 055 2 78 88 or ☎ 147 86 56 43) is at Lungarno degli Acciaiuoli 10–12r; TWA (Map 6; ☎ 055 239 68 56) is at Via de' Vecchietti 4 and Lufthansa (Map 6; ☎ 055 21 79 36) is c/o City Center Intertravel, Via de' Lamberti 39r.

Bus

The SITA bus station (Map 3; ☎ 055 21 47 21), Via Santa Caterina da Siena 15, is just to the west of Stazione di Santa Maria Novella. There is a direct, rapid service t Siena, and buses leave here for Pogg bonsi, where there are connecting buse for San Gimignano. Direct buses serv Arezzo, Castellina in the Chianti regio and other smaller cities throughou Tuscany.

Several bus companies, including CA (☎ 055 24 46 37) and COPIT (☎ 055 21 5 51), operate from Largo Fratelli Alinari, the southern end of Via Nazionale (Map 3 with services to nearby towns includin Prato and Pistoia.

Lazzi (Map 3; ☎ 166 84 50 10), Piazz Adua 1, next to the train station, runs se vices to Rome, Pistoia and Lucca.

Lazzi forms part of the Eurolines ne work of international bus services. You ca for instance, catch a bus from Paris, Pragu or Barcelona to Florence. A detaile brochure of all Eurolines services is avai able from their ticket office.

Train

Florence is on the Rome–Milan line, whic means that most of the trains from Rome Bologna and Milan are intercities or th *pendolino*, for which you have to pay a sup plement. There are also regular trains to an from Venice (three hours) and Trieste. From Verona you will generally need to change a Bologna. To get to Florence from Genoa an Torino, a change at Pisa is often necessary

The train information office is in front o platform 5 at Stazione di Santa Mari Novella – it's open from 7 am to 9 pm daily A porter service (Map 3; ☎ 055 21 23 19 operates from the train station; they charge L4500 per article to ferry your luggage to your hotel.

Car & Motorcycle

Florence is connected by the A1 to Bologna and Milan in the north, and Rome and Naples in the south. The Autostrada de Mare (A11) connects Florence with Prato Lucca, Pisa and the coast. Alternatively from Pisa or Livorno take the toll-free SGC *superstrada* (also known as the Fi-Pi-Li) Another toll-free superstrada connects the city with Siena.

Exits from these roads into Florence are well signposted and there are tourist offices on the A1 both north and south of the city. From the north on the A1, exit at Firenze Nord and then simply follow the bulls-eye '*centro*' signs. If approaching from Rome, exit at Firenze Sud. The more picturesque SS67 connects the city with Pisa to the west and Forlì and Ravenna to the east.

For car rental details, see the following Getting Around section.

GETTING AROUND
The Airports
The No 62 bus runs approximately every 20 minutes between the Stazione di Santa Maria Novella and Amerigo Vespucci airport. The service from the airport runs from 5.30 am to 10.45 pm; from the train station it runs from 6 am to 10.20 pm. The trip takes 15 minutes (although it can take much longer with traffic). Buy a normal city bus ticket (L1500).

Regular trains leave from platform No 5 at Stazione di Santa Maria Novella for Galileo Galilei airport in Pisa. Check in your luggage 15 minutes before the train departs. Services are roughly hourly from 7.51 am to 5.05 pm from Florence, and from 10.44 am to 5.44 pm from the airport (only until 4.44 pm at the weekend). The trip takes an hour and 20 minutes. A couple of bus services run to meet flights for which no trains run. Two of these are run by SITA (VOLAinBUS), departing at 11.15 am and 9.20 pm from near the taxi rank. The fare is L20,000 and you are dropped at the SITA terminal in Via Santa Caterina di Siena, just by the train station. The railways run a third bus at 12.49 am for late arrivals.

Bus
ATAF (Azienda Trasporti Area Fiorentina) buses service the city centre, Fiesole and other areas in the city's periphery. For information, call ☎ 055 565 02 22.

You'll find several bus stops for most routes around the Stazione di Santa Maria Novella. Some of the most useful lines operate from a stop just outside the south-east

exit of the train station below Piazza Adua. Buses leaving from here include:

No 7, for Fiesole
No 13, for Piazzale Michelangelo
No 62, for Amerigo Vespucci airport
No 70, night bus for the Duomo and the Uffizi

Bus tickets can be bought at tobacconists or automatic vending machines at major bus stops before you get on the bus and must be validated in the machine as you enter. You can buy tickets and pick up a useful routes brochure at the ticket office in among the series of ATAF bus stops on Largo Alinari just outside the south-east exit of the train station. Tickets cost L1500 for 60 minutes and L2500 for three hours. A 24-hour ticket costs L6000.

Car & Motorcycle
Traffic is restricted in the city centre and parking is prohibited. Non-residents may only drive into the centre to drop off or pick up luggage from hotels or to park in hotel or public garages (the latter will cost you a fortune).

There are several major car parks and numerous smaller parking areas around the fringes of the city centre. If you are planning to spend the day in Florence, your best option is to park at the Fortezza da Basso, which costs L1500 per hour.

If your car is towed, call ☎ 055 30 82 49. You will have to pay L90,000 to recover it plus whatever fine you are charged.

Rental Avis (Map 3; ☎ 055 239 88 26) is at Borgo Ognissanti 128r, Europcar (Map 5; ☎ 055 29 04 38) at Borgo Ognissanti 53r and Hertz (Map 3; ☎ 055 239 82 05), at Via Maso Finiguerra 33r.

Alinari (Map 3; ☎ 055 28 05 00), Via Guelfa 85r, rents scooters, larger mopeds and bicycles. In summer it also sets up shop at several camp sites – check at the APT tourist office for details. Mopeds/scooters cost from L28,000 to L50,000 for five hours, or from L35,000 to L80,000 per day. Motorbikes cost up to L180,000 per day. You can rent a bicycle for L12,000

FLORENCE

for five hours, L20,000 per day or L40,000 per weekend.

Taxi

Taxis can be found outside Stazione di Santa Maria Novella. Alternatively, you could call ☎ 055 42 42, 055 47 98 or 055 43 90. The flagfall is L3000 and then around L2500 per kilometre within the city limits. You are also charged at a slower rate for waiting time (at lights and so on) and L1000 per item of luggage.

Around Florence

ne of the beauties of Florence, believe it
not, is leaving it behind. Whether it's just
make a delicious lunchtime assault on the
arby towns of Fiesole and Settignano, ex-
ore the hilly wine region of the Chianti to
e south or check out less-visited towns to
e north and west, there's no shortage of
ings to do. Public transport, while often
ow, enables you to get to most places
sted in this chapter without excessive dif-
culty, although you shouldn't be overly
mbitious about how much you try to get
one. With your own motor, the world, as
ey say, is your oyster (which is fine if you
ke oysters).

IESOLE

erched in hills about 8km north-east of
lorence, between the valleys of the Arno
nd Mugnone rivers, Fiesole has attracted
e likes of Boccaccio, Carducci, Giovanni
Dupré, Marcel Proust, Gertrude Stein and
rank Lloyd Wright, all drawn by the lush
live groves and valleys – not to mention
e spectacular view of Florence. Fiesole
vas founded in the 7th century BC by the
Etruscans and remained the most important
ity in northern Etruria. The views and
resh air alone make it worth your trouble to
ome up. It makes a fabulous spot for a pic-
ic and a short walk, and there's even a
ttle sightseeing to be done.

The APT tourist office in Florence, or its
counterpart in Fiesole (☎ 055 59 87 20), Pizza Mino da Fiesole 36, can assist with in-
ormation about the town, accommodation,
valks and other activities. Most other services – including a bank, an ATM and a
post office – are located around the tourist
office.

Things to See & Do

Opposite the tourist office in Piazza Mino
da Fiesole is the **cathedral**, started in the
11th century and altered in the 13th cen-
ury, although a 19th-century renovation
has eradicated many earlier features. Be-

Highlights

- Tuck into a hearty serving of *bistecca alla fiorentina* in one of the fine restaurants of Fiesole and Settignano
- Visit the Roman amphitheatre of Fiesole
- Explore the Chianti region in search of enticing country towns like Greve and some of Italy's best-known wines
- Seek out Leonardo da Vinci's home town, Vinci
- Go ceramic shopping in the town of Montelupo

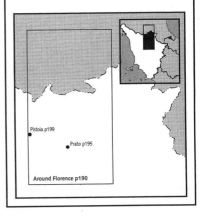

Pistoia p199

Prato p195

Around Florence p190

hind the cathedral is the **Museo Bandini**,
featuring an impressive collection of early
Tuscan Renaissance works, including
Taddeo Gaddi's *Annunciazione* and Petrarch's beautifully illustrated *Trionfi* (Tri-
umphs).

Opposite the entrance to the museum on
Via Portigiana, the **Zona Archeologica** features a 1st-century BC Roman theatre that
is used from June to August for the Estate
Fiesolana, a series of concerts and performances. Also in the complex are a small
Etruscan temple and Roman baths, which
date from the same period. The small

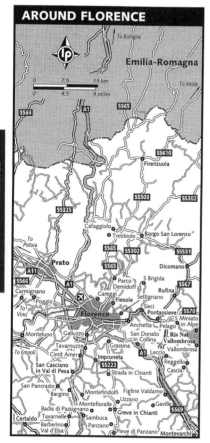

Places to Stay & Eat

The camping ground at Fiesole is t **Campeggio Panoramico** (☎ 055 59 90 (*Via Peramonda 1*), which also has bung lows for hire. Take bus No 70 from Piaz Mino da Fiesole.

The city has several hotels but most a quite expensive. **Bencistà** (☎ 055 5 91 6 *Via Benedetto da Maiano 4*), about 1k short of Fiesole just off the road from Flc ence, is an old villa and from its terra there is a magnificent view of Florenc Half board is compulsory at L130,000 p person. It might bust the budget, but for o or two days it's well worth it. Ask for room with a view (couldn't resist it).

One of the best places to eat in Fiesole the **Trattoria Cave di Maiano** (☎ 055 5 9 *33, Via Cave di Maiano 16*). In summer yo can sit in the pleasant garden. Count o about L70,000 for good Florentine coo ing. Getting here without a car is a litt tricky as the restaurant is actually in Maian a *frazione* of Fiesole, and off the bus route You could try getting a taxi from centr Fiesole (or indeed Florence if you're n counting the pennies too closely). Th restaurant is closed on Monday lunchtim

Otherwise, there are several restauran of varying quality around Piazza Mino d Fiesole. If you're thirsty, you might wa to have a pint at **JJ Hill Irish Pub** (☎ 05 55 93 24, Piazza Mino da Fiesole 40 which is popular and opens nightly unt 1.30 am.

Getting There & Away

Fiesole is easily reached from Florence ATAF bus No 7 from the Stazione di San Maria Novella in Florence connects wit Piazza Mino da Fiesole, the centre of thi small town. If you are driving, find you way to Piazza della Libertà, north of th Duomo, and then follow the signs t Fiesole.

SETTIGNANO

Just 6km south-east of Fiesole along a de lightful back-country lane, Settignan offers even more splendid views of Flor ence than Fiesole (come in the morning, a

archaeological museum is worth a look, as it includes exhibits from the Bronze Age to the Roman period. Both museums open from 9 am to 7 pm (5 pm in winter) daily except the first Tuesday of each month. The L10,000 ticket gives entry to both museums and the archaeological zone.

If you are planning a picnic, or just want a refreshing walk, head uphill along the main street from Piazza Mino da Fiesole to Via Corsica. Take Via Pelagaccio, which eventually becomes a dirt track as it weaves around the mountain overlooking Florence and winds back into Fiesole.

y early afternoon all you can see is glare). is a pleasant little *borgo* worth visiting for ne dining opportunity alone. **La Cap-oncina** (*☎ 055 69 70 37, Via San Romano 7r*) is one of the city's better-known estaurants, up in the hills overlooking Florence to the north-east. The kitchen is known n particular for its *tagliata di manzo*, succulent beef fillets sliced up and served on a ed of rocket. Sitting in the garden is a true pleasure in summer. You are sure of being several degrees cooler than down in Florence. Count on paying about L70,000 a lead for a full meal.

You can get bus No 10 from the Stazione li Santa Maria Novella or Piazza San Marco in Florence (this service is replaced rom 9 pm by the No 67). The restaurant is a few steps off the central Piazza San Tommaseo, where the bus terminates. It is closed on Monday.

THE MEDICI VILLAS

The Medici built several opulent villas in he countryside around Florence as their wealth and prosperity grew during the 15th and 16th centuries. Most of the villas are now enclosed by the city's suburbs and industrial sprawl, and are easily reached by taking ATAF buses from the train station. Ask at the APT tourist office in Florence for details of bus numbers and opening times.

The **Villa Medicea La Petraia**, about 3.5km north of the city, is one of the finest. Commissioned by Cardinal Ferdinando de' Medici in 1576, this former castle was converted by Buontalenti and features a magnificent garden. It's on Via della Petraia and opens from 9 am daily except the second and third Mondays of the month. Closing time varies from 4.30 pm in the winter months to 7.30 pm from June to August. Admission is L4000.

Farther north of the city, the **Villa Medicea di Castello** was the summer home of Lorenzo the Magnificent. You may only visit the park. Admission details are the same as for the Villa Medicea La Petraia.

The **Villa Medicea di Careggi** (*☎ 055 427 97 55*), Viale Pieraccini 17, is open from 8 am to 6 pm daily except Sunday (groups

must book ahead). Entry to the villa where Lorenzo the Magnificent breathed his last in 1492 is free, but access is limited as it is used as administration offices for the local hospital.

Another Medici getaway was the **Villa di Poggio a Caiano**, about 15km from Florence on the old road to Pistoia. Set in magnificent sprawling gardens, the interior of the villa is sumptuously decorated in frescoes and furnished much as it was early in the 20th century as a royal residence of the Savoys. Visits inside (L4000) are permitted every hour from 9.30 am to 6.30 pm (5.30 pm from mid-September to May). You can wander around the grounds for free. The easiest way here without your own transport is with the COPIT bus service running between Florence and Pistoia – there is a bus stop right outside the villa.

THE MUGELLO

The area north-east of Florence leading up to Firenzuola, near the border with Emilia-Romagna, is known as the Mugello and features some of the most traditional villages in Tuscany. The Sieve river winds through the area and its valley is one of Tuscany's premier wine areas.

Start with the APT tourist office in Florence, or contact the Comunità Montana del Mugello (*☎ 055 849 53 46*), Via P Togliatti 45, Borgo San Lorenzo. Promo Mugello (*☎ 055 849 42 20*), Piazza Martin Luther King 5-6, Borgo San Lorenzo, can help with hotel information and bookings.

The Medici originated from the Mugello and held extensive property in the area. Some of their family castles, villas and palaces are open to the public, while others can be visited with a guide.

Just outside Pratolino, the **Parco della Villa Medici-Demidoff** was the focal point of one of the Medici family's villas, which was demolished in 1824. The Demidoff family acquired the land and transformed the property into a fine romantic garden. If you keep following the SS65 for another 13km you will reach a turn-off (east) for **Trebbiolo** and, a few kilometres further on, another for **Cafaggiolo**, both sites of

AROUND FLORENCE

Medici villas. The APT tourist office in Florence has more details, otherwise contact the Associazione Turismo Ambiente (☎ 055 845 87 93), Piazza Dante 29, Borgo San Lorenzo.

If you're interested in a wineries tour, there is a so-called *strada del vino* (wine road) mapped out, which will take you through the areas producing Chianti Rufino and Colli Fiorentini. Again, the Florence APT tourist office has details. Also ask about the various walking trails through the Mugello.

EAST OF FLORENCE
Vallombrosa

An interesting little excursion, most easily accomplished with your own transport, has as its prime objective the cool forest of Vallombrosa and the *abbazia* of the same name. Although you can get to many of the following spots by bus, doing things this way could turn the following enterprise into a project of several days!

Exiting Florence eastwards along the SS67 (follow the blues signs for Arezzo), you first strike a Commonwealth war cemetery half a kilometre short of **Anchetta**. It is sobering to stop here and think of the soldiers who died in and around Florence in 1944.

You follow the road to **Sieci**, whose Romanesque church is accompanied by a graceful, slender bell tower. A detour north (signposted) would take you up to the one-time Pazzi family's **Castello del Trebbio**, a typical 12th-century fortified rural outpost that now operates as an *agriturismo*. You can go horse riding here and/or stock up on wine.

Back on the SS67, you next pass through **Pontassieve**, a busy little town picturesquely set on the Sieve river. Shortly after, take the SS70 for a short distance, turning off for **Pelago**, which is perched high on a ledge overlooking farming valleys. From here it's another 12km to **Vallombrosa**. As you wind higher, the forest thickens with the fir trees planted over the centuries by the Vallombrosan monks and the air freshens noticeably (it's a great little escape in summer).

The abbey is almost 1000m above se level. Back in the 11th century, San Giovanni Gualberto formed this branch of th Benedictine order in the midst of what n doubt was an even more impressive fores The monks set themselves the task of wip ing out simony and corruption in th Church in Florence and eventually th abbey came to play an important role in th city's politics. The monks were booted ou by Napoleon and only since the 1950s hav they returned to get the monastery back i working order. The church is open from 9 am to noon and 3 to 6 pm. You can wan der into the grounds any time.

The surrounding area is great for picnic and walks, including one up to **Monte Sec chieta** (1449m). At the abbey and i **Saltino**, 2km further down the road, yo will find a few restaurants and places t stay. From here we follow the road south t **Reggello** and **Cascia** (which has a small Ro manesque church) and finally on to **Figlin Valdarno**. The centre of this town, onc known as Florence's granary, has a coupl of interesting buildings, including the 14th century Palazzo Pretorio, the seat of loca power. Much of the city wall and its tower still stand.

Another detour here would see you head ing 6km south-west to **Gaville** (you coul catch the local Maddii bus) to see the 11th century Romanesque Pieve di San Romolo set in olive groves.

Back in Figline Valdarno, you can follow the SS69 back up to Florence.

THE CHIANTI REGION

The hills and valleys spreading out betweer Firenze and Siena are known as 'Il Chianti' Since the area's home to some of the country's best-marketed wines, they don't call i Chiantishire for nothing. In some of the small-town tourist offices they just assume everyone who wanders in speaks English Of the wines, Chianti Classico is the mos well known. It is a blend of white and red grapes and sold under the Gallo Nerc (Black Cockerel) symbol.

Now the Chianti is indeed very pleasant – lots of rolling hills, olive groves and vine-ards. In among them stand the many cas-les of Florentine and Sienese warlords and Romanesque churches known as *pievi*. But perhaps the hype has been just a trifle over-done. In Tuscany alone there is plenty of more spectacular country to be seen (around Pitigliano, for instance, or up in the Apuan Alps). Not that we want to put you off, but the Tuscan countryside by no means begins and ends in the Chianti.

It is possible to catch buses around the Chianti countryside, but the best way to ex-plore the area is by car. However, you might also like to do it by bicycle, or even on foot. You could take a few days to travel along the state road SS222, known as the Strada Chiantigiana, which runs between Florence and Siena.

Budget accommodation is not the area's strong point, and you'll need to book well ahead, since it is a popular area for tourists year-round. However, if you have some extra funds and you're in search of a romantic spot, you shouldn't pass the Chianti by.

Getting information about the area is easy. Virtually every tourist office in Tus-cany has good information, but the best is at Radda in Chianti. The tourist office there also has a Web site (see under Radda in Chianti in the Central Tuscany chapter). For more details about Chianti wines, and Tus-can wines in general, see the special section 'The Tuscan Table'.

Chianti Fiorentino

South of Florence If you are heading down from Florence under your own steam, you might want to call in at the **Castello di Verrazzano** along the way. It's about 1.5km west of the Strada Chiantigiana, just before Greti. The word castle, as often in this area, is a little overplayed – these places tend to be fortified manors. This one is well known for its wine. You can drop by to taste and buy and even have a meal on the terrace, from where you have fine views across the valleys. Ring ahead (☎ 055 85 42 43) to check the restaurant's opening hours. An-other castle, **Uzzano**, lies a little further south. Follow the signs east of the Strada Chiantigiana.

Greve in Chianti About 20km south of Florence on the Chiantigiana is Greve in Chianti, a good base for exploring the area. You can get there easily from Florence on a SITA bus. The unusual triangular 'square', Piazza Matteotti, is the old centre of the town. An interesting provincial version of a Flor-entine piazza, it is surrounded by porticoes.

The tourist office (☎ 055 854 52 43) at Via L Cini 1, 500m east of the piazza, opens from 10 am to 1 pm and 4 to 7 pm in sum-mer. It can provide maps and information in several languages, including English. If you're looking for a place to stay, try *Gio-vanni da Verrazzano* (☎ 055 85 31 89, Pi-azza Matteotti 28), with singles/doubles for L110,000/130,000. The *Del Chianti* (☎ 055 85 37 63, Piazza Matteotti 86) is less inter-esting and charges L160,000/ 180,000.

Montefioralle is an ancient castle-village, only 2km west of Greve. It's worth the walk, particularly to see its church of Santo Stefano, which contains precious medieval paintings. From Montefioralle, follow the dirt road for a few hundred metres, then turn off to the right to reach the simple **Pieve di San Cresci**. From here you can descend directly to Greve.

Badia di Passignano About 7km west, in a magnificent setting of olive groves and vineyards, is the mighty Badia di Passig-nano, founded in 1049 by Benedictine monks of the Vallombrosan order. The abbey is a massive towered castle encircled by cypresses.

The abbey church of San Michele has early 17th-century frescoes by Passignano (so called because he was born here). In the refectory there's an *Ultima Cena* done by Domenico and Davide Ghirlandaio in 1476. Take a look at the huge medieval chimney in the kitchen. It is possible to visit the abbey (☎ 055 807 16 22) from 3 to 5 pm on Saturday and Sunday, but you can try to persuade the monks to let you in at other times. Food and drinks are available in the tiny village surrounding the abbey.

Panzano Travelling south along the Chian-tigiana you will pass the medieval village of

AROUND FLORENCE

Panzano; after about 1km, turn off for the Chiesa di San Leolino at **Pieve di Panzano**. Built in the 10th century, it was rebuilt in Romanesque style in the 13th century. You can then continue south into the Chianti Senese (see the Central Tuscany chapter).

Florence to the Val d'Elsa

Another route south from Florence could start from the Certosa di Galluzzo (see the Florence chapter). You could take the SS2 *superstrada* that connects Florence with Siena or the more tortuous and windy road that runs alongside it. Follow the latter to **Tavarnuzze**, where you could make a detour for **Impruneta**, about 8km south-east.

Impruneta is famed for its production of terracotta – from roof tiles to more imaginative garden decorations. The centre of town is Piazza Buondelmonti. Not the most fascinating of Chianti towns by any stretch, it has been around since the 8th century. Its importance historically was due above all to an image of the Madonna dell'Impruneta, supposedly miraculous, now housed in the Basilica di Santa Maria, which looks onto the piazza.

Back at Tavarnuzze, you head south past the **US war cemetery** to **San Casciano in Val di Pesa**. An important wine centre, the town came under Florentine control in the 13th century and was later equipped with a defensive wall, parts of which remain intact. The town centre itself is not overly interesting, however, so you could drink in the views and hit the road again.

Just before Bargino, take the side road east for **Montefiridolfi**. It's one of those charming little detours that takes you winding up on to a high ridge through vineyards and olive groves. Along the way you pass the **Castello di Bibbione**, a ponderous stone manor house. Another 1.5km brings you to a large Etruscan tomb. You can keep going until you hit a crossroads. From there turn west for **Tavarnelle Val di Pesa**, from where you can reach the charming little medieval borgo of **Barberino Val d'Elsa**, which is worth a stop for a brief stroll along the main street.

At Tavarnelle you have the option of staying in a youth hostel, the **Ostello de Chianti** (☎ *055 807 70 09, fax 055 805 0 04, Via Roma 137*). It costs L16,000 a nigh including breakfast, and L14,000 for mai meals. They also have family rooms. Th building is a rather characterless moder job and is open from March to the end c October.

Heading directly south from Barberin would take you to Poggibonsi, from whe you can make bus connections for Sa Gimignano (see the Central Tuscany chap ter). Some of the spots indicated above ca be reached by bus (especially with the SIT. company) from Florence, but it can b painfully slow going making progress th way.

Certaldo

About 15km west of Barberino lies thi pretty hilltop town, well worth the effort c a detour, although this move takes you ou of Chianti territory. The upper town (Cer taldo Alto) is particularly captivating in th warm glow of the late-afternoon sun. Th high town has Etruscan origins, while th low town in the valley sprang up in the 13t century – by which time both had been ab sorbed into the Florentine republic.

The upper town was the seat of the Boc caccio family. Giovanni Boccaccio died an was buried here in 1375. You can visit th largely reconstructed version of his hous (it was severely damaged in WWII) alon Via Boccaccio, the upper town's mai street, from 10 am to 12.30 pm and 2.30 t 6 pm daily. Admission is free. The librar inside contains several precious copies o Boccaccio's *Decameron*. A couple of door up, the Chiesa di SS Jacopo e Filipp houses a cenotaph to the writer.

The whole walled borgo of the uppe town is commanded by the stout figure o the Palazzo Pretorio, the seat of powe whose 14th-century facade is richly decor ated with family coats of arms. You ca wander inside from 10 am to 1 pm and 2.3 to 7.30 pm daily, for L5000. Frescoed hall lead off the Renaissance courtyard.

A real find if you need a place to stay i **Fattoria Bassetto** (☎ *0571 66 83 42*

bassetto@dedalo.com), 2km east of Cer-
aldo on the road to Siena. A 14th-century
enedictine convent, it was transformed
ato a farm by the Guicciardini counts. It is
arrounded by a garden complete with
wimming pool and offers dorm-style
ccommodation for L30,000 a night. In the
djacent 19th-century manor house, roman-
c rooms with antique furniture cost
100,000 per person. Book in advance.

See Lonely Planet's *Walking in Italy* for
etails of a three-day walk from Certaldo to
an Gimignano and on to Volterra.

PRATO

ostcode 59100 • pop 171,100

irtually enclosed in the urban and indus-
ial sprawl of Florence, 17km to the south-
ast, Prato is one of Italy's main centres for
extile production. Founded by the Liguri-
is, the city fell to the Etruscans and later
ie Romans, and by the 11th century was an
nportant centre for wool production. It is

worth visiting on your way to the more picturesque cities of Pistoia, Lucca and Pisa to
the west.

Orientation & Information

The old centre is small and is surrounded by
the city wall. The main train station, on Piazza della Stazione, is to the east of the city
centre.

The APT tourist office (☎ 0547 2 41 12)
is at Via B Cairoli 48–52, two blocks east
of the central Piazza del Comune, and is
open from 9 am to 1 pm and 4 to 7 pm (2.30
to 6 pm in winter), Monday to Saturday.

The main post office is at Via Arci-
vescovo Martini 8.

The police station (*questura*; ☎ 0547 55
55) is well out of the centre at Via Cino 10,
but operates a small station at Via B Cairoli
29. For medical emergencies, the Ospedale
Misericordia e Dolce (☎ 0547 43 41) is in
Piazza dell'Ospedale, south-west of Piazza
del Comune.

AROUND FLORENCE

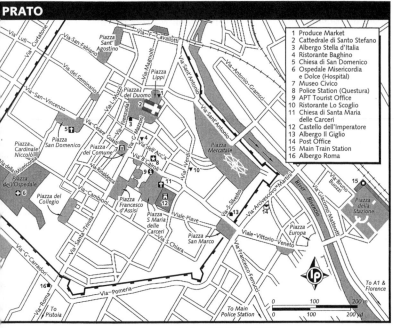

PRATO

1 Produce Market
2 Cattedrale di Santo Stefano
3 Albergo Stella d'Italia
4 Ristorante Baghino
5 Chiesa di San Domenico
6 Ospedale Misericordia
   e Dolce (Hospital)
7 Museo Civico
8 Police Station (Questura)
9 APT Tourist Office
10 Ristorante Lo Scoglio
11 Chiesa di Santa Maria
   delle Carceri
12 Castello dell'Imperatore
13 Albergo Il Giglio
14 Post Office
15 Main Train Station
16 Albergo Roma

euro currency converter L10,000 = €5.16

Museo Civico

This museum, with its small but impressive collection of largely Tuscan paintings, is housed in the imposing medieval Palazzo Pretorio on Piazza del Comune. Among the artists represented are Filippo Lippi and Vasari. The museum is open from 10 am to 7 pm, daily except Tuesday (morning only on Sunday). Admission is L10,000.

Cattedrale di Santo Stefano

Along Via Mazzoni from Piazza del Comune is Piazza del Duomo and the 12th-century Cattedrale di Santo Stefano. The rather simple Pisan-Romanesque facade features a lunette by Andrea della Robbia and the white-and-green marble banding you will find elsewhere in Tuscany (Siena, Pistoia, Lucca). The most extraordinary element, however, is the oddly protruding **Pulpito della Sacra Cintola** jutting out over the piazza on the right-hand side of the main entrance. The eroded panels of the pulpit, designed by Donatello and Michelozzo in the 1430s, are in the **Museo dell' Opera del Duomo** next door. The pulpit was expressly added on so that the *sacra cintola* (sacred girdle) could be displayed to the people five times a year (Easter, 1 May, 15 August, 8 September and 25 December). It is believed the girdle (or belt) was given to St Thomas by the Virgin, and brought to the city from Jerusalem after the Second Crusade.

In medieval times great importance was attached to such holy relics, but just how many girdles did Mary have? Another, declared the real thing in 1953 by the Orthodox Patriarch of Antioch, is stored in the Syrian city of Homs.

Among the magnificent frescoes inside the church look for those behind the high altar by Filippo Lippi, depicting the martyrdoms of John the Baptist and St Stephen, and Agnolo Gaddi's *Legend of the Holy Girdle* in the chapel to the left of the entrance.

Chiesa di Santa Maria delle Carceri

Built by Giuliano da Sangallo towards the end of the 15th century, the interior of this church is considered a Renaissance masterpiece, with a frieze and medallions of the Evangelists by the workshop of Andrea della Robbia.

Also on Piazza Santa Maria delle Carceri is the **Castello dell'Imperatore**, built in the 13th century by the Holy Roman Emperor Frederick II. The castle is open from 9.30 to 11.30 am and 3.30 to 7 pm (3 to 5.30 pm in winter), daily except Tuesday and Sunday afternoon.

Chiesa di San Domenico

The main reason for dropping by this church is to have a look at the **Museo di Pittura Murale**, a collection of 14th- to 17th-century frescoes and graffiti, reached through the church's cloister. It is open from 10 am to 1 pm and 3.30 to 7 pm, daily except Tuesday (morning only on Sunday). Entry costs L8000.

Special Events

Outside town in Poggio a Caiano they have been celebrating the Festival delle Colline since 1979. The concert series brings together class acts of world music from late June to late July. In 1999 they included Portugal's Madredeus and the UK's Billy Bragg.

Places to Stay & Eat

The *Albergo Stella d'Italia* (☎ 0547 2 79 10, Piazza del Duomo 8), looking across to the cathedral, has singles/doubles from L60,000/90,000 (or L90,000/115,000 with private bath). *Albergo Roma* (☎ 0547 3 13 77, Via G Carradori 1) has singles/doubles from L75,000/90,000. The same people run *Albergo Il Giglio* (☎ 0547 3 70 49, Piazza San Marco 14), where they charge L85,000/110,000 for pleasant singles/doubles with bathroom (or L20,000 less for rooms without their own bath). They are disposed to a little horse trading in slow periods 'in the interest of customer relations' – whatever that means.

There is a produce market in Piazza Lippi, open from 8 am to 1 pm, daily except Sunday. A most pleasant spot for a meal is *Ristorante Lo Scoglio* (☎ 0547 2 27 60, Via Verdi 40), where the whole deal will cost

The Merchant of Prato

'Fate has so willed that, from the day of my birth, I should never know a whole happy day...' So wrote one of Prato's most celebrated sons, Francesco di Marco Datini, in the 1390s.

Datini, to whom a statue was erected in the shadow of the Palazzo Pretorio after his death in August 1410, was neither a hero of the battlefield nor a great statesman. Nor was he a man of learning or an inventor. Born in 1335 to a poor innkeeper, Datini grew up to become a highly successful international merchant.

Although he never reached the dizzy heights of the great Florentine trading families, Datini carved out for himself a respectable business empire that stretched from Prato and Florence to Avignon, Barcelona and the Balearic Islands. Not bad for a 15-year-old boy who arrived in Avignon, then a thriving political and trading centre by virtue of the Pope's presence, with 150 florins from a small land sale.

JANE SMITH

From rags to riches – Datini went on to become the richest man in Prato.

Prato was (and remains) a town of shopkeepers and small businesses. Datini rose above this and, by the time of his return from Avignon 33 years later, was the richest man in town. For the people of Prato, this made him something of a hero. In the following years he put his wealth to work in the creation of, well, more wealth. Basing himself principally in Florence, he traded in just about anything that looked likely to turn a profit. Indeed, in those years he and most other traders frequently headed up their letters and business papers with the pious exclamation: 'In the name of God and Profit'. At one stage he ran what was considered one of the most modern banking houses in Europe.

Through his branches in Italy, France and Spain, and agents in London, Flanders and elsewhere, he moved cloth, raw materials, arms, slaves, primary produce – you name it, he had an interest in it.

Datini knew how to have fun, and the stories of his banquets, luxury possessions and womanising demonstrate he was no aesthete. On the other hand, he worked like a slave himself, often sleeping no more than four hours a night. Only at the end of his life did he seem to give thought to things other than the accumulation of money. In his will he left all his wealth (after bequests) to a new charitable foundation established in his name in his fine house on Via Rinaldesca.

It is not so much Datini's financial exploits that make him interesting today. Something of a control freak, he spent long hours every day writing correspondence, not only to his branches but to his wife Margherita and friends too. He was meticulous about keeping all mail that came to him and ordered his branch managers to do the same. His charity, the Ceppo di Francesco di Marco (housed in his former home), has kept the archive of this correspondence in one piece for more than 500 years. It provides a rare glimpse not only into the business life of a late medieval trader, but also into the daily life of middle-class Tuscans, especially in Prato and Florence.

Iris Origo distilled this wealth of material into a fascinating account of medieval life, predictably entitled *The Merchant of Prato*.

you around L40,000 a head. It is closed Monday. **Ristorante Baghino** (☎ 0547 2 79 20, Via dell'Accademia 9) is in much the same vein. It's closed Sunday and Monday lunchtime.

Getting There & Around

CAP and Lazzi buses operate regular services to Florence (L3500, 45 minutes) and Pistoia from in front of the train station, on Piazza della Stazione. Prato is on the Florence–Bologna and Florence–Lucca lines. By car, take the A1 from Florence and exit at Calenzano, or the A11 and exit at Prato Est or Ovest. The SS325 connects Prato with Bologna. Several buses, including the No 5, connect the train station with the cathedral.

PISTOIA

postcode 51100 • pop 90,200

A pleasant city at the foot of the Apennines and a half-hour west of Florence by train, Pistoia has grown beyond its well-preserved medieval ramparts and is today a world centre for the manufacture of trains. In the 16th century the city's metalworkers created the pistol, named after the city.

Orientation & Information

Although spread out, the old city centre is easy to negotiate. From the train station in Piazza Dante Alighieri, head north along Via XX Settembre, through Piazza Treviso, and continue heading north to turn right into Via Cavour. Via Roma, branching off the north side of Via Cavour, takes you to Piazza del Duomo and the APT tourist office (☎ 0573 2 16 22), which is open from 9 am to 1 pm and 3 to 6 pm, Monday to Saturday (year round). You can hire a 'Cityphone', a handheld gismo that looks like a big phone and gives you a running commentary along a set route through the city. It costs L15,000.

The main post office is at Via Roma 5, and an unstaffed Telecom phone booth is on Corso Antonio Gramsci, near Via della Madonna.

The police station (questura; ☎ 0573 2 67 05) is out of the centre at Via Macallé

23. The public hospital (Ospedale Riuniti ☎ 0573 35 21) is off Viale Giacomo Matteotti, behind the old Ospedale del Ceppo. If you need a doctor fast, call ☎ 057 36 36.

Piazza del Duomo

Much of Pistoia's visual wealth is concentrated on this central square. The Pisan Romanesque facade of the **Cattedrale** **San Zeno** boasts a lunette of the Madonna col Bambino fra due Angeli (Madonna and Child with two Angels) by Andrea della Robbia, who also made the terracotta tile that line the barrel vault of the main porch. Inside, in the Cappella di San Jacopo, is the remarkable silver Dossale di San Jacopo (Altarpiece of St James). It was begun in the 13th century, with artisans adding to it over the ensuing two centuries until Brunelleschi contributed the final touch, the two half figures on the left side.

The venerable building between the cathedral and Via Roma is the **Antico Palazzo dei Vescovi**. Guided tours four times a day take you through what little remains of an original Roman-era structure on this site as well as displays of artefacts dating as far back as Etruscan times, which were discovered during restoration work.

Across Via Roma is the **Battistero** (Baptistry). Elegantly banded in green-and-white marble, it was started in 1337 to design by Andrea Pisano.

Dominating the eastern flank of the piazza, the Gothic Palazzo del Comune houses the **Museo Civico**, with works by Tuscan artists from the 13th to 19th centuries. The museum is open from 10 am to 6 pm, Tuesday to Saturday (9 am to 12.30 pm on Sunday and on holidays). Admission is L6000 (free on Saturday afternoon).

The portico of the nearby **Ospedale del Ceppo** will stop even the more monument weary in their tracks, for the terracotta frieze by Giovanni della Robbia is quite unique. It depicts the Virtù Teologali (Theological Virtues) and the Sette Opere di Misericordia (Seven Works of Mercy) and is one of the best examples to come from the della Robbia family workshops.

Special Events

For a weekend in mid-July Pistoia hosts Pistoia Blues, one of Italy's bigger music events. Patti Smith, Jethro Tull and even Deep Purple (!) performed in 1999. Tickets range from L38,000 for one night to L90,000 for all three.

Places to Stay

There are a couple of cheap places to stay here. *Hotel Firenze* (☎ 0573 2 31 41, Via Curtatone e Montanara) has singles/doubles for up to L50,000/80,000, or L65,000/100,000 with bathroom. These

prices should include breakfast, and without the grub you may be able to talk them down a little. You can pick up a pokey single/double at *Albergo Autisti* (☎ 0573 2 17 71, Via Antonio Pacinotti 89) for L30,000/50,000, or a slightly better double with its own bathroom for L70,000.

Places to Eat

A produce market is open most days in Piazza della Sala, west of the cathedral. *Pizzeria Tonino* (☎ 0573 3 33 30, Corso Antonio Gramsci 159) is a pleasant trattoria where a meal could cost L25,000. It's closed on

AROUND FLORENCE

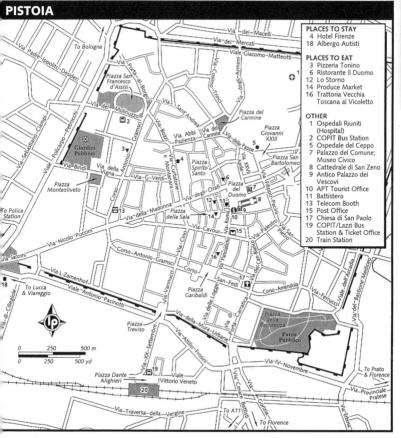

PISTOIA

PLACES TO STAY
4 Hotel Firenze
18 Albergo Autisti

PLACES TO EAT
3 Pizzeria Tonino
6 Ristorante Il Duomo
12 Lo Storno
14 Produce Market
16 Trattoria Vecchia Toscana al Vicoletto

OTHER
1 Ospedali Riuniti (Hospital)
2 COPIT Bus Station
5 Ospedale del Ceppo
7 Palazzo del Comune; Museo Civico
8 Cattedrale di San Zeno
9 Antico Palazzo dei Vescovi
10 APT Tourist Office
11 Battistero
13 Telecom Booth
15 Post Office
17 Chiesa di San Paolo
19 COPIT/Lazzi Bus Station & Ticket Office
20 Train Station

Monday. *Trattoria Vecchia Toscana al Vicoletto* (☎ *0573 2 92 30, Via Panciatichi 4*) is good but slightly more expensive, with pasta from L10,000. It's closed on Sunday. *Ristorante Il Duomo* (☎ *0573 3 19 48, Via Bracciolini 5)*, also closed on Sunday, is a cheap self-service buffet place open for lunch only from noon to 3 pm.

If you are looking for something a little special but still affordable, try your luck at *Lo Storno* (☎ *0573 2 61 93, Via del Lastrone 8)*. An *osteria* of one sort or another has been documented on this site for the past 600 years! Today the chef prepares a continually changing array of dishes. You are unlikely to spend more than L50,000 a head for a full meal. The restaurant is closed on Sunday.

Getting There & Around

Buses connect Pistoia with most towns in Tuscany. The main ticket office for COPIT and Lazzi buses is on the corner of Viale Vittorio Veneto and Via XX Settembre, near the train station, and most buses leave from just outside (those for Florence depart from Piazza Treviso, at the other end of Via XX Settembre – tickets cost L5000 and the journey takes 50 minutes). Other COPIT buses leave from Via del Molinuzzo, off Piazza San Francesco d'Assisi.

Trains connect Pistoia with Florence (L4200, 40 minutes), Bologna, Lucca and Viareggio. By car, the city is on the A11, and the SS64 and SS66, which head northeast for Bologna and north-west for Parma respectively. Bus Nos 10 and 12 connect the train station with the cathedral, although the city is easily explored on foot.

WEST OF FLORENCE

West of Florence and south of Pistoia lie several towns of secondary interest. If time is on your side you could include them in a trip between Pistoia and Florence. There is little reason to stay in any of these places, but all have hotels if you get stuck.

Vinci

A small country road (the SP13) leads south out of Pistoia towards Empoli. After a long series of winding curves through the forested high country of the Monte Alban you come across a sign pointing left to the Casa di Leonardo (Leonardo's House) Anchiano. It's about 1km up the hill. Here it is believed, Leonardo da Vinci was bor the bastard child of a Florentine solicitc Piero. Whether or not it is the real thin you can poke your nose around inside fro 9.30 am to 7 pm (6 pm in winter) for fre

Back down at the SP13, you are abo 1.5km short of arriving in Vinci itself. Th town is dominated by the Castello d Guidi, named after the feudal family th lorded it over this town and the surroundi area until Florence took control in the 13 century. Inside the castle nowadays is th **Museo Leonardiano**. This contains an i triguing set of more than 50 models base on Leonardo's far-sighted designs. Th hours are the same as for his house and a mission is L7000. Down below the castle the **Museo Ideale Leonardo da Vinci**, a pr vate competitor to the above museum and little on the silly side. It opens from 9 am 1 pm and 3 to 7 pm daily. Admission L5000 and not really worth it.

COPIT buses run regularly between Er poli and Vinci. To get to/from Pistoia y need to change at Crocifisso for the Pi toia–Lamporecchio bus. The drive fro Pistoia is lovely, as indeed is the ride b tween Poggio a Caiano (see the Medici Vi las section above) and Vinci via the wi centre of **Carmignano**.

Empoli

From Vinci you can connect south by reg lar COPIT bus to Empoli, a busy provinci centre of 43,000 on the Arno. It's a fair nondescript sort of a place, although th small centre is pleasant enough. The R manesque white-and-green-marble façac (reminiscent of what you can see at the Ba tistero in Florence) of the **Collegiata Sant'Andrea** in Piazza Uberti is testimor that the medieval settlement that emerg from a place called Emporium must ha been of some importance. Subject to th Guidi lords, in the 12th century the city w allowed to raise defensive walls. In 1182

ʌose to join Florence to escape the feudal
ɔke.

On the western edge of town rises the
ɪmewhat worn profile of the 12th-century
hiesa di Santa Maria a Ripa. The original
ʌwn, documented in the 8th century, lay
ʲre.

The bus from Florence to Empoli costs
ʲ5000 and takes 70 minutes.

ʌontelupo

ɔp on a train on the Pisa–Florence line to
ʲad back towards Florence. If you have
ʲne and the inclination, you could get out
. Montelupo, a market town on the conflu-
ʲce of the Arno and Pesa. The town has
ʲen a well-known centre of Tuscan ceram-
ʲs production since medieval times and
ʲere is no shortage of shops here in which
. browse or part with money.

Before you do buy anything, you might
ʲant to inspect the **Museo Archeologico e
ʲlla Ceramica**, opposite the tourist office

at Via Baccio da Montelupo 43. It houses
examples of pottery from prehistoric times
right up to the 18th century. The museum,
housed in the 14th-century Palazzo del
Podestà, opens from 9 am to noon and 2.30
to 7 pm, daily except Monday. Admission is
L5000.

Across the Pesa stream, the Medici villa
known as the **Ambrogiana** and built for Ferdinando I is now a psychiatric hospital.

In the third week of every month a pottery market is held in an exposition centre
in Corso Garibaldi. In the last week of June,
Montelupo hosts an international pottery
fair, which might be a good time for ceramics fans to turn up for a day. If you want
to visit ceramics workshops, you may need
to make an appointment. Call ☎ 0571 91 75
27 for more information.

To get to Florence (or head west towards
Pisa) the easiest bet is the train, although
there is a bus that costs L4200 and takes 55
minutes.

AROUND FLORENCE

North-Western Tuscany

While the bulk of tourists in Tuscany battle their way through hordes of their confreres in Florence, Siena and the hill towns of the Chianti region and around, considerably fewer bother with the north-west.

Admittedly, a good number of day-trippers pour into Pisa (usually from Florence or en route to or from the nearby international airport) to get the obligatory look at the Leaning Tower but they tend to ignore the rest of the city. Lucca, a gracious medieval enclave sheltered behind impressive bulwarks, has certainly not been left untouched by the busloads, but the numbers remain manageable.

The curious wanderer aspiring to taste lesser known parts of the 'real Tuscany' has no shortage of options here. Walkers can get some serious mountain walking done in the Apuan Alps, known to Italians but largely ignored by foreigners.

Need to fit a spot of skiing in during a winter sojourn in Tuscany? Head for Abetone. It's not quite the Dolomites, but then the Dolomites are a mighty way off, aren't they?

In the rural Garfagnana and more rugged Lunigiana territories you can be pretty sure not to stumble across too many Hawaiian shirts and tour leaders waving little flags.

And this is marble territory. The business is centred above all on the town of Carrara, whose name is synonymous throughout the world with the best in exquisite white stone. To this day sculptors from all over the world (among many other less artistically inclined customers) seek their raw materials here, just as Michelangelo did four centuries ago.

You can even have a dip in the sea if you're in the area in summer. The seaside resorts are not terribly exciting (except when Viareggio puts on its party clothes for Carnevale in February), but quite acceptable. Locals clearly love 'em, to judge by the summertime crowds.

Highlights

- Take a walk in the Apuan Alps
- Relax in the walled town of Lucca, one of the most attractive in northern Tuscany
- Scratch your head in bewilderment at Pisa's Leaning Tower – will it stay up?
- Party at Viareggio's Carnevale in February and March
- Look around at the most famous marble quarries in the world – Carrara
- Explore the rural Garfagnana region and its towns, especially Barga

Carrara p226

Viareggio p222

Lucca p205

Ligurian Sea

Pisa p215

North Western Tuscany p203

LUCCA

postcode 55100 • pop 87,000

Hidden behind imposing Renaissance walls, Lucca is a pretty base from which explore the Apuan Alps and the Garfagnana, and is well worth a visit in its own right.

Founded by the Etruscans, Lucca became a Roman colony in 180 BC and a free commune during the 12th century, initiating a period of prosperity based on the silk trade. In 1314 it fell to Pisa but, under the leadership of local adventurer Castruccio

NORTH-WESTERN TUSCANY

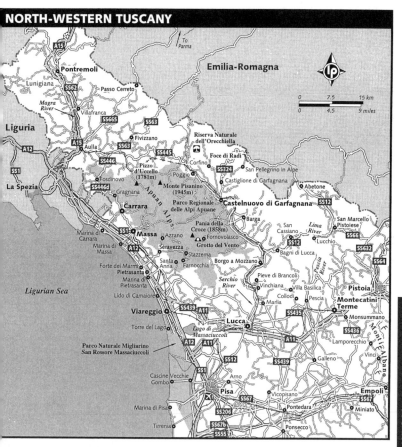

NORTH-WESTERN TUSCANY

astracani degli Anterminelli, the city re-
ained its independence and began to
nass territories in western Tuscany. Car-
ra was among these acquisitions, and the
onopoly of control over its marble trade
as a powerful element in the prosperity of
e city and the maintenance of its inde-
endence. Castruccio died in 1325 but
ucca remained an independent republic
r almost 500 years.

Napoleon ended all this in 1805 when he
eated the principality of Lucca. Unswerv-
g in his democratic values, he placed one
the seemingly countless members of his

family in need of an Italian fiefdom (this
time his sister Elisa, who in 1809 was entrusted with all of Tuscany) in control.
Twelve years later the city became a Bourbon duchy before being incorporated first
into the grand duchy of Tuscany in 1847
and subsequently into the Kingdom of
Italy.

Lucca remains a strong agricultural centre, although shoes and paper products are
also important to the city's economy.

The long periods of peace it enjoyed explain the almost perfect preservation of the
city walls: they were rarely put to the test.

Orientation

From the train station in Piazza Ricasoli, just outside the city walls to the south, walk north-west to Piazza Risorgimento and through Porta San Pietro. Head north along Via Vittorio Veneto to the immense Piazza Napoleone and on to Piazza San Michele – the centre of town.

Information

Tourist Offices The main APT tourist office (☎ 0583 41 96 89) is in Piazzale Verdi, on the western edge of the walled city. It is open from 9 am to 7 pm daily from about Easter to October. During the rest of the year opening times tend to be shorter, but vary from year to year. You can be fairly sure to find it closed on Sunday and public holidays in the off season.

On Piazza Santa Maria a smaller booth opens from 10 am to noon in the summer months only.

At the main office you can pick up an audio-tour of the city. The gizmo looks like a clumsy mobile phone and the commentary, which you listen to as you follow its directions around the town (this works here since the old centre is so compact), lasts two hours. You hire it for about four hours (thus giving you time to interrupt the thing and go and get a coffee or lunch) for L15,000 (L10,000 per person if there is more than one of you). It appears to be very popular.

Money The Deutsche Bank at Via Fillungo 76 has a user-friendly ATM, or you can change money over the counter. Several other banks with ATMs are scattered about town.

Post & Communications The main post office is in Via Vallisneri 2, just north of the cathedral, and the unstaffed Telecom phone centre is at Via Cenami 19. The latter has phonebooks for all of Italy, an increasingly rare thing.

Rinascimento (☎ 0583 46 98 73), Via C Battisti 58/60 is a higgledy-piggledy store with a few computers in it. They will let you go online under the following original conditions. Pay a L10,000 annual fee and you can get up to 30 minutes a day free. Sound pretty good if you hang about for a coup of days or more. Check out their Web site www.macciosoft.it/rinascimento.

Medical Services & Emergency T main hospital (☎ 0583 97 01) is on Via de Ospedale, beyond the city walls to t north-east. The police station (*questur* ☎ 0583 45 51) is at Viale Cavour 38, ne the train station.

Cathedral

Lucca's Romanesque cathedral, dedicat to St Martin, dates from the 11th centur The exquisite facade, in the Lucca-Pis style, was designed to accommodate t pre-existing bell tower. Each of the colum in the upper part of the facade was carv by a local artisan and all are quite differe from one another. The reliefs over the l doorway of the portico are believed to be Nicola Pisano.

The interior was rebuilt in the 14th a 15th centuries with a Gothic flourish. Ma teo Civitali designed the pulpit and, in t north aisle, the 15th-century *tempiet* (small temple) that contains the **Vol Santo**, an image of Christ on a wooden cr cifix said to have been carved by Nicod mus, who witnessed the crucifixion. It i major object of pilgrimage and each year 13 September is carried through the stre in a procession at dusk.

In the sacristy the tomb of Ilaria del Ca retto (wife of the 15th-century lord Lucca, Paolo Guinigi) is a masterpiece funerary sculpture executed (if you'll f give the expression) by Jacopo della Que cia. The church contains numerous oth artworks, including a magnificent *Ultir Cena* (Last Supper) by Tintoretto, over third altar of the south aisle.

Next to the cathedral is the **Museo de Cattedrale**, which houses religious mainly of the 15th and 16th centuri sculpture from the cathedral and illun nated manuscripts. Opening times for cathedral and museum are 10 am to 6 daily (to 2 pm between November a March). Admission to the museum and

LUCCA

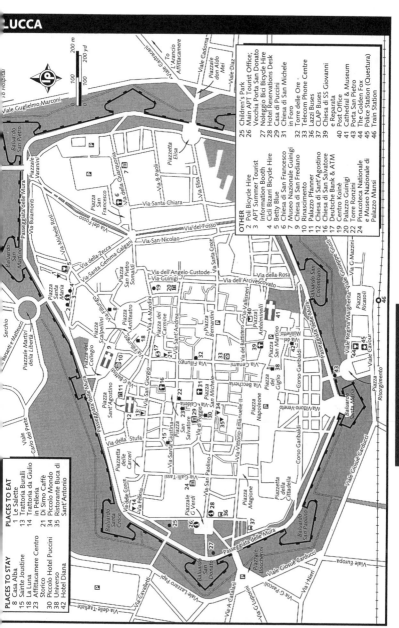

PLACES TO STAY
8 Casa Alba
15 Sainte Joustine
18 La Luna
23 Affittacamere Centro Storico
30 Piccolo Hotel Puccini
38 Universo
42 Hotel Diana

PLACES TO EAT
1 Le Salette
13 Trattoria Buralli
14 Trattoria da Giulio in Pelleria
21 Di Simo Caffè
34 Piccolo Mondo
35 Ristorante Buca di Sant'Antonio

OTHER
2 Poli Bicycle Hire
3 APT Summer Tourist Information Booth
4 Cicli Bizarri Bicycle Hire
5 Betty Blue
6 Chiesa di San Francesco
7 Museo Nazionale Guinigi
9 Chiesa di San Frediano
10 Rinascimento
11 Palazzo Pfanner
12 Chiesa di Sant'Agostino
16 Chiesa di San Salvatore
17 Deutsche Bank & ATM
19 Centro Koinè
20 Palazzo Guinigi
22 Torre Ronzini
24 Pinacoteca Nazionale e Museo Nazionale di Palazzo Mansi
25 Children's Park
26 Main APT Tourist Office; Vecchia Porta San Donato
27 Noleggio Bici Bicycle Hire
28 Hotel Reservations Desk
29 Casa di Puccini
31 Chiesa di San Michele in Foro
32 Torre delle Ore
33 Telecom Phone Centre
36 Lazzi Buses
37 CLAP Buses
39 Chiesa di SS Giovanni e Reparata
40 Post Office
41 Cathedral & Museum
43 Porta San Pietro
44 The Golden Fox
45 Police Station (Questura)
46 Train Station

euro currency converter L10,000 = €5.16

see the tomb of Ilaria del Carretto costs L5000.

Chiesa di SS Giovanni e Reparata

The 17th-century facade of this one-time cathedral of Lucca hides more than 1000 years of history. Parts of its *area archeologica* have even been dated to the 2nd century BC. Remains of the original early-Christian church and baptistry, built in the 5th century, are visible in the present Gothic baptistry. Roman remains of preceding buildings have been revealed below floor level and can be viewed. The church as you see it today is largely the 12th-century remodelling of its 5th-century predecessor, although some restructuring took place in later centuries. The church is open from 10 am to 6 pm daily (to 2 pm from November to March). Admission costs L2000.

Chiesa di San Michele in Foro

As dazzling as the cathedral is this Romanesque church, built on the site of its 8th-century precursor over a period of nearly 300 years from the 11th century. The wedding-cake facade is topped by a figure of the Archangel Michael slaying a dragon. Look for Andrea della Robbia's *Madonna e Bambino* (Madonna and Child) in the south aisle.

Near the church, off Via di Poggio, is the **Casa di Puccini**, where the composer was born. It houses a small museum dedicated to his life, which is open from 10 am to 1 pm and 3 to 6 pm (closed Monday). Admission costs L5000.

Via Fillungo

Lucca's busiest street, Via Fillungo, threads its way through the medieval heart of the old city and is lined with fascinating, centuries-old buildings. The **Torre delle Ore**, or city clock tower, is about halfway along. In medieval days its possession was hotly contested by rival families.

East of Via Fillungo

You would never know it by simply parading north along Via Fillungo, but just off to the east (accessed from Piazza Scalpellini)

is the place where local Thespians regular gathered in Roman days for a spot of ou door theatre. Centuries later the ov shaped theatre became **Piazza Anfiteatro** houses were built on the foundations of t imperial amphitheatre. In some respects i a bit of a theatre even today. Arty shops a cool cafes jostle to accommodate one a other around the edges of the one-tin stage.

A short walk farther east is **Piazza S Francesco** and the attractive 13th-centu church of the same name. Along Via de Quarquonia is the Villa Guinigi, whi houses the **Museo Nazionale Guinigi** a the city's art collection. It is open from 9 a to 7 pm (to 2 pm on Sunday and holiday closed Monday). Admission costs L4000

West of Via Fillungo

Another example of Lucca's adaptation Pisan Romanesque, the facade of t **Chiesa di San Frediano** features a uniq (and much-restored) 13th-century mosa The main feature of the beautiful basilic interior is the **Fontana Lustrale**, a 12 century baptismal font decorated wi sculpted reliefs. Behind it is an *Annun azione* by Andrea della Robbia.

Of some interest are the interior and a works of the **Pinacoteca Nazionale e Mus di Palazzo Mansi on** Via Galli Tassi. It open from 9 am to 7 pm (2 pm on Sund and holidays; closed Monday). Admissi costs L8000.

Palazzo Pfanner

Erected in the late 17th century, the palaz is a fine example of how the other half liv in Lucca. A sweeping flight of stairs lea up to the baroque residence, but most v itors are here for the ornate 18th-centu garden. It opens from 10 am to 6 pm dai between 1 March and 15 November. A mission costs L3000.

City Walls

If you have the time, do the 4km walk jog) along the top of the city walls. The ramparts were raised in the 16th and 1 centuries and are similar to the defens stems later developed by the French military engineer Vauban. When you have finished torturing any kids you may have with urches and high culture you could take em to the swings and things near the Vecia Porta San Donato.

ourses

he Centro Koinè (☎ 0583 49 30 40), Via Mordini 60, offers Italian courses for forgners. A two-week summer course costs 550,000, while month-long courses, availle year-round, cost nearly L900,000. The hool can also arrange accommodation.

pecial Events

ucca has hosted the Summer Festival since ●98, a concert series that, if 1999 was anying to go by, hosts an impressive series of ts. Elton John, Bill Wyman, Backstreet ɔys and James Taylor were among the ɔrformers in action in the city's Piazza Aneatro and Piazza Napoleone that year. It is ɔld in July and tickets cost from L40,000 L60,000 for the whole festival. Ask at the ain APT tourist office for further details.

laces to Stay

is always advisable to book ahead, but if ɔu're in a spot try the city's hotel associaɔn, the Sindacato Lucchese Albergatori ● 0583 49 41 81), at Via Fillungo 121, ay be able to help you find a room. If they ɪl, there is another hotel reservation desk ● 0583 31 22 62) at Piazzale G Verdi 1.

The city's HI youth hostel, Ostello Il Serio (☎ 0583 34 18 11, Via del Brennero ′3), is outside the walls to the north; take AP bus No 1 or 2 from Piazzale G Verdi. &B costs L18,000. It is open from 10 arch to 31 October.

Only four of the city's hotels are actually ːated within the walls of the old city. You n add to this a handful of affittacamere ɔoms to rent). It really makes a difference stay within the old city if possible, alough some of the extramural options are mittedly only a quick stroll away.

A good budget option smack in the heart town is Affittacamere Centro Storico 0583 49 07 48, Corte Portici 16). It

charges L70,000 for doubles and will discount for singles in slack periods. They don't accept newcomers after 8 pm. Another perfectly acceptable one to bed down in is Sainte Joustine (☎ 0583 58 79 64, Via Santa Giustina 30). The doubles are all much the same and cost up to L90,000. There is one single room for L70,000, but when business is slow they'll rent out doubles to lone travellers for the same price. Breakfast is included and bathrooms are in the corridor.

Another option is Casa Alba (☎ 0583 49 53 61, Via Fillungo 142), where you will be charged up to L60,000/80,000 for good, clean single/double rooms. Hotel Diana (☎ 0583 49 22 02, Via del Molinetto 11) has singles for L60,000 and doubles with bathroom for up to L105,000.

If you can afford the extra, the three-star Piccolo Hotel Puccini (☎ 0583 5 54 21, fax 0583 5 34 87, Via di Poggio 9) is a better deal: singles/doubles with bathroom cost L90,000/125,000. La Luna (☎ 0583 49 36 34, fax 0583 49 00 21, Corte Compagni 12) doesn't really have that much more going for it except for the guest parking. Here you will pay L140,000/200,000.

Another three-star place within the city walls is Universo (☎ 0583 49 36 78, fax 0583 95 48 54, Piazza del Giglio 1). It's on a charming square and with luck the prices may not be too exorbitant. When business is brisk you could be required to hand over as much as L195,000/260,000.

If you don't mind being outside the city walls, you could try L'Arancio Affittacamere (☎ 0583 49 65 17, Via Romana 57). Singles/doubles go for L70,000/90,000. The latter have private bathroom and TV and are quite pleasant.

Places to Eat

Lucca boasts a good selection of relatively reasonable trattorie (cheap restaurants). Piccolo Mondo (☎ 0583 5 52 65, Piazza dei Cocomeri 5) is a good spot for a cheap meal – there's a filling if basic set lunch menu for L12,500. It is closed Thursday and Friday evening.

Just around the corner, Ristorante Buca

Sant'Antonio (☎ *0583 5 58 81, Via della Cervia 3*) is a rather classier affair where you'll need about L50,000 per person for a full meal. It's closed Sunday evening and Monday.

Trattoria Buralli (☎ *0583 95 06 11, Piazza Sant'Agostino 9*) offers a simple but filling tourist menu for L18,000. It's closed Wednesday.

You'll also find several reasonably priced restaurants and pizza joints, including *Le Salette* (☎ *0583 46 78 47, Piazza Santa Maria)*. It is closed Wednesday.

One of the best compromises in town is *Trattoria da Giulio in Pelleria* (☎ *0583 5 59 48, Via delle Conce 45)*. A somewhat impersonal barn of a place, they serve up high quality food at very affordable prices. Service is efficient and just for once you should not let the multilingual menu put you off. The *maccheroni tortellati* are a particularly good first course. This place shuts its doors on Sunday and Monday.

Di Simo Caffè (☎ *0583 49 62 34, Via Fillungo 58)* is a grand bar and *gelateria* (ice-cream parlour) serving local specialities such as *buccellato*, a kind of sweet bun typical of Lucca. It is closed Monday.

Entertainment

Lucca doesn't exactly rock your soul, but you can down a pint at the *The Golden Fox* (☎ *0583 49 16 19, Viale Regina Margherita 207)* near the train station. It's closed Monday.

Otherwise one local mecca for a drink and, on Wednesdays and Fridays, some live music (jazz and rock respectively), is *Betty Blue* (☎ *0583 49 21 66, Via del Gonfalone 16/18)*. You can also get a good breakfast here. It's open until 1 am nightly.

Getting There & Away

CLAP buses (☎ *0583 58 78 97*) serve the region, including the Garfagnana. Lazzi (☎ *0583 58 48 77*) operates buses to Florence (L8600, 1¼ hours), La Spezia, Carrara and Pisa. Both companies operate from near Piazzale G Verdi.

Lucca is on the train line between Florence (L7300, 1¼ hours) and Viareggio, and

there are also services into the Garfagnan By car, the A11 passes to the south of t city, connecting it with Pisa and Viareggi The SS12, which becomes the SS445 Barga, connects the city with the Garfagnan

Getting Around

Most cars are banned from the city centr although tourists are allowed to drive in the walled city and park in the resident spaces (yellow lines) if they have a perm from one of the hotels. There are parki areas (not free) in piazzas Bernardini, Sa Martino, Napoleone and Boccherini. A some points along the road running th length of the walls you will find free par ing areas.

CLAP buses connect the train station, P azza del Giglio (near Piazza Napoleon and Piazzale G Verdi, but it is just as eas and more pleasurable, to walk.

You can hire bicycles from several ou lets. There is one near the main APT touri office (look for the Noleggio Bici sign Others, including Poli and Cicli Bizarri, a huddled together on Piazza Santa Mari Rates are similar wherever you go. A no mal bicycle costs L4000 per hour or L600 for a mountain bike (which you don't nee in town). Day rates are around L18,00 You can hire tandems too (but do you rea want to?).

For a taxi, call ☎ 0583 49 49 89.

EAST OF LUCCA
Villas

From the 16th to the 19th centuries, Lucc businessmen who had finally arrived bu themselves country residences – some 30 of them all told. Today most have gon have been abandoned or are inaccessib but a dozen fine examples still dot the cou tryside to the north-east of Lucca.

The **Villa Reale** at Marlia, about 12k from Lucca, is the most striking. Much its present look, and that of the metic lously planned gardens, is owed to t tastes of Elisa Baciocchi, Napoleon's sist and short-lived ruler of Tuscany. You c visit the gardens from March to Novemb You must join a guided tour (there are s

...m 10 am to 6 pm) which costs L9000. ...e grounds are closed Monday.

Not far off to the east but less engaging ...the **Villa Mansi**, at Segromigno in Monte. ...s, however, open year-round from 10 am ...12.30 pm and 3 to 5 pm (until 7 pm in ...mmer; closed Monday), and you can ...ter the villa buildings too. The gardens ...e a not entirely happy mix of rigid French ...sign and the intentionally haphazard Eng-...h style. Admission costs L9000.

A couple of kilometres farther on is the ...la Torrigiani** in Camigliano, whose gar-...ns stick more to the English taste. Some ...the *giochi d'acqua* (water games) still ...ork. Guests would be sprayed when they ...ast suspected it by a series of water-...urting mechanisms. The house is fronted ...a baroque facade, said to be among the ...st examples of the style in all of Tuscany. ...opens from 10 am to 12.30 pm and 3 pm ...sunset from March to early November ...losed Tuesday). Admission to the park ...d villa costs L15,000, or L10,000 to the ...rk alone.

To get to the villas, take the SS435 to-...ards Pescia then turn north for Marlia ...gnposted 7km east of Lucca). It's slow ...it possible with public transport (CLAP ...ses) and the Lucca APT tourist office can ...lp you with timetables. If you have your ...vn wheels (even of the hired bicycle vari-...y), so much the better.

...ollodi

...you stick to the SS435 you will, after an-...her 8km, reach a turn-off north to this ...vn. It is moderately interesting in its own ...ght, if only for the **Villa Garzoni**, whose ...ajestic gardens rise away from the en-...nce on the town's main road. The ...roque building, richly frescoed inside, is ...ite impressive, but the gardens are more ...sorbing. It's open from 9 am to sunset ...ily and admission costs L10,000. You ...uld also wander the steep lanes at the ...rthern end of town.

The **Parco di Pinocchio** (☎ 0572 42 93 ...) might be one for the kids. Pinocchio is ...ite a phenomenon in Italian literature ...d considerably more meaningful than the

Disney version – see the boxed text 'The Real Adventures of Pinocchio'). The Flor-entine Carlo Lorenzini, who spent some time when he was a child in Collodi, took the hamlet's name for a pseudonym, so the town felt it should repay the compliment with the park. It started off in 1956 as a monument to the writer and his creation and consisted of a bronze statue symbolising the moment when Pinocchio becomes a boy and a set of mosaics recounting the main episodes of the puppet's adventures. Later other elements were added, including Toy-land (Il Paese dei Balocchi), with bronze statues of characters out of the book. The park opens 8.30 am to sunset daily. Admis-sion costs L12,000 (L7000 for children).

Getting here can be a bit of a pain with-out your own car, as buses between Lucca and Montecatini Terme don't stop that often in Collodi. If you happen to have your own wheels, head north about 5km until you strike a sharp turn-off to the left for **Villa Basilica**, a high mountain town with a re-markable Romanesque church.

Pescia

Pescia is the self-proclaimed Tuscan flower capital. Three-quarters of all Tuscany's flori-culture businesses operate in and around here and the flower trade, including national and international exports, is worth some L250 billion annually. Every second September (even-numbered years) a flower fair is held in Pescia. The town, split by the north-south flow of the Pescia river, is quite an interest-ing place for a bit of a wander too.

The medieval heart of town is the unusu-ally long and uneven Piazza Mazzini, which gets busy on Saturday with the weekly mar-ket. The northern end is capped by the Palazzo Comunale and the Palazzo del Vic-ario – the latter dates back to the 13th cen-tury. A couple of streets to the west is the Chiesa di SS Stefano e Niccolao, dating partly to the 14th century. A couple of other fine palazzi around the church complete the picture on the western bank. The eastern bank is dominated above all by the Gothic Chiesa di San Francesco and the less inter-esting baroque cathedral.

NORTH-WESTERN TUSCANY

The Real Adventures of Pinocchio

No, the story of Pinocchio, the wooden puppet that eventually turns into a boy, is not a Walt Disney invention. It is rather one of the most widely read and internationally popular pieces of literature ever to emerge from Italy. Back in the early 1880s Carlo Collodi, a Florentine journalist, could hardly have guessed that the series he was writing for one of united Italy's first children's periodicals, *Storia di un Burattino* (Story of a Puppet), would become an international classic.

JANE SMITH

Later collated under the title *of Le Avventure di Pinocchio (The Adventures of Pinocchio)*, the tale would have made Collodi (a pseudonym taken from a town north-west of Florence where Carlo's family spent some time when he was a child) a multi-millionaire had he lived to exploit film and translation rights!

Collodi (his real name was Lorenzini) did not merely intend to pen an amusing child's tale. Literary critics have been trawling the text for the past century in search of ever more evidence to show that it was as much aimed at adult readers as kiddies.

The character of Pinocchio is a frustrating mix of the likeable and the odious. At his worst he is a wilful, obnoxious and deceitful little devil who deserves just about everything he gets. Humble and blubbering when things go wrong, he has the oh-so-human tendency to return to his dismissive ways when he thinks he's in the clear. The wooden puppet is a prime example of flesh-and-blood failings. You thought Jiminy Cricket was cute? Pinocchio thought him such a pain he splattered him against the wall (in the real, not the Disney version).

Pinocchio spends a good deal of the tale playing truant and one of Collodi's central messages seems to be that only good, diligent school-children have a hope of getting anywhere (or in this case of turning into a fine human lad). But Collodi was not merely taking a middle-class swipe at naughty-boyish behaviour. He was convinced that the recently united Italy was in urgent need of a decent education system to help the country out of its poverty and lethargy. His text can be read in part as criticism of a society as yet incapable of meeting that need.

Indeed the tale, weaving between fantasy and reality, is a mine of references, some more veiled than others, to the society of late-19th-century Italy – a troubled country with enormous socioeconomic problems and little apparent will to do much about them. Pinocchio waits the length of the story to become a real boy. But while his persona might provoke laughter, his encounters with poverty, petty crime, skewed justice and just plain bad luck constitute a painful education in the machinations of the 'real' world.

For those English-speaking adults curious enough to rediscover this little classic, the bilingual edition translated and prefaced by Nicolas J Perella and published by the University of California Press is a handsome tool for better understanding and enjoying the tale.

There's no need to stay overnight. About
e only people who do are those in the
ower business. On the eating front, head
r *Boutique del Cibo (Borgo della Vittoria*
. They do all sorts of cheap snacks and
ll meals that will cost about L35,000 all
including wine. It's closed Thursday.

CLAP buses connect Pescia with Lucca
,4300, 45 minutes, 18 buses daily). Plenty
' buses head east to Montecatini Terme
o. You can also make connections for
ollodi.

lontecatini Terme & Around

ain't the most exciting place in Tuscany
it if you are in need of spa baths, mud
icks and other related activities for beauty
· health reasons, Montecatini Terme is
ady for you. Grand Duke Pietro Leopoldo
ot the ball rolling, but the value of the
rings was known in Roman times. The
irliest bathing centres were built as early
; the 15th century.

The APT tourist office (☎ 0572 77 22 44),
iale Verdi 66 (actually the entrance is
ound the corner on Via Manzoni), is open
om 9 am to 12.30 pm and 3 to 6 pm Monay to Saturday (9 am to noon Sunday). It
is general information on the town and sur-
ounding area. For more specifics on the hot
oring centres and the various treatments
vailable, head next door to the Terme di
Iontecatini information office (☎ 0572 77
) at Viale Verdi 41. It's open similar hours
› the main APT tourist office and has a
Veb site at www.termemontecatini.it.

The springs are the thing. Nine separate
rme operate, many of them encased in
rand late-19th-century buildings ranging
om the moderately ornate to the rather
lly. They work from May to October, al-
iough some services in some of the baths
› on longer. The Excelsior is open year-
ound. The baths cater to beauty concerns
; much as health problems. At the Excel-
or's Centro di Benessere (Thermal Well-
eing Centre), you can have anything from
facial hair removal session (for the girls
L5000) through to a body and facial with
iud and bath (L100,000). The range of ser-
ces, treatments and medical tests avail-

able is staggering. You could spend a week
here and go broke, but at least you'd feel
good for a while.

A pleasant distraction is to take the late-
19th-century funicular railway *(funicolare)*
uphill to Montecatini Alto. This small quiet
borgo has inevitably ceded to temptation
and the pretty central square is given over
to cafes that probably could not exist without the passing thermal tourist trade. Afi-
cionados of Montecatini's waters, such as
Giuseppe Verdi, have been keeping those
very cafes in business for quite some time.
Such visitors are considerably more benign
than was Cosimo I de' Medici, who had the
medieval town largely destroyed and its
walls pulled down after it had been taken
and used by Henri II of France in his campaign against Medici Florence.

The funicular railway operates from
10 am to midnight (until 7.30 pm Monday)
every 30 minutes (with a lunch break from
1 to 3 pm). It costs L8000 return or L4500
one way (you can also get up and down by
local bus).

Montecatini is crawling with hotels. If you
do decide to stay, try to get into *L'Etrusco*
(☎ 0572 7 96 45, Via Talenti 2) up in Montecatini Alto. In the high season you will probably be obliged to pay full board, which
comes to L90,000 per person, but at other
times you should be able to negotiate for a
room alone. It also has a good, mid-priced
restaurant (closed Wednesday). Again, there
are plenty of places to choose from to satisfy
your hunger in the main town.

Montecatini Terme is on the train line between Lucca and Florence. Regular buses,
running from the station next to the train
station, service Florence (L5800, 50 minutes), Pistoia, Lucca, Pescia, Monsummano
(L1600) and other nearby locations.

Monsummano

Diehard lovers of spa complexes could also
wander over to Monsummano, a few kilometres away from Montecatini Terme by
bus (L1600). There's really nothing much
here apart from the Grotta Giusti Terme,
just outside town. It is a spa complex and
hotel, but non-guests are welcome to pay

NORTH-WESTERN TUSCANY

for use of the facilities. You can sit in the heat of Inferno, one of three caves steamed up with hot spa water. Again, a long list of health and beauty treatments is available. The centre opens from 9 am to 1 pm and 3 to 7 pm Monday to Saturday, between 22 March and 13 November. The bus goes right to the complex.

THE GARFAGNANA

The heart of the Garfagnana is in the valley formed by the Serchio river and its tributaries. This is a good area for trekking, horse riding and a host of other outdoor pursuits, and the region is well geared for tourism. The tourist offices in Lucca or Pisa can advise, or you can approach the tourist offices in Castelnuovo di Garfagnana. Pro Loco tourist offices in several smaller villages can help with details on hotels and *rifugi*. Many use this area as a launch pad for treks into the Apuan Alps (see the 'Tuscany on Foot' special section at the end of the Facts for the Visitor chapter).

The SS12 sneaks away from the north walls of Lucca (follow the signs for Abetone) and proceeds to follow the Serchio river valley northwards. It is a fairly uneventful route but hides a few surprises off to the sides. If you turn east at **Vinchiana** and follow the narrow winding road a few kilometres you will arrive at the **Pieve di Brancoli**, a fine 12th-century Romanesque church.

Farther upstream you hit **Borgo a Mozzano**, where you cannot fail to miss the extraordinary medieval Ponte della Maddalena (also known as Ponte del Diavolo, or Devil's Bridge). Each of its five arches is different, and the engineer must have been on interesting drugs. Typical of the era, the bridge rises to a midpoint and then descends to the other side of the Serchio – only the 'midpoint' here is well off centre!

Bagni di Lucca

A few kilometres farther on as the SS12 curves east and just past the turn-off north for Barga (where we return shortly) is Bagni di Lucca. Since Roman days the thermal waters have been much appreci-

ated and an 11th-century document co tains instructions on how best to use t waters for cures. In the early 19th centu the place became particularly well know both to the gentry of Lucca and to an inte national set. Byron, Shelley, Heinri Heine and Giacomo Puccini were amoi the celebrity guests to take the waters. T dignified neoclassical buildings are a r minder that the town's heyday belongs times gone by.

The town straggles along the Lima riv and seems to have two focal points. At t end farthest from Lucca are clustered couple of reasonable hotels and the rath splendid old *Circolo dei Forestieri (☎ 058 8 60 38, Viale Umberto I)*. This 'Foreigne Club' seems to have straight out of Victorian time You can dine well here for a steal if y take the set menu at L20,000. It's close Monday and Tuesday lunchtime.

The hotels in question include *Hot Roma (☎/fax 0583 8 72 78, Viale Umber I 110)*, where decent singles/doubles wi bath will cost L55,000/75,000, and t slightly more upmarket *Hotel Svizzer (☎/fax 0583 80 53 15, Via Casalini 30* about a five-minute walk away. Here the charge anything up to L65,000/90,000.

Lazzi buses from Lucca run here seve times daily (fewer on Sunday and hol days).

The Lima Valley & Abetone

The SS12 proceeds in a north-easterly d rection away from the Garfagnana into Pi toia province. If you felt the urge to do som skiing, then this would be the way to go.

En route, those with vehicles could ta a couple of small detours. **San Cassian** 10km from Bagni di Lucca, boasts a 12t century church, while **Lucchio**, anoth 10km farther on, is spectacular for its pos tion. A muddle of grey stone houses tight hugging the north-eastern slope of a gid high wooded ridge, which is topped by th ruins of a one-time fortress, this is one those places that seems to have stood still another epoch. Don't misunderstand, the is really nothing here beyond what is a ready described, but after the long windir

cent you feel you have entered another
scany. Try to compare in your mind the
lendours of Renaissance Florence with
e cold stark simplicity of this mountain
mlet.

Back down to earth, the SS12 passes
rough **San Marcello Pistoiese**. From here
e road banks north to gain altitude on its
cturesque way up to **Abetone**.

This latter is the centre of Tuscany's
ain skiing resort. It is not the Alps, but
s not bad. About 30 pistes ranging from
rely 500m to 3km will keep you amused
ough, with 28 lifts and tow-ropes to get
u around. One day's skiing costs
42,000 (L50,000 at weekends). A three-
y pass for weekdays costs L110,000,
hile a seven-day pass costs L195,000.
u can obtain tickets at the Ufficio Cen-
le Biglietti (☎ 0573 6 05 56) at Piazza
ramidi in Abetone. It's open from 8 am
1 pm and 3 to 7 pm daily. You can also
gn up for lessons with a couple of ski
hools.

The cheapest place to stay (by far) is the
stello della Gioventù (☎ 0573 6 01 17, Via
ennero 157), where you'll pay L18,000 a
ght for a dorm bed and breakfast. Full
oard costs L46,000 per person. Otherwise
e town has 15 hotels in which the cheap-
t rates for a single/double hover around
e L70,000/100,000 mark. Bear in mind
at at the height of the ski season the ho-
ls tend to prefer bookings of at least three
ys and may also make half board obliga-
ry. Another dozen or so hotels are strung
t in nearby towns. For those without their
vn transport, the easiest way up is to catch
bus from Pistoia (see the Around Florence
apter).

arga

he high point of the steep old town of
arga is quite literally the high point. Climb
the top of town for panoramic views and
ke a look inside the cathedral, built be-
veen the 10th and 14th centuries. The pul-
t is the prime object of curiosity,
quisitely carved and resting on four red
arble pillars. Look at them more closely.
he two front ones rest on lions dominating

a dragon and a heretic. One of the back pillars rests on an unhappy looking dwarf!

A fairly decent lower mid-range hotel not
too far from the old town is *La Pergola*
(☎ 0583 71 12 39, fax 0583 71 04 33, Via
San Antonio 46), where singles/doubles
with bathroom, TV and phone cost L78,000/
99,000. Another option that isn't bad is *Albergo Alpino* (☎ 0583 72 33 36, fax 0583
72 37 92, Via Pascoli 41), where you'll pay
L60,000/110,000. Both have their own
restaurants.

CLAP buses from Lucca run up to 11
times daily (L5000, 1¼ hours). The buses
stop in Piazzale del Fosso by Porta Man-
cianella, the main gate into the old city.
Other buses run to Castelnuovo di Garfagnana (as many as eight on school days; as
few as one otherwise) and Bagni di Lucca.

Castelnuovo di Garfagnana

Apart from the formidable 14th-century
Rocca, a castle built for the Este dukes of
Ferrara, there is not an awful lot to see here.
This is, however, one of the best centres to
get information on walking in the Apuan
Alps (for more information see the 'Tus-
cany on Foot' special section).

The Pro Loco tourist office (☎ 0583 64
10 07) at Loggiato Porta 10 is open from
9 am to noon and 3.30 to 6.30 pm Monday
to Saturday. A second tourist office (☎ 0583
64 42 42), at Piazza delle Erbe 1, concentrates on walking information. You can
stock up on maps and get information on
rifugi, walking trails and other tips.

Walkers should pick up a copy of
Garfagnana Trekking, which details a specific signposted and well-maintained 10-
day walk around the area and extending into
the western Apuan Alps. Another booklet,
Garfagnana a Cavallo, details guided horse
treks that cost around L20,000 per hour or
L90,000 per day. If you can't get the information you need, you could also try the
Azienda Agrituristica La Garfagnana
(☎ 0583 6 87 05), Località Prade 25, in
Castiglione di Garfagnana.

If you decide to make this a base or initial stop, about the best bet is *Da Carlino*
(☎ 0583 64 42 70, fax 0583 6 55 75, Via

Garibaldi 15). Rooms without private bath start at L45,000/75,000 and range up to L60,000/100,000 with.

CLAP buses from Lucca run about a dozen times a day (L5600, 1½ hours).

Around Castelnuovo di Garfagnana

Several scenic roads fan out from Castelnuovo, so if you have your own transport plenty of options open themselves up to you. If you are relying on public transport things get considerably slower and sometimes impossible, but you can still enjoy the area.

One option is to follow the concertina of hair-pin bends that constitute the road leading via Castiglione to the Foce di Radici pass across the Apennines into Emilia-Romagna. The scenery in parts is splendid. Occasional buses run this route. With your own car you may want to take the minor parallel road to the south that leads you to **San Pellegrino in Alpe**, site of a fine monastery. A few *pensioni* and hotels at San Pellegrino and along the main road give you the option to stay if need be.

Walkers will want to head for the small **Riserva Naturale dell'Orecchiella** park on the narrow road via **Corfino**, itself a pleasant village with three hotels. Seven kilometres farther north is the park's visitors centre. Here you can pick up information and maps for walks inside the reserve. One of the most scenic routes to follow to get here is to start on the main road that takes you through Castiglione. Shortly after a tiny road leads off to the west (left) to Villa Collemandine, after which you turn right along the road for Corfino.

The SS445 road follows the Serchio valley to the east of the Apuan Alps and into the Lunigiana region that occupies the northern end of Tuscany (for more on the Lunigiana see that section later in this chapter). About 8km north along this road from Castelnuovo at Poggio is a pretty turn-off to the artificial Lago Vagli along the Torrente Edron stream. You can undertake some pleasant little walks in the area, or simply some circular driving routes that can lead you back to Castelnuovo.

PISA
postcode 56100 • pop 98,000

Once, if briefly, a maritime power to riv Genoa (Genova) and Venice (Venezi Pisa now draws its fame from an architec tural project gone terribly wrong: its Lea ing Tower. But the city offers quite a de more. Indeed, the tower is only one e ement of the trio of Romanesque beaut astride the green carpet of the Campo d Miracoli – along with Piazza San Marco Venice, one of Italy's most memorab squares.

Pisa has a centuries-old tradition as university town and even today is full young students. A perhaps unexpected beautiful city, it really deserves more th the usual one-day stopover planned by t average tourist.

History

Possibly of Greek origin, Pisa became important naval base under Rome and r mained a significant port for many ce turies. The city's so-called Golden Da began late in the 11th century when it b came an independent maritime republic ar a rival of Genoa and Venice. The goc times rolled on into the 13th century, b which time Pisa controlled Corsica, Sa dinia and all of the Tuscan coast. The m jority of the city's finest buildings date fro this period, as does the distinctive Pisa Romanesque architectural style.

Pisa's support for the Ghibellines durir the tussles between the Holy Roman En peror and the pope brought the city int conflict with its mostly Guelph Tusca neighbours, in particular Florence but als Lucca. The real blow, however, came whe Genoa's fleet inflicted a devastating defe on Pisa in the Battle of Meloria in 128 The city fell to Florence in 1406 and, as by way of compensation, the Medici en couraged artistic, literary and scientif endeavour and re-established Pisa's unive sity. The city's most famous son, Galile Galilei, later taught at the university.

The medieval city underwent profoun change under the grand dukes of Tuscan who began a process of demolition to mak

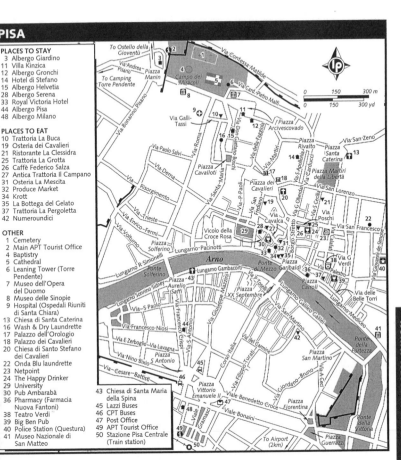

PISA

PLACES TO STAY
3 Albergo Giardino
11 Villa Kinzica
12 Albergo Gronchi
14 Hotel di Stefano
15 Albergo Helvetia
28 Albergo Serena
33 Royal Victoria Hotel
44 Albergo Pisa
48 Albergo Milano

PLACES TO EAT
10 Trattoria La Buca
19 Osteria dei Cavalieri
21 Ristorante La Clessidra
25 Trattoria La Grotta
26 Caffè Federico Salza
27 Antica Trattoria Il Campano
31 Osteria La Mescita
32 Produce Market
34 Krott
35 La Bottega del Gelato
37 Trattoria La Pergoletta
42 Numeroundici

OTHER
1 Cemetery
2 Main APT Tourist Office
4 Baptistry
5 Cathedral
6 Leaning Tower (Torre Pendente)
7 Museo dell'Opera del Duomo
8 Museo delle Sinopie
9 Hospital (Ospedali Riuniti di Santa Chiara)
13 Chiesa di Santa Caterina
16 Wash & Dry Laundrette
17 Palazzo dell'Orologio
18 Palazzo dei Cavalieri
20 Chiesa di Santo Stefano dei Cavalieri
22 Onda Blu laundrette
23 Netpoint
24 The Happy Drinker
29 University
30 Pub Ambarabà
36 Pharmacy (Farmacia Nuova Fantoni)
38 Teatro Verdi
39 Big Ben Pub
40 Police Station (Questura)
41 Museo Nazionale di San Matteo
43 Chiesa di Santa Maria della Spina
45 Lazzi Buses
46 CPT Buses
47 Post Office
49 APT Tourist Office
50 Stazione Pisa Centrale (Train station)

NORTH-WESTERN TUSCANY

... vay for wider boulevards and so ease traf-
ic. The single heaviest blow came in
WWII, during the course of which about
30% of old Pisa was destroyed.

Orientation

By train you'll arrive at Stazione Pisa Centrale, at the southern edge of the old city
centre. The main intercity bus terminus is
Piazza Vittorio Emanuele II, a short walk
north along Viale Gramsci. The medieval
centre is about a 15-minute walk north,
across the Arno river, and Campo dei Miracoli (also known as Piazza del Duomo) is

about another 10-minute walk north-west. It
is quicker to catch a city bus from outside
the station (see Getting Around later in this
section).

Information

Tourist Offices The main APT tourist
office (☎ 050 56 04 64) is housed in a little
cube of a building just outside the city
walls. It opens from 8 am to 8 pm Monday
to Saturday (9.30 am to midday and 3 to
5.30 pm in the low season) and 10 am to
4 pm Sunday. The office at the train station
(☎ 050 4 22 91) keeps different hours

Low & Dry

In the 19th century, the arrival of the railway in Pisa represented the death blow to river transport along the Arno. It will strike some as a little ironic that the State Railways (FS) should stumble across one of the greatest archaeological finds of the 20th century – a veritable port of ancient Roman shipwrecks.

While digging on a building site near the San Rossore train station, a couple of kilometres west of Campo dei Miracoli, in 1998, FS contractors came across the vessels. Six months later excavators, whose work is partly subsidised by the FS, had uncovered 10 boats, but digging continues in the hope of finding more.

Archaeologists could hardly believe their eyes. From a small warship through to cargo vessels of various kinds, a squadron of ships wrecked in storms at ancient Pisa's port had come to light. Up to 700 years of ancient maritime history was unveiled, as the wrecks clearly date to different epochs between the 3rd century BC and the 4th century AD.

On board some of the vessels rigging and sailing instruments were discovered, which will doubtless shed light on Roman-era seafaring. Just as important were the goods being transported. Hundreds of amphorae used to carry wine, fish, cherries, chestnuts, walnuts, olives and so on have been discovered, some actually containing remains of their contents.

Ceramics and other materials found on board these ships will provide clues to trade routes and communications in the ancient Mediterranean world.

How was all this preserved? It appears that, after sinking, the vessels were slowly buried deep in an airtight sepulchre of mud. That very mud preserved this precious archaeological treasure for 2000 years.

(9.30 am to 3 pm) but has little more than a map and a list of hotels.

Money Avoid the exchange booths near the cathedral. Change money at banks along Corso Italia, or at the train station.

Post & Communications The main post office is on Piazza Vittorio Emanuele II. You'll find phones scattered about all over town. If you need to go online you could head for Netpoint (☎ 050 97 00 13) at Piazza San Paolo all'Orto 11. It opens from 10 am to 1.30 pm and 2.30 to 7.30 pm Monday to Friday.

Laundry There's an Onda Blu self-service laundrette at Via San Francesco 8a. A Wash & Dry laundrette is at Via Santa Maria 105. The latter is slightly more expensive.

Medical Services & Emergency The Ospedali Riuniti di Santa Chiara (☎ 050 99 21 11) is a hospital complex at Via Roma 67. The Farmacia Nuova Fantoni (pharmacy), Lungarno Mediceo 51, is open 2 hours. The police station (*questura*; ☎ 05 58 35 11) is on Via Mario Lalli.

Campo dei Miracoli

The Pisans can justly claim that the Campo dei Miracoli is one of the most beautiful squares in the world. Set among its sprawling lawns is surely one of the most extraordinary concentrations of Romanesque splendour – the cathedral, the baptistry (*battistero*) and the Leaning Tower (Torre Pendente). On any day the piazza is teeming with people – students studying or at play, tourists wandering and local workers eating lunch.

A staggered pricing system operates for tickets to enter one or more of the monuments in and around the square. L10,000 gets you admission to two monuments, or L15,000 to four – the two museums, baptistry and cemetery (*cimitero*). The cathedral itself is not included and costs an extra L3000.

Opening times are complex. In some cases there are summer, autumn and winter mes. What follows gives the summer and inter 'extremes'.

athedral The majesty of Pisa's cathedral ade it a model for Romanesque churches roughout Tuscany and even in Sardinia. egun in 1064, it is covered inside and out ith the alternating bands of (now somehat faded) dark green and cream marble at were to become characteristic of the isan-Romanesque style.

The main facade, when not hidden by affolding, is a sight to behold, adorned as is with four tiers of columns. The bronze oors of the transept, facing the Leaning ower, are by Bonanno Pisano. The 16th-entury bronze doors of the main entrance ere designed by the school of Gianbologna to replace the wooden originals, estroyed in a fire in 1596.

The huge interior is lined with 68 olumns in classical style. This unusual feare is a remarkable reminder of the fact at among the many artisans at work on is church were also Arabs. The forest of olumns is reminiscent of many a great iddle Eastern mosque.

After the 1596 fire, much of the inside as redecorated. Important works to surive the blaze include Giovanni Pisano's rly-14th-century pulpit and an apse moic of *Il Redentore fra la Vergine e San iovanni Evangelista* (Christ between the irgin Mary and St John the Evangelist) ompleted by Cimabue in 1302.

The cathedral is open from 10 am to 8 pm n weekdays and 1 to 8 pm at weekends. In inter it opens from 10 am to 1 pm and to 5 pm.

eaning Tower Welcome to one of the orld's great cockups. The cathedral's bell ower *(campanile)* was in trouble from the art: its architect, Bonanno Pisano, maned to complete only three tiers before the ower started to lean on the south side. The roblem is generally believed to have been aused by shifting soil, and the 'leaning ower' has continued to lean by an average f 1mm per year ever since.

Galileo supposedly climbed its 294 steps to experiment with gravity, but today it is no longer possible to follow in his footsteps. The tower has been closed since 1990 while the experts try to work out how to stop its inexorable lean towards the ground – it now leans almost 4.5m off the perpendicular.

Several solutions have been tried and failed (for more on which see the boxed text 'Brace, Brace, Brace'). Some believe all the meddling is a mistake. The controversial Italian art historian, Vittorio Sgarbi, once said it would be 'better to see it fall and remember it leaning than see it straightened by mistake'. Was he saying that two wrongs won't set it upright?

Baptistry The unusual, round baptistry was started in 1153 by Diotisalvi, remodelled and continued by Nicola and Giovanni Pisano more than a century later, and finally completed in the 14th century – which explains the mix of architectural styles. At the time of writing it was shrouded in cleaners' scaffolding. The lower level of arcades is in the Pisan-Romanesque style and the pinnacled upper section and dome are a Gothic add-on. Inside, the beautiful pulpit was carved by Nicola Pisano and signed in 1260, and the white marble font was carved by Guido da Como in 1246. The acoustics beneath the dome are quite remarkable too. It is open from 8 am to 9 pm daily (9 am to 5 pm in winter).

Cemetery Located behind the white wall to the north of the cathedral, this exquisite cemetery (also known as the Camposanto) is said to contain soil shipped across from Calvary during the Crusades. Many precious frescoes in the cloisters were badly damaged or destroyed during WWII Allied bombing raids. Among those saved were the *Trionfo della Morte* (Triumph of Death) and *Giudizio Universale* (Last Judgement), attributed to an anonymous 14th-century painter known as 'The Master of the Triumph of Death'. The cemetery is open from 8 am to 8 pm daily (9 am to 5 pm in winter).

Around Campo dei Miracoli

The **Museo delle Sinopie** houses some

Brace, Brace, Brace

When architect Bonanno Pisano undertook construction work on the *campanile*, or bell tower, for the Romanesque cathedral in 1173, he was on shaky ground. Barely 2m above sea level, what lies below the deep green lawns of the Campo dei Miracoli is hardly ideal for major building. A treacherous sand and clay mix sits atop a series of alternate strata of clay and sand to a depth of more than 40m – not exactly rock solid.

Pisano had barely begun to build when the earth below the southern foundations started to give. By the time construction ground to a halt five years later, with only three storeys completed, Pisano's stump of a tower already had a noticeable lean.

A new band of artisans and masons set to work on it again almost 100 years later – in 1272. They attempted to bolster the foundations, but could not right the tower. Their solution was to keep going, compensating for the lean by gradually building straight up from the lower storeys, creating a slight but definite banana curve. The bell chamber at the top was built in 1370. At some point the process came to a halt and until the 18th century the lean remained stable.

Over the following centuries, the banana solution showed it was no solution, as the tower continued to lean a further 1mm each year. By 1993 it was 4.47m out of plumb, more than 5° from the vertical.

In addition to the problems down on the ground floor, the structure is itself a little on the dodgy side. The tower is basically a pretty but hollow cylinder, cased on the inside and out with layers of marble. Between those layers is a loosely packed mix of rubble and mortar, very unevenly distributed. The stresses caused by the lean have led some observers to fear they might be too much and simply cause the casing to crack and crumble.

In 1990 the tower was closed to the public. Two years later the government in Rome assembled a panel of experts to debate a solution. In 1993 engineers placed 1000 tonnes of lead ingots on the northern side in a bid to counteract the subsidence on the southern side. Steel bands were wrapped around the 2nd storey to try to keep it all together. For a while it seemed to have worked, until in 1995 it slipped a whole 2.5mm.

In 1999, a new solution was being tried. Steel braces were slung around the 3rd storey and attached to heavy hydraulic A-frame anchors some way from the northern side. These frames were later replaced by steel cables attached to neighbouring buildings. The tower thus held in place, engineers began gingerly to remove soil from below the northern foundations. The aim is to correct the lean by about 10% and return the tower to where it was in the 18th century. No-one wants to straighten the tower – least of all the town fathers, who realise that much of Pisa's tourist lolly (however unfairly) is attracted wholly and solely by the Leaning Tower. The Straight Tower of Pisa just wouldn't have the same ring about it.

The plan was devised by a British geotechnical engineer but many experts have contributed to finding a solution. By August 1999 the lean had been corrected by 4cm. The aim is to pull it back 40cm. This, say the experts, would guarantee the tower's future for three centuries.

JANE SMITH

ddish-brown sketches drawn onto walls as e base for frescoes, discovered in the metery after the WWII bombing raids. he *sinopie* have been restored and provide fascinating insight into the process of eating a fresco, although they are really ly worth visiting if you have a particular terest in the subject. The museum is open om 8 am to 8 pm daily (9 am to 1 pm and to 5 pm in winter).

The **Museo dell'Opera del Duomo** in azza Arcivescovado, near the Leaning wer, features many artworks from the wer, cathedral and baptistry, including a agnificent ivory carving of the *Madonna Crocifisso* by Giovanni Pisano. Another ghlight is the bust known as the *Madonna l Colloquio*, by the same artist, taken om the exterior of the baptistry. The mu-um is open from 9 am to 1 pm and 3 to 30 pm daily (to 5.30 pm in winter).

he City

ead south along Via Santa Maria from the ampo dei Miracoli and turn left at Piazza avallotti for the splendid **Piazza dei Cav-ieri**, the centre of temporal power in the ty remodelled by Vasari in the 16th cen-ry. The **Palazzo dell'Orologio**, on the orthern side of the piazza, occupies the site f a tower where, in 1288, Count Ugolino ella Gherardesca, his sons and grandsons, ere starved to death on suspicion of hav-g helped the Genoese enemy at the Battle f Meloria. The incident was recorded in ante's *Inferno*.

The **Palazzo dei Cavalieri** on the north-stern side of the piazza was redesigned by asari and features remarkable graffiti dec-ration. The piazza and palace are named ter the Knights of St Stephen, a religious d military order founded by Cosimo I de' ledici. Their church, **Chiesa di Santo Ste-ano dei Cavalieri**, was also designed by asari.

The **Chiesa di Santa Caterina**, off Via an Lorenzo on Piazza Martiri della Lib-tà, is a fine example of Pisan Gothic rchitecture and contains works by Nino isano.

Wander south to the area around **Borgo Stretto**, the city's medieval heart. East along the waterfront boulevard, the Lungarno Mediceo, is the **Museo Nazionale di San Matteo**, an interesting enough art gallery housing mostly religious art, particularly from the 14th century. It features works by Giovanni and Nicola Pisano, Masaccio and Donatello. The gallery is open from 9 am to 7 pm Tuesday to Saturday and until 1 pm Sunday. Admission costs L8000.

Cross the Arno and head west to reach the **Chiesa di Santa Maria della Spina**, oddly perched on the road along the Arno and built in the early 14th century to house a thorn purportedly from Christ's crown. It opens from 11 am to sunset daily. Admis-sion costs L2000.

Places to Stay

Pisa has a reasonable number of budget ho-tels for a small town, but many double as residences for students during the school year so it can be difficult to find a cheap room.

Camping Torre Pendente (☎ 050 56 17 04, Via delle Cascine 86) is west of the cathedral, and is open all year. The non-HI *Ostello della Gioventù* (☎ 050 89 06 22, Via Pietrasantina 15) is a long hike north-west of the cathedral. A bed costs L22,000 in a quad. Take bus No 3 from the train station (walking it from Campo dei Miracoli is a huge pain).

Albergo Serena (☎ 050 58 08 09, Via D Cavalca 45), just off Piazza Dante Alighieri, has singles/doubles for up to L45,000/65,000. *Albergo Helvetia* (☎ 050 55 30 84, Via Don Gaetano Boschi 31), just south of the cathedral, offers pleasant rooms with shared bath for L50,000/65,000 and doubles with bath for L95,000 (prices drop in low season). *Hotel di Stefano* (☎ 050 55 35 59, Via Sant'Apollonia 35), has good rooms with private bath for up to L80,000/115,000 (about L20,000 less with-out private bath).

Albergo Gronchi (☎ 050 56 18 23, Pi-azza Arcivescovado 1) is a steal for its po-sition alone, and offers singles/doubles for L30,000/54,000. *Albergo Giardino* (☎ 050 56 21 01, Piazza Manin 1), just west of

NORTH-WESTERN TUSCANY

Campo dei Miracoli, was refurbished in early 1999 and charges around L90,000/120,000 for sparkling rooms with private bath.

More upmarket is **Villa Kinzica** (☎ 050 56 04 19, fax 050 55 12 04, Piazza Arcivescovado 2), with views of the Leaning Tower and singles/doubles with bathroom and breakfast for L105,000/140,000.

Near the train station, **Albergo Milano** (☎ 050 2 31 62, Via Mascagni 14) has simple rooms for L45,000/77,000 (doubles with bath can cost up to L105,000). The two-star **Albergo Pisa** (☎ 050 4 45 51, Via Manzoni 22), near .Via Francesco Crispi, has a variety of rooms starting at L48,000/64,000.

For a little old world luxury by the river, the only choice is the **Royal Victoria Hotel** (☎ 050 94 01 11, fax 050 94 01 80, Lungarno Pacinotti 12), where attractively maintained rooms will set you back up to L130,000/160,000. It goes without saying that rooms with river views are sought after.

Places to Eat

Being a university town, Pisa has a good range of cheap eating places. Head for the area north of the river around Borgo Stretto and the university. There is an open-air **produce market** in Piazza delle Vettovaglie, off Borgo Stretto.

Antica Trattoria il Campano (☎ 050 58 05 85, Via Cavalca 44), in an old tower, is full of atmosphere; a full meal is likely to set you back L40,000. It is closed Wednesday. Nearby is a more modest little eatery where the food is good – **Osteria la Mescita** (☎ 050 54 42 94, Via Cavalca 2) is well worth a look. A one-time wine purveyor (mescita), the tiny eatery still has its 15th-century brick vaulted ceilings. It is closed Monday. **Trattoria la Grotta** (☎ 050 57 81 05, Via San Francesco 103) is another good choice and similarly priced. It is, as the name suggests, suitably cavern-like. It is closed Sunday.

Ristorante la Clessidra (☎ 050 54 01 60, Via Santa Cecilia 34) has excellent food and if the prices look a little steep you can settle for the set meals at L30,000 (meat main course) or L35,000 (seafood). It is closed f Saturday lunch and on Sunday. A wonderf sprawling place is **Trattoria la Pergolet** (☎ 050 54 24 58, Via delle Belle Torri 4(tucked away out of sight just north of th river. Expect to pay about L40,000 per pe son. Doors shut on Monday.

At **Osteria dei Cavalieri** (☎ 050 58 12 5 Via San Frediano 16) you can opt for a sir gle dish (piatto unico) for less than L20,0(or choose from a mouth-watering menu. closes on Sunday.

Trattoria la Buca (☎ 050 56 06 60, V Galli Tassi 6/b) has pizzas from L8000, e: cept on Friday, when it shuts.

A wonderfully exuberant spot for coffe gelati (ice-creams), a cocktail or some fir foccacia (soft bread) is **Krott** (☎ 050 58 (80, Lungarno Pacinotti 2).

If only for the low prices and the fa they open nonstop from noon to 10 pm, **N** meroundici (Via San Martino 47) is wor knowing. They serve up great salads, f caccine (a kind of filled bread) and othe delights. You could eat a light lunch for ni more than L10,000. It is closed Saturda lunchtime and on Sunday.

One of the city's finest bars is the **Caf** **Federico Salza** (☎ 050 58 01 44, Borg Stretto 46), offering cakes, gelati an chocolates. Prices inside are one-third those charged if you eat at the tables ou side. It is closed Monday. For great gelat head for **La Bottega del Gelato** (☎ 050 5 54 67, Piazza Garibaldi 11), just north c the river. It is closed Wednesday.

Entertainment

Pisa can hardly be described as a clu mecca, in spite of the student populatio Still, a few watering holes in the centre sug gest themselves. The tourist office may b able to make suggestions on the club fror farther out of town, although (relativel nearby Viareggio is a better option.

A couple of UK-style pubs hav emerged, which can be quite pleasant i you're in the mood for a soothing pint. On is **Big Ben Pub** (☎ 050 58 11 85, Via Pale stro 11). It is closed Monday. Another i **The Happy Drinker** (☎ 050 57 85 55, V

lo del Poschi 11), which is closed Tues-
ay. For a somewhat quieter atmosphere
nd the option of a meal try **Pub Ambarabà**
☎ 050 57 67 97, Vicolo della Croce Rossa
), also closed Tuesday.

Opera and ballet are staged at the **Teatro
erdi** (☎ 050 94 11 11, Via Palestro 40)
om September to November. Cultural and
storic events include the Gioco del Ponte,
festival of traditional costume held on the
st Sunday in June. On 16 and 17 June, the
rno river comes to life with the Regata
torica di San Ranieri, a rowing competi-
on commemorating the city's patron saint.

etting There & Away

ir The city's Galileo Galilei airport (☎ 050
0 07 07), about 2km south of the city cen-
e, is Tuscany's main international airport
nd handles flights to major cities in Eur-
pe. Alitalia (☎ 800 050 350) and other
ajor airlines are based at the airport.

us Lazzi (☎ 050 4 62 88), Piazza Vittorio
manuele II, operates regular services to
ucca, Florence (via Montecatini; L5800,
hours) and Viareggio. Less frequent runs
rve Prato, Pistoia, Massa and Carrara.

CPT (☎ 050 50 55 11), Piazza Sant'An-
nio, also near the train station, serves
olterra, Livorno (Leghorn), Marina di Pisa
nd Tirrenia.

rain The train station, Stazione Pisa Cen-
ale, is on Piazza della Stazione at the
outhern edge of town. The city is connected
 Florence (via Empoli; L8000, 65 min-
tes) and is also on the Rome–La Spezia
ne, with frequent services in all directions.

ar & Motorcycle Pisa is close to the
12, which connects Parma to Livorno and
 being extended south to Rome, although
at may yet take some years to complete.
he city is also close to the A11 (tollway)
nd SS67 to Florence, while the north-south
S1, the Via Aurelia, connects the city with
a Spezia and Rome.

Large car parks abound in Pisa. The one
st north of the cathedral is perfect for day-
rippers.

Getting Around

To get to the airport, take a train from the
main station for the four-minute journey to
Stazione FS Pisa Aeroporto, or CPT city
bus No 3, which passes through the city
centre and past the train station on its way
to the airport (it also goes to the Ostello
della Gioventù).

To get from the train station to the cathedral, take CPT bus No 4 or walk 1.5km. Bus
tickets cost L1500 for an hour, L2000 for
two hours or L13,500 for a book of 10 one-
hour tickets (you can change as often as
you like within the validity of the ticket).

Trattoria La Buca (see Places to Eat earlier in this section) rents out bicycles.

For a taxi, call ☎ 050 54 16 00.

VIAREGGIO
postcode 55049 • pop 57,800

Funny that Italy's second Carnevale capital
after Venice should also begin with 'v'.
That's about where the comparisons between the two cities end, however. Viareggio is the not unpleasant leading resort town
on the northern Tuscan coast, an area
known as La Versilia. The town's architectural wonders are limited to some pleasing
Liberty (Art Nouveau) edifices, mostly on
or a block or two back from the palm-lined
Passeggiata, the (almost) waterfront boulevard.

Orientation

It's a 10-minute walk (if that) from the train
station to the waterfront and the main APT
tourist office. The city is ranged roughly
north to south on a grid pattern. South from
the pleasure-boat-lined Canale Burlamacca
stretch the enticing woods of the Pineta di
Levante. Another smaller wood, the Pineta
di Ponente, occupies a large chunk of the
northern end of town. Beyond it Viareggio
blends seamlessly into the next beach resort
of Lido di Camaiore.

Information

Tourist Offices The main APT tourist
office (☎ 0584 96 22 33, fax 0584 4 73 36,
🖃 viareggio@versilia.turismo.Tuscany.it)
is at Viale Carducci 10. There's an abundance

NORTH-WESTERN TUSCANY

VIAREGGIO

Tyrrhanian Sea

To Agorà Café,
Lido di Camaiore,
A12, SS1 &
Forte dei Marmi

To Pineta di Levante;
Sergio, Campeggio dei
Tigli, Torre del Lago,
Lago di Massaciuccoli

Pineta di Ponente

Piazza Mazzini

Piazza Shelley

Piazza d'Azeglio

Piazza Garibaldi

Piazza Nieri Paolini

Piazza S Antonio

Piazza Mercato Vecchio

Largo Risorgimento

Canale Burlamacca

0   200   400 m
0   200   400 yd
Approximate Scale

PLACES TO STAY
6 Albergo Villa Bruna
7 Hotel Garden

PLACES TO EAT
10 Brasserie Stuzzichino
14 Barcobestia

OTHER
1 Hospital (Ospedale G Tabaracci)
2 Idea Virtuale
3 Police Station (Questura)
4 Train Station
5 APT Tourist Office
8 Gran Caffè Margherita
9 Patchouly
11 Lazzi & CLAP Buses
12 Post Office
13 Scorpion Pub

of info on the town and surrounding area and staff speak several languages, but they do not make hotel bookings. The office opens from 9 am to 1 pm and 4 to 7 pm Monday to Saturday, from Easter to the end of September. For the rest of the year (except the excitable time of Carnevale – see under Special Events later in this section) they open only in the morning. In summer a smaller office also operates at the train station from 9 am to 1 pm daily.

Money You can change money at the main post office and most banks, of which plenty are scattered about town.

Post & Communications The main post office, on Corso Garibaldi, opens from 8.15 am to 7 pm Monday to Friday, and until noon Saturday. For a Web fix, try Idea Virtuale at Via Pacinotti 57. It opens from 11 am to 1 pm and 5 to 8 pm daily (closed Tuesday and Sunday). Surfing costs L5000 per half hour.

Medical Services & Emergency Th[e] main hospital, the Ospedale G Tabarac[ci] (☎ 0584 94 91, accident & emergenc[y] ☎ 0584 94 92 80) is at Via Antonio Fra[tti] 530. The police station (*questura*; ☎ 0584 [94] 27 41) is at Via Fratelli Cervi 32.

Things to See & Do
Apart from strolling along the tracks in th[e] Pineta di Levante, around the Canale Burla[ve] macca and along Via Regina Margherita[,] there's not much to occupy your time b[ut] the beach.

A good deal of the waterfront as it is no[w] went up in the 1920s and '30s, and some [of] the buildings, such as Puccini's favourit[e,] the Gran Caffè Margherita, retain some[-] thing of their Liberty stylishness.

The beach costs. It has been divided u[p] into *stabilimenti*, individual lots where yo[u] can hire change cabins, umbrellas, recline[rs] and the like. You have to avail yourself [of] at least a recliner, which will set you bac[k]

NORTH-WESTERN TUSCANY

out L20,000 per person. To get to free beaches you have to leave town.

Special Events
Viareggio's moment of glory comes for about three weeks in February and March when the city lets its hair down for Carnevale – a festival of floats (usually with giant and rarely flattering effigies of political and other topical figures), fireworks and fun. They have been doing this here since 1873. In 2000 it ran from 20 February to 12 March. For more information see Special Events in the Facts for the Visitor chapter.

Places to Stay
Camping You have a choice of about half a dozen camping grounds spread out between Viareggio and Torre del Lago in the Pineta di Levante woods. Most open from April to September. *Campeggio dei Tigli* (☎/fax 0584 34 12 78, Viale dei Tigli) is one of the biggest sites. It costs about L12,000 per adult, with extra charges per tent site and car. Without a car from Viareggio, take CLAP bus No 1 or 3 from Piazza d'Azeglio.

Hotels Viareggio boasts more than 120 hotels of all classes, along with affittacamere, villas and the like. They mostly jostle for space on, or a couple of blocks in from, the waterfront and it seems unfair to single any out, as they are mostly much of a muchness.

In high summer, especially July, many hotels charge at least half board (*mezza pensione*) and often full board (*pensione completa*).

A quiet little place is *Albergo Villa Bruna* (☎ 0584 3 10 38, Via Michelangelo Buonarroti 10). It charges L40,000 per person for straightforward, clean rooms, but insists you take full board (L80,000 per person) in July and August.

You can be confident of the quality at *Hotel Garden* (☎ 0584 4 40 25, fax 0584 4 44 45, Viale Foscolo 70), where good rooms with TV, phone and minibar cost L150,000/220,000 for singles/doubles. In high summer they like you to take full board, costing L180,000 per person, but don't necessarily insist on it.

Places to Eat
If you dodge full board in the hotels, there are plenty of restaurant options around town. The waterfront places tend to be expensive and uninspiring.

For all sorts of snacks, salads and full meals if you are so inclined, try *Brasserie Stuzzichino* (☎ 0584 4 50 85, Viale Foscolo 3). The speciality of the house is the amazing range of salads. It is closed Wednesday.

Sergio (☎ 0584 96 37 50, Via Zanardelli 151) is Viareggio's favourite roast chicken joint, but you can also get other meals and they offer a decent selection of wines to try. It's closed Monday. Take CLAP bus No 1 or 3 from Piazza d'Azeglio.

For fish specialities, head to *Barcobestia* (☎ 0584 38 44 16, Via Copponi 289). The decor is modern seafarer (with portholes and the like) but the food is very good. Expect to pay around L60,000 a head. Book ahead. It is closed Monday.

Entertainment
Viareggio is one of Tuscany's better places for a night out on the tiles. Which is not necessarily saying an awful lot, but you can find a few bars and clubs to keep you occupied. To get started pick up a copy of *Note*, a monthly events listing brochure, from the tourist office.

For cocktails and New Age music, float into *Patchouly* (☎ 0368 353 99 00, Viale Foscolo 17). The fairly boisterous disco/bar *Scorpion Pub* (☎ 0584 3 10 06, Largo Risorgimento) is in a crass-looking building overlooking a petrol station. You can drink and dine, and at weekends dance into the wee hours. Admission costs L10,000 on Friday and Saturday unless you eat. It is closed Monday.

Catch live music of varying types at *Agorà Café* (☎ 0584 61 04 88, Viale Colombo 666) in Lido di Camaiore. Later in the evening it converts into a disco – the standard musical fare is house and its relatives.

Getting There & Around
Bus Lazzi (☎ 0584 4 62 34) and CLAP (☎ 0584 5 37 04) buses run from Piazza

NORTH-WESTERN TUSCANY

d'Azeglio to destinations throughout the north-west of Tuscany. The Lazzi service to Florence takes about two hours and costs L10,600.

CLAP has fairly regular buses up the coast to Pietrasanta and Forte dei Marmi, as well as up to 12 daily to Lucca and from three to six a day to Massa. CLAP also runs the town's local buses.

In summer, long-distance buses run to such destinations as Milan (L42,000).

Train Local trains run to Livorno (one hour) and Pisa (20 minutes), and to La Spezia (45 minutes) via Massa and Carrara. Regular Florence-bound trains run via Lucca. A couple of Eurostar Italia trains bound for Rome, Genoa and Turin stop here.

Taxi Several taxi companies operate in Viareggio. You can order one on ☎ 0584 4 54 54, operating 24 hours.

Boat In summer, Navigazione Golfo dei Poeti (☎ 0187 73 29 87), based at Via Mazzini 21 in La Spezia in the region of Liguria, puts on boats connecting Viareggio (along with Forte dei Marmi, Marina di Carrara and Marina di Massa) with coastal destinations in Liguria such as the Cinque Terre and Portofino. Call the boat company or inquire at the tourist office for more information. The same company also operates day excursions from Viareggio to the island of Capraia (see the Central Coast chapter). Boats leave at 9.30 am and return at 6.15 pm. The round trip costs L60,000.

SOUTH OF VIAREGGIO
Torre del Lago
A couple of kilometres south of Viareggio on the other side of the Pineta di Levante, Torre del Lago is a quiet continuation of the seaside theme. With one important difference. The **Lago di Massaciuccoli** spreads out a couple of kilometres inland, a shallow lagoon forming part of the **Parco Naturale Migliarino San Rossore Massaciuccoli** (see the following section). The lagoon hosts more than 100 species of permanent, migratory and nesting birds, including heron,

egret, wild duck and moor buzzard. Boat excursions run out across the lagoon for about an hour and cost L8000 per person (minimum eight people).

The composer Puccini had a villa built here by the lake. You can visit the spot where he hammered out some of his operas from 10 am to 12.30 pm and 3 to 6 pm (closed Monday morning). Admission costs L7000. In July and August the open-air theatre by the lagoon is one of the stages for the Festival Pucciniano, in which his operas are performed (contact the Viareggio APT for details).

A couple of modest hotels here could make a nice calming base to stay – although you'd really want wheels to get around unless you want to rely on CLAP buses No 1 and 3 to get into central Viareggio.

Parco Naturale Migliarino San Rossore Massaciuccoli
Covering 24,000 hectares and stretching from Viareggio in the north to Livorno in the south, this park is one of the rare stretches of protected coastline in Tuscany.

Part swamp, part pine forest, the park plays host to a particularly diverse birdlife, especially during the migratory periods. Several species of falcon, duck, heron, cormorant and a series of other waterbirds call the area home for some or part of the year. Deer, wild boar and goats constitute the bulk of the land-going critter contingent.

You can get more information at the Centro Visite in Cascine Vecchie, a cluster of buildings dating to the first half of the 19th century. To get to it, take the road west from Pisa off the SS1, which ends on the coast at Gombo. The centre is open from 8.30 am to 7.30 pm (until 5.30 pm in winter) at weekends only. You can also call ☎ 050 52 55 00 or ☎ 050 53 91 11.

A sliver of coast between the Arno river and Livorno is not part of the park, and for Pisans the small seaside towns of **Marina di Pisa** and **Tirrenia** are the hub of the weekend beach-going experience. Of the two, Tirrenia is marginally more attractive. Regular CPT buses run to both towns from Pisa en route for Livorno.

Beyond the park, the next stop south on

popular Porto Ercole on Monte Argentario still retains some of its fishing-village character.

Renaissance Palazzo Ricci, Montepulciano

Gateway to Massa Marittima, southern Tuscan

GEOFF STRINGER

The Palazzo del Popolo's tower in San Gimignano

DAMIEN SIMONIS

A view of the Chiesa di San Domenico in Sie

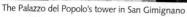

JON DAVISON

The dazzling interior of Siena's cathedral, one of Italy's great Gothic churches

e coast is the sprawling port town of
vorno (covered in the Central Coast
apter).

A VERSILIA

ne coastal area from Viareggio north to the
gional border with Liguria is known as La
ersilia. Although popular with local
oliday-makers in the summer and surpris-
gly with a good number of foreigners
iermans, French and Brits), it is hardly the
iediterranean's premier beach resort. Strip
velopment that would do some of the less
lustrious coastal suburbs of Australia or
e States proud is fronted by sandy
eaches, many of them in private hands
which means you have to pay to use them).
In short, the area is only worth including
your itinerary if you simply want to in-
lude a little summer beach fun in a more
ide-ranging tour of Tuscany. If *all* you
ant is sand, sun and sea, Tuscany is not for
»u.

ietrasanta & Around

essing up the coast from Viareggio you
oss a municipal boundary into **Lido di Ca-
aiore**. The only thing to suggest any dif-
rence from what you have left behind is
e sign. The development becomes sparser
you head north, and on slower days at
ast the beaches are a little less crowded.
When you reach **Marina di Pietrasanta**
rn inland 3.5km for the town of
etrasanta itself. The centre of the old
wn is Piazza Duomo, which represents
e sum total of this town's attraction. If it's
»en, pop into the Chiesa di Sant'Agostino.
ne church has a rather stark Gothic facade
at won't necessarily appeal, but the clois-
r inside is pleasant. Other structures of
ite on the square are the cathedral (13th
ntury) and the Palazzo Moroni, which
uses a modest archaeological museum.
With a car (or indeed a circle line CLAP
is from Piazza Matteotti) you could push
rther inland to **Seravezza**, since the 16th
ntury an important centre for marble ex-
action (Michelangelo spent some time
ere looking for raw materials) and now a
ateway to the Parco delle Alpi Apuane

(see the Apuan Alps section later in this
chapter). Set on the confluence of the rivers
Serra and Vezza into La Versilia, and with
the Apuan Alps rising behind it, Seravezza
is a pleasant little spot although with few
particularly arresting sights. You could have
a look at the cathedral and, about 4.5km
north, the Pieve della Cappella (parish
church) in Azzano. Also worth a look is the
Palazzo Mediceo, built by Cosimo I de'
Medici as a summer getaway.

While in this area you could proceed
south-east along the Vezza river (also by
CLAP bus from Piazza Matteotti) to the
picturesque hamlet *(frazione)* of **Stazzema**.
The village entrance is marked by the Romanesque Chiesa di Santa Maria Assunta,
but for many people the name Stazzema is
synonymous with a massacre carried out
nearby by German troops in 1944. A
memorial and small museum dedicated to
the memory of the 561 victims in Santa
Anna, a tiny settlement to the south-west, is
a sobering reminder of the nastiness that
went on here not so long ago. There is no
direct road, so you would need to drive to
the hamlet of Farnocchia and then walk
(there are trails) a couple of kilometres.
Several buses to Stazzema run from
Pietrasanta and Seravezza.

If all this has raised an uncomfortable
sweat and you feel like a dip in the briny,
you could return to Seravezza and then take
a direct road to **Forte dei Marmi**. It's in
much the same league as Viareggio, with
plenty of places to eat and drink scattered
along and just in behind the waterfront. Oh,
and if you feel the urge to stay, some 100
hotels offer their services. Ask for a list at
the APT tourist office (☎ 0584 8 00 91), Via
Franceschi 8/b.

Between Forte dei Marmi and the regional border with Liguria the seaside becomes less attractive. Indeed, if you are
moving around under your own steam you
would be better off heading straight into
Liguria in search of coastal delights.

Massa

Inland, the next town of note is Massa, the
administrative centre of the province of the

NORTH-WESTERN TUSCANY

same name (the province is also known as Massa Carrara).

The main tourist office (☎ 0585 24 00 63) at Viale Vespucci 24 is on the coast in Marina di Massa. There is precious little reason for calling in to Massa, where hardly anything remains of the old core of the town apart from the cathedral, itself of slight interest. Dominating the town and quite a sight from a distance is the **Castello Malaspina**. The Malaspina family was in charge here for hundreds of years from the mid-15th century on. From this high point they could keep a watch on the surrounding territory. At the time of writing it was closed.

There are only two hotels in Massa itself, should you for some strange reason want to stay. You are better off trying your luck on the coast at Marina di Massa – again if you really feel the need. The youth hostel, or *Ostello della Gioventù (☎ 0585 78 00 34, Via delle Pinete 237)*, which charges L15,000 for a bed, is on the seafront north of Marina di Massa. It opens from April to September. About 70 hotels of all categories compete for business down here too. Buses for a good number of destinations around the north-west of Tuscany leave from the train station, which is in Massa itself. The bus to Lucca runs five times daily (L5600, 1½ hours).

Carrara

Carrara, about 8km north-west of Massa, is a more attractive spot. If your idea of a good time is staring at marble quarries perhaps you should hang out for a wee while in Carrara.

Indeed, Carrara is thought of as the world capital of both the extraction and working of white marble. Michelangelo made frequent trips to Carrara and other marble-producing centres in the area to select the best-quality material for his commissions. Watching the trucks rumble down from the quarries today makes you wonder just how back-breaking and treacherous a business the extraction and transport of marble must have been in Michelangelo's day. No doubt the concept of danger money had not yet occurred to anyone.

The marble quarries up in the hills behind Carrara were already being worked under the Romans, so the tradition is a long one. In 1442 the town came under the control of the Malaspina family, and shared the fate of Massa farther south. Apart from a couple of Napoleonic interludes, the town remained in the Malaspinas' control until handed over to the Estense family in the early 19th century. Quarrying marble is no child's game and a monument to workers who have lost their lives in the quarries can be seen in Piazza XXVII Aprile. The tough men who worked these stone faces formed the backbone of a strong leftist and anarchist tradition in Carrara, something that won them no friends among the Fascists or, later, the occupying German forces.

The gracious little old centre of Carrara is tucked away in the north-western corner of the town, almost 10km inland from its coastal counterpart, Marina di Carrara, and nuzzling up the first hills of the Apuan

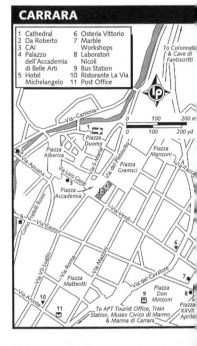

CARRARA

1 Cathedral
2 Da Roberto
3 CAI
4 Palazzo dell'Accademia di Belle Arti
5 Hotel Michelangelo
6 Osteria Vittorio
7 Marble Workshops
8 Laboratori Nicoli
9 Bus Station
10 Ristorante La Via
11 Post Office

Alps, some of them visibly scarred by years of marble extraction.

Information The APT office (☎ 0585 84 49 72), Via Settembre XX, is about 2km south of the town centre on the way to the coast. It opens from 10 am to 1 pm and 2 to 5 pm Monday to Saturday. They can hand you a useful map and outdated hotel lists. If you are interested in visiting the *laboratori*, or marble workshops, ask them for the relevant map. As you will see from this, they are spread out between Carrara and Marina di Carrara. The office also has information about walking in the Apuan Alps. There is another tourist office down in Marina di Carrara (☎ 0585 63 25 19) at Piazza Menoni 6B. The main post office is on the corner of Via Mazzini and Via Aronte.

Things to See The **cathedral**, at the heart of the old town, is one of the earliest medieval buildings to have been constructed entirely of Apuan marble. Building began in the 11th century, but it dragged on for two centuries. The facade, a mix of Romanesque (the lower half) and Gothic, was largely inspired by Pisan models. The rose window is especially noteworthy. Admission is free, and the cathedral closes at lunchtime (exact times vary).

The prettiest square in the town, with its festively painted houses, is without doubt **Piazza Alberica**, created in the 15th century.

The 'castle' on Piazza Gramsci started life as a fortified residence of the Malaspina clan and is now the **Palazzo dell'Accademia di Belle Arti**. Inside you can cast a glance at a collection of Roman sculptural fragments and other odds and ends.

South of the centre on Via Settembre XX towards Marina di Carrara is the **Museo Civico di Marmo**. Here you can find out everything you wanted to know about marble and were afraid to ask. On display are examples of no less than 310 types of marble, granite and other decorative stones found in Italy. They also have a modest modern sculpture collection. It opens from 10 am to 8 pm Monday to Saturday from June to September (until 5 pm during May

and October). For the rest of the year it opens from 8.30 am to 1.30 pm. Admission costs L6000. Buses running between Marina di Carrara and Carrara will drop you off – it's near the stadium *(stadio)*.

Many visitors feel drawn to marble quarries; here you can get a look at several. Roads run north into the hills to **Colonnata** and the **Cave di Fantiscritti**, among others. If you are driving, follow the yellow signs for the *cave* (quarries). Local buses make regular runs to Colonnata. It appears this latter town was home to Roman slaves used to extract marble down below. Nowadays they use mechanical saws to carve out great blocks of the white stone. At the Cave di Fantiscritti, a chap called Walter Danesi has installed a private museum, where you can see the kinds of tools quarriers used to struggle with. To get to this spot you cross the Ponti di Vara, a viaduct built in the 19th century for the railways. At the time it was considered one of the great feats of modern engineering.

If you've still not had enough, you could consider visiting some of the marble laboratori where the stuff is worked into all sorts of shapes. The commissions can range from the banal to the bizarre. Artists frequently instruct the workshops on how they want a piece executed, or at least begun – thus cleverly avoiding the hard and dusty work themselves. A handy one is **Laboratori Nicoli** on Piazza XXVII Aprile. If nothing else you could poke your nose into the dust-filled air of the workshops on either side of the square.

Places to Stay & Eat To sleep over in Carrara you have two choices. The fairly basic *Da Roberto* (☎ 0585 7 06 34, Via Apuana 5/b) offers singles/doubles costing up to L60,000/90,000. Slightly more luxurious is *Hotel Michelangelo* (☎ 0585 77 71 61, fax 0585 7 45 45, Corso Fratelli Rossi 3). Comfortable rooms with phone and TV cost as much as L100,000/140,000 in high season. Otherwise you can head down through the chaotic traffic to Marina di Carrara and choose from a dozen or so places in this utterly unenticing seaside shambles.

NORTH-WESTERN TUSCANY

One of the only serious vegetarian restaurants in northern Tuscany, if not the whole region, is *Ristorante La Via (☎ 0585 77 94 23, Via Roma 17/c)*. They are strict about this, so carnivores should wait outside. Ingredients used are at least 90% organically produced, and they offer two set meals in which you can taste a range of small portions, one for L27,000 and one for L35,000. The menu changes regularly. They also do fruit shakes and a selection of teas. It is closed Saturday lunchtime and Sunday.

On an altogether more prosaic local front, *Osteria Vittorio (☎ 0585 7 21 34, Via del Cavatore)* serves up hearty no-nonsense meals. There's nothing spectacular about it, but you can eat your fill for around L30,000. It is closed Wednesday.

Getting There & Away The bus station is on Piazza Don Minzoni. From here you can get CLAP buses (☎ 0585 7 14 92) to various spots in the vicinity, such as Florence (L12,000, 2¾ hours), Massa to the south and, in the Lunigiana area, Fivizzano, Aulla and Pontremoli.

Trains along the coastal line (from Genoa, Rome, Viareggio and so on) stop nearer Marina di Carrara, from where local buses shuttle into Carrara itself.

LUNIGIANA

To the west of Carrara and Massa spread the mountains of the Apuan Alps (see later in the chapter and the 'Tuscany on Foot' special section) but for now we proceed farther north into one of the least explored pockets of Tuscany. The Lunigiana, a landlocked enclave of Tuscan territory bordered to the north and east by Emilia-Romagna, to the west by Liguria and the south by the Apuan Alps, caters little to tourism. Its main towns, with the exception of Pontremoli, are scarcely inviting.

The pleasure of the area comes from pottering about the back roads and small villages, using a combination of motorised propulsion and walking. The rugged territory abutting the mountains in Parma province to the north is great to explore. The medieval Via Francigena, a vital route

connecting northern and central Italy i Roman days and again a key to armies an Rome-bound pilgrims alike, roughly fo lows the modern A15 autostrada from th Passo della Cisa south to Sarzana (in Lig uria) on the coast.

Our route is one of several you could tak From Carrara take the provincial SP446 road north (if you pass through Gragnar you know you are headed in the right direc tion) and follow the signs to **Fosdinovo**.

The only reason for calling in here is i take a closer look at the formidable castl Owned by the Malaspina clan since 1340 (still belongs to a branch of the family), i defensive walls and towers were graduall modified from the 16th century on as th family converted it into a residence. opens daily (except Tuesday) for hourl guided visits. For the latest information o times and prices call ☎ 0187 6 88 91.

From Fosdinovo you can follow th SS446 to a T-junction with the SS63. Head ing right (east) will bring you to **Fivizzan** (buses serve this route). You could stop fo a food break in this largely modern farmin centre before proceeding up to the bord with Emilia-Romagna and the Apennine Apart from the vaguely charming Piazz Medicea there is precious little to keep yo here. On or near the square are clustered few bars and restaurants.

CAT buses run regularly to Aulla and le so to Massa, Carrara, Fosdinovo and Pass Cerreto (the pass over the Apennines int Emilia). Indeed, beyond Fivizzano th mountain road offers wonderfully prett country deep into Emilia-Romagna.

Heading in the opposite direction, south west from Fivizzano, you would hit **Aull** Blasted to smithereens in WWII, it offe little incentive to do anything but driv straight past. The only possible temptatio for the castle-collector is the 16th-centur Fortezza on a bluff outside the town centr

Just north of the town, the SS665 roa leads to Parma in Emilia-Romagna. Agai if you are looking for some beautiful cou try, you could do worse than follow th road across the regional border, from whe the driving becomes quite breathtaking.

Proceeding north from Aulla, you arrive **Villafranca**, a one-time way station on the la Francigena and, according to the stor- s, something of a medieval tourist trap, here the difference between local tax col- ctors and plain old thieves was vague to y the least. The northern end of what is sentially a one-street medieval settlement dominated by a mill (now housing a local hnographic museum) and bridge over the agra river.

Albergo Manganelli (*☎/fax 0187 49 30* *2, Piazza San Nicolò 5*) is at the southern d of the old village and offers single/ ouble rooms with bath for about L50,000/ 0,000. They also have a few without for a tle less.

ontremoli

his is the most winsome of the Lunigiana's ain towns. A primary halting place along e Via Francigena, the original old town is long sliver of a place stretched north to uth between the Magra and Verde rivers. hese watercourses served as natural de- nsive barriers in this, a key position for e control of traffic between northern and ntral Italy. After it was absorbed into the and duchy of Tuscany in the 17th century, e town enjoyed a boom. Much of the ace of Pontremoli dates to the fine resi- ences built in those times.

The Pro Loco tourist office (☎ 0187 460 41) is in the Palazzo Comunale in a urtyard off Piazza della Repubblica. It's en from 9 am to noon and 3 to 5 pm Mon- ay to Friday.

From the central Piazza della Repubblica d Piazza del Duomo (the latter is flanked y the 17th-century cathedral with its neo- assical facade) a steep and winding way kes you to the **Castello del Piagnaro**. Al- ough originally raised in the 9th century, hat you see today is largely the result of th- and 15th-century reconstruction. The ews across the town are enchanting and side you can visit the museum, given over prehistoric finds in the area. It opens om 9 am to noon and 3 to 6 pm (2 to 5 pm om October to March) Tuesday to Sunday d admission costs L5000.

There are only two not overly cheap hotel options here. *Hotel Napoleon* (*☎/fax 0187* *83 05 44, Piazza Italia 2/b*) offers sin- gles/doubles for around L90,000/135,000. You are actually better off staying down the road at Villafranca (see above). Your stom- ach, however, may be pleased to stick around. In the shadow of the cathedral is *Trattoria Da Bussè* (*☎ 0187 83 13 71, Pi-* *azza Duomo 31*), where you can dine on ex- cellent local specialities and spend around L45,000. It is well worth stopping for, ex- cept on Friday, when it is shut.

CAT buses run regularly south to Aulla and other destinations around the Luni- giana. You can also get to La Spezia (an im- portant coastal town in Liguria).

APUAN ALPS

This mountain range is bordered on one side by the Versilia coastline and on the other by the vast valley of the Garfagnana. Altitudes are relatively low (the highest peak, Monte Pisanino, is 1945m) in com- parison with the Alps farther north, but the Apuan Alps are certainly not lacking in great walking possibilities: some trails afford spectacular views to the coast and the Ligurian Sea.

The landscape in some areas has been utterly destroyed by marble mining, an in- dustry that has exploited these mountains since Roman times. No environmental laws have been in place to prevent mining com- panies from literally removing entire peaks in some places. But, in the end, the extent of interference in the natural landscape has created a new environment that has a cer- tain, slightly bizarre, aesthetic appeal.

The heartland of the mountains was con- stituted as the 543 sq km Parco Regionale delle Alpi Apuane in 1985. Some 22,000 people live within its boundaries.

There is a good network of marked trails, as well as several rifugi in the Apuan Alps, making walking in the region a popular choice. For further details of walking in this region, see the special section 'Tuscany on Foot'.

Apart from the walking opportunities, one of the main attractions in the area is the

NORTH-WESTERN TUSCANY

Grotta del Vento, caves with stalagmites, stalactites and crystal-encrusted lakes. Most visitors arrive by car. Barga to the east and Castelnuovo di Garfagnana to the north make possible bases. Lucca, to the south, is about an hour away by car. By bus it's more of an ordeal. From Lucca you take a bus for Gallicano, where you have to change and wait for one of the not-too-frequent connections to Fornovalasco, from where you have another 1km on foot, on the road north towards Trimpello.

The caves are open year-round, and the possible guided itineraries are offered (ranging in length from one to three hours). The first groups start at 10 am. Tours cost from L10,000 to L25,000, depending on which of the itineraries you choose to follow. From October to March only the one-hour walk is available from Monday to Saturday.

For more information call ☎ 0583 72 24 or you could check out their Web site www.grottadelvento.com.

Central Coast

The Medici grand dukes first gave life to the little town of Livorno on the central Tuscan coast, and it remains a busy port to this day. Eager for a little naval grandeur, the masters of Florence chose Livorno because it is close to Pisa, but also because it was one of the few handy coastal positions not surrounded by malarial swamps.

For much of the coast south of Livorno as far as Piombino, known as the Maremma Pisana, was indeed unpleasantly damp and mosquito-infested. Although initial attempts to dry out these swamps were carried out in the 18th century, it was really only under Leopoldo II that serious land reclamation took place. As a result, agricultural and industrial activity grew, old roads were rebuilt and new ones laid out. The Maremma Pisana only formally became a part of Livorno province in 1925.

Although some of the inland mountain towns are definitely worth some exploration and the occasional beach (especially on the southern Golfo di Baratti) is pleasant enough, this is not the most riveting part of Tuscany to hang about in. For those into searching out remnants of Etruscan civilisation, Populonia and its medieval twin, Populonia Alta, make a pleasant diversion. Livorno and Piombino are also departure points for ferries to the Tuscan islands and points beyond (such as Corsica), so you may well find yourself passing through the area anyway. If so, and you have time to spare, a few of the options below will make your travels here more enjoyable.

LIVORNO (LEGHORN)
postcode 57100 • pop 173,000

Tuscany's second-largest city, Livorno is not really worth a visit unless you are catching a ferry to Sardinia or Corsica. This modern port and industrial centre was heavily bombed during WWII and there is something unnervingly melancholy about the centre of town.

There may have been a time when the

Highlights

- Chow down to a generous helping of *cacciucco*, a kind of seafood hotpot

- Sail out to the charming island of Capraia from Livorno

- Visit the historic towns of Campiglia Marittima and Suvereto

- Combine a rest on the beach of the Golfo di Baratti with an exploration of the Etruscan and medieval settlements of Populonia

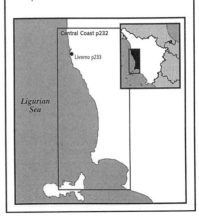

story was quite different. Earliest references to the town date to 1017 and the port was in the hands of Pisa and then Genoa for centuries. Florence, in need of an opening onto the sea, bought it in 1421. It was still tiny – indeed by the 1550s it boasted a grand total of 480 permanent residents! All that changed under Cosimo I de' Medici, who converted the scrawny settlement into a heavily fortified coastal bastion. It is quite extraordinary that by the end of the 18th century 80,000 people lived in Livorno, a busy port that had become one of the main staging posts for British and Dutch merchants operating between Western Europe

231

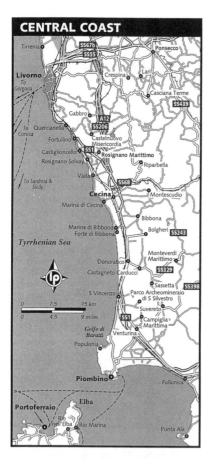

CENTRAL COAST

(map showing: Tirrenia, Ponsecco, SS67b, SS555, Livorno, To Gorgona, Crespina, Lari, Casciana Terme, SS439, Gabbro, A12, SS206, To Corsica, Quercianella, Fortullino, Castelnuovo Misericordia, Castiglioncello, SS1, Rosignano Marittimo, Rosignano Solvay, Riparbella, Vada, SS68, To Sardinia & Sicily, Cecina, Montescudio, Marina di Cecina, Bibbona, Marina di Bibbona, Forte di Bibbona, Bolgheri, SS243, Tyrrhenian Sea, Monteverdi Marittimo, Donoratico, SS329, Castagneto Carducci, Sassetta, SS398, S Vincenzo, Parco Archeominerario di S Silvestro, Suvereto, SS1, Campiglia Marittima, Golfo di Baratti, Venturina, Populonia, Piombino, Follonica, Elba, Portoferraio, Rio nell'Elba, Rio Marina, Punta Ala)

Scale: 0 — 7.5 — 15 km / 0 — 4.5 — 9 miles

cooked in white wine, tomato and broth and eaten with slices of toasted bread.

Orientation & Information

From the train station in Piazza Dante, east of the city centre, walk west along Viale Carducci and then Via Grande into the central Piazza Grande. The main APT tourist office (☎ 0586 89 81 11) is at Piazza Cavour 6 (2nd floor) to the south. From Piazza Grande, continue west towards the waterfront, through Piazza Micheli, Piazza Arsenale and towards a smaller APT (☎ 0586 89 53 20). A third APT is near the main ferry terminal, known as Calata Carrara, near Stazione Marittima. The main office is open from 9 am to 1 pm, Monday to Friday (also from 3 to 5 pm, Tuesday and Thursday). The smaller offices are open mornings and afternoons during summer only.

The main post office is at Via Cairoli 46 and the unstaffed Telecom office at Largo Duomo 14 opens from 8 am to 9.45 pm daily.

The police station (*questura*; ☎ 0586 2 51 11) is in the Palazzo del Governo, Piazza Unità d'Italia. The hospital (Ospedale Civile ☎ 0586 40 11 29) is at Viale Alfieri 36, between the centre and the main train station.

Things to See

The city does have a few worthy sights. The **Fortezza Nuova** (New Fort), in the area known as Piccola Venezia (oh please) because of its small canals, was built for the Medici in the late 16th century. The resemblance to Venice is notable by its absence – why is that whenever someone builds a canal or two in a city they are inevitably drawn to call it Little Venice? In this case there is some small excuse – the methods used to reclaim the land from the sea to extend the city northwards in the 17th century were based on the tried and tested practice of the Venetians. The fort, built under the Medici, is now a pleasant public park.

Close to the waterfront is the city's other fort, the **Fortezza Vecchia** (Old Fort), built 60 years earlier on the site of an 11th century building. It is in pretty bad shape, some amazing subsidence must be happening

and the Middle East. In the following century it was declared a free port, no doubt stimulating further growth and prosperity.

One of fascist Italy's main naval bases, Livorno took a hammering in unrelenting air raids in 1943 and on into 1944 (when it was under direct German occupation). The postwar rebuilding programme may be charitably described as unimaginative.

Livornese cuisine is, as you might expect, seafood based. If you find yourself here (or in any of the middling beach 'resorts' farther down the coast), try to tuck into a *cacciucco*, a quite remarkable mixed seafood stew

g judging by the yawning chasms that
me might be tempted by politeness to call
acks in the wall.

Livorno has a couple of extremely mod-
t museums. Perhaps the only one worth
ur time (if you have some of the latter to
ll) is the **Museo Civico Giovanni Fattori**.
's located in a villa in a pretty park south
 the centre at Via San Jacopo 65, and fea-
res works by the 19th-century Macchi-
oli movement led by the artist Giovanni
attori. The gallery, where temporary exhi-
tions are also occasionally held, is open
om 9 am to 1 pm, Tuesday to Sunday. Ad-

mission costs L6000. The city's unspectacular **Cathedral** is just off Piazza Grande.

South of town the so-called Etruscan
Coast (Costa degli Etruschi) begins. The
town beaches stretch for some way south,
but they are pebbly and generally nothing
special. The grand old seaside villas are a
bit of a sight. The No 1 bus from the main
train station heads down the coast road via
the town centre and Porto Mediceo.

Places to Stay & Eat

Finding accommodation shouldn't be a
problem. *Albergo L'Amico Fritz* (☎ *0586*

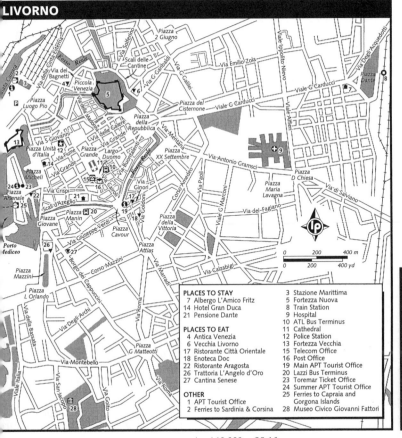

PLACES TO STAY
7 Albergo L'Amico Fritz
14 Hotel Gran Duca
21 Pensione Dante

PLACES TO EAT
4 Antica Venezia
6 Vecchia Livorno
17 Ristorante Città Orientale
18 Enoteca Doc
22 Ristorante Aragosta
26 Trattoria L'Angelo d'Oro
27 Cantina Senese

OTHER
1 APT Tourist Office
2 Ferries to Sardinia & Corsica

3 Stazione Marittima
5 Fortezza Nuova
8 Train Station
9 Hospital
10 ATL Bus Terminus
11 Cathedral
12 Police Station
13 Fortezza Vecchia
15 Telecom Office
16 Post Office
19 Main APT Tourist Office
20 Lazzi Bus Terminus
23 Toremar Ticket Office
24 Summer APT Tourist Office
25 Ferries to Capraia and
   Gorgona Islands
28 Museo Civico Giovanni Fattori

Amedeo Does Paris

Among the most striking nudes painted in the 20th century have to be those of Amedeo Modigliani. Born in Livorno in 1884, he showed talent as an artist at an early age and trained under the influence of the former Macchiaioli who had shaken up the Florentine, and indeed Italian, art scene in the years before and after Italian Unity. Livorno's own Giovanni Fattori had been a leading light among the Macchiaioli.

Modigliani was soon drawn away from his home town. He headed first to Florence, where he studied in 1902, but this was not enough. A year in Venice, where he became more closely acquainted with Austrian painters such as Gustav Klimt and the Jugendstil, was followed finally by a move to Paris in 1906.

Fauvism and cubism were taking off and Paris was the epicentre of the art world. It was here that Modigliani's particular style, marked but not swamped by the exciting new influences with which he now surrounded himself, came to life.

JANE SMITH

Modigliani returned to Italy briefly in 1909, but from then until the end of his life in 1920 remained in Montparnasse in Paris. For the next five years he turned to sculpture, rapidly accelerating the process of simplification – seeking to emphasise the contours. This period was then reflected in his subsequent paintings – the long faces typical of his later work are a result of his venture into sculpture. In 1914 and 1915 he concentrated on portraiture, and then in the last years of his life produced the series of nudes that figure among his best-known works. These nudes ooze a sultry, voluptuous sensuality, bursting with rich, warm colour. Yet they are painted with remarkable simplicity. His figures are infused with a touching, imperfect humanity.

Predictably, his work really only began to receive critical acclaim after his death, particularly in the wake of an exhibition of his paintings at the Venice Biennale in 1930. The bulk of his work has been scattered across art galleries in various parts of Italy and from Switzerland to France, Britain, the USA and beyond.

---

40 11 49, Viale G Carducci 180) is near the station and offers singles/doubles without own bath for L60,000/80,000 and others with bath for L80,000/110,000. Near the waterfront, *Pensione Dante* (☎ 0586 89 34 61, Scali d'Azeglio 28) has modest rooms without private bath for L40,000/58,000. For greater comfort you could try the *Hotel Gran Duca* (☎ 0586 89 10 24, Piazza Micheli), where rooms with all mod cons cost L140,000/210,000 including breakfast.

For produce, the *market* is on Via Buo talenti, and the area around Piazza XX S tembre is encouraging for *bars* and *caf* For seafood try *Ristorante Aragos* (☎ 0586 89 53 95, Piazza Arsenale (closed Sunday, right on the waterfront. Fi main courses cost from L12,000 L20,000. *L'Angelo d'Oro* (☎ 0586 88 95, Piazza Mazzini 15), closed Wednesda is an inexpensive trattoria with pasta fr L7000. The *Cantina Senese* (☎ 0586 89

, *Borgo dei Cappuccini 95)* is also a pop-
ar local eatery and just as inexpensive. It
closed Sunday.

The menu changes weekly at ***Enoteca***
oc (☎ 0586 88 75 83, Via Goldoni 40–44)
d you can enjoy fresh pasta dishes and
od *carpaccio*, as well as snacks. As with
y *enoteca* (wine bar), the main attraction
the wine, of which there is a broad selec-
on, along with grappas and whiskies. It is
osed Monday.

Fronting the Fortezza Nuova, ***Vecchia***
*vorno (☎ 0586 88 40 48, Scali delle Can-
e 34)* is a family-run place of disarming
mplicity, which is closed Tuesday. When
u are quite comfortably seated at your
ooden table, go for the seafood dishes.
xpect to pay around L45,000 for a full
eal with wine.

Not far off in the heart of the so-called
enice quarter, ***Antica Venezia (☎ 0586 88***
3 53, Via dei Bagnetti 1) is another good
cal seafood eatery, which is closed Sun-
ay and Monday. Prices are much the same
at Vecchia Livorno.

There's Chinese at the ***Ristorante Città***
rientale (☎ 0586 88 82 66, Via Ginori 23).

etting There & Away

us ATL buses (☎ 0586 88 42 62) depart
om Largo Duomo for Cecina, Piombino
d Pisa. Lazzi buses (☎ 0586 89 95 62) de-
art from Piazza Manin for Florence, Pisa,
ucca and Viareggio.

rain The main train station in Piazza Dante
on the Rome-La Spezia line and the city
also connected to Florence and Pisa.
rains are less frequent to Stazione Marit-
ma, the second station near the main port.
is usually easier to catch a train to the
ain train station and then a bus to the ports.

ar & Motorbike The A12 runs past the
ty and the SS1 connects Livorno with
ome. There are several car parks near the
aterfront.

oat Livorno is a major west-coast port.
egular departures for Sardinia and Cor-
ica leave from the Stazione Marittima (in

an area called Calata Carrara, just north of
Fortezza Vecchia). In addition, ferries also
depart from a smaller terminal known as
Porto Mediceo, near Piazza Arsenale, and
occasionally from the Porto Nuovo. The
first two can be easily reached by bus from
the main train station. The Toremar ticket
office, for ferries to the islands of Capraia
and Gorgona, is the opposite side of Piazza
Arsenale to the ferry terminal. The third is
several kilometres north of the city along
Via Salvatore Orlando and not well served
by public transport. Ask at the tourist office
for directions.

Ferry services from Livorno include:

Stazione Marittima

Corsica Ferries (☎ 0586 88 13 80) Regular services to Corsica (one-way daytime deck-class
fares to Bastia range from L29,000 to L47,000
plus L4000 taxes).

Corsica Marittima (☎ 0586 21 11 01) Services
to Corsica (Bastia and Porto Vecchio).

Sardinia Ferries (☎ 0586 88 13 80) Regular services to Sardinia (one-way deck-class fares to
Golfo Aranci, near Olbia, range from L38,000
to L84,000 – the latter fares on summer weekends only).

Moby Lines (☎ 0586 82 68 23/4/5) Services to
Corsica (one-way deck-class fares to Bastia
range from L32,000 to L50,000 depending on
the season) and Sardinia (one-way deck-class
fares to Olbia range from L33,000 to L86,000).

Porto Mediceo

Toremar (☎ 0586 89 61 13) Services to Gorgona
and Capraia.

Porto Nuovo

Compagnia Sarda Navigazione Marittima
(☎ 0586 40 99 25) Located at Varco Galvani,
Calata Tripoli, with ferries to Olbia (Sardinia).

Grandi Navi Veloci (☎ 0586 40 98 04) Located
at Varco Galvani, Calata Tripoli, Darsena 1,
with boats to Palermo in Sicily (one-way seats
range from L103,000 to L161,000).

Getting Around

To get from the train station to Piazza Arsenale and the Porto Mediceo, take ATL bus
No 1. To reach the Stazione Marittima take
bus No 7. Both these and several others pass
through Piazza Grande in the centre. Tickets cost L1500.

CENTRAL COAST

AROUND LIVORNO
Capraia & Gorgona

As you will have noticed above, Toremar operates boats to the islands of Capraia and Gorgona from Livorno. Along with their big sister to the south, Elba, and four others farther south still (Pianosa, Montecristo, Giglio and Giannutri), they form the Parco Nazionale dell'Arcipelago Toscano.

The tiny island of **Gorgona** is the greenest and northernmost of the islands. At just 2.23 sq km in area, there's not much to it. The two towers were built respectively by the Pisans and Medicis of Florence. Part of the island is off limits as a low-security prison farm. You can effectively only visit the island on Tuesday, when the 8.30 am Toremar ferry from Livorno stops there on the way to and from Capraia, giving you about five hours from arrival time at 10 am. Other days of the week, some ferries stop on the way out to Capraia, but none stops on the way back, which would leave you in a pickle.

The elliptical, volcanic island of **Capraia** lies 65km from Livorno. It is hilly (the highest point is Monte Castello at 447m) and covered mainly in *macchia*, various types of Mediterranean scrub. It has changed hands several times over the course of its history, belonging at one stage or another to Genoa, Sardinia, the Saracens from North Africa and Napoleon.

You can sign up for boat trips around the 30km coastline of the island (for which you will pay around L20,000 per person) or trek across the island. The most popular walk is to the **Stagnone**, a small lake in the south. The only beach worthy of the name is **Cala della Mortola**, a few kilometres north of the island's town, **Capraia Isola**. The town is a 1km walk from the little port.

Accommodation on the island is tight. You can check into the camping ground, *Le Sughere* (☎/fax 0586 90 50 66, Via delle Sughere), which opens from May to the end of September. Otherwise you choose between two expensive hotels, *Il Saracino* (☎ 0586 90 50 18, fax 0586 90 50 62, Via Cibo 40) or *Da Beppone* (☎/fax 0586 90 50 01, Via della Assunzione 78). The latter is

the cheaper at L100,000/130,000 for single doubles and also is a good place to eat. T former charges L185,000/250,000 in hi season.

A daily boat to Capraia with Torem sails from Livorno. On most days there also a return trip, but triple check befo you go. The one-way trip costs L20,00 whether you go to Capraia or Gorgona. summer, excursions from Elba to Capra are also organised.

THE ETRUSCAN COAST

The province of Livorno stretches down th coast to a little way beyond Piombino, fro where you catch the ferry to the island Elba (see the Elba chapter for more detai on this island).

Tuscany is never going to win any prize as great beach territory, but if you a trundling around in the area and fancy a d in the briny, some of the beaches are OK.

A handful of little towns of some intere are scattered about in the hilly hinterland this slender province. A couple of archaeo logical parks and the possibility of discove ing some of Tuscany's lesser known, bu often very good, wines complete the pictur

Livorno to Cecina

You can chug down the coast from Livorn by train, bus or car. As usual, your ow transport makes life a lot easier.

There's a cute little beach a couple o kilometres short of **Quercianella**, but de scribing how to find it ain't easy. Keep watch out for a tower and castle atop promontory before you (assuming you ar heading south from Livorno). The inlet di rectly north of that promontory is where th beach is. As you round a curve into the inle you may notice a small sign for a path dow to the beach. Limited parking is available i a lay-by just to the right of the road a littl further on.

In Quercianella itself you'll find a coupl of little grey stone affairs. At the norther end of the town surfers gather even when a adverse wind is up. It's a leafy, sleepy littl place. Another 5km or so down the roa you will see a sign for the **Parco Comunal**

Fortullino. If you can find a place to leave your vehicle and walk down to the water's edge, the park is pleasant and a bar operates in summer. But again, the beach is a disappointing rocky affair.

Comparatively cute is the high northern end of **Castiglioncello**, which sits on a small promontory a few kilometres farther on from Fortullino. The small sandy beaches (for a spot on which you will have to fork out around L15,000) on the north side of the town are the nicest. On the south side the backdrop is flat and dominated by the smokestacks of the industrial plant at Rosignano Solvay just beyond.

You could do worse than stay in the high part of Castiglioncello. It's a pleasant, leafy spot with a few restaurants scattered about to keep your jaws happy. *Pensione Bartoli* (☎ *0586 75 20 51, Via Martelli 9*) is not a bad little choice, with single/double rooms for up to L70,000/90,000 with own bath. In July and August you may be obliged to pay up to L100,000 per person for full board. Their restaurant offers vegetarian food.

Inland from Rosignano Solvay, perched on a hill, is **Rosignano Marittimo**. Already a small settlement in Lombard times, Rosignano was one of Lorenzo the Magnificent's preferred bases for hunting. Although there has been a castle here since the 8th century, the fortifications you see today date to the times of Cosimo I de' Medici.

Back down on the coast, **Vada** is a typically characterless seaside spot. At least the beaches have sand. Another 8km and you reach **Marina di Cecina**, where the story is much the same, although being a bigger place there is a little life. About halfway between the sea and the modern centre of Cecina you can visit the Parco Archeologico, which preserves Etruscan remains. It opens from 10 am to 1 pm and 4.30 to 7.30 pm daily, from mid-July to the end of August. It is closed altogether from mid-December to mid-February and open weekends for the rest of the year. Admission is free. For an assortment of ancient artefacts dug up in these parts you could pop into the Museo Archeologico at the Villa Cinquatina, Via Guerrazzi. For info on opening times (irregular at best), call ☎ 0586 66 04 11.

Places to stay, some open only in summer, abound here and in places such as Vada. Cecina is encircled by five camping grounds. At the southern end of Marina di Cecina, *Le Tamerici* (☎ *0586 62 06 29, Località Il Paiolo*) has all the facilities you are likely to need. You pay up to L13,000 per person and L22,000 for a tent.

You can get the train or ATL bus to Cecina from Livorno. The latter costs L5000, but makes so many stops that it can be a little slow.

Cecina to Piombino

From Cecina you could follow the SS1 or minor coast roads south, but even the latter aren't too loaded with excitement. A more enticing idea is to head inland. Livorno's tourist office has come up with a wine route (Strada del Vino) that moves inland from Cecina to **Montescudaio**. This is a pretty drive and as good as any for moving away from the relatively drab coastal flats. Along the following route towards Piombino you will pass the odd vineyard where you can taste and purchase local wines. There is a particular concentration of them around Castagneto Carducci (see later in this section). You can pick up a map and comprehensive list of outlets from the tourist office in Livorno.

Head south from Montescudaio and you soon reach **Bibbona**, a medieval hill town that dominates the plain running below to the coast. A little farther south and on the coast is **Marina di Bibbona**, south of which stretches a narrow strip of sandy beach backed by macchia and pine woods. A couple of accommodation options present themselves, including the *Hotel Paradiso Verde* (☎*/fax 0586 60 00 22, Via del Forte 9*), where doubles cost up to L110,000.

A short way south of Marina di Bibbona is the small but important **Rifugio Faunistico di Bolgheri**. This nature reserve is a key stop for migratory birds. The number of birds is greatest from November to March, and the best time for seeing them is from December to January. Visits are severely limited. Never more than 15 people are allowed in at any time and you need to arrange it beforehand. For information, call ☎ 0565 77 71 25, or inquire at the local police (Vigili Urbani) in the village of **Donoratico**. The entrance to the park is just west off the SS1, a short way south of the cypress-lined, arrow-straight road that leads eastwards to the pretty little settlement of **Bolgheri**. The castle that takes in the city gate and Romanesque Chiesa di SS Giacomo e Cristoro, and so serves as the village entrance, was restructured towards the end of the 19th century. You can get a bite to eat or do a little low-key tourist shopping for local food products and wine.

So far we have assumed you will have some form of transport of your own, as getting about here with buses is extremely tedious. That also goes for the next stretch of the Strada del Vino, which takes you initially through dense woodland along a minor road due south of Bolgheri. The route becomes less interesting towards the end until you climb up into the hills to reach **Castagneto Carducci**.

Behind the town walls here lies a web of steep narrow lanes crowded in by brooding houses and dominated by the castle (turned into a mansion in the 18th century) of the Gherardesca clan that once controlled the surrounding area. The 19th-century poet Giosuë Carducci spent much of his childhood here.

If you want to stay you might try *Marcella Niccolai* (☎ 0565 76 34 34, Via Cavour 6), a small *affittacamere* in the centre of the town. It has simple doubles for L50,000 and opens from May to September. A pleasing little restaurant with a garden dining area is *Ristorante Glorione* (☎ 0565 76 33 22, Via Carducci 6), which is closed Tuesday. To pick up some local liqueurs and other hooch, try the 100-year-old L'Elixir (☎ 0565 76 60 17) at Via Garibaldi 7. By the way, some of the country's finest olive oil is said to come from here.

Next stop on the winding hill road, which runs through cool woods, is the tiny hamlet of **Sassetta**. Coming at it from Castagneto, its houses seem to be hanging on to their perches for dear life. There's not an awful lot to it, but it's pleasant enough and you could stay comfortably in the *Albergo La Selva* (☎/fax 0565 79 42 39, Via Fornace 32), just outside the town on the road to Castagneto Carducci.

Suvereto This next stop is a surprise packet. The tortuous streets and steep stairways of Suvereto have constituted a busy little centre since well before the year 1000. For a while it was even the seat of a bishopric and was only incorporated into the Tuscan grand duchy in 1815. The town has maintained much of its Gothic feel and would make a great base (if you could find anywhere to stay) for exploring this area for a day or two. A tourist office (☎ 0565 82 93 04) opens on Piazza Gramsci from about May to September. At the time of writing it opened from 10 am to 12.30 pm on Sunday and every other day but Wednesday from 3.30 to 6 pm. They can provide info on walking in the surrounding hills.

Apart from a handful of affittacamere and *agriturismo* options scattered about in the vicinity, the accommodation options are scarce. *Il Chiostro* (☎ 0565 82 81 33, Via del Crocifisso 2), right in the centre, offers small apartments that can cost anything from L92,000 to L162,000 for two.

Another possibility is the *Casa per le Ferie La Rocca* (☎ 0565 82 98 82, Via della Rocca), which is right up at the top of the town near the Rocca, the old (and now largely ruined) fort. They have doubles only for L80,000, although in low season you can probably bargain them down a little for single occupancy.

An atmospheric spot for a meal and, more critically, a drink, is *Enoteca dei Difficili* (☎ 0565 82 80 18, Via San Leonardo), which is closed Monday. Alongside an array of delightful snacks and a limited serving of salads and main courses, you can sip your favourite Tuscan tipple or enjoy the rare opportunity (in this part of the world) to make comparisons with foreign competitors. Here they offer a few selected Australian, Californian, Chilean and French wines.

If you are here in mid-August, you may catch the traditional Corsa delle Botte, when townfolk race each other to push huge tumbling wine barrels along the cobbled lanes of the town. In December the people of Suvereto tuck in for their Sagra del Cinghiale (Wild Boar Festival).

Campiglia Marittima to the Coast

From Suvereto you drop down onto the plains along the SS398 road to Piombino for about 5km before turning off right to head back into the hills, in which nestle the dun-coloured stone houses of **Campiglia Marittima**, another surprisingly intact medieval town.

The other principal hue, spattered about across the town, is the fern green of the doors and shutters, which appears to be standard issue. From the central Piazza della Repubblica, fronted by centuries-old mansions, you walk up to the Palazzo Pretorio, long the seat of government. Its main facade, covered in an assortment of coats-of-arms, is akin to the bulky bemedalled chest of many a modern-day general. Campiglia belonged to the Pisan republic and then, from 1406, to Florence, but the location has been inhabited since Etruscan times. There's nowhere to stay in the town itself, although several affittacamere and agriturismo options can be located in the immediately surrounding area.

A few kilometres north-west of Campiglia on the road to San Vincenzo is the **Parco Archeominerario di San Silvestro**. Just before you reach the turn-off (on the right) you pass the church of Madonna di Fucinaia, right by which you can inspect Etruscan smelting ovens used for copper production.

The park is dedicated to the 3000-year mining history of the area. The highlight for most is Rocca di San Silvestro, a medieval mining town which was abandoned in the 14th century. The Temperino mines around it produced copper and lead, some used for the mints of Lucca and later Pisa.

You can make two guided tours, one of Rocca di San Silvestro and the other of part of the Temperino mine and museum. The mine and museum (the latter in the same building as the ticket office) are near the entrance, while Rocca di San Silvestro is about a half hour walk away (or take the park shuttle). Tours of each location take place every hour or so (timetables vary throughout the year). You pay L20,000 for both or L12,000 for just one.

The park opens from 9 am to sunset, Tuesday to Sunday, from May to September. For the rest of the year it opens only at weekends and public holidays. The occasional bus runs from San Vincenzo, about 6km down the road.

If you get back on the road leading away from Campiglia, you would end up on the coast at the rather bland but popular seaside town of **San Vincenzo**. Yachties can park their vessels here but there's not much to do after that. Sandy beaches stretch to the north and south of the town. Those to the south are the more tempting, backed by macchia and pine plantations. Although there are quite a few hotels, getting a room in summer is challenging. And so are the prices. There is only one camping ground.

If you get hungry while on the beach to the south of town, you could tuck into a seaside pizza for about L10,000 at ***Ristorante La Barcaccina*** (*☎ 0565 70 19 11, Via Tridentina*). The restaurant is on the beach, and is closed Wednesday. From the coast road (not the SS1), look for the parking area and sign for the Parco Comunale and walk through the pines to the beach.

Golfo di Baratti & Populonia Twenty-three kilometres south of San Vincenzo along the coast road a minor road leads off to the south-west and the Golfo di Baratti. This must be one of the mainland Tuscan coast's prettiest beaches, although as the weird and wonderful postures of the trees attest, it is often a shade windy – handy for windsurfers though.

Inland from the gulf is the **Parco Archeologico di Baratti e Populonia**, where Etruscan tombs of varying interest have been unearthed. The most interesting are the circular ones in the Necropoli di San Cerbone, between the coast road and the visitors'

CENTRAL COAST

centre. You have several choices when you enter. You can get the L20,000 ticket that permits you to walk all over the park (an exercise that will take several hours at a leisurely pace). Otherwise you can pay L12,000 and visit one of the two set areas. The first is the Necropoli di San Cerbone. The second includes quarries and underground tombs along the so-called Via delle Cave. Frankly, especially if your time is limited, you could content yourself with the necropolis. Clattering down steps to stare into the gloom of a small underground tomb is, save for experts, of limited interest for the average punter. Repeating the operation can most kindly be described as tedious. Still, maybe you'll be in it just for some pleasant walking.

Opening times change all the time. In August it's open from 9 am to 8 pm daily, but otherwise the hours start to reduce and some days it may be closed altogether (most likely Monday). The only way to be sure is to call ahead on ☎ 0565 2 91 07.

You probably have already espied the crenellations of a castle and town walls up among the woods farther down the road. Your curiosity is worth following as medieval **Populonia Alta** is a rather fetching little three-street hamlet, walled in and protected by the castle. Built in the 15th century, the hamlet grew up on the site of a Pisan watchtower. You can visit the small Etruscan Museum for an inspection of a few local finds. Admission costs L2500. Opening times seem flexible – to wit: '*Il brutto tempo, l'umore e la fame potrebbero influenzare l'orario di apertura e chiusura*' ('Bad weather, mood and hunger could affect opening and closing times').

Virtually across the road, near the car park, is the Etruscan acropolis of ancient **Populonia** (Popluna to the Etruscans). From 1980 to 1990 it was excavated and you can now enter free of charge. If your Italian is up to it join a short guided visit (every half hour). In a nutshell, the digs have revealed the foundations of an Etruscan temple dating to the 2nd century BC, along with its adjacent buildings. The acropolis grounds are open daily from 9 am to 7 pm.

There's an expensive restaurant and an inordinate amount of souvenir shopping options, but no place to stay in Populonia. It appears the only way up here from the Golfo di Baratti (which can be reached by ATL buses from Piombino and San Vincenzo) is under your own steam (parking costs L1500 for two hours).

Piombino Poor old Piombino, it really gets a lot of lousy press. Unfortunately it is largely true for the busy visitor that the best thing to come out of Piombino is the Elba ferry. A Roman-era port and from the late 19th century a centre of steel production, the city was heavily damaged during WWII and precious little remains of the walled historical centre.

That said, the more indulgent might want to give it a quick shufti. The centre, whose focal point is the 15th-century **Torrione Rivellino**, and fishing port are not without a little charm. Those with wheels might want to follow the signs just out of town for the scruffy **Parco di Punta Alcone**. You can follow a couple of brief trails to wartime German bunkers and gun emplacements and gaze out across to Elba.

Farther to the north (along the coast in the direction of Populonia) are a couple of modest beaches (don't bother if you are going to Elba).

Should you need, for whatever emergency, to stay, the *Hotel Roma* (☎ 0565 3 43 41, fax 0565 3 43 48, Via San Francesco 43) is a reasonable central choice with singles/doubles costing up to L70,000/110,000 with private bathroom.

Piombino is on the Rome–Genoa train line. There are fairly regular connections to Florence too. ATM buses (☎ 0565 22 21 18) leave from the centre of town at Via Leonardo da Vinci 13. See immediately below for some general transport tips in the area.

For Elba ferry information see the Elba chapter.

Getting Around

With enormous reserves of patience you can get pretty much anywhere mentioned above y bus. Piombino-based ATM buses running between Piombino and Cecina, for instance, stop (in some cases – ask before boarding) at Castagneto Carducci, Sassetta, an Vincenzo and Golfo di Baratti. Another ne serves Suvereto a few times a day on its ay to Sassetta and Monteverdi Marittimo. et another connects Piombino with Suvereto and Campiglia Marittima. For coastal stops such as San Vincenzo, the train is probably a better bet, but the hill towns are generally a long distance from the nearest train station in the plains below. Remember also that ATL buses from Livorno make quite a few stops along the coast on their way south to Piombino.

Elba

postcode 57307 • pop 29,400

Napoleon should have considered himself lucky to be shunted off to such a pretty spot. He arrived in May 1814 and lasted a year – he just had to have another shot at imperial greatness. Well, he met his Waterloo and the rest is histrionics.

Don't come in August (the best thing any level-headed human can do in August anywhere in Europe is leave altogether or stay at home and wait for better days), as it gets unpleasantly crowded and everything costs even more than usual.

Nowadays people would willingly be exiled here, and the island attracts more than one million tourists a year. They come to swim in its glorious blue waters, lie on the beaches, eat fine (if often pricey) food and generally loll about.

Elba is growing in popularity among walkers. Its mountainous terrain can provide some tough treks, although there are better places to walk elsewhere in Tuscany.

Just 28km long and 19km across at its widest point, Elba is well equipped for tourists, with plenty of hotels and camping grounds. The hordes have arrived only in recent years, so the island is not (as yet) overdeveloped. The main towns are Portoferraio on the northern side and Marina di Campo on the southern.

History

Elba has been inhabited since the Iron Age. Funny we should mention that, because the extraction of iron ore and metallurgy were, until the second half of the 20th century, the island's principal sources of economic wellbeing (the last of the mines closed in 1981). In fact, Elba is something of a geologist's dream. It fairly reeks of mineral wealth – so much so that you can even fossick around in museums dedicated to rocks.

Ligurian tribespeople were the island's first inhabitants, followed later by Etruscans and Greeks from Magna Graecia. The iron business was well established by this point

Highlights

- Relax on some of the little beaches and coves in the north-west and south of the island
- Indulge in good food and late-night drinks in the island's prettiest town, Capoliveri
- Put on your walking boots or saddle up on a mountain bike to explore the western heights of the island around Monte Capanne

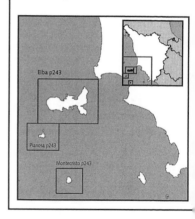

and no doubt made the island doubly attractive to the Romans, the richer of whom took to building holiday villas on the island.

Centuries of peace under the Pax Romana gave way to more uncertain times during the barbarian invasions, when Elba and the other Tuscan islands became refuges for those fleeing mainland marauders. By the 11th century, Pisa (and later Piombino) was in control and built fortresses to help ward off attacks by Muslim raiders and pirates operating out of North Africa. These raids remained a constant problem.

In the 16th century, Cosimo I de' Medici obtained territory in the north of the island, where he founded the port town of

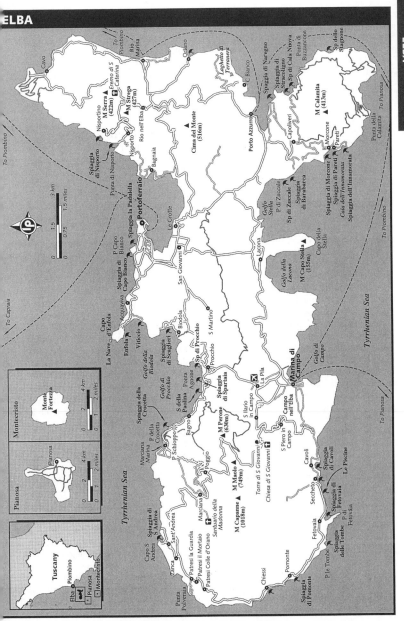

ELBA

Cosmopolis (today Portoferraio). At the same time, the Spanish acquired control of the south-eastern strip of the island.

Grand Duke Pietro Leopoldo II encouraged land reform, the drainage of swamps and greater agricultural production on the island in the 18th century. Nevertheless, iron remained the major industry. In 1917 some 840,000 tonnes were produced, but during WWII the industry was hit hard by the Allies and never recovered. By the beginning of the 1980s production was down to 100,000 tonnes. The writing was on the wall, but tourism had arrived to take the place of mining and smelting.

Orientation & Information

Most ferries arrive at Portoferraio, Elba's capital and its main transport hub. Ferries from Piombino travel less frequently to Rio Marina, Marina di Campo and Porto Azzurro.

The main APT tourist office (☎ 0565 91 46 71), Calata Italia 26, Portoferraio, can assist with accommodation. If you plan to visit in summer, book ahead – the Associazione Albergatori Isola d'Elba (☎ 0565 91 47 54), Calata Italia 20, will find you a room. Should you choose to roam around the island without booking rooms ahead, look out for 'camere' or 'affittacamere' signs, which indicate rooms for rent in private houses. They can come in handy when hotels are full and often represent reasonable value for money.

A tourist medical service operates during summer at: Portoferraio (☎ 0565 91 42 12) at the public hospital, Località San Rocco; Marina di Campo (☎ 0565 97 60 61), Piazza Dante Alighieri 3; Rio Marina (☎ 0565 96 24 07), Via Principe Amadeo; Marciana Marina (☎ 0565 90 44 36), Viale Regina Margherita; and Capoliveri (☎ 0565 96 89 95), Via Soprana.

Activities

Elba has some excellent walks, and is growing in popularity as a walkers' venue. For further information, see the 'Tuscany on Foot' special section at the end of the Facts for the Visitor chapter.

Other popular activities on the island include mountain biking, windsurfing, diving and sailing. Schools offering courses or hiring out equipment abound in the main coastal resorts on the island, particularly Portoferraio, Marina di Campo and Porto Azzurro. Given the scope of this book would be a little unfair to single out one or two outlets – they are always easy to find.

Getting There & Away

In the summer months Lufthansa and several minor airlines operate regular flights from Munich, Stuttgart, Vienna, Zürich, Berne, Brescia, Bergamo and Rome to Elba's tiny aerodrome at La Pila. Charter flights also operate to the island.

Unless you have your own boat, the only other way to get to Elba is by ferry from Piombino. If you arrive in Piombino by train get a connecting train to the port. Several companies (Moby Lines, Toremar and Elba Ferries) operate ferries and have offices in Piombino and Portoferraio. Unless it is the middle of August, you shouldn't have any trouble buying a ticket at the port. Prices are competitive at around L11,000 per person or L51,500 for a small car plus driver (other passengers extra). All lines offer a special deal on certain runs (indicated in timetables). The ferry trip takes an hour.

Elba Ferries has a faster catamaran, which carries cars and makes the trip in 25 minutes. Prices on most days are from L12,000 per person and L54,500 for a small car.

Getting Around

Bus The island's bus company, ATL (☎ 0565 91 43 92), runs regular service across the island. From Portoferraio, for instance, you can reach all of the main towns including Marciana Marina, Marina di Campo, Capoliveri and Porto Azzurro, as well as smaller resorts and beaches such as Sant'Andrea, Cavo and Fetovaia. Ask at the tourist office for an updated timetable.

Car, Motorcycle & Bicycle The best way to get around Elba is to rent a mountain bike (be aware that the island is hilly – some would say mountainous – and cycling an be a real pain in the legs), scooter or motorcycle. In high season mountain bikes start at L20,000 a day and L100,000 for one week, mopeds (50cc) are from L35,000 to 50,000 a day, and motorbikes start at about L100,000 a day. TWN (Two Wheels Network; ☎ 0565 91 46 66), Viale Elba 32, Portoferraio (branches at Marciana Marina, Marina di Campo, Porto Azzurro and several other locations) is one of several car/bike/motorbike rental outlets. Happy Rent (☎ 0565 91 46 65), Viale Elba 5, is another, although there are plenty of others.

PORTOFERRAIO

Known to the Romans as Fabricia and later Ferraia (on account of its use as a port for iron exports), this small port was acquired by Cosimo I de' Medici in the mid-16th century. It was from this time that the fortifications and town you see today took shape. The walls link two forts (Stella and Falcone) on high points and a third tower closing the port (Linguella). In 1814 Napoleon took up residence here as he began his exile on Elba, which his enemies had generously turned into a Napoleonic statelet (see the boxed text 'Napoleon in Early Retirement'). Steelworks began operating in 1902 but were destroyed by the Allies in 1943.

The new part of Portoferraio encompasses the modern ferry port, but otherwise is of little interest, so head around to the old town, gathered in picturesquely around the fishing and pleasure port built under Cosimo I de' Medici and enclosed by the above-mentioned walls. You can wander around the Falcone (L3000) and Stella (L2000) **forts** from 9 am to 7 pm (later in summer). Down from the walls leading to Forte Falcone is a narrow but rather fetching little sliver of beach.

In the old town, up on the bastions between the two forts, you'll also encounter the **Villa dei Mulini**, one of the residences where Napoleon mooched about. It features a splendid terraced garden and his library, and is open from 9 am to 7 pm Monday to Saturday and from 9 am to 1 pm on Sunday. Admission costs L8000.

The ticket also allows you admission to the **Villa Napoleonica di San Martino**, Napoleon's summer residence, set in hills about 5km south-west of the town. The villa houses a modest collection of Napoleonic paraphernalia and also hosts an annual exhibition based on a Napoleonic theme. The villa is open the same hours as the museum.

The Linguella fortifications down by the port house the modest **Museo Civico Archeologico**. It opens from 9.30 am to 12.30 pm and 4 to 7 pm daily except Thursday, Sunday and holidays (6 pm to midnight in July and August). Admission costs L4000.

Places to Stay & Eat
The closest camping grounds are about 4km west of Portoferraio, in Acquaviva. *Campeggio La Sorgente (☎ 0565 91 71 39)* and *Acquaviva (☎ 0565 91 55 92)* are easily found.

Albergo Ape Elbana (☎ 0565 91 42 45, Salita de' Medici 2), in the old town, has singles/doubles with bathroom starting at L65,000 a head including breakfast. They climb to L90,000/125,000 for singles/doubles in high season. The *Villa Ombrosa (☎ 0565 91 43 63, Via De Gasperi 3)* has singles/doubles with bathroom for around L120,000/150,000. They may insist that you take half board, which is OK as their *Ristorante Villa Ombrosa* serves good Tuscan dishes. A full meal will cost around L40,000.

In the old town, you could do worse than the Neapolitan *Trattoria da Zucchetta (☎ 0565 91 53 31, Piazza della Repubblica 40)*, which has been in business since 1891. You can eat a full meal for around L45,000. It is closed Tuesday. If it's a little too full of foreigners for your tastes, try *Stella Marina (☎ 0565 91 59 83, Banchina Alto Fondale)*, nearer the ferry terminal on the waterfront. It ain't cheap, but the loud and contrary (with each other!) staff serve some good local and Genoese (!) dishes. Seafood takes centre stage. It is closed Wednesday.

Entertainment
A nice little harbourside bar where you can sip decent cocktails and mixed drinks is

Napoleon in Early Retirement

At 6 pm on 3 May 1814, the English frigate *Undaunted* dropped anchor in the Medici harbour of Portoferraio. The cargo was unusual to say the least. Under the Treaty of Fontainebleau, the Emperor who since the beginning of the century had held all Europe in his thrall, campaigning with superhuman energy from Spain to Russia, was exiled to the island of Elba.

It could have been a lot worse for the Emperor, but the Allies decided on a soft option, partly to short-circuit any possible adverse reaction in France. Napoleon was awarded the island as his private fiefdom, to hold until the end of his days.

His arrival was greeted with considerable pomp. The guns of Portoferraio shot off a 100-round salute, to which the English frigate replied. That at least is Alexandre Dumas' version. Others say the guns were actually firing *at* the frigate.

Whatever may have been the case, Elba would never be quite the same again. Although no doubt watching the situation in Europe with a hawk's eye, Napoleon threw himself into frenetic activity in his new, somewhat humbler domain.

After touring the island and making all the right noises to its inhabitants, he undertook a long series of public works. They included improving operations in the island's iron-ore mines (whose revenue now went to Napoleon), boosting agriculture, initiating a road-building program, draining marshes, overhauling the legal and education systems and so on. On some of the programs he often set members of his faithful 500 guardsmen to work.

A great deal of ink has been spilled over the Corsican's dictatorial style and seemingly impossible ambitions, but he can't have been all bad. To this day they still say a Mass for his soul in the Chiesa della Misericordia in May!

Napoleon had by now installed himself in the bastions of the city wall, in what became known as the Residenza dei Mulini. His so-called country or summer home, outside town in San Martino, he used as an occasional stopover on excursions – he never slept there. Some weeks after his arrival Napoleon was joined by his mother Letizia and sister Paolina. But he remained separated from his wife Maria Luisa and was visited for just two days by his lover Maria Walewska.

On the Continent, things were hotting up. Rumours were rife that Napoleon's really rather comfortable exile might be curtailed. At the Congress of Vienna, France called for Napoleon's removal to a more distant location. Austria, too, was nervous. Some suggested Malta, but Britain objected. London then suggested the South Atlantic islet of St Helena.

Napoleon could not be sure which rumours to believe. According to some he would sooner or later be moved. Others suggested such reports were designed to induce him to some rash act in breach of the Treaty of Fontainebleau that would provide the Allies with the excuse they needed to get rid of him, for they were not keen to be seen to break what they could claim had been the generous terms of the treaty. The congress broke up with no official decision, although the Allies were well aware that Napoleon still had many supporters in and beyond France and could easily raise a new army should he be of a mind to try.

He was. Under no circumstances was he going to allow himself to be meekly shipped off to some rocky speck in the middle of the Atlantic. A lifelong risk-taker, he decided to have another roll of the dice. Perhaps, during his time on Elba, he always knew he would. For months he had sent out a couple of vessels flying his Elban flag on 'routine' trips around the Mediterranean. When one of them, the *Incostante*, set sail early in the morning of 26 February 1815 (a Sunday), no-one suspected he might be hidden on board. Sir Neil Campbell, his English jail warden, had only returned to Livorno the previous day under the impression that Napoleon was, as ever, fully immersed in the business of the island.

Elba lost its emperor and Napoleon his gilded cage. He had embarked on the Hundred Days that would culminate in defeat at Waterloo – he got the Atlantic exile after all, but at least he had tried.

Baretto (☎ *0565 91 46 13, Calata Mazzni 21*). Most drinks cost around L10,000.

AROUND PORTOFERRAIO
West to Capo d'Enfola

Several modest little beaches spread west from Portoferraio. Quite nice, although narrow and shelly, are **Spiaggia La Padulella** and its counterpart just west of Capo Bianco, **Spiaggia di Capo Bianco**. A couple of similar beaches dot the coast along the km stretch out to **Capo d'Enfola**. Presided over by a derelict tuna factory *(tonnara)*, you can have a dip here or head south down the coast a few kilometres to **Viticcio**, a more pleasant little place. The area is quieter than much of the rest of the island and is served by ATL buses. It is possible to walk around from Viticcio to the pleasant beaches of the **Golfo della Biodola**.

At Viticcio you could stay in one of a couple of places. The cheaper is the *Hotel Scoglio Bianco* (☎ *0565 93 90 36, fax 0565 93 90 31*). It's open from late May to mid-September, and it offers half board at anything from L64,000 to L120,000 per person, depending on when you come.

A great little restaurant is *Emanuel* (☎ *0565 93 90 03, Località Enfola*). For years it has been serving up consistently good Elban dishes – probably the best way to go is the *menù di degustazione* at L45,000, which gives you a rounded experience of the local cuisine. It is closed Wednesday except in summer.

WEST TO MARCIANA MARINA

From Portoferraio, a provincial road heads south and then forks westwards along the coast to Marciana Marina via Procchio.

The pick of the beaches are the sandy strands lining the **Golfo della Biodola**. When the *Hermitage* (☎ *0565 93 69 11, fax 0565 96 99 84*) opened its doors in 1951, there were only five small *pensioni* scattered elsewhere on the island. Since then a succession of other hotels and camping grounds has followed on this little gulf. It's reasonably low key and tasteful, but most of the beach is for hotel guests only. Half board in the rather exclusive Hermitage

will cost you up to L280,000 per person per day.

Procchio, a little farther on, is an unlovely road junction, but the beaches are still sandy and at least you can get on to them! On the road just outside Procchio heading towards Marciana Marina is the unassuming *Osteria del Piano* (☎ *0565 90 72 92, Via Provinciale 24*). Looks aren't everything. Here they make all their own pasta and serve up some astonishing concoctions, such as black-and-white spaghetti in a crab sauce. It's not dirt cheap, but you get what you pay for. It is closed Wednesday.

West from Procchio, the road hugs the cliffs, presenting you with an endless parade of fine views along the winding coast. If you can tie up your steed somewhere, **Spiaggia di Spartaia** and **Spiaggia della Paolina** are part of a series of beautiful little beaches (all requiring a steep walk down from the highway).

MARCIANA MARINA & THE WEST

Almost 20km west of Portoferraio, Marciana Marina is slightly less crowded with tourists and is fronted by some pleasant pebble beaches. It makes a fine base for some of the island's best walking trails too.

About the cheapest hotel is *Casa Lupi* (☎ *0565 9 91 43, Viale Amedeo*), about half a kilometre inland on the road to Marciana. Here you shouldn't pay more than L45,000 a head for a room with breakfast.

Poggio & the Interior

Following the inland road up into the mountains is especially advisable for those who are getting a little sick of sweating on the coast. The first town you reach is Poggio, an enchanting little place with a medieval core that is famed for its spring water.

Chill out a little at the *Pensione Monte Capanne* (☎ *0565 9 90 83*) up in Poggio. Singles/doubles are around L70,000/110,000, depending on the time of year. They may insist on half board. If you want to spill money on a great meal, try *Publius* (☎ *0565 9 92 08*), just at the entrance to the village. The breathtaking views down to the

ELBA

coast (you feel as if you are suspended in mid-air) should keep your mind off the fact that you are likely to emerge about L70,000 lighter. It is closed Monday.

From Poggio you have two choices. You can proceed west to Marciana and then head around the coast (see the next section) or opt for the narrow SP37 road that winds up into some of the highest and most densely wooded country on the island. This latter option is comparatively neglected by most sun-and-sand-obsessed tourists.

The vegetation is so dense in parts you could be forgiven for thinking you are about to enter rainforest. Stop at the picnic site at the foot of Monte Perone (you can't miss it). If you have a car, this is the best place to park it. Mountain bikers should proceed with caution. To the left (east) you can wander up to **Monte Perone** (630m), which offers spectacular views across much of the island. To the right (west) you can scramble fairly quickly to a height that affords broad vistas down to Poggio, Marciana and Marciana Marina. From there you could press on to **Monte Maolo** (749m).

The road descends from this location into the southern flank of the island. On the way you will notice the granite shell of the Romanesque **Chiesa di San Giovanni** and, shortly after, the ruined **tower** named after the same saint.

Those with their own transport should give a little time to two small hamlets here, **Sant'Ilario in Campo** and **San Piero in Campo**. The latter is a little larger and boasts a few *osterie* and snack bars, although you can pick up a quick pizza at the former. If you want to stay, *Albergo La Rosa* (☎ *0565 98 31 91*), in San Piero, offers half board for between L60,000 and L90,000 per person depending on the season (open year-round). The hamlets lie on separate routes that lead around to Marina di Campo (see later in this chapter) and for those on mountain bikes or with some motorised form of transport they are easily reached. Short on sights, they are pleasant enough and little affected by tourism. Up to seven buses a day link both with Marina di Campo, and five with Portoferraio.

MARCIANA & THE WEST COAST

From Poggio, the other possibility is to continue west to Marciana, the most engaging of the western interior towns. Once an important defensive position under Pisan rule, subsequently passed to Piombino, the French and finally to the grand duchy of Tuscany.

The **Fortezza Pisana** (which is closed) is a reminder of the town's medieval days, while about a 40-minute walk west out of town is the **Santuario della Madonna**, the most important object of pilgrimage on the island. A much-altered 11th-century church houses a stone upon which a divine hand is said to have painted an image of the Virgin.

From Marciana you can also take a cable car to the summit of **Monte Capanne** (1018m), the island's highest summit, from where you can see across Elba and as far as Corsica to the west. Alternatively you can walk up (about three hours).

The road west out of Marciana pursues a course around the island, maintaining a prudent distance and altitude from the often precipitous coastline.

An increasingly popular coastal hangout is **Sant'Andrea**, which now has an astounding concentration of nine hotels and other assorted accommodation options winding back up the hill to the main road. *Bambù* (☎ *0565 90 80 12*) is one of the cheapest and a spit from the tiny beach. A bed will cost you L50,000 to L60,000. In August they charge L110,000 for obligatory half board.

A series of small beaches follows as you follow the road round to the south side of the island. **Chiessi** and **Pomonte** have pebbly beaches, but the water is beautiful. **Spiaggia delle Tombe** is one of the only spots on the island where nude bathing is OK. It is a nice protected sandy number.

At **Fetovaia**, **Seccheto** and **Cavoli** you will find further protected sand beaches, accommodation and restaurants. West of Seccheto **Le Piscine** is another mostly nudist stretch.

ATL buses run around the coast to all these points, connecting with Marina di Campo and ultimately Portoferraio.

MARINA DI CAMPO

Elba's second-largest town, Marina di

ampo is on Golfo di Campo to the island's outh. The beaches are not bad at all (although if you venture farther west you will find a few less crowded ones). Many amping grounds are located around the own and along the coastline. The *Albergo Thomas* (☎ 0565 97 77 32, Viale degli Etruschi) is one of the cheapest hotels here and has doubles from L100,000 in low season. In high season they will ask around 95,000 per person for half board. This is a standard story around here. The place gets ridiculously packed in high summer, but this is where some of the island's action can e found too – a few bars and discos keep young holiday-makers happy through the hot months.

CAPOLIVERI & THE SOUTH-EAST

It's hard to keep anything a secret in a place like Elba, so it's no surprise really that at least one Italian newspaper writer remarked tartly that one may as well hoist the German flag at Capoliveri.

This town, high up on a majestic ridge-back in the south-eastern pocket of the island, is an enchanting village, all steep, narrow alleys and interlocking houses. At the height of the season it is jammed with tourists (and not just Germans – the whole UN seems to move in here in summer). Come out of season and you can rediscover some of the peace of this hamlet, which used to live off iron-ore mining in the Punta della Calamita area.

There's nowhere to stay in the town itself, although several possibilities suggest themselves around the coast to either side of the town.

The tourists have brought an eating-and-drinking culture to Capoliveri, however, and it's quite astounding just how many eateries and the like have been crammed in.

One of the best restaurants in town is *Il Chiasso* (☎ 0565 96 87 09, Via Sauro), where a meal could cost you L80,000. It is closed Tuesday. Another good place is *Summertime* (☎ 0565 93 51 80, Via Roma 6), where you can get good local dishes such as *sarde ripiene* (stuffed sardines). A full

meal will come in at around L40,000, including local wine. At *Fandango* (☎ 0565 96 83 29, Piazza Matteotti) you can taste fine Tuscan wines and snacks – it's actually located downstairs just below the main square. It is closed Monday.

After munching, you can move on to drinking at a few places such as *Charlie's Pub* (☎ 0565 93 51 02, Via Cavour 44), which opens from 10.30 pm to 4 am – extraordinary by local standards!

Around Capoliveri

If you have your own transport you can visit a series of pleasant little beaches. By bus it's possible, but not easy. Directly west of Capoliveri (take the Portoferraio road and watch for the signs) are the beaches of **Zuccale** and **Barabarca**. You end up on a dirt track – leave your vehicle in the car park and walk the final stretch.

If you take the road heading south from Capoliveri, another three charming sandy little coves come in quick succession: **Morcone**, **Pareti** and **Spiaggia dell'Innamorata**. The 'woman in love' *(innamorata)* of the last of these was apparently an orphan girl of Capoliveri in love with a young man of means. When the latter's parents finally consented to marriage, they went down to the seaside to give vent to their joy. Pirates spoiled the party and captured the man, killing him. The girl, beside herself with sorrow, threw herself off the cliffs to where she had managed to escape.

There are several hotel options at these beaches, and at Morcone you can do diving and windsurfing courses. Simple restaurants keep people's tummies from rumbling too hard.

To the east of Capoliveri, you have two choices. One road takes you to the comparatively long (for this part of the island) stretch of beach at **Naregno**, fronted by a series of discreet hotels.

The more adventurous will follow the signs for **Stracoligno**. This is one of the first in a series of beaches down the east coast here. The road at this point becomes a dirt track and if you don't mind dusting up your vehicle somewhat, you can push on to a couple of less-frequented beaches. **Cala Nuova** is a nice enough little beach with a good restaurant. ***Ristorante Calanova*** (☎ *0565 96 89 58*) will charge you about L60,000 per person for a meal. It closes Tuesday and from November to Easter.

Another 4 or 5km and you reach a path down to the **Spiaggia dello Stagnone**, which even in summer you should not find too crowded, if only because of the effort required to rattle down this far.

PORTO AZZURRO

Dominated by its fort, which was built in 1603 by Philip III of Spain and is now used as a prison, Porto Azzurro is a pleasant resort town, close to some good beaches.

Albergo Villa Italia (☎ *0565 9 51 19, Viale Italia)* has singles/doubles for L55,000/85,000. At the more cheerful ***Hotel Belmare*** (☎ *0565 9 50 12, fax 0565 95 82 45, Banchina IV Novembre)* you will pay L70,000/130,000.

If you can loosen the purse strings a little around dinner time, try ***Ristorante Cutty Sark*** (☎ *0565 95 78 21, Piazza del Mercato 25).* The *ravioloni alla Cutty Sark* are big ravioli filled with *zucchini* and shrimp meat and layered in a shrimp and tomato sauce. You get to wrestle with seafood critters too to extract a sliver of extra flesh. It is closed Tuesday. Otherwise, two of the portside restaurants are stock favourites. ***Delfino Verde*** (☎ *0565 9 51 97, Lungomare Vitaliani 1)* and ***La Lanterna Magica*** (☎ *0565 95 83 94, Lungomare Vitaliani 5)* offer menus of similar quality and price – you can expect to part with about L65,000 per person for a full meal. They are closed Tuesday and Monday respectively.

THE NORTH-EAST

If, on leaving Portoferraio, you were to swing around to the east and head for Rio nell'Elba and beyond, you would be opting to explore the least-touristed part of the island. There is a simple enough reason for this – the beaches are generally not so hot. Although in some cases the locations are pretty, sand tends to contend with pebbles, shingle and shells. If you don't mind that, it

can be quite an intriguing corner to poke around in for a couple of days.

The road out of Portoferraio hugs the coast on its way around to Bagnaia, the first worthwhile stop. En route you will scoot by **San Giovanni**, home to a rather expensive and dull mud spa and **Le Grotte**, where few stones still managing to stand one on top of the other are all that remain of a Roman villa. At the fork in the road for Porto Azzurro and Bagnaia is a possible last resort to keep stressed small kids happy. Yes, it's Elbaland! Sorry folks, this is where the anklebiters get to take their revenge. It's all very low-key, more like an outsize park with swings and other such amusements. It opens from noon to 7 pm Tuesday to Sunday and costs L10,000/5000 for adults/kids under 12 years of age.

That behind you, swing northward to **Bagnaia**. The beach is attractive and there are a few places to stay. The modest ***Hotel Punta Pina*** (☎ *0565 96 10 09, fax 0565 9 11 91)* does bed and breakfast for L40,000 to L80,000 per person, depending on the season. It opens from late March to late October. Eat at ***Pizzeria Sunset*** (☎ *0565 93 0 86).* The views across the gulf to Portoferraio are wonderful, the sunset especially. It is closed from mid-October to April.

From Bagnaia you have the option of following the partly dirt road to **Nisporto**, and then on farther up the coast to **Nisportino**. The views along the way are quite spectacular in parts and in each of the settlements you will find a small beach and, in summer, snack stands and one or two restaurants. From Nisportino you head back down a few kilometres to the junction with the road that links Nisporto and Rio nell'Elba. About halfway along this road you can stop to take a short stroll to what little is left of the **Eremo di Santa Caterina**, a tiny stone hermitage. The views around here are extensive.

The road plunges down to the inland basin of **Rio nell'Elba**, which lay at the heart of the island's iron-mining operations. It's a little gloomy, but the simple fact that it caters little to tourism is almost attractive. Actually, it's not quite accurate to say that

Rio nell'Elba ignores tourism altogether. After all, there's the Museo di Minerali Elbani, with 700 rare mineral specimens from the east of the island and also Monte Capanne. Amateur geologists should have a field day. It opens from 10 am to 1 pm and 4 to 7.30 pm daily except on Monday and on Wednesday afternoon, from May to September. Admission costs L5000. You are unlikely to want to hang around too long, but you can get lunch at one of a handful of restaurants on and around the central Piazza del Popolo.

You could take another road back north from Rio nell'Elba to **Cavo** on the north-eastern coast, but no obvious reasons spring to mind for making the effort. Easier is the short run downhill to Rio nell'Elba's coastal outlet, **Rio Marina**. Oh goody, there's yet another mineral museum here! Apart from that, not a lot will hold you up here either. If

you feel the need to stay over, *Hotel Rio* (☎ *0565 92 42 25, fax 0565 92 41 62, Via Palestro*) charges from L65,000 to L100,000 per person depending on the season. It is closed from early October to April. Lunch might be an idea at *Da Oreste La Strega* (☎ *0565 96 22 11, Via Vittorio Emanuele 6*), a seafood restaurant with a certain distinction and where a meal will cost you around L60,000. The restaurant is closed Tuesday.

The best beach choice around here is a little way south at **Ortano**. To get there you need to head back a couple of kilometres towards Rio nell'Elba and then swing south. It's a nice location, but again the beach is that far-from-ideal part-sand part-pebble mix. If you want to stay you can choose between camping at *Campeggio Canapei* (☎/fax *0565 93 91 65*) or a sprawling hotel complex.

The Count of Montecristo

Alexandre Dumas could hardly have known, when he penned the swash-buckling adventures of the much wronged Edmond Dantès in the mid-19th century, just how much success his character would have.

The dashing officer of the French merchant marine, incarcerated in the Château d'If, near Marseille, for 'Bonapartism', had been set up and wasn't very happy about it. But life is a funny thing, as they say, and never funnier than in a good read. So it is that Abbot Faria clues the seething Dantès in to the existence of a fabulous treasure in the caves of the little island of Montecristo.

Itching to get rich and revenge, Dantès manages the daring escape from the castle and heads off for Italy. As his boat glides past Elba Dantès can see Pianosa before him and, in the distance, his objective – the island of Montecristo.

JANE SMITH

Alexandre Dumas

Well, through much adventure and jolly japes, our man wins all the prizes really – getting rich, becoming the Count of Montecristo and exacting a full measure of revenge on those who had framed him.

Of course, it's all a tall tale. No-one has ever found any treasure on Montecristo, but this particular yarn has made a lot of loot for a lot of people. In the 20th century at least 25 film and TV versions of the story have been made, with greater or lesser skill. Among the better ones are the oldies. Rowland Lee's 1935 film and the 1943 flick by Robert Vernay were equally good tales in the spirit of Dumas' writing. In Italy, Andrea Giordana had women swooning at their TV sets in the 1966 series by Edmo Fenoglio. Richard Chamberlain had a go at the lead role in David Greene's 1975 *The Count of Montecristo*, as did Gérard Depardieu in *Montecristo* (1997).

MINOR ISLANDS

Elba is part of what is now called the Parco Nazionale dell'Arcipelago Toscano. For reasons of logic in terms of travel and access, two of the seven islands, Capraia and Gorgona, are dealt with in the section on Livorno in the Central Coast chapter (note that in summer you can join boat excursions to Capraia from Elba). The islands of Giglio and Giannutri are discussed in the Southern Tuscany chapter. That leaves Elba, Pianosa and Montecristo.

Pianosa, 14km west of Elba, is a remarkably flat, triangular affair measuring about 5.8km by 4.6km. From 1858 until the mid-1990s it was a penal colony, but it is now part of the national park. In 1999 the first excursions began to operate from Marina di Campo. A maximum of 100 people a day can go on a day trip for L110,000 per person. Ask at Agenzia Margherita Viaggi (☎ 0565 97 80 04), Via Puccini 3, in Marina di Campo. They run in summer only. Otherwise, the island can be reached on Tuesday only by Toremar ferry from Porto Azzurro. Unless you want to be stranded for a week, you have about two hours to poke around before heading back! And if you go this way, you are not allowed into the grounds of the former prison (so the two hours will probably be more than sufficient).

There are no ferry services to Montecristo, 40km south of Elba. Montecristo was also at one stage a prison island, but that role was short-lived. Since 1979 it has been a marine biological reserve and can be seen only as part of an organised visit. You need special permission from the Ufficio Forestale in Follonica (on the Italian mainland). Call ☎ 0566 4 00 19 if you are interested.

e area known as the Maremma (really st an extension of the Maremma Pisana) etches southward from Piombino and its it hinterland until Tuscany's border with izio.

As in the Maremma Pisana (see the Cen-l Coast chapter), serious land reclama-n and the drying out of the extensive amps that characterised the whole area ly began at the end of the 18th and start the 19th centuries under the direction of e Lorraine grand dukes. This went hand hand with a series of reforms aimed at osening the grip of the feudal-style land-lders on the bulk of this previously un-oductive land. Roads were built and nals dug, agriculture was stimulated and iry production encouraged – in a region hilly and mountainous as Tuscany, the ains of the newly 'cleansed' Maremma ere ideal for grazing. Sheep farming also ew.

For the sake of simplicity, the area cov-ed in this chapter roughly corresponds to rosseto, the southernmost of the Tuscan ovinces.

Several of Tuscany's most important ruscan sites (and a host of minor ones too) in be found in this area. Touring the wild gh country towns of Vetulonia, Sovana, rano and Pitigliano allows you to com-ne the hunt for Etruscan sites with some ectacular medieval towns neglected by e majority of tourists swanning about far-er north in Tuscany.

Along the coast, the highlights are the rco Naturale della Maremma, incorporat-g the Monti dell'Uccellina, and the Monte rgentario peninsula. Otherwise, several cceptable beaches allow for some relief om the summertime heat.

Lovers of hot water should make for the rings and thermal baths at Saturnia, once so an Etruscan settlement.

Many towns in the area have small tourist formation offices that open daily only ring summer.

Highlights

- Explore the extraordinary town of Pitigliano, rising dramatically from a rocky outcrop
- Follow in the footsteps of the Etruscans in the necropolises around Sovana
- Bathe in the natural hot springs of Saturnia
- Get up early for some birdwatching along the Tombolo della Feniglia, in the Monte Argentario peninsula
- Take a boat trip to the island of Giglio

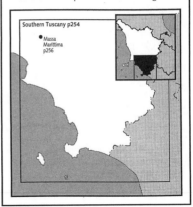

GROSSETO
postcode 58100 • pop 71,600

Precious little about this place – provincial capital and the biggest town in the Maremma – draws attention to it. If for whatever you reason you wind up here (and it will almost always be because you are waiting for a transport connection), you could kill a couple of hours in what's left of the old walled town.

Information

The APT tourist office (☎ 0564 45 45 10) is at Via Fucini 43c, a block from the train station. Information about the Parco Naturale

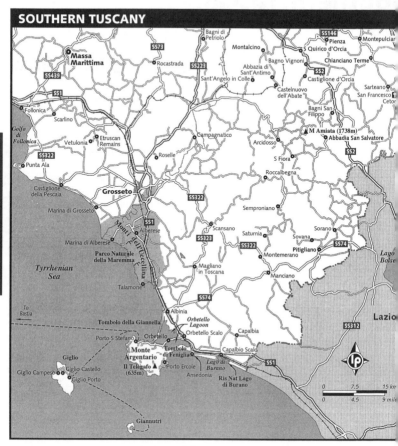

SOUTHERN TUSCANY

della Maremma can be obtained there or at Marina di Alberese, on the northern edge of the park (see later in this chapter). The Associazione Albergatori (☎ 0564 2 63 15), next door to the APT at Via Fucini 43, can help you find a bed in the province.

Things to See

Grosseto was the last of the Siena-dominated towns to fall into Medici hands, in 1559. The walls, bastions and fortress that you see today were built on the orders of Florence to protect what was then an important grain and salt depot for the grand duchy.

Within the walls, the **cathedral** w begun in the late 13th century and has distinctive Sienese touch. Much of the cade was renewed along neo-Romanesq lines in the 19th century. Overall, t styles are a mix of the original R manesque and Gothic. The bell tower a now stands was built in the early 1900 The other interesting-looking building the not unpleasant Piazza Dante, t Palazzo della Provincia, seems to Sienese Gothic, which is exactly what early-20th-century architects hoped y might think.

laces to Stay & Eat

you are stranded here for the night, *Al-rgo Appennino* (☎ 0564 2 30 09, *Via ameli 1*) has the advantage of being handy r the train station and old centre. Sin-es/doubles with own shower cost 48,000/75,000.

Il Canto del Gallo (☎ 0564 41 45 89, *Via azzini 29*), located in the old town, pre-nts all sorts of options on the menu. Try e gnocchi, which are home-made and ry good. It is closed Sunday.

etting There & Away

us Rama buses (☎ 0564 2 52 15), Via ameli 14, leave for points throughout the ovince. Most of the buses depart from in ont of the train station. There are fairly gular buses for Siena, some of them run the Sienese company Tra-in. From Siena u can then connect with either Tra-in or TA buses to Florence. Direct services to orence are less frequent – no more than ree a day. Strangely there is only one bus day to Massa Marittima (none on Sun-y). Other destinations include: Piombino, agliano in Toscana, Follonica, Cas-glione della Pescia and Pitigliano.

ain Grosseto is on the main coastal train ne between Rome and Livorno. For places ch as Pisa, Florence or Siena (L10,100, 5 minutes) train is probably a smarter bet.

ROUND GROSSETO
oselle

pulated as early as the 7th century BC, oselle was a middle-ranking Etruscan wn which came under Roman control in e 3rd century BC.

Although no great monuments are left anding, the extensive site retains defen-ve walls, an oddly elliptical amphitheatre, aces of houses, the forum and streets. uch of it is attributable to periods after the rival of the Romans but is interesting onetheless. It is of course no match for ompei and other more famous Italian ar-aeological sights. But its high position in seemingly hidden basin affords wonderful ews down to the plains and out to sea.

The site is open daily from 9 am to sun-set and admission costs L8000. Getting there is easiest by private means. Otherwise you have to get the bus driver to let you off at the appropriate spot on the Siena–Grosseto run and then walk a few kilometres.

NORTH TO MASSA MARITTIMA
Vetulonia

This chilly mountain town seems to rise out of nothing from the surrounding plains. You can see the sea from here, but it seems to belong to another time dimension. A pleas-ing enough distraction for a brief stroll, most of Vetulonia's visitors come in search of Etruscan remains. In the town itself are what are purported to be some blocks from the ancient Etruscan town's wall. Just out-side in two separate locations (the more ex-tensive is just below the town as you leave by the only road), excavations have re-vealed bits and bobs of the Etruscan settle-ment. The sites are open daily from 9 am to dusk. Entry is supposed to cost L4000 but the ticket office had an abandoned look when we went through.

A couple of kilometres farther downhill, a turn-off leads to three Etruscan tombs. The most interesting of these is the last, which is about 1km down a rough dirt track. Admission to the tombs is free and they are open daily from 9 am to dusk. An automatic gate slams shut in the evening, so check the posted closing time before you go inside.

A couple of restaurants will keep you fed at lunch and if you get stuck the *Taverna Etrusca* on the central square has a few rooms. Buses run twice a day to Castiglione della Pescia and once to Grosseto. The for-mer makes the more sensible base.

MASSA MARITTIMA
postcode 58024 • pop 9300

With little doubt this is about the most in-teresting town in the Maremma. Dating back to the 8th century, the walled nucleus of the old town was already in place by the 12th. For a while under Pisan domination, the medieval town thrived on the local metal mining industry. In 1225 it became

SOUTHERN TUSCANY

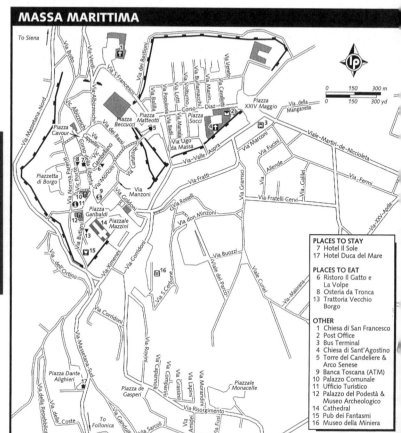

MASSA MARITTIMA

an independent commune but was swallowed up by Siena a century later. The plague in 1348 and the end of mining 50 years later reduced the city almost to extinction. Only in the 18th century, with the draining of marshes and re-establishment of mining, did Massa Marittima come back to life.

Information

The Ufficio Turistico (☎ 0566 90 27 56), Via Norma Parenti 22, opens from 9 am to 12.30 pm and 3.30 to 6 pm, Monday to Saturday (from 9 am to 1.30 pm Sunday).

The post office is on Corso Diaz and th Banca Toscana at Piazza Garibaldi 17 ha an ATM.

Things to See

The heart of medieval Massa is Piazz Garibaldi, dominated by the imposing bul of the **cathedral**, in Pisan Romanesqu style. It is thought Giovanni Pisano de signed the church, although much of th work may have been carried out by Sienes workmen. The inside is graced with sub stantial remnants of frescoes and severa paintings, including a *Madonna delle Gr*

e precariously-perched monastery, Volterra

A wine cellar near the Val di Pesa in Chianti

ird's-eye view of the cathedral in Siena

The striking bell tower of Siena's cathedral

Elegant motif, Piazza dei Priori, Volterra

Ring any bells? Ceramics for sale, Siena

Pick up a bargain at the antiques market in Piazza Grande, Arezzo.

by the workshop of Siena's Duccio di
oninsegna. It opens daily from 8 am to
on and 3.30 to 7 pm.

Opposite is the **Palazzo Comunale**, his-
ic seat of government in the city. The
oud coat of arms of Florence's Medici
mily does not quite distract attention from
e earlier symbol of rival Siena's one-time
cendancy here – the wolf with Romulus
d Remus.

The 13th-century **Palazzo del Podesta**
wadays houses the **Museo Archeologico**,
sited above all for Ambrogio Lorenzetti's
aestà. Paling into comparative insignifi-
nce is a modest collection of ancient
oman and Etruscan artefacts dug up
ound Massa. The museum opens from 10
n to 12.30 pm and 3.30 to 7 pm, Tuesday
Sunday (April to October). The rest of
e year the hours drop to 11 am to noon
d 3 to 5 pm. Admission costs L5000.

The Città Nuova (New Town) is domi-
ted by the **Torre del Candeliere**, in turn
ined to defensive bastions in the wall by
e so-called **Arco Senese** (Sienese Arch).
u can enter the tower and bestride the
ch for L3000 – the views over the Città
cchia (Old Town) are best in the early
orning. Access to the tower is from 10 am
1 pm and 2.30 to 5.30 pm, Tuesday to
nday.

At the **Museo della Miniera** you can ex-
nine (if you really want to) the city's min-
g history. The display includes a replica of
length of mine. Guided tours go through
to seven times (loosely on the hour) from
.15 am to 5.45 pm daily (except Mon-
y). Tickets cost L10,000.

aces to Stay

vernight options are thin on the ground. In
assa itself your only choice is *Hotel Il*
le (☎ 0566 90 19 71, fax 0566 90 19 59,
rso della Libertà 43), where decent
oms with TV, phone and heating cost
0,000/110,000.

A few kilometres south on the road to
llonica is *Hotel Duca del Mare* (☎ 0566
22 84, fax 0566 90 19 05, Piazza Dante
ighieri 1/2), where you'll pay L70,000/
0,000. On the road to Siena, *Hotel Il Gir-*

ifalco (☎/fax 0566 90 21 77, Via Massetana
Nord 25) offers doubles only at L110,000.

If, as is quite possible, you find them all
full, the tourist office may be able to help
organise something else in the surrounding
area.

Places to Eat

As surprising as the lack of accommodation
is the concentration of above-average
restaurants. Even the touristy places on Piazza Garibaldi aren't bad.

Trattoria Vecchio Borgo (☎ 0566 90 39
50, Via Butigni 12) does an appetising *tris
di primi* (smaller portions of three first
courses) for L30,000 for two people. At
Ristoro Il Gatto e La Volpe (☎ 0566 90 35
75, Vicolo Ciambellano 12) try the divine
filetto tartufato (filet steak prepared with
truffles) for L22,000. Your average main
course costs a more modest L15,000. Both
are closed Monday.

Finally, *Osteria da Tronca* (☎ 0566 90
19 91, Vicolo Porte 5) is another quality address where a full meal should not cost
more than about L45,000. It is closed
Wednesday.

Entertainment

If you are feeling a little frisky after dinner,
head for *Pub dei Fantasmi* (☎ 0566 94 02
74, Via Parenti 2/4) where you can tipple
until 3 am at the weekend (2 am during the
week). It is closed Wednesday.

Getting There & Away

Getting in and out of Massa requires some
patience. Irregular bus services connect
Massa with Siena and Volterra to the north.
Only one goes to Grosseto. The bus termi-
nal is south of the new town on Via Valle
Aspra.

The nearest train station is at Follonica
on the coastal Rome–Livorno line. Up to 20
FMF buses connect Massa with the train
station each weekday.

THE COAST

Don't get your hopes too high when cruis-
ing the coast from Piombino south. Occasional stretches of pine-backed beach are

SOUTHERN TUSCANY

pleasant without being breath-taking. The best that this southern stretch of mainland Tuscan coast has to offer is down in the Parco Naturale della Maremma.

Golfo di Follonica

Picture yourself in your car or on a bike disembarking in Piombino from Elba. Just take in the reassuring picture of chimney stacks and industry at work. All quite necessary, to be sure, but no reason to hang about. Hit the road, and if heading south, hit it for a while. The first town of note you will reach is **Follonica**. It is interesting if only because it leaves you wondering what kind of town planning rules they have that allow all that cheap and tacky high-rise building. Right up on the beach too. But this ain't Surfers' Paradise (it's not even *that* good), so the best advice, unless you need a dip in the sea right now, is to not even bother entering town. On a slightly less nasty note, the beach improves, with a pleasant pinewood backdrop, if you proceed a few kilometres farther around the gulf – about where you see the turn-off signs inland for **Scarlino**.

You will find a couple of camping grounds in the same vicinity. If you are obliged by fate to spend a night in Follonica, there is no shortage of hotels and eateries to keep your spirits up. On the tummy front, head for *Osteria Santarino* (☎ *0564 4 16 65, Piazza XXIV Maggio*). For around L40,000 you will get excellent home-cooking – book ahead, because it's no secret locally. It's closed Tuesday.

A very annoying committee must have been hard at work in **Punta Ala** to devise the most Kafkaesque road system imaginable when it set to designing this leafy but rather fake getaway for the filthy rich. On the plus side, the promontory is green and rather sparingly brutalised by building development. Along the north flank and hidden from view by the serried ranks of inevitable pines is a long if narrow stretch of beach, quite a lot of it open to the public. On the down side, most of the accommodation for blow-ins (many people here own villas, timeshares or whatever) is in the interstellar price range. Most infuriating of all is

finding anything. The odd bus dares make an appearance here from Grosseto but the obvious way in is with your own wheels. That's the easy part. Roundabout follows roundabout, each with dozens of signs pointing you in the direction of everything from minigolf to estate agents. But the beaches? The port? Huh? Round and round you go, skirting horse-riding circuits and enclaves of shady private housing or, if the search for the port (and you are foolish enough to follow the roundabout indications), up a series of gentle switchbacks leading ever upwards (upwards to the port?!) to ... a dead end. The rich and factious can have it (but to be fair the public beaches on a slow mid-week day are quite pleasant – assuming you stumble on them). The easiest way to get wet is to ditch the car while still on the straight stretch of road (or jump off the bus) just before entering the labyrinth of roundabouts and follow your nose through the pinewoods.

Castiglione della Pescaia

At last, something seriously worth stopping for on the mad rush southwards. You almost get the feeling someone must have built a hill here on purpose so they could erect a medieval stone village of the kind one more readily associates with its confreres in the interior (about which more later in the chapter).

The modern sprawl around its feet is not too disturbing. In fact, the point where old meets new is quite contagious with its bustle. The clink of cutlery and tinkle of wine glasses sets the mood as holiday-making weekenders up from Rome and day-trippers from the hinterland join in to celebrate the good things (which after cavorting in the Tyrrhenian Sea can only mean eating, drinking and perhaps a digestive stroll). When most of the rest of the coast around here is all but deserted on a mid-October weekend, this place is still bustling.

The walled old town, brooding in stoney quiet, has no specific monuments of interest, but the views out to sea are majestic and a wander is as pleasing as tends to be the case in such places.

A tourist office (☎ 0564 93 36 78) is on azza Garibaldi.

aces to Stay Castiglione has the advan-ge that it is fairly liberally blessed with tels and other sleeping options. Of the lf-dozen camping grounds around the wn (four of which are actually near Le cchette, itself closer to Punta Ala than astiglione), *Camping Etruria (☎ 0564 93 83)* in Le Marze, a few kilometres south town off the road to Marina di Grosseto, a reasonable choice. You pay L10,000 r adult and L18,000 for a pitch.

If you are looking for a cheap doss, *otel Bologna (☎ 0564 93 37 46, Piaza aribaldi 8)* is nothing special but in the art of the action and a steal (by local stan-rds) at L45,000/75,000 for basic sin-es/doubles. Quite a number of places erage around L70,000/120,000.

laces to Eat Whether or not you want ay, this place does boast some rather recom-endable places where you can get your andibles into gear.

Osteria nel Buco (☎ 0564 93 44 60, Via l Recinto 11) is a lively little hole in the all (as its name and position just inside the d town walls suggest). They serve up typ-al dishes of the Maremma, including a od *zuppa di porri* (leek soup) and a crab rsion too. If it's packed, try *Ristorante La ortezza (☎ 0564 93 61 00, Via del Recinto 3)*, a more ample spot that also serves od local cuisine. Both are closed Monday.

etting There & Away Rama buses run irly regularly to/from Grosseto and con-ct with other places on the coast. Up to ven buses a day connect with Follonica ain station, one of the main stops around re.

larina di Grosseto
es, by Tuscan standards the beach is broad d sandy. But that's about it folks. Luckily e grid-like town with its thoughtlessly apped-together housing is rendered less of eyesore by the fact that it is spread out d low, and well camouflaged by the um-

brella pines typical of the Maremma coast. It's a nice spot for locals to come and splash in the sea, but there are more interesting places to be, even on this coastline (see the entries on Castiglione della Pescaia and Parco Naturale della Maremma, either side of this section)!

If for whatever reason you get stuck or actually like the place, there is a fair range of places to stay and you won't go hungry. About the most economical digs are at *Tre Stelle (☎ 0564 3 45 38, Via dei Platani 15)*, where you are looking at L60,000/80,000 for singles/doubles. Should you (for some even less comprehensible reason) have elected to become a temporary resident of Grosseto, this place has the benefit of being a short and comparatively regular bus ride away.

Parco Naturale della Maremma
Along the entire coastline from Piombino to Rome, this has to be the main attraction. The park incorporates the Monti dell'Uc-cellina and a magnificent stretch of un-spoiled coastline.

Entry to the park is limited and cars must be left in designated parking areas. Certain areas can be visited only on certain days and excursions into the park are limited to set itineraries. Depending on your chosen route, you may see plenty of native animals (including deer, wild boar, foxes and hawks). Certain routes also provide access to the sea.

You must buy tickets at the visitors' cen-tre in Alberese – they cost L10,000 (which includes bus transport from Alberese to the starting point for some walks) or L7000. A couple of the itineraries (including one from Talamone at the southern end of the park) are free and accessible daily.

There are no shelters or bars (with the ex-ception of a couple at Marina di Alberese) within the park, so make sure you carry water and are properly dressed. Cycling is an option (if you bring your own). The park gets crowded in summer, especially at the weekend.

The Centro Visite del Parco (visitors' centre) at Alberese (☎ 0564 40 70 98) opens

SOUTHERN TUSCANY

euro currency converter L10,000 = €5.16

daily from 9 am to sunset in summer and from 8 am to 1 pm from October to May. **Talamone**, just outside the southern extremity of the park, is a fetching little fortress village with several hotel and restaurant options.

MONTE ARGENTARIO

Once an island, this promontory came to be linked to the mainland by an accumulation of sand that is now the isthmus of Orbetello. Further sandy bulwarks form the Tombolo della Giannella and the Tombolo di Feniglia to the north and south. They enclose a lagoon that is now a protected nature reserve. Intense building has spoiled the northern side of the promontory, but the south and centre have been left in peace (forest fires aside). It is something of a weekend getaway fave with Romans in summer.

Orbetello

Orbetello's main attraction is its **cathedral**, which has retained its 14th-century Gothic facade despite being remodelled in the Spanish style in the 16th century. Other reminders of the Spanish garrison *(presidio)* that was stationed in the city include the fort and city wall. Parts of the latter belong to the original Etruscan wall.

The best place for observing the birdlife (as many as 140 species have been identified) on Orbetello's lagoon is out along the **Tombolo della Feniglia**, the southern strip of land linking Monte Argentario to the mainland. It is blocked to traffic – you can park your car near the camping ground and proceed on foot. The beach on the seaward side is quite popular too (indeed it is about the nicest on the peninsula).

Around the Peninsula

Monte Argentario is popular with Romans, but not many tourists go there. **Porto Santo Stefano** and **Porto Ercole** are resort towns for the wealthy, but Porto Ercole, in a picturesque position between two Spanish forts, retains some of its fishing village character. The main tourist office (☎ 0564 81 42 08) is in Porto Santo Stefano, in the Monte dei Paschi di Siena building, at

Corso Umberto 55. It opens from 9 am 1 pm and 4 to 6 pm, Monday to Saturday

For a pleasant drive, follow the signs to Telegrafo, one of the highest mountains the region, and turn off at the **Convento** **Frati Passionisti**, a church and convent w sensational views across to the mainlar Another good drive is the *via panoramica* circuit running out from Porto Santo Stefan

There are several good beaches, mair of the pebbly or rocky (rather than sand variety. Near Porto Ercole the beach is s viced, which means it's clean but clutter with deck chairs and umbrellas for rent. you move farther away the beach becom less crowded but, as with most publ beaches in Italy, it also gets dirtier.

Places to Stay

Accommodation on the peninsula is gene ally expensive, although there is a *campi* *ground* (☎ 0564 83 10 90) near Porto E cole, on the northern fringe at the Fenigl beach.

Orbetello If it's no-frills cheap you a looking for (well, cheapish), *Albergo I* *Perla* (☎ 0564 86 35 46, Via Volontari a Sangue 10), just outside the old town on t road back to the mainland, has pokey si gles without own bath for as little L40,000 or up to L60,000 depending on t season. Doubles with own bathroom co L100,000.

Porto Santo Stefano A cosy place *Pensione Weekend* (☎ 0564 81 25 80, V Martiri d'Ungheria 3), with doubles wi bathroom from L100,000. *Albergo Be* *vedere* (☎ 0564 81 26 34, Via del Fortir 51) is a luxurious complex overlooking tl water shortly before you enter the tov proper, where fine singles/doubles co L120,000/L160,000 in the high seaso breakfast included. It also has a priva beach.

For splendid isolation and views over tl sea, open your wallets and head for tl *Torre di Cala Piccola* (☎ 0564 82 51 11, f 0564 82 53 25, Località Cala Piccola). I out on the via panoramica.

laces to Eat

he peninsula is full of its fair share of staurants and, unsurprisingly, seafood les OK. Remember, however, that at the eekend freshly caught fish is hard to come y – there are simply too many people eating their way through the peninsula then!

rbetello While in Tuscany, why not eat cilian? If you haven't had the chance to ck into true Sicilian cooking, justifiably nown for its imaginativeness and often uite spicy (an Arab legacy), you will be eased you sauntered into *Osteria del Luicante* (☎ *0564 86 76 18, Corso Italia)3). The spaghetti alla messinese* (Messina yle) comes with swordfish meat, tomato, eppers, sunflower seeds and spices. A full eal could be pricey, but the pasta courses e generous and will satisfy the average apetite. Count on a minimum spend of about 40,000. It is closed Tuesday.

Another excellent choice here, and with out as much seating capacity as a gloried matchbox, is *Osteria il Nocchino* ☎ *0564 86 03 29, Via dei Mille 64).* Prices re moderate and the food is like mamma sed to make. It is closed Wednesday.

orto Santo Stefano At *Il Veliero* ☎ *0564 81 22 26, Via Panoramica 149),* losed Monday, an excellent meal will cost ound L50,000. *Trattoria Da Siro* (☎ *0564 1 25 38, Corso Umberto I 100),* just off the aterfront, is a good bet for fine seafood. 's also closed Monday. Cheaper is *Lo Sfizio* ☎ *0564 81 99 52, Corso Umberto I 26)* on e waterfront. You can have *bruschette,* izza or seafood, such as *sauté di cozze e von- ole veraci* (sauteed mussels and clams). It closed Tuesday.

A handful of restaurants along the via anoramica offer fine views while you dine.

orto Ercole For good pizza try *El Pirata* ☎ *0564 83 11 78, Lungomare Andrea Doria 4),* which is closed Wednesday.

etting There & Around

ama buses connect most towns on the Monte Argentario with Orbetello Scalo (co-

inciding with the arrival of trains) and Grosseto. By car, follow the signs to Monte Argentario from the SS1, which connects Grosseto with Rome.

THE ISLANDS

More than a few locals skip Monte Argentario altogether and choose to head off on excursions to one of two islands off the coast. The islands of Giglio and Giannutri are both part of the Parco Nazionale dell'Arcipelago Toscano.

Giglio

The hilly island of Giglio lies 14km off Monte Argentario. Regular boat services from Porto Santo Stefano make getting to this pretty little spot easy. You arrive at Giglio Porto, once a Roman port and now the best spot to find a room. A local bus service will take you 6km to the inland fastness of Giglio Castello, dominated by a Pisan castle.

The only beaches are on the western side of the island, and the best of them is now fronted by the modern resort of Giglio Campese. It's relatively low key and the beach is protected.

About a dozen hotels and a sprinkling of *affittacamere* offer accommodation options. If you don't have a list from the tourist office get a morning boat over and do the rounds. That way if you are out of luck (probable on summer weekends) you can always get back to the mainland.

Toremar (☎ 0564 81 08 03) and Navalgiglio (☎ 0564 81 29 20) run boats to the island. Toremar has three or four a day year-round, while Navalgiglio drops its service to three or so a day on weekends and Monday only, out of season. The one-way trip costs L10,000.

Giannutri This tiny islet is the southern-most of the archipelago and is a flat and relatively lacklustre affair with just two tiny beaches barely worthy of the name. Still, the curious can get over on a day tour from Porto Santo Stefano (via Giglio) from May to September. Ask at the tourist office about times and prices. It may run on weekends out of season too.

THE ROAD TO ROME
Lago di Burano
Little more than 10km farther east along the coast, and about 5km short of the regional frontier with Lazio, this saltwater flat has been a WWF-run nature reserve – the Riserva Naturale Lago di Burano – since 1980. Covering 410 hectares, it is typical of the Maremma in its flora, but interesting above all for its migratory bird life. Tens of thousands of birds of many species winter here, including several kinds of duck and even falcons. Among the animals, the most precious is the beaver. A path dotted with seven observation points winds its way through the park.

It opens on Thursday and Sunday only from September to April. Visits, which last about two hours, start at 10 am and 2.30 pm. For more information call ☎ 0564 89 88 29. To get there you take the Capalbio Scalo exit from the SS1 (the odd train stops at the station here too).

INLAND & ETRUSCAN SITES
On the assumption that you might have decided to hang about the Monte Argentario area for a bit, a seriously worthwhile inland route suggests itself. You can explore the relatively untouristed 'deep south' of Tuscany by bus, although as usual your own wheels make life easier.

Magliano & Scansano
From **Albinia**, at the northern tip of the Orbetello lagoon, take the SS74 in the direction of Manciano (where we will arrive a little later on) and make a detour up the SS323.

First stop is **Magliano in Toscana**, impressive above all for its largely intact city walls. Some date to the 14th century, while the bulk were raised by Siena in the 16th century. The town is a little scrappy on the inside, but lunch is a good idea at the *Antica Trattoria Aurora* (☎ *0564 59 20 30, Via Chiasso Lavagnini 12/14*). They stop serving at 1.30 pm and they are closed Wednesday. A few buses connect with Grosseto, Scansano and Orbetello.

Next proceed up to **Scansano**. Although there are no monuments of great impor-

tance, the old centre is a pleasure to wander around, all narrow lanes and archways, with some great views over the surrounding country.

A couple of Rama buses from Grosseto trundle through Scansano on their way to Manciano via Montemerano.

Montemerano, Manciano & Saturnia
Heading towards Manciano, you first hit the small walled medieval town of **Montemerano**, where you can buy outstanding Tuscan olive oil at *La Piaggia*, an agriturismo establishment. Visit the town's Chiesa San Giorgio, which is decorated with 15th-century frescoes of the Sienese school.

From here it is a 6km hike or occasional bus or car ride to **Saturnia** and its sulphur spring and thermal baths at **Terme di Saturnia**, just outside the village. Bring along bathing costume and towel for a restorative dip. You have two options here. You can fork out for the hi-tech private spa with all the services typical of such establishment, or go for a hot shower under the sulphurous waterfall. A small lane leads off to the waterfall, a pleasantly secluded spot sometimes jammed with an international motley crew of hippies and all sorts.

Saturnia's Etruscan remains, including part of the town wall, are worth a diversion if you are into that sort of thing. A tomb at **Sede di Carlo**, just north-east of the town, is one of the area's best preserved.

Getting here by bus is a real hassle and virtually impossible on our route, as about the only service is by the odd bus running between Grosseto and Pitigliano.

Another former Sienese fortress, Manciano could end up being a compulsory transport stop on your travels around here. Apart from the much interfered with Rocca (the fortress) there is not an awful lot to hold you up.

Pitigliano
From Manciano head east along the SS74 for Pitigliano. The visual impact of this town is hard to forget. It seems to grow organically out of a high volcanic rocky out-

op that towers over the surrounding coun-
y. The gorges that surround the town on
ree sides constitute a natural bastion,
mpleted to the east by the man-made fort.
Originally built by the Etruscans, the
wn remained beyond the orbit of the great
uscan city states, such as Florence and
ena, until it was finally absorbed into the
and duchy under Cosimo I de' Medici.

In the course of the 15th century a Jew-
h community began to grow here, a ten-
ency that accelerated when Pope Pius IV
anned Jews from Rome in 1569. Perhaps
ey felt themselves still too close to the
ockpit of Catholicism, for in subsequent
ears they began to move away, to Livorno,
lorence and often farther afield still, such
s to Venice. Maybe it was just that there
as no room, for in 1622 the Jews of Pit-
gliano were obliged to move into a tiny
hetto, where they remained until 1772.
rom then until well into the following cen-
ury, the local community of 400 flourished
nd Pitigliano was dubbed Little Jerusalem.
y the time the Fascists introduced their
ace laws in 1938, most Jews had moved
way (only 80 or so were left, precious few
f whom survived the war).

nformation The tourist information of-
ice (☎ 0564 61 44 33, 0564 61 57 88) is at
Via Roma 6, just off Piazza della Repub-
lica, and is supposedly open from 10 am to
oon and 3 to 5 pm, Monday to Friday
from 10 am to noon on Sunday). It is not
ncommon to find it well shut in the winter
months.

hings to See Apart from the spectacle of
iewing the town from the Manciano ap-
roach road (arrive at night and you see it
ll lit up – quite breathtaking), it is a joy to
wander around its narrow little lanes.
Perched as it is on a sharp outcrop surrounded by gorges, the place seems like it
could have inspired Escher. Twisting stairways disappear around corners, cobbled alleys bend out of sight down beneath arches
and the stone houses seem to have been
piled up one on top of the other by a giant
drunk playing with building blocks.

As you enter the town, the first intriguing
sight is the aqueduct, built in the 16th century. Keeping watch over the interlocking
Piazza Garibaldi and Piazza Petruccioli is
the 13th-century **Palazzo Orsini**. Much of
what you see was built over the following
centuries. Now seat of the local bishopric,
it is a true citadel, a city within a city –
fortress, residence and supply dump. Inside
you will find the **Museo Archeologico**, with
an instructive display rather than just the
usual glass containers full of all sorts of un-
explained ancient odds and sods. It opens
from 10 am to 1 pm and 3 to 5 pm daily except Wednesday. Admission costs L5000.

If you wander down Via Zuccarelli deep
into the town, you will after a few minutes
(Pitigliano cannot claim to be huge) see a
sign pointing left off to the **synagogue**, at
the heart of the town's once busy little
ghetto. It had largely gone to seed until
1995, when it was restored using old photos and other material to reconstruct it. If
you want to visit (unless you get lucky and
it's open when you happen by), call Dottore
Luigi Cerroni on ☎ 0347 789 20 33. It is not
possible to visit on Saturdays and Jewish
holidays.

The town's cathedral dates back to the
Middle Ages, but its facade is baroque and
its interior has been modernised. Older is
the oddly shaped **Chiesa di Santa Maria**.

Places to Stay & Eat For a place to stay,
try *Albergo Guastini* (☎ *0564 61 60 65, Piazza Petruccioli 4*), with singles/doubles
with own bathroom for L55,000/85,000 (although the price can rise to L110,000 for
the latter). The rooms are clean and comfortable, if unimaginative. They also have a
reasonable restaurant.

Hotel Valle Orientina (☎ *0564 61 66 11,
Località Valle Orientina*) is 3km outside
town on the road to Orvieto. Rooms are fine
and cost L60,000/90,000 for singles/doubles.
Several affittacamere operate in and about
the town too. You'll see the occasional sign
or you can get information from the tourist
office.

The place to eat is definitely the *Osteria
Il Tufo Allegro* (☎ *0564 61 61 92, Vico*

SOUTHERN TUSCANY

della Costituzione 2), just off Via Zuccar-elli. You would pay about L45,000 for a full meal with wine and dessert. The *gnocchi di zucca al tartufo bianco* (pumpkin gnocchi with white truffle) are a delight (although a rather pricey first course at L35,000). The aromas emanating from the kitchen into the street should be enough to persuade you. The restaurant is closed Tuesday. Someone in the family rents out four rooms for L60,000 each in an old cartmakers' house just outside the town (ask at the restaurant).

If you feel like a night out, all the local young persons seem to gather at the *Jerry Lee Bar* (Via Roma 28).

Getting There & Away The Rama bus terminus is about 1km down the hill from the centre on the road to Sorano. Up to five buses a day run to Grosseto via Manciano Monday to Saturday, but drop off to nothing on Sunday. Quite a few buses run to Sorano, while only two go to Sovana. To get to Saturnia you need to go to Manciano and connect. Inquire at the terminus in advance to make sure of the connections.

Sovana

This pretty little town has more than its fair share of important Etruscan sites and his-torical monuments. There's an information office (☎ 0564 61 40 74) in the Palazzetto dell'Archivio in Piazza del Pretorio.

Pope Gregory VII was born here. Medi-eval mansions and the remains of a fortress belonging to his family are at the eastern end of the town, where you enter. Proceed west along the main street (this is essen-tially a one-street town) and you emerge in the broad Piazza del Pretorio. Here the **Chiesa di Santa Maria** is a starkly simple Romanesque church (although interfered with in parts in later centuries) featuring a magnificent 9th-century ciborium in white marble, one of the last remaining pre-Romanesque works left in Tuscany. It is a highly curious piece of work placed over the altar. In the church there are also some early-16th-century frescoes.

Walk along the Via del Duomo to reach the imposing Gothic-Romanesque cathedral, at the far western end of the town. The ori-ginal construction dates back to the 9th cen-tury, although it was largely rebuilt in the 12th and 13th centuries. Of particular note are the cathedral's marble portal and the capitals of the columns that divide the in-terior into three naves. Several of the cap-itals feature biblical scenes and are thought to be the work of the Lombard school, dat-ing from the 11th century.

A couple of kilometres out of town pro-ceeding west along the road to Saturnia (if you have no vehicle, walking is the only real choice) you will come to a series of ar-chaeological sites harbouring the most sig-nificant Etruscan tombs in Tuscany. Look for the yellow sign on the left for the **Tomba della Sirena**. You pay L5000 to enter the site, which is open from 10 am to 5 pm (or you can get a combined L10,000 ticket in Sorano for the necropolis and the sites in that town – see later in this chapter). The same ticket is valid for the second area, a few kilometres farther west along the same road.

At the first site you can follow a trail run-ning alongside a series of monumental tomb facades cut from the rock face, as well as walk along a *via cava*, one of the so-called 'sunken roads' the Etruscans carved into the rock in this area. No-one is quite sure why they bothered to create these artificial pedestrian gorges.

The second area is dominated by the **Tomba di Ildebranda**, by far the grandest of Etruscan tombs, still preserving traces of the columns and stairs that made up this majestic resting place.

You could easily devote a good day to ex-ploring these sites and/or other less obvious ones in the area. It makes for some pleasant walking.

Places to Stay & Eat If you'd like to stay in Sovana, try the *Taverna Etrusca* (☎ 0564 61 61 83, Piazza Pretorio 16), which has attractive singles/doubles for L80,000/140,000 with bathroom. They also have a fine restaurant, where you are likely to pay about L50,000 a head (but enjoy the experi-ence). It is closed Monday.

The *Scilla (☎ 0564 61 65 31, Via del uomo 5)*, just off the piazza, has cheaper oms, starting at L45,000/70,000 without vn bathroom, or L50,000/75,000 with. hey also boast a classy restaurant, glassed and well worth the L60,000 you are kely to spend. It is closed Tuesday.

orano

om Sovana we turn back down the road e arrived on and past the turn-off for Pitliano to proceed north-east to Sorano. A w kilometres before Sorano is the **Neopoli di San Rocco**, an Etruscan burial site. High on a rocky spur, the small medieval wn of Sorano has largely retained its orinal form. Its houses seem to huddle tother in an effort not to shove one another f their precarious perch. There's a small urist information office (☎ 0546 63 30) on Piazza Busati.

The town's main attraction is the partly renovated **Fortezza Orsini**. It opens from 10 am to 7 pm daily, from April to September. During the rest of the year it opens from 10 am to 4 pm, Friday, weekends and holidays. Admission costs L3000, and guided visits to the underground cellars and quarters of the castle cost L7000.

You could also climb up **Masso Leopoldino** for a spectacular view of the surrounding countryside. The gate is opened at the same times as the Fortezza Orsini.

If you like the fortress so much you want to stay there, you can do – at *Hotel della Fortezza (☎ 0564 63 20 10, fax 0564 63 32 09)*. You'll pay L120,000/200,000 for the privilege.

Otherwise, the accommodation options are more promising at Pitigliano and Sovana (especially if you hunt around for an affittacamere).

Central Tuscany

The hottest frontier in medieval Tuscany was the demarcation line that separated Florence and its possessions from the county of Siena. This proud Gothic hilltop city, although long ago swallowed up by Florence into what became the grand duchy of Tuscany, even today maintains a separate identity. In some respects the Sienese have neither forgiven nor forgotten.

Siena province and the rest of central Tuscany is predominantly hill country, its peaks and ridges dotted with some of the most enchanting towns and villages in the entire region. From the steep straggling Montepulciano to the one-time defensive bulwark of Monteriggioni, the traveller with time to explore will stumble across numerous gems.

Moving westwards, the pilgrim route bastion of San Gimignano, with its ranks of medieval towers, gives us insight into the pomp and circumstance even relatively small towns enjoyed in the Middle Ages. Volterra, the brooding medieval successor to an Etruscan settlement, stands aloof watch over lunar expanses to the south.

Within the patchwork quilt of countryside stretching from Chianti Senese in the north to Montalcino and Montepulciano in the south you will find yourself continually reminded of two of the principal vocations of the area – wine and olive oil. Here you will have the chance to try some of Tuscany's most prized drops, like Brunello, on their home turf.

South of Siena hot springs bubble forth in various spots. A hot outdoor bath in the depths of winter is a unique experience.

For the energetic, central Tuscany offers plenty of walking options. Indeed the most satisfying way to come to know the small medieval towns and Romanesque *pievi* (parish churches) scattered about the area is by following the country lanes.

SIENA
postcode 53100 • pop 59,200

Siena is without doubt one of Italy's most

Highlights

- Visit the great Gothic feast that is Siena's cathedral

- Climb the Torre del Mangia for extensive views and follow up with a coffee in the unique Piazza del Campo, the heart of medieval Siena

- Tour around the Crete and visit the imposing monasteries of Sant'Antimo and the Abbazia di Monte Oliveto Maggiore

- Marvel at the 'medieval Manhattan' formed by the towers of the town of San Gimignano

- Sip on a glass of Brunello in its home, Montalcino

- Wander the streets of Montepulciano, one of the prettiest of the area's hill towns

- Seek out of the captivating walled hamlet of Monteriggioni

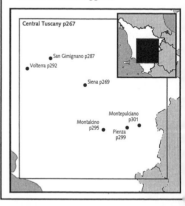

enchanting cities. Its medieval centre bri- tles with majestic Gothic buildings, such the Palazzo Pubblico on the main squar Piazza del Campo, while the churches, m seums and public buildings are home to a extraordinary treasure trove of art.

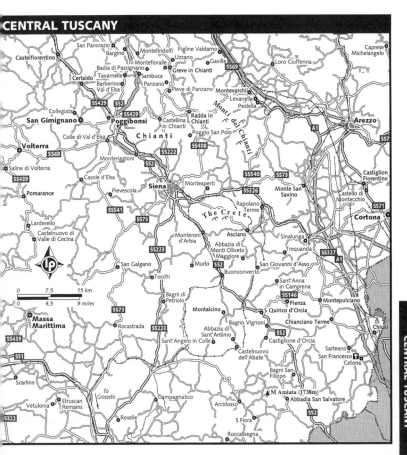

CENTRAL TUSCANY

Like Florence, Siena offers an incredible concentration of things to see, which simply can't be appreciated in a day trip. Try to plan at least one night's stay, or better still allow yourself a few days to properly take in the richness of the city's Gothic architecture and the art of the Sienese school.

Siena actually makes a good base from which to explore central Tuscany, in particular the medieval towns of San Gimignano and Volterra (see later in the chapter). Note, however, that it can be difficult to find budget accommodation in Siena unless you book ahead. In August and during the city's twice-yearly festival, 'Il Palio', it is impossible to find accommodation without a reservation.

History

According to legend Siena was founded by the son of Remus, Senius, and the symbol of the wolf feeding the twins Romulus and Remus is as ubiquitous in Siena as it is in Rome. In reality the city was probably of Etruscan origin, although it wasn't until the 1st century BC, when the Romans established a military colony called Saena Julia, that it began to grow into a proper town.

It remained a minor outpost until the arrival of the Lombards in the 6th century AD. Under them Siena became a key point along the main route from northern Italy to Rome, the Via Francigena. The medieval town was an amalgamation of three areas (Città, Camollia and San Martino) that would come to be known as the *terzi* (thirds). From Lombard hands the city passed under the control of local bishops and then a first line of locally elected administrators, the *consoli* (consuls).

By the 13th century, Siena had become a wealthy trading city, the pillars of whose riches lay in the production of textiles, saffron, wine, spices and wax. International traders and bankers (the Piccolomini, Chigi, Malavolti and Buonsignori families to name a few) were increasingly active.

The parallel with Florence is hard to miss and it is hardly surprising that their rivalry grew. Both cities were also bent on occupying more and more Tuscan territory, so war between the two was inevitable. Ghibelline Siena defeated Guelph Florence at the Battle of Monteaperti in 1260, but it was a short-lived victory. Only nine years later the Tuscan Ghibellines were defeated by Charles of Anjou and for almost a century Siena was obliged to toe the Florentine line in international affairs, becoming a member of the Tuscan Guelph League (supporters of the pope).

During this period Siena reached its peak under the republican rule of the Consiglio dei Nove (Council of Nine), an elected executive dominated by the rising mercantile class. Many of the finest buildings in the Sienese Gothic style, which give the city its striking appearance, were constructed under the direction of the Consiglio, including the cathedral, the Palazzo Pubblico and the Piazza del Campo. The Sienese school of painting had its beginnings at this time with Guido da Siena and reached its peak in the early 14th century with the works of artists including Duccio di Buoninsegna, Simone Martini and Pietro and Ambrogio Lorenzetti.

A plague outbreak in 1348 killed two-thirds of the city's 100,000 inhabitants and led to a period of decline for Siena. The plague also put an end to an ambitious plan to dramatically enlarge the cathedral.

At the end of the 14th century, Siena came under the control of Milano's Visconti family, followed the century after by the autocratic patrician Pandolfo Petrucci. Under the power of Petrucci, the city's fortunes improved, but the Holy Roman Emperor Charles V conquered Siena in 1555 after a two-year siege that left thousands dead. Consequently, the city was handed over to Cosimo I de' Medici, who for a while even barred the inhabitants from operating banks and thus curtailed Siena's power for good.

Siena was home to St Catherine (Santa Caterina), one of Italy's most venerated saints. But saints don't make money. Siena today relies for its prosperity on tourism and the success of its Monte dei Paschi di Siena bank, founded in 1472 and now one of the city's largest employers.

That Siena has remained largely intact as a Gothic city is the silver lining in what was for the people of this city a particularly dark cloud. Its decline in the wake of the Medici takeover was so complete that no one gave thought to demolition and/or new construction. As the population again finally grew in the years after WWII (it had dropped to 16,000 in the latter half of the 18th century), the city became the first in Italy (in 1965) to ban motorised traffic in the old centre.

Orientation

Historic Siena, still largely surrounded by its medieval walls, is small and easily tackled on foot, although the way in which streets swirl in semicircles around the city's heart, Piazza del Campo (also known as 'Il Campo'), may confuse you.

That the city once thrived on banking is evident by the name of two of its main central streets, the Banchi di Sopra and Banchi di Sotto. Together they form part of the medieval Via Francigena pilgrims road from the north to Rome. Another artery is the Via di Città, which runs into the others just behind Piazza del Campo.

SIENA

PLACES TO STAY
2 Piccolo Hotel il Palio
14 Albergo Cannon d'Oro
20 Chiusarelli
25 Albergo Bernini
30 Albergo La Perla
33 Albergo La Toscana
34 Hotel Le Tre Donzelle
35 Piccolo Hotel Etruria
58 Locanda Garibaldi
74 Albergo Duomo

PLACES TO EAT
1 Da Titti
10 Trattoria Tullio (Tre Cristi)
26 La Chiacchiera
32 Crai Supermarket
36 Nannini
45 Grotta del Gallo Nero
48 Spizzico-Ciao
51 Ristorante da Mugolone
60 Hostaria il Carroccio

65 Taverna del Capitano
66 Crai Supermarket
68 Al Marsili
73 Osteria del Castelvecchio

OTHER
3 Società Dante Alighieri
4 Enoteca Italiana
5 Local Bus Terminus
6 The Dublin Rose
7 Chiesa di San Francesco
8 Economics Faculty Library
9 Oratorio di San Bernardino
11 Palazzo Salimbeni
12 ATMs
13 Monte dei Paschi
   di Siena Bank
15 Bus Stop
16 Post Office
17 Vigil Urbani
18 Internet Point
19 Scuola Leonarda da Vinci

21 Siena Hotels Promotion
22 Bus Terminus
23 Bus Ticket Office
24 Chiesa di San Domenico
27 Feltrinelli bookshop
28 Telecom Office
29 Casa di Santa Caterina
31 Exact Change
37 APT Tourist Office
38 Palazzo Piccolomini
39 Logge del Papa
40 Exòdisco
41 Università per Stranieri
42 Telecom Office
43 Al Cambio
44 Internet Train
46 Chiesa di San Martino
47 Synagogue
49 Fonte Gaia
50 Loggia dei Mercanti
52 Battistero di San
   Giovanni (Baptistery)

53 Cathedral
54 Museo dell'Opera
   Metropolitana
55 Exact Change
56 Palazzo Pubblico;
   Torre del Mangia
57 Casa del Boia
59 Onda Blu laundrette
61 Siena Ricama
62 Police Station (Questura)
63 Complesso Museale di
   Santa Maria della Scala
64 Museo Archeologico
67 Telecom Office
69 Palazzo delle Papesse
70 Palazzo Chigi-Saracini;
   Accademia Musicale Chigiana
71 Basilica di Santa Maria
   dei Servi
72 Pinacoteca Nazionale;
   Palazzo Buonsignori
75 Chiesa di Sant'Agostino

CENTRAL TUSCANY

By bus you will arrive at Piazza San Domenico, which affords a panoramic view of the city. Walk east along Via della Sapienza and turn right into Banchi di Sopra to reach Piazza del Campo.

From the train station you will need to catch a bus to Piazza Matteotti. From there walk south-east out of the piazza along Via Pianigiani to reach Banchi di Sopra, turn right and follow it to Piazza del Campo.

Drivers note that streets within the walls are blocked to normal traffic – even if you are staying at a hotel in the centre of town you will be required to leave your car in a car park after dropping off your bags.

You can enter Siena through any of eight city gates; probably the most convenient is Porta San Marco, south-west of the city centre, as it has a well signposted route to the centre. See Getting There & Away later in the chapter for details.

Information

Tourist Office The APT office (☎ 0577 28 05 51, fax 0577 27 06 76) is at Piazza del Campo 56 and is open from 8.30 am to 7.30 pm Monday to Saturday and from 9 am to 2 pm on Sunday in the summer. The hours are 8.30 am to 1 pm and 3.30 to 6.30 pm Monday to Friday (to midday on Saturday) for the rest of the year.

Money Several banks ply their trade near Piazza del Campo in Piazza Tolomei, Banchi di Sopra, Banchi di Sotto and Via di Città. The main branch of the Monte dei Paschi di Siena bank is in Piazza Salimbeni. It offers an automatic exchange service at Banchi di Sopra 92, and ATMs at No 84.

The Exact Change exchange bureau (☎ 0577 28 81 15) is at Via di Città 80–82. There's another branch (☎ 0577 22 61 33) at Via Banchi di Sopra 33.

Post & Communications The main post office is at Piazza Matteotti 1. It is open from 8.15 am to 6 pm Monday to Saturday. Unstaffed Telecom phone offices are at Via dei Termini 40, Via di Città 113 and Via di Pantaneto 44.

You can go online at Internet Tra (☎ 0577 24 74 60) at Via di Pantaneto 5 It is open seven days a week. Their Web si is at www.sienaweb.com. An hour onli costs L12,000 (L10,000 for students). A other option is Internet Point (☎ 0577 24 7 47), Via del Paradiso 10. An hour onlir costs L9600. They are open from 9.30 a to 1 pm and 2.30 to 8 pm (mornings only c Saturday).

Laundry At the self-service laundry Ond Blu, Via del Casato di Sotto 17, you ca wash and dry 6.5 kilos for L10,000.

Medical Services The public hospita (☎ 0577 58 51 11) is in Viale Bracci, ju north of Siena at Le Scotte.

Police The police station (☎ 0577 20 11 1 is at Via del Castoro (open 24 hours a day between the cathedral and Via di Città. Th Foreigners Office (*Ufficio Stranieri*) is i Piazza Jacopo della Quercia, facing th cathedral. It is open from 10 am to midda Monday to Saturday and also from 4.30 t 6.30 pm on Wednesday.

Piazza del Campo

This shell-shaped, slanting square has bee the city's civic centre since it was laid ou by the Council of Nine in the mid-14th cen tury. Siena's republican government in tended that the public life of the city shoul run its course on this spot, once the Roma market place.

Today tourists and locals alike gather i the square to take a break from the day's er rands or sightseeing – backpackers and stu dents lounge on the pavement in the square's centre, while the more well-heele drink expensive coffee or beer at the out door cafes around the periphery.

The square's paving is divided into nin sectors, representing the number of mem bers of the ruling council. In 1346 water firs bubbled forth from the **Fonte Gaia** (Happy Fountain) in the upper part of the square – i took its name from the evident pleasure o locals at this new source of water. The foun tain's panels are reproductions of those don y Jacopo della Quercia in the early 15th century. The much-worn originals can be een in the Palazzo Pubblico.

alazzo Pubblico At the lowest point of e square, this impressive building is also nown as the Palazzo Comunale (town all). Its bell tower, the **Torre del Mangia**, 102m high and was built in 1344.

Dating from 1297, the palazzo itself is ne of the most graceful Gothic buildings in taly. Its construction as the nerve centre of epublican government was planned as an ntegral part of the project for the piazza beore it – the whole creates the effect of an mphitheatre with the Palazzo Pubblico as entral stage.

The Council of Nine wanted to unite the ffices of government and the courts in one entral building, thus further removing the nstruments of power, symbolically and factally, from the hands of the feudal nobles vho had once called the shots here.

The lower level of its facade (*facciatone*) eatures a characteristic Sienese Gothic rcade.

Inside is the **Museo Civico**, a series of ooms on an upper floor of the palazzo with rescoes by artists of the Sienese school. As ou will soon come to notice, the Sienese enchant for frescoes is quite unique. Here s in other great buildings of Siena, and indeed elsewhere in the province (the Palazzo el Popolo and Collegiata in San Gimignano re sufficient confirmation), the decoration, ften with a foundation of deep-blue hues on he ceiling, tends to be rich and full, leaving scarcely a millimetre uncovered.

After buying your ticket you head up two flights of stairs and are obliged to turn left to have your ticket stamped. Here you are in the first of five rather nondescript rooms filled with equally unarresting paintings, mostly by Sienese artists of the 16th to the 18th centuries. Do the anticlockwise circuit or turn immediately left into the **Sala del Risorgimento**, which is bedecked by a series of late-19th-century frescoes serialising key events in the campaign to unite Italy.

A door from this room crosses the central corridor into the **Sala di Balia** (or Sala dei

> ## Tickets Please
>
> If you plan to visit every last monument in sight, you should consider a seven-day cumulative ticket, or *biglietto unico*. Between 16 March and 31 October it costs L32,000 and gives you access to the Museo Civico, Complesso Museale di Santa Maria della Scala, Museo d'Arte Contemporanea, Museo dell'Opera, Libreria Piccolomini, Battistero di San Giovanni, Chiesa di Sant'Agostino and the Oratorio di San Bernardino. For the rest of the year it costs L7000 less as the last two of these monuments are shut.

Priori). The 15 scenes depicted in frescoes around the walls recount episodes in the life of Pope Alexander III (the Sienese Rolando Bandinelli), including his clashes with the Holy Roman Emperor Frederick Barbarossa.

You then pass into the **Anticamera del Concistoro**, remarkable above all for the fresco (moved here in the 19th century) of *Santi Caterina d'Alessandria, Giovanni e Agostino*, executed by Ambrogio Lorenzetti.

The following hall, the **Sala del Concistoro**, is dominated by the allegorical ceiling frescoes by the Mannerist Domenico Beccafumi.

Back in the Anticamera del Concistoro, you pass to your right into the **Vestibolo** (Vestibule), whose star attraction is a bronze wolf, symbol of the city. Above the doorway is a Lorenzetti fresco of the *Madonna col Bambino*. Next door in the **Anticappella** are frescoes of scenes from Greco-Roman mythology and history, while the **Cappella** (Chapel), sealed off by a heavy wrought-iron screen, contains a fine *Sacra Famiglia e San Leonardo* by Sodoma.

The best is saved till last. From the Cappella you emerge in the **Sala del Mappamondo**, so-called because it was once adorned with a circular map fresco, in which you can admire the masterpiece of the building, the *Maestà* by Simone Martini. The striking fresco is his earliest-known work and depicts the Virgin Mary

CENTRAL TUSCANY

enthroned with the Christ child, surrounded by angels, saints and other figures. It is one of the most important works of the Sienese school.

On the opposite wall, the equestrian fresco of *Guidoriccio da Fogliano* has also long been attributed to Martini, although there is some doubt about it now. Other large frescoes along the inside long wall depict famous Sienese victories.

The next room, the **Sala dei Nove** (or Sala della Pace) is dominated by Ambrogio Lorenzetti's fresco series depicting the *Effetti del Buon e del Cattivo Governo* (Allegories of Good and Bad Government), which are among the most significant to survive from the Middle Ages. On the party wall with the Sala del Mappamondo are scenes of a charming serenity that happen to lend a little insight into everyday life in medieval Siena and its countryside. This sunlit idyll is the result of good and wise government, symbolised by the figures on the narrow inner wall. Turning to the next long wall you see the symbolic figures of all the nasty vices that can come to rule the hearts of princes and lead to the misery depicted next to them. Unfortunately, this fresco has been much damaged.

You can wind up the visit by leaping up the stairs to the **loggia** that looks out north over Piazza del Mercato and the countryside. It is here that some of the original panels of the Fonte Gaia sit leaning against the wall.

The opening hours for the Palazzo Pubblico and museum vary throughout the year: they open from 10 am to 11 pm Monday to Saturday (from 9 am to 1.30 pm on Sunday) in July and August. They close as early as 4 pm at other times of the year. Admission costs L8000 (L4000 for students). You can hire an audio guide to the palazzo for L7000 – ask at the bookshop.

Torre del Mangia You can climb the graceful bell tower for splendid views across the city. This exercise can be undertaken from 10 am to 4 pm (6 pm in summer, except July and August, when it stays open until 11 pm). It opens only from 9.30 am to 1.30 pm on Sunday. Note that the tick office closes 45 minutes before the tow shuts and only 30 people are allowed up any time. You may find yourself queuing a wooden door waiting for people to con down. On rainy days you're not allowed climb the 400 steps (there is no lift) at al Admission costs L7000.

Cathedral

Despite the retention of some Romanesqu elements, the cathedral is one of Italy great Gothic churches. Begun in 1196, was largely completed by 1215, althoug work continued on features such as the aps and dome well into the 13th century.

Exterior Work then began on changing, er larging and embellishing the structure. Th magnificent facade of white, green and re polychrome marble was begun by Giovann Pisano, who completed only the lower sec tion, and was finished towards the end c the 14th century. The mosaics in the gable were added in the 19th century. The statue of philosophers and prophets by Giovann Pisano above the lower section are copies the originals being preserved in the adjacen Museo dell'Opera Metropolitana. The bel tower is Romanesque, although the exac date of its completion is uncertain.

In 1339, the city's leaders launched plan to enlarge the cathedral and create on of Italy's largest churches. Known as th Duomo Nuovo (New Cathedral), the re mains of this unrealised project can be see in Piazza Jacopo della Quercia, on the east ern side of the main cathedral. According t the ambitious plan, an immense new nav would rise and the present church woul have become the transept. The plague o 1348, which devastated the city, put a sto to this formidable scheme. The main facad is interesting as it clearly combines ele ments of Gothic and Renaissance (look a the top central arch). You can climb to th top for great views from the Museo dell' Opera del Duomo (see later in the chapter)

Interior The cathedral's interior is ric with artworks and warrants an hour or more f your time. It's a pity about the classical music they play in here. One assumes it is upposed to be atmospheric but the building tself does quite well on its own without the xtra cheese. Walls and pillars continue the lack-and-white-stripe theme of the exterior, while the vaults are painted blue with old stars (a common device in Sienese territory). High along the walls of the nave is a long series of papal busts.

After looking up, look down...unfortuately all you will probably see is cardboard nd masking tape. Beneath these lie the athedral's most precious feature – the inlaid-narble floor, which is decorated with 56 anels depicting historical and biblical subects. The earliest panels are graffiti designs n simple black-and-white marble, dating rom the mid-14th century. The latest panels were completed in the 16th century. Most of them are kept covered throughout he year, except for a period of a few weeks etween August and September, when you ave to pay to enter the church. Typically he panels have been revealed from 7 to 22 August, but you should check with the APT or the latest timetable and admission harges. If you don't get to see them and vould like to depress yourself with an idea f what you have missed, make sure you inpect the 19th-century drawings in the Museo dell'Opera del Duomo (see the following section).

After the floor, the most exquisite item in he church is, however, the beautiful octagonal pulpit carved in marble and porphyry y Nicola Pisano in the 13th century. Among his helpers on this project were his on, Giovanni, and Arnolfo di Cambio. Often compared with Pisano's hexagonal ulpit in the Baptistry in Pisa, this is if anything better still and is one of the outstanding masterpieces of Gothic sculpture. The more you behold the seven panels, laden vith crowd scenes of remarkable reality, the nore they seem to come to life. Unfortuately you can't inch as close as you might ike as barriers keep you at a respectful disance. To shed a little light on the subject, tick coins into the machine (L500 gets you a generous one minute of illumination).

Other significant artworks include a bronze statue of St John the Baptist by Donatello, in the north transept.

Libreria Piccolomini Through a door off the north aisle, this is another of the cathedral's great treasures. Pope Pius III (pope in 1503) built this compact hall to house the books of his uncle, Enea Silvio Piccolomini, who was Pope Pius II. Of the books, only a series of huge choral tomes belonging to the cathedral remains on display.

You are not here for the books, but for the walls. They are covered by an impressive series of richly coloured frescoes by Bernardino Pinturicchio. They depict events in the life of Piccolomini, starting from his early career days as a secretary to an Italian bishop on a mission to Basle, through to his ordination as pope and eventually his death in Ancona while trying to get a crusade against the Turks off the ground.

In the centre of the hall is a group of statues known as the *Tre Grazie* (Three Graces), a 3rd-century-AD Roman copy of an earlier Hellenistic work.

The libreria is open from 9 am to 7.30 pm from mid-March to the end of October; it opens from 10 am to 1 pm and 2.30 to 5 pm at other times of the year. Admission costs L2000 (if you don't have the combined ticket).

Museo dell'Opera Metropolitana

This museum is next to the cathedral, in what would have been the south aisle of the nave of the new cathedral. Its great artworks formerly adorned the cathedral, including the 12 statues of prophets and philosophers by Giovanni Pisano that decorated the facade. These stand on the ground floor. If you are wondering why they look so distorted (they all crane uncomfortably forward) it is explained by the fact that their creator designed them with a view to how they would best be seen from ground level.

However, the museum's main draw card is Duccio di Buoninsegna's striking early 14th-century *Maestà*, painted on both sides as a screen for the cathedral's high altar.

CENTRAL TUSCANY

euro currency converter   L10,000 = €5.16

The front and back have now been separated and the panels depicting the *Passione* (Story of Christ's Passion) hang opposite the *Maestà*. It is interesting to compare Buoninsegna's work with Martini's slightly later *Maestà* in the Palazzo Pubblico. The closer you look at the Passion scenes the more you are absorbed into the story. It is important to remember that this kind of art was above all didactic. The 'pretty pictures' tell the story of the Scriptures, which the largely illiterate masses could not read. Duccio's narrative genius is impressive. Take the lower half of the bottom big middle panel. In one 'shot' three scenes take place: Christ preaches to the Apostles in the Garden of Gethsemane; he then asks them to wait up for him; and then is portrayed while in prayer. In the half panel above, he is kissed by Judas while Peter lops off a soldier's ear and the remaining Apostles flee.

To the right of the *Maestà* a door leads into a back room with statues by Jacopo della Quercia, while the door to the left leads to a room with 19th-century illustrations of the entire collection of marble floor panels in the cathedral.

On the upper floors other artists represented in the museum are Ambrogio Lorenzetti, Simone Martini and Taddeo di Bartolo. The collection also includes tapestries and manuscripts.

Follow the signs to the **Panorama del Facciatone** (which involves a claustrophobic climb up winding stairs) to come out on top of the facade of what would have been the huge extension of the cathedral. The views over all Siena are marvellous.

The museum is open from 9 am to 7.30 pm daily from 16 March to 31 October, until 6 pm for the rest of October and until 1.30 pm during the rest of the year. Admission costs L6000 without the combined ticket.

Battistero di San Giovanni

Behind the cathedral and down a flight of stairs is the Battistero di San Giovanni (Baptistry of St John). Its Gothic facade is unfinished at the upper levels but is nonetheless a quite remarkable extravagance in marble.

Inside, the ceiling and vaults are bedecked with predictable lavishness in frescoes depicting the Apostles, sibyls, and series devoted to the articles of the cree The life of Jesus is portrayed in frescoes the apse of this oddly shaped rectangula baptistry. The lower illustrations are by Vecchietta – the one on the right showin Christ carrying the Cross of particular in terest. If you look at the city from which appears he and the crowd have come, it hard to escape the feeling that, among th imaginary buildings have been illustrate Brunelleschi's dome and Giotto's Cam panile in Florence. Is this a nasty little ant Florentine dig suggesting Siena's rival a the source of Christ's tribulations?

The real attraction is, however, a marb font by Jacopo della Quercia, decorate with bronze panels in relief depicting th life of St John the Baptist. The panels wer carried out by several top-notch artists an include Lorenzo Ghiberti's *Battesimo Gesù* (Baptism of Christ) and *Cattura d Battista* (St John in Prison), and Donatello *Banchetto di Erode* (Herod's Feast).

The baptistry has the same opening hou as the Museo dell'Opera Metropolitana, ex cept that it also opens from 2.30 to 5 p during the winter months. Admission cos L3000 (without the combined ticket).

Complesso Museale di Santa Maria della Scala

Until a few years ago a working hospita with almost a millennium of history, th immense space is being transformed (rathe slowly by all appearances) into a major art centre. Located on the south-west side c Piazza del Duomo, the main attraction re mains the extraordinary series of frescoe by Domenico di Bartolo in what was th main ward.

First references to the hospital date to th 11th century. It appears it was initially mor of a hospice for pilgrims on the Via Franci gena. The medical aspects of the work don by sisters and later doctors here only be came paramount some time farther on.

From the ticket office you turn right into the **Cappella del Manto**, decorated with frescoes of which the most striking is that by Beccafumi (done in 1514) portraying the *Incontro di San Gioacchino con Santa Anna* (St Joaquim and St Anna), the supposed parents of the Virgin Mary.

Next you pass into a long hall and turn left again into the room of principal interest in the complex, the remarkable 14th-century **Sala del Pellegrinaio**. As its name suggests, it was initially more like a dorm for tired pilgrims. With time it became the hospital's main ward. Try to imagine it full of the sick and dying over the centuries. Let's hope there were some joyful moments of recovery for some.

One can only wonder whether patients were uplifted by the frescoes celebrating the charitable nature of bringing succour to the ill and needy. The bulk of the series was carried out by Domenico di Bartolo in the 1440s. The first panel, by Il Vecchietta, depicts orphans *(gettatelli)* ascending to heaven. Taking in orphans was frequently one of the routine tasks of hospitals throughout Tuscany. Later panels show wet-nurses *(balie)* suckling orphans and other needy children – for which they were either paid in kind or hard cash. Panels on the opposite wall depict the tending of the sick, distribution of alms and other charitable deeds.

As you pass out of the ward you are directed to the **Chiesa della Santissima Annunziata**, a church built into the complex in the 13th century and remodelled two centuries later. At the time of writing you could not get into the body of the church proper, only the **Sagrestia Vecchia** (Old Sacristy), which is decorated with complex frescoes explaining the articles of the creed. Next door is the little baroque **Cappella della Madonna** through which you would normally be able to get into the church.

Downstairs you pass through the **Fienile**, storage space for the hospital, to the **Oratorio di Santa Caterina della Notte**, a gloomy little chapel for sending up a prayer or two for the unwell upstairs.

The complex is open from 10 am to 6.30 pm in summer, with reduced hours during the rest of the year. Admission costs L8000 (without the combined ticket).

Museo Archeologico

Also housed in the former hospital is this modest collection of ancient artefacts dug up in the region surrounding Siena, mostly in the 19th century. It is no match for Florence's Museo Archeologico, but worth a quick look if you are particularly interested in this sort of thing. Objects on show range from elaborate Etruscan alabaster funerary urns to gold Roman coins. In between you'll see some statuary (much of it Etruscan and dating from several centuries BC), a variety of household items, votive statuettes in bronze and even a pair of playing dice.

The museum opens from 9 am to 2 pm Monday to Saturday and from 9 am to 1 pm on Sunday (closed the second and fourth Sunday of the month). Admission supposedly costs L4000, although the last time we wandered in it was free.

Palazzo delle Papesse

This is a pot-luck art gallery on Via di Città, where you come to see the latest itinerant contemporary art exhibitions. These usually last several months. The gallery is open from noon to 7 pm daily and admission usually costs L5000 (without the combined ticket). Unless of course you have the kind of luck we had and try to visit on the day they are changing over from one exhibition to another.

Palazzo Chigo-Saracini

The magnificent curving Gothic facade of this palazzo on Via di Città is in part a travesty, the result of 'restoration' in the 18th and 19th centuries to re-create the medieval feel. From the tower, which is the genuine article, they say a young boy with particularly good eyesight watched the Battle of Monteaperti in 1260 and shouted down details of the home side's progress against the Florentines to eager crowds in the streets below (as you may remember, the home side won this round).

euro currency converter L10,000 = €5.16

The palazzo is now home to the Accademia Musicale Chigiana and not generally open to the public. You can however, by making an appointment with the Monte dei Paschi di Siena bank, arrange to make a visit. Inside you can see sumptuously furnished rooms and an interesting collection of principally Sienese art. Ask at the APT for the latest contact details. This is really only for those who are spending some time in Siena and wish to get to know it in more depth.

Pinacoteca Nazionale

Located in the 15th-century Palazzo Buonsignori, a short walk south of the cathedral at Via San Pietro 29, this gallery *(pinacoteca)* constitutes the greatest concentration of Sienese art in the city. This means, in particular, an excursion into the Gothic masterpieces of the Sienese school. As you progress through the collection, you can only marvel at the gulf that lay between artistic life in Siena and Florence in the 15th century. While the Renaissance flourished 70km to the north, Siena's masters and their patrons remained firmly rooted in the Byzantine and Gothic precepts that had stood them in such good stead from the early 13th century. Stock religious images and episodes predominate, typically lavishly filled with gold and generally lacking any of the advances in painting (such as perspective, emotion or movement) that artists in Florence were indulging in.

Follow the gallery's advice and start your tour on the 2nd floor, which is where the Sienese masters from the early 13th through to the 15th century are on show.

In the first two rooms you can see some of the earliest surviving, pre-Gothic works of the Sienese school, including pieces by Guida da Siena. Rooms 3 and 4 are given over to a few works by Duccio di Buoninsegna (to see him at his best you need to go to the Museo dell'Opera del Duomo) and his followers. The most striking exhibit in Room 5 is Simone Martini's *Madonna della Misericordia*, in which the Virgin Mary seems to take the whole of society protectively under her wings.

The brothers Pietro and Ambrogio Lorenzetti dominate Rooms 7 and 8, while the following three rooms contain works by several early-15th-century artists, including Taddeo di Bartolo, who is responsible for massive *Crocifisso*.

Giovanni di Paolo dominates most of Rooms 12 and 13, and a couple of his paintings show refreshing signs of a break from strict tradition. His two versions of the *Presentazione nel Tempio* (The Presentation of Jesus in the Temple) introduce new architectural themes, a hint of perspective, virtually no gold and a discernible trace of human emotion in the characters depicted. A few of the radical ideas unleashed in Florence were clearly filtering through. From here to the end of the floor, however the themes and styles remain remarkably faithful to the old formulae.

The small **Collezione Spannochi** on the 3rd floor is a motley group of paintings with a few highlights, including a Dürer and a nativity scene by Lorenzo Lotto in which all the light emanates from the Christ child.

Down on the 1st floor, the Sienese roll call continues, and although there are some exceptions, the interest starts to fade. The rooms to spend time in include Nos 27 to 32 and 37, which are dominated by works of the Mannerist Domenico Beccafumi and Il Sodoma. Of all these, Sodoma's *Cristo alla Colonna* (Christ Tied to the Pillar) in Room 32 is the most disturbing. Christ's tears are a heart-rending human touch. Beccafumi's *Discesa di Cristo al Limbo* (Christ's Descent into Limbo) in Room 37 is also worth close inspection.

The gallery is open from 9 am to 7 pm Tuesday to Saturday, from 8 am to 1 pm on Sunday and from 8.30 am to 1.30 pm on Monday. The hours are 8.30 am to 1.30 pm and 2.30 to 5.30 pm Tuesday to Saturday in winter. Admission costs L8000. In winter the 1st floor is closed (and admission reduced to L4000) in the afternoon session.

Chiesa di San Domenico

This imposing Gothic church was started in the early 13th century, but has been much altered over the centuries.

The bare, barn-like interior surprises by s sheer emptiness, although this was in eeping with the Dominican order's spartan utlook. At the bottom end of the church near the door where you enter) is the raised Cappella delle Volte, where St Catherine ook her vows as a Dominican and suppos-dly performed some of her miracles. In the hapel is a portrait of the saint painted dur-ng her lifetime.

In the Cappella di Santa Caterina, on the outh side of the church, are frescoes by odoma depicting events in the saint's life. St Catherine died in Rome and most of her ody is preserved there in the Chiesa di Santa Maria Sopra Minerva. In line with he bizarre practice of collecting relics of lead saints, her head was given back to Siena. It is contained in a tabernacle on the ltar of the Cappella di Santa Caterina.

Another bit of her that managed to find ts way here is a thumb, on display in a mall window box to the right of the chapel. Also on show is a rather nasty-looking hain whip with which she used to apply a good flogging to herself every now and hen for the well-being of the souls of the aithful.

Fortezza Medicea

A short walk west of the Chiesa di San Domenico, this fortress is typical of those built in major cities in the early years of the grand duchy. Also known as the Forte di Santa Barbara, the Sienese could have been given little more obvious a reminder of who was in charge than this huge Medici bas-ion, raised on the orders of Cosimo I de' Medici in 1560. It was built on the site of a ormer Spanish fort, which had had much he same function as watchdog over the estive folk of Siena.

Casa di Santa Caterina

The house where St Catherine was born s on Via delle Terme, off Via della Sap-enza. The rooms inside the house were converted into small chapels in the 15th century and are decorated with frescoes and paintings by Sienese artists, including Sodoma. The house is open from 9 am to 12.30 pm and 2.30 to 6 pm daily. Admission is free (it was actually closed at the time of writing).

Piazza del Campo to Porta Romana

The Loggia dei Mercanti, finished in the early 15th century and designed to give merchants a central place to do their deals, is inserted among the row of palazzi that form the backdrop to Piazza del Campo.

From here take Banchi di Sotto to the east for the Palazzo Piccolomini, Siena's finest Renaissance palace built by Pope Pius II, the leading figure of the Piccolo-mini family. It houses the city's archives and a small museum open from 9 am to 1 pm Monday to Saturday. Admission is free, and you will be guided through the building.

A block east are the Logge del Papa, an-other of Pius II's Renaissance contributions to the city. On the same intersection you see the Mannerist facade of the Chiesa di San Martino, a makeover that disguises the fact that this is one of the oldest churches in Siena. The original building went up here in the 8th century. Siena's only synagogue is just near here down the narrow Vicolo delle Scotte.

Proceed east along Via del Porrione (which becomes Via San Martino) and you will run into the 13th-century Basilica di Santa Maria dei Servi. Inside you can see Pietro Lorenzetti's depiction of the *Strage degli Innocenti* (Massacre of the Innocents) and a painting of the *Madonna del Bordone* by Coppo di Marcovaldo, done after the Florentine artist was captured during the Battle of Monteaperti in 1260.

A short stroll south of the church is the massive 14th-century Porta Romana, one of the city's main gates. As the name sug-gests, the road to Rome once went directly from this gate.

Piazza del Campo to Chiesa di San Francesco

Return to the Loggia dei Mercanti and head north along Banchi di Sopra and past Piazza Tolomei, dominated by the 13th-century

Palazzo Tolomei. Farther along there's the Piazza Salimbeni, featuring the **Palazzo Tantucci** to the north, the Gothic **Palazzo Salimbeni** to the east, the head office of the Monte dei Paschi di Siena bank and the Renaissance **Palazzo Spannocchi**.

North-east of here, along Via dei Rossi, is the **Chiesa di San Francesco**, which is every bit as big and bare as its Dominican rival. The two orders had a habit of competing in the construction of gargantuan Gothic churches (see Santa Croce and Santa Maria Novella in Florence) but in Siena they seemed to outdo themselves in the creation of unadorned empty space. The cloister next door is now part of the Università di Siena.

Also facing Piazza San Francesco is the **Oratorio di San Bernardino**, notable for its frescoes, particularly those by Sodoma. It is open from 10.30 am to 1.30 pm and 3 to 5.30 pm daily from mid-March to the end of October. Admission costs L4000 (without the combined ticket).

Courses

Language Siena's Università per Stranieri (University for Foreigners; ☎ 0577 24 01 11, fax 0577 28 10 30) is in Piazzetta Grassi 2, 53100 Siena, and has a Web site at www.unistrasi.it. The school is open all year and the only requirement for enrolment is a high-school graduation/pass certificate. (The four-week summer courses have no prerequisites.) There are several areas of study and courses cost L1,100,000 for 10 weeks. Brochures can be obtained by making a request to the secretary of the university, or from the Istituto Italiano di Cultura in your country (see also Useful Organisations in the Facts for the Visitor chapter).

The Scuola Leonardo da Vinci (☎ 0577 24 90 97, fax 0577 24 90 96, @ leonardo .siena@si.nettuno.it) is at Via del Paradiso 16. Or you could try the Società Dante Alighieri (☎ 0577 4 95 33, fax 0577 27 06 46, @ dantesi@iol.it) Piazza La Lizza 10, 53100 Siena. Their Web site is at www .dantealighieri.com. They also run culture and cookery courses.

Non-EU students are usually required t obtain a study visa in their own country; is important to check with an Italian con sulate. See Study Visas under Visas & Docu ments in the Facts for the Visitor chapter fo more details.

Music The Accademia Musicale Chigian (☎ 0577 4 61 52, fax 0577 28 81 24), Via d Città 89, offers classical music classe every summer, as well as seminars and con certs performed by visiting musicians teachers and students as part of the Setti mana Musicale Senese. Classes are offere for most classical instruments and price range from L280,000 to L1,200,000.

The Associazione Siena Jazz (☎ 0577 2 14 01, fax 0577 28 14 04), Via di Vallerozz 77, offers courses in jazz which start a L380,000. It's one of Europe's foremost in stitutions of its type.

Organised Tour

The Treno Natura is a great way to see th stunning scenery of the Crete south o Siena. The train line extends in a rin from Siena, through Asciano, across to th Val d'Orcia and the Monte Antico station before heading back towards Siena. Th line, which opened in the early 1800s, wa closed in 1994 and trains now run exclu sively for tourists.

Trains run on some Sundays during May June, September and the first half of Oct ober. There are usually three per day, stop ping at Asciano and Monte Antico, and they are generally met by connecting trains from Florence. Tickets cost L20,000. Check a the Siena APT or at Siena's train station fo precise details.

Special Events

The Accademia Musicale Chigiana hold the Settimana Musicale Senese each July as well as the Estate Musicale Chigiana i July, August and September. Concerts i these series are frequently held at the Ab bazia di San Galgano (a former abbey about 20km south-west of the city and re garded as one of Italy's finest Gothi buildings) and at Sant'Antimo, near Mon

Il Palio

This spectacular event, held twice yearly on 2 July and 16 August in honour of the Virgin Mary, dates back to the Middle Ages and features a series of colourful pageants, a wild horse race around Piazza del Campo and much eating, drinking and celebrating in the streets.

Il Palio is probably one of the only major medieval spectacles of the type in Italy that has survived through the sheer tenacity of Sienese traditionalism. Most of the other charming displays of medieval nostalgia, although doubtless pleasing, have in fact been brought back to life in the 20th century out of a combination of nostalgia and the desire to earn a few more tourist bucks.

Ten of Siena's 17 town districts, or *contrade*, compete for the coveted *palio*, a silk banner. Each of the contrade has its own traditions, symbol and colours, and its own church and palio museum. The centuries-old local rivalries make the festival very much an event for the Sienese, although the horse race and pageantry predictably attract larger crowds of tourists.

Local allegiance to the contrade is much in evidence all year around. As you wander the streets you will be hard-pressed to miss the various flags and plaques delineating these quarters, each with a name and symbol related to an animal.

The contrade were first noted unofficially in the 14th century but it was only in 1729 that they were given judicial recognition as tiny units of local administration.

On festival days Piazza del Campo becomes a racetrack, with a ring of packed dirt around its perimeter serving as the course. From about 5 pm representatives of each *contrada* parade in historical costume, each bearing their individual banners.

The race is run at 7.45 pm in July and 7 pm in August. For not much more than one exhilarating minute, the 10 horses and their bareback riders tear three times around Piazza del Campo with a speed and violence that makes your hair stand on end.

Even if a horse loses its rider it is still eligible to win and since many riders fall each year, it is the horses in the end who are the focus of the event. There is only one rule: that riders are not to interfere with the reins of other horses. The Sienese place incredible demands on the national TV network, RAI, for rights to televise the event.

Book well in advance if you want to stay in Siena at this time, and join the crowds in the centre of Piazza del Campo at least four hours before the start, or even earlier if you want a place on the barrier lining the track. If you can't find a good vantage point, don't despair – the race is televised live and then repeated throughout the evening on TV.

If you happen to be in town in the few days immediately preceding the race, you may get to see the jockeys and horses trying out in Piazza del Campo – almost as good as the real thing.

JANE SMITH

...alcino. Concerts are also held throughout the year. For information, call ☎ 0577 4 51 52. See also Abbazia di San Galgano and Abbazia di Sant'Antimo later in the chapter.

The city hosts Siena Jazz, an international festival each July and August, with concerts at the Fortezza Medicea, as well as various sites throughout the city. For information, call ☎ 0577 27 14 01.

euro currency converter L10,000 = €5.16

Places to Stay

Siena offers a good range of accommodation but budget hotels generally fill quickly, so it is advisable year-round to book in advance if you want to pay less than about L130,000 per double. Forget about finding a room during the Palio unless you have a booking. For assistance in finding a room, contact the APT (☎ 0577 28 05 51) or Siena Hotels Promotion (☎ 0577 28 80 84, fax 0577 28 02 90), Piazza San Domenico. The latter is open from 9 am to 8 pm Monday to Saturday in summer and 9 am to 7 pm in winter.

If you are having trouble with the hotels, don't despair. The tourist office has a list of about 120 *affittacamere* in town, private households letting out rooms. *Agriturismo* (tourist rooms on farms) is well organised around Siena, and the tourist office has a list of establishments that rent rooms by the week or month.

The *Colleverde* camp site (☎ 0577 28 00 44, fax 0577 33 32 98, Strada di Scacciapensieri 47) is north of the historical centre (take bus No 3 from Piazza Gramsci) and opens from late March to early November. The cost for one night is L20,000 for adults, L10,000 for children and L25,000 for a pitch. The non-HI youth hostel *Guidoriccio* (☎ 0577 5 22 12, fax 0577 5 61 72, Via Fiorentina 89, Località Stellino) is about 2km north-west of the city centre. Bed and breakfast costs L23,000 and a full meal L14,000. It's a little awkwardly placed and not the best of the Italian hostel crop – you are better off with a pensione room in town. If you want to stay here anyway, take bus No 3 from Piazza Gramsci. If driving, leave the city by Via Vittorio Emanuele II, which is an extension of Via di Camollia.

In town, try the *Hotel Le Tre Donzelle* (☎ 0577 28 03 58, fax 0577 22 39 33, Via delle Donzelle 5), off Banchi di Sotto north of Piazza del Campo. It has clean, simple singles/doubles for L45,000/75,000. A double with bathroom costs L95,000. The *Piccolo Hotel Etruria* (☎ 0577 28 80 88, fax 0577 28 84 61, Via delle Donzelle 3) has pleasant rooms for up to L65,000/103,000

with bathroom. The *Locanda Garibal*... (☎ 0577 28 42 04, fax 0577 28 42 04, V... Giovanni Duprè 18), just south of Piazz... del Campo, has singles/doubles for L45,00... 85,000.

Albergo Bernini (☎ 0577 28 90 47, V... della Sapienza 15) is not a good deal f... loners but not bad for people in pairs... doubles with own bathrooms cost L130,00... or L110,000 without. *Albergo La Per*... (☎ 0577 4 71 44, Via delle Terme 25) is... short walk north-west of Piazza del Camp... Small but clean rooms with shower co... L60,000/90,000.

Albergo La Toscana (☎ 0577 4 60 9... fax 0577 27 06 34, Via Cecco Angioleri 1... has a variety of rooms. The singles... L60,000 are OK but nothing to write hom... about. The doubles for L90,000, withou... own shower, are fine. If you want your ow... bathroom you pay L90,000/130,000. Room... have TV and phone.

A good 15-minute walk from Piazza d... Campo, the *Piccolo Hotel il Palio* (☎ 057... 28 11 31, fax 0577 28 11 42, Piazza del Sal... 19) has rooms with bathroom for L130,00... 160,000. The *Albergo Cannon d'Or*... (☎ 0577 4 43 21, fax 0577 28 08 68, Via d... Montanini 28) has rooms with bathroom fo... L115,000/135,000.

The three-star *Albergo Duomo* (☎ 057... 28 90 88, fax 0577 4 30 43, Via di Stal... loreggi 38) has lovely rooms, many wit... views, which cost from L150,000/220,00... Just off Piazza San Domenico is th... *Chiusarelli* (☎ 0577 28 05 62, fax 0577 2... 11 77, Viale Curtatone 15), which has pleas... ant singles/doubles with bathroom fo... L97,000/135,000. It is in a handy location i... you have a car.

A bit of a way out to the south is *Hote*... *Santa Caterina* (☎ 0577 22 11 05, fax 057... 27 10 87, Via Enea Silvio Piccolomini 7)... is small and friendly with good service. Yo... will pay L175,000/220,000.

If you are thinking about hanging aroun... long-term and want to share a flat with stu... dents, check out the noticeboards at the uni... versity (such as the one at the economic... faculty library in the cloister of the Chies... di San Francesco).

Places to Eat

Local Cuisine The Sienese claim that most Tuscan cuisine has its origins in Siena, where the locals still use methods introduced to the area by the Etruscans.

Tuscans elsewhere may well dispute such claims, but the Sienese maintain that such dishes as *ribollita*, *panzanella* and *pappardelle al sugo di lepre* (hare sauce) are their own. *Pici*, a kind of bloated rough spaghetti, definitely are. *Panforte*, a rich cake of almonds, honey and candied melon or citrus fruit, has its origins in the city. Loosely translated, panforte is 'strong bread', and it was created as sustenance for the crusaders to the Holy Land.

Restaurants At the cheap self-service *Spizzico-Ciao* (☎ 0577 74 01 87, Piazza del Campo 77–81) you can eat solidly for L20,000 or even less. *Hostaria il Carroccio* (☎ 0577 4 11 65, Via Casato di Sotto 32), off Piazza del Campo, has excellent pasta for around L10,000. Try the pici followed by the *friselle di pollo ai zucchini* (bite-sized juicy chicken bits with a zucchini side). It is closed on Wednesday.

Taverna del Capitano (☎ 0577 28 80 94, Via del Capitano 8) is a good little spot for local food. A full meal will probably cost you about L35,000. More expensive but highly regarded by locals is the nearby *Osteria del Castelvecchio* (☎ 0577 4 95 86, Via di Castelvecchio 65). You are advised to book ahead at both, and they both shut on Tuesday.

La Chiacchiera (☎ 0577 28 42 95, Costa di Sant'Antonio 4), off Via Santa Caterina, is tiny but has a good menu with local specialities. Pasta costs from L8000. A full meal will cost about L35,000. It is closed on Wednesday.

Al Marsili (☎ 0577 4 71 54, Via del Castoro 3) is one of the city's better-known restaurants and has dishes from L8000 for a first course and from L15,000 for a second. The doors close on Monday. *Ristorante da Mugolone* (☎ 0577 28 32 35, Via dei Pellegrini 8) is another excellent restaurant, with local specialities. Pasta costs from L10,000 and second courses cost between L15,000

and L25,000. The setting is a little on the starched-collar side, with besuited waiters gliding noiselessly about the tables and the well-dressed customers. The foyer feels more like a hotel reception area. It is closed on Thursday.

About a 10-minute walk north of Piazza del Campo, in a less frenetic neighbourhood, are several trattorie and alimentari. *Da Titti* (☎ 0577 4 80 87, Via di Camollia 193) is a no-frills establishment with big wooden benches where full meals with wine cost around L25,000. It is closed on Saturday.

At *Grotta del Gallo Nero* (☎ 0577 28 43 56, Via del Porrione 67) you can feast at a medieval banquet. It appears some research has gone into the meals, so your five or six courses will be a departure from the average Italian fare. The musical accompaniment may not be to everyone's taste. Banquets cost from L60,000 to 80,000 a head. It is closed on Monday.

Returning to modern times, *Trattoria Tullio (Tre Cristi)* (☎ 0577 28 06 08, Vicolo di Provenzano 1) is tucked away on a small lane not far from the Chiesa di San Francesco. Beneath the brick vaults of this restaurant, which has been operating in one way or another since the early 19th century, you can expect to pay around L40,000 for a full meal.

Nannini (☎ 0577 74 15 91, Banchi di Sopra 22) is one of the city's finest cafes and *pasticcerie* (cake and pastry shops).

There are *Crai* supermarkets scattered around the town centre, including at Via di Città 152–156 and in Via Cecco Angiolieri, opposite Albergo La Toscana.

Entertainment
Although a little too much publicised, an interesting place to taste a wide range of fine Tuscan wines is the *Enoteca Italiana* (☎ 0577 28 84 97), just inside the Fortezza Medicea. It closes on Sunday and on Monday evening.

Och, if you feel in need of a UK ale, you could always pop over to *Robert the Bruce* (Via Montesanto 1). It opens until 2 am, except on Wednesday when it doesn't open at

CENTRAL TUSCANY

all. It is on the west side of the Fortezza Medicea. Another in this line, but with a pseudo-Irish lilt, is **The Dublin Rose** (☎ *0577 28 90 89, Piazza Gramsci 20–21).* It opens daily until 1 am and you can get snack food (panini and the like).

Exòdisco (☎ *0577 28 53 10, Via di Pantaneto 22)* is one of the few dance locations in Siena keeping the young students busy. On occasion it stages live music. Just down the road, **Al Cambio** *(Via di Pantaneto 48)* is an alternative dance venue.

Casa del Boia (☎ *0577 22 68 20, Piazza del Mercato 34–36)* stages Latin nights on Tuesday, Thursday and Saturday. In compensation, happy hour from 9 pm on the alternative evenings is designed to warm you up for more mainstream music. It is closed on Sunday.

As elsewhere in Italy, the big dance venues are generally well outside town. **Bombo** (☎ *0577 4 55 54)* is about 25km south of Siena on the SS223. Look for La Locanda del Ponte near the turn off for Monticiano. Admission costs L30,000, which includes a drink. Another is **Papillon** in Monteroni d'Arbia, about 15km south-east of Siena on the SS2. You should check ads for these places, for instance at the uni noticeboard in the cloister of the Chiesa di San Francesco, for details of what is happening – often one or more bars in Siena are selected as meeting points.

Shopping

Siena Ricama, a shop at Via di Città 61, promotes the crafts of Siena, in particular embroidery, and is worth a visit. Via di Città is a chic shopping street (with a clear leaning to selling products to tourists) where you can buy ceramics, food items, antiques, jewellery and so on. For clothes there are more shops on Banchi di Sopra.

Feltrinelli (☎ 0577 27 11 04), Banchi di Sopra 54 and 64, is a good bookshop.

Getting There & Away

Bus From Siena, bus is generally the way to go. Up to seven SENA buses leave Piazza San Domenico for Rome. The trip takes about three hours and costs L26,000.

Regular SITA buses race up the super strada to Florence (L7800, 130 minutes *rapido* service L11,000, 75 minutes) whil LFI buses (as many as seven a day) connec to Arezzo (L8000).

Tra-in buses connect Siena with destin ations around its province. Connections t Poggibonsi (for San Gimignano) and Col di Val d'Elsa (for Volterra) are frequen Other destinations include Monterrigion Chianciano, Pienza, Radda in Chianti, Rap olano, Montalcino, Montepulciano, Sa Quirico d'Orcia and Grosseto.

At Piazza Gramsci, Tra-in operates a underground ticket sales and informatio service, along with left luggage and eve public showers (L5000). Several sets c signposted stairs lead you to the office.

Train Siena is not on a major train line, s from Rome it is necessary to change a Chiusi, and from Florence at Empoli, mak ing buses a better alternative. Trains arrive a Piazza F Rosselli, north of the city centre.

Car & Motorcycle Take the SS2 whic connects Florence and Siena. Alternativel take the SS222 ('la Chiantigiana'), whic meanders its way through the Chianti hill From the Florence–Siena superstrada, th least confusing exit to take is Porta Sa Marco. From there follow the signs for th 'centro'.

Getting Around

Bus Tra-in operates city bus services fro a base in Piazza Gramsci. From the trai station, catch bus No 3 to Piazza Gramsc about a 10-minute walk from the Piazza d Campo.

Car & Motorcycle No cars, apart fro those of residents, are allowed in the ci centre. There are large car parks at the Sta dio Comunale and around the Fortezz Medicea; both are just north of Piazza Sa Domenico. Technically, even to just dr off your luggage at your hotel it is nece sary to get a special permit to enter the ci by car. This can be obtained from the *vig urbani* in Viale Federico Tozzi, but only ou have a hotel booking. Otherwise, phone our hotel for advice.

Taxi For a taxi, call ☎ 0577 4 92 22, or after pm, ☎ 0577 28 93 50. The flagfall is 6300 (of which L2900 covers the first km) and thereafter you pay L1450 per ilometre or about L500 per minute when at standstill. Extra charges include L600 per tem of luggage, L2500 for trips between 0 pm and 6 am, L2100 on public holidays nd a L2100 snow charge.

At Centro Bici (☎/fax 0577 28 25 50, ✉ centrobici@iol.it), Viale Toselli 110, you an hire bicycles.

AROUND SIENA
Chianti Senese

With lots of hotels and restaurants, **Castellina in Chianti** is one of the best organised Chianti towns for tourists. Its information ffice (☎ 0577 74 02 01) is at the central Pizza del Comune 1.

You might prefer to head east to **Radda in Chianti**, which has retained much of its harm despite the tourist influx. It is also a andy jumping-off point to many of Chinti's most beautiful spots. The excellent nformation office (☎ 0577 73 84 94) at Pizza Ferrucci 1 has an enthusiastic and elpful staff. They have loads of informaon about places to stay and eat in Chianti, s well as things to see and do, including uggestions for independent walking or oranised tours to wineries, where you can try ne local wines before enjoying a traditional unch. The tourist office has a site on the Veb at www.chiantinet.it. Their email adress is ✉ proradda@chiantinet.it.

For cooking courses in this area, you ould consider trying Posere le Rose (☎ 055 9 45 11), in the village of Poggio San Polo, bout 10km from Radda. One week costs 900,000 (excluding accommodation).

One of the cheapest forms of accommoation is a room in a private house. *Da Gioannino (☎ 0577 73 80 56, Via Roma 6–8)* a real family house in the centre of adda. You'll pay L50,000/80,000 for a ngle/double. The Radda tourist office can rovide details about the apartments and

the numerous farms and wineries offering accommodation. Prices start at around L100,000 a double.

Getting Around Buses connect Florence (L6200, 100 minutes) and Siena, passing through Castellina and Radda, as well as other small towns. The fare from Siena to Radda, for example, is L4700.

The Crete

Just south-east of Siena, this area of rolling clay hills is a feast of classic Tuscan images – bare ridges topped by a solitary cypress tree flanking a medieval farmhouse, four hills silhouetted one against the other as they fade off into the misty distance. The area of the Crete changes colour according to the season – from the creamy violet of the ploughed clay to the green of the young wheat, which then turns to gold. If you have the funds to spare, hire a car in Florence or Siena and spend a few days exploring the Crete. Another option is the Treno Natura, a tourist train which runs from Siena through Asciano and along the Val d'Orcia (see Organised Tour under Siena earlier in the chapter).

Rapolano Terme This is a relatively modern spa town that holds little interest for anyone not intent on taking an old-fashioned cure in the hot bubbling waters here. Two bathing establishments operate from about April to October. There are more interesting places to take a sulphur bath elsewhere in central and southern Tuscany (such as Bagni di San Filippo, Bagno Vignoni and Saturnia – for the latter see the Southern Tuscany chapter).

Asciano This pretty little hamlet is home to a trio of small museums dedicated to Sienese art and Etruscan finds in the area. It is most easily reached along the scenic SP438 road running south-east from Siena. The occasional slow local train passes through from Siena. While the town and its museums are interesting enough, the travelling is more rewarding than the arriving. Asciano is at the heart of the Crete, so the trip there and beyond (such as south to the Abbazia di Monte Oliveto Maggiore) is a real treat.

Abbazia di Monte Oliveto Maggiore

This 14th-century Olivetan monastery is famous for the frescoes by Signorelli and Sodoma that decorate its **Choistro Grande** (Great Cloister). They illustrate events in the life of St Benedict. About 40 monks still live in the monastery.

The fresco cycle begins with Sodoma's work on the east wall (immediately to the right of the entrance into the church from the cloisters), and continues along the south wall of the cloisters. The nine frescoes by Signorelli line the west side of the cloisters and Sodoma picks up again on the north wall. Sodoma's frescoes offer some ambiguous food for thought. Just why this artist was known as 'the Sodomite' has never been confirmed, although it is not too hard to guess that it may have been a reference to his sexual preferences. At any rate, careful inspection of his frescoes reveals rather effeminate traits in many of the male figures represented. Part of the second fresco along the east wall (on the bulging column), in which a potential new acolyte kneels before the severe St Benedict, who is holding up part of his habit, has a suspect air about it. Even if the sexual allusion is imaginary, it seems odd that the monastery's abbot should not have objected to the image. Farther around on the south wall, St Benedict is depicted giving a fellow friar a sound thrashing to exorcise a demon – again a rather kinky image.

Note the decorations on the pillars between some of Sodoma's frescoes – they are among the earliest examples of 'grotesque' art, copied from decorations found in the then newly excavated Domus Aurea of Nero, in Rome.

After the frescoes you can wander into the **church** off the cloister. The baroque interior is a pleasingly sober play of perspective and shape. You can also see further works by Sodoma here. Also off the cloister is a staircase leading up to the Renaissance **library**, which you are allowed to

view only through small windows in the door.

The monastery is open from 9.15 am to 12.15 pm and 3.15 to 6 pm daily (to 5 pm in winter). It is possible to stay at the monastery from Easter to the end of September, although as a rule this possibility (a L30,000 a head) is reserved for priests, families and laypersons intending to remain for spiritual purposes. Call ☎ 0577 70 70 61 for information. They don't take bookings, so it's a case of first in, best dressed.

From the monastery, if you have your own transport, head for **San Giovanni d'Asso**, where there's an interesting 11th century church with a Lombard-Tuscan facade, and a picturesque *borghetto* with the remains of a castle. Continue on to Montisi and Castelmuzio. Along a side road just outside Castelmuzio is the **Pieve di Santo Stefano in Cennano**, an abandoned 13th century church. Ask for the key at the adjacent farm buildings.

Two kilometres past Castelmuzio on the road to Pienza is the 14th-century Olivetan monastery of **Sant'Anna in Camprena**. In the refectory there are frescoes by Sodoma that can occasionally be visited. Phone ☎ 0755 74 83 03 for further information or take your chances by turning up (if you have a vehicle). Some restoration work is in progress.

The route from Monte Oliveto Maggiore to Pienza runs almost entirely along a high ridge, with great views of the Crete.

Buonconvento On first approaching Buonconvento down the SS2 highway, you could almost be forgiven for thinking it a large roadside rest stop. Lying perfectly flat in a rare stretch of plain, the low-slung fortified walls of this farming centre hide from view a quiet little town of medieval origin. One of its biggest moments in history came when the Holy Roman Emperor Henry VII, having shortly before captured it, expired in Buonconvento in August 1313 and so put an end to any hopes the Empire might have had of reasserting direct control over Tuscany. About the only sight here is the local **Museo d'Arte Sacra** in the main street. It contains eligious art collected in the town and from neighbouring churches and hamlets.

Handy as it is for the highway, Buonconvento makes an easy stop for a cup of coffee or stretch of the legs while touring the area. It is also on the Siena–Grosseto bus route. If you are looking for a place to stay, San Quirico d'Orcia, just down the road, is a prettier location.

San Galgano & Around

Abbazia di San Galgano About 20km south-west of Siena, just off the SS73, is the ruined 13th-century San Galgano abbey, one of the country's finest Gothic buildings in its day and now an atmospheric ruin.

A former Cistercian abbey, its monks were among Tuscany's most powerful, forming the judiciary and acting as accountants for the *comuni* (councils) of Volterra and Siena. They presided over disputes between the cities, played a significant role in the construction of the cathedral in Siena and built for themselves an opulent church.

As early as the 14th century Sir John Hawkwood, the feared English mercenary, sacked the abbey on at least two occasions. Things went from bad to worse and by the 16th century the monks' wealth and importance had declined and the church had deteriorated to the point of ruin. An attempt at restoration was made towards the end of the 16th century, but the rot had set in. In 1786 the bell tower simply collapsed, followed by the vaults of the ceiling a few years later.

The great roofless stone and brick monolith stands silent in the fields. Come on a rainy winter's day and you feel more like you are in France or England, surrounded by glistening green fields and confronted by this classic grey Gothic ruin. The French reference is no coincidence, since the style of building is reminiscent of French Gothic.

Next door to the church are what remain of the monastery buildings, as well as a brief stretch of cloister. You can wander in at will.

The abbey is definitely worth a diversion if you are driving, but visiting by public transport is quite difficult. The only option is the bus service between Siena and Massa Marittima, a little farther south-west.

The Accademia Musicale Chigiana in Siena sponsors concerts at the abbey during summer. See Special Events under Siena earlier in the chapter.

On a hill overlooking the abbey is the tiny, round Romanesque **Cappella di Monte Siepi**. This is where the original Cistercian settlement lived – from it came the impulse to build the great abbey below. Inside the chapel are badly preserved frescoes by Ambrogio Lorenzetti depicting the life of St Galgano, a local soldier who had a vision of St Michael on this site. A real-life 'sword in the stone' is under glass in the floor of the chapel, put there, legend has it, by San Galgano.

Murlo You could continue across the valley towards this interesting medieval fortified village. This was once an important Etruscan settlement and experts claim that DNA tests show the locals are close relatives of these ancient people.

Bagni di Petrioli About halfway down the SS322 highway between Siena and Grosseto, a side road leads down to the hot sulphur springs of Bagni di Petrioli. Scorching-hot spring water cascades into a few small natural basins. Anyone can come and sit in them, but they are not what they used to be. The nearby mega-bath-and-hotel complex has detracted a great deal from the charm of the place.

About the only way to get here is with your own transport, since the 9km walk from the highway (along which run several buses between Siena and Grosseto) won't appeal to everyone.

Val d'Elsa

Monteriggioni This captivating walled medieval stronghold is just off the SS2 about 12km north of Siena.

Established in 1203 as a forward defensive position against Florence, the walls and towers today constitute one of the most complete examples of such a fortified bastion in Tuscany. The walls were rebuilt in

CENTRAL TUSCANY

the 1260s and seven of the 14 towers were reconstructed in the 20th century. It appears from Dante's descriptions that they were considerably higher when the Florentines had reason to fear them and their defenders.

Once inside the small town, there is really precious little to it. Should the quiet of the place appeal, you could opt to stay a while in the rather expensive *Hotel Monterriggioni* (☎ 0577 30 50 09, fax 0577 30 50 11, Via Primo Maggio 4), where enticing rooms will cost you L200,000/340,000. Perhaps you'd prefer just to hang about for a meal. If you can loosen the purse strings a little, you will be pleased you sat down at the *Ristorante Il Pozzo* (☎ 0577 30 41 27, Piazza Roma 20). Delicious meals, often with a game base, will cost around L60,000 all in. They are closed on Sunday evening and Monday.

Regular buses run from Siena (L2600).

Colle di Val d'Elsa All most 'visitors' do here is change buses for Volterra. That's a shame, because the town is worth a little exploration time. Florentine forces won a telling victory over the Sienese in 1269 in the plains below the town. The great medieval architect, Arnolfo di Cambio, was born here. From the Middle Ages on it was a bustling little town and had long been an important centre of Italian crystal production.

The most engaging part of town is Colle Alta, the old centre perched up on a ridge. From Piazza Arnolfo, where you will arrive, it is about a 10-minute climb up along Via San Sebastiano.

Eventually you will find yourself walking along Via Castello, the main drag through Colle Alta. At its eastern end is a medieval *casa-torre* (tower house) where they say Arnolfo di Cambio was born. About halfway along the road is Piazza del Duomo, dominated by the rather unprepossessing neoclassical facade of the cathedral itself.

Three little museums cluster around the cathedral. The **Museo Civico** and **Museo d'Arte Sacra** are housed together at Via del Castello 31, while the **Museo Archeologico** is right on Piazza del Duomo. The most in-teresting is the Museo d'Arte Sacra, wit some good paintings by Sienese masters Admission costs L5000 (which includes th Museo Civico). It is open from 10 am t noon and 4 to 7 pm daily except Monda from April to October. They open only a the weekend and public holidays for the res of the year.

You have a choice of three hotels, two i the lower part of town (Colle Bassa). Th pick is the *Hotel Arnolfo* (☎ 0577 92 20 20 fax 0577 92 26 88, Via Campana 8) in Coll Alta, where you will pay L93,000/130,000

Regular buses run here from Sien (L4200). Up to five connecting buses wit the CPT company head west to Volterra.

Casole d'Elsa & Around South-west c Colle di Val d'Elsa, this quiet fortifie backwater was once a key part of Siena' western defences. In the course of the Mid dle Ages, Sienese troops found themselve squaring off on several occasions wit enemy units from rivals Volterra and Flor ence. Little remains to detain you for mor than a cursory inspection but those with ro mantic tastes and a Swiss bank accoun could stick to the tiny road that winds sout out of town to **Mensano** (a pretty littl borgo) and swing east to **Pievescola**. Her an exquisite former castle and Renaissanc villa is now the *Relais La Suvera* (☎ 057 96 03 00, fax 0577 96 02 20). Aside fror centuries of now well-manicured charm rooms here offer all the comforts you coul want, along with a pool. Doubles cos L500,000, unless you take the Villa Ponti icia, which will cost you a cool L1 millior

Poggibonsi WWII managed to take care c what little that was interesting about Poggi bonsi, which takes line honours as one c the ugliest places in central Tuscany. If yo are travelling by bus between Florence c Siena and San Gimignano you will have t pass through. Should you get stuck, th cheapest hotel is *Albergo Italia* (☎ 0577 9 61 42, fax 0577 93 99 70, Via Trento 36 where singles/doubles cost L60,000/90,000 You will have no trouble finding places t eat or have a coffee.

AN GIMIGNANO
ostcode 53037 • pop 7100

As you crest the hill coming from the east, the 14 towers of this medieval walled town look in the distance for all the world like some medieval Manhattan. And when you arrive you might feel half of Manhattan's population has moved in – San Gimignano (San Jimmy to some of the Anglos who have opted to live in the area) is quite a tourist magnet. Come in the dead of winter, preferably when it's raining, to indulge your imagination a little. In summer most of your attention will probably be focused on dodging fellow visitors!

There is a reason for all this of course. The towers were symbols of the power and wealth of the city's medieval families, and once numbered 72. San Gimignano delle Belle Torri ('of the Fine Towers') is surrounded by lush and productive land and the setting is altogether enchanting.

Originally an Etruscan village, the town later took its name from the Bishop of Modena, St Gimignano, who is said to have saved the city from a barbarian assault. It became a comune in 1199, but fought frequently with neighbouring Volterra and the internal battles between the Ardinghelli family (Guelph) and the Salvucci family (Ghibelline) over the next two centuries caused deep divisions. Most towers were built during this period – in the 13th century the *podestà* (town chief) forbade the building of towers higher than his (51m).

In 1348, the plague decimated the town's population and weakened the power of its nobles, leading to the town's submission to Florence in 1353. Today, not even the plague would dent the summer swarms!

Orientation

The manicured gardens of Piazzale dei Martiri di Montemaggio, at the southern end of the town, lie just outside the medieval wall and next to the main gate, the Porta San Giovanni. From the gate, Via San Giovanni heads north to Piazza della Cisterna and the connecting Piazza del Duomo, the city centre. The other major thoroughfare, Via San Matteo, leaves Piazza del

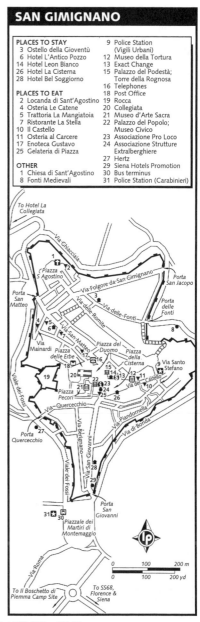

SAN GIMIGNANO

PLACES TO STAY
3 Ostello della Gioventù
6 Hotel L'Antico Pozzo
14 Hotel Leon Bianco
26 Hotel La Cisterna
28 Hotel Bel Soggiorno

PLACES TO EAT
2 Locanda di Sant'Agostino
4 Osteria Le Catene
5 Trattoria La Mangiatoia
7 Ristorante La Stella
10 Il Castello
11 Osteria al Carcere
17 Enoteca Gustavo
25 Gelateria di Piazza

OTHER
1 Chiesa di Sant'Agostino
8 Fonti Medievali

9 Police Station
   (Vigili Urbani)
12 Museo della Tortura
13 Exact Change
15 Palazzo del Podestà;
   Torre della Rognosa
16 Telephones
18 Post Office
19 Rocca
20 Collegiata
21 Museo d'Arte Sacra
22 Palazzo del Popolo;
   Museo Civico
23 Associazione Pro Loco
24 Associazione Strutture
   Extralberghiere
27 Hertz
29 Siena Hotels Promotion
30 Bus terminus
31 Police Station (Carabinieri)

CENTRAL TUSCANY

Duomo for the main northern gate, Porta San Matteo.

Information

Tourist Office The Associazione Pro Loco (☎ 0577 94 00 08, fax 0577 94 09 03, @ prolocsg@tin.it) is at Piazza del Duomo 1, on the left as you approach the cathedral. It is open from 9 am to 1 pm and 3 to 7 pm daily (closing at 6 pm from November to the end of February). The office closes only on Christmas Day and New Year's Eve. Their Web site is at www.sangimignano .com.

Money Exact Change (☎ 0577 94 32 38) operates a change office at Piazza della Cisterna 16. A couple of banks also operate in the town centre.

Post & Communications The post office is in Piazza delle Erbe 8, on the northern side of the cathedral. It opens from 8.15 am to 6 pm Monday to Friday, and to 12.30 pm on Saturday. You can make telephone calls from an unstaffed office on the northern side of Piazza del Duomo.

Police The carabinieri (☎ 0577 94 03 13) are behind the bus stop in Piazzale dei Martiri di Montemaggio. The vigili urbani (☎ 0577 94 03 46) are on Via Santo Stefano.

Things to See & Do

If you intend to visit everything, buy the L18,000 ticket, which allows admission into most of San Gimignano's museums, from the ticket offices of any of the city's sights.

Start in the triangular Piazza della Cisterna, named after the 13th-century cistern in its centre. The square is lined with houses and towers dating from the 13th and 14th centuries. In the adjoining Piazza del Duomo, the Collegiata (cathedral) looks across to the late-13th-century **Palazzo del Podestà** and its tower, known as the **Torre della Rognosa**. The Palazzo del Popolo, left of the cathedral, still operates as the town hall.

Collegiata Up a flight of steps from the square is the town's Romanesque cathedral, its simple facade belying the remarkable frescoes covering the walls of its interior. There are three main cycles.

You get your ticket at an office in the little square (Piazza Pecori) off the southern flank of the church, which you are then obliged to enter via a turnstile. You thus enter the church by the southern (left) flank and near the transept. The first look at this feast of (much restored) frescoes amid the black-and-white striped arches and columns separating three naves is likely to be a bit of a shock.

Pull yourself together and head to the end of the church to the main entrance (where visitors now exit through another turnstile). The fresco by Taddeo di Bartolo covering the top half of the rear wall depicts the Last Judgement, while below Benozzo Gozzoli's rendering of the martyrdom St Sebastian dominates. From either side of these frescoes walls extend into the interior of the church. On the right side are frescoes depicting *Paradiso* (Heaven) and on the left *Inferno* (Hell). Both are by Taddeo di Bartolo, who seems to have taken particular delight in presenting the horror of the underworld – remember that many of the faithful in these times would have taken such images pretty much at face value.

Along the left (southern) wall are scenes from Genesis and the Old Testament by Bartolo di Fredi, dating from around 1367. The top row runs from the creation of the world through to forbidden fruit, the eating of which leads to the first scene of the following level – the expulsion of Adam and Eve from Heaven. Further scenes on this level include Cain killing Abel, the story of Noah's ark, and Joseph's coat. The last level picks up this story, the tale of Moses leading the Jews out of Egypt and the story of Job.

On the right (northern) wall are scenes from the New Testament by Barna da Siena, completed in 1381. Again, the frescoes are spread over three levels, starting in the six lunettes at the top. Commencing with the Annunciation, the panels proceed through isodes such as the Epiphany, the presentation of Christ in the temple and the massacre of the innocents on Herod's orders. he subsequent panels on the lower levels mmarise the life and death of Christ, the esurrection and so on. Some of these are poor condition.

One of the delights of the church is the **appella di Santa Fina**, a Renaissance apel off the right wall. Apart from enedetto da Maiano's tomb-altar to the int, two beautiful frescoes by Domenico hirlandaio depicting events in her life and out.

The cathedral and chapel are open from 30 am to 12.30 pm and 3 to 5.30 pm daily, it tourists cannot enter during Mass. Without the L18,000 general ticket, admission osts L6000.

Museo d'Arte Sacra An interesting collection of religious art, including sculpture nd an assortment of paintings by lesser-nown artists, can be seen in this museum n the Piazza Pecori. It opens from 9.30 am 7.30 pm daily (until 5 pm from November to March). Admission without the combined ticket costs L5000. It was closed for estoration at the time of writing.

alazzo del Popolo To balance the religious, the other principal sight in San imignano is this seat of secular power. ince 1288 the comune has sat here, although the present building is the result of xpansion in the 14th century. The neo-othic facade was actually added late in the 9th century.

From the internal courtyard, which contains frescoes and heralds, climb the stairs the **Museo Civico**.

After purchasing your ticket you follow he signs into the museum, whose main oom is known as the **Sala di Dante**. The reat poet is said to have addressed the own's council here, imploring it to join a lorentine-led Guelph League. Your attention is captured above all by the *Maestà*, a nasterful fresco by Lippo Memmi dating to 317 and depicting the enthroned Virgin lary and Christ child with angels and

saints. Other frescoes portray jousts, hunting scenes, castles and other medieval goings-on.

Upstairs to the right is the small **Pinacoteca**, in whose rooms you can admire a limited collection of medieval religious works, including a *Crocifisso* by Coppo di Marcovaldo and a pair of remarkable tondi by Filippino Lippi, the *Angelo Annunciante* (Angel Gabriel) and *Vergine Annunciata*, which depicts the Virgin receiving Gabriel's news.

Opposite the Pinacoteca is a small frescoed room. Opinion on what these frescoes showing wedding scenes are all about is divided. It all looks like great fun, with the newly weds taking a bath together and then hopping into the sack.

When you have had enough off the art you can climb the stairs to the top of the **Torre Grossa** for a spectacular view of the town and surrounding countryside.

The palace, tower and museum are open from 9.30 am to 7.30 pm daily (10.30 am to 4.30 pm from November to February; it is also closed on Friday at this time). Combined entry to the museum and tower costs L12,000 (without the all-in ticket). Otherwise it costs L7000 for the museum alone or L8000 for the tower alone.

Museo della Tortura Sadomasochists in need of a few new ideas should pop along to this rather gruesome little museum. It's all here, from gibbets to thumbscrews – 99 ways to inflict unspeakable pain on your neighbour. There is no doubt that people really knew how to live in the Middle Ages!

Admission to this chamber of historical horrors, at Via del Castello 1–3, costs L15,000. It's open daily, with a variable timetable. In the depths of winter it opens from 10 am to 7 pm. Hours lengthen as the year proceeds. It's open from 9 am to midnight from mid-July to mid-September.

Other Sights The **Rocca**, a short walk to the west of Piazza del Duomo, is the atmospheric ruin of the town's fortress from where you have great views across the valley. There's little left but the crumbling shell, and at the foot of it on the southern side are a few swings for bored children.

At the northern end of the town is the **Chiesa di Sant'Agostino**, whose main attraction is the fresco cycle by Benozzo Gozzoli in the apse, depicting the life of St Augustine.

If you head out of the town walls to the east you will be guided by signs to the **Fonti Medievali**, ruined arches around one-time springs.

Places to Stay

Inside the walls of San Gimignano you will find only a handful of hotels, all with eye-popping prices. Coming to the rescue are, apart from the hostel and a camp site, numerous affittacamere (rooms for rent) at reasonable prices. The tourist office will provide details, but will not make bookings (this may change from the year 2000).

The Siena Hotels Promotion (☎/fax 0577 94 08 09, Via San Giovanni, 🅔 hotsang @tin.it), just inside the gate of the same name, can place you in a hotel. It will make arrangements months in advance and charges a L3000 fee. You can check out their Web site at www.sangimignano.com. Bear in mind that most hotels give themselves up to two months off between November and March. They generally make an exception for the Christmas and New Year period.

The camp site, *Il Boschetto di Piemma* (☎ 0577 94 03 52, fax 0577 94 19 82), is at Santa Lucia, a couple of kilometres south of the Porta San Giovanni, and is open from Easter to 15 October. Buses leave from Piazzale dei Martiri di Montemaggio. The non-HI *Ostello della Gioventù* (☎ 0577 94 19 91, Via delle Fonti 1) is at the northern edge of town inside the wall. Bed and breakfast is L24,000.

While on cheaper options, there were 17 affittacamere within the town walls at last count. They often only have a few rooms and prices vary considerably. You can pretty safely assume the cheapest it will get is L50,000/80,000 for singles/doubles with use of a shared bathroom in the corridor. Further options are scattered about outside the town

walls, which is not so romantic, or even o[] into the surrounding countryside. In th[] case you need your own wheels and shou[] consider instead the agriturismo option. G[] lists from the Associazione Pro Loco. Alte[] natively, for any of these non-hotel optio[] contact the Associazione Strutture Extra[] berghiere (☎ 0577 94 31 11, fax 0577 94 [] 90) at Piazza della Cisterna 6.

Hotel La Cisterna (☎ 0577 94 03 28, f[] 0577 94 20 80, Piazza della Cisterna 24[] right in the heart of the old town, has single[] doubles from L95,000/170,000. Ask for [] room in the medieval section, with a vie[] across the valley. Across the square, th[] *Hotel Leon Bianco* (☎ 0577 94 12 94, f[] 0577 94 21 23, Piazza della Cisterna 13[] marginally more expensive (they charg[] about L110,000 a head) and offers muc[] the same standards, plus parking.

Hotel L'Antico Pozzo (☎ 0577 94 20 1[] fax 0577 94 21 17, Via San Matteo 87) [] pricier still at L155,000/260,000, while [] the opposite end of town you could try th[] *Hotel Bel Soggiorno* (☎/fax 0577 94 03 7[] Via San Giovanni 91), where doubles co[] L220,000 (no singles).

If the bank has given you a generou[] overdraft you may be tempted to stay ou[] side the town at *Hotel La Collegiat[] (☎ 0577 94 32 01, fax 0577 94 05 66, L[] calità Strada 27). The assumption is yo[] will have a car to get to and from this mag[] nificent old country residence, where on[] disburses around L500,000/800,000 for [] single/double. Elegantly appointed room[] have all the mod cons and outside you ca[] splash about in the pool. They have a fin[] restaurant too.

Places to Eat

An excellent place to sip wines with snac[] food is *Enoteca Gustavo* (☎ 0577 94 00 5[] Via San Matteo 29). It closes on Friday.

Try the wines at *Il Castello* (☎ 0577 9[] 08 78, Via del Castello 20), a wine bar an[] restaurant that stays open until midnigh[] pasta starts at L10,000. *Ristorante La Stell[] (☎ 0577 94 04 44, Via San Matteo 77) ha[] reasonable food, although they tend to ex[] ploit the tourists by providing small ser[]

gs. A meal could cost L25,000. It is osed on Wednesday.

Trattoria La Mangiatoia (☎ 0577 94 15 8, *Via Mainardi 5*) is one of the city's bet-r restaurants, a romantic spot where you at to the accompaniment of slow classical music. A full meal will cost around 50,000. It's closed on Tuesday.

Virtually across the road, *Osteria Le atene* (☎ 0577 94 19 66, *Via Mainardi 18*) an interesting option. Alongside many Tuscan stalwarts they also experiment a lit-e, for instance using saffron, a standard ice in medieval cooking, in dishes like *ppa medievale*. It's closed on Wednesday.

A relative newcomer offering fine food at moderate prices is the *Osteria al Carcere* (☎ 0577 94 19 05, *Via Castello 5*). They ave an original menu including a half-ozen soups, each for L11,000. It's closed n Wednesday. For a relatively quiet drink nd a sampling of one or two of 49 *ruschette*, try *Locanda di Sant'Agostino* (☎ 0577 94 31 41, *Piazza Sant'Agostino*). t L11,000 they are a tad overpriced but uite delicious and filling – they a make a ood light lunch option.

Gelateria di Piazza (☎ 0577 94 22 44, *Pi-zza della Cisterna 4*) is great and turns the ocal wine, Vernaccia, into a delicious ice ream.

A *produce market* is held on Thursday mornings in Piazza della Cisterna and Pi-zza del Duomo.

Getting There & Around

Bus San Gimignano is accessible from lorence and Siena by regular buses, but ou need to change at Poggibonsi. For ome and towns such as Perugia and As-isi, you need to get to Siena first. There's lso a bus to Volterra and another to Cer-aldo. Buses arrive in Piazzale dei Martiri di Montemaggio at Porta San Giovanni. Re-member that Sunday is a bad day for doing his trip, in that connections are reduced. ive trips are possible from Florence – two f them at the crack of dawn and the next ot until 3.40 pm. Depending on connec-ons, the trip can take up to 1½ hours. The rip is easier from Siena.

The closest train station to San Gimig-nano is in Poggibonsi.

Car & Motorcycle Various roads lead to San Gimignano – it all depends on where you are coming from. From Florence, the easiest is to take the SS2 to Poggibonsi and follow the signs. You could also approach by taking the SS68 from Colle di Val d'Elsa. From Volterra, take the SS68 east and follow the turn-off signs north to San Gimignano.

When you arrive, signs direct you to var-ious car parks where you pay L2000 an hour. Some car parks are for residents only. It is possible to find free parking in the new parts of town that sprawl north-west of the old centre.

You can hire a car at Hertz (☎ 0577 94 22 20) on Viale dei Fossi.

VOLTERRA
postcode 56048 • pop 13,400
Straggling high on a rocky plateau, Vol-terra's well-preserved medieval ramparts give the windswept ridge town a proud and forbidding air.

The Etruscan settlement of Velathri was an important trading centre and senior part-ner of the Dodecapolis. It is believed as many as 25,000 people lived here in its Etruscan heyday. Partly because of the difficult ter-rain of which it was master, the city was one of the last to succumb to Rome – it was absorbed into the Roman confederation around 260 BC and renamed Volaterrae.

The bulk of the old city as it stands today was raised in the 12th and 13th centuries under a fiercely independent free comune. The city first entered into Florence's orbit in 1361, but it was some time before the Arno city took full control. When this was threat-ened in 1472, Lorenzo the Magnificent made one of his few big mistakes and last-ing enemies of the people of Volterra when he marched in and ruthlessly snuffed out every vestige of potential opposition to dir-ect Florentine rule.

Since Etruscan times Volterra has been a centre of alabaster extraction and work-manship. The quarries lay fallow for several

CENTRAL TUSCANY

centuries till the Renaissance brought renewed interest in the material for sculpture. To this day, the traditions have been maintained and passed from generation to generation.

Orientation & Information
Driving and parking inside the walled town are more or less prohibited. Park in one of the designated parking areas and enter the nearest city gate – all the main streets lead to the central Piazza dei Priori.

The tourist office (☎ 0588 8 61 50) is at Piazza dei Priori 20. You can exchange money at the Cassa di Risparmio di Firenze bank on the corner of Via dei Marchesi and Via Giacoma Matteotti, or at Exact Change (☎ 0588 8 89 99) on Piazza Martiri della Libertà (the latter shuts down in December and January for lack of tourist interest). The post office and Telecom office face the tourist office on the northern side of Piazza dei Priori. Next door to them is the police station in the Palazzo Pretorio.

Things to See & Do
A L12,000 ticket, valid for a year, cove visits to the Museo Etrusco Guarnacci, t Pinacoteca Comunale and Museo Dioc sano di Arte Sacra. Access to the Rom theatre and Parco Archeologico is free.

Piazza dei Priori & Around Piazza c Priori is surrounded by austere mediev mansions. The 13th-century **Palazzo d Priori** is the oldest seat of local governme in Tuscany and is believed to have been model for Florence's Palazzo Vecchio. T **Palazzo Pretorio**, also dating from the 13 century, is dominated by the Piglet's Tow so named because of the wild boar sculpt on its upper section.

Behind the Palazzo dei Priori, along V Turazza, is the **cathedral**, built in the 12 and 13th centuries. Inside, highlights i clude a small fresco by Benozzo Gozzo the *Adorazione dei Magi*, behind a nativi group in the oratory at the beginning of t

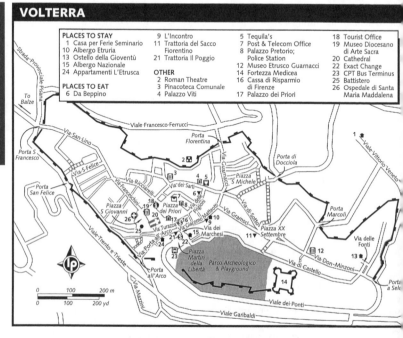

VOLTERRA

PLACES TO STAY
1 Casa per Ferie Seminario
10 Albergo Etruria
13 Ostello della Gioventù
15 Albergo Nazionale
24 Appartamenti L'Etrusca

PLACES TO EAT
6 Da Beppino

9 L'Incontro
11 Trattoria del Sacco Fiorentino
21 Trattoria Il Poggio

OTHER
2 Roman Theatre
3 Pinacoteca Comunale
4 Palazzo Viti

5 Tequila's
7 Post & Telecom Office
8 Palazzo Pretorio; Police Station
12 Museo Etrusco Guarnacci
14 Fortezza Medicea
16 Cassa di Risparmio di Firenze
17 Palazzo dei Priori

18 Tourist Office
19 Museo Diocesano di Arte Sacra
20 Cathedral
22 Exact Change
23 CPT Bus Terminus
25 Battistero
26 Ospedale di Santa Maria Maddalena

ft aisle. The 15th-century tabernacle on the high altar is by Mino da Fiesole. The black-and-white marble banding on the inside and the Renaissance coffered ceiling are unusual touches.

Facing the cathedral is the 13th-century baptistry (battistero), which features a font by Andrea Sansovino. On the western side of the square you can tell the porticoed Ospedale di Santa Maria Maddalena was once a foundlings hospital by the robbiane depicting infants in swaddling clothes. Next to the cathedral you can see works of religious art, sculpture in particular, collected in the Museo Diocesano di Arte Sacra. It opens from 9 am to 1 pm and 3 to 6 pm daily (mornings only from November to mid-March).

The Pinacoteca Comunale in the Palazzo Minucci Solaini, Via dei Sarti 1, houses a modest collection of local, Sienese and Florentine art, including some works by Rosso Fiorentino and Luca Signorelli. It opens from 9 am to 7 pm daily (until 2 pm from November to mid-March).

Museo Etrusco Guarnacci All the exhibits in this fascinating Etruscan museum were unearthed locally, including a vast collection of some 600 funerary urns carved from alabaster, tufa and other materials.

The urns are displayed according to the subjects depicted on their bas-reliefs and the period from which they date. Be selective, as they all start to look the same after a while. The best examples – those dating from later periods – are on the 2nd and 3rd floors.

Most significant are the *Ombra della Sera* sculpture, a strange, elongated nude figure that would fit in well in any museum of modern art; and the urn of the *Sposi*, featuring an elderly couple, their faces depicted in portrait fashion rather than the stylised method usually employed. The museum has the same opening times as the Pinacoteca.

Fortezza Medicea & Parco Archeologico Farther along Via Minzoni is the entrance to the Fortezza Medicea, built in the 14th century and altered by Lorenzo the Magnificent, and now used as a prison (you cannot enter unless you would like to stay for a while).

Near the fort is the pleasant Parco Archeologico, whose archaeological remains have suffered with the passage of time. This is where the heart of the ancient city, the Acropolis, was located. Little has survived, but the park has swings and things for kids and is a good place for a picnic.

Palazzo Viti Built at the end of the 16th century and completely renovated by a successful alabaster merchant, Benedetto Viti, in the 1850s, Palazzo Viti affords you a glance into the luxury enjoyed by the wealthy business class in Tuscany. The great halls are richly decorated, sometimes too much so (the impression of parvenu wealth seeps through the place). It is open from 9 am to 1 pm daily, as well as 3 to 5.30 pm at the weekend. Admission costs L5000.

Other Sights On the city's northern edge is a Roman theatre, a well preserved complex that includes a Roman bath.

The Balze, a deep ravine created by erosion, about a 20-minute walk north-west of the city centre, has claimed several churches since the Middle Ages, the buildings having fallen into its deep gullies. A 14th-century monastery is perched close to the precipice and is in danger of toppling into the ravine. To get there, head out of the north-west end of the city along Via San Lino and follow its continuation, Borgo Santo Stefano and then Borgo San Giusto.

Places to Stay

The best deal is at the non-HI *Ostello della Gioventù* (☎ 0588 8 55 77, Via del Poggetto 3), near the Museo Etrusco Guarnacci; it has beds for L30,000. The *Casa per Ferie Seminario* (☎ 0588 8 60 28, Viale Vittorio Veneto), in the Monastero di Sant'Andrea, is an excellent deal. Rooms are large, clean and have bathrooms. They cost L64,000 for a double. The *Albergo Etruria* (☎/fax 0588 8 73 77, Via Giacomo Matteotti 32) offers singles/doubles with own bathroom for L80,000/120,000. The *Albergo Nazionale* (☎ *0588 8 62 84, fax 0588 8 40 97, Via dei Marchesi 11)* is similar.

If you would prefer to have an apartment, *Appartamenti L'Etrusca* (☎ *0588 8 00 34, fax 0588 8 72 84, Via Porta all'Arco 37–41)*. Single/double/triple self-contained apartments cost L55,000/90,000/110,000 per day (the rate comes down marginally if you rent for a week or more).

Places to Eat

A cheerful and rather cavernous place for breakfast, a coffee during the day or even a drink or two in the evening is *L'Incontro* (☎ *0588 8 05 00, Via Giacoma Matteotti 18)*. It is closed on Wednesday.

The restaurant *Da Beppino* (☎ *0588 8 60 51, Via delle Prigioni 13)* has good pasta from L10,000. It also closes on Wednesday.

Trattoria del Sacco Fiorentino (☎ *0588 8 85 37, Piazza XX Settembre)* is a nice little eatery serving up fine food with a happy selection of local wines. Try the *coniglio in salsa di aglio e Vin Santo*, rabbit cooked in a garlic dessert-wine sauce. It is closed on Friday.

Not quite as good but pleasant enough is the *Trattoria Il Poggio* (☎ *0588 8 52 57, Via Porta all'Arco 7)*. The pizzas are fine and cost up to L10,000. It closes on Tuesday.

If you have wheels and would like to venture out of town a little, drive down to Saline di Volterra and then take the SS439 road south heading to Pomarance. About 3km out of Saline di Volterra you enter the tiny settlement of San Lorenzo, home to the *Osteria San Lorenzo* (☎ *0588 4 41 60, Via Massetana)*, where you can get simple home-style cooking. A full meal might cost L30,000 with wine. It is closed on Tuesday.

Entertainment

Tequila's (☎ *0588 8 00 33, Via dei Sarti 37a)* is the local disco-bar where you can get in a Guinness and occasionally even catch live acts on the weekend. This is about as much as old Volterra hops.

Getting There & Away

Bus Volterra is a little bit of a pain to get t If you are coming from Florence (L780, 130 minutes; rapido service L11,000, 7 minutes) or Siena you need to reach Col di Val d'Elsa first and change buses. Fro Monday to Saturday CPT has five connec tions between Volterra (Piazza Martiri del Liberta) and Colle di Val d'Elsa (L3800 These drop to three on Sunday and publi holidays. Bear in mind that on Sunday an holidays there is only one bus (at 7.10 am from Florence and there are two afternoo possibilities for the return trip. The journe takes two hours when you make the righ connections. As with San Gimignano, thi trip is easier to Siena.

Several buses a day run to Pisa (L950C and plenty to Montecatini (L4000). If yo are stuck and need to get back to, say, Flor ence or Pisa, it might be worth considerin the trip to Montecatini, from where ther are plenty of bus and train links to Florenc and Lucca (and some to Pisa). Other buse head south in the direction of Massa Marit tima, but only go as far as Pomarance an Castelnuovo di Val di Cecina.

Train From the small train station in Salin di Volterra, 9km to the south-west o Volterra, you can get a train to Cecina o the coast (see the Central Coast chapter) from where you can catch trains on th Rome–Pisa line. Up to six CPT buses a da run between Volterra and the train station.

Car & Motorcycle By car, take the SS68 which runs between Cecina and Colle d Val d'Elsa. A couple of back routes to Sar Gimignano (see the San Gimignano sectio earlier in the chapter) are signposted nort off the SS68.

SOUTH OF VOLTERRA

If you have a car and want to head fo Massa Marittima (a worthwhile objective – see the Southern Tuscany chapter), the ride south from Volterra is interesting enough.

The SS68 drops away to the south-wes from Volterra towards Cecina. At Saline d Volterra (where you'll find the nearest trair

ation for Volterra), the SS439 intersects
e SS68 on its way from Lucca south to-
ards Massa Marittima. **Saline di Volterra**
kes its name from the nearby saltmines,
hich were the source of its wealth in the
9th century.

The lunar-landscape ride south is enga-
ing in its own way. You can pass straight
rough **Pomarance**, a largely industrial
wn. To the south, take the hilly road for
arderello, which has the strange honour of
eing Italy's most important boric acid pro-
ucer. The road out of here keeps winding
s way south to Massa.

OUTHERN SIENA PROVINCE

'ou may already have had a taste of the
trange undulating countryside of the Crete
see earlier in the chapter). For a while sim-
ar countryside persists as you roam south,
radually giving away to more unruly terri-
ory as you get farther away from the more
ouristed centres. This part of the province
ffers everything from the haughty hilltop
nedieval wine centres of Montalcino and
Montepulciano to hot sulphurous baths in
pots like Bagno Vignoni. From the Roman-
sque splendours of the Abbazia di Sant'
Antimo you can transfer to the Renaissance
race of Pienza, an early example of ideal-
sed town planning.

Montalcino

ostcode 53024 • pop 5100

A pretty town perched high above the Orcia
valley, Montalcino is best known for its
wine, the Brunello. Produced only in the
vineyards surrounding the town, it is said to
be one of Italy's best reds and has gained
considerable international fame.

Plenty of *enoteche* (wine cellars) around
own provide you with the chance to taste
and buy Brunello, as well as the other main
local wine, the Rosso di Montalcino, al-
hough you'll pay a minimum of L25,000
for a Brunello. Top names in excellent years
can come with price tags heading up to the
L200,000 mark. Price alone is not necessarily an indication of the wine's quality.
Bear in mind that all Brunello is made to
strict regulations so that, in some respects,

price differences are often as much a matter
of marketing as of drinking quality.

There is a Pro Loco tourist office (☎ 0577
84 93 21) at Costa Municipio 8, just off Piazza del Popolo, the town's main square. It
is open from 10 am to 1 pm and 2 to 6 pm
from Tuesday to Sunday throughout the
year.

Things to See The **Fortezza**, an impressive 14th-century fortress that was later
expanded under the Medici dukes, dominates the town from a high point at its
southern end. It can be visited from 9 am

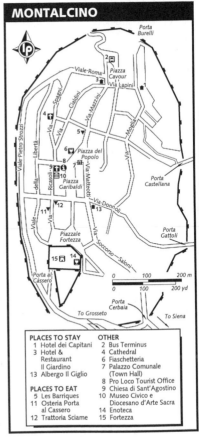

MONTALCINO

PLACES TO STAY	OTHER
1 Hotel dei Capitani	2 Bus Terminus
3 Hotel &	4 Cathedral
Restaurant	6 Fiaschetteria
Il Giardino	7 Palazzo Comunale
13 Albergo Il Giglio	(Town Hall)
	8 Pro Loco Tourist Office
PLACES TO EAT	9 Chiesa di Sant'Agostino
5 Les Barriques	10 Museo Civico e
11 Osteria Porta	Diocesano d'Arte Sacra
al Cassero	14 Enoteca
12 Trattoria Sciame	15 Fortezza

CENTRAL TUSCANY

to 8 pm daily in summer and from 9 am to 6 pm Tuesday to Sunday in winter. Entry to the empty courtyard of the fort is free. You can sample and buy local wines in the *enoteca* inside, from where you can also climb up to the ramparts of the fort (L3500).

The **Museo Civico e Diocesano d'Arte Sacra** on Via Ricasoli, housed in the former convent of the neighbouring **Chiesa di Sant' Agostino**, contains an important collection of religious art from the town and surrounding region. Among the items on show are a tryptich by Duccio di Buoninsegna and a *Madonna col Bambino* by Simone Martini. Other artists represented include the Lorenzetti brothers, Giovanni di Paolo, Bartolo di Fredi and Sano di Pietro.

The museum is open from 10 am to 1 pm and 2 to 6 pm daily except Monday. Admission costs L8000.

Several churches dot the town, but none are of especial interest. The **cathedral** in particular is a rather awful 19th-century neoclassical travesty of what was probably once a fine Romanesque church.

If you want to visit vineyards in the Montalcino area, you should start by getting a list of those generally open to visitors from the tourist office. As a rule they only open at the weekend and may require a booking. The office can also provide a full list of Brunello producers (many smaller ones have little more than a hectare or two of land) and information on good and mediocre years.

Places to Stay The hotel front in Montalcino is limited, so try not to arrive at night when everything is taken. Try *Il Giardino* (*☎/fax 0577 84 82 57, Piazza Cavour 4*), which has doubles with bathroom for up to L100,000.

Albergo Il Giglio (*☎/fax 0577 84 81 67, Via Soccorso Saloni 5*) is probably the pick of the crop, with comfortable singles/doubles coming in at L80,000/120,000. The only other such option in town is *Hotel dei Capitani* (*☎ 0577 84 72 27, fax 0577 84 72 39, Via Lapini 6*). It is also perfectly comfortable, if a little lacking in atmosphere.

They have a small off-street parking area. Singles/doubles cost L120,000/170,000.

If you have no luck with the hotels get a list of affittacamere, of which there are a dozen in the town. Should that option fail all is not lost, as the surrounding countryside is dotted with agriturismo possibilities. The tourist office has full lists.

Places to Eat At *Ristorante Il Giardino* (*☎ 0577 84 90 76, Piazza Cavour 1*), in the hotel of the same name, you can expect to eat well for around L40,000 – the *coniglio alla paesana* (rabbit) is prepared in a pleasingly tangy sauce. It is closed Wednesday.

Trattoria Sciame (*☎ 0577 84 80 17, Via Ricasoli 9*) is an unassuming place where you can eat fairly straightforward but well prepared meals at surprisingly low prices. Many mains costs around L13,000. It is closed on Tuesday.

For homemade pasta at reasonable prices you should make a beeline for *Osteria Porta al Cassero* (*☎ 0577 84 71 96, Via della Libertà 9*). It is closed on Wednesday.

The *Enoteca* in the Fortezza is a wonderful place to try out one of countless varieties of Brunello, buy a bottle and/or climb up on to the ramparts (L3500). It is open from 9 am to 6 pm every day except Monday.

Fiaschetteria (*☎ 0577 84 90 43, Piazza del Popolo 6*) is a fine old cafe where you can get yourself a glass of wine or pot of tea and read the paper. It is closed on Thursday.

Several bars near the Fiaschetteria are perfectly good for trying out the local wines. A particularly attractive one is *Les Barriques* (*☎ 0577 84 84 11, Piazza del Popolo 20–22*). You can also dine here.

Getting There & Away Montalcino is accessible from Siena by up to nine buses (L5500) a day. Buses leave from Piazza Cavour for the return journey.

Abbazia di Sant'Antimo

It is best to visit this superb Romanesque church in the morning, when the sun shines through the east windows to create an almost surreal atmosphere. At night, it is lit p impressively and shines like a beacon into the darkness. Set in a broad valley, just below the village of **Castelnuovo dell' Abate**, the 12th-century church in pale travertine stone is notable for its simplicity and unusual grandeur – the style is clearly influenced by northern European versions of Romanesque, especially that of the Cistercians.

They say Charlemagne founded the original monastery here in 781. In subsequent centuries the Benedictine monks became among the most powerful feudal landlords in southern Tuscany, until they came into conflict with Siena in the 13th century, when the monastery went into decline. Until the mid-1990s, the church and abbey lay pretty much abandoned. Then seven monks moved in at the local bishop's wish. They have supervised restoration work and hold daily prayers and Masses in the church, which anyone is welcome to attend. This is a worthwhile exercise as the monks sing Gregorian chants. If you can't make any of the services, they have some CDs on sale in the church.

Among the decorative features note the stone carvings of the bell tower and the apse windows, which include a *Madonna col Bambino* and the various fantastic animals typical of the Romanesque style. Inside, take the time to study the capitals of the columns lining the nave, including one representing Daniel in the lion's den (second on the right as you enter).

Ask the attendant to let you into the **sacristy**, where there are monochrome frescoes depicting the life of St Benedict. They probably date to the 15th century. The 11th-century crypt beneath the chapel is closed to the public, but you can get a murky glimpse of it through the small round window at the base of the exterior of the chapel's apse. The church is open from 10.30 am to 12.30 pm and 3 to 6.30 pm daily.

Concerts are sometimes held here as part of Siena's Estate Musicale Chigiana (see Special Events under Siena earlier in this chapter).

If you're planning a visit to Sant'Antimo, stop for lunch at *Osteria Bassomondo*

(☎ *0577 83 56 19, Via Bassomondo 7*), less than 1km away at Castelnuovo dell'Abate. You will spend about L35,000 a head. It closes on Monday.

Three buses a day run from Montalcino (Azienda Consorziale Trasporto–Siena) to Castelnuovo dell'Abate, from where you can walk to the church.

If you have your own transport, you may want to consider an alternative lunch or dinner excursion west along a mostly dirt road to **Sant'Angelo in Colle**. The views from the little settlement are wonderful, and you can eat fine home-cooked food at the *Trattoria Il Pozzo* (☎ *0577 84 40 15*), in the middle of the village just off the square. It is closed on Tuesday. Those without a car can get here by bus (three or four times a day Monday to Saturday; nothing on Sunday) from Montalcino.

San Quirico d'Orcia

This fortified medieval town on the Via Cassia (SS2) is well worth a stopover. Its Romanesque **Collegiata**, dating from the 12th century, is notable for its unusual three doorways, decorated with extraordinary stone carvings. Inside is a triptych by Sano di Pietro. Wander through the **Horti Leononi**, a lovely Italian Renaissance garden at the other end of town. It is a pleasant little town and doesn't make a bad base for exploring the area, sitting just off the highway and at a crossroads between the more touristy (but highly worthwhile) Montalcino and Pienza.

Places to Stay & Eat If you're interested in staying in the area, try the *Agriturismo Aiole* (☎ *0577 88 74 54, Strada Provinciale 22 della Grossola*), near Castiglione d'Orcia. Bed and breakfast costs L50,000 per person and dinner L25,000. You must book ahead.

Right in the centre of town is a fine little affittacamere, *Affittacamere L'Orcia* (☎ *0577 89 76 77, Via Dante Alighieri 49*). Immaculately kept doubles with own bathroom and TV cost L75,000. The owner, Signore Bisdomini, likes a chat and will happily send you off to his pals to buy

CENTRAL TUSCANY

virgin olive oil and local wines. He shakes his head in disapproval when he hears of out-of-towners paying top dollar for such items in towns like Pienza and Montalcino.

You will eat well indeed at the *Trattoria Al Vecchio Forno* (☎ *0577 89 73 80, Via Piazzola 8)*, a few steps away from Via Dante Alighieri. Try the *pappardelle al sugo d'anatra* (pasta in a duck sauce) and the *brasato al Brunello* (beef slices cooked in Brunello wine). Expect to pay around L50,000 a head for a full meal. It is closed on Wednesday.

Getting There & Away San Quirico is accessible by bus from Siena (L5500), Buonconvento, Pienza and Montepulciano.

Bagno Vignoni

About 5km from San Quirico along the SS2 towards Rome, this tiny spa town dates back to Roman times. The hot sulphurous water bubbles up into a picturesque pool, built by the Medici in the town's main square. Some 36 springs cook at up to 51°C to collect in the pool, although in winter the water is considerably cooler.

Unfortunately you are not allowed to bathe in the pool, but it is such a picturesque sight that it is merits a quick stop regardless. If you do wish to take the waters you have to pay for the pleasure at the nearby Hotel Posta Marcucci (☎ 0577 87 29 82, fax 0577 87 26 84). Their open-air **Piscina del Sole** is open from 9 am to 1 pm and 2.30 to 8 pm daily. A day ticket costs L18,000, or you can pay L12,000 for the afternoon session.

If you want to stay, the cheapest hotel is the *Hotel Le Terme* (☎ *0577 88 71 50, fax 0577 88 74 97)*, where rooms start at L95,000/140,000. Or try the *Affittacamere Casagni* (☎ *0577 87 26 19)*, where you can get a simple double for about L60,000.

Whether you choose to stay or not, a fine choice for a lunch or dinner stop is the *Osteria del Leone* (☎ *0577 88 73 00)*, just back a block from the pool. In a pleasantly lit rustic building with a heavy-beamed ceiling you can eat solid Tuscan country fare, such as *faraona al Vin Santo* (pheasant cooked in Vin Santo). Expect to shell out about L45,000.

Buses servicing the Siena–Grosseto rou call in here.

Bagni San Filippo

While on the subject of baths, those wh prefer not to pay for their hot-water frolic could press on south along the SS2 highwa about 15km to Bagni San Filippo (whic lies a couple of kilometres west of the SS2 Most Siena–Grosseto buses call in here too A park is signposted off the village's onl road just a little uphill from the hotel an paying baths. A short stroll down the lan brings you to a set of hot little tumbling ca cades where you can plant yourself for a re laxing soak. It is best in winter, which i off-season for the hotel and when the wate pressure is greatest.

Pienza
postcode 53026 • pop 2400

A superb example of Renaissance architec ture, this town was designed and built i the mid-15th century by the Florentine a chitect Bernardo Rossellino on the order of Pope Pius II, Aeneas Silvius Piccolo mini, who was born there in 1405. Th pope even had the town's name change from Corsignano. The town had been modest medieval village since the 8th cen tury, but was transformed by the pope projects. Inspired in part by Leon Battist Alberti, who was busy elaborating a whol philosophy of the ideal city, Pius II en trusted Rossellino with the experimenta project.

Information The tourist information of fice (☎ 0578 74 90 71) is in the Palazz Pubblico, on the town's main square, Piazz Pio II. It opens from 9.30 am to 1 pm and to 6.30 pm daily.

Things to See & Do The most importan buildings are grouped around Piazza Pio II a short walk from the town's entrance alon Corso Rossellino. The square was designe by Rossellino, who left nothing to chance The available space was limited, so to in crease the sense of perspective and dignity of the great edifices that would grace the

PIENZA

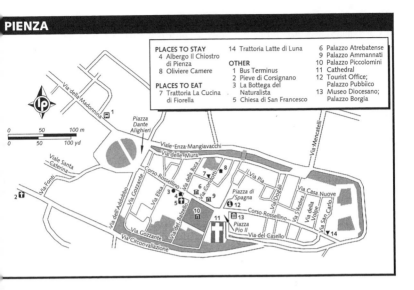

PLACES TO STAY
4 Albergo II Chiostro di Pienza
8 Oliviere Camere

PLACES TO EAT
7 Trattoria La Cucina di Fiorella

14 Trattoria Latte di Luna

OTHER
1 Bus Terminus
2 Pieve di Corsignano
3 La Bottega del Naturalista
5 Chiesa di San Francesco

6 Palazzo Atrebatense
9 Palazzo Ammannati
10 Palazzo Piccolomini
11 Cathedral
12 Tourist Office; Palazzo Pubblico
13 Museo Diocesano; Palazzo Borgia

square, Rossellino set the Palazzo Borgia and Palazzo Piccolomini off at angles to the cathedral.

The **cathedral** was built on the site of the Romanesque Chiesa di Santa Maria, of which little remains. The Renaissance facade in travertine stone is of clear Albertian inspiration.

The interior of the building is itself a strange mix of Gothic and Renaissance, and contains a collection of five altarpieces painted by Sienese artists of the period, as well as a superb marble tabernacle by Rossellino.

Perhaps the most bizarre aspect of the building is the state of collapse of the transept and apse. Built on dodgy ground, the top end of the church seems to be breaking off. The huge cracks in the wall and floor are matched by the crazy downward slant of this part of the church floor. Various attempts to prop it all up have failed to solve the problem, as is quite clear from the major cracking in the walls and floor. The cathedral is open from 7 am to 1 pm and 2 to 6 pm daily.

The **Palazzo Piccolomini**, to your right as you face the cathedral, was the pope's residence and is considered Rossellino's masterpiece. Built on the site of former Piccolomini family houses, the building demonstrates some indebtedness on Rossellino's part to Alberti, whose Palazzo Rucellai in Florence it appears in part to emulate.

Inside you enter a fine courtyard, from where stairs lead you up into the papal apartments, now filled with an assortment of period furnishings, minor art and the like. To the rear a three-level loggia facing out over the countryside afforded Pius II and his guests splendid vistas.

The palazzo is open from 10 am to 12.30 pm and 3 to 6 pm Tuesday to Sunday; entry is with a guide only and costs L5000. Opposite is the Palazzo Ammannati.

To the left of the cathedral is the **Palazzo Borgia**, built by Cardinal Borgia, later Pope Alexander VI. The building is now more commonly known as the Palazzo Vescovile and contains the **Museo Diocesano**. The museum contains an intriguing miscellany of art works, illuminated manuscripts, tapestries and miniatures. The museum is open from 10 am to 1 pm and 2 to 6 pm daily except Tuesday (it opens only at the weekend in winter).

Make time to visit the Romanesque **Pieve di Corsignano**, less than 1km out of town along Via Fonti from Piazza Dante Alighieri. It dates to the 10th century and boasts a strange circular bell tower. Ask at the tourist office in town where you can get a hold of the key.

Places to Stay At the *Oliviere Camere* (☎ 0578 74 82 74, Via Condotti 4) you can get simple but attractive little rooms for L40,000 per person.

Albergo Il Chiostro di Pienza (☎/fax 0578 74 84 00, Corso Rossellino 26) is in the former convent and cloister of the adjacent Chiesa di San Francesco. Singles/doubles can cost as much as L170,000/250,000.

Places to Eat At *Trattoria La Cucina di Fiorella* (☎ 0578 74 90 95, Via Condotti 11) you'll eat well for around L45,000 a head. It closes on Wednesday.

Trattoria Latte di Luna (☎ 0578 74 86 06, Via San Carlo 6), on a kind of squarette where the street splits off from Corso Rossellino, is a charming little spot to eat outside. Try the *anatra arrosto alle olive* (roast duck with olives; L13,000). It is closed on Tuesday and sometimes on Monday evening.

Pienza is renowned as a centre for that ever-so-Tuscan cheese, *pecorino*. If you want to get an idea of all the varieties available (from fresh to well aged and smelly, from the classic pecorino to ones lightly infused with peppers or truffles), pop into La Bottega del Naturalista (☎ 0578 74 80 81) at Corso Rossellino 16. They have a truly mouth-watering choice of cheeses, but you should possibly use it as a learning experience and do your actual shopping elsewhere, as the products are all a little expensive.

Getting There & Away Up to seven buses run on weekdays from Siena to Pienza (L5900). You can also make connections to San Quirico d'Orcia and Montepulciano. The buses stop just a short way off Piazza Dante Alighieri.

Montepulciano
postcode 53045 • pop 14,000

Set atop a narrow ridge of volcanic rock Montepulciano combines Tuscany's superb countryside with some of the region's finest wines. This medieval town is the perfect place to spend a few quiet days. Stop by the various enoteche to sample the local wines.

A late Etruscan castrum was the first in a series of settlements here. During the Middle Ages it was a constant bone of contention between Florence and Siena until in 1404 the city finally passed under the permanent jurisdiction of the former. And so the Marzocco, or lion of Florence, came to replace the she-wolf of Siena as the city's symbol on a column just off Piazza Savonarola. The new administration brought a new wind of construction taste as Michelozzo, Sangallo il Vecchio and others were invited in to do some innovative spring cleaning, lending this Gothic stronghold a fresh wind of Renaissance vigour. That mix alone makes the town an intriguing place for a stopover.

Orientation & Information However you arrive, you will probably end up at the Porta al Prato (also known as the Porta al Bacco) on the town's northern edge. From here, buses take you through the town to Piazza Grande. Alternatively, the 15-minute walk is mostly uphill but well worth the exercise.

The Pro Loco tourist office (☎ 0578 75 73 91) is on Via Gracciano nel Corso, next door to the Chiesa di Sant'Agostino at the lower end of town. The office opens from 9 am to 12.30 pm and 3 to 8 pm daily (to 6 pm in winter). It opens in the morning only on Sunday and holidays.

The post office is at Via delle Erbe 12 and opens from 8.15 am to 6 pm Monday to Saturday. You'll find a couple of banks with ATMs scattered about the town. A reliable one is the Banca Nazionale di Lavoro at Piazza Savonarola 14.

The *carabinieri* have a barracks on Piazza Savonarola.

Things to See & Do Most of the main sights are clustered around Piazza Grande, though the town's streets boast a wealth of palazzos and other fine buildings.

On the assumption you arrive by bus or park your car near Porta al Prato, you'll see the bee-like banding that is the facade of the **Chiesa di Sant'Agnese**. The original church was built in the early 14th century, but this version was the result of a remake by Antonio da Sangallo il Vecchio in 1511. He may also have restructured the medieval gate leading into the city proper, the **Porta al Prato**.

To the left shortly after you enter the gate, you'll see the 18th-century **Chiesa di San Bernardo**. Nearby is the late Renaissance **Palazzo Avignonesi** by Giacomo da Vignola. Several other **mansions** line Via di Gracciano nel Corso including the **Palazzo di Bucelli** at No 73, whose facade features Etruscan and Latin inscriptions. Sangallo also designed **Palazzo Cocconi** at No 70.

Piazza Michelozzo is dominated by the striking Renaissance facade of Michelozzo's **Chiesa di Sant'Agostino**. Directly in front is a medieval tower house, **Torre di Pulcinella**, topped by the town clock and the bizarre figure Pulcinella (Punch of Punch & Judy fame), who strikes the hours.

Continue up the hill and take the first left past the **Loggia di Mercato** for Via del Poggiolo, which eventually becomes Via Ricci. On the Renaissance **Palazzo Ricci** is one of the town's wine *cantine* (wine cellars), the Cantina Redi. The town's **Museo Civico** is opposite in the Gothic Palazzo Neri-Orselli. The small collection features terracotta reliefs by the della Robbia family and some Gothic and Renaissance paintings. It was closed at the time of writing.

Piazza Grande marks the highest point of the town and features the austere **Palazzo Comunale**, a 13th-century Gothic building remodelled in the 15th century by Michelozzo (the comparison with the Palazzo Vecchio in Florence, in form if not in colour, is hard to avoid). From the top of the 14th-century tower, on a clear day, you can see the Monti Sibillini to the east and, they say, Siena to the north-west. The tower is open from 9 am to 1.30 pm Monday to Saturday

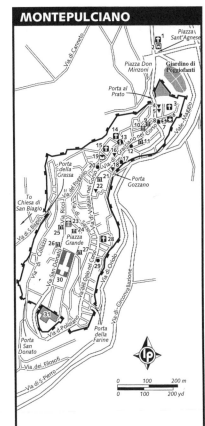

MONTEPULCIANO

PLACES TO STAY
8 Albergo Il Marzocco
17 Albergo Il Borghetto

PLACES TO EAT
4 Trattoria Il Pulcino
5 Trattoria Diva e Marceo
16 Lo Spuntino
18 Borgo Buio
22 Caffè Poliziano

OTHER
1 Chiesa di Sant'Agnese
2 Bus Terminus
3 Chiesa di San Bernardo
6 Police Station (Carabinieri); Piazza Savonarola
7 Banca Nazionale di Lavoro
9 Palazzo Avignonesi
10 Palazzo di Bucelli
11 Palazzo Cocconi
12 Torre di Pulcinella
13 Pro Loco Tourist Office; Piazza Michelozzo
14 Chiesa di Sant'Agostino
15 Chiesa di Santa Lucia
19 Post Office
20 Loggia di Mercato
21 Palazzo Cervini
23 Museo Civico; Palazzo Neri-Orselli
24 Palazzo Tarugi
25 Palazzo Ricci; Cantina del Redi
26 Palazzo Comunale
27 Palazzo Contucci; Le Cantine Contucci
28 Chiesa del Gesù
29 Il Sasso
30 Cathedral
31 Fortezza

CENTRAL TUSCANY

and the climb is free. You'll need to clear it with the guardian.

The other palaces in the piazza are the **Palazzo Contucci**, now a wine cellar, and the Palazzo Tarugi, attributed to Giacomo da Vignola, near the fountain. The **cathedral**, whose facade is noticeable by its absence, dates to the 16th century. Inside there is a lovely triptych above the high altar, depicting the Assumption, by Taddeo da Bartolo.

If from Piazza Michelozzi you were to take the low road and follow Via di Voltaia nel Corso, you would pass first, on your left, the Renaissance **Palazzo Cervini**, built for Cardinal Marcello Cervini, the future Pope Marcellus II. The unusual U-shape at the front, including a courtyard into the facade design, appears to have been another Sangallo creation. A few blocks farther along you reach, again on the left, the **Chiesa del Gesù**, a baroque job.

Outside the town wall, about 1km from the Porta della Grassa, stands the **Chiesa di San Biagio**, a fine Renaissance church built by (yet again) Antonio da Sangallo il Vecchio and consecrated in 1529 by the Medici pope Clement VII.

Courses It is possible to organise language courses through Il Sasso (☎ 0578 75 83 11, fax 0578 75 75 47) at Via dell'Opio nel Corso 3. One-on-one lessons of one hour start at L45,000, but you are better off organising a program of classes. Four hours a day over two weeks will cost you L600,000. The same place can also organise you into mosaic- and gold-jewellery-making classes. By happy coincidence, the organisation doubles as an estate agency specialising in the rental of apartments, villas and the like to foreigners.

Places to Stay You might consider visiting Montepulciano on a day trip when you discover the hotel prices. The *Albergo Il Marzocco* (☎ 0578 75 72 62, fax 0578 75 75 30, Piazza Savonarola 18) has singles/doubles with bathroom from L70,000/100,000. The *Albergo Il Borghetto* (☎ 0578 75 75 35, fax 0578 75 73 54, Via Borgo

Buio 5) is appealing and has rooms fo L100,000/135,000.

Otherwise, several affittacamere are scat tered about town. Get a list of them from th tourist office and expect to pay anything u to L150,000 for a double.

Places to Eat You can buy pizza by th slice at *Lo Spuntino* (☎ 0578 75 77 68, Vi Gracciano nel Corso 25). It is closed o Tuesday.

You'll eat well at either *Trattoria Il Pul cino* (☎ 0578 757907, Via Gracciano ne Corso 108)*, which closes on Friday, or *Trat toria Diva e Marceo* (☎ 0578 71 65 91, Vi Gracciano nel Corso 92)*, which is shut o Tuesday. You should get away with payin around L40,000 at either.

Borgo Buio (☎ 0578 71 74 97, Via Borg Buio 10) is a rustic, low-lit sort of a place where you can enjoy good Tuscan meals a reasonable prices. In addition, it function as an enoteca (you can tipple from 10.30 an to midnight) with a good selection of wines This place also organises wine and food tastings with various Italian personalities along with occasional courses in wine tasting. It usually closes on Thursday, al though they shut on Sunday evening and Monday lunchtime in the winter months.

Other places to get your palate wet on the local red, Vino Nobile, include the several long-established cantinas around town. *Cantina del Redi* is downhill from Piazza Grande along Via Ricci. *Le Cantine Contucci* is in the Palazzo Contucci on Piazza Grande.

If you just want a good old-fashioned coffee, a fine place to procure one is *Caffè Poliziano* (☎ 0578 75 86 15, Via di Voltaia nel Corso 27)*. The views are magnificent and the interior a pleasure. You can also eat here if the fancy should take you.

Getting There & Around Tra-in operates eight bus services daily between Montepulciano and Siena (L8000), via Pienza. Regular LFI buses connect with Chiusi (up to 17 a day). One direct LFI bus goes to Siena, while two travel to Florence. Four buses make the run to Arezzo (change at Bettolle).

It is possible to pick up the occasional bus to Rome here too. Buses leave from Piazza Sant'Agnese, outside the Porta al Prato at the northern end of town.

The most convenient train station is at Chiusi-Chianciano Terme, 10km south-east, on the main Rome-Florence line. Buses for Montepulciano meet each train, so it is the best way to get there from Florence or Rome. Stazione di Montepulciano, about 5km to the north-east, has less frequent local services.

By car, if you are not coming from Pienza, take the Chianciano Terme exit off the A1 and follow the SS166 for the 18km trip to Montepulciano.

Most cars are banned from the town centre and there are car parks near the Porta al Prato. Small town buses weave their way from here to Piazza Grande.

Chianciano Terme

A short trip south from Montepulciano by bus or car, you can probably skip Chianciano Terme unless you think a local spa-water treatment for your liver is in order. The town is blessed with a small conical medieval core, which seems to recoil at all the surrounding development. Given its proximity to Montepulciano, it does make an alternative accommodation possibility if you really can't find a thing in Montepulciano. Some 200 hotels cater to spa guests, so finding a room shouldn't be that difficult.

Chiusi

postcode 53043 • pop 9000

One of the most important of the 12 cities of the Etruscan League, Chiusi was once powerful enough to attack Rome, under the leadership of the Etruscan king Porsenna. These days it is a fairly sleepy country town, but highly recommended as a stopover. There is a Pro Loco information office (☎ 0578 22 76 67) at Via Porsenna 67, on the corner of the main square. It is open from 9.30 am to 12.30 pm daily (and 3 to 5 pm in summer).

Things to See & Do Chiusi's main attractions are the **Etruscan tombs** that dot the countryside around the town. Chiusi is noted as having the most painted tombs after Tarquinia – unfortunately, almost all are in a serious state of disrepair and are closed to the public. Visits to accessible tombs are with a guide only; ask at the **Museo Archeologico Nazionale**. The museum has a reasonably interesting collection of artefacts found in the local tombs. The museum is open from 9 am to 2 pm daily – closing time is generally later in the summer.

Also take a look at the Romanesque **cathedral** and the adjacent **Museo della Cattedrale**, which has an important collection of 22 illustrated antiphonals (psalm books). The **Labirinto di Porsenna** is a series of tunnels underneath the Piazza del Duomo, which date back to Etruscan times and formed part of the town's water supply system.

Since ancient times, legend has associated the labyrinth with the Etruscan king Porsenna – it supposedly hid his grand tomb. A section of the labyrinth was excavated in the 1980s and can be visited with a guide. It's well worth a visit, and tickets can be bought at the Museo della Cattedrale. The museum is open from 9.30 am to 12.45 pm and 4 to 7 pm daily from June to mid-October. From then to the end of May it opens in the morning only, except on Sunday and holidays, when it opens from 3 to 6 pm too.

Places to Stay & Eat The *Albergo La Sfinge* (☎ 0578 2 01 57, fax 0578 22 21 53, Via Marconi 2) is the only hotel in Chiusi's historical centre. It has singles/doubles for L70,000/100,000 with bathroom. There are several agriturismo establishments in the countryside near Chiusi; contact the Pro Loco for details.

Two options for a good meal are *Il Bucchero* (☎ 0578 22 20 92, Via Bonci 28), off Via Porsenna, where you can eat a good meal for about L40,000 a head. It is closed on Wednesday. At *La Solita Zuppa* (☎ 0578 2 10 06, Via Porsenna 21), just near the Albergo La Sfinge, you can start off with a wide range of soup options, the place's forte. Things continue well with other first-course

euro currency converter L10,000 = €5.16

CENTRAL TUSCANY

options, such as pici, and solid mains. Expect to pay around L45,000 with wine. It is closed on Tuesday.

Getting There & Away Chiusi is easily accessible by public transport. Its train station, in the valley below the town, is on the main Rome-Florence line. The town is just off the Autostrada del Sole (A1).

Sarteano & Cetona

Heading into this part of the province you definitely feel you have left the last of the tour buses well and truly behind you. This quiet rural territory is best explored with your own wheels. Both Sarteano and Cetona are curious little medieval settlements, the former topped by a brooding castle. No specific outstanding sights present themselves, but they are both fun to wander for a little while. At the camp site at Via Campo dei Fiori 30 in Sarteano you can luxuriate in the warm waters of the Piscina Bagno Santo. Near Cetona is the modest mountain of the same name, which invites to some vigorous meanderings in the clean country air.

Those with wads of money and a desire for a special retreat might like to consider the *Frateria di San Francesco* (☎ 0578 23 82 61, fax 0578 23 92 20, Via di San Francesco, ❷ frateria@ftbcc.it). A couple of kilometres along a side road (which leads up to Monte Cetona) outside the northern entrance to Cetona, this former convent has been lovingly restored and converted into a top-class restaurant with a few rooms added. A double costs from L360,000 to L410,000. A five-course dining experience of world-class standing will set you back L140,000 excluding wine. The restaurant is closed on Tuesday and the whole place for about a month from early November. Look for the Mondo X signs when driving up. Up to five buses a day (Monday to Saturday) head down to both towns from Montepulciano (some involve a change at Chianciano Terme).

Abbadia San Salvatore & Monte Amiata

A largely rather ugly mining town that gre rapidly and tastelessly from the late 19t century, Abbadia San Salvatore has a coup of saving graces. The old town, a sombr stone affair entered off the main Piazzal XX Settembre, is curious enough althoug perhaps not really worth an excursion on i own.

The **Abbazia di San Salvatore**, off Vi Cavour (about 500m off Piazzale X Settembre) was founded in 743 by th Lombard Erfo. It eventually passed int the hands of Cistercian monks, who sti occupy it today. Of the monastery littl remains, but the church is extremely inter esting (for people into churches and archi tecture at any rate). Built in the 11th centur and Romanesque in style, it was recon structed in a curious manner in the late 16t century, when the whole area from th transept to the apse was raised and adorne with broad, frescoed arches. Best of all however, if you can find someone to ope it, is the Lombard crypt, a remarkable ston forest of 36 columns. No-one is sure wha purpose this hall served.

The town lies in the shadow of Mont Amiata (1736m) and serves as a base fo local holidaymakers getting in a little skiin on one run on the peak (snow permitting) i winter or some walking in summer. You can for instance, walk right around the mountai following a 30km trail known as the Anell della Montagna. The path is signposted an maps are available. For this reason there ar plenty of hotels in Abbadia San Salvator and several others in towns dotted about th broad expanse of the mountain, so yo should not have too much trouble finding place to sleep should the need arise.

A handful of RAMA buses running be tween Grosseto and Bagni San Filippo ca in at Abbadia San Salvatore. It is also pos sible to get down from Siena (two buses ru a day).

Eastern Tuscany

An easy train ride from Florence puts the capital of this region, Arezzo, within tempting reach even of many fleeting tourists in Tuscany, but relatively few get beyond this former Etruscan city. The old centre, dominated by one of the most inspiring examples of Tuscan Romanesque construction, certainly makes the trip worth every lira, even if much of the rest of the town is a little scrappy. The only other seriously sought out destination is Cortona, the spectacularly located hilltop eyrie that looks out over the surrounding Tuscan and Umbrian plains.

Art lovers will no doubt be attracted by what could be called the Piero della Francesca trail. Starting with his fresco cycles in Arezzo itself, you can head out into the country in search of other of his masterpieces in towns such as Monterchi and Sansepolcro.

Beyond the towns, one of the least visited corners of Tuscany are the forests and hill country of the Casentino farther east en route for the Apennine frontier with the region of Emilia-Romagna.

AREZZO
postcode 52100 • pop 91,700

Heavily bombed during WWII, Arezzo is not the prettiest city in Tuscany. That said, the small medieval centre retains some inspiring highlights. The sloping Piazza Grande and the Romanesque jewel that is the Pieve di Santa Maria are lesser known perhaps than the fresco cycle by Piero della Francesca in the Chiesa di San Francesco. In all, though, it is well worth a visit, easily accomplished as a day trip from Florence.

An important Etruscan town, Arezzo was later absorbed into the Roman Empire, of which it was an important and flourishing centre. It became a free republic from the 10th century and supported the Ghibelline cause in the awful battles between pope and emperor. Arezzo was eventually subjugated by Guelph Florence in 1384, when Florence effectively bought the place. Conquering could be done like that more often.

Highlights

- Follow the Piero della Francesca trail from Arezzo to Sansepolcro
- Take a load off your feet and enjoy a drink on Arezzo's Piazza Grande while you admire the Romanesque Pieve di Santa Maria
- Turn up for the monthly antiques market in Arezzo
- Embark on a back road journey through the little-visited Casentino region
- Walk in the footsteps of St Francis of Assisi at the Santuario di San Francesco
- Wander the steep medieval streets of Cortona and soak up the splendid views across the Tuscan and Umbrian countryside

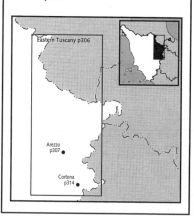

Sons of whom Arezzo can be justly proud include the poet Petrarch, the writer Pietro Aretino and the artist Vasari, most famous for his book *Lives of the Artists*.

A widely known antiques fair is held in Piazza Grande and the surrounding streets on the first Sunday of every month, which means accommodation can be difficult to find unless you book well ahead.

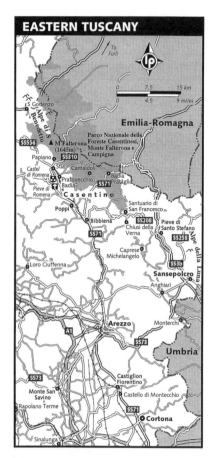

EASTERN TUSCANY

69 64) is outside the city walls on Via A⟨
Gasperi. The police station *(questur⟨*
☎ 0575 92 21) is on Via Fra Guittone.

Chiesa di San Francesco

The apse of this 14th-century Gothic churc⟨
houses one of the greatest works of Itali⟨
art, Piero della Francesca's fresco cycle ⟨
the *Leggenda della Vera Croce* (Legend ⟨
the True Cross). This masterpiece, painte⟨
between 1452 and 1456, relates in ⟨
episodes the story of Christ's death.

This Renaissance 'cartoon strip' bring⟨
an uncommonly human element to the me⟨
ieval tale, which involves characters fro⟨
the Old and New Testaments.

You can visit the church from 8.30 am ⟨
noon and 2.30 to 6.30 pm daily. Unfort⟨
nately, the frescoes were badly damaged ⟨
damp and were under restoration for som⟨
years. At the time of writing, the only wa⟨
to see those frescoes that were restored wa⟨
by guided tour. The restoration work ha⟨
now finished and the frescoes were due to ⟨
officially unveiled in the spring of 2000. ⟨
was not certain what format visits wou⟨
take once restoration was completed but, ⟨
a guide, during restoration a maximum of ⟨
people were guided for the close-up inspe⟨
tion every half hour or so (the timetable va⟨
ied with the season) which cost L10,000. T⟨
ticket office is right (west) of the main e⟨
trance to the church. Otherwise simply tak⟨
a pew and view from afar. The nave of th⟨
church is richly decorated in frescoes b⟨
lesser mortals.

Orientation & Information

From the train station on the southern edge
of the walled city, walk north-east along Via
Guido Monaco to the garden piazza of the
same name. The old city is to the north-east
and the modern part to the south-east along
Via Roma.

The APT tourist office (☎ 0575 37 76
78), near the train station in Piazza della
Repubblica, is open from 9 am to 1 pm
and 3 to 6.30 pm Monday to Friday, and
from 9 am to 1 pm on Saturday. The post
office is at Via Guido Monaco 34.

The Ospedale Civile (hospital; ☎ 0575 2

Pieve di Santa Maria

This 12th-century church has a magnifice⟨
Romanesque arcaded facade reminiscent ⟨
the cathedral at Pisa (but without the gloriou⟨
marble facing). Each column is of a differe⟨
design. Over the central doorway (hidden b⟨
scaffolding at the time of writing) are carve⟨
reliefs representing the months. The 14t⟨
century bell tower, with its 40 windows, ⟨
something of an emblem for the city. Th⟨
stark interior of the church shows a Goth⟨
influence, the only colour coming from th⟨
polyptych by Pietro Lorenzetti on the raise⟨
sanctuary at the rear of the church.

AREZZO

AREZZO

PLACES TO STAY		19	Caffé dei Costanti	12	Pieve di Santa Maria
1	La Toscana	20	La Buca di San Francesco	14	Fortezza Medicea
15	Villa Severi	30	Antica Trattoria da Guido	18	Enoteca Vinodivino
23	Astoria			21	Chiesa di San
24	Albergo Milano	**OTHER**			Francesco
25	Cecco	2	Chiesa di San Domenico	22	Post Office
		3	Casa di Vasari	26	Museo Archeologico
PLACES TO EAT		4	Museo Statale d'Arte	27	Crispi's Pub
5	Afroteranga		Medioevale e Moderna	28	Roman Amphitheatre
9	Caffé Vasari	6	Cathedral	29	Chiesa di San Bernardo
10	Trattoria Lancia dell'Oro	7	Casa di Petrarca	31	APT Tourist Office
13	La Torre di Gnicche	8	Palazzo Logge Vasariane	32	Bus Station
16	Osteria L'Agania	11	Palazzo della Fraternità dei	33	Bus Ticket Office
17	Trattoria Il Saraceno		Laici	34	Train Station

Piazza Grande & Around

The high end of this lumpy sloping piazza is lined by the porticoes of the **Palazzo delle Logge Vasariane**, completed in 1573. The **Palazzo della Fraternità dei Laici** on the western flank dates from 1375. It was started in the Gothic style and finished after the onset of the Renaissance. The south-east flank of the square is lined by a huddle of medieval houses.

Via dei Pileati leads to **Casa di Petrarca**, former home of the poet, which contains a small museum and the Accademia Petrarca. Visits are by appointment and really only for serious Petrarch fans. Enquire at the tourist office for further details.

Cathedral & Around

At the top of the hill on Via Ricasoli is the cathedral, started in the 13th century and not completed until the 15th century. The Gothic interior houses several artworks of note, the most important of which is easily the fresco of the *Maddalena* (Mary Magdalene) by Piero della Francesca. The church has a rather gaunt feel about it.

Virtually in front of the cathedral is the seat of the city's secular power, the **Palazzo dei Priori** on Piazza della Libertà. It retains relatively little of its original 14th-century grandeur. To the south-east of the cathedral, across the peaceful gardens of the **Passeggio del Prato** lies the hulk of the **Fortezza Medicea**, built in 1538.

Chiesa di San Domenico & Around

It is worth the walk to the rather odd-looking Gothic Chiesa di San Domenico to see the crucifix painted by Cimabue (once it comes out of restoration), which hangs above the main altar.

South on Via XX Settembre, the **Casa di Vasari** was built and sumptuously decorated by the architect himself. The house is open from 9 am to 7 pm Monday to Saturday and to 1 pm on Sunday. Admission is free.

Down the hill on Via di San Lorentino, the **Museo Statale d'Arte Medioevale e Moderna** houses works by local artists, including Luca Signorelli and Vasari, spanning the 13th to 18th centuries. A small sculpture gallery (mostly pieces from churches in the surrounding area) occupies the ground floor. The first floor is taken up with paintings from the 13th to 15th centuries. There is also an extensive porcelain collection. Upstairs the art continues into the 19th century. The gallery is open from 9 am to 7 pm daily. Admission costs L8000.

Museo Archeologico & Roman Amphitheatre

Not far from the train station, the museum is in a convent overlooking the remains of the Roman amphitheatre (*anfiteatro Romano*). It houses an interesting collection of Etruscan and Roman artefacts, including lo-

cally produced ceramics, bronzeware and the like. It opens from 9 am to 2 pm Monday to Saturday. Admission costs L8000.

Special Events

Over four or five days in late June/early July the town hosts Arezzo Wave, a music festival featuring named artists and bands from Italy and abroad and a range of new and emerging bands.

Good old medieval jousting fun happens on the second to last Sunday of June and again on the first Sunday of September. For the Giostro del Saracino (Joust of the Saracen), the four medieval quarters of the city present teams of knights, who aim to score as many points as they can by charging with their lances at an effigy of a Saracen warrior in Piazza Grande. The jousts are preceded by parades in period costume accompanied by lots of trumpet blowing and general clamour.

The first Sunday of every month sees the centre of Arezzo converted into one of Tuscany's biggest antique fairs.

JANE SMITH

Arezzo's Joust of the Saracen is preceded by parades in period costume.

laces to Stay

he non-HI youth hostel, the **Villa Severi** */fax 0575 29 90 47, Via F Redi 13)* offers &B for up to L26,000 in a wonderfully re- ored villa overlooking the countryside.

La Toscana *(☎ 0575 2 16 92, Via M rennio 56)* has simple single/double rooms om L40,000/75,000. **Astoria** *(☎ 0575 2 61, Via Guido Monaco 54)* has OK oms for L50,000/80,000. The Soviet-style ifice that is the **Cecco** *(☎ 0575 2 09 86, x 0575 35 67 30, Corso Italia 215)*, near e train station, has soulless but clean oms for L50,000/75,000, or L65,000/ ,000 with bathroom and TV.

Albergo Milano *(☎ 0575 2 68 36, fax 75 2 19 25, Via della Madonna del Prato)* is between the train station and the old ntre, near Piazza Guido Monaco. It offers od singles/doubles costing L100,000/ 0,000.

laces to Eat

azza Sant'Agostino comes to life each esday, Thursday and Saturday with the y's produce market. One of the best- lue *trattorie* in town is the unassuming **tica Trattoria da Guido** *(☎ 0575 2 37 60, a della Madonna del Prato 85)*, next to bergo Milano (see Places to Stay). Here u'll eat excellent, home-style food: try e *penne agli asparagi* (pasta with aspara- s). A full meal should come to less than 5,000. **La Buca di San Francesco** * 0575 2 32 71, Via San Francesco 1)*, ar the church of the same name, is one of e city's better restaurants, where you'll y up to L50,000 for a full meal. It is osed Monday evening and Tuesday.

Not far off the Piazza Grande, **La Torre Gnicche** *(☎ 0575 35 20 35, Piaggia San artino 8)* is a fine old osteria. It is closed ednesday.

At **Trattoria Lancia dell'Oro** *(☎ 0575 2 33, Logge Vasariane)* the food is not ite as good, but it is hard to beat the com- anding position over Piazza Grande. It is osed Monday. Or sip a drink at **Caffè sari** *(☎ 0575 2 19 45, Logge Vasariane)*, ouple of doors up. It is closed Sunday. Via G Mazzini hosts a few places that

will tickle your fancy. **Trattoria Il Sara- ceno** *(☎ 0575 2 76 44, Via G Mazzini 6)* is recommended by locals for no-nonsense Tuscan food at moderate prices. It is closed Wednesday. **Osteria L'Agania** *(☎ 0575 2 53 81, Via G Mazzini 10)* is another reliable choice. The cooking is again earthy and solid and much appreciated by locals. Main courses range from about L10,000 to L15,000. It is closed Monday.

Afroteranga *(☎ 0575 35 53 93, Via di San Lorentino 9–13)* is an overpriced 'African' restaurant where you can indulge in a range of dishes of more or less African origin. You can snack on things such as samosas (huh?) instead of having a full meal. The main virtue of the food is simply that it makes a change if, for whatever reason, you are a little sick of the local stuff. It is closed Wednesday.

One of Arezzo's fine cafes is **Caffè dei Costanti** *(☎ 0575 2 16 60, Piazza di San Francesco 19)*. It is closed Monday.

Entertainment

For an evening tipple with young people, try **Crispi's Pub** *(☎ 0575 2 28 73, Via Francesco Crispi 10)*. It's not very pub-like but quite fun on a weekend.

For something a little more refined, drop into **Enoteca Vinodivino** *(Via Andrea Ces- alpino 10)*, where you can try out a nice range of drinks. There is seating out the back and snacks are served. It is open until midnight except on Sunday and Monday, when the doors are kept well shut.

Getting There & Away

Buses depart from and arrive at Piazza della Repubblica, serving Cortona, Sansepolcro, Monterchi, Siena, San Giovanni Valdarno, Florence (L9900, 130 minutes) and other local towns. The city is on the Florence (L8000, 85 minutes) to Rome train line. Arezzo is a few kilometres east of the A1, and the SS73 heads east to Sansepolcro.

NORTH-EAST OF AREZZO

The art lovers' trail in search of master- pieces by Piero della Francesca leads away to the north-east of Arezzo to the towns of

EASTERN TUSCANY

Monterchi and Sansepolcro, both of them easy day trips from Arezzo.

Monterchi & Anghiari

Visit Monterchi to see Piero della Francesca's fresco *Madonna del Parto* (The Pregnant Madonna). It was removed from its original home in the local cemetery for restoration and is currently on display in a former primary school in Via Reglia. It is planned to eventually return it to its original location. The Madonna is considered one of the key works of 15th-century Italian art. Opening hours are between 9 am and 1 pm and 2 to 7 pm daily (closed Monday). Admission costs L5000.

A few kilometres north of Monterchi along the way to Sansepolcro lies the still-compact medieval centre of **Anghiari**, which is worth a brief stopover just to meander along its narrow twisting lanes. A local bus occasionally runs the 17km north to **Caprese Michelangelo**, birthplace of the painter of the Sistine Chapel (a clue – the artist's name was not Caprese!).

The closest camping ground is *Camping Michelangelo* (☎ *0575 79 38 86, fax 0575 79 11 83*). It opens from mid-March to the end of October. There is a fairly basic non-HI youth hostel here, the *Ostello Michelangelo* (☎ *0575 79 20 92, fax 0575 79 39 94, Località Fragaiola*). It opens from May to September only and beds cost up to L20,000.

Sansepolcro

Piero della Francesca was born in Sansepolcro. He left the town when he was quite young and returned when he was in his 70s to work on his treatises, which included *On Perspective in Painting*. Although most visitors give little thought to the town itself, Sansepolcro as it stands now dates largely to the 15th century, although it is thought possible an earlier medieval settlement grew up where once there had been a Roman castrum. Today it is a centre of light industry whose sprawl can hardly be said to enhance the upper Tiber valley countryside in which it is located.

The small tourist office (☎ 0575 74 05 36), at Piazza Garibaldi 2, can assist with some local information. The itinerary ‹ della Francesca's work takes in other tow in Tuscany and The Marches, includir Rimini, Urbino, Perugia and Florence. Y‹ can pick up a copy of *Following in Pie della Francesca's Footsteps in Tuscar Marches, Umbria & Romagna* in Arezzo ‹ Sansepolcro.

The **Museo Civico**, in the former tow hall at Via Aggiunti 65, just outside t‹ main city gate, is the pride of Sansepolc‹ and features a couple of Piero del Francesca's masterpieces. The most cel‹ brated of them is doubtless the *Risurrezior* (Resurrection), but other important worl by the master include the *Misericordia*, a impressive polyptych. The museum is op‹ from 9 am to 1.30 pm and 2.30 to 7.30 p daily (from 9.30 am to 1 pm and 2.30 6 pm between October and May). Admi sion costs L10,000.

Beyond the museum, the old town pleasant enough to wander around for while. The cathedral and a handful of oth‹ churches are scattered about the tow while just beyond the city walls looms t‹ forbidding hulk of the inevitable 16t‹ century Fortezza Medicea.

If you need to stay in the town, there a several hotels, including the budget *Orf‹* (☎ *0575 74 20 61, Viale A Diaz 12*), whic charges L45,000/80,000 for a single/doub‹ room. *Albergo Fiorentino* (☎ *0575 74 (50, fax 0575 74 03 70, Via Luca Pacioli 6* has rooms with bathroom for L65,00‹ 95,000 in high season. The latter is easi the pick of the crop, and boasts an atmo pheric restaurant up on the first floor. Mea are taken in a spacious dining area, a heavy exposed beams and chunky table and prices are moderate. It is closed Frida‹

SITA buses connect Arezzo with Sa‹ sepolcro hourly, and the town is on the Terr‹ Perugia train line.

THE CASENTINO REGION

A driving tour through the remote fore‹ and farming region of Casentino will tal‹ you through a little-visited area boastir two of Tuscany's most important mona‹ teries and some wonderful walking in t‹

arco Nazionale delle Foreste Casentinesi,
Monte Falterona e Campigna.

We start this route as though you were
coming from Florence, but it (or variations
in it) could just as easily be accomplished
from Arezzo, making your initial stops in
Monterchi, Anghiari and Sansepolcro (see
the previous sections).

Buses and a private train line from
Arezzo make it possible to get around the
Casentino region slowly, but ideally you
would have your own transport.

ratovecchio & Around

From Florence, follow the Arezzo road
(SS67) east along the northern bank of the
Arno (see also the Vallombrosa section of
the Around Florence chapter). From Vallombrosa you could head north to the SS70
highway via San Miniato in Alpe or take
another route through **Montemignaio**, a
pretty country town. Either way, it is worth
getting to the SS70 (which you can follow
all the way from Pontassieve rather than
making the Vallombrosa detour if you so
wish). The point is that, as you climb across
the Pratomagno range and head east, you
have wonderful views of the sparsely populated countryside to the north and south of
this winding hill road.

Once over the Consuma pass, you could
follow the road to Poppi and beyond (it becomes the SS71) down to Arezzo, but about
9km short of Poppi we detour off to the
north along the SS310 to Stia. Follow the
town signs for the **Castello di Romena** and
the Romanesque **Pieve di Romena**. Both are
well worth the visit (the only way here is by
car or your own feet – a CAI walking
trail meanders through the area).

The castle, still in private hands, is a
shadow of its former self. Erected around
the year 1000 on the site of an Etruscan settlement, the castle in its heyday was an
enormous complex surrounded by three sets
of defensive walls. The Guidi counts were
the local feudal lords until Florence took
over. All around it slope green fields of such
peacefulness it is hard to imagine the chaos
and carnage that medieval armies might
have wrought while fighting over the

stronghold. Normally it is open for visits
from 10 am to noon and 2 to 5 pm, but was
closed at the time of writing – check at the
tourist office in Arezzo. You generally have
to ask the custodian to show you around,
should you find it open.

About 1km downhill on a side road that
eventually slithers into Pratovecchio stands
one of the mightiest examples of Romanesque church-building in the Casentino.
The dark (and much weather-beaten) stone
of the church, with its heavy triple apse, has
been here since the 12th century.

Pratovecchio itself is of minimal interest.
The spacious porticoed Piazza Garibaldi is
about all there is to it. However, the LFI private train line runs through here with regular trains that connect Arezzo (via Bibbiena
and Poppi) with Stia. The trip between
Arezzo and Stia takes about an hour. If you
are approaching this way, you can stock up
on supplies and then walk out to the Romena castle and church.

Also in Pratovecchio is an information
office (☎ 0575 5 03 01, fax 0575 50 44 97)
for the Parco Nazionale delle Foreste Casentinesi, Monte Falterona e Campigna. It's
at Via Brochi in the centre of the town and
is open year-round.

Stia, a couple of kilometres up the road,
marks the end of the train line. Like Pratovecchio, there is really nothing of extraordinary interest here, although the porticoed
central square is pretty.

Parco Nazionale delle Foreste Casentinesi, Monte Falterona e Campigna

The park, instituted in 1993, spreads over
both sides of the frontier between Tuscany
and Emilia-Romagna, taking in some of the
most scenic stretches of the Apennines. The
Tuscan half is gentler territory than on the
Emilian side and if you have a few days to
spend in this part of Tuscany you should get
information on all of the park.

One of the highest peaks, Monte Falterona
(1654m) marks the source of the Arno river.
The park authorities have laid out nine *sentieri natura*, easy to cover short nature walks.
Apart from the human population, which

includes the inhabitants of two monasteries (see the following sections), the park is also home to some 160 species of animal, from squirrel and fox to wolves, deer and wild boar. They are accompanied by about 80 bird species and some 30 kinds of fish and reptiles. The dense forests are a cool summer refuge and ideal for walking. The Grande Escursione Appenninica (GEA) passes through here, and several other walking paths (such as those marked by the CAI) criss-cross the park area. Approach the park office in Pratovecchio (see under the previous Pratovecchio & Around section) for more details.

Camaldoli

A winding hill road sneaks west out of Pratovecchio (crossing the train line on the north side of the station) towards Camaldoli. Where it emerges at a crossroads you are pointed left to the **Eremo di Camaldoli** and right to the **Monastero di Camaldoli**. The distance between the two is 3km.

According to the story, Conte Maldolo handed the land for this isolated retreat to St Romualdo in 1012. From the name of the count came that of the location, and Romualdo set about building the monastery. He founded the hermitage *(eremo)* around 1023. The Camaldolesi, a branch of the Benedictines, came to be one of the most powerful forces in medieval Tuscany. What you can see today is the result of a mix of developments. The baroque church stands on the same spot as the original (built in 1027). Through a fence you can see 20 small tiled houses – they are the cells of the monks who still live here to this day. Opposite the church you can visit St Romualdo's cell.

Follow the road the 3km downhill and you come to the monastery. Originally designed as a *hospitium* for passing pilgrims, it evolved into a fully fledged monastery and centre of learning. The monks cultivated the forests that still stand around the monastery and developed all sorts of medicinal and herbal products. Take a look inside the Antica Farmacia. As you can see, the monks still make all sorts of liqueurs, honey,

chocolate, essences and (if you'll pardon th expression) God knows what else. If it i closed, the bar in the Hotel Camaldoli ha some of their products for sale.

On the subject of hotels, there are thre around here. The two cheapies stand righ opposite the monastery. **Albergo Camaldo** *(☎/fax 0575 55 60 19)* and the adjacent **L Foresta** *(☎/fax 0575 55 60 15)* both hav simple single/double rooms for L45,00 70,000. The former also has a restaurant.

Two or three LFI buses a day run up t the monastery and hermitage from Pop and Bibbiena.

Poppi & Bibbiena

Easily the most striking town of th Casentino is Poppi, perched up on a hill i the Arno plain and topped by the broodin hulk of the Palazzo dei Conti Guidi (th same counts who raised the Romena castle Speculation surrounds the origins of th fortified medieval residence. Vasari attri utes it to the father of Arnolfo di Cambi who subsequently used it as a model for th Palazzo Vecchio in Florence. Others clai Arnolfo built this one here and modelled on his own work in Florence. A hard one t call. It is open from 9.30 am to 12.30 p and 3 to 6 pm daily (Thursday to Sunda only from mid-October to mid-March). A mission costs L5000.

You can stay within sight of the palace **Hotel Casentino** *(☎ 0575 52 90 90, f 0575 52 90 67, Piazza Repubblica 6).* Plea ant singles/doubles cost up to L70,00 90,000.

Poppi is on the LFI train line betwe Arezzo and Stia. LFI buses also conne with several destinations throughout t province.

Santuario di San Francesco (Verna)

Of more interest than the Camaldoli mo astery to many modern pilgrims is t Franciscan monastic complex 23km east Bibbiena. It marks the southern edge of national park, 5km uphill from Chiusi de Verna at a spot called Verna. This is wh St Francis of Assisi is said to have recei e stigmata and lived other key episodes in s life. In a sense, this place is closer to the sence of the saint than Assisi itself.

When you enter the dark stone complex llow the signs around to the sanctuary *antuario*). You will find yourself first at e Chiesa Maggiore (also known as the asilica), decorated with some remarkable amelled ceramics by Andrea della Rob- a. Also on display are various reliquaries ontaining items associated with the saint, cluding his walking stick and a 'discipline' r castigating himself (self-flagellation and e like played a large part in the religiosity many in the Middle Ages).

By the entrance to the basilica is the Cap- lla della Pietà (another ceramic from the lla Robbia family), off which the Corri- io dell Stimmate (with frescoes recount- g the saint's life) leads you to the core of e sanctuary – a series of chapels associ- ed with St Francis' life. The masterpiece the Cappella delle Stimmate, beautifully corated with ceramic works by Luca and ndrea della Robbia. In the older church, iesa di Santa Maria degli Angeli, ad- cent to the basilica (which was mostly ilt in the 15th century), is a further mas- piece by Andrea della Robbia. The sanc- ary is open from 6 am to 8.30 pm daily. dmission is free.

Pilgrims can stay in the Foresteria of the onastery. For more information, contact e Direzione Pastor Angelicus del Santu- io della Verna, 52010 Chiusi della Verna R). Or call ☎ 0575 59 90 25 (summer) or 0575 53 42 49 (winter).

A few LFI buses run to the complex from bbiena and Pieve di Santo Stefano.

OUTH OF AREZZO
astiglion Fiorentino
ost visitors to the area make a beeline om Arezzo to Cortona or vice-versa, arcely giving this steep hillside town a ught. It deserves slightly better attention an that, and given the frequent bus that nnects south to Cortona and north to ezzo, is an easy stop-off.

A fortified settlement has existed here ce Etruscan times. In the Middle Ages it

changed owners several times, belonging at one time or another to, among others, Arezzo and Perugia. It finally fell under Florence's sway in 1384. The old town has changed little since that day.

A stroll up through the steep streets brings you to the central square, whose main feature is a stylish loggia supposedly by Vasari. Just up the hill behind the Palazzo Comunale (town hall) is the Pina- coteca. It is housed in the town fortifica- tions, or Cassero, along with the Chiesa di Sant'Angelo. The Pinacoteca contains mostly paintings from the 13th to the 15th centuries. It opens from 10 am to 12.30 pm and 3.30 to 6 pm, Tuesday to Sunday. Ad- mission costs L5000. Several churches dot- ted about the town are worth poking your nose into if you have time to kill.

There is no reason to stay, since the bus connections on to Arezzo and Cortona are frequent. The only hotel is a fairly sad op- tion by the highway, and the town isn't ex- actly overloaded with quality eateries either.

A few kilometres farther south along the road to Cortona, you will hardly fail to no- tice rising proudly on the left the **Castello di Montecchio**, a formidable redoubt that a somewhat intimidated Florence gave to the English mercenary John Hawkwood in re- turn for his military services.

Cortona
postcode 52044 • pop 22,500
Set into the side of a hill covered with olive groves, Cortona offers stunning views across the Tuscan countryside and has changed little since the Middle Ages. It was a small settlement when the Etruscans moved in during the 8th century BC and it later became a Roman town. In the late 14th century, it attracted the likes of Fra An- gelico, who lived and worked in the city for about 10 years. Luca Signorelli and the artist known as Pietro da Cortona were born here. The city is small, easily seen in a couple of hours, and well worth visiting for the sensational view alone.

One might almost have thought that was the explanation for the booming trade the

EASTERN TUSCANY

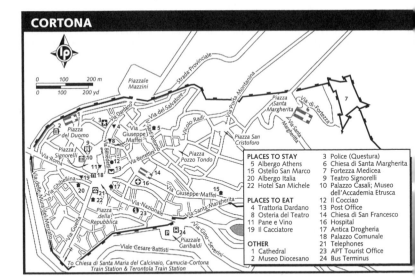

CORTONA

PLACES TO STAY
5 Albergo Athens
15 Ostello San Marco
20 Albergo Italia
22 Hotel San Michele

PLACES TO EAT
4 Trattoria Dardano
8 Osteria del Teatro
11 Pane e Vino
19 Il Cacciatore

OTHER
1 Cathedral
2 Museo Diocesano

3 Police (Questura)
6 Chiesa di Santa Margherita
7 Fortezza Medicea
9 Teatro Signorelli
10 Palazzo Casali; Museo
   dell'Accademia Etrusca
12 Il Cocciaio
13 Post Office
14 Chiesa di San Francesco
16 Hospital
17 Antica Drogheria
18 Palazzo Comunale
21 Telephones
23 APT Tourist Office
24 Bus Terminus

town is doing. But no, it's all thanks to Frances Mayes and her saccharine accounts of life in Tuscany, *Under the Tuscan Sun* (yawn). You know the story: Americans seized by a sense of romance battle the inscrutable but always slightly comical bureaucrats to buy dream house in Tuscany (in this case just outside Cortona) and live idyllically ever after – mostly on the earnings of the inevitable treacly book describing these non-events. It appears some intrepid visitors to Cortona go to the extreme of tracking the house down, ringing the bell and wandering about uninvited in the yards.

Orientation Buses arrive at Piazzale Garibaldi, on the south-eastern edge of the walled city, after a long winding climb out of the valley. The square has a large car park, and also offers some of the best views from the city over the surrounding Tuscan and Umbrian countryside. From the piazza, walk straight up Via Nazionale to Piazza della Repubblica, the centre of town.

Information The APT tourist office (☎ 0575 63 03 52), Via Nazionale 42, can assist with a hotel list and the useful *Cor-*

tona brochure, a complete guide to touri essentials. It is open from 8 am to 1 pm an 3 to 7 pm Monday to Saturday, and from 9 am to 1 pm on Sunday from May to Sep tember. The rest of the year it shuts on Sun day and Saturday afternoon, and at 6 p during the week.

The post office is on the corner of V Benedetti and Piazza Pescheria. It open from 8.15 am to 7 pm Monday to Frida and until 12.30 pm on Saturday. You ca find some phones in a little office just o Piazza della Repubblica on Via Guelfa.

The Ospedale Civico (hospital; ☎ 057 63 91) is high up in the old town on V Giuseppe Maffei. For a night locum yo can call ☎ 0575 6 28 93. The police (*ques tura*; ☎ 0575 60 36 90) are on the corner Via Dardano and Piazza Tommasi.

Things to See Start in Piazza della R pubblica with the crenellated **Palazzo Con unale**, which was renovated in the 16 century and again, unhappily, in the 19th

To the north is Piazza Signorelli, name after the artist and dominated by the 13t century **Palazzo Casali** (which in mediev times was known as the Palazzo Pretoric ay hint of its medieval grandeur has been obscured by the rather unimaginative façade added in the 17th century. Inside is the **Museo dell'Accademia Etrusca**, which across about a dozen rooms displays a substantial haul of Etruscan artefacts dug up in the area around Cortona. One of the single most intriguing pieces is an elaborate 5th-century BC oil lamp. The collection also includes jewellery, funerary urns, some ancient Egyptian artefacts, bronzeware and household implements.

The museum is open from 10 am to 7 pm, Tuesday to Sunday. Admission costs L8000.

Little is left of the Romanesque character of the **cathedral** north-west of Piazza Signorelli. It was completely rebuilt late in the Renaissance and again in the 18th century. The result can most tactfully be described as indifferent. Opposite is the **Museo Diocesano** in the former church of Gesù. It contains a fine if limited collection of artworks. Room 1 contains a remarkable Roman-era sarcophagus made of Carrara marble, along with a series of paintings by Luca Signorelli and his workshop. These continue into the adjoining Room 4. Of Signorelli's personal contributions, *Compianto su Cristo Morto* (Grief at Christ's Death) is possibly the most interesting. Easily the star work of the collection is to be found in Room 3. Fra Angelico's *Annunciazione* is a triumph and by its sheer luminosity leaves the surrounding works in the shade. Downstairs in the Oratorio del Gesù you can see frescoes carried out by Vasari.

The museum is open from 9.30 am to 1 pm and 3.30 to 7 pm daily (10 am to 1 pm and 3 to 5 pm in winter). Admission costs L5000.

At the eastern edge of the city centre is **Chiesa di Santa Margherita**, which features the Gothic tomb of St Margaret. Farther up the hill is the 16th-century **Fortezza Medicea**, built for the Medici by Laparelli, who designed the fortress city of Valletta in Malta.

If you care for a walk of a few kilometres south out of the old town, you could inspect the rather weather-beaten **Chiesa di Santa Maria del Calcinaio**. Francesco di Giorgio's original approach to Renaissance architecture will intrigue students of the subject. Note how the main body of the church is free of columns and basically a two-storey structure topped with tabernacle windows – all unusual elements. If it's open you can just push the door and wander inside.

Special Events Every year for about a week from late August into the first days of September, Cortona becomes a big Mostra Antiquaria, one of Italy's main antique fairs. If you are interested in antique furniture, this will interest you. Of course getting a room in Cortona around then is virtually impossible without a reservation.

Places to Stay The city has several cheap hotels and a hostel, and finding a room shouldn't be a problem. The attractive HI *Ostello San Marco (☎/fax 0575 60 13 92, Via Guiseppe Maffei 57)*, a short but uphill walk east of Piazzale Garibaldi, has B&B for L18,000. It is open from 15 March to 15 October.

About the next cheapest option is a further stretch in the uphill luggage-lugging stakes. *Albergo Athens (☎ 0575 63 05 08, fax 0575 60 44 57, Via Sant'Antonio 12)* has smallish, straightforward singles/doubles for L45,000/65,000.

The *Albergo Italia (☎ 0575 63 02 54, fax 0575 63 05 64, Via Ghibellina 5)*, just off Piazza della Repubblica, is in an old mansion and has singles/doubles with private bathroom, TV and phone for up to L90,000/130,000 in high season.

The luxury option in town is *Hotel San Michele (☎ 0575 60 43 48, fax 0575 63 01 47 Via Guelfa 15)*. Comfortable rooms come with phone, TV and minibar at L160,000/220,000. They have guest parking.

Places to Eat Piazza della Repubblica hosts a produce market each Saturday and several grocery shops dot the area. At *Trattoria Dardano (☎ 0575 60 19 44, Via Dardano 24)* try the *ravioli al burro e salvia* (butter and sage ravioli). A full meal can come in at around L30,000. It is closed Wednesday. *Il Cacciatore (☎ 0575 63 05 52,*

EASTERN TUSCANY

Via Roma 11) is one of the city's better restaurants and offers local specialities. Count on paying about L45,000 for a full meal and wine. Also closed Wednesday.

Pane e Vino (☎ 055 63 10 10, *Piazza Signorelli 27*) is a huge and hugely popular dining hall in the heart of Cortona. You may find you have to queue. Expect to pay around L35,000 per person for a meal.

The pick of the crop is probably *Osteria del Teatro* (☎ 055 63 05 56, *Via Giuseppe Maffei 5)*. It is the latest incarnation of what was probably the last genuine osteria in Cortona. You will probably pay about L45,000 for a full meal that could include *ravioli ai fiori di zucca* (pumpkin-flower ravioli). It is closed Wednesday.

Shopping Il Cocciaio (☎ 0575 60 12 46), at Via Benedetti 24, tucked away from the madding crowds is a friendly little store where you can buy ceramics. It has a Web site at www.toscumbria.com/cocciaio. If you want specialist and handmade food products from around the province, try An-

tica Drogheria at Via Nazionale 1. Amon other comestibles, the owner brings stu down from the Antica Farmacia at th Camaldoli monastery in the north of th province (see the earlier Camaldoli sec tion). This street is lined with all sorts o shops, from antiques to tacky souvenirs.

Getting There & Around LFI buses con nect Cortona frequently (at least 13 a day o work days) with Arezzo (via Castiglio Fiorentino) from Piazzale Garibaldi.

Two train stations serve the town. Trai from Arezzo stop at the Camucia-Corton station, in the valley below Cortona, a trains for Rome stop at Terontola, abo 5km to the south of the Camucia-Corton station. Shuttle buses connect both statio with Piazzale Garibaldi, and a board in shop window on the north side of V Nazionale, about 50m in from Piazza Garibaldi, details schedules.

By car, the city is on the north-south SS7 which runs to Arezzo, and it is close to t *superstrada* that connects Perugia to the A

lian is a Romance language related to ench, Spanish, Portuguese and Romian. The Romance languages belong to e Indo-European group of languages, hich include English. Indeed, as English d Italian share common roots in Latin, u will recognise many Italian words.

Modern literary Italian began to develop the 13th and 14th centuries, preminantly through the works of Dante, trarch and Boccaccio, who wrote chiefly the Florentine dialect. The language drew its Latin heritage and many dialects to velop into the standard Italian of today. lthough many dialects are spoken in eryday conversation, standard Italian is e national language of schools, media and erature and is understood throughout the untry.

Florentines may argue that their dialect *is* e national language, and it's true it formed e basis of 'standard' Italian (due mainly to e status of Florence as Italy's major politi-l, economic and cultural power base in the nturies leading up to unification in 1861). owever, even those with a reasonable ounding in Italian may find many orentines surprisingly hard to understand, least at first. No-one can deny the pecu-rity of the local accent. Here and in other rts of Tuscany you're bound to hear the rd 'c' pronounced as a heavily aspirated '. *Voglio una Coca Cola con cannuccia* (I nt a Coca Cola with a straw) in Florence unds more like *Voglio una Hoha Hola hon nnuccia*!

In Tuscany (and throughout Central ly), 'c' before 'e' and 'i' is pronounced as '' – for example, the standard Italian for , *dieci*, is pronounced as *dieshi*. Often, ere standard Italian has 'nd', 'mb' or 'ld', Central dialect has 'nn', 'mm' or 'll' unds. Therefore 'hot' would sound more e *callo* than the standard Italian *caldo*.

There are 58 million speakers of Italian Italy; 500,000 in Switzerland, where Italian is one of the official languages; and 1.5 million speakers in France, Slovenia and Croatia. As a result of migration, Italian is also spoken in the USA, Argentina, Brazil and Australia.

Visitors to Italy with more than the most fundamental grasp of the language need to be aware that many older Italians still expect to be addressed by the third person formal, ie *lei* instead of *tu*. Also, it is not considered polite to use the greeting *ciao* when addressing strangers, unless they use it first; it's better to say *buon giorno* (or *buona sera*, as the case may be) and *arrivederci* (or the more polite form, *arrivederla*). We have used the formal address for most of the phrases in this guide. Use of the informal address is indicated by 'inf' in brackets. Italian also has both masculine and feminine forms (they usually end in 'o' and 'a' respectively). Where both forms are given in this guide, they are separated by a slash, the masculine form first.

If you'd like a more comprehensive guide to the language, get a copy of Lonely Planet's *Italian phrasebook*.

Pronunciation

Italian pronunciation isn't difficult to master once you learn a few easy rules. Although some of the more clipped vowels, and stress on double letters, require careful practice for English speakers, it is easy enough to make yourself understood.

Vowels

Vowels are generally more clipped than in English:

a	as in 'art', eg *caro* (dear); sometimes short, eg *amico/a* (friend)
e	as in 'tell', eg *mettere* (to put)
i	as in 'inn', eg *inizio* (start)
o	as in 'dot', eg *donna* (woman); as in 'port', eg *dormire* (to sleep)
u	as the 'oo' in 'book', eg *puro* (pure)

Consonants

The pronunciation of many Italian consonants is similar to that of their English counterparts. Pronunciation of some consonants depends on certain rules:

c	as 'k' before 'a', 'o' and 'u'; as the 'ch' in 'choose' before 'e' and 'i'
ch	as the 'k' in 'kit'
g	as the 'g' in 'get' before 'a', 'o', 'u' and 'h'; as the 'j' in 'jet' before 'e' and 'i'
gli	as the 'lli' in 'million'
gn	as the 'ny' in 'canyon'
h	always silent
r	a rolled 'rr' sound
sc	as the 'sh' in 'sheep' before 'e' and 'i'; as 'sk' before 'a', 'o', 'u' and 'h'
z	as the 'ts' in 'lights', except at the beginning of a word, when it's as the 'ds' in 'suds'

Note that when **ci**, **gi** and **sci** are followed by **a**, **o** or **u**, the 'i' is not pronounced unless the accent falls on the 'i'. Thus the name 'Giovanni' is pronounced 'joh-**vahn**-nee'.

Word Stress

A double consonant is pronounced as a longer, more forceful sound than a single consonant.

Stress generally falls on the second-last syllable, as in spa-**ghet**-ti. When a word has an accent, the stress falls on that syllable, as in cit-**tà** (city).

Greetings & Civilities

Hello.	*Buongiorno.*
	Ciao. (inf)
Goodbye.	*Arrivederci.*
	Ciao. (inf)
Yes.	*Sì.*
No.	*No.*
Please.	*Per favore/Per piacere.*
Thank you.	*Grazie.*
That's fine/	*Prego.*
You're welcome.	
Excuse me.	*Mi scusi.*
Sorry (forgive me).	*Mi scusi/Mi perdoni.*

Small Talk

What's your name?	*Come si chiama?*
	Come ti chiami? (inf)
My name is ...	*Mi chiamo ...*
Where are you from?	*Di dov'è?*
	Di dove sei? (inf)
I'm from ...	*Sono di ...*
I (don't) like ...	*(Non) Mi piace ...*
Just a minute.	*Un momento.*

Language Difficulties

Please write it down.	*Può scriverlo, per favore?*
Can you show me (on the map)?	*Può mostrarmelo (sulla carta/pianta)*
I understand.	*Capisco.*
I don't understand.	*Non capisco.*
Do you speak English?	*Parla inglese?*
	Parli inglese? (inf)
Does anyone here speak English?	*C'è qualcuno che parla inglese?*
How do you say ... in Italian?	*Come si dice ... in italiano?*
What does ... mean?	*Che vuole dire ...?*

Paperwork

name	*nome*
nationality	*nazionalità*
date of birth	*data di nascita*
place of birth	*luogo di nascita*
sex (gender)	*sesso*
passport	*passaporto*
visa	*visto*

Getting Around

What time does ... leave/arrive?	*A che ora parte/ arriva ...?*
the aeroplane	*l'aereo*
the boat	*la barca*
the (city) bus	*l'autobus*
the (intercity) bus	*il pullman*
the train	*il treno*
I'd like a ... ticket.	*Vorrei un biglietto ..*
one-way	*di solo andata*
return	*di andata e ritorn*
1st class	*prima classe*
2nd class	*seconda classe*
I want to go to ...	*Voglio andare a ...*

Signs

INGRESSO/ ENTRATA	ENTRANCE
USCITA	EXIT
INFORMAZIONE	INFORMATION
APERTO/CHIUSO	OPEN/CLOSED
PROIBITO/ VIETATO	PROHIBITED
POLIZIA/ CARABINIERI	POLICE
QUESTURA	POLICE STATION
CAMERE LIBERE	ROOMS AVAILABLE
COMPLETO	FULL/NO VACANCIES
GABINETTI/BAGNI	TOILETS
UOMINI	MEN
DONNE	WOMEN

The train has been cancelled/delayed.	*Il treno è soppresso/ in ritardo.*
the first	*il primo*
the last	*l'ultimo*
platform number	*binario numero*
ticket office	*biglietteria*
timetable	*orario*
train station	*stazione*

I'd like to hire ...	*Vorrei noleggiare ...*
a bicycle	*una bicicletta*
a car	*una macchina*
a motorcycle	*una motocicletta*

Around Town

I'm looking for ...	*Cerco ...*
a bank	*un banco*
the church	*la chiesa*
the city centre	*il centro (città)*
the ... embassy	*l'ambasciata di ...*
my hotel	*il mio albergo*
the market	*il mercato*
the museum	*il museo*
the post office	*la posta*
a public toilet	*un gabinetto/ bagno pubblico*
the telephone centre	*il centro telefonico*
the tourist office	*l'ufficio di turismo/ d'informazione*

I want to change ...	*Voglio cambiare ...*
money	*del denaro*
travellers cheques	*degli assegni per viaggiatori*

beach	*la spiaggia*
bridge	*il ponte*
castle	*il castello*
cathedral	*il duomo/ la cattedrale*
church	*la chiesa*
island	*l'isola*
main square	*la piazza principale*
market	*il mercato*
mosque	*la moschea*
old city	*il centro storico*
palace	*il palazzo*
ruins	*le rovine*
sea	*il mare*
square	*la piazza*
tower	*la torre*

Directions

Where is ...?	*Dov'è ...?*
Go straight ahead.	*Si va sempre diritto.*
	Vai sempre diritto. (inf)
Turn left.	*Giri a sinistra.*
Turn right.	*Giri a destra.*
at the next corner	*al prossimo angolo*
at the traffic lights	*al semaforo*
behind	*dietro*
in front of	*davanti*
far	*lontano*
near	*vicino*
opposite	*di fronte a*

Accommodation

I'm looking for ...	*Cerco ...*
a guesthouse	*una pensione*
a hotel	*un albergo*
a youth hostel	*un ostello per la gioventù*

Where is a cheap hotel?	*Dov'è un albergo che costa poco?*
What is the address?	*Cos'è l'indirizzo?*
Could you write the address, please?	*Può scrivere l'indirizzo, per favore?*

Do you have any rooms available?	Ha camere libere/C'è una camera libera?
I'd like ...	Vorrei ...
a bed	un letto
a single room	una camera singola
a double room	una camera matrimoniale
a room with two beds	una camera doppia
a room with a bathroom	una camera con bagno
to share a dorm	un letto in dormitorio
How much is it ...?	Quanto costa ...?
per night	per la notte
per person	per ciascuno
May I see it?	Posso vederla?
Where is the bathroom?	Dov'è il bagno?
I'm/We're leaving today.	Parto/Partiamo oggi.

Shopping

I'd like to buy ...	Vorrei comprare ...
How much is it?	Quanto costa?
I don't like it.	Non mi piace.
May I look at it?	Posso dare un'occhiata?
I'm just looking.	Sto solo guardando.
It's cheap.	Non è caro/a.
It's too expensive.	È troppo caro/a.
I'll take it.	Lo/La compro.

Do you accept ...?	Accettate ...?
credit cards	carte di credito
travellers cheques	assegni per viaggiatori

more	più
less	meno
smaller	più piccolo/a
bigger	più grande

Time, Date & Numbers

What time is it?	Che (ora è/ore sono)?
It's (8 o'clock).	Sono (le otto).
in the morning	di mattina

in the afternoon	di pomeriggio
in the evening	di sera
When?	Quando?
today	oggi
tomorrow	domani
yesterday	ieri

Monday	lunedì
Tuesday	martedì
Wednesday	mercoledì
Thursday	giovedì
Friday	venerdì
Saturday	sabato
Sunday	domenica

January	gennaio
February	febbraio
March	marzo
April	aprile
May	maggio
June	giugno
July	luglio
August	agosto
September	settembre
October	ottobre
November	novembre
December	dicembre

0	zero
1	uno
2	due
3	tre
4	quattro
5	cinque
6	sei

Emergencies

Help!	Aiuto!
Call ...!	Chiami ...!
	Chiama ...! (inf)
a doctor	un dottore/ un medico
the police	la polizia
There's been an accident	C'è stato un incidente!
I'm lost.	Mi sono perso/a.
Go away!	Lasciami in pace! Vai via! (inf)

7	sette
8	otto
9	nove
10	dieci
11	undici
12	dodici
13	tredici
14	quattordici
15	quindici
16	sedici
17	diciassette
18	diciotto
19	diciannove
20	venti
21	ventuno
22	ventidue
30	trenta
40	quaranta
50	cinquanta
60	sessanta
70	settanta
80	ottanta
90	novanta
00	cento
•00	mille
•00	due mila

| e million | un milione |

ealth

n ill.	Mi sento male.
hurts here.	Mi fa male qui.
n ...	Sono ...
asthmatic	asmatico/a
diabetic	diabetico/a
epileptic	epilettico/a
n allergic ...	Sono allergico/a ...
to antibiotics	agli antibiotici
to penicillin	alla penicillina
tiseptic	antisettico
pirin	aspirina
ndoms	preservativi
ntraceptive	anticoncezionale
arrhoea	diarrea
edicine	medicina
nblock cream	crema/latte solare (per protezione)
npons	tamponi

FOOD

Basics

breakfast	prima colazione
lunch	pranzo
dinner	cena
restaurant	ristorante
grocery store	un alimentari

What is this?	(Che) cos'è?
I'd like the set lunch.	Vorrei il menù turistico.
Is service included in the bill?	È compreso il servizio?
I'm a ...	Sono ...
vegetarian.	vegetariano/a.
vegan	vegetaliano/a.

Menu

This glossary is intended as a brief guide to some of the basics and by no means covers all of the dishes you're likely to encounter in Tuscany. Most travellers to the region will already be well acquainted with the various Italian pastas, which include spaghetti, fettucine, penne, rigatoni, gnocchi, lasagne, tortellini and ravioli. The names are the same in Italy and no further definitions are given here.

Useful Words

affumicato	smoked
al dente	firm (as all good pasta should be)
alla brace	cooked over hot coals
alla griglia	grilled
arrosto	roasted
ben cotto	well done (cooked)
bollito	boiled
cameriere/a	waiter/waitress
coltello	knife
conto	bill/cheque
cotto	cooked
crudo	raw
cucchiaino	teaspoon
cucchiaio	spoon
forchetta	fork
fritto	fried
menù	menu
piatto	plate
ristorante	restaurant

Staples

aceto	vinegar
burro	butter
formaggio	cheese
limone	lemon
marmellata	jam
miele	honey
olio	oil
olive	olives
pane	bread
pane integrale	wholemeal bread
panna	cream
pepe	pepper
peperoncino	chilli
polenta	cooked cornmeal
riso	rice
risotto	rice cooked with wine and stock
sale	salt
uovo/uova	egg/eggs
zucchero	sugar

Meat & Fish

acciughe	anchovies
agnello	lamb
aragosta	lobster
bistecca	steak
calamari	squid
coniglio	rabbit
cotoletta	cutlet or thin cut of meat, usually crumbed and fried
cozze	mussels
dentice	dentex (type of fish)
fegato	liver
gamberi	prawns
granchio	crab
manzo	beef
merluzzo	cod
ostriche	oysters
pesce spada	swordfish
pollo	chicken
polpo	octopus
salsiccia	sausage
sarde	sardines
sgombro	mackerel
sogliola	sole
tacchino	turkey
tonno	tuna
trippa	tripe
vitello	veal
vongole	clams

Vegetables

asparagi	asparagus
carciofi	artichokes
carote	carrots
cavolo/verza	cabbage
cicoria	chicory
cipolla	onion
fagiolini	string beans
melanzane	aubergines
patate	potatoes
peperoni	peppers
piselli	peas
spinaci	spinach

Fruit

arance	oranges
banane	bananas
ciliegie	cherries
fragole	strawberries
mele	apples
pere	pears
pesche	peaches
uva	grapes

Soups & Antipasti

brodo – broth
carpaccio – very fine slices of raw meat
insalata caprese – sliced tomatoes with mozzarella and basil
insalata di mare – seafood, generally crustaceans
minestrina in brodo – pasta in broth
minestrone – vegetable soup
olive ascolane – stuffed, deep-fried olives
prosciutto e melone – cured ham with melon
ripieni – stuffed, oven-baked vegetables
stracciatella – egg in broth

Pasta Sauces

alla matriciana – tomato and bacon
al ragù – meat sauce (bolognese)
arrabbiata – tomato and chilli
carbonara – egg, bacon and black pepper
napoletana – tomato and basil
panna – cream, prosciutto and sometimes peas

sto – basil, garlic and oil, often with pine nuts

ngole – clams, garlic, oil and sometimes with tomato

izzas

ll of the pizzas included in the following st have a tomato (and sometimes mozzalla) base.

pricciosa – olives, prosciutto, mushrooms and artichokes

frutti di mare – seafood

funghi – mushrooms

margherita – oregano

napoletana – anchovies

pugliese – tomato, mozzarella and onions

quattro formaggi – with four types of cheese

quattro stagioni – like a capricciosa, but sometimes with egg

verdura – mixed vegetables; usually courgette (zucchini) and aubergine (eggplant), sometimes carrot and spinach

Glossary

ACI – Automobile Club Italiano, the Italian automobile club
aereo – aeroplane
affittacamere – rooms for rent (cheaper than a *pensione*, and not part of the classification system)
affresco – fresco; the painting method in which watercolour paint is applied to wet plaster
agriturismo – tourist accommodation on farms
AIG – Associazione Italiana Alberghi per la Gioventù, Italy's youth hostel association
albergo – hotel (up to five stars)
alimentari – grocery shop or delicatessen
aliscafo – hydrofoil
alloggio – lodging (cheaper than a *pensione*, and not part of the classification system)
alto – high
ambasciata – embassy
ambulanza – ambulance
anfiteatro – amphitheatre
Annunciazione – Annunciation
appartamento – apartment, flat
apse – (English) domed or arched area at the altar end of a church
APT – Azienda di Promozione Turistica, the provincial tourist office
arco – arch
assicurato/a – insured
atrium – (Latin) forecourt of a Roman house or a Christian basilica
autobus – bus
autostazione – bus station/terminal
autostop – hitchhiking
autostrada – freeway, motorway

bagno – bathroom; also toilet
balia – emergency committee (historical)
bancomat – Automatic Teller Machine
basilica – in ancient Rome, a building used for public administration, with a rectangular hall flanked by aisles and an *apse* at the end; later, a Christian church built in the same style

battistero – baptistry
benzina – petrol
bicicletta – bicycle
biglietto – ticket
binario – (train) platform
bivacco – unattended hut, bivouac
borgo – ancient town or village, sometime used to mean equivalent of *via*
brioche – pastry
busta – envelope

cabinovia – two-seater cable car
cacciucco – mixed seafood stew
CAI – Club Alpino Italiano, for informatio on hiking and mountain refuges
camera – room
camera doppia – double room with twi beds
camera matrimoniale – double roo with a double bed
camera singola – single room
campanile – bell tower
campeggio – camp site
cappella – chapel
carabinieri – police under the jurisdictio of the Ministry of Defence (see *polizia*)
carta d'identità – ID card
carta telefonica – phonecard (also *sched telefonica*)
cartoleria – stationery shop
cartolina (postale) – postcard
casa – house
casa dello studente – accommodatio for students available on campus durir holidays
castello – castle
cattedrale – cathedral
cava – quarry (as in the marble quarri around Carrara)
cena – evening meal
cenacolo – refectory
centro – centre
centro storico – old town (literally, h torical centre)
chiesa – church
chiostro – cloister; covered walkwa

ually enclosed by columns, around a
ıadrangle
n cin – cheers (a drinking toast)
ınquecento – 16th century
T – Compagnia Italiana di Turismo, the
ılian national tourist/travel agency
ıdice fiscale – tax number
ılazione – breakfast
ılonna – column
ımune – equivalent to a municipality or
ıunty; town or city council; historically, a
ımmune (self-governing town or city)
ıntado – district around a major town
ıntorno – side dish
ıntrada – town district
ınvalida – ticket stamping machine
ıperto – cover charge
ırso – main street, avenue
ırtile – courtyard
ıocifissione – Crucifixion
ΓS – Centro Turistico Studentesco e
ıovanile, the student/youth travel agency
ıccetta – couchette
ıpola – dome

ɛposito bagagli – left luggage
gestivo – after-dinner liqueur
stributore di benzina – petrol pump
ɛe *stazione di servizio*)
ıomo – cathedral

NIT – Ente Nazionale Italiano per il
ırismo, the Italian state tourist office
ıoteca – wine shop, nowadays often a
ısic restaurant with a range of fine wines
 taste
ıpresso – express mail; express train;
ıort black coffee

ırmacia (di turno) – pharmacy (open
ɛe)
ırmo posta – poste restante
ırrovia – train station
ısta – festival
ıume – river
ıntana – fountain
ıro – forum
ırtezza – fortress
ıancobollo – postage stamp
ıesco – (English) see *affresco*

FS – Ferrovie dello Stato, the Italian state
railway
funicolare – funicular railway
funivia – cable car

gabinetto – toilet, WC
gelato – ice cream
gasolio – diesel
golfo – gulf
grotta – cave
guardia di finanza – fiscal police

intarsia – inlaid wood, marble or metal
intonaco – whitewash
isola – island

laboratori – marble workshops
lago – lake
largo – (small) square
lavanderia – laundrette
lavasecco – dry-cleaning
lettera – letter
locanda – inn, small hotel
loggia – covered area on the side of a
building; porch
lungomare – seafront road; promenade

macchia – Mediterranean scrub
Madonna col Bambino – Madonna with
Baby Jesus (often the subject of paintings,
drawings and sculptures)
Maestà – depiction of the Trinity, Christ or
Mary enthroned (often the subject of paintings, drawings and sculptures)
mare – sea
menù del giorno – menu of the day
mercato – market
mescita di vini – wine outlet
mezza pensione – half board
monte – mountain, mount
motorino – moped
municipio – town hall
museo – museum

necropolis – (English) ancient cemetery,
burial site
Novecento – 20th century

oggetti smarriti – lost property
ospedale – hospital

ostello – hostel
ostello per la gioventù – youth hostel
osteria – snack bar/cheap restaurant

pacchetto – package, parcel
pacco – package, parcel
pala – altarpiece
palazzo – palace or mansion; a large building of any type, including an apartment block
panino – bread roll with filling
parco – park
parlamento – people's plebiscite (historical)
partenze – departures
passaggio ponte – deck class
passeggiata – traditional evening stroll
pasta – cake; pasta; pastry or dough
pasticceria – shop selling cakes, pastries and biscuits
pedaggio – toll
pensione – small hotel, often with board
pensione completa – full board
permesso di soggiorno – residence permit
piazza – square
piazzale – (large) open square
pietà – (literally, pity or compassion) sculpture, drawing or painting of the dead Christ supported (usually) by the Madonna
pietre dure – semiprecious 'hard stone', often cut, used to decorate many Tuscan buildings
pietra forte – dun-coloured 'strong stone' characteristic of the exterior of many Tuscan buildings
pietra serena – grey 'tranquil stone' used to great effect by Brunelleschi and others in the interiors of Renaissance churches, alternated with *intonaco* surfaces
pievi – parish church
pinacoteca – gallery
podestà – external martial
polizia – police
polyptych – altarpiece consisting of more than three panels (see *triptych*)
ponte – bridge
porta – gate
portico – portico; covered walkway, usually attached to the outside of buildings

porto – port
post area – airmail
pranzo – lunch
priori – governors (historical)
pronto soccorso – first aid, casualty wa⊓
pullman – (English) long-distance bus

Quattrocento – 15th century
questura – police station

raccolta – collection
raccomandata – registered mail
ribollita – vegetable stew
rifugio – mountain refuge
rocca – fortress
rustication – (English) rough-hewn, pr⊓ tuding blocks of stone used in building

sagra – festival (generally dedicated to o⊓ food item or theme)
sagrestia – sacristy
sala – room
salumeria – delicatessen that sells main⊓ cheeses and sausage meats
santuario – sanctuary
scheda telefonica – phonecard (als⊓ *carta telefonica*)
Seicento – 17th century
servizio – service charge
signoria – government (historical)
sindaco – mayor
spiaggia (libera) – (public) beach
stazione – station
stazione di servizio – service/petrol sta⊓ tion
stazione marittima – ferry terminal
strada – street, road
superstrada – expressway; highway wi⊓ divided lanes

teatro – theatre
telamoni – large statues of men, used ⊓ columns in temples
telegramma – telegram
tempio – temple
terme – thermal baths
torrone – stream
tessera – membership card
tondo – circular painting
torre – tower

orrente – stream
raghetto – ferry
ramezzini – sandwiches
rattoria – cheap restaurant
reno – train
rinità – Trinity
riptych – painting or carving on three anels, hinged so that the outer panels fold ver the middle one, often used as an altariece (see *polyptych*)
rompe l'oeil – painting or other illustraon designed to 'deceive the eye', creating ne impression that the image is real

fficio postale – post office

ufficio stranieri – (police) foreigners bureau
Ultima Cena – The Last Supper (often the subject of paintings, drawings and sculptures)

via – street, road
via aerea – airmail
via ferrata – climbing trail with permanent steel cables to aid walkers
vin santo – type of sweet white wine, often used in Mass
villa – town house or country house; also the park surrounding the house
vinai – wine bar or shop

LONELY PLANET

You already know that Lonely Planet publishes more than this one guidebook, but you might not be aware of the other products we have on this region. Here is a selection of titles that you may want to check out as well:

Europe on a shoestring
ISBN 0 86442 648 8
US$24.95 • UK£14.99 • 180FF

Florence
ISBN 0 86442 785 9
US$14.95 • UK£8.99 • 110FF

Italian phrasebook
ISBN 0 86442 456 6
US$5.95 • UK£3.99 • 40FF

Italy
ISBN 0 86442 692 5
US$21.95 • UK£13.99 • 170FF

Mediterrean Europe
ISBN 0 86442 619 4
US$25.95 • UK£15.99 • 190FF

Read This First: Europe
ISBN 1 86450 136 7
US$14.99 • UK£8.99 • 99FF

Rome
ISBN 0 86442 626 7
US$15.95 • UK£9.99 • 120FF

Venice
ISBN 0 86442 786 7
US$14.95 • UK£8.99 • 110FF

Walking in Italy
ISBN 0 86442 542 2
US$17.95 • UK£11.99 • 140FF

Western Europe
ISBN 0 86442 639 9
US$25.95 • UK£15.99 • 190FF

World Food Italy
ISBN 1 86450 022 0
US$12.95 • UK£7.99 • 110FF

Available wherever books are sold.

LONELY PLANET

Guides by Region

L onely Planet is known worldwide for publishing practical, reliable and no-nonsense travel information in our guides and on our web site. The Lonely Planet list covers just about every accessible part of the world. Currently there are fifteen series: travel guides, Shoestrings, Condensed, Phrasebooks, Read This First, Healthy Travel, Walking guides, Cycling guides, Pisces Diving & Snorkeling guides, City Maps, Travel Atlases, Out to Eat, World Food, Journeys travel literature and Pictorials.

AFRICA Africa on a shoestring • Africa – the South • Arabic (Egyptian) phrasebook • Arabic (Moroccan) phrasebook • Cairo • Cape Town • Cape Town city map • Central Africa • East Africa • Egypt • Egypt travel atlas • Ethiopian (Amharic) phrasebook • The Gambia & Senegal • Healthy Travel Africa • Kenya • Kenya travel atlas • Malawi, Mozambique & Zambia • Morocco • North Africa • Read This First Africa • South Africa, Lesotho & Swaziland • South Africa, Lesotho & Swaziland travel atlas • Swahili phrasebook • Tanzania, Zanzibar & Pemba • Trekking in East Africa • Tunisia • West Africa • Zimbabwe, Botswana & Namibia • Zimbabwe, Botswana & Nambia Travel Atlas • World Food Morocco
Travel Literature: The Rainbird: A Central African Journey • Songs to an African Sunset: A Zimbabwean Story • Mali Blues: Traveling to an African Beat

AUSTRALIA & THE PACIFIC Auckland • Australia • Australian phrasebook • Bushwalking in Australia • Bushwalking in Papua New Guinea • Fiji • Fijian phrasebook • Healthy Travel Australia, NZ and the Pacific • Islands of Australia's Great Barrier Reef • Melbourne • Melbourne city map • Micronesia • New Caledonia • New South Wales & the ACT • New Zealand • Northern Territory • Outback Australia • Out To Eat – Melbourne • Out to Eat – Sydney • Papua New Guinea • Pidgin phrasebook • Queensland • Rarotonga & the Cook Islands • Samoa • Solomon Islands • South Australia • South Pacific • South Pacific Languages phrasebook • Sydney • Sydney city map • Sydney Condensed • Tahiti & French Polynesia • Tasmania • Tonga • Tramping in New Zealand • Vanuatu • Victoria • Western Australia
Travel Literature: Islands in the Clouds • Kiwi Tracks: A New Zealand Journey • Sean & David's Long Drive

CENTRAL AMERICA & THE CARIBBEAN Bahamas, Turks & Caicos • Bermuda • Central America on a shoestring • Costa Rica • Cuba • Dominican Republic & Haiti • Eastern Caribbean • Guatemala, Belize & Yucatán: La Ruta Maya • Jamaica • Mexico • Mexico City • Panama • Puerto Rico • Read This First Central & South America • World Food Mexico
Travel Literature: Green Dreams: Travels in Central America

EUROPE Amsterdam • Amsterdam city map • Andalucía • Austria • Baltic States phrasebook • Barcelona • Berlin • Berlin city map • Britain • British phrasebook • Brussels, Bruges & Antwerp • Budapest city map • Canary Islands • Central Europe • Central Europe phrasebook • Corfu & Ionians • Corsica • Crete • Crete Condensed • Croatia • Cyprus • Czech & Slovak Republics • Denmark • Dublin • Eastern Europe • Eastern Europe phrasebook • Edinburgh • Estonia, Latvia & Lithuania • Europe on a shoestring • Finland • Florence • France • French phrasebook • Germany • German phrasebook • Greece • Greek Islands • Greek phrasebook • Hungary • Iceland, Greenland & the Faroe Islands • Istanbul City Map • Ireland • Italian phrasebook • Italy • Krakow •Lisbon • London • London city map • London Condensed • Mediterranean Europe • Mediterranean Europe phrasebook • Munich • Norway • Paris • Paris city map • Paris Condensed • Poland • Portugal • Portugese phrasebook • Portugal travel atlas • Prague • Prague city map • Provence & the Côte d'Azur • Read This First Europe • Romania & Moldova • Rome • Russia, Ukraine & Belarus • Russian phrasebook • Scandinavian & Baltic Europe • Scandinavian Europe phrasebook • Scotland • Slovenia • Spain • Spanish phrasebook • St Petersburg • Switzerland • Trekking in Spain • Ukrainian phrasebook • Venice • Vienna • Walking in Britain • Walking in Ireland • Walking in Italy • Walking in Spain • Walking in Switzerland • Western Europe • Western Europe phrasebook • World Food Italy • World Food Spain
Travel Literature: The Olive Grove: Travels in Greece

INDIAN SUBCONTINENT Bangladesh • Bengali phrasebook • Bhutan • Delhi • Goa • Hindi & Urdu phrasebook • India • India & Bangladesh travel atlas • Indian Himalaya • Karakoram Highway • Kerala • Mumbai (Bombay) • Nepal • Nepali phrasebook • Pakistan • Rajasthan • Read This First: Asia & India • South India • Sri Lanka • Sri Lanka phrasebook • Trekking in the Indian Himalaya • Trekking in the Karakoram & Hindukush • Trekking in the Nepal Himalaya
Travel Literature: In Rajasthan • Shopping for Buddhas • The Age Of Kali

LONELY PLANET

Mail Order

Lonely Planet products are distributed worldwide. They are also available by mail order from Lonely Planet, so if you have difficulty finding a title please write to us. North and South American residents should write to 150 Linden St, Oakland CA 94607, USA; European and African residents should write to 10a Spring Place, London, NW5 3BH; and residents of other countries to PO Box 617, Hawthorn, Victoria 3122, Australia.

ISLANDS OF THE INDIAN OCEAN Madagascar & Comoros • Maldives • Mauritius, Réunion & Seychelles

MIDDLE EAST & CENTRAL ASIA Bahrain, Kuwait & Qatar • Central Asia • Central Asia phrasebook • Dubai • Hebrew phrasebook • Iran • Israel & the Palestinian Territories • Israel & the Palestinian Territories travel atlas • Istanbul • Istanbul to Cairo on a shoestring • Jerusalem • Jerusalem City Map • Jordan • Jordan, Syria & Lebanon travel atlas • Lebanon • Middle East • Oman & the United Arab Emirates • Syria • Turkey • Turkey travel atlas • Turkish phrasebook • Yemen
Travel Literature: The Gates of Damascus • Kingdom of the Film Stars: Journey into Jordan • Black on Black: Iran Revisited

NORTH AMERICA Alaska • Backpacking in Alaska • Baja California • California & Nevada • California Condensed • Canada • Chicago • Chicago city map • Deep South • Florida • Hawaii • Honolulu • Las Vegas • Los Angeles • Miami • New England • New Orleans • New York City • New York city map • New York Condensed • New York, New Jersey & Pennsylvania • Oahu • Pacific Northwest USA • Puerto Rico • Rocky Mountain • San Francisco • San Francisco city map • Seattle • Southwest USA • Texas • USA • USA phrasebook • Vancouver • Washington, DC & the Capital Region • Washington DC city map
Travel Literature: Drive Thru America

NORTH-EAST ASIA Beijing • Cantonese phrasebook • China • Hong Kong • Hong Kong city map • Hong Kong, Macau & Guangzhou • Japan • Japanese phrasebook • Japanese audio pack • Korea • Korean phrasebook • Kyoto • Mandarin phrasebook • Mongolia • Mongolian phrasebook • North-East Asia on a shoestring • Seoul • South-West China • Taiwan • Tibet • Tibetan phrasebook • Tokyo
Travel Literature: Lost Japan • In Xanadu

SOUTH AMERICA Argentina, Uruguay & Paraguay • Bolivia • Brazil • Brazilian phrasebook • Buenos Aires • Chile & Easter Island • Chile & Easter Island travel atlas • Colombia • Ecuador & the Galapagos Islands • Healthy Travel Central & South America • Latin American Spanish phrasebook • Peru • Quechua phrasebook • Rio de Janeiro • Rio de Janeiro city map • South America on a shoestring • Trekking in the Patagonian Andes • Venezuela
Travel Literature: Full Circle: A South American Journey

SOUTH-EAST ASIA Bali & Lombok • Bangkok • Bangkok city map • Burmese phrasebook • Cambodia • Hanoi • Healthy Travel Asia & India • Hill Tribes phrasebook • Ho Chi Minh City • Indonesia • Indonesia's Eastern Islands • Indonesian phrasebook • Indonesian audio pack • Jakarta • Java • Laos • Lao phrasebook • Laos travel atlas • Malay phrasebook • Malaysia, Singapore & Brunei • Myanmar (Burma) • Philippines • Pilipino (Tagalog) phrasebook • Read This First Asia & India • Singapore • South-East Asia on a shoestring • South-East Asia phrasebook • Thailand • Thailand's Islands & Beaches • Thailand travel atlas • Thai phrasebook • Thai audio pack • Vietnam • Vietnamese phrasebook • Vietnam travel atlas • World Food Thailand • World Food Vietnam

ALSO AVAILABLE: Antarctica • The Arctic • Brief Encounters: Stories of Love, Sex & Travel • Chasing Rickshaws • Lonely Planet Unpacked • Not the Only Planet: Travel Stories from Science Fiction • Sacred India • Travel with Children • Traveller's Tales

Index

Text

Boxed Text

Bold indicates maps.

MAP LEGEND

BOUNDARIES

························· Provincial

HYDROGRAPHY

················· Coastline
················· River, Creek
······················ Lake
······················ Canal

ROUTES & TRANSPORT

······················ Freeway
················· Primary Road
················· Secondary Road
················· Tertiary Road
················· Unsealed Road
················· City Freeway
················· City Highway

······················ City Road
················· City Street, Lane
················· Pedestrian Mall
······················ Tunnel
······ Train Route & Station
······················ Tramway
····· Cable Car or Chairlift

AREA FEATURES

······················ Building
························· Hotel
················· Urban Area

················· Park, Gardens
······················ Cemetery
······················ Market

······················ Forest
························· Beach
························· Rocks

MAP SYMBOLS

🐾 **FLORENCE** ························· City
⊙ **Lucca** ············ Large Town
⊙ Miniato ················· Town
⊙ Galleno ················· Village

• ··········· Point of Interest

★ ················· Place to Stay
⬛ ··················· Camp Site
🚐 ··············· Caravan Park
⬛ ·············· Hut or Chalet

▼ ················· Place to Eat
⬛ ··················· Pub or Bar

🛬 ························· Airport
······ Ancient or City Wall
⊖ ························· Bank
⊼ ·························· Beach
🚌 🚏 ····· Bus Station, Bus Stop
🏰 ················· Castle or Fort
⛰ ·········· Cave or Cavern
⛪ 🏛 ········ Church, Cathedral
🎬 ························· Cinema
📷 ··· Embassy or Consulate
⛴ ··························· Ferry
⛲ ······················· Fountain
⊕ ·········· Hospital or Clinic
ℹ ················· Information

⬛ ··············· Internet Cafe
▲ ··················· Mountain
⛰ ·········· Mountain Range
🏛 ······················ Museum
🏞 ················ National Park
🏛 ····················· Palazzo
🅿 ··············· Parking Area
➕ ··············· Police Station
✉ ················· Post Office
⬛ ························· Ruins
🏊 ············ Swimming Pool
☎ ··················· Telephone
🎭 ····················· Theatre
⬛ ··················· Transport

Note: not all symbols displayed above appear in this book

LONELY PLANET OFFICES

Australia
PO Box 617, Hawthorn, Victoria 3122
☎ 03 9819 1877 fax 03 9819 6459
email: talk2us@lonelyplanet.com.au

USA
150 Linden St, Oakland, CA 94607
☎ 510 893 8555 TOLL FREE: 800 275 8555
fax 510 893 8572
email: info@lonelyplanet.com

UK
10a Spring Place, London NW5 3BH
☎ 020 7428 4800 fax 020 7428 4828
email: go@lonelyplanet.co.uk

France
1 rue du Dahomey, 75011 Paris
☎ 01 55 25 33 00 fax 01 55 25 33 01
email: bip@lonelyplanet.fr
www.lonelyplanet.fr

World Wide Web: www.lonelyplanet.com *or* AOL keyword: lp
Lonely Planet Images: lpi@lonelyplanet.com.au